Database Systems
Handbook

Other McGraw-Hill Books of Interest

ISBN	AUTHOR	TITLE
0-07-000748-9	Aiken	*Data Reverse Engineering*
0-07-005996-9	Allen, Bambara, Bambara	*Informix: Client / Server Application Development*
0-07-001697-6	Anderson	*Client / Server Database Design with SYBASE*
0-07-001974-6	Andriole	*Managing Systems Requirements: Methods, Tools, and Cases*
0-07-005779-6	Bigus	*Data Mining with Neural Networks: Solving Business Problems from Application Development to Decision Support*
0-07-036929-1	Leach	*Software Reuse: Methods, Models, and Costs*
0-07-041034-8	Mattison	*Data Warehousing: Strategies, Technologies, and Techniques*
0-07-057725-0	Sanders	*The Developer's Guide to DB2 / 2 and DB2 / 6000*

Database Systems Handbook

Paul J. Fortier, Ph.D.
Editor

McGraw-Hill

New York San Francisco Washington, D.C. Auckland Bogotá
Caracas Lisbon London Madrid Mexico City Milan
Montreal New Delhi San Juan Singapore
Sydney Tokyo Toronto

Library of Congress Cataloging-in-Publication Data

Database systems handbook / Paul J. Fortier, editor.
  p.   cm.
  Includes bibliographical references and index.
  ISBN 0-07-021626-6
  1. Database management. 2. Distributed databases. I. Fortier,
Paul J.
  QA76.9.03035886   1997
  005.74—dc20   96-33407
                                                          CIP

McGraw-Hill

A Division of The **McGraw·Hill** Companies

1 2 3 4 5 6 7 8 9 0 DOC/DOC 9 0 1 0 9 8 7 6

ISBN 0-07-021626-6

The sponsoring editor for this book was Steven Elliot and the production supervisor was Suzanne W. B. Rapcavage. It was set in New Century Schoolbook by Multiscience Press Inc.

Printed and bound by R. R. Donnelley & Sons Company.

This book is printed on acid-free paper.

McGraw-Hill books are available at special quantity discounts to use as premiums and sales promotion, or for use in corporate training programs. For more information, please write to the Director of Special Sales, McGraw-Hill, 11 West 19th Street, New York, NY 10011. Or contact your local bookstore.

Contents

Contributors

Anitha Basavaraj
Department of Electrical and Computer Engineering
University of Massachusetts Dartmouth
North Dartmouth, MA 02747-2300   (Chapter 19)

Son K. Dao
Hughes Research laboratories Inc.
Malibu, CA 90265   (Chapter 15)

Lisa Cingiser DiPippo
Department of Computer Science
University of Rhode Island
Kingston, RI 02881-0816   (Chapters 1, 11)

Donna K. Fisher
NCCOSC RDTE DIV 412
49180 Transmitter Road, Rm 2
San Diego, CA 92152-7341   (Chapter 18)

Paul J. Fortier
Department of Electrical and Computer Engineering
University of Massachusetts Dartmouth
North Dartmouth, MA 02747-2300   (Chapters 1–5, 7–10,
                                                   14, 16, 17, 19)

David K. Hsiao
Department of Computer Science
Naval Post Graduate School
Monterey, CA 93943   (Chapter 12)

Bonnie MacKellar
Department of Mathematics and Computer Science
Western Connecticut State University
Westside Campus
Danbury, CT 06810   (Chapters 6, 17)

Joan Peckham
Department of Computer Science
University of Rhode Island
Kingston, RI 02881-0816   (Chapters 6, 17)

Janet J. Prichard
Department of Mathematics and Computer Science
East Carolina University
Greenville, NC 27859   (Chapter 18)

David Rasikan
Department of Computer Science
University of Virginia
Charlottesville, VA 22903   (Chapter 13)

Sang H. Son
Department of Computer Science
University of Virginia
Charlottesville, VA 22903   (Chapter 13)

Bhavani Thuraisingham
The MITRE Corporation
Burlington Road
Bedford, MA 01730   (Chapters 13, 15)

Victor Fay Wolfe
Department of Computer Science
University of Rhode Island
Kingston, RI 02881-0816   (Chapter 11)

About the Editor

Paul J. Fortier is an associate professor of Electrical and Computer Engineering specializing in databases and real-time systems. A faculty member at the University of Massachusetts at Dartmouth, he holds a doctorate in computer science and a master of science degree in electrical engineering. An active member of several ANSI/ISO standards committees, including X3H2, Fortier is also a best-selling author. His previous books include *Handbook of Local Area Networks Technology* and *Design of Distributed Operating Systems*.

Preface

The field of database systems is relatively new, having only been around for about 40 years. Database technology began with the network and hierarchical database systems. The relational paradigm (about 20 to 25 years ago) was followed by a long period of stability, where the science and technology of database systems was refined and solidified. The last 15 years have seen another major shift in the database systems field with the advent of the object-oriented database system. Object-oriented database technology introduced a variety of changes within the database systems community. Theories of correctness are being revisited, altered states of operations are evolving, and the database system is becoming a part of a wider range of applications every day.

The network and relational database systems evolved to a point where U.S. and international standards for a database language interface were developed. The recent object-oriented database systems are evolving in a more ad hoc fashion than SmallTalk and C++ programming languages and have resulted in numerous variations and dialects, none of which has emerged as a de facto or de jure standard. In recent years the object-oriented database community has focused on generating a proposed nonsanctioned standard, which should eventually result in more interoperability among the various object-oriented database systems. In conjunction with this, the relational database community has embraced object concepts as being fundamental to the next relational database system standards evolution. The resulting ANSI and ISO standards will be a hybrid database system based on the relational/object-oriented paradigms.

The result of all these efforts has been the incorporation of database management systems into a wider range of application domains. Databases have advanced from simple recordkeeping applications to more complex data and processing domains. Databases are being applied to medical information management; medical monitoring systems; manufacturing control; highly fault-tolerant environments; high-performance systems, such as end-user sales; stock market trading and analysis; real-time control; multimedia; and many other specialized and diverse application domains, all of which require specialized features from a database management system.

These activities have resulted in a flood of new and evolving database management system features that are being researched, designed, developed, and integrated into both existing and new database systems. Because of this there are now numerous database systems specifically designed and fielded to support unique market niches—for example, to support real-time command and control environments, real-time database management systems have been developed and marketed to support temporal constraints on data and transactions and to deliver predictable performance. To support other specializations such as security, fault tolerance, high performance, heterogeneous, and multimedia applications, databases with specific support for these applications' unique needs have also been developed.

The text addresses the variety of database classes by providing an understanding of the differences as well as the similarities among these systems. In addition to these new database systems, the text also discusses fundamental concepts in database structure, design, and management. The book is not a programmer's guide but focuses instead on understanding the composition and operations of general and specialized database systems. It is tutorial in nature and as such can be used as a general reference on database systems technology or as a single-term or multiterm course text on database systems.

USE OF THE BOOK

If you are new to the area of database systems, this book provides a comprehensive introduction to the specification, selection, design, and operations of database management systems. If you are already familiar with the fundamentals of database systems, but wish to examine specialized database system concepts, this book will introduce you to a number of advanced database systems and their domain of applicability. The goal is to provide a foundation in database systems technology and to present specialized applications so that readers can expand their understanding of database systems and discover new ways in which database systems can be applied to applications' information management needs.

The book has been designed based on teaching an introductory course in database systems and an advanced course in database and transaction systems. The book could be used as a one- or two-semester course in database systems, augmented with material from a specific database system if practical programming exercises are desired. The presentation moves from basic theory and concepts of a database and database management system, through a presentation of database design concepts and four main database design models, followed by chapters on advanced database management system concepts, such as distributed database technology, secure database system concepts, fault-tolerant database system concepts, real-time database systems, heterogeneous database systems, database machines, and multimedia database management system concepts. The text concludes with a review of the state of standards with the database area and short reviews of example database management systems.

Acknowledgments

This book would not have been possible were it not for the contributions of the many authors involved. The book represents a collaborative effort and is an acknowledgment of their contributions to the field of database systems. The contributors have endured the long duration of this project, almost two years, without faltering. Through the many iterations they maintained their sense of dedication and professionalism to an admirable end goal.

A second note of thanks goes to the many graduate database students who were used as the test cases for numerous first drafts of chapters and for the testing of examples included. Without prodding the students to finish the text it may have taken longer to accomplish.

Special thanks to the staff of Intertext Publications for their support in seeing this project to completion and making the final production as painless as possible. I further wish to thank Anitha Basavaraj for her work in producing the numerous figures used throughout this text and my son Daniel for his efforts in completing and proofing the art. The idea for writing this book rests squarely in the hands of the members of several database standards committees and study groups, who urged me to publish a text dealing with new applications of database systems and their technology.

This book would not have been possible without the financial support I received from the University of Massachusetts College of Engineering, the U.S. Navy's Next-Generation Computer Resources Database Management Interface Standards Working Group, and from my publisher.

Finally, I wish to thank my wife, Kathleen, always an inspiration, and my three children, Daniel, Brian, and Nicole, for their assistance and support during the writing and production of this book.

1

Introduction to Database Systems

Paul Fortier
Lisa Cingiser DiPippo

1.1 INTRODUCTION

Database management systems are finding their way into more end-user applications every day. We use databases daily in our normal activities and do not even think much about where or how the data are being accessed and managed. Databases come in many flavors. We find databases in use when we purchase products using a credit card or debit card. Databases provide the basis for the use of on-line transaction processing systems being more widely applied to debit purchases. We use databases when we make airline reservations and when we look for a book in the library using the computer card catalog. Databases are being applied in the automobile industry for advanced positioning systems and for control of the automobile's various systems. Designers in the clothing, automobile, and toy industries, as well as architects, use computers and databases to assist in the design process. We have begun to apply database technology to time-critical systems and to personal-safety systems. In such environments the databases have widely different requirements as to how data are represented, stored, managed, and accessed by users.

In this book we will investigate the many ways in which a database can be used in various industries, how the information to be managed by the database is logically represented, how the logical data are physically represented, how the database manages this stored data, how the data are maintained correctly, and how database management systems have evolved and will continue to evolve as the demands on them escalate.

1.2 EVOLUTION OF COMPUTERS AND COMPUTER DATA PROCESSING

Database management systems followed the development of computers and advanced operating systems for these computers. Computers came into being with the development of the ENIAC computer system in the late 1940s. The early ENIAC and subsequent computers were constructed of vacuum tubes and filled a large room. These early computer systems were dedicated to a single task and had no operating system or database management system.

The power of these early computers was less than that of the handheld calculators in use today. These computers were used mainly for ballistic missile trajectory projections and military research. The architecture of these early computers was based on the von Neumann stored program, single-stream instruction flow architecture (Figure 1.1). This basic architecture and philosophy is still in use today in most computer systems.

These early computer systems had no databases or sophisticated operating systems to simplify their operations. They stored program instructions and data needed for computation in the same place. Instructions were read from memory one at a time and were mostly associated with the loading and storage of program data from memory to registers where the data were to be operated on. Data in these early systems were not shared by programs. If a program needed data produced by another program, these data were typically copied into a region near the end of a program's space, and the end addresses were hard-coded for use by the application program in which they were embedded.

Database systems evolved as the need for shared data increased. The evolution of operating systems to allow for multiple processes to share computer resources led to their development (Figure 1.2). The advent of multiprocess operating systems led to programs that could now share information. In the early systems data were shared by the

Figure 1.1 Von Neumann programming paradigm

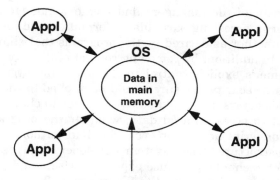

Figure 1.2   Early data access control

operating systems or explicitly through a programmer's instructions. Programmers could use methods such as aliasing data regions that allowed for one program to leave data in memory for another to use at a later time. The problem was that there were no controls over how the data were to be passed from program to program or how the access or alteration of the data from one program to the other program was to be accomplished.

As more problems were defined for these systems, and as the need for persistent data storage increased, users demanded general-purpose solutions for memory and data sharing provided through an operating system's service. This memory-sharing issue was addressed by

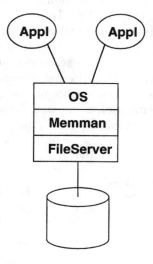

Figure 1.3   Computer storage hierarchy

the development of file managers and memory managers that could work together in accessing particular information and moving it from one place to another as desired by the programs that shared the data (Figure 1.3). In addition, by removing control of the stored data from the programmer's explicit control to the operating system's control, additional data security measures could be applied to the data's management. File servers developed access schemes to check if a program had the right to access shared data, whether the program had only read access or write access, or even if it had authority to alter the data's basic structure. Once system developers and users saw the benefit of such technology, its use expanded. Users and programmers demanded more services from the file systems. These requirements led to the development of the first database systems based on the network, or CODASYL database language. Early databases provided control over access, as well as the ability to construct and specify the database and to guarantee correct and consistent database use. These capabilities will be discussed in more detail, as the book progresses through the presentation of each main component of a database system.

1.3 WHAT IS A DATABASE?

Before we can define a database management system, we must first define the basic element of such a system: the database, or data storage repository.

A database consists of four main elements: data, relationships, constraints, and a schema (Figure 1.4). Data are a binary computer representation of stored logical entities, relationships represent a correspondence among data items, constraints are predicates that define correct database states, and a schema describes the organization of data and relationships within the database.

The schema defines various views of the database for database management system components' use and for applications' security. A schema separates the physical aspects of data storage from the logical

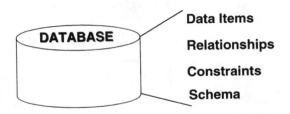

Figure 1.4   Database components

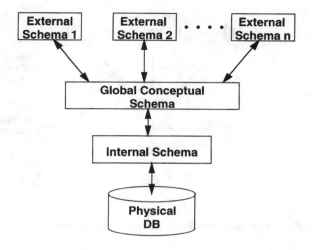

Figure 1.5 Database schema concept

aspects of data representation (Figure 1.5). The internal schema defines how and where data are organized in physical data storage. The conceptual schema model defines the stored data structures in terms of the database data model in place (e.g., the relational or object model). The external schema defines a view or views of the database for particular user(s). A data model is an abstract definition or model of the database and provides a notation for describing data.

A database management system provides services for accessing the database while maintaining the required correctness and consistency features of the stored data (Figure 1.6).

The operational unit of work in a database management system upon which consistency and correctness is defined is the transaction. A transaction is required to support the *ACID* properties. The *ACID* properties include: Atomic, Consistent, Isolation, and Durability of transaction execution. Atomicity ensures that a transaction is treated as an all-or-nothing unit of operation. Consistency of a transaction's operations ensures correctness of transformation of the database from an initial consistent state to a new consistent state, where the consistency is defined by predicates on data items defined over the database. Isolation is the property of transactions that defines what they are allowed to view. An isolated transaction sees a view of the database as if the transaction were being performed alone on the database. Finally, durability is the property of transactions that ensures that once a transaction is committed its results are permanent and cannot be removed from the database.

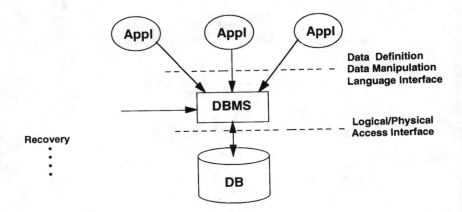

Figure 1.6   Services of a database management system

1.4 FEATURES OF DATA IN A DATABASE

The following is a list of features that data in a database are required to have.

1. *Shared*: Data in a database are shared among several users and application programs.

2. *Persistence*: Data in a database exist permanently; that is, a data item can live beyond the scope of the process that created it.

3. *Security*: Data in a database are protected from unauthorized disclosure, alteration, or destruction. The decision regarding authorization of database access is determined by a system administrator based on the usefulness and sensitivity of the data with respect to each user or group of users.

4. *Validity*: Also referred to as data *integrity* or *correctness*, data in a database should be correct with respect to the real-world entity that they represent.

5. *Consistency*: Whenever more than one data item in a database represents related real-world values, the values should be consistent with respect to the relationship.

6. *Nonredundancy*: No two data items in a database represent the same real-world entity.

7. *Independence*: The three levels in the three-schema model should be independent of each other so that changes in the schema at one level should not affect either of the other two levels. *Physical data independence* implies that the internal schema can be changed

without altering the conceptual or external schema. Therefore, programs that access the data are independent of *how* and *where* the data are stored; that is, a change in the physical storage of the database should have no effect on any application programs that access that data. *Logical data independence* indicates that modifications to the conceptual schema require no change (or possibly only a redefinition of the mapping) to the external schema. Of course, if the modification involved is a deletion of a data item (at any level), then the other levels are affected, but this can be controlled.

1.5 WHAT IS A DATABASE MANAGEMENT SYSTEM?

A database management system (DBMS), Figure 1.7, is software that provides services for accessing a database, while maintaining all of the required features of the data. The following services are provided by a database management system in support of applications' program access and manipulation of data in the database.

1. *Transaction Processing:* A *transaction* is a partially ordered sequence of *database operations* that represents a logical unit of work and that accesses a shared database. A transaction transforms the database from one consistent state to another consistent state. Database operations fall into two categories: data access operations and transaction operations. There are three specific transaction operations—*start* indicates that a new transaction is about to begin, *commit* indicates that the transaction has terminated normally and that its effects should be made permanent, and *abort* indicates that the transaction has terminated abnormally and that all of its effects should be obliterated.

   Transactions traditionally are required to have the *ACID* properties previously described.

   A *schedule* or *history* indicates the partial order in which the operations of one or more transactions are executed relative to each other.

   Transaction processing involves applying transaction operations coming from various sources (users, application programs, etc.) to the database in such a way that the above desired properties of transactions are maintained. As a part of transaction processing, access to resources such as the CPU and to data items is scheduled to meet the requirements of the transactions. The next two services in this list, concurrency control and recovery, are closely related to transaction processing because they help maintain the *ACID* properties of transactions.

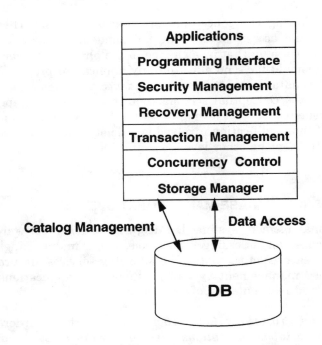

Figure 1.7   Database system's management components

2. *Concurrency Control:* Concurrency control is the database management activity of coordinating the actions of database manipulation processes that operate concurrently, access shared data, and therefore potentially interfere with each other. The goal of a concurrency control mechanism is to allow concurrency while maintaining the consistency of the shared data. The unit of concurrency in a database system is a transaction.

Varying degrees of concurrency may be allowed or required by a database system. Most techniques follow some given *correctness criterion*, which dictates the maximum amount of concurrency allowed among transactions. The amount of concurrency is defined by the degree of interleaving among concurrent transactions and the number of transactions that run concurrently. The simplest correctness criterion is *mutual exclusion,* which requires that each transaction run from start to finish without interruption from any other transaction. This execution criterion produces *serial* schedules—that is, schedules in which all operations of a transaction are executed consecutively. Many traditional concurrency control techniques use *serializability* as their correctness criterion—that is, these techniques produce serializable schedules. A schedule is serializable if it produces the same output and has the same effect on the database as a serial schedule of the same transactions. Other, less restrictive, correctness criteria have been suggested that carefully relax serializability in order to increase concurrency.

3. *Recovery:* The goal of recovery in a database is to ensure that aborted or failed transactions produce no adverse effects on the database or the other transactions. There are two effects of an aborted transaction: effects on data and effects on other transactions. The effects on the data are any changes made to the data by the transaction. Recovery makes sure that the database is returned to a consistent state after a transaction abort. One transaction may affect another transaction if the second transaction reads data that were changed by the first transaction. The database recovery mechanism ensures that these conflicting transactions view consistent data or else they are aborted. Recovery is closely related to concurrency control, because the more concurrency that is allowed, the more likely it is that an aborted transaction will affect other transactions.

4. *Security:* Security refers to the protection of data against unauthorized disclosure, alteration, or destruction. Each individual user and application program have specific data access privileges. These privileges may be defined by the external schema; that is, each user may be given a different view of the data based on the data that he or she is allowed to access and/or change. The security system provides some means of determining what view a particular user or application program may access. Security also has the function of limiting initial access to the database through the use of authorization and authentication procedures. The most common of these procedures are the login name and the password protection services, which most computer users already are familiar with.

5. *Language Interface:* The DBMS provides support for languages used for definition of data and for manipulation of data. The conceptual schema is specified in a data definition language (DDL). This component of a database language is a notation for describing the data, the relationships among the data, and the constraints on the data and relationships. The DDL is used initially when the database is designed and later to modify the schema.

The data manipulation language (DML) is used to express operations on the database. The DML is sometimes referred to as a query language. The DBMS provides the DML so that users and application programmers can access data in the database without having to know how or where the data are stored.

6. *Fault Tolerance:* The ability to remain available to provide reliable DBMS service despite faults is called *fault tolerance*. A failed database component produces a fault to other components that interact with it. Typical database faults include constraint violations and transaction timing faults. Recovery, as described above, is closely related to fault tolerance, because recovery is a mechanism that ensures that faults causing transaction aborts are tolerated.

7. *Data Catalog:* The data catalog (sometimes called the data dictionary) is a system database that contains descriptions of the data in the main database (sometimes referred to as metadata). It contains information about the data, relationships, constraints, and all of the schemata that organize these features into a unified database. The catalog is considered a database because it can be queried to get information about the structure of the main database.

8. *Storage Management:* The DBMS provides a mechanism for management of permanent storage of the data. The internal schema defines how the data should be stored by the storage management mechanism. The storage manager interfaces with the operating system in order to access physical storage.

1.6 WHY USE A DATABASE MANAGEMENT SYSTEM?

Why do applications choose to use a database and database management system? A database provides a secure and survivable medium for the storage of shared persistent data. If users have no need for data to be persistent beyond their boundaries, then a database will not provide a value-added service to such users. On the other hand, if data have a life beyond the boundaries of a program or application, then a database is an appropriate place to maintain these persistent data. But the maintenance of persistent data alone does not imply the use or need for a database management system. To determine if a database is appropriate we must also determine if the data to be managed have structure, relationships, and constraints. If the data do not have these qualities, then possibly a file system is more appropriate—for example, if we wish to store programs, these may be better held in a file system. Likewise, if we wish to keep track of the parts inventory of an automobile factory a database is very appropriate. The decision regarding a file system or database must be made based on the data to be stored and how they are to be used. Database management systems provide functions to query the database to find interrelated data items—for example, we could use the parts inventory database for the automobile factory to determine if we have all the parts needed to construct a particular car. The simplicity of the query is dependent on the database manipulation language available, the logical database structure in use, and the granularity of the data items stored.

1.7   WHERE ARE DATABASE MANAGEMENT SYSTEMS USED?

Database management systems are finding their way into a wider range of end-user applications as we become more dependent on the access and use of information in all facets of our lives. We use databases to access our bank account information, thereby increasing the availability of access to our money. We use databases to transfer funds from our bank account to our stock fund to purchase stocks. The stock traders use databases to acquire the stock for us, to sell stock, or to get information on an offered stock. Databases provide the means to perform many of the common everyday information access and manipulation operations.

Databases are being used in our educational systems for more varied purposes. Educators use databases to store libraries of information, to inquire about the information, and to retrieve the information on demand. Databases are finding their way into the early childhood educational systems, where they support the access and storage of learning tools and information to drive these tools. The data need not be stored directly at the site of use, but can be acquired on a demand basis by a database management system.

Our manufacturing businesses are relying on databases to assist in the management of a continually growing array of information. Manufacturers use databases to maintain data about products in their initial research or design phase (e.g., computer-aided design systems); to produce complete designs of a product, down to the smallest component; to maintain information about the inventory of components for manufacturing use; to collect data regarding the manufacturing, storage, ordering, and shipping of a product; and to monitor the satisfaction of the consumer. (See Figure 1.8.)

The legal system is beginning to use databases to store case histories and provide quick location and access to copious amounts of information. The database facilitates the definition of interrelations between data and the maintenance of these relationships over time, thus allowing for the retrieval of such information as needed. An example of such use includes querying the database to locate past case histories that match specific keywords or relationships defined on the stored data.

The medical and scientific community uses databases to store interrelated information about diseases and/or scientific findings so present and future researchers can quickly access this information. This

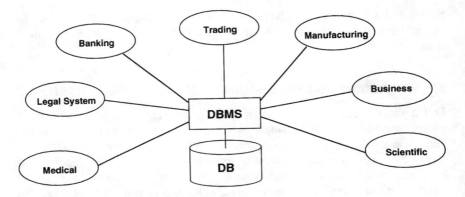

Figure 1.8   Database management system uses

has led to better, more comprehensive research about diseases and other scientific findings.

1.8 CLASSES OF COMPUTER SYSTEMS AND DATABASE SYSTEMS

Database systems do not come in one form. There are many types of databases that have been developed. We have seen distributed databases, multidatabase systems, real-time databases, fault-tolerant databases, secure databases, and federated databases. Each of these database system classes was developed for a particular purpose. Each supports the application environment it was designed for.

In the following sections we will examine each of these systems separately.

1.8.1 Distributed Database Management System

A distributed database system does not simply imply data distribution. The definition of distributed database also implies a cohesion of knowledge, actions, and control over the distributed components that make up the distributed computer system (Figure 1.9). To understand what a distributed database management system is we must first examine why distribution and control over this system is required by applications developers. Most distributed computing systems are developed to off-load and distribute the workload of an enterprise or, conversely, to move data processing functions closer to the physical site performing the function. The goal in both cases is not simply to move the data processing function or distribute its computing, but to do these in such a way that the distribution is invisible. The intent is

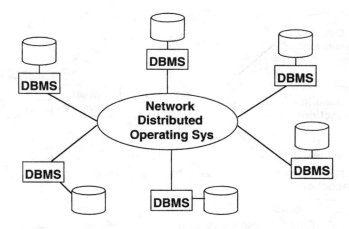

Figure 1.9   Distributed database system

still to provide the view of a single computer system to users. This means that all resource management functions must be coordinated across the sites in a seamless fashion. Chapter 10 looks at the issues involved in distributed data management that result from these requirements.

1.8.2 Real-Time Database Management System

A real-time system is not simply a fast system. Real time refers to the temporal interaction of the computing system and the real world the system is interacting with. A real-time control system can be centralized, federated, or distributed. The distinguishing feature of a real-time system is its use of time in all aspects of operations. (See Figure 1.10.)

Real-time computing systems have historically been applied to physical control applications where the computer extracts information about the physical system, computes some response (control action) based on the derived information, and performs the computed control action. All these activities are done in such a way that the input, computing, and output function responses are all predefined, have bounded response times, and are optimized in such a way that each input condition has a predictable output condition that will always occur at the same time and in the same way.

This is not to say that real-time computing is just limited to control applications. The best definition of a real-time system is defined by predictable response to real-world activities within time frames so that corrective control can be performed. The correctness of a real-

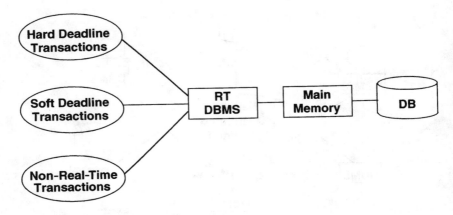

Figure 1.10   Real-time database system

time system is thus defined not just by the computed response, but by the timeliness of the response.

Chapter 11 will examine in further detail what makes up a real-time system and how databases can be constructed to provide adequate support for real-time systems information management.

1.8.3 Fault-Tolerant Database Management System

A fault-tolerant system is one that maintains some designed degree of service in the face of failure of hardware and software components. A fault-tolerant system has features similar to those of a real-time system. Fault-tolerant systems must be preanalyzed to delineate all possible failure points in the system and to design means into the system to detect, fix, and/or recover from these failures. All this should be done in a way that minimizes the impact on running applications. (See Figure 1.11.)

Fault-tolerant systems must address a variety of faults coming from numerous system elements. A fault can be generated by a hardware element, a software element, a combination of the two elements, or by an external condition applied to the system. A fault can be intermittent, transient, or permanent. The fault-tolerant system must have the capability to monitor the system, detect faults, isolate the condition causing the fault, and either fix the fault or make recommendations to a higher authority to recover the system to some acceptable state.

Chapter 14 will address fault-tolerant systems and how database management systems can be designed and constructed to support fault tolerance.

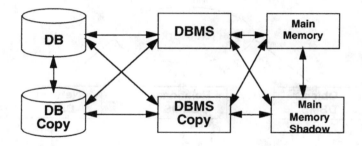

Figure 1.11   Fault-tolerant database system

1.8.4 Secure Database Management System

A secure system is one where users and applications are controlled as to what, when, and to what extent they are allowed to perform operations within the system. An example is a company's personnel system. It would be desirable to allow all users access to check on their own personnel history and to extract information pertinent to their job. It is not desirable though to allow them to access other employees' personnel history or possibly even some of their own. To deliver such service a database system must build in capabilities to define access rights and to check these rights against the users trying to access data. This is just a very simple example of security. (See Figure 1.12.)

Security can go way beyond this simple access authorization level and begin to get into detailed security checks. We may wish to limit the ability of users to be able to *infer* some further piece of information by the simple access to uncorrelated data searches. Or we may need to provide detailed control over access to subparts of data or relationships between data. Chapter 13 will examine issues in database security ranging from simple login control and access authorization up to multilevel secure systems.

1.8.5 Heterogeneous Database Management System

A heterogeneous system is one composed of numerous unique subsystems (Figure 1.13). For example, each department of a company has

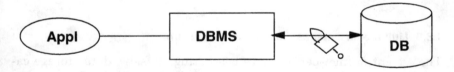

Figure 1.12   Secure database system

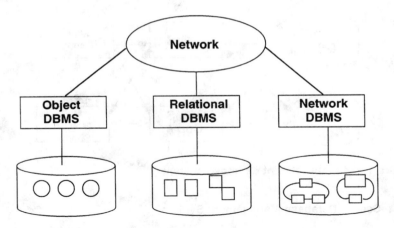

Figure 1.13   Heterogeneous database management system

its own data processing needs. The personnel department has one set of needs, engineering another set of needs, and manufacturing yet another. Each of these separate departments may go out and acquire its own unique computer system with unique hardware and software. If there is a need for these unique systems to interact and we manage to link them via some communications medium, we now have a heterogeneous system. Such systems have unique problems to solve. A basic problem concerns the lowest hardware data representation. If one computer uses 8-bit words, another 16-bit words, and yet another 32-bit words, how do we rectify the differences so that these systems can exchange useful data?

Heterogeneous database systems have evolved due to the example discussed previously. Databases were purchased, they were populated with a company's departmental data, and numerous applications were written using this stored shared data. When these databases were then required to share their data with other departments, we found a problem. Heterogeneous database systems are being developed to solve some of these legacy database problems. Chapter 12 will examine in further detail the problems with heterogeneous database systems and some solutions for integrating and making these databases interoperable.

1.8.6 Multimedia Database Management System

The advent of high-performance computing, massive data storage capabilities, and the promise of the national information infrastructure (the information highway) has and will facilitate the use and growth

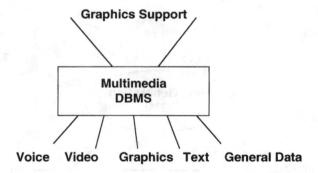

Figure 1.14 Multimedia database system

of multimedia computing systems that will require multimedia database management systems. Multimedia computing systems use and intermix a variety of data sources, such as graphics, video images, voice, sounds, and text, into a growing array of applications and products. These complex data sources must be readily accessible to the computing system and presented in such a way that facilitates its interleaved use. A multimedia computing system will require the information access and presentations to be synchronized and accessed for real-time support of possible interactive user applications. (See Figure 1.14.)

A multimedia database management system will combine the requirements of a real-time database with those of interactive graphics systems. Chapter 15 will further define what a multimedia computing system is, what it can be used for, and what comprises the structure, design, and operations of a multimedia database management system.

1.8.7 The Future of Database Management

As the need for information has grown, so has the role of database systems. Database systems have evolved to fill the needs of shared information users. Future database systems will do the same. Databases and database management systems are finding their way into previously unthought of application domains. Database systems are being used for medical monitoring, medical diagnostics, medical research, computer-aided design, computer-aided engineering, computer-aided manufacturing, power management, library management, information dissemination, avionics systems, space systems, defense-oriented systems, automobiles, navigation, weather forecasting, transportation reservations, hotel reservations, and in many other fields. (See Figure 1.15.)

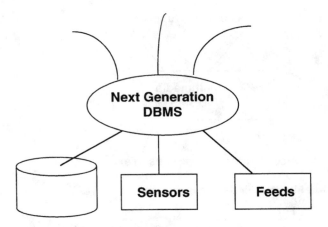

Figure 1.15   Next-generation database systems

As more information goes on line and more users wish to access such information, new database management systems geared toward application support will be developed and produced. Chapter 16 will examine the trends in database systems research and development, looking at the future of this technology.

1.9 OVERVIEW OF THE TEXT

The text is broken into five main parts. Each of these focuses on some aspect of database systems technology or application. This first part introduces the basic concepts and technology required to understand what a database is, what a database management system is, how it operates, and how it is used in the management of shared information resources.

The second part examines the database structural models used to describe how data are stored in the database. These models express the means through which data items are related to each other and how these related data items are organized in the database. The four major database structuring models are addressed: relational, network, object, and functional (entity-relationship) data models.

The third part examines the variety of database management systems available. Each major class of database management systems was constructed to meet the needs of a specific application domain. In this part we review the features, technology, and architectures for each major class of database management system. These classes include distributed databases, real-time databases, heterogeneous databases, secure databases, fault-tolerant databases, multimedia databases, database machines, and advanced databases.

The fourth part of the text covers database management system standards. Standards play an important role in the database management marketplace, as both a means to provide products that easily can be integrated into a client's computer system and for the interoperability of the database with other database management systems. This part of the text looks at where standards for databases are coming from, what standards exist for database management systems, where standardization efforts are headed in the future, and what products exist that have been constructed to the standards.

The fifth part of the text looks to the future. Given what has happened in the past and what is occurring now in computer technology and the evolving national information infrastructure, we examine where database systems are heading.

2

Computer Data Processing Hardware Architecture

Paul Fortier

This chapter defines the hardware components used in computer and database management systems. Included here are the fundamental composition of computers (CPU, memory, I/O), secondary storage devices, other peripheral input and output devices, and networks. Our discussions are tailored to focus on the architecture and use of these components as they relate to computer management of persistent data.

2.1 INTRODUCTION

A database system resides on a computer system. The computer system provides the physical medium upon which the data are stored and the processing capacity to manipulate stored data. A processing unit of a computer system consists of five main elements: the memory, an arithmetic logic unit, an input unit, an output unit, and a control element. The memory unit stores both the data for programs and the instructions of a program that manipulates stored data.

The program's individual elements or instructions are fetched from the memory one at a time and are interpreted by the control unit. The control unit, depending on the interpretation of the instruction, determines what computer operation to perform next. If the instruction requires no additional data, the control indicates to the arithmetic

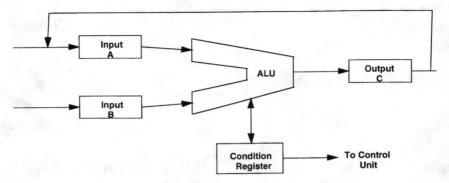

Figure 2.1   Arithmetic logic unit control and operations

logic unit what operation to perform and with what registers. (See Figure 2.1.)

If the instruction requires additional data, the control unit passes the appropriate command to the memory (MAR, memory address register) to fetch a data item from memory (MDR, memory data register) and to place it in an appropriate register in the ALU (data register bank) (Figure 2.2). This continues until all required operands are in the appropriate registers of the ALU. Once all operands are in place the control unit commands the ALU to perform the appropriate instruction—for example, multiplication, addition, or subtraction. If the instruction indicated an input or output were required, the control element would transmit a word from the input unit to the memory or ALU, depending on the instruction. If an output instruction were decoded, the control unit would command the transmission of the appropriate memory word or register to the output channel indicated. These

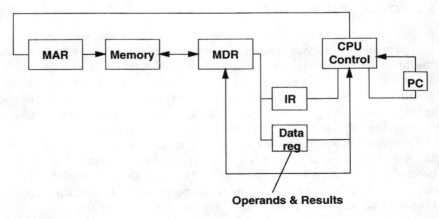

Figure 2.2   Control, instruction, and data access

five elements comprise the fundamental building blocks used in the original von Neumann computer system and which are found in most contemporary systems in some form or another.

In this chapter we will examine these fundamental building blocks and see how they are used to form a variety of computer architectures.

2.2 COMPUTER HARDWARE ARCHITECTURE

A computer system is comprised of the five building blocks described in the introduction and additional peripheral support devices, which aid in data movement and processing. These basic building blocks are used to form the general processing, control, storage, and input and output units that make up modern computer systems. Devices typically are organized in a fashion that supports the application processing for which the computer system is intended—for example, if massive amounts of data need to be stored, then additional peripheral storage devices such as disks or tape units are required along with their required controllers or data channels.

A computer system's architecture is constructed using basic building blocks, such as CPUs, memories, disks, I/O, and other devices as needed. To better describe the variations within architectures we will discuss some details briefly—for example, the arithmetic logic unit and the control unit are merged together into a central processing unit or CPU. The CPU controls the flow of instructions and data in the computer system. Memories can be broken down into hierarchies based on nearness to the CPU and speed of access—for example, cache memory is small, extremely fast memory used for instructions and data actively executing and being used by the CPU. The primary memory is slower, but it is also cheaper and contains much more memory locations. It is used to store data and instructions that will be used during the execution of applications presently running on the CPU—for example, if you boot up your word processing program on your personal computer, the operating system will attempt to place the entire word processing program in primary memory. If there is insufficient space the operating system will partition the program into segments and pull them in as needed. The portion of the program that cannot be stored in memory is maintained on a secondary storage device, typically a disk drive. This device has a much greater storage capacity than the primary memory, typically costs much less per unit of storage, and has data access times that are much slower than the primary memory. An additional secondary storage device is the tape drive unit. A tape drive is a simple storage device that can store massive amounts of data—again, at less cost than the disk units, but at a reduced access speed. Other components of a computer system are input and output units. These are used to extract data from the computer and provide them to external devices or to input data from the external device. The external devices could be end-user terminals, sensors, information network ports, video, voice, or other computers.

In the following sections we will examine each of the components of a computer system in more detail, as we examine how these devices can be interconnected to support data processing applications.

2.3 CPU ARCHITECTURES

The Central Processing Unit (CPU) is the brains of a computer system. The CPU consists of the arithmetic logic unit and the control unit, as indicated previously. The ALU can come in a variety of configurations—from a single simple unit, shown in Figure 2.1, that performs simple adds, subtracts, increments, decrements, load, and store, up to extremely complex units that perform operations such as multiply, divide, exponentiation, sine, cosine, and so on. The primary operation of the ALU is to take zero or more operands and perform the function called for in the instruction. In addition to the ALU the CPU consists of a set of registers to store operands and intermediate results and to maintain information used by the CPU to determine the state of its computations. There are registers for the status of the ALU's operation, for keeping count of the instruction to be performed next, to keep data flowing in from memory or out to memory, to maintain the instruction being executed, and for the location of operands being operated on by the CPU.

These registers each have a unique function within the CPU, and each is necessary for various classes of computer architectures. A typical minimal architecture for a CPU and its registers is shown in Figure 2.3. This architecture consists of a primary memory connected to the CPU via buses that use a memory address register and memory data register to address a location in memory and transfer the contents of the location from the memory into the memory data register. There are registers in the CPU for instructions (the instruction or IR register), for instruction operands (the A and B registers), for results of operations (the C and D registers), a location counter (which contains either the location in memory for instructions or operands depending on the decoding of instructions), and a program counter (which maintains the location of the next instruction to perform). The CPU also contains the control unit. The control unit uses the status registers and instructions in the instruction register to determine what functions the CPU must perform on the registers, ALU, and data paths that make up the CPU.

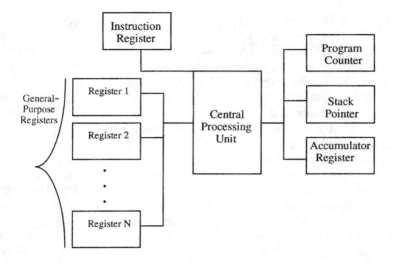

Figure 2.3   Central processing unit register configuration

The basic operation of the CPU follows a simple loop (unless interrupts occur that alter the flow of execution). This loop is called the instruction execution cycle (Figure 2.4). There are six basic functions performed in the instruction loop: instruction fetch, instruction decode, operand effective address calculation, operand fetch, operation execution, and next address calculation.

Instruction fetch uses the instruction pointer register to point to the next instruction stored in memory to acquire. The address is placed in the memory address register and the instruction is then gated (electronically signaled by the CPU control element to transfer the data) from the data memory into the memory data register. The instruction then flows into the instruction register under the direction of the control unit.

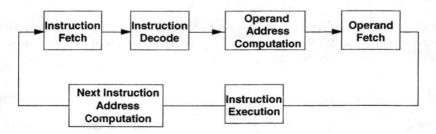

Figure 2.4   Instruction execution cycle

Once an instruction is in the instruction register the second cycle in instruction execution can be performed—decode. To decode the instruction the control unit must recognize what type of instruction is being requested—for example, does the instruction require additional data from memory to perform its intended function, or does the instruction involve only ALU resident registers. Once the type and number of operands is determined the ALU can acquire the operands and is then set up to perform the decoded instruction.

The third cycle within instruction execution is the operand effective address calculation. This phase of instruction execution operates by extracting operand address information from the instruction then performing some form of calculation (e.g., base plus offset) with this information to form a physical address in memory. We will discuss the various types of addressing in later sections of this chapter.

Once we have a physical address, we can fetch the operand (the fourth function of the instruction execution cycle). To fetch the operand the effective address is placed in the memory address register, and the control gates the contents pointed to by the memory address register into the memory data register. The extracted operand is then gated from the memory data register into an ALU register. If an additional operand is needed, the two cycle steps for operand fetch would be repeated to get the remaining operand.

With all required operands in ALU registers the instruction requested can now be performed. The instruction execution is controlled by the CPU control unit. The control unit signals to the ALU to perform the instruction—for example, if an add is requested the ALU would add the A and B registers and place the result in the C register. After the instruction is completed the last step in the instruction execution cycle can proceed.

The next address calculation uses the instruction pointer and/or any pertinent computation result (such as a go to–type instruction) to determine where in the memory the next instruction is to be found. The normal mode of address calculation is to increment the contents of the instruction pointer. With the new address the instruction cycle begins once more.

This execution sequence represents the basic functions found in all computer systems. Variations in the number of steps are found based on the type and length of the instruction.

2.3.1 Instruction Types

Based on the number of registers available and the configuration of these registers a variety of instruction types are possible—for example, if many registers are available, as would be the case in a stack computer, no address computations are needed and the instruction therefore can be much shorter both in format and execution time required. On the other hand, if there are no general registers and all computations are performed by memory movements of data, then instructions will be longer and require more time due to operand fetching and storage. The following are representative of instruction types.

0-address instructions—This type of instruction is found in machines where many general-purpose registers are available. This is the case in stack machines and in some reduced instruction set machines. Instructions of this type perform their function totally using registers. Given that we have three general registers, A, B, and C, a typical format would have the form:

```
R[A] --> R[B] operator R[C]
```

which indicates that the contents of registers B and C have the operator (such as add, subtract, multiply, etc.) performed on them, with the result stored in general register C. Similarly we could describe instructions that use just one or two registers as follows:

```
R[B] --> R[B] operator R[C]
```

or

```
operator R[C]
```

which represent two-register and one-register instructions, respectively. In the two-register case one of the operand registers is also used as the result register. In the single-register case the operand register is also the result register. The increment instruction is an example of one-register instruction. This type of instruction is found in all machines.

1-address instructions—In this type of instruction a single memory address is found in the instruction. If another operand is used it is typically an accumulator or the top of a stack in a stack computer. The typical format of these instructions has the form:

```
operator M[address]
```

where the contents of the named memory address have the named operator performed on them in conjunction with an implied special register. An example of such an instruction could be:

```
Move M[100]
```

or

```
Add M[100]
```

which moves the contents of memory location 100 into the ALU's accumulator or adds the contents of memory address 100 with the accumulator and stores the result in the accumulator. If the result must be stored in memory, we would need a store instruction:

```
Store M[100].
```

1-and-1/2-address instructions—Once we have an architecture that has some general-purpose registers we can provide more advanced operations combining memory contents and the general registers. The typical instruction performs an operation on a memory location's contents with that of a general register—for example, we could add the contents of a memory location with the contents of a general register A as shown:

```
Add R[A], M[100].
```

This instruction typically stores the result in the first named location or register in the instruction. In this example it is register A.

2-address instructions—Two address instructions utilize two memory locations to perform an instruction—for example, a block move of N words from one location in memory to another, or a block add. The move may look like:

```
Move N, M[100], M[1000].
```

2-and-1/2-address instructions—This format uses two memory locations and a general register in the instruction. Typical of this type of instruction is an operation involving two memory locations storing the result in a register, or an operation with a general register and a memory location storing the result on another memory location as shown:

```
R[A] --> M[100] operator M[1000]

M[1000] --> M[100] operator R[A].
```

3-address instructions—Another less common form of instruction format is the three-address instruction. These instructions involve three memory locations—two used for operands and one as the results location. A typical format is shown:

```
M[200] --> M[100] operator M[300].
```

2.3.2 Instruction Architectures

There are numerous ideas on how to organize computer systems around the instruction set. One form, which has come of age with the new powerful workstations, is the reduced instruction set architecture. These machines typically have a small number of instructions that are simple and that take a relatively short equal number of clock cycles per instruction. Each of the instructions is highly optimized and operates efficiently. Machine-coded programs are typically longer, but the actual code may run faster due to the highly optimized and regular code.

On the other side of the spectrum are architectures built around complex instructions. These computers are referred to as complex instruction set computers, or CISC. These machines use instructions that each perform some complex function—for example, a matrix multiply or a complex number manipulation trigonometric function. Each instruction may take numerous machine cycles to perform and may itself be coded in lower-level microcode. Programs written in this type of architecture may be shorter, but may not take any less time and in some cases even take more time due to their complexity.

2.3.3 Memory-Addressing Schemes

Just as there are a variety of instruction formats, there are also numerous ways in which to determine the address of an operand from an instruction. Each form of address computation has its benefits in terms of instruction design flexibility. There are six major types of addressing computation schemes found in computers: immediate, direct, index, base, indirect, and two-operand. We will briefly examine these.

Immediate—Immediate addressing is not really an addressing mode into memory; rather, it is an instruction format that directly includes the data to be acted on as part of the instruction. This form of operand access simplifies the instruction execution cycle since no fetches are required.

Direct—For direct addressing there is no operand address decoding required. The instruction operand address field contains the physical address of the operand. The control simply places the operand address field into the memory address field and the operand is fetched from memory.

Index—A refinement of direct addressing is indexed addressing. In this form of operand address decoding the operand address field is added to the contents of a designated register to compute the effective physical address.

Base—Base addressing expands on this concept further. A base register contains an address base, which is added to the indexed address to form an effective physical address. This scheme is used in computer systems for addressing and partitioning the memory into *segments*. When more than one base register is available in an architecture we can more easily manage partitioned memory for multiple users and systems control software.

Indirect—For this address computation scheme we use the contents of a specified memory location as the effective address. The control fetches the contents of the named memory location and uses this as the memory address register pointer to extract the actual operand.

Two-Operand Addressing—In two-operand addressing any combination of the above schemes could be used together to access multiple operands for an instruction.

2.3.4 Memory Architectures

Memory storage can also have an architecture (configuration) that can aid in the storing and fetching of memory contents. Generally a memory is organized as a regular structure that can be addressed using the memory address register and have data transferred through the memory data register (Figure 2.5). The memory is accessed through the combination of addressing and either drivers or sensors to write or read data from or to the memory data register. Memory structures are built based on the organization of the memory words. The simplest form is a linear two-dimensional structure. Each memory location has a unique word line, which, when energized, gates the N-bit lines' (where N is the size of a data word in the computer) contents into the memory data register.

A second organization is the two-and-a-half-dimension architecture. In this memory structure the memory words are broken up into sepa-

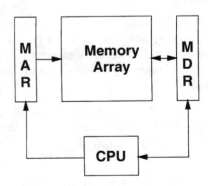

Figure 2.5 Memory access architecture

rate data planes, each consisting of one bit for all memory locations. To access a word the n planes must be energized with the composite X and Y coordinates, which correspond to the wanted memory word. The individual plane drivers gate the proper bit into the memory data register for the addressed memory word. Other data organizations have been derived and we leave it to the interested reader to investigate these.

2.4 I/O ARCHITECTURES

Input and output mechanisms are used by computer systems to move information into or out of the computer's main memory. A typical sequence for performing this movement of information from or to an input and output device is:

1. Select an I/O device

2. Busy Wait until the device is ready

3. Transfer a word from the device I/O buffer into the CPU accumulator

4. Transfer the contents of the accumulator into a memory location

5. Compute the next memory location for I/O data

6. Go back to step 2 and repeat until all data are transferred

The above sequence assumes that all data must pass through the CPU to control the flow. If instead we have the ability to place or extract data directly to or from memory without passing through the CPU, we can get further improvements in performance and a refined architecture. To allow for the CPU to be taken out of the I/O loop we need an additional control element. For I/O to be controlled directly and bypass the CPU en route to memory requires added control; this controller is referred to as a direct memory access (DMA) device. The DMA device allows us to alter what the CPU must do. The CPU issues a begin I/O command to the DMA control unit with the address of the data block to be transferred. The CPU is now free from added input and output overhead and can be relieved to do some other processing or simply wait until the DMA responds that the transfer is complete. To effectively provide this function an added feature is required of the CPU: an interrupt capability. The interrupts can be of several types.

Interrupts can be immediate, causing the CPU to halt and service the interrupt.

Interrupts can be deferred, allowing the CPU to service them when it is ready.

Interrupts can be prioritized, allowing for prompt service to critical actions occurring in the system.

2.5 SECONDARY STORAGE AND PERIPHERAL DEVICES ARCHITECTURES

Memory storage volume is always looked at as an important feature when one looks at acquiring a computer system. Whether the system is a desktop personal computer, a workstation, or a large special-purpose processor, data storage has always been a major selling point and a requested feature. As the price of memory has come down, the size of memory purchased for all classes of computers has gone up. One nonchanging feature is the general structure of the memory hierarchy. No matter how sophisticated or how simple the systems are, we will find that they all have something in common. The designers of the systems have organized data storage to maximize performance and provide adequate information volume storage.

The storage hierarchy (Figure 2.6) consists of a variety of data storage types that respond to the information needs of the system. From the highest-speed element (a cache) to the slowest-speed elements (archival devices), the tradeoff is the cost and speed of the storage me-

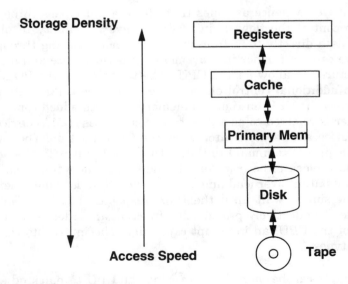

Figure 2.6   The storage hierarchy

dium per unit of memory. What is being attempted is to match the speed of the computer processor with the highest-speed devices within a reasonable cost curve. In the following sections we will examine the information storage devices outside of the central processing unit realm. This leaves out the high-speed expensive cache memories and primary memory. We will begin our review by looking at tape devices, magnetic disks, and archival devices.

2.6 TAPE STORAGE DEVICES

Magnetic tape information storage provides a low-cost, high-density storage medium for low-access or slow-access data. A tape unit consists of the storage medium (a spool of magnetic material formed into a tape), access electronics, and mechanical components (see Figure 2.7). A tape unit operates in a simple fashion. Data on a tape can only be accessed in sequential form. Data must be located on the tape and then removed from the tape. A tape drive mechanically can rewind a tape, sequentially search the tape, and stop the tape. To access data stored on a tape an I/O program would have to command the tape unit to rewind the tape and then sequentially search the tape from the beginning until a match is found. Once found the addressed data can be removed. To improve the performance of tape units additional storage semantic access schemes have been devised. The beginning of the tape is reserved to maintain pointers to the start points of files stored on the tape. Instead of sequentially searching the entire tape the controller searches the tape's directory, finds out where on the tape (e.g., how many feet from the directory region) the data are stored, and then uses this information to fast forward to the general location where linear search can resume. This allows for a speedup in the ac-

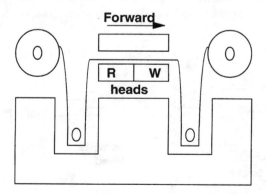

Figure 2.7   Tape storage device

cess and transfer of the data stored on the device—an important feature when a database management system is involved.

2.7 MAGNETIC AND OPTICAL DISK STORAGE DEVICES

An improvement over tape storage is the random access disk units, which most users of computers are aware of. The disks can be of the removable or internal fixed forms. A disk unit is typically comprised of one or more of the following: a controller, a movable access arm, and a magnetic storage medium in the form of a rotating platter (see Figure 2.8). The platter(s) is mounted on a spindle, which rotates at some given speed. The platter is organized into a set of rings called tracks and a partitioning of these tracks called sectors. The movable arm contains the sensing and driving hardware to allow for the reading and writing of the magnetic data stored on the platter. The controller orchestrates the access of the stored data based on a variety of access algorithms, only the simplest of which we will discuss here. The simplest form of disk access is that found in the sequential search paradigm. The disk controller knows on what sector and track a data file is stored and using this information the disk controller must perform some simple functions, such as moving the access arm out to the track the data are stored on (this is called seeking and the time it takes is called the seek time).

Once on the proper track the controller must find the proper sector that the data are stored on. This requires the controller to recognize the start of the sector markers on the track and to find the appropriate sector as it passes under the access arm's sensors. The time required for this is called the rotation time. Once the arm is over the proper sector and track the data can be transferred from the medium to the controller. This time is called the transfer time.

So for the average access of a data file on a disk we must take the following time:

$$T = t_{seek} + t_{search} + t_{transfer}$$

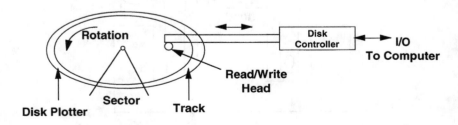

Figure 2.8   Disk storage device

One can readily see from this that the time to access data on a disk unit is greater than that of the primary memory and would typically be less than the time to extract a similar amount of data from a tape unit.

The density of the disk is based on the medium used to store the data. Disk units built on a magnetic medium are getting fairly dense, but they are approaching their limits. In addition the medium is susceptible to failures due to airborne pollutants and magnetic fields. To improve this the industry has developed optical disk technology. This technology replaces the magnetic medium with an optical medium where data are stored as reflective optical media. The medium is similar to what is seen in television optical disk players. The advantage of these devices is their higher density and faster transfer speeds. A drawback, which is being addressed, is their read-only capability. New devices will emerge that have both the read and write capability.

2.8 ARCHIVAL STORAGE DEVICES

Even with all of the disk and tape technology available, not all wanted or required data for a computer system can be kept on line. To keep data that are only occasionally needed we require archival storage devices. Archival storage devices typically have removable media. If you have access to the new multimedia systems or have a personal computer or workstation for use, you have interacted with a form of archival device: the removable disk or tape cartridge. This represents the most visible form of archival storage device. Data are loaded into the system as needed and removed when completed. Other more elaborate archival systems have been developed that use a combination of mechanical and electrical systems to port media on line and off line. These are similar to compact disk magazines and resemble jukeboxes. When a particular data item is needed, its physical storage location is found, and the medium is placed into the active storage hierarchy on line where the archived data can now be accessed. Again, this is a useful feature when we are talking about a very large database.

2.9 NETWORK ARCHITECTURES

Not all systems consist of one computer. Modern systems used in academia, business, and government are more frequently being interconnected to form information-sharing systems. These networks are constructed by providing yet another input and output path for the computer to receive or send information. The input and output unit and controller for the network peripheral device is called a network interface unit, or NIU. The function of these interface units is to provide a seamless (typically) way for one computer to interact with another as if they were located in the same machine. Networks come in a variety of configurations—for example, the NIUs can be configured as a single global bus topology, as a central star or hub topology, as a ring topology, or as some hybrid. When interconnected in such ways over a relatively small distance (a single floor, building, or small organization), we have what is referred to as a local area network, or LAN. A LAN is used to interconnect a subunit of some larger organization or to interconnect a small number of users who need to share information. Beyond a LAN we have the emerging national information infrastructure and its national networks.

2.9.1 Computer to Network Interface Elements

The network can be formed in many ways: It could have a central switching element, which could be a stand-alone computer acting as a router (see Figure 2.9a); it could share a central storage repository (see Figure 2.9b); or it could be connected using intelligent interface units into a communications medium. The configuration used depends on the degree of synchronization and control required, as well as the distribution between computers.

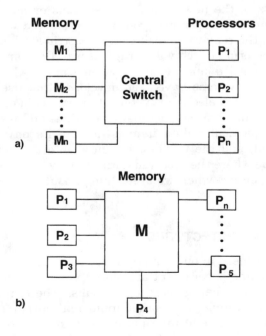

Figure 2.9   Network architectures

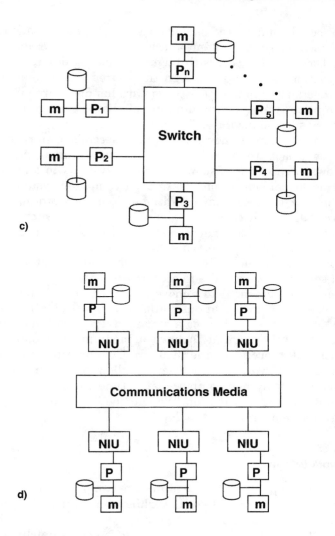

Figure 2.9 *(continued)*

The tightly coupled multiprocessor uses a shared central memory as the interconnection device. All processors on the network use the central memory to access and pass data among the interconnected processors. This distributed architecture provides an easy means to coordinate actions between processors. A distinction is that each processor does not have any local memory; all instructions and data are acquired from the shared memory bank. An improvement over this architecture is the loosely coupled multiprocessor (see Figure 2.9b). In this architecture each processor has some primary local memory and is interconnected via a shared secondary storage system. Each processor has its own operating system and local storage for programs and local data. Coordination occurs through the passing of data from one computer system to another through the shared storage device. The data exchange and signaling of transfers are handled through mechanisms such as messages or coordination of shared storage regions in the secondary storage medium.

A further refinement removes the shared secondary storage device and replaces this with a communications switching element. The switch allows each of the disjoint computer systems to address and send information among themselves. Each computer system has its own local memory and can have additional secondary storage devices (see Figure 2.9c). Each computer communicates with interconnected systems by addressing the called system, forming a connection, and then initiating a conversation. This is analogous to how we converse over a phone system. The switching-based distributed system requires additional software at each site to coordinate access.

A further enhancement is to remove the central switch and replace it with a shared communications path (see Figure 2.9d). The path could be a shared bus, a ring, or a star medium. The interconnected computers are each required to have a medium interconnect unit, which controls the access to the medium. This architecture requires further control software and policies to allow for control over the shared medium. Only one computer at a time can be accessing the medium and sending information. We will see in subsequent sections how this software operates.

2.9.2 Network Bridges

We can further expand on the local area network or multiprocessing systems by introducing another networking control unit. To interconnect multiple networks or multiprocessing systems requires a bridge. (See Figure 2.10.) A bridge can be viewed as a speed-matching device to synchronize the traffic between networks. Bridges typically contain software and hardware to buffer incoming messages, to determine and rectify variances in addresses on interconnected networks, and to forward messages to the addressed unit.

2.10 NETWORK TOPOLOGIES

As mentioned earlier there are a variety of interconnection topologies used in local area networks. They are the global bus, the ring, and the star topologies.

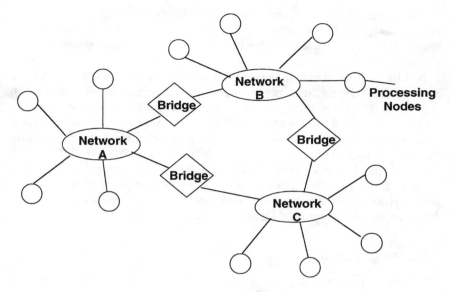

Figure 2.10 Bridges interconnect multiple networks

2.10.1 Bus Topology

A global bus is a single shared medium, which can only be used by one device at a time. The global bus is controlled by a variety of schemes. One of the simplest is the carrier sense multiple access scheme. This protocol works by using two principles: first, the delay taken to send a bit from one end of the bus to the other and second, the ability to send and then listen to the medium. The protocol in its simplest form operates as follows.

- Listen to the bus—if busy wait, if clear send data.
- Once data have been sent continue to listen and compare what is heard against what was sent.
- If what was sent matches what is heard for the entire end-to-end communications time, then I control the bus and can continue sending a message (the assumption here is that if I wait an end-to-end transfer time then all other nodes must have heard my message and will now delay if they wish to transmit).
- When complete go back into listen mode.
- If I do not hear the same message that I sent, then a collision occurred on the bus. I immediately stop transmission and delay before trying to send again.

Using this simple protocol devices on the network can send and receive messages fairly efficiently. The problem with this protocol is that it inherently wastes media bandwidth in the sending and sensing process.

A different approach to control access to a global bus is based on a reservation scheme. In a reservation scheme the available bandwidth is broken up into chunks, which are then allocated to various devices on the network. To access the medium to transmit data a device must first wait until its reservation slot becomes available. There are numerous schemes through which the slots can be allocated and controlled. The problem with this approach is that it is inherently static. The slots cannot be reallocated easily from one system to another. Numerous variations on this protocol have been developed and implemented in systems with varying degrees of success.

2.10.2 Ring Topology

The ring topology links the computer systems in the network in a continuous ring. Messages flow around the network from one computer system to another until they return to the sender. (See Figure 2.11.) This topology allows for better utilization of the medium. The medium can be broken into slots that flow around the network. The

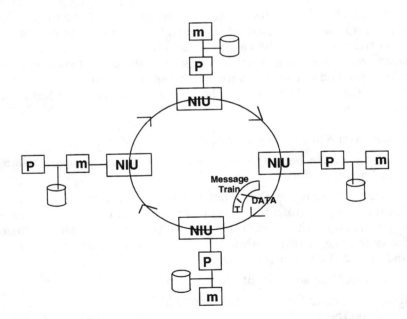

Figure 2.11   Ring topology

slots are marked as either empty or full depending on whether or not a message is present in the slot. To send a message a computer senses the slot beginning and checks whether it is full or empty. If the slot is full the sender waits for the next slot. If the slot is empty the sender inserts its message. The problem with this scheme is that the slot size limits the size of messages that can be sent in a single slot. Variations on this protocol have alleviated this problem, but have their own set of problems. A different protocol that allows for variable size messages is the insertion ring protocol. This protocol requires hardware support to buffer incoming messages that would interfere with a sender's message. A computer that wants to send a message on the network can simply send the message if no other message traffic is sensed by the sender. If another message should then arrive at the sender's input during the transmission of its own message, the sender simply queues up the arriving message and appends it to the sending message when it has completed.

2.11 COMPUTER ARCHITECTURES

To continue our earlier discussion of computer configurations we will examine how the various components can be interconnected to form a computer system. The basic premise of these architectures is to speed up the movement of data to allow for increased processing. The basic architecture has the CPU at the core with a main memory and input/output system on either side of the CPU (see Figure 2.12). In this architecture all data flow into, out of, and through the CPU under the control of the CPU. This represents the basic von Neumann architecture described earlier. Refinements of this architecture have been designed to remove the CPU from the burden of controlling all data movement.

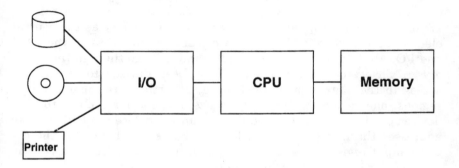

Figure 2.12   Central CPU architecture

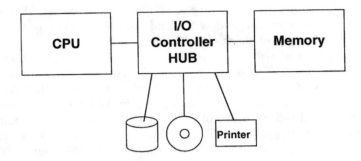

Figure 2.13   Central IOC architecture

2.11.1 Central IOC Architectures

To remove the CPU from the central function of coordinating all data flow the central input/output controller architecture was developed (see Figure 2.13). This architecture has the IOC at the core of the system with the CPU, main memory, and I/O devices connected to the IOC hub. To transfer data from the main memory to an I/O device the CPU would command the IOC to initiate the transfer. The data would flow under control of the IOC from the main memory through the IOC to the named output device. The problem with this architecture is that the CPU must also use the IOC to transfer data from the main memory to the CPU. This results in potential reduction in CPU performance. Variations of this architecture have a secondary path to the main memory for better service to the CPU.

2.11.2 Memory-Mapped Architectures

The main memory is the location in the computer system where all data and instructions flow in and out. As a consequence of this an architecture was proposed that had the main memory as the central element (see Figure 2.14). The main memory sits between the CPU and I/O. All data flow between the I/O and CPU go through the memory. A variety of control schemes have been devised to control the access to the shared memory. One is to partition the memory into regions: one region for the CPU to use and one for each of the I/O devices on the system. To send data to an I/O device the CPU simply addresses the memory location for the device. By doing this the device's input register is directly loaded with the data. To the CPU the I/O transfer is the same as a write to main memory.

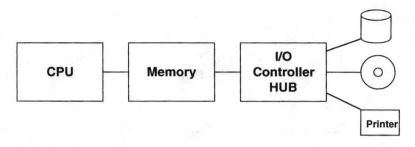

Figure 2.14   Central memory architecture

2.11.3 Common Bus Architecture

An architecture that is similar to the global network architecture previously described is the unibus architecture. The unibus or global bus architecture uses a single communications bus to interconnect memory, CPU, and I/O devices (see Figure 2.15). These elements are connected to the bus and communicate with each other using addresses over the bus. As in the network case this design will result in reduced utilization if conflicts between bus access are frequent. This architecture was successfully used in numerous early digital equipment computers and still is in use in many systems.

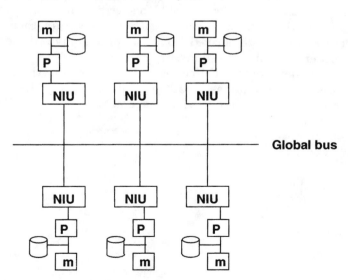

Figure 2.15   Central bus architecture

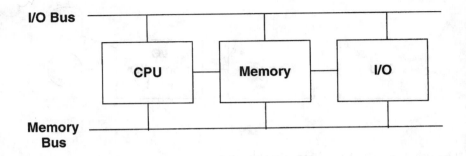

Figure 2.16 Dual bus architecture

2.11.4 Dual Bus Architecture

A refinement on the single bus architecture is the dual bus architecture (Figure 2.16). In this architecture the central hub of the computer is a dual bus configuration: one bus for memory traffic and one for I/O traffic. All devices, CPU, main memory, disks, tapes, terminals, and direct memory access devices are connected to both buses. This architecture removed some of the contention between the CPU memory accesses and I/O transfers. The CPU and memory were free to actively move data to and from memory, as were the I/O devices, without conflict. An I/O device could be writing into one region of memory while the CPU was concurrently accessing another section. Architectures that have derived from this philosophy are more common in modern computer systems.

We will see how these architectures and elements of the computer system are used by database management systems as we continue with our discussion of database management system architectures and operations.

3

Computer Systems Support Software Architecture

Paul Fortier

3.1 INTRODUCTION

A database management system requires services and cooperative support from computer hardware and software to perform its designated function. The database management system requires a computational platform consisting of a CPU, memory, and secondary data storage and a supporting operational infrastructure consisting of an operating system, network management, and additional process and resource management components. To understand how a database utilizes these components we must first understand the operation of these software infrastructure elements.

The central processing unit (CPU) and the main memory make up the basic computational engine for the database management system and support the execution of all software within this computer. The CPU is composed of a collection of registers, computational subunits, data paths, and status registers that are used to move data about and to perform basic manipulations on these data (Figure 3.1). For example, a CPU can add, subtract, multiply, divide, and compare values or simply move them from one location to another. These are basic operations, which the remainder of the system's infrastructure is built upon and where it resides. The CPU also includes some additional support hardware, such as timers, interrupt registers and latches, in-

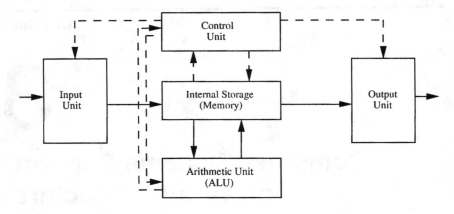

Figure 3.1   Central processing unit (CPU)

put and output registers, and interconnections. For additional details on these elements refer to Chapter 2.

In addition to the CPU the other primary element within the basic system is the memory. A memory hierarchy is typically comprised of high-speed data registers, fast cache memory, primary memory, and secondary storage (Figure 3.2). The memory hierarchy at the closest point to the CPU hardware is populated with very expensive and limited high-speed registers. These registers are used to move a very limited number of data items into and out of the CPU for actual processing. The second level of the hierarchy is the cache memory. A cache memory is a bank of high-speed memory organized in a fashion that allows for rapid retrieval of data; it executes at nearly the speed of on-chip or CPU registers. A cache memory is used to keep data most likely to be used next in close proximity to the CPU and in fast storage. The problem with cache memory and registers is that they are very expensive, thereby limiting the amount of either that may be found in an architecture. This type of storage hardware requires additional infrastructure support from the operating system and hardware to maintain the most appropriate piece of data in the most appropriate level of the hierarchy.

This control has typically been performed by a memory management hardware and software combination that uses locality of reference and locality of use principles to determine what information to place into the appropriate level and what information to remove.

The third element of the memory hierarchy is the primary memory. The primary memory in most machines today is sized in the tens of megabytes of storage range. This volume of storage allows for large

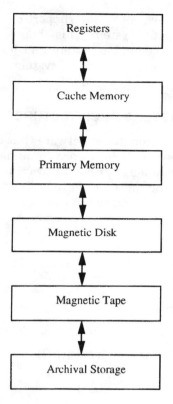

Figure 3.2 Memory hierarchy

portions of a data processing task to be memory resident during processing for small data processing applications. This is not to say that there is no swapping of information between the primary memory and the bulk secondary storage disk units. The volume of storage on such units is now in the 100 megabyte to the gigabyte range. The main emphasis in a database system is on how and what performs the management of this hierarchy. The database manager could do the best job for the database, but at a cost to all other applications of the operating system, of which the database is considered just one.

For the collection of computer hardware elements described above and in Chapter 2, to become a working computer system requires policies and mechanisms for control of these resources and coordination between them to exist. This has typically been the function of a computer's operating system. An operating system consists of specialized software with hardware support to manage the interaction of the CPU and all other hardware elements supporting applications software running on the computer system. This chapter looks at the software control elements of a computer system and how these interface and interact with a database management system.

3.2 OPERATING SYSTEMS ARCHITECTURE

An operating system is computer software that interacts at a low level with the computer system's hardware to manage the sharing of the computer's resources among various software applications. An operating system runs as the most privileged of software elements on the system and requires basic hardware support for interrupts and timers to effect control over executing programs. An operating system provides the following services.

1. Hardware management (interrupt handling, timer management)

2. Semaphores

3. Process management

4. Resource allocation (scheduling, dispatching)

5. Storage management and access (I/O)

6. Memory management

7. File management

8. Protection of system and user resources

An operating system begins with the management of a computer system's hardware. Hardware management requires the ability to set limits on the holding of resources and the ability to transfer control from an executing program back to the operating system. These functions are realized through the use of hardware timers and interrupt services. A hardware timer is a counter that can be set to a specific count (time period). When the time expires, an interrupt signal is released, which stops the processor, saves the processor's state (saves all active register contents, ALU registers, status registers, stack pointers, program counters, instruction registers, etc.), and turns control over to an interrupt service routine. The interrupt service routine examines the contents of predefined registers (e.g., the CPU status register or a predefined interrupt register) or set memory locations and determines what operations are to be performed next. Typically, control is immediately turned over to the operating system's kernel for servicing of the interrupt.

3.3 INTERRUPT MANAGEMENT AND SEMAPHORES

The use of interrupts is one means for an operating system to effect control over the hardware of the system. Another means is through the use of cooperative software and control actions or instructions. The notion described here is *mutual exclusion*. An operating system, to guarantee singular, noninterfering access to a resource, must have a means to limit the access to a resource or a resource allocation mechanism via some mutually exclusive operator. A mutual exclusion primitive must possess, the ability to limit access to a region or resource by only one element at a time, even when concurrent access is being attempted (atomic action). This notion of an *atomic* action is not foreign to database systems. The all-or-nothing operation of an atomic function is required for the guaranteed, nonconflicting access and control over system resources by the operating system. A specific hardware instruction called *test-and-set* is provided in many computer systems to support this mutual exclusion primitive. The instruction in a single atomic instruction cycle reads a variable specified, tests its value against some basic value, and sets the variable to a new value if the condition tested for is valid.

The test-and-set instruction forms the basis for constructing *semaphores*. A semaphore is a system variable that can exist in only one of two states, either true or false, with no other valid states holding for the variable. The semaphore variables have atomic operations that can be performed on them, with no other operations outside of these being valid operations. The valid operations are of two types. The first operation is a request to set the variable, sometimes referred to as *P(S)*. The second operation is a request to reset the variable and is sometimes referred to as *V(S)*. These act much like a flip-flop in a logic circuit. The flip-flop can be set or reset, holding a zero or one value only. The set and reset operations of a semaphore variable are used to construct lock and unlock operations on resources or to hold and release operations on the resources. Semaphores are used to construct *monitors*, which encase the control of an operating system's controlled resource. For example, a monitor could be used as a means to limit the access to a tape unit to one process at a time by constructing a queue of waiting processes and one service routine. The operation would be to build an outside shell around the tape service routine to allow only one process access to it at a time. The P and V operators can be used for this function.

P(S) If $S = 0$ THEN $S: = 1$ ELSE *Enqueue* requester;

Tape Service Routine

V(S) $S: = 0$; If Queue $<>$ null the *Dequeue*;

The processes that wish to use the tape service routine request service by first requesting the set function (P[S]). If no process is presently using the tape, then the S variable is zero. If it is free the variable gets set, and the process is allowed to enter the *critical section* of code reserved for the tape service routine and use the routine. If the tape routine is already being used (indicated by the S semaphore variable being set to one), the request is enqueued awaiting the release of the resource. Once a process finishes with the tape service routine, the V(S) or reset operation is requested. The reset operator resets the value of the semaphore back to zero and tests the queue of waiting processes to see if any processes still require service. If there are waiting processes, the top of the queue is removed and a P(S) request is issued for the process, starting over the entire process.

In this fashion, using semaphores, complex monitors can be constructed to control access to a variety of system hardware and software resources. Monitors and semaphores have been used as a means to construct synchronization mechanisms to coordinate the actions of cooperating resources. For example, using the simple P and V semaphores described above, one could construct two cooperative resource management routines by using two semaphore variables and the P and V operators as follows:

$P(S)$ If $S = 0$ THEN $S: = 1$; $P(S1)$ If $S1 = 0$ THEN $S1: = 1$;

Resource A Service Routine   Resource B Service Routine

$V(S1)$ $S1: = 0$; $V(S)$ $S: = 0$;

The two semaphores would provide for the synchronous operation of the two resources in such a way that they would toggle back and forth—either the resource A service routine first followed by the resource B service routine or the resource B service routine followed by the resource A routine. They could not, however, be executed concurrently due to the use of the semaphores. One can see from this example some of the rudimentary needs of the database management system's functions being implemented using similar concepts to guarantee mutual restricted access to database-stored information and management routines.

3.4 PROCESS MANAGEMENT

A process is typically viewed as the lowest executable level of software recognized by the operating system. Processes themselves can have additional internal management layers that are outside the domain of the operating system. The process does not, however, equate equally to a user program. A user program may be partitioned into multiple processes, or it could be a single process. The process does not have to be a fixed-size image in the system. It can take a variety of shapes and forms. The important aspect of a process is that there exists a measurable entity that the operating system knows about and has information about, at least in terms of how this process interacts with and fits into the resources being managed.

Process management performs the task of managing software processes on a computer system. The operating system provides the services to create a process (build and populate a process control block for a new process), to kill a process (remove its process control block), to fork a process into tasks, to join tasks, and to dispatch processes. A process is described in the operating system using a process control block, or PCB. The PCB is created for a process upon its initial instantiation in the system. A typical process control block contains information such as a process identifier, a process type (user, system, database, network, etc.), process priority, process state information, process resource requirements (memory, disks, peripherals, other processes, etc.), and the state of required resources, process size, and present process memory load location. This is only a representative set of information and is by no means complete.

The operating system uses the process control block information from all processes within the system to coordinate the execution of all of the processes in order to meet some operating system's goal, such as fair execution, equal execution times, or some minimum average execution time. Processes run at a variety of levels within the operating system. Some processes are *privileged* and can therefore access protected regions of memory or hidden routines. Application processes may have no outside access other than the programmer's immediate load image. Others, such as the database management system, have some form of access rights in-between these two extremes. Processes exist within the system in many different degrees of completion, called states. A process within the system can be in one of these four states: ready to run, running, suspended or blocked, and terminated or dead (Figure 3.3).

The ready state refers to the state a process is in when it is prepared to run on the hardware, but is awaiting the go-ahead from the operating system. To be in this state the process must have all the resources it requires to run allocated or at least fully specified, and it must have a known state for the resources stored in the PCB. Transitions from the ready state include *terminate*, *dispatch*, or *block*. Terminating the process can be the result of a user action to kill the process or a command from another process, such as an operating sys-

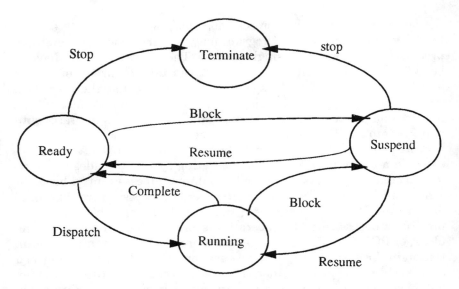

Figure 3.3   Process state transition diagram

tem command due to resource removal or an error condition (e.g., a bad control word for a printer). Dispatching a process moves a process from the ready state to the running state due to a scheduling action. The block transition moves a process from the ready state to the waiting state and is due to the removal of an acquired resource by the operating system or to some other deficiency that will not allow the process to go forward.

The running state refers to the point when the process has control of the CPU and is executing its instructions on the bare machine. The process has control of the hardware at this level and is only removed from execution by an interrupt from the operating system or an error condition. Transitions to this state only occur under control of the operating system and are due to scheduling actions. Transitions out of this state are due to a variety of conditions. A process can go from the running state to the termination state upon completion of execution, or a process can go back to the ready state due to an input/output request (which is serviced by another process) or due to an interrupt from the operating system for some other condition.

The waiting or suspended state for a process is used to hold processes that have not acquired the needed resources to execute or that have been removed from active execution due to some blocking action. A waiting action could be due to the transfer of data from the disk into memory or the completion of a cooperating process. Transitions to the

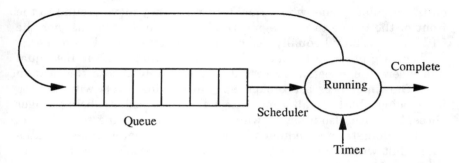

Figure 3.4   Process round-robin, time-slice scheduling

waiting state are typically caused by requests for added resources, the removal or reallocation of some needed resources waiting for a cooperating process to finish its service, or waiting for resources to be freed up for other requests.

The termination or dead state is the state from which all processes originate and finally return to for exiting the system. This state is where a process is originally given basic assets, such as a process control block, initial memory load space, and so forth. In addition, this is the state where processes that have been terminated for whatever reason are returned. The functions here deallocate held resources and remove the process from the system.

Processes are moved from state to state based on the actions of various operating system support routines, such as the scheduler, dispatcher, and allocation routines. These routines have the job of determining when to move a process from one state to another, which process to move from one state to another, how to move the process, and where to move it to. All these decisions are based on the interpretation of the operating system's managed process control block and the state of the system resources.

To determine which one of a set of ready processes to move from the ready state to the running state requires a scheduling policy and supporting mechanism to implement this policy. Traditional time-sharing systems use simple FIFO scheduling, where the next process in a list (queue, linked list, or some other data structure of PCBs) is the process scheduled for transition from the ready state to the running state. Other scheduling techniques try to be more fair and break up running processes into chunks of time called quantums. One such scheduler is the round-robin technique, where processes are moved from running to blocked or suspended states once they exceed their allotted quantum of time (a time slice or period). Suspended processes are placed on the circular queue, where they wait until they move around to the front of the queue to once again receive service. In this manner the CPU time is shared equally among all active processes (Figure 3.4).

There are other techniques where the quantum time is not equal and where the selection process does not simply choose the next in line. The time slices are broken up into varying levels with the top level being short, small time slices; the intermediate being longer slices, but with also a longer wait time between getting service; and, finally, a long-term scheduler where there is a greater time slice allocated, but where the time between service intervals is even greater (Figure 3.5).

A variety of other schedulers have been constructed for almost every conceivable measurable system quantity. For example, schedulers have been constructed that use priority (from a few levels to thousands of levels), execution time remaining, fixed deadline time scheduling, priority ceiling, and other techniques to select which process will get serviced next.

Once a process has been scheduled for service, it still must be moved from the inactive process control block state to a state where it is being prepared to execute upon the hardware. The task of preparing the process for actual execution falls on the operating system dis-

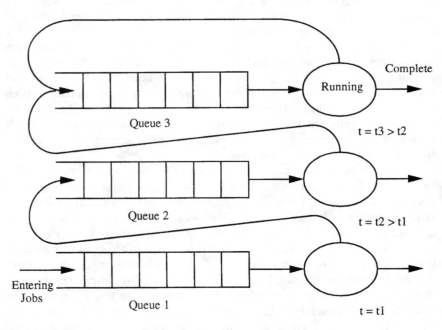

Figure 3.5   Process multilevel time-slice scheduling

patcher. The dispatcher accepts the given process control block from the scheduler and proceeds to perform tasks required to ready the CPU for execution of the provided process. The dispatcher loads the stored CPU register values for the process into the appropriate registers, restores the CPU status registers, the stored program counter for the process is loaded into the CPU's program counter register, and the proper physical addressing information for the process is loaded into the appropriate memory-addressing registers and data structures. Once all of the parameters are in place, the dispatcher turns over control to the process by making the program counter for the process the next jump address from which to acquire the following instruction. The dispatcher may also have the task of resetting timers and interrupt flags before it turns over execution control of the CPU. The setting of interrupt timers is essential if the operating system is to reacquire control of the CPU at a later time.

Another operating system function responsible for the movement of processes from one state to another state is the memory allocation service. This will be discussed in more detail in the following section. Additional features that the operating system must provide for process management include error management and deadlock detection, both of which are also important to a database management system, but not in the form used within an operating system. The error management services provide functions to detect, correct, avoid, and prevent errors, depending on the class of service required and the cost the operating system and serviced applications are willing to pay.

Deadlock detection is performed for the processes and for the resources required by the processes running within the system. Deadlock occurs when one process is holding a resource another requires and a resource this process needs is held by the other (Figure 3.6). Deadlock management can take many forms. We may wish to detect deadlock and correct it by removing some of the offenders. We may wish to prevent deadlock from occurring by guaranteeing ahead of time that the allocation of requested resources cannot result in a deadlock. One way to realize this is to preallocate all of the resources needed for an executing process before it is allowed to begin. This is a safe algorithm, but one that has an enormous amount of built-in holding time on resources, and one that will directly result in longer waiting time by processes, resulting in longer overall execution times and lower system process throughput. Another means to deadlock management is to avoid deadlock altogether. Avoidance can be achieved by setting up resources in a specific order of access, which must be followed by all processes. In this way processes can only access resources in order and cannot hold a resource held by another that you are waiting for. The circular wait is removed in this approach.

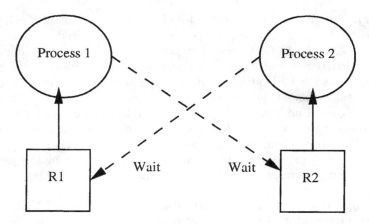

Figure 3.6   Deadlocked processes

3.5 RESOURCE MANAGEMENT

Resource management requires that the operating system coordinate the access and transmission of information from resources connected to the computer. Typical of functions handled by the resource management function of the operating system are: memory management, peripheral device initialization, device setup, control over the data transfer, and closing of the peripheral device. In early systems the operating system controlled these devices down to a low level. In more modern systems the operating system sets up the parameters of a transfer and leaves the details of the data transfer to the device controllers and to direct memory transfer control devices. This leaves the operating system and CPU free to do other required resource management tasks.

3.5.1 Memory Management

An operating system's storage manager manages the memory hierarchy of the computer. The operating system in particular must coordinate the movement of information into and out of the computer's primary memory and cache memory, as well as the maintenance of the memory's free space. To perform these functions an operating system typically uses a scheme where the primary memory is broken up into pieces called pages. The operating system then manages the movement of pages in memory based on policies in use. The memory manager must allocate space for processes upon initiation, deallocate space when a process completes, and periodically clean up the mem-

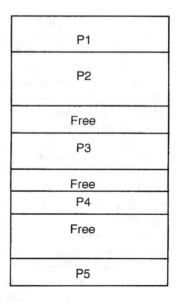

| P1 |
| P2 |
| Free |
| P3 |
| Free |
| P4 |
| Free |
| P5 |

Figure 3.7   Memory map

ory space when the pages within the memory become fragmented due to allocation and deallocation of uneven partitions.

The memory allocation problem is directly tied to the memory map (Figure 3.7). The memory map indicates which pages in memory are allocated to a process and which pages are free to be allocated to a new process. This memory map can be managed in a variety of ways to help the allocation manager. The list of free pages can be organized into a free list, where the blocks are structured as a tree of increasing block size, or as a heap, with the largest block always toward the top of the heap. Memory allocation then becomes a function of selecting a block of appropriate size based on the selection policy in place. Some policies include first fit, where the first block encountered that fits this process is selected. Another policy is best fit, where the blocks are scanned until one is found that best fits the size of the process to be loaded into the memory. There are numerous other schemes, but they are beyond the scope of this chapter.

Hand in hand with allocation is deallocation of the memory pages. As pages are released by processes leaving the running state, pages must be removed from the allocated list and replaced into the free list of free pages. The deallocated pages are restored to the list in a block equal to the size of the allocated process that held them. These free pages are then placed into the free list in a location appropriate to the size of the free pages being restored. However, not all page replace-

ments are done in such a nice fashion on process execution boundaries. Most are performed on a full or near-full primary memory with
few free pages. In order to still allow processes to move forward in
their execution, we must reorder the active pages by some policy that
will allow us to remove some active pages and let them be reallocated
to other more demanding or starved-out processes. The most common
page replacement algorithm and deallocation policy is based on the
LRU (least recently used) principle. This principle indicates that the
least recently used page is most likely to stay that way for the foresee-
able future and therefore is a prime candidate to be removed and replaced by a waiting process. Other schemes used for page replacement
include most recently used, least frequently used, and random removal. All of these policies have been examined in detail in the past
and have merits for certain process activities, although for database
systems some of these are downright disastrous. The database process
acts in a way that is not typical of most applications and, therefore,
will not react the same to a certain policy.

Another job for memory management is to maintain a map of free
memory areas and to periodically clean up memory to free up larger
contiguous chunks to make allocation easier. This process is called
garbage collection and reallocation. The allocation and deallocation
policies discussed previously result in memory becoming periodically
fragmented. When memory is fragmented into very fine fragments, it
may become impossible to find contiguous blocks of free memory to
allocate to incoming processes requiring pages (Figure 3.8). To rectify
this problem, memory management services periodically check the
map of memory to determine if cleaning up the loose fragmented free

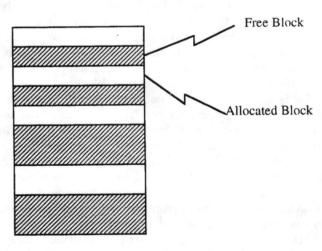

Figure 3.8 Memory fragmentation

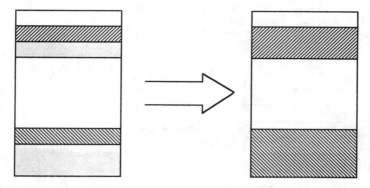

Figure 3.9   Coalescing memory holes

blocks into larger segments will result in significant increases in free contiguous blocks of sufficient size.

One technique scans all marked free pages and coalesces adjacent holes into marked, larger free segments. These are then added to the free list with the coalesced disjoint holes removed from the free list (Figure 3.9).

This in itself may not result in sufficient free space of adequate size. To get larger free blocks it may be necessary to periodically scan the entire memory and reallocate where processes are stored to clean up the memory allocation map into two areas—one a contiguous area consisting of all allocated memory pages and the other all free memory pages. The process by which all allocated pages are moved and reallocated to one end of memory is called compaction, and the process for reallocating all of the newly freed space into the free list is referred to as garbage collection (Figure 3.10). Like a garbage truck, compac-

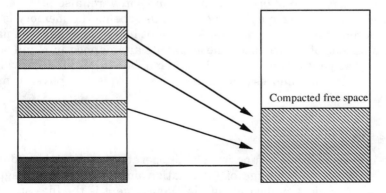

Figure 3.10   Memory compaction and garbage collection

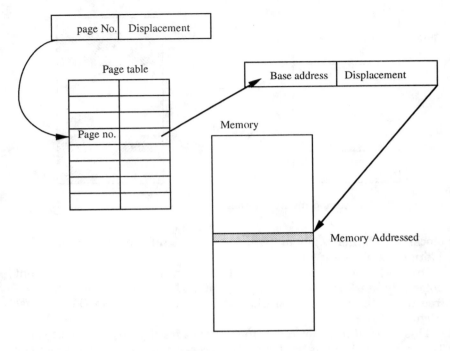

Figure 3.11   Virtual memory-mapping scheme

tion strives to compress the contents into one end of the container, freeing up the remainder of the space for more garbage. The process requires the reallocation and movement of processes and their addresses (all references must be changed in PCB and physical load segments).

Beyond these basic memory management schemes the operating system, along with support hardware and software, also provides *virtual memory* management support. In this scheme the memory is further decomposed into segments. A segment has some number of pages and a page is of a fixed size. The segments are mapped into and out of memory as pages were in the first scheme, but this system provides a way to map more address space into a smaller piece of physical memory (Figure 3.11).

3.5.2 File Management

File management is a function of the operating system that controls the structure and storage of information on nonprimary storage resources. A typical application of file management is the files stored on a disk drive or tape drive. Files are collections of data and/or programs that are moved to or from memory. To perform this movement requires that the file's structure, format, and location be known to the operating system (see Chapter 2). The file manager uses this information to request memory space from the memory manager to move a file from storage into the memory. When ready to move back into storage, the file system uses information from the memory manager to determine if any changes have been made to the file. If no changes have been made, then the file can simply be discarded. If changes have been made, the file manager needs to determine if more space than the file originally occupied is required. If it is, the file is stored possibly in a different location or requires fragmentation on the device. Like the memory manager the file manager may periodically be required to reallocate storage space and move files to free up larger contiguous areas.

The file manager provides additional services to the applications. File management provides functions to create, delete, and insert information into files; append information to the end of a file; and alter the contents of a file. File control mechanisms support the sharing of files among users in order to control the form of access allowed, to structure files for optimal space and time usage, and to name or rename files, and to copy and replicate files as needed for system support.

Management of the location and contents of a file system is controlled by the use of a file directory service. A file directory can be used as the means to facilitate access to files and to limit the use of a file as specified by the owner or the operating system. The file manager organizes files by type, such as .EXE for executables, .TXT for text files, .FOR for FORTRAN files, .PAS for Pascal files, and .C for C files. To aid in the management of files the file manager maintains a file control block with information about the files under its control. This information can facilitate the maintenance and use of the files.

3.5.3 Protection

Protection is an operating system function that manages access to controlled resources. Protection typically consists of access authorization, access authentication, and access restrictions. The operating system checks the authorization rights of a service requester before the service is performed. If the proper rights exist the access is allowed, if not the requester is blocked from access.

Access authorization is a process through which the operating system determines that a process has the right to execute on this system. The most common form of this control is the user name, which we are all familiar with when we log on to a computer. The second form of operating system protection is authentication. Authentication deals with the problem of a user being verified as to who he or she claims to be. The most common form of authentication is the *password*. The combination of user authorization through a stored user name and user authentication through a password has proven adequate for most noncritical computer systems' access restriction management. If necessary, these two methods can be applied to the access of any resource to limit access to it. The problem to be addressed is the degree of protection required and the amount of overhead we are willing to pay for it.

Access control is a more involved issue and deals with how to control the use of information and programs by users who have authorization to be on a system. To control who uses software on the system and how it is used, an operating system must provide mechanisms to limit the execution rights of controlled software. To do this operating systems use some form of access control. The most common are access control lists, access control matrixes, and capabilities. Access control lists provide a means to list all software elements to be controlled in the system and provide a list of users or processes that have the right to use these software elements. The control can also limit the type of execution rights the process or user may have. For example, we may only allow for the invocation of a process, not the freeing of the CPU to the calling process. We may allow only read access to a region of a software process or insert rights, or we may give unrestricted rights. The main mechanism (the comparison of a user identifier against a list of rights) for an access control list is performed in a centralized site, possibly within a separate operating system service or within the controlled software itself. Capabilities perform a similar function, but do it in a distributed fashion. Capabilities are created for each controlled element and are requested by processes that wish to use the controlled element. If the capability is appropriate for a process, it is given to the process. The process can then use the capability like a ticket to access and use the controlled element.

The typical operating system may get in the way of a database management system's best performance, since the operating system is optimized to give fair service to all processes, of which the database process is just one. The operating system's functionality must be modified to meet database management system needs. More cooperation is needed with more on par functionality if a database is to fully utilize a system's assets to manage database-stored information.

3.5.4 Peripheral Device Management

Input/output and peripheral device management services were created to remove the physical details of use from user processes and to provide for more seamless and fair management of the resources. The goal of peripheral device management services is to make access clear, clean, and transparent to users. Management should remove all physical dependencies from users' access requirements and replace these with logical mechanisms that are already common in programming environments. The control is to make access device independent. The user should not have to know what type of device or where the device is located to access data or service software.

Management for peripheral devices is bound into two classes of operating systems' service routines: I/O and device managers. The operating system strives to make all accesses appear the same. The typical method is to make all accesses have the look and feel of a file access. The I/O management process has the function to set up and maintain the logical channels or paths between CPU-resident processes and the outside world. The functions provided by this element include channel allocation and deallocation, channel setup, channel coordination, and remote data transfer and control. Included in this may be error detection and correction over the channel. In concert with this function is the device management function. Device management services provide mechanisms to perform device-dependent setup, allocation, control, synchronization, deallocation, and data transfer (Figure 3.12).

I/O and device management create the physical link and control the transfer. Included in this function is the request for buffer assets for the channel to utilize in transferring information from the secondary storage to the internal computer's memory. The buffers are used as the intermediary between the devices and the CPU. They allow for the concurrent operation of the I/O with applications processing within the system. The I/O channel control and device control are typically handled in an operating system as an independent process.

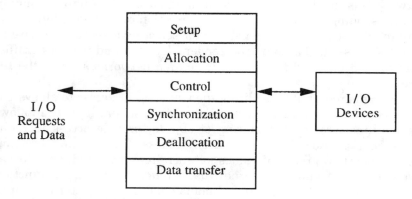

Figure 3.12   Input/output and device management

The operating system initiates the I/O or device operation and departs, allowing the device and I/O managers to perform the task and when completed interrupt the operating system to indicate the completion of the task. The interrupt can be active, where it stops the operating system for immediate service, or it can be message oriented, where it sets some status indicator, which the operating system will check at its leisure.

When integrated with the operating system's file manager, these routines form a seamless link between the stored programs, data, and the run-time system. The file manager is used for the direct access of *logical* storage elements by the operating system and controlled processes. The file manager provides services to name files, address files, control access, select and coordinate access paths, perform background copying and backup for recovery, coordinate the allocation and deallocation of resources where file information is located, and manage the placement (logical) of stored information. An important function of the file management system from a database's perspective is lock management. File managers create, issue, and control the locking and unlocking of files and records within files. This service is extremely important to databases for concurrency control and maintenance of transaction ACID properties.

3.6 NETWORK CONTROL SOFTWARE

Network management software manages the sending and receiving of information over a communications medium. Typical functions include message routing, naming, addressing, protection, media access, error detection and correction, communications setup, and management.

Routing is a system network management function needed to coordinate the movement of information over a network(s). In a local area network this function is not needed in all cases. Routing may simply require sending the data in a certain direction over the medium, or it may require more elaborate policies for selecting a channel or wire to send the message, based on the sender's location and network traffic. Routing is a required function in wide area networks such as the Internet.

Naming is required to facilitate the transparent access to all system resources, local or remote. A naming scheme should have the following features: provide for sharing of objects, provide access to replicants, and provide fully transparent access. The naming function must support two types of names for each item managed: an internal (systems) name and en external (user) name. The naming function must manage the translation and management of the external names with internal (unique) names.

Addressing is the means through which the system determines where a named item is located. Addressing schemes may be broken up into hierarchies, where local computers have their own set of names, which may not be unique between systems. The combination of the system's address (a node on the network) and the local name is sufficient to provide a system's unique name. Likewise we could have a unique name and address for each network in a collection of interconnected networks.

Access control over a network deals with policies and mechanisms to limit the mode of access given to network users. Access limitations could be as simple as login privilege or more complex, such as limiting the type of connections one can acquire or the type of access to remote information. The mechanism for limiting access may be embedded in software accessing the network or may be explicitly provided by the user of the software accessing the network.

Protection is a function of the operating system that deals with the management of resources from malicious or accidental access that may deadlock the system. There are two major classes of protection schemes: The first tries to avoid the problem by preallocating resources; the second allows deadlock to occur but provides means to detect and correct problems. Avoidance builds access to resources in a methodical fashion. One scheme requires a process to acquire all resources it will need ahead of time and hold them for the duration of its access. This is highly restrictive and may cause excessive delays for other resources that may need the held resources. Deadlock detection allows for more concurrent access of resources, but at the cost of potential deadlocks. One scheme requires the construction of waits for graphs, which allow for the detection of potential and actual deadlocks and provide mechanisms to remove deadlock by aborting conflicting processes.

One can see from this simple description the possible problems from a database's perspective. The operating system may limit the sharing of resources between processes, even if the database would allow it.

Media access software controls the interaction of users and software processes with the network. Typical mechanisms deal with the recognition and login interaction with a network node. Media access software deals with the connection to the communications medium and the setup of communications sessions. Access allows a process to log in with the network and be recognized by others over the network.

Communications setup and management acts in conjunction with media access software to interact with remote nodes and set up a link. Typically one node requests a linkup with a remote node. If the remote node can support an additional session, it creates a control block to hold information about the setup. The requesting node is signaled that a session was successfully created. Once created the interacting processes can send and receive information using their preallocated parameters.

3.6.1 Client/Server Policies and Mechanisms

The client/server mode of remote resource access and control has been gaining a great deal of support. One just has to open up a trade magazine to find advertisements for systems claiming client/server processing. The technique provides some of the benefits of distributed systems but without the added control overhead. Client/server participants operate by requesting and receiving services as needed. Servers hold resources and can provide service to clients. Clients require held resources and can request service from the server. The server grants service to the clients based on the present usage and the sharing policy in place at the server. The methodology does not offer the tight synchronization one would find with distributed systems, but it does offer a simple means to access and share remote resources in a uniform fashion. Its simplicity has added to its popularity and growth.

3.6.2 Remote Procedure Call Policies and Mechanisms

A similar remote access mechanism is the remote procedure call mechanism. As with local procedures, a requester must know the procedure's name and the proper parameters. The requester calls the remote procedure and the blocks awaiting the remote procedure's response. The called procedure performs the requested service, and, on return of control to the caller, the caller unblocks and continues processing. The procedure is exactly the same as the conventional procedure call except that the call is over a remote channel to another site. Further details of network software and specifics related to databases will be described in Chapter 10.

3.7 FAULT DETECTION AND RECOVERY

An operating system has a requirement to monitor the system for errors, faults, and failures and to provide mechanisms to correct these conditions or to reconfigure around them. To detect errors or faults in the first place an operating system uses a few basic functions. The first relies on hardware detection of errors—for example, parity check bits, cyclic redundancy checks, and computational checks such as overflows and divide by zero. These provide for detection of intermittent or hard errors within the communications and computational infrastructure of the machine. To check for more subtle or buried errors requires the periodic initiation of fault-monitoring software. This software collects information from these basic hardware elements and from running software using predefined test points. These collected data are then periodically analyzed for patterns that may indicate software or hardware errors present in the system. This software is referred to as program monitoring software.

Once an error condition has been detected using the operating system's error-monitoring mechanisms, the next job is to determine where the error is coming from and then to isolate the error down to some predetermined hardware or software granularity—for example, for hardware down to a replaceable board or a component such as an integrated circuit; for software down to a module, process, function, or possibly a block or line of code; for data within the file, down to the record or data item level. The level of isolation provided will depend on the overhead and cost the system is willing to pay for the detection and isolation. This mechanism is typically called *fault localization*. Fault localization operates by using known test drivers and known reponses to walk through system hardware and software elements testing for erroneous outputs. It is not, however, sufficient to simply detect an erroneous output condition and assume this is the component at fault. Errors can propagate through numerous layers of hardware and software, only showing up in later stages. The goal of fault localization is to detect an error, and then test back through all interacting elements to isolate the fault or error to the appropriate culprit.

On isolation of a faulty hardware or software element, the operating system must determine an appropriate action to relieve the system of the error. The process of performing this function is called recovery and reconfiguration. The most common method is to perform some recovery action first. The recovery may be as simple as reload and restart or simply resetting the already loaded software. More elaborate techniques include maintaining partial execution history (register status, computation state) and to reset and restart from some intermediary point in the software. If an error is more elaborate, it may require the removal and replacement of the software or hardware element to effect recovery.

If redundant hardware and software are available, the recovery can take on a more global perspective. Recovery can look to other assets available within the system to work around the errors or failures. This form of recovery requires the reallocation of resources (both hardware and software) to fill the gap left by the failed elements. This form of recovery is referred to as *reconfiguration*. Reconfiguration will be discussed in further detail in Chapter 10.

3.8 SUMMARY

The operating system and related support infrastructure services are used by a database management system to organize, maintain, and manipulate information. The database and operating system's needs and priorities do not always match. Due to this impedance mismatch, database systems have in the past tried to work around the operating system instead of working with it. The operating system's management of the memory hierarchy may be fair and reasonably optimal for the average application running on the system, but may not match the needs of the database management system. The operating system strives to maintain a reasonable set of data pages in memory for the application's use, but it does not attempt to go beyond its own measures of effectiveness. The concept today is to engineer systems so that they operate optimally based on the semantic needs and intent of the applications, which may go against the operating system's average response time and fairness goals.

The operating system migrates storage from primary memory to secondary storage, based on the operating system's perspective on when this should be done. Demand paging and limited storage dictate that this be performed on a page fault basis. The database, however, may not wish the page to be written back to secondary memory due to concurrency control and atomicity issues. The database may wish to hold pages in memory until transaction commit time and then flush to secondary storage. This would allow the database to not require undo of transactions on failure, simply abort and restart.

Related to this is I/O management and device management. The database may wish to order access based on the queries being presented to it in order to maintain ACID execution, whereas the operating system simply will order the accesses to deliver the greatest throughput of data back to the CPU. The order in which it returns information may be counterproductive to the database, to the point where the database has waited so long for needed data that when the data do come the operating system pages out the database software to make room for the data, or it removes the data that the new information is to be processed against. In either case this is not conducive to optimal database processing.

The problem with the operating system for this type of problem is the I/O buffer management policies and mechanisms. The database wishes to use and optimize buffers to maximize transaction throughput, while the operating system wants to maximize average process response.

The control of the processor itself by the operating system may block essential functions that the database must perform—for example, the database requires that the log of database actions be flushed to secondary storage at specific points and in an uninterruptable manner in order to guarantee recovery and correct execution. Likewise, to keep the database as consistent as possible requires the database to flush committed data to the persistent store when necessary and in an atomic operation. The operating system in its wish to be fair may time-out a database function doing specifically this operation. On another related issue, if a database is sorting and processing two large data files against each other, it may wish to maintain direct control over how and when data traverse the boundaries from the storage to the processor and back. Without direct control over the allocation and deallocation mechanisms, the database could be removed from one resource while still holding another, causing a loss of the intended operation's continuity.

The operating system's locking mechanism works well for simple file management, and for the majority of applications this is sufficient. But a database needs better control over locking to allow locking at possibly a data item level only. The reason for this is to allow more concurrency and less blocking of data. The intent is to increase data availability by only locking what is being used, not an entire file. To rectify this databases are forced to use direct addressing and direct file management features to allow for their own control over the file level of locking. However, in some operating systems the database still suffers under the control of the operating system's lock manager, regardless of what mode is used.

An operating system's interprocess communication mechanisms may be too expensive to use within a database system. Many operating systems use a form of message passing involving interrupt processing. Such mechanisms may have a high cost in terms of overhead. A database may wish to provide more simple IPC mechanisms using shared memory or semaphores, especially since a database is only another process within the operating system.

Scheduling in an operating system looks to maximize overall average response time and to share resources fairly. Scheduling only deals with the selection of a process to place onto the executing hardware. A database, on the other hand, has a multilevel scheduling problem—not only must it select which transaction to place into service at any point in time, but it must also schedule which operation to perform on the underlying database to meet concurrency control requirements. An operating system's scheduler will not and does not provide such a service.

A database requires the use of copying, backup, and recovery services of the underlying infrastructure to aid in constructing database recovery protocols. The problem is that many of the other features of an operating system may get in the way and hinder the easy operation of database recovery. The database wishes to dictate how and when it will force information out to persistent storage. This is done in order to minimize the work (UNDO and REDO, Chapter 4) that must be done to recover the database to a known consistent state. The operating system, on the other hand, will do this based on its needs to reallocate storage for processes in execution. The operating system will not take into account that this least recently used page will actually be the next page to be used by the database. It will simply choose this page and force it out immediately, based on its needs.

To make the operating system and database interface more compatible it is desirable that the operating system use *semantic* information, which can be provided by the database to make sound, informed decisions. This is not to say that the database should overtake or dictate the moves of the operating system. Instead it should act in a cooperative fashion to maximize the system-oriented needs of a database, which are more diverse than those of a typical application.

4

Database Management Systems Architecture

Paul Fortier

4.1 INTRODUCTION

A database management system is composed of five elements: computer hardware, software, data, people (users), and operations procedures. The computer hardware consists of processing elements, volatile memory, secondary storage components, archival storage devices, input and output devices, and possibly specialized computational devices and input sensors. The software for a database can be broken up into three categories: infrastructure support software, database software, and applications software. The infrastructure support software includes the operating system and network communications software. The database management system software includes components for storage management, concurrency control, transaction processing, database manipulation interface, database definition interface, and database control interface. Applications software is dependent on user needs. Data are the commodity the database system is managing. People and applications programs, as users, manipulate the stored data and, as database administrators, examine and maintain the database for the users. Operations procedures are developed and put into practice to provide additional support to the database system. Operations procedures include backing up the database onto nonvolatile mass storage, such as tapes, on a scheduled basis, and collection

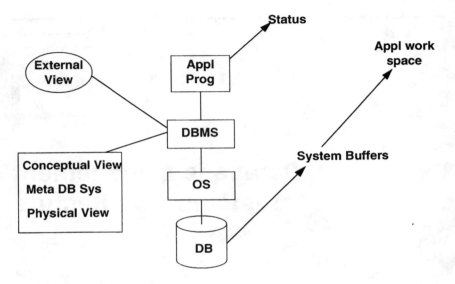

Figure 4.1   Database system

of operational statistics for use in tuning the database's structure and performance.

A database management system performs as an applications process under the control of the operating system. The database manager uses the operating system's file management and memory management services to store and retrieve the data in the database. Interface to the database management system is through three distinct paths: the database definition language, database control language, and database manipulation language (Figure 4.1).

4.1.1 Database Definition Language

A database is constructed to manage data that must be maintained for future use. The data in the database are organized into structured collections based on applications' informational needs. Data are placed in the database in these predefined data structures. These data structures are defined using data definition primitives within the database's language. Data definition primitives allow the database designer to specify individual data item composition as well as more complex data structures composed of these low-level data items.

A data item represents the smallest identifiable piece of information managed within the database. These data items, or attributes, are given a unique name and their physical structure and type are specified using data types available within the given language. In the

Structured Query Language (SQL) used to define relational databases, a data item is defined at the same time that a relation is defined. As an example, to define a person relation in SQL we could use the following code:

```
CREATE TABLE person
    ( name          VARCHAR(30) NOT NULL,
    ssnum           INT(9) NOT NULL,
    bdate           DATE NOT NULL,
    saddr           VARCHAR(20) NOT NULL,
    city            VARCHAR(20) NOT NULL,
    state           VARCHAR(20) NOT NULL,
    zcode           INT(9) NOT NULL,
    PRIMARY KEY (ssnum) )
```

This example defines a person data entity to be composed of seven distinct data items. Each data item is given an explicit data type and a maximum size for the data item—for example, the name can be from one to 30 characters long; the birthday is of type date. Date is defined in SQL as having the form year-month-day and is comprised of four integers for year and two integers for both the month and day entities.

Database definition typically uses a compilation process to build and generate the database schema or data description model. The database definition process results in descriptions of the database in both logical and physical terms and the generation of a mapping between the two.

```
CREATE TABLE customer
    ( cname         VARCHAR(10) NOT NULL,
    cnum            INT(3) NOT NULL,
    credlim         DECIMAL(6, 2),
    PRIMARY KEY (cnum) )


CREATE TABLE order
    ( onum          DECIMAL(5) NOT NULL,
    cnum            DECIMAL(3) NOT NULL,
    spnum           SMALL INT NOT NULL,
    date            DECIMAL(6),
    amount          DECIMAL(6, 2),
    PRIMARY KEY (onum) )
```

The above data definition constructs are from the structured query language (SQL) and specify two relations. One is a customer relation and the other is an order relation. The customer relation is specified as having three attributes: a customer name, a customer number, and a credit limit. The key attribute for the relation is defined as the customer number attribute. The second relation is a customer order relation. The customer order relation is composed of five attributes: order number, customer number, supplier part number, date of the order, and dollar amount for the order. The primary key for this relation is defined as the order number. Also notice that since the customer number in the order relation is the same as the customer number in the customer relation, this attribute constitutes a foreign key into the customer relation. By using techniques such as this the relations are linked together in an informational sense.

For all database models, there exists a language for the specification of the database's structure and content. The specification is called the schema design and represents the logical view of information that is to be managed by a particular database management system. The specification gives the designer the ability to map disjoint logical user views of information into a comprehensive global view of information and finally into a mapping to physical storage structures. This separation of the logical and physical database structures results in transparency from the physical and logical dependencies of the data from the users. By doing this the database designer has the ability to alter the physical storage structure and organization in order to optimize low-level storage and retrieval efficiency without the need to alter the logical user view and its application's code.

The database design language, beyond the basic ability to define data, must also have the ability to alter specified data structures and their physical representations after the database has been specified. Features to drop a structure from the database, to insert a new structure, or to alter an existing structure need to be built into the language for completeness and for the maintenance of a database. Keep in mind that most databases will not be constructed, put in service, and removed over a short period of time. When enterprises construct and populate a database, they do so continually over the lifetime of their system. The lifetime of a database system in such an enterprise may span decades, implying that growth and change are inevitable and must be designed for up front. A database within such an environment is initially specified and put into service. After using the database, some initial adjustments will be required. In addition, as the enterprise grows and possibly changes the focus of its activities, so must its information base change in order to stay competitive. One can see that a rigid, unchangeable specification and operational structure will lead to obsolescence and degradation of performance to the very applications the database was initially specified to support. A database specification language and implementation must be flexible in order to be useful and enduring.

4.1.2 Database Manipulation Language

The component of the database most visible and recognizable by database professionals, as well as applications developers and possibly applications users, is the data manipulation language. This component of the database can take on many forms, the most common being a programming language–like interface, which provides the ability to retrieve and store information within the database previously specified by the database design language.

The data manipulation language need not, however, take on a textual and procedural view only. The data manipulation language can be visual as in the spatial data management system, where information is described using icons and is retrieved using pictures that can be zoomed in on for greater detail about an item—for example, given that we have a map of the United States used as the top-level view for the querying of business information, we may wish to find out what universities are within the southern region of Massachusetts closest to Cape Cod. We would first select the type of icons we wish depicted—for example, only show regions with universities by selecting the university icons. The visual display would then highlight cities where major universities are located. To isolate a particular university or to find out more about the area where a university is located, we begin by selecting the area, say southeastern New England around Cape Cod, by encircling the region. The display would then expand this area, again only depicting the universities. To select a particular university select a university icon (Figure 4.2). If we selected the University of Massachusetts at Dartmouth, we may next get an aerial view of the university. To discover more information we could select a building, then a department, possibly even a particular professor or course offering. In such a way the majority of information wanted could be extracted and displayed in visual form. There are however limitations in this method. Not all information lends itself to visual-only representation. We may be forced to place only a subset of the totally available information in such a system and use a separate database interface for more textual information.

A second type of interface is related more toward business uses of databases. This type of interface uses a company's typical paper forms for information about inventory, sales, employee records, and so forth as the interface presented to the users of the database. An application

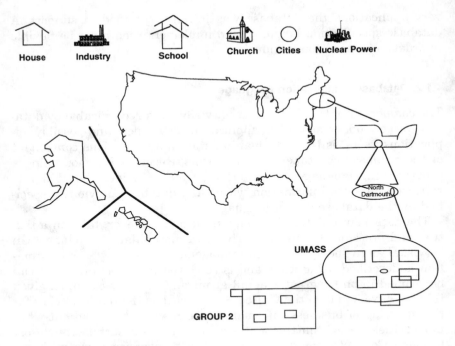

Figure 4.2   Spatial database manipulation example

or user simply selects the proper form, say an employee record form, and selects which employee or group of employee records to look at by typing in information on the form.

Figure 4.3 shows a form that may be used by a business to represent customers or suppliers. The form shows the company's major information, such as the company's name, address, phone number, fax machine number, and e-mail address, and possibly some information about the type of product or service it produces or supplies. In addition, the form may include some extra fields that can be used to aid in the finding of information. In the example screen of Figure 4.3, there is a separate field called FIND on the bottom of the screen. In this field a user could input parameters to be looked for or qualifiers to aid in a search—for example, if we wished to select all companies in Boston, Massachusetts, that are stored in our database, there are two potential ways to do this. The first is to enter the names Boston and Massachusetts in the appropriate city and state fields and select GO on the bottom right of the screen. This would indicate to the database to match any records that have these qualities in these particular fields. To find additional entries with the same fields one would select the NEXT field on the lower-right corner. An additional means to re-

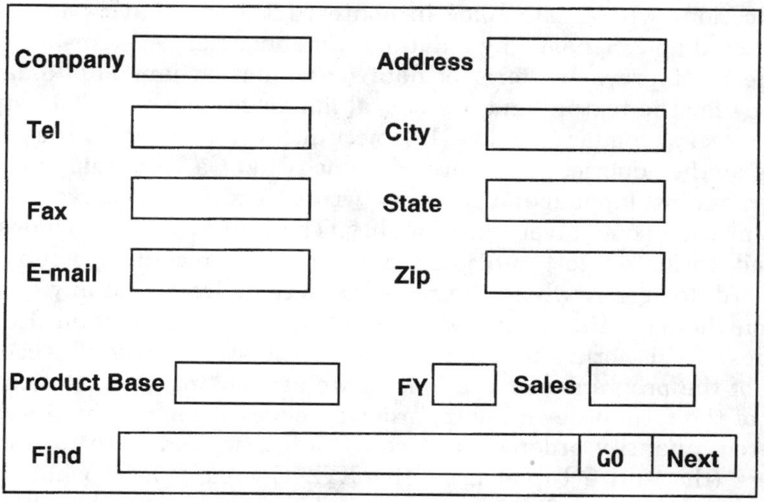

Figure 4.3   Forms database manipulation example

cover the same records is to type All, Boston, and Massachusetts in the FIND field of the form.

A third form of nontraditional data manipulation language is the Query by Example or QBE type of facility. In a query by example environment the user requests basic information about a record of interest, for example, a company name. The system then returns some template that may or may not fit what is being requested. This template can then be used by the user to further refine the query and to receive further examples to use in formulating a more precise query. The QBE interface developed for the relational model is closely tied to the forms-based interface. The examples come back in the form of tables, and the user fills in known quantities. The database then attempts to fill in a response table using this information as the restriction information.

Other data manipulation languages are based on functional evaluation. In these types of languages the users request information from the database through the use of function calls. The function calls may return text, graphics, video, sound, or a variety of data formats. The form returned is dependent on the data formats of the function called and the parameters' data types. This form of query interface is most prevalent in object-oriented databases and in multimedia and hypermedia databases. The information that is passed between the database and the applications is in the native form of the application, not in the base form of the database. This type of interface is desirable in applications where data come in nontextual forms that nevertheless are stored and managed by a database management system.

The most prevalent form of data manipulation language today is still by far the textual and procedural languages, such as SQL (structured query language) and OQL (object query language). In these languages the queries are formed much like a program in any programming language. The query writer has some reserved words that provide some given functionality. The typical query includes reserved words to select multiple records, a single record, or a subset of a record; to specify where the record is to come from; and any qualifiers on the access and retrieval of the requested information. In languages of this form the queries take on the structure and execution flow of the program—for example, if we are looking at a relation Order, of the form order number, order date, customer number, product ordered, quantity ordered, unit cost, total cost, and wish to find all orders (the entire tuple) from the XYZ Company for bookbindings since May 1995, the following query could be used, given that the XYZ Company has the customer number I101.

```
Range of O is order;
    SELECT  O.onum, O.odate, O.cnum, O.pname, O.qty, O.uic, O.ttl
    FROM Orders
    WHERE O.cnum := 'C101' and O.odate > '4-30-95' and O.pname :=
    'bindings';
```

In this query we first set an internal variable to range over all values of the search relation. Second, we request the search look to retrieve all of the attributes of the relation Order in the same order they are stored in. Third, we specify where to look for these attributes, namely in relation Order. And finally, we restrict the selection to find and copy into our result relation only those tuples that have the company number attribute stored with the value of 'C101', the value for attribute order date greater than the end of April (odate > '4-30-95'), and only the parts named 'binding'.

The procedural languages such as SQL also have operators to insert new tuples in the database, to create new relations, to modify existing relations, to delete relations, and to update the contents of a relation. An insert of a tuple into the relation above could be readily performed by issuing the following instruction.

```
Range of O is order;
    INSERT INTO Orders
    VALUES ('O100', '5-21-95', 'C101', 'binding', '100', '1.25',
    '125.00') ;
```

To delete the same tuple from the database requires that we first find the proper tuple, then remove it from the relation. The code may look something like the following.

```
Range of O is order;
  DELETE FROM Orders
  Where O.cnum := '0100' AND  O.odate := '5-21-95', AND O.cnum,
  := 'C101' AND
  O.pname := 'binding' AND O.qty := '100' AND O.uic := '1.25'
AND O.ttl := '125.00';
```

A simpler means would be to refer to the intended tuple by its *primary key* only. Since in a relational database the primary key by definition must uniquely define a tuple in a relation, then this alone can be used to find and delete the proper tuple. The reformed deletion operation would be as follows.

```
Range of O is order;
  DELETE FROM Orders
  Where O.onum := '0100';
```

What the reader should realize from this discussion is that there is no one correct means of retrieving information from a database. There are however standard means, as discussed in Chapter 18. The important concept is that database retrieval is different from conventional programming language processes. There is a language of informational access, which has evolved and continues to evolve along with database technology. These languages however will continue to be different in some fashion from their programming language counterparts primarily due to the differences in the requirements for persistent data beyond the point of a program's existence and the requirements for consistency and correctness of information beyond the scope of any single process or program.

4.1.3 Database Control Language

The last component of the language interface to a database management system is the data control language. This is also sometimes included as part of the data definition language in some descriptions. We decompose it here to help focus on some of the differences. In particular this component of a database interface is typically used by the database administrator. Typical functions provided at this layer are tools to monitor database operations, restructure underlying physical storage, reset constraint values on data items, rename relations, create additional indexes, archive data, and to grant, alter, or revoke privileges. The typical interface at this level is textual-oriented with specialized analysis tools used to analyze collected information.

The database administrator could for example examine a set of range constraints on an attribute value and determine, based on the user's requirements, to alter them to increase the possible domain of values considered correct by this attribute—for example, if the database administrator feels that there is not a sufficient range of values to represent the job categories in a company, he or she could elect to increase the number of jobs and their titles as needed. If originally there were only three titles in the company,

```
jobtitle IN {welding, management, sales}
```

but it is determined that the data structure must expanded to more fully meet the need of more job categories, the data administrator simply extends the list of valid items as shown below. This instruction simply adds three new categories to the list of allowable job titles. These new titles can now be used by applications querying or modifying the database.

```
jobtitle IN (welding, management, metal cutter,
machinist, glass cutter, sales)
```

Constraints for the range of values of a data item can be altered by increasing the values assigned to boundary values—for example, if an initial constraint indicates that the customer number ranges from 1 to 500, but we now find ourselves with 501 customers, the constraint must be altered to allow storage of the new customer record. To change the constraint, simply set RANGE OF Customer.cnum 1 .. 750. Constraints on when to perform testing functions can be altered also—for example, test constraints on reads, writes, or commit.

Beyond the alteration of constraints, database data control languages provide instructions and constructs to grant additional privileges to users, or to revoke privileges. The GRANT statement is used to allow a user to perform certain manipulations—for example, to allow user Tom to read values from the Customer relation can be done by

```
GRANT SELECT ON Customer TO Tom;
```

One could also grant the rights to multiple operations within one statement.

```
GRANT SELECT, UPDATE, INSERTION ON Customer TO Tom;
```

This statement grants selection, update, and insertion rights to the user Tom on the relation Customer. In this manner the database administrator can alter, add, or remove access rights to any items within the database. Not all database systems and models support a wide variety of data control language features. In several languages, many of these features would necessitate bringing the database off line for alteration.

4.2 COMPONENTS OF A DATABASE SYSTEM

A database system is composed of much more than just the data definition language, data manipulation language, and data control language. These simply represent the interface into the actual database system. The core of a database management system is the collection of services that provide the persistence of data in the database and the functionality to guarantee the consistency and correctness of data and the adherence to ACID properties by transactions (Figure 4.4). The ACID properties include the atomic, consistent, independent, and durable execution of a transaction on the database. We will discuss these in more detail later in this chapter.

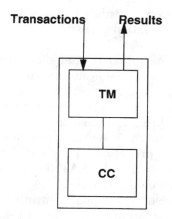

Figure 4.4   Database systems architecture

The architecture of a database system is comprised of a set of services built on top of basic operating system services, system file storage services, and primary memory buffer management services. The file manager is the database's interface to the persistent stored information. The information managed for the database by the file system includes the internal, conceptual, and external schema for the stored information (metadatabase); the actual database; and the database log file. The log files include before images (buffer values), after images, redo records (actions of committed transactions), undo records (actions of uncommitted transactions), commit records, abort records, and transaction begin records.

Through the basic features of process management, interprocess communications, synchronization, buffer management, and file management the database systems services can be constructed. These services include catalog management, integrity management, transaction management, concurrency control, lock management, deadlock management, recovery management, security management, query processing, communications management, and log management. On top of the database services the user's applications operate through the input/output view manager and the data manipulation manager. In the next few paragraphs we will briefly review each of these. Following these brief overviews, we will additionally review some of these in greater detail.

Catalog Manager—The catalog manager maintains information about the database's maintained information. This metadata forms the schema for the database. The database administrator, using data control language and data definition language interfaces, can alter the schema. As an example, in SQL this portion of the database would keep the definition for all relations, constraints, security assertions, and mappings to physical storage.

Integrity Manager—The integrity manager aids in the maintenance of the database's data items' accuracy, correctness, and validity—for example, the integrity manager may check that a data item is of the proper type through a mechanism that determines when to do the check, how to do the check, and how to recover, reject, or fix the condition when encountered. The integrity manager may check to see that a data item is within a predefined domain of correct values, such as DOMAIN FIXED (5) or Weight GREATER THAN 0 AND Weight LESS THAN 2000. These would test the ranges of values a data item may span. Integrity checks can span multiple entities or relations—for example, a referential integrity check in SQL can be used to see that the relationship of many objects has a property that must hold for them to be considered valid. Such a check could be that the SUM of all account balances at a bank must equal the bank's balance.

An important aspect of this management is when to perform the specified checks—for example, there is a different cost if the checks are done at database definition time, on access to the data item, on update of a data item, on an event such as a timer, or on the commit of a transaction. The tradeoff is accuracy and validity of the data versus performance. Checks done during run time will slow down the database's processing throughput.

Transaction Manager—The transaction manager controls and coordinates the execution of transactions within the database. For now just assume that a transaction is a collection of operations on the database that are bound together into a single run-time unit. The transaction manager must perform tasks to initiate transactions (scheduling); synchronize transaction execution with the database, other transactions, and the operating system; coordinate intertransaction communications; commit (completion) processing; and abort (failure) processing, transaction constraint checking and condition handling, and transaction recovery (error) management. A transaction typically is of the form

```
TRANSACTION T (Optional Input Parameters)
   Specification Part
      BEGIN

      BODY of T

      COMMIT or ABORT of T
      RECOVERY PART of T
   END
END TRANSACTION T
```

The initial statement names the transaction, allowing it to be possibly precompiled and stored for later execution. The initial statement also leaves space for transferring input parameters to the transaction, such as the location of data to be executed. The specification part of the transaction is the area where local variables for the transaction's workspace are specified, as are preconditions and postconditions on transaction execution, recovery conditions, isolation level, access modes, and the diagnostic size to allocate. The body contains the executable code for the transaction. The commit and abort statements indicate the success or failure of the transaction. Finally, the recovery part specifies user- or system-supplied recovery or condition handlers for error processing and transaction completion processing.

Concurrency Control Manager—The concurrency control manager coordinates the actions of interactive access to the database by concurrently running transactions. The goal of concurrency control is to coordinate execution such that the *VIEW* or effect from the database's perspective is the same as if the concurrently executing transactions were executed in a serial fashion. This scheme is referred to as the *serializable* execution of transactions. Concurrency control's serializability theory has two basic modes: The simplest concerns the serializable execution of the read and write sets from conflicting transactions and is based on either locking, timestamp ordering, or optimistic read and write conflict resolution. The second concurrency control concept is more complex and uses *semantic* knowledge of a transaction's execution to aid in coordination. The major difference is that the granularity of the serialization operator is not the read and write, but rather complex functions and procedures as well as complex data objects. The criterion of correct execution, however, is nevertheless serialization across concurrent transactions.

Lock Manager—The lock manager is designed to control the access to the database lock table. The lock table of the database maintains the status of locks (read lock, write lock, share lock, semantic lock, etc.) for each item of the database that has been accessed. The lock manager isolates users from accessing the lock table directly. To acquire access to lock status, the lock manager provides lock and unlock primitives to database and user code. The lock can be a read lock, which is granted (if no one holds a conflicting write lock) when a transaction attempts to read a data item. A write lock can only be granted if no other transaction holds a read or write lock on the data item. Locks in a database can be viewed like semaphores in an operating system; they are used as a means to guarantee exclusive use to an item within the database's control.

Deadlock Manager—When a locking protocol is being used, a lock held by one transaction can block a lock request from another transaction. If there are no circular waits for a lock, then the lock will ultimately be granted. If there are circular waits, then deadlock occurs. Deadlock is the condition where two or more transactions wait for resources held by another transaction that is waiting for a resource you hold. Since no one can move forward, the system cannot get any useful work done. The deadlock manager must detect when a deadlock condition holds and decide how to handle the condition. Typically one of the involved transactions is aborted and its locks released, thus allowing other transactions to go on.

Recovery Manager—The recovery manager must ensure that the database is always in a state that is *recoverable* consistently and correctly. This is done by ensuring that the database contains all or none of the effects of committed transactions and none from aborted or running transactions. The recovery manager uses the notion of a checkpoint (snapshot of the present state of the database) and a log file (file of operations on the database) to aid in the recovery. For conventional databases recovery attempts to bring the database *back* to an old state of the database and initiate processing from there. To bring the database back to a past state the recovery manager uses both *undo*, where uncommitted or active transaction past views are restored, and *redo*, where committed transactions not written to the database have their new states restored to the persistent store. These undo and redo records are applied to a checkpoint state to bring the database to some intermediate acceptable *consistent* state. A second form of recovery attempts to move the database *forward* by applying compensating transactions (to change committed effects to acceptable forms based on semantic needs), by applying extrapolations (to compute new acceptably correct and consistent future states), and by applying condition handlers to user or system semantic actions at a variety of levels within the database.

Security Manager—The security manager has the task of limiting access, modification, and malicious intrusion to the database. To perform these control actions the security manager requires that users be identified, authenticated, and authorized for the access and control over a data item being requested. Identification is much like typical login capabilities, where the security manager asks the users to identify themselves. To make sure that not just anybody attempts access the database may also ask a user to authenticate his or her identity. This can be done with a password or by a variety of fairly elaborate mechanisms. Once the user is allowed access, he or she is further restricted to what can be viewed and altered. Authorization performs the function of limiting access to only a desirable predefined level—for example, read only, write only, alter capability, view restriction, and numerous other restrictions on access.

Query Processing Support Manager—The query processor of a database system has the function of determining how to answer the requests for information from a user in the most optimal manner. The idea is that a query can be answered by a database system in a variety of ways. The most straightforward is the brute-force approach. This however is typically the most expensive in terms of time and resources consumed—for example, the cost to join two tables will be the cost of scanning each item of the first with each item of the second, or on the order of N times N or N squared if we assume they are the same size. On the other hand, if we could reduce the size of each by a factor of 2, then the cost drops by one-half. This is easily accomplished if we perform a select first on each before a join. If the size of N is large, this reduction can become significant and have a meaningful result on the database's performance. To reduce the cost of queries we look at heuristics on the order of access of relations and their combinations, relation reductions via selections and projections, preprocessing (sorting), iteration order, relation operator precedence ordering, and numerous other factors.

Communications Manager—The communications manager has the role of traffic cop in the database. This service must coordinate the transfer of database data as well as status information to aid in the processing of data. Communications may be between database services, different databases, different processors, different transactions, or within a transaction. Mechanisms such as simple message-passing schemes, client/server protocols, and others have been implemented.

Log Manager—The log manager has the job of coordinating the transfer of information from the active database into secondary persistent storage to aid in the recoverability of the database and to effectively mitigate the problems with the operating system paging out information prematurely. The log maintains a history of data flow in and out of the database, as well as actions that can affect the database's state. This includes transactions before images, after images, undo records, and redo records.

4.3 TRANSACTION MANAGEMENT

The transaction manager has the job of providing a bounded framework around which to guarantee that the database stays consistent while concurrent operations execute on the database. The database manager, without concurrency, can guarantee this with no problem—but this is not very interesting to study, nor is it very practical in the real world. The real world of database processing typically deals with a large database with a high degree of multiprocessing (concurrently executing transactions).

The execution of a transaction is similar to making a contract; both sides are involved in the contract, they negotiate for a while, and then they either come to a consensus and sign the contract, or they both walk away. A transaction is thus either *all or nothing*. A transaction must complete totally or must not complete at all. Now that's a concept.

The transaction is meant to be used as a consistent and reliable unit of work for the database system. A transaction interacts with the application's environment and the database's concurrency control protocols to perform its intended function (Figure 4.5a). A transaction is required to guarantee four properties when executing on a consistent database. These four properties are called the transaction's ACID properties; they include atomic, consistent, independent, and durable executions of transactions on the database.

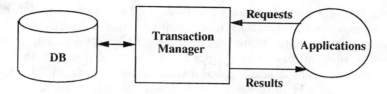

Figure 4.5a Transaction manager's main database interfaces

An ACID transaction guarantees that the database the transaction begins with and the database it finishes with are consistent, that the data are durable, that the transaction acted alone on the database, and that the transaction completely finished its actions on the database (Figure 4.5b).

The transaction ACID properties imply:

Atomic—The atomic property implies that a transaction is an indivisible unit of execution that either completely performs its designed function or else its effect on the database is as if the transaction never began; that is, the database state an atomic transaction leaves if the transaction does not totally commit is the same database state that the transaction began with. On the other hand, if an atomic transaction completes, then the database state it leaves has *all* of the changes the transaction computed with no others installed.

Consistent—Consistent execution of a transaction requires that a transaction transform an initial consistent database state to another new consistent database state. The basic concept behind this transaction property is that the database is comprised of a set of

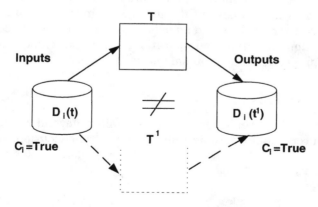

Figure 4.5b Database state transition by transaction execution

data items, which have constraints defined on them. The database, to be considered consistent at any point in time, requires that these constraints on data items within the database all evaluate to true; that is, none of these constraints can be violated if we are to have a *consistent* database state. A valid transaction, which initially sees a database that is consistent, must, upon commit, leave a database that is still consistent.

Independent—Independence, sometimes referred to as the isolation property of transactions, requires that each transaction accessing shared data acts alone, without being affected by other concurrently running transactions. This property basically indicates that a transaction's effect on the database is as if it and it alone were executing on the database. The function of this property is to require the removal of any dependence of a transaction's execution on any other transaction's execution.

Durable—The durability of a transaction's execution requires that once a transaction is committed, its effects remain permanent in the database. What this property implies is that the changes a transaction makes to the database do not disappear when the transaction terminates. Data produced by a transaction and written to the database become *permanent*. Data once written to the database can only be altered by another transaction that reads and/or writes over this data item.

These transaction properties must hold for all transactions that execute within a database management system if consistency, correctness, and validity of the database is to be maintained. The properties must hold even when other transactions execute along with each other concurrently. In addition, if adhered to, the properties will guarantee a correct and consistent database even in the face of failures or errors. It is when we begin to envision what policies and mechanisms for transaction execution and operations can be developed to guarantee these properties that problems arise.

4.3.1 Transaction Basics

A transaction is a collection of applications code and database manipulation code bound into an indivisible unit of execution.

```
BEGIN-TRANSACTION Name

    Applications Code
```

```
DB-Code
Applications Code
DB-Code
DB-Code
   .
   .
   .
Applications Code

END TRANSACTION Name
```

A transaction is framed by the **BEGIN TRANSACTION** and **END TRANSACTION** markers delineating the boundaries of the transaction—for example, if we have the following three relations

FLIGHT(Fno, Date, Source, Destination, Seats-Sold, Capacity)

CUSTOMER(Cname, Address, Balance)

FlghtCust(FNO, Date, Cname, Special)

that describe an airline reservation system. The first relation depicts the flight information—flight number, the date of the flight, the city of origin, the destination city, the number of seats sold for this flight, and the capacity of this plane. The second relation describes the customers who will be flying on a flight; it gives their names, addresses, and the balances owed on the tickets. The third relation describes the relationship between the flights and the customers. This relation in particular indicates which flight, which passengers are flying on what date, and any special requirements for these passengers—for example, maybe someone wants a McDonald's Happy Meal or a vegetarian meal.

To generate a simple transaction on these database relations, which make a reservation for a customer, we could write the following pseudocoded relational structured query language request or *query*:

```
BEGIN TRANSACTION Reservation
  BEGIN
    Input (FlightNo, date, customer, specl)
    EXEX SQL UPDATE FLIGHT;
      SET Seats-Sold = Seats-Sold + 1;
      WHERE Fno = 'FlightNo';
      AND Date = 'date';
```

```
EXEX SQL INSERT;
    INTO FlightCust (FNO, Date, Cname, Special)
    VALUES (FlightNo, date, customer, specl)
    OUTPUT("Transaction Completed")
END TRANSACTION Reservation;
```

This transaction looks for input from the keyboard for the flight number, date of the flight, the customer's name, and any special requirements the customer may have. These are input to transaction variables: FlightNo, date, customer, and specl, respectively. The contents of these variables are then inserted into the proper places within the relation through the VALUES function. We update the count of seats sold for this flight by incrementing the value by one and then updating the value in the relation. The transaction then updates the FlghtCust relation with the new information. To be complete we should also update the customer relation; this will be left as an exercise for the reader. This represents a simple transaction; however, as it stands it will not guarantee the transaction ACID properties alone.

To guarantee the transaction ACID properties we need some additional features within this simple transaction model. To meet the needs of *atomic* execution we require a means to determine the conditions for termination of a transaction, correct or otherwise. The first concept required for correct execution and termination is the commit. Commit is used to indicate the correct and atomic termination of a transaction. It includes the processing necessary to ensure proper updating and marking of the database. The second concept, called abort, is necessary for transactions that fail or stop execution for some reason. Abort conditions will include erroneous operations, conflicts in accessing stored information, or the inability to meet the ACID requirements on transaction processing. An abort requires that all of the effects of a transaction are removed from the database before any other transaction has a chance to see them. These two added features are necessary to facilitate atomic execution, although not in isolation.

The commit action is necessary in order to synchronize the actions of other elements of the database management system to make changes to the database permanent—for example, this command may be used to cause the database buffers and activity log to be flushed (force written) to the permanent storage subsystem, thereby making the changes durable.

```
BEGIN TRANSACTION Reservation
    BEGIN
        Input(FlightNo, date, customer,specl)
        SELECT Seats-Sold, Capacity FROM FLIGHT ;
```

```
IF Seats-Sold  < Capacity THEN
  BEGIN
  EXEX SQL UPDATE FLIGHT;
  SET Seats-Sold = Seats-Sold + 1;
    WHERE Fno = 'FlightNo';
    AND Date = 'date';
   EXEX SQL INSERT;
    INTO FlightCust(FNO, Date, Cname, Special)
    VALUES(FlightNo, date, customer, specl)
    OUTPUT("Transaction Completed")
  COMMIT Reservation;
  ELSE
  ABORT Reservation;
  END
END TRANSACTION Reservation;
```

This altered transaction now allows us to either go on with the transaction if it has a chance to succeed, or abort the transaction if we cannot complete it. In this example we would abort the transaction if we did not have a seat remaining in the plane to give to this customer. If there is a seat, we sell this customer a seat and commit the transaction.

4.3.2 Transaction Formalization

A transaction, Ti, is composed of a set of operations, $Oj \in \{Read, Write\}$, where Oj is some operation from a transaction i on data items from the database D.

Let $Osi = \cup j\ Oij$ represent the union of the set of all operations j from a transaction i.

Finally, let $Ni \in \{Abort, Commit\}$ represent the set of termination conditions on a transaction, either commit or abort.

A transaction is modeled as a partial ordering over its operations and end conditions. The partial ordering is represented by $P = \{\Sigma, <\}$, which indicates that the partial order P is composed of a set of operations, denoted Σ, and an ordering relation that holds between the elements in Σ denoted $<$.

With these definitions we can formally describe a transaction, Ti, as a partial ordering of its composite operations as follows.

$$Ti = \{\ \Sigma i, <i\ \}$$

where

1. $\Sigma i = OSi \cup Ni$

2. For any two operations from Ti

   $Oij, Oik \in OSi$ If $Oij = R(X)$ and $Oik = W(X)$
   Then for any X, Either $Oij <i Oik$ or $Oik <i Oij$

3. $\forall Oij \in OSi, Oij <i Ni$

What all this says is that a transaction is made up of reads, writes, and a commit or an abort operation, and that there exists an explicit ordering in a transaction such that if a conflicting read precedes a conflicting write in the history, a strict sequential ordering must always hold in this transaction for these conflicting operations. In addition, all operations from the transactions must precede the commit or the abort statements. This is an important notion for developing correctness criteria for transaction executions, especially when concurrency comes into play. The transaction ordering must not be violated, to ensure that the transaction can perform the intended operation.

To illustrate the conflict of notions and transaction ordering concepts described above, a simple example will be presented. In this example we look at one transaction, Ti, which is made up of two reads, a simple computation, a write, and a commit.

```
BEGIN TRANSACTION T
  Read(X);
  Read(Y);
    X := X + Y;
  Write(X);
COMMIT (T);
END TRANSACTION T
```

The set of operations for this transaction is shown as:

$$\Sigma = \{ R(X), \ R(Y), \ W(X), \ C\}$$

and

$$<i = \{((RX), W(X)), (R(Y),W(Y)), (W(X),C), (R(X),C), (R(Y),C)\}$$

where (Oi, Oj) represent an element of $<i$ and indicate that the operation (Oi) precedes $(<i)$ operation (Oj) in the transaction's structure and therefore must also maintain this order when the transaction is executed. The ordering in the relationship $<i$ indicates that the reads on data items X and Y must precede the write on data item X and that all of these operations must precede the commit operation. However, the ordering relationship does not specify the ordering for all pairs of operations in a transaction, only for the *conflicting* or *dependent* pairs of operations.

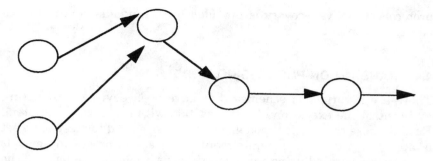

Figure 4.6 Directed acyclic graph representation for transaction relative ordering

Another representation for the partial ordering within a transaction utilizes a directed acyclic graph (Figure 4.6). This represents a shorthand for depicting the operations and ordering relationships in a more compact form. The operations are represented as the nodes in the graph and the ordering relationships as the edges—for example, the nodes R(X) and W(X) represent the read and write operations on data item X, and the directed edge, (R(X), W(X)), represents the ordering relationship, indicating that the read of data item X must precede the write on data item X.

A compact shorthand notation for $Ti = \{\Sigma i, <i\}$ is also used in numerous discussions dealing with the ordering relationships in transactions. This notation simply uses the operators and a relative sequential ordering to show precedence. In the simple transaction above this shorthand reduces to:

$$Ti = \{ R(X), R(Y), W(X), C \}$$

This represents one possible sequence for this transaction; another simply switches the read of X and Y:

$$Ti = \{ R(Y), R(X), W(X), C \}$$

This is still a valid representation, since the switching of the two reads will not alter the validity of the final result of the transaction.

Transaction processing in a database system strives for guaranteeing the ACID properties, while delivering a high degree of data availability, no loss of updates, avoidance of cascading aborts, and recoverability of the database and transactions. A high degree of data availability is realized through reduced blocking of read and write requests. No loss of updates is guaranteed by correct commit processing. The avoidance of cascading aborts is provided for by robust recovery protocols. Finally, recovery is provided by redundancy and the rules governing commit.

4.4 TRANSACTION PROCESSING MODELS

There are a variety of schemes that have been devised to structure and control the execution of a transaction within a database system. Each of these transaction models has been developed to meet some set of application or system requirement. Transaction processing models have been classified using three metrics: the applications domain, the relative duration of transactions, and the structure of transactions. Each of these metrics will be briefly discussed below.

Application—The applications domain is defined by the class of applications the database must support—for example, a distributed application that is partitioned over some set of hardware assets will require different transaction services than a centralized application. An application can be *distributed, real-time, fault-tolerant, secure,* or operate on *multimedia* data. Each of these applications has unique processing needs that define what a database serving these applications must provide.

Duration—The second metric for defining a transaction processing model is the duration of a transaction's execution. Most conventional systems had transactions that varied in duration deterministically about some average median value. Transactions in evolving database systems go beyond simple query processing into applications support. Some transaction systems must support applications that are long-lived, such as computer-aided design and manufacturing, while others must support applications that are bursty, such as end transaction sales systems. Finally, some databases are being required to support applications where the duration is variable, but the timeliness of the response is critical. Applications such as medical monitoring systems and real-time command and control systems are such environments. The important measure here is in terms of the average duration of a transaction and its restrictions on when and how it must complete operations.

Structure—The third metric for classification of transaction models is based on the structure of transactions within a system. Transactions can and should be organized to support the application's processing framework within which they operate. Some transaction structures mimic programming language structures' straight code segments and are referred to as *uniform* or regular structures. Partitioned application environments or programming languages require transactions that support partitioned transaction structures. Partitioned transactions should be organized such that the transaction is broken up into separate segments. The segments can be executed in sequence or as parallel elements if the application's domain requires this feature. Partitioned structure may or may not imply partitioned or *early* commit. Transaction structure can be *nested*. Nested transactions are those where transactions may have subtransactions embedded within them. A subtransaction may take on the properties of the parent. Transaction structure may be decomposed into separate *synchronous* components, or into *cooperative* interleaved components. Each of these potential structuring models has an impact on the processing and commit strategies for transactions and the database system they support.

4.5 EXAMPLE TRANSACTION MODELS

4.5.1 Nested Transactions

Nested transactions were first introduced in the mid-1970s by Elliott Moss. In this transaction model a transaction consists of one *parent* and one or more transaction fragments. A fragment may be at the same level or *nested* within another fragment (Figure 4.7). A top-level fragment is called a *parent*. Parents have *children* embedded within them. The children of the parent transaction are controlled by the

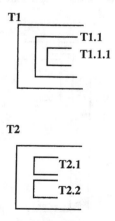

Figure 4.7   Nested transaction structure

parent in terms of commit and aborts. The parent transaction cannot commit before the children subtransactions have completed and are ready to commit. This implies that a child transaction must begin after the parent and complete before the parent completes. A child's commit is dependent on the parent's commit. If the parent fails to commit for some reason, then the child likewise must fail and be aborted. The child cannot commit without the parent in the classical nested transaction model.

The children can use the locks held by a parent, but not the locks held by another child of the parent. The parent controls the execution ordering of children to guarantee the execution as specified by the transaction's structure, although the parent can execute child transactions in a parallel mode if supported. Upon the failure of a child, the parent determines how to perform the recovery. The parent may decide to restart the child, or to abort the child and the parent transaction along with any siblings.

An example of a nested transaction is shown in Figure 4.8. In this figure there are three nested transactions within the parent transaction. The subtransactions are organized such that subtransaction $S1$ has a child $S2$ and subtransaction $S3$ does not have any children, but is at the same nesting level as $S1$. If $S1$ and $S3$ are assumed to be ordered for a purpose, then $S3$ cannot begin execution until $S1$ has completed its execution. Subtransaction $S2$ must begin execution after $S1$ and cannot commit until $S1$ is also ready to commit. Likewise, the subtransaction $S1$ must wait until $S2$ is ready to commit until it can prepare to commit. The subtransactions of transaction T, the parent, must all wait to commit until the parent signals all are ready. Updates only become visible outside of transaction T when T commits.

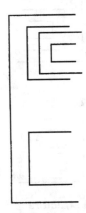

Figure 4.8   Example nested transaction structure

4.5.2 Long Duration Transactions

Transactions that support applications having a relatively long life, compared to traditional applications, have developed the long duration transaction model (Figure 4.9). This transaction model requires the partitioning of transactions into *well-formed*, relatively independent transaction steps. The criterion for this partitioning is that the transaction steps cannot have data or execution dependencies between them; that is, one step must not rely on the execution or results of the other to continue. The results of these steps are *committed* to the database and are visible from outside the long duration transaction. This requirement implies that the relationship between the steps of the long duration transaction is the same as if they were independent transactions themselves. Therefore, intermediate results from one step to the other cannot be seen; only the end results are seen. This guarantees that the transaction steps are ACID.

For reliability and recoverability, each of the subtransactions or steps must have a *compensating* transaction step that goes with this transaction step and no others. A compensating transaction is designed to *remove* the effect of a committed transaction from the database, although it does not guarantee a return to the same *pretransaction* state as is the case with traditional undo and redo recovery protocols. As an example of a compensating transaction step, say we have a transaction step that withdraws ten dollars from a bank account. A compensating transaction step for the withdrawal transaction step may be to deposit the ten dollars back into the account. This is not to say that some other transaction step may have used the value of the account with the ten dollars removed and possibly may have failed because of this. The goal is to remove the effect of the transaction being compensated for.

The parent transaction can only commit when all of the transaction steps have committed. Upon a failure of a transaction step the parent transaction may decide to undo and restart a failed transaction, or simply compensate the failed transaction step. If the parent transaction chooses the latter recovery option, it must then perform the compensating transaction steps for all committed transaction steps of this transaction. The more desirable approach is to recover the failed transaction step only and continue on. This is the normal mode that would typically be used within a long duration transaction.

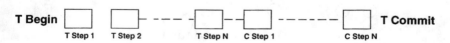

Figure 4.9   Long duration transaction structure

As an example of a long duration transaction we could have a transaction with n parts, as shown in Figure 4.9. This transaction will also be comprised of n compensating transaction steps, one for each of the n original transaction steps. The n parts may be a string of reservations on an airline or for car rentals or stock trades. If any of the reservations or trades fail we wish to cancel them all, since this is the intent of the transaction. The compensators would be required to release the seats ticketed or release the stocks acquired back into the pool of available tickets or stocks.

The advantage of this transaction model is that it loosens the isolation requirement of the ACID properties, allowing subresults to be visible by other transactions. If few failures occur, then this model will deliver higher service. The benefits are also visible in the area of data availability. By allowing locks on transaction steps to be released before the parent transaction commits, we increase the chance for other transactions to acquire data and commit themselves, thereby decreasing waiting queues on long duration locks. One added expense of this transaction model is that transactions must be well formed into disjoint isolated transaction steps that can be committed independently.

4.5.3 Cooperative Transaction Hierarchy

In the cooperative transaction hierarchy model transactions are organized in a manner that enables them to share common data at specific points in execution or through the use of allowable operations on shared objects.

Transactions form a hierarchical tree that defines which transactions can cooperate with other transactions and when they can do this (Figure 4.10). In addition, the cooperation points may have specific operations defined for this sharing. What this implies is that not all operations on the shared objects may be allowed. An object that is being shared may have some set of rules specified for the sharing—for

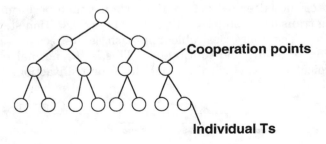

Figure 4.10   Cooperative transaction hierarchy example

example, the owner may read and write an object, but all others can only read. Such transactions may be useful for computer-aided design environments, where designers need to share information with each other regarding boundary information for their designs or functional information for their design fragments. The transactions *cooperate* through the sharing of common data, which are formed into a rooted tree. The individual transactions operate as the leaves of the tree and can cooperate with other transactions through the access and manipulation of connected data at the cooperation points. The cooperation points are defined by a set of *rules*, which indicate how the common data are to be shared. These rules may define the set of allowable operations over the shared set of objects. In addition, the rules may indicate what other conditions must hold for the sharing to be allowed.

4.5.4 Distributed Object Model

The distributed object transaction model has the features described for the nested transaction model, but these features are extended to allow a greater degree of freedom in determining commit requirements. In the distributed object model there are two types of transactions: closed nested and open nested. The closed nested transactions are the same as those described for the nested database system model. Transactions are organized into parent transactions and children transactions with multiple levels of nesting supported. As in the prior version of the nested model, a child transaction commit is bound to the commit of the parent. Likewise, the parent cannot commit unless the children can also commit. The open transactions, on the other hand, are less restricted. There is no top-level atomicity supported; that is, there is no requirement that the parents and the children commit in a bundled unit. Due to this feature there is also a need for compensating transactions, as in the long duration transaction model.

This alone however does not gain us much in the way of added flexibility. We would merely have nested transactions with compensating transactions for them. To provide further flexibility the parent transactions have different classifications and execution policies. There are two types of parents defined in this model. The first is referred to as *vital*. A vital parent is one that is tightly bound to its children. If a child fails or cannot commit for some reason, the parent must follow the same path. This implies that a vital transaction within this model is the same as the nested transactions of the previous model. The second type of parent is called *nonvital*. A nonvital parent transaction does not have to follow the path of a child transaction—for example, if a child fails for some reason, the parent need not follow the same path. The parent can follow its own design and continue, or perform some user-defined operation.

This model and the previous cooperative transaction model are best suited to computer-aided design databases. They have not been proven correct for non-computer-aided design systems, although there appears to be a trend toward proving the correctness of nontraditional transaction processing systems in the literature.

4.5.5 Open Publication Model

The open publications environment was developed to support both long and short duration transactions that have the need to cooperate at a variety of levels. The transactions are not recognizable as the traditional models depict them. This model was developed to operate on higher-level objects and with higher-level operators. The model is composed of three components: assistants, agents, and tools. The tools are those that would be required in a publications environment: text editors, information systems, graphics systems, and the like. The assistants are used to coordinate access to local tools. The agents coordinate access to nonlocal tools. These elements are similar to the communications agents in a distributed system that coordinate the remote and local access to programs and data in a distributed system.

This model strives to reduce the conflict rate of information access by using more *semantic* information about the nature of conflicting transaction access. Transactions that are concurrently accessing information must still coordinate their conflicting access to information if the ACID properties are to be preserved, although this model allows more concurrency by extending operations beyond the simple read and write operations to more complex operations. Conflicting operations must still be serialized, although there is some leeway in how to perform this. If operations from two conflicting operations *commute*, then they are allowed to execute in any order. The commute operation implies that the switching of one operation with the other has no erroneous effect on the database. The use of semantic information to increase concurrency will be discussed further in subsequent chapters.

4.5.6 Contract Model and Split Transaction Model

The basic concept with both the contract model and the split transaction model is the same. The transaction is broken into discrete pieces so that they can commit independently. In the contract model the transaction is broken into discrete steps. Each of these steps is constructed in such a way that it is forward recoverable; that is, the failure of any step does not require the reinitiation or failure of the entire transaction. Each of the steps can be reset to its initiation point and restarted. This allows transactions to be written that will always ultimately commit. The drawback is that the transaction writer must construct well-formed transactions that can operate in this manner. The burden of guaranteeing the correctness of the database is on the transaction writer, not on the database system.

The split transaction model is constructed so that transactions are broken up into separate pieces, allowing each of the pieces to commit independently. The transaction writer sets breakpoints in the transaction to define the points that the writer considers as being good points for subcommits. This model was developed for the benefit of adaptive recovery and for reducing transactions' isolation levels. Transaction recovery can be decomposed into pieces just like the transaction, thereby reducing the effort required in recovering a transaction and speeding its reinitiation. In addition, the split transaction may allow for earlier release of held data items, although this was not an initial goal of the model. The early release of interim results to the outside world was considered important, and this model does allow for this to occur.

4.5.7 Flexible Transaction Model

The flexible transaction model is an attempt to construct transactions that are tuned to the needs of the applications they are supporting. Transactions are decomposed into subtransactions, which have a variety of relationships that can be defined on them (Figure 4.11)—for example, a subtransaction can have an initiation dependency indicating that this subtransaction cannot initiate execution until the defined condition is satisfied. The condition can be the completion of another subtransaction or transaction; the initiation of a subtransaction; a data item's value being set; an event occurring in the system, such as a read or write or flag getting set, the time reaching a predefined boundary point, the successful completion of an action, or the failure of an action; or some other application-defined condition. The flexible transaction model uses various constraints on transaction and data processing and manipulation to determine how to proceed.

Transaction correctness is defined by two metrics: The first is a set of preconditions, which define the initiation conditions that will provide the start point for a correct execution, and the second is the postcondition, which defines the conditions that must be met for the transaction to commit correctly and consistently. This model provides for user-defined semantic recovery using condition handlers from the system for generic errors or faults and from the users for user-defined errors and faults. This model appears to be matched to multimedia

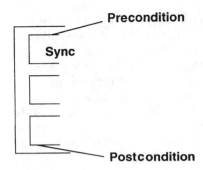

Figure 4.11   Flexible transaction example

and real-time database system needs. The correctness of the model's execution has not as yet been formally proved, although it does appear to adhere to epsilon serializability.

4.5.8 ACTA Model

The ACTA model was developed as a framework upon which other transaction models could be constructed. ACTA consists of a set of transaction initiation constructs, as well as termination, coordination, and commit constructs. Each of these structures has a variety of rules that can be applied to them, defining the policies to follow in executing the construct—for example, initiation conditions can be predicated on the completion of other statements or transactions. Commit could be based on the commit of other transactions or the preparation to commit from subparts of the same transaction. This model has already been used to construct the conventional transaction model, the nested transaction model, and the long duration transaction model. More experience with this type of model may provide further evidence as to the validity of other models, as well as highlight the differences with them based on shared constructs.

4.5.9 Early Commit Model

The early commit model was developed to meet the needs of real-time databases, where high data availability and low blocking delays are essential to meet timing requirements on data access. The model has two parts: The first places constraints on the database structure and manipulation, while the second places constraints on the transaction structure and operations. In the first part, the database is partitioned into *consistency preserving partitions*. These partitions are constructed in one of two ways—one method is to determine the partitions by the

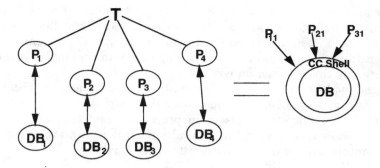

Figure 4.12   Early commit transaction example

closure of constraints defined on the database, while the second method uses the boundaries defined on objects in an object-oriented database along with constraints that bind objects together. In either case the result is a database that consists of multiple disjoint elements, whose consistency and correctness can be maintained in isolation from each other.

With the partitioned database the transactions themselves can now be partitioned across the disjoint database partitions (Figure 4.12). The partitioning of the transactions can be done in a variety of ways. The first and simplest method is to have the transaction writer form the transaction partitions as disjoint entities, each of which execute on only one partition of the database. The more general case is to allow the database management system to determine the partitions on the fly. As statements are executed, the database system determines which database partition it is executing on. This database partition becomes the transaction partition with which to associate this statement. This would be nice if it were that simple, but in addition the database system must check for data uses and definitions within other transaction partitions that may have used derived information from the other database partitions to determine *dependencies*. If a dependency exists, the transaction partitions are merged into larger consistency preserving execution units. In this manner the model forms the transaction into pieces, which can be committed separately, and, more importantly, earlier than the parent transaction in such a way that the ACID properties (albeit loosely defined) can be guaranteed.

This model coordinates the execution of separate transaction partitions on the database partitions in such a way as to guarantee the setwise serializable execution of the partitions on each of the database partitions in the system. This model increases concurrency by isolating commit to a database partition's requirements in isolation instead of for an entire transaction on a monolithic database. The early commit model includes constructs for transaction and subtransaction initiation and boundary marking, as well as dependencies for cooperation, data, commit, and recovery based on the degree of ACID required by the transaction writer.

These models do not by far define all of the transaction processing systems that have been developed over the years. Complete and comprehensive coverage of transaction processing and transaction processing models can be found in several publications, and it will be left to the interested reader to investigate these further.

4.6 CONCURRENCY CONTROL MANAGEMENT

Concurrency control is a mechanism in the database system that handles the *scheduling* of operations on the underlying database's persistent storage subsystem. This scheduler provides the policies and mechanisms necessary to schedule the execution ordering of the operations of multiple concurrently executing transactions. One can think of this element of the database management system as being similar to the task scheduler for an operating system. The scheduler determines how to present the operations for execution on the actual data store in order to guarantee the ACID properties.

The transaction manager within a database system is dependent on the concurrency control protocol and algorithm to order the execution of transaction operations on the underlying database system. The concurrency control manager is the interface to the physical database (Figure 4.13). The goal of this interface is to separate the transaction execution from the persistent store and to order the execution to guarantee the *serializability* of executions on the database.

If we have N transactions, as shown in Figure 4.14, that wish to execute on the database, the concurrency control manager acts as the funnel to transform the stream of parallel database accesses from the N transactions and form them into a serial stream of accesses on the database. The goal of this funneling operation is to select and order the operations presented to the concurrency control scheduler in such a way that the effect of the ordering is as if the concurrent transaction

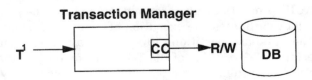

Figure 4.13   Transaction manager and concurrency control interface

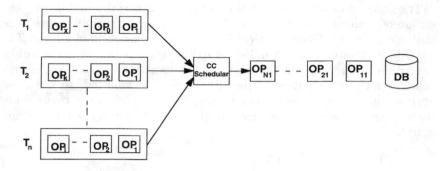

Figure 4.14   Concurrency control scheduler example

operations were executed one entire transaction at a time in serial order.

The concept of *serial* order is important as a correctness criterion for transaction execution in order to guarantee the ACID properties of transactions. In our example we wish the effect of the concurrent transactions to be:

$$T1 > T2 > T3 > T4 \ldots TN$$

or any other ordering that is the same as if a strict serial execution of the transactions occurred. This serialization ordering must be adhered to for all *conflicting* operations from the set of transactions. Other nonconflicting operations do not have to adhere to the same strict ordering, since their execution has no effect on the other transactions. In reality the transactions have their nonconflicting operations interleaved. The conflicting operations, on the other hand, must be strictly ordered. In addition, once an ordering has been determined, all conflicting operations from the same transactions must be ordered in the same way—for example, if transaction 1 and transaction 2 have conflicting operations, then either all conflicting operations from transaction 1 precede those from transaction 2 or all of the operations from transaction 2 precede those from transaction 1. In other words, for all conflicting operations from $T1$ and $T2$, either

$$T1 > T2$$

or

$$T2 > T1$$

and the structural ordering of $T1$ and $T2$ must be consistent.

The concept of adherence to the allusion of a serial schedule or execution of transactions is referred to as *serializability*; that is, the executions of *T*1 and *T*2 are equivalent to a serial execution of *T*1 and *T*2.

Why is it important to adhere to this strict policy of serializable execution of operations? To illustrate the reasons we will look at the results of three executions where this policy is violated. In the first case we have two transactions *T*1 and *T*2, each of which reads data item X, then performs some computations, and then writes data item X back to the database.

*T*1	*T*2
BOT *T*1	
R(X)	
	BOT *T*2
	R(X)
W(X)	
EOT *T*1	W(X) -> *Causes Lost Update from T1*
	EOT *T*2

The first transaction *T*1 reads X. This is followed in the next time frame by the beginning of transaction *T*2 and the read of data item X by *T*2. At this point both *T*1 and *T*2 have the same value for data item X in their work areas. Transaction *T*1 then writes a new value for data item X into the database and then completes execution. Data item X now has a new value for X stored in the database. In the next step, transaction *T*2 now writes a different value over the value for data item X. This value will replace the value stored by *T*1, resulting in the effect of the write from *T*1 being *lost*. This is referred to as the lost update problem. To correct this problem, if we require either *T*1 or *T*2 to wait until the other has performed its write of data item X before it can be read, the results would not be lost, since the trailing transaction *sees* the value written by the leading transaction upon its read.

The second problem deals with failures and their effects on serialization order and the correctness of data. In this example transaction,

*T*1	*T*2
BOT *T*1	
R(X)	
W(X)	
	BOT *T*2
	R(X) -> *T*2 *reads update of* X

Abort *T*1 -> *T1's failure causes dirty read of* X *from T*1

W(X)

*T*1 initially reads data item X and then updates data item X. *T*2 follows this in the proper order and reads the update from *T*1 on data item X. *T*1 then fails, resulting in the abort of the effect of *T*1 on the database. Since *T*2 has read this value before *T*1 had committed, it now has a data value that is invalid due to the abort. This read is called a dirty read, since it cannot be repeated and is not permanent in the database. To rectify this situation a transaction cannot read the values of data items written by another transaction until the commit of these values to the database. The commit guarantees the permanence of the changes to the database, removing the possibility of the data item becoming invalid after reading it.

The third problem deals with allowing transactions to see intermediate values from each other's execution and the anomaly that results from this. In this example we have two transactions, *T*1 and *T*2, as follows:

*T*1	*T*2
BOT *T*1	
Sum := 0	
R(X)	
R(Y)	
Sum := Sum + X	
Sum := Sum + Y	
	BOT *T*2
	R(Z)
	Z := Z − 10
	W(Z)
	R(X)
	X := X + 10
	W(X)
	Commit
	EOT *T*2

R(Z) -> *Reads updated value for* Z

Sum := Sum + Z -> *Sum now not correct—110 instead of the correct 120*

EOT *T*1	W(X) -> Lost Update from T1

Assuming the initial values for the data items were X = 40, Y = 50, and Z = 30, the results of these two transactions produce Sum by adding X and Y together, resulting in a value of 90, followed by transaction $T2$ altering Z from 30 to 20 and X from 40 to 50. Transaction $T1$ then reads the updated value for Z, which is 20, and adds this to 90, resulting in a value of 110 for Sum. This value is easily shown to be wrong, since the second transaction moved 10 from Z to X, not altering the actual Sum, but altering the value for Z to be read by $T1$. This problem of reading data from another transaction's commit, which altered the data already read by the transaction, is called the *phantom* or unrepeatable read problem. To rectify this form of concurrency control problem requires that transactions first acquire all the data items they need for their operation in *exclusive* mode before they perform their computations on the data. All of these problems can be corrected if conflicting operations are correctly ordered and no viewing of any intermediate data values is allowed.

4.6.1 Serializability

We have already defined a transaction as a partial ordering of its own operations such that the following conditions hold.

- $Ti = \{\Sigma i \, <i \, \}$

where

- $\Sigma i = OSi \cup Ni$

For any two operations from Ti

$$\{Oij, Oik\} \in OSi \text{ If } Oij = R(X) \text{ and } Oik = W(X)$$

Then for any X, either

$$Oij <i Oik$$

or

$$Oik <i Oij$$

$$\forall \, Oij \in OSi, Oij <i Ni$$

But when more than one transaction acts concurrently on the database, we need an expanded definition of correctness, which must include the ordering of these conflicting operations over some period of time. The definition used is based on the history of execution for a set of transaction operations on a database. The history reflects how the concurrency control scheduler executed the operations from the set of transactions. A history of concurrent transaction operations is defined as:

1. $H = \cup i = 1, N\ Ti$
2. $<H \subset \cup i = 1, N <i$
3. For conflicting operations $P, Q \in H$ either

   $-P <H\ Q$ or $Q <H\ P$

What this extended definition indicates is that a history, H, is comprised of the union of all transactions that have executed. Second, the order of the operations in the history does not violate any of the ordering relationships for any transaction within the history. Third, for all conflicting operations within the history, all operations from conflicting transactions are strictly ordered.

The history or schedule for a set of transactions as defined above is used as the means to determine or prove the correctness of execution for a set of concurrently executing transactions. A schedule for a set of transactions is an execution of the set with specified orderings—for example, given four transactions as shown:

1. $t0 = W0(X), W0(Z), W0(Y)$
2. $t1 = W1(X), W1(Z), W1(Y)$
3. $t2 = R2(X), W2(Y)$
4. $t3 = R3(Z), W3(Z), W3(Y)$

A strict serial schedule, $S1$, for these transactions in the order

$$S1 = t0 > t1 > t2 > t3$$

would represent the sequence of operations as:

$$S1 = W0(X), W0(Z), W0(Y), W1(X), W1(Z), W1(Y), R2(X), W2(Y),$$
$$R3(Z), W3(Z), W3(Y)$$

This is a *strict* serial scheduling of these transaction operations and by definition is a correct execution and will result in a new consistent database state.

Another way to show the schedule of operations in a schedule S is to use a directed acyclic graph, or DAG representation (Figure 4.15). This, however, is not the only schedule that can be generated that will result in a correct execution. Any serial ordering of the four transac-

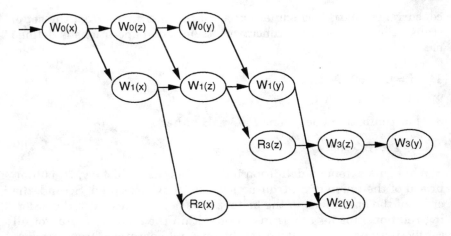

Figure 4.15 DAG schedule example

tions and a strict serial execution of these will also be correct. Therefore, the schedules

1. $S1 = t0 > t1 > t2 > t3$
2. $S2 = t1 > t0 > t2 > t3$
3. $S3 = t1 > t2 > t0 > t3$
4. $S4 = t1 > t2 > t3 > t0$
5. $S5 = t2 > t0 > t1 > t3$
6. $S6 = t2 > t3 > t0 > t1$
7. $S7 = t2 > t1 > t3 > t0$
8. $S8 = t3 > t0 > t1 > t2$
9. $S9 = t3 > t1 > t2 > t0$
10. $S10 = t3 > t0 > t1 > t2$
11. $S11 = t3 > t2 > t0 > t1$
12. $S12 = t0 > t2 > t3 > t1$
13. $S13 = t0 > t3 > t1 > t2$

are also strictly correct, since they represent strict serial executions of
the operations from the four transactions. The problem is that this is
not that interesting and it does not increase the ability to perform a
greater volume of transactions in a unit of time. Strict serial execution
will result in excessive waiting and a loss in performance.

To improve this situation we look at what is not strictly serial, but
what nonetheless produces correct and consistent results. The method

of serial equivalence is used. A serial equivalent schedule is a schedule whose effect on the database is the same as if the transactions involved had actually executed in some serial fashion—for example, the schedule $S14$ = W0(X), R1(X), W0(Z), R1(Z), W1(X), W0(Y), R2(X), R3(Z), W3(Z), W2(Y), W3(Y) can be shown to be e*quivalent* to the serial schedule $S1$ = W0(X), W0(Z), W0(Y), R1(X), R1(Z), W1(X), R2(X), W2(Y), R3(Z), W3(Z), W3(Y), since the conflicting operations in $S14$ are ordered in the same way as those in $S1$. In particular notice the conflicts between $t0$ and $t1$—W0(X) precedes R1(X) and W1(X), and the W0(Z) in $t0$ precedes the conflicting R1(Z) in transaction $t1$. Likewise, conflicts between $t1$ and $t2$ follow the same pattern. The conflicting read of X follows the writes of $t0$ and $t1$ and the conflicting write of data item Y in $t2$ follows the write on Y from $t0$. Finally, the conflicting read and write of data item Z in transaction $t3$ follows all previous reads and writes on data item Z from $t0$ and $t1$.

The test for equivalence is to check that all conflicting operations in one serial schedule match those in the tested schedule. If all conflicting operations are ordered in a compatible manner, then the two schedules are equivalent. Since a serial schedule is correct, then an equivalent serializable schedule is also correct.

Other forms of correctness criteria have been postulated and are presented here for completeness. The first alternate form of correctness is called *view serializable*. A view serializable schedule is one where two schedules, S and S', are view serializable if and only if all reads in S and S' follow the same writes in both S and S'. This implies that all read actions will read the value of the last write viewable. For both schedules all such reads and writes follow the same pattern—for example, in schedule $S1$ W1(Z) is followed by R3(Z), followed by W2(Z), and finally R4(Z). To be view equivalent both schedules must order the reads and writes in the same way. This will result in both transactions arriving at the same final writes and, therefore, results. Two view equivalent schedules are view serializable if there exists some *serial* schedule S'' such that $S'' \equiv S$. View equivalence and serializability are not equivalent to strict serializability.

The second alternative form of serialization testing looks at conflict equivalence and conflict serializability. Conflict equivalence is derived from the ordering of conflicting operations within a schedule. Two schedules are conflict equivalent if, for all pairs of operations that are in conflict, the order in S for these operations is equivalent to the order of the same conflicting operations in schedule S'—for example, if there are two operations Ai and Bj from transactions i and j, respectively, that are in conflict with each other, then for the two schedules S and S', of which Ai and Bj are elements, either Ai precedes Bj in S and in S' or Bj precedes Ai in S and S'. Only if the same order of conflict follows in both schedules are the schedules *conflict* equivalent.

Two schedules that are conflict equivalent can also be conflict serializable if and only if one of the schedules is a serial schedule of transactions i and j. Since the schedules are defined as conflict equivalent, and since one of the schedules is also serial, then the schedules are conflict serializable.

With a correctness criterion in place that has been proven correct, we must next examine how this technique can be applied in a realistic environment at a reasonable cost. Three major techniques have been developed to guarantee serializability in an operational environment. These techniques are called locking, timestamp ordering, and optimistic concurrency control protocols. These techniques can be classified as either pessimistic or optimistic. Pessimistic protocols assume problems will occur and therefore specify means to avoid the problems, whereas optimistic techniques assume conflicts will be rare and use methods to discover problems before the database is committed.

The first protocol is a pessimistic protocol and is based on the use of locks. The locking protocol operates in two phases of lock manipulation. In the first phase of operation a transaction acquires all the locks it needs as they are needed. Once a lock is acquired it is held until the transaction ends its processing. This phase of transaction processing is called the growing phase, where all locks needed are acquired. At the end of transaction processing, the transaction begins releasing locks. Once a lock has been released, the transaction is said to be in the shrinking phase and cannot acquire any additional locks. This protocol requires only a few simple primitives to implement: a lock table, and read and write locks. The lock table is used to indicate what locks are held on what data items by which transaction. A lock can be either a read lock (sometimes called a shared lock) or a write lock (sometimes referred to as an exclusive lock). When a read lock is requested the lock manager must examine the lock table to see if a lock is already held on the requested data item. If no lock is held the request is granted. If a read lock is held by any other transaction or by this transaction, the lock is granted (read locks do not conflict). If a write lock is held by any transaction, other than the requester, the lock request is rejected, but it can be queued for future granting. If a write lock is requested, the lock table is again checked for conflicting locks. The write lock can only be granted if no other transactions hold a read or a write lock on this object. If a write lock is rejected the request is queued for future checking on the data item.

The problem with locking is that if one transaction, $t1$, holds a lock on a data item, say X, being requested by another transaction, $t2$, and $t2$ holds a lock on a data item, say Y, which $t1$ is requesting, we have a situation called deadlock.

$t1$ $t2$

Wlock(X)

Wlock(Y)

Wlock(Y) -> $t1$ *waits on* $t2$

Wlock(X) -> $t2$ *waits on* $t1$

DEADLOCK

Deadlock is the condition where all involved transactions cannot move forward and are forced to wait for a condition that will never be satisfied. Deadlock can be a major problem in systems where locking is employed and there are high rates of contention for data resources. To guarantee that the database system can still perform useful work, the database manager must possess the ability to discover when deadlock exists and to recover from deadlock when it is found. To detect deadlock requires the construction and maintenance of a directed graph.

The directed graph consists of nodes representing transactions and arcs representing the waiting on resources held by another transaction. The graph is scanned for cycles (fully connected path, where the traversing of the arcs leads from the beginning back to itself over some number of intermediary nodes, as shown in Figure 4.16). If a cycle in the graph has been detected, then deadlock is present. To recover from deadlock a victim must be chosen from the waiting transactions within the graph. The victim chosen has its locks removed and returned to the pool for the waiting transactions to acquire. The choice of a victim can be based on a variety of conditions, such as the

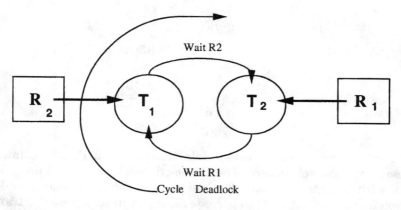

Figure 4.16 Deadlock detection using directed graph

transaction that has been running the shortest time, one that has been running the longest time, and so forth.

The second form of concurrency control protocol scheduler is based on the use of timestamps and the ordering of accesses based on the timestamp of the transactions and the timestamps on data items. A timestamp can be derived in a number of ways: It can come from the system's time clock or from some artificial counter that assigns a monotonically increasing value. In any case, the timestamp is viewed as a unique value and cannot be the same for any two transactions. In a concurrency control protocol using timestamp ordering transactions a timestamp is acquired at initiation (the beginning of the transaction). This timestamp is then used by the transaction to order accesses in timestamp order. Each data item in the system initially begins with a timestamp of zero. On a read or write access the timestamp of the data item is updated based on the application of the following tests. If the write timestamp stored at the data item is less than the read timestamp of the requesting transaction, then the request is okay, and the transaction's timestamp becomes the data item's new stored read timestamp. On the other hand, if a transaction finds that the stored timestamp is greater than the transaction's timestamp, the request fails. The transaction is aborted and it restarts by acquiring a new timestamp. The restarted transaction can now begin again with a new value for its timestamp. On a write the transaction checks if the read and write timestamps are less than the transaction's timestamp. If the test succeeds the transaction updates the write timestamp and continues on.

$$\text{Ts}(t1) = 300, \text{Ts}(t2) = 100, \text{Ts}(t3) = 200$$

$t1$	$t2$	$t3$
	R2(A)	
		R3(A)
		W3(A)
R1(B)		
	R2(B)	
	W2(B)	

In this example we have two data items, A and B, whose initial timestamps are set at zero. The transactions $t1$, $t2$, and $t3$ are initiated with timestamps 300, 100, and 200, respectively. The intended action is for transaction $t2$ to precede $t3$, which in turn precedes transaction $t1$, based on the initial timestamps provided. If we assume the operations are provided to the concurrency control system, as indicated above, the following actions will occur. On the read of data item A by transaction $t2$, the check finds that the timestamp of A is less than the timestamp of $t2$, so the action is allowed and data item B's read timestamp is set to 100. On transaction $t3$'s read of data item A the test determines that the read and write timestamps for A are less than the transaction's timestamp so the action is allowed, and the read timestamp for A is changed to 200. On the write of A by $t3$ the test finds that the write timestamp of A and the read timestamp of A are less than or equal to the transaction's timestamp. The test succeeds and the operation is allowed. The write timestamp of A is then set to 200, the timestamp of transaction $t3$. The action in the timeline is the read of data item B by transaction $t1$. On the test transaction $t1$ finds that the timestamps of data item B are both at zero, so the test suceeds and the operation is allowed to occur. The read timestamp for B is updated to 300. The next operation is a read of data item B by transaction $t2$. On the test the stored read timestamp is found to be greater than the read timestamp of the transaction. The test fails and the transaction cannot go on. The transaction is aborted since its test failed.

In this protocol the conflicts are possibly found earlier than the locking protocol, since this protocol is more pessimistic in the sense that it immediately halts execution on detecting a conflict, whereas the locking protocols form the contending locks into waiting chains, which may not be found to be in error until later in execution.

The final concurrency control protocol is the optimistic protocol. The optimistic concurrency control protocol operates by letting all actions occur (in private space) and then validating that they are correct before installing them on the database. A transaction's reads and writes are allowed to occur uncontrolled during transaction execution. Initial reads come from the database. All secondary access to data items (reads or writes) is directed to the working space of the transaction and occurs there. At the end of the transaction's execution, but before commit, the set of all reads and writes to the database is validated against all other validated or pending transaction reads or writes to see if any conflicts arose during execution. If no conflicts were found (validation succeeded), then the transaction's changes are installed into the database. If any conflicts were detected (validation failed), the transaction is aborted and its working space deleted.

One form of validation in optimistic protocols uses the read and write sets of a transaction and compares these to any other transaction's read and write sets in the validation phase. The test performed uses two timestamps—an initial timestamp and a final timestamp. The validation examines all transactions within this frame of time. For all reads in the transaction, test if the read set of T's timestamp is greater than or equal to the write set of all other validating transactions. For the writes in the write set of transaction T, test if the write timestamp is greater than or equal to the read and write timestamps for all other validating transactions.

$$Ts(t1) = 200, \ Ts(t2) = 150, \ Ts(t3) = 175$$

$t1$	$t2$	$t3$	A	B	C
R(B)			r = 0,w = 0	r = 200,w = 0	r = 0,w = 0
	R(A)		r = 150,w = 0		
		R(C)			r = 175,w = 0
W(B)				r = 200,w = 200	
W(A)			r = 150,w = 200		
		W(C)			r = 150,w = 175
		W(A)			

In the example above, upon validation of transaction 1, we find that transaction 1's read set and write set indicate that all active transactions have read and write timestamps before my timestamps, so this transaction's validation succeeds. This is not the case for the other two transactions. Since transaction 1 reached validation first and succeeded, its timestamps are inserted as the basis timestamps against which the validation reads and writes will be compared. Transaction 2 enters validation next and finds that its read timestamp is less than the basis read timestamp and that its write set has conflict with transaction 3's write set. When transaction 3 validates, it finds its write set intersects transaction 1's write set. Transaction 3 would be aborted and restarted. Some extension protocols allow transaction 3 to commit, by indicating that transaction 3's write would have been overwritten by transaction 1's in time; therefore, it can be ignored and allowed to commit, although not writing its changes to the database.

There are numerous other concurrency control protocols that are variations on these basic protocols and will not be mentioned here. In addition, there are even more specialized concurrency control protocols for the specialized systems to be discussed in subsequent chapters. Some of these protocols will be discussed, but it will be left to the interested reader to explore beyond these boundaries for more specialized implementations and concepts.

4.7 QUERY PROCESSING

The function of query processing is to find a way to provide the answer to the user in a more efficient and timely manner. The problem is that most database languages tell the system *what* is being looked for, not *how* to most efficiently find it and retrieve it. There are exceptions to this rule. The early network database languages provided the *how* through the requirement to navigate the network, although the user-provided navigation through the database may not have been optimal.

There are a few techniques worth mentioning here, although most are applicable to the relational model. It has not yet been proven if these or other techniques are applicable to object database systems. The first method discussed is the brute-force method. This bounds the lower end of performance for query processing protocols. In the brute-force method, no optimization is attempted. The query is processed as it arrives: in the same form, with no modification. In this case the cost of answering a query is proportional to the magnitudes of the involved relations, objects, or entities modified by the operation being performed—for example, if a join is being performed the cost is proportional to the multiplicative values of the magnitudes; that is, if the size of two involved relations is 100 tuples, the relative cost is 100 times 100, or 10,000 units. If the operation is a union or selection type of operation, then the relative cost is the additive value of the magnitudes of the involved relations. In general the cost is proportional to some additive or multiplicative factor with the involved relations, which can become a very large value with relatively small relations.

This proportionality cost, however, can be reduced. By the proper and selective application of reductions, the factor can be greatly trimmed down. Some possible reductions include the following.

1. Attempt to reduce the secondary storage accesses—only get what is needed; find a way to reduce the data flowing from the disks.

2. Find a way to reduce the size of accessed data structures—for example, by applying some reduction operations during initial access.

3. Try to improve access to stored data (presort, multiple keys sorted on access keys). Reorder the access pattern to minimize some form of cost function.

The last option is the most typical for reducing cost on line. The other metrics can be used a priori to aid in the reduction function. To illustrate the cost differences we will examine a relational database system example. Given that we have two relations, A and B, the query is to project a from A joined with B, where x.A is equal to y.B and y.B is equal to 99. The first approach is to try to perform the query by brute-force methods. This would operate as follows.

1. Join relation A with relation B.
2. Select those tuples that meet x.A = y.B.
3. Select from the resultant tuples those that meet y.B = 99.
4. Project column with attribute equal to a.

The cost of this brute-force approach, assuming first that all relations can fit in memory, includes:

- Read relation A then relation B, at a cost of the magnitude of A plus B (I A + B I).
- For all A over B concatenate relation A tuples to those of relation B at a cost of the magnitudes of A times B (I A * B I).
- Scan the results of A joined with B for condition x.A = y.B at a cost of the magnitude of A times B (I A * B I).
- Scan the results of the previous reduction for y.B = 99 at a cost of somewhat less than the cost of the magnitude of A times B (I A * B I).
- Copy the result of the reductions at a cost of less than the magnitude of A times B < (I A * B I).
- Copy the column needed for the final result at a cost of less than the magnitude of A times B < (I A * B I).

The total cost for the brute-force method is approximately the aggregate cost of the magnitude of ((A + B) + 5 (AB)).

If the relations, objects, or entities involved in the query are large, then the brute-force approach is unacceptable. This cost gets even worse if we cannot fit the entire relation in memory. To rectify this problem requires reorganizing how a query is to be answered. The main goal of optimization is to reduce the size of the relations involved in answering a query at each step of the process. Pushing down reductions to the earliest point of the query process is possible, thereby reducing the overall cost proportionally.

To aid in this process queries are formed into a tree structure. The initial tree is constructed using the brute-force approach, representing each operation as either a branching limb (a binary operation) or a leaf operation (a unary operation) (Figure 4.17). The initial tree makes no attempt to limit cost at any step. It represents each step in simple form.

To make this tree optimal we must apply the simple rules listed earlier. The most important optimization is to reduce all base rela-

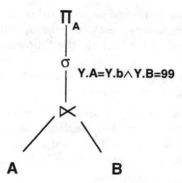

Figure 4.17   Initial query tree

tions to the smallest degree possible. This is accomplished by pushing down any selections or projections that only require information from a single relation. In the example above this would be represented by moving the selection of all tuples that meet the criterion of x.B = 99 down to the leaf node that includes relation B (Figure 4.18). This moves the reduction below the Cartesian product, which will result in a smaller result than if the reduction were not applied. A second reduction is possible where the Cartesian product is performed. By using the cross-equality that x.A = y.B, we can form the Cartesian product into an equijoin by pushing this selection into the Cartesian product operation. This operation causes a resulting relation much smaller than would have occurred through simply applying the Cartesian product without the selection conditions being applied (Figure 4.18).

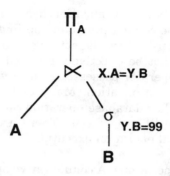

Figure 4.18   Optimized query tree

From this discussion some general rules, which will result in significant reductions in query costs, can be specified. General reductions that should be looked for include the following.

1. Perform all selection operations as early as possible to reduce the initial input to binary operations.

2. Preprocess files appropriately before joins to reduce the volume of data to be viewed. Prudent sorting may allow the selection to cut off before the end of file, for example. Preprocessing includes sorting, adding extra indexes, and so forth.

3. Look for common subexpressions within a query stream—for example, similar selections or projections. These may allow the reduction to be formed into a range of values instead of a simple less than or greater than selection.

4. Cascade selections and projections in a string to further reduce the size of relations involved in binary operations. Perform these operations in parallel during a *single* scan to reduce the cost of preprocessing a file.

5. Combine projections with binary operations that precede or follow them—for example, apply projections on relations before a union, difference, and so on to reduce the size of resulting relations.

6. Combine selections with Cartesian products before operations—for example, perform selections on relations to reduce the number of tuples to be involved in a binary relation such as a join operation before the join is begun.

4.8 RELATIONAL OPTIMIZATION AND PROPERTIES

Many of the concepts for optimization use basic properties of the operations to aid in the computation of an optimal execution plan. Without the ability to reorder how the actual operation is to be performed, optimization could not be effectively pursued and implemented. The relational model's operator possesses a variety of properties that lend themselves well to optimization. Many of these properties are also applicable to the other database operation models, such as the object model, although in differing forms. There are nine basic properties defined for relational operation executions.

1. Commutative operations: A commutative operation is one that can be switched and performed in another order, but will still result in the same result. The join is such an operation. The join of two relations, R1 and R2, can be performed with R1 first and then R2,

or R2 first and then R1. Either form will result in the same result, since the operation is commutative. The add operation is a similar form of operation that possesses the commutative property.

2. Associative operations: An associative operation is one that can have its relationships reordered, resulting in a different order of operation, yet the final result is still the same. In basic math the addition operation is associative—for example, given $(10 + 5) + 6$, the operation indicates add 10 with 5, get a result, and then add 6. The 10 and 5 are *associated* together by the parentheses. Associativity indicates that we can reassociate the operators and still get the same result; therefore, we can perform $10 + (5 + 6)$ and expect the same result if associativity holds, which it does. The join operation is associative, thus allowing a string of joins to be ordered arbitrarily to provide a minimum cost function result. The selection of which order to perform the operations in becomes the optimization function for associative operators.

3. Cascade unary operations: The projection in the relational model is a unary operation, which can be grouped together and performed in parallel—for example, given the order N squared operation of $\Pi a_i \ldots \Pi a_n (\Pi b_j \ldots \Pi b_m (R))$ by the combining of the projections from two cascading levels into one level, Πa_i , $\Pi b_j \ldots$ $\Pi a_n, \Pi b_m (R)$, executed once in unison on the relation, the cost can be reduced to order N operations, since we are not iterating twice over the same relation trying to project the same column(s).

4. Cascading selections: As with the projections, if multiple selections are being sequentially applied to a relation in a nested fashion $\sigma_{f1}, \sigma_{f2} (\ldots \sigma_{fn} (R))$, these costs can be grouped and performed in unison during a single iteration. This will alter the cost of the operation from N raised to the power of N to an order N operational cost.

5. Commuting selections with projections: This optimization property deals with reordering accesses to reduce the volume of tuples to be operated on by following stages of the query—for example, if we have a query of the form $\sigma_{f1} (\Pi a_i \ldots \Pi a_n (R))$, we can possibly reduce the cost of this operation by first applying the selection to reduce the number of tuples and then perform the projection to get only those tuples and attributes wanted. The saving here is mostly in the copying cost of a relation, but still is a cost of order N savings. The altered sequence of query steps looks like $\Pi a_i \ldots \Pi a_n$ $(\sigma_{f1} (R))$.

6. Commuting selection with products (joins): The same type of optimization is possible by commuting selections through all join participants before the join operation is performed. This type of

optimization results in smaller relations being joined at a lower cost than if the initial unreduced relations were used—for example, the query σ_{f1} (R1 × R2) can be rewritten to reduce the volume of both relations before the join by commuting the selection to σ_{f1} (R1) × σ_{f1} (R2). The cost is reduced from order N * N to something much smaller on the order of n * n, where n << N.

7. Commuting selection with general binary operations: The selection operator is a basic reduction operator for use in optimization. It should be used in all possible cases to reduce the number of tuples to be scanned in a binary operation. In the relational model we can apply commuting of selection reductions on the binary relational operations of difference, intersect, and union. For the difference a query of the form σ_{f1} (R1 − R2) can be optimized by commuting the selection to the two relations separately, σ_{f1} (R1) − Σ_{f1} (R2). This will result in a cost somewhat lower than the initial cost without commuting the selection. For the intersect a query of the form σ_{f1} (R1 ∩ R2) can be optimized by commuting the selection to the two relations separately, σ_{f1} (R1) intersect σ_{f1} (R2). This will result in a cost lower than the initial cost without commuting the selection. Finally for the union a query of the form σ_{f1} (R1 ∪ R2) can be optimized by commuting the selection to the two relations separately: σ_{f1} (R1) ∪ σ_{f1} (R2). This will result in a reduced cost lower than the initial cost without commuting the selection.

8. Commuting projection with joins: The function of this property and optimization is to commute the projections of attributes to the relations before the join is performed in order to reduce the size of the relation being generated through the join. The initial general query, Π_{a_i} ... Π_{a_n} (R1 × R2), is reduced to the form Π_{a_i} ... Π_{a_n} (R1) × Π_{a_i} ... Π_{a_n} (R2).

9. Commuting projections with binary operations of difference, union, and intersect: This operation, like the previous ones, will result in a smaller volume of storage needed to copy the relations and reduce the size of the intermediate relations that must be manipulated in performing these binary operations. For the difference, a query of the form Π_{a_i} ... Π_{a_n} (R1 − R2) can be optimized by commuting the selection to the two relations separately: Π_{a_i} ... Π_{a_n} (R1) − Π_{a_i} ... Π_{a_n} (R2). This will result in a cost somewhat lower than the initial cost without commuting the selection.

For the intersect, a query of the form Π_{a_i} ... Π_{a_n} (R1 ∩ R2) can be optimized by commuting the selection to the two relations separately, Π_{a_i} ... Π_{a_n} (R1) Π_{a_i} ... Π_{a_n} (R2). This will result in a cost lower than the initial cost without commuting the selection. Finally, for the union a query of the form $\Pi a_i \ldots \Pi a_n$ (R1) $\cup$ (R2) can be optimized by commuting the selection to the two relations separately: $\Pi a_i \ldots \Pi a_n$ (R1) $\cup$ $\Pi a_i \ldots \Pi a_n$ (R2). This will result in a reduced cost lower than the initial cost without commuting the selection.

The optimization of a given query must use the above properties to reduce the cost based on some given optimization policy. The general process for optimizing a query begins with a brute-force query tree as the start point. This represents a worst-case cost for most queries. The process for optimization first looks to distribute selections to the base relations, where possible, to reduce the size of all relations involved. Once a set of selections is associated with a relation or relations in the tree, the next step is to push selections down the query tree as low as possible, with the optimum being the leaves. With all possible selection reductions in place, the next operation is to move projections from the root of the tree down to the branches and leaves of the tree. The final optimization recombines projections and selections into singular operation sequences on relations to reduce the need for multiple scanning of relations to perform multiple unary operations on the same relation.

As an example, given the three relations

1. Frequents (diner, restaurant)
2. Serves (restaurant, cuisine)
3. Likes (diner, cuisine)

we wish to ask the query: *Find the diners who frequent a restaurant serving food they like.* The query looks like:

Π diner,restaurant,cuisine
    (σServes.restaurant = Frequents.restaurant and
    Serves.cuisine = Likes.cuisine
    (Frequents $\times$ Serves $\times$ Likes)

The initial query tree for this query is shown in Figure 4.19a. In this query tree one should notice that the operations are exactly as specified, with the leaves of the tree having the base relations, the first-level branch nodes are the joins, and the trunk has the selection and projection operations, respectively.

The optimization of this tree begins by pushing the selections down the tree as low as possible. In this example the selections amount to equijoin conditions and can therefore be pushed down to the branch-

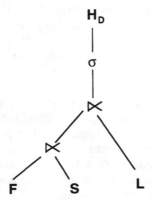

Figure 4.19a   Initial query tree

ing nodes of the tree, transforming the Cartesian products into equi-joins. After this step in the optimization is completed, the next step is to push the projection operations down the tree as low as possible. In this example we can push the projection of the cuisine and diners down to the node trunk, before the equijoin of frequents and diner. The final projection remains at the top of the tree to extract the diners who meet our query specifications (Figure 4.19b). A further optimization would be to examine the cost functions associated with the order of evaluation for the three relations within the join operations. If the reordering of which join to do when results in a lower cost, the joins should be reordered.

Π Diner (σ F.Diner=S.Diner$\wedge$ S.Cuisine=L.Cuisine $\wedge$F.Restaurant=S.Rest FreqX Ser XL.Res)

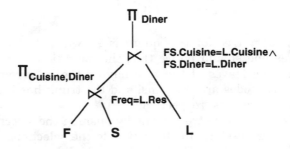

Figure 4.19b   Optimized query tree

4.9 FAULT AND FAILURE RECOVERY

A database must have the ability to recover from error or fault conditions within the system. A failure can take on many forms and be derived from a variety of sources—for example, a failure can be caused due to a transaction that does not terminate normally due to deadlock, inconsistency in the database, or a fault in the software of the transaction or database system. A failure could be caused by a system-related problem, such as a loss of power or a failed memory chip or data path. A failure may be caused by the loss of the secondary storage system due to a disk crash or driver failure. Whatever the cause, the database manager must possess the means to recover the database to a stable place in order that correct execution can continue. The failures the database manager must be concerned with are:

- Transaction failure: any problem that causes an abnormal termination of a transaction

- System failure: any problem that causes a loss of main memory or access to main memory.

- Medium failure: any problem that causes loss of the persistent database storage medium.

We will focus here on the errors that cause transaction failures. Other failures, such as medium and hardware failure, must be dealt with through fault-tolerant hardware features. These will be covered in greater detail in Chapter 15.

When a systems failure occurs, transactions are in one of two states (Figure 4.20):

1. Transactions *committed* before crash

2. Transactions *not committed* before crash

For transactions that have committed before a crash, transaction recovery uses the *REDO* protocol. For transactions that have not committed before the crash, transaction recovery is performed using the *UNDO* protocol.

Before we discuss the undo and redo protocols let's examine some of the basic needs of a database system for recovery to be provided. Recovery is required for both committed and uncommitted transactions due to the operating system's operations that page information into and out of memory. Some committed transactions may not have been written yet to persistent storage and at other times some uncommitted transaction information may have been written to persistent stor-

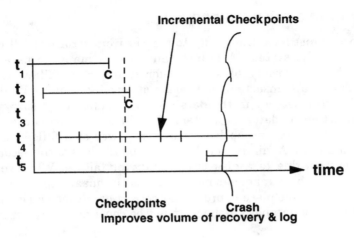

Figure 4.20   Transaction states on failure

age before it completed. These forced writes to the database result in a database that may not be 100 percent accurate. Due to these issues recovery of transactions must take into account the possibility of a corrupted database state.

The most fundamental requirement for recovery policies and implementations is redundancy. Redundancy at all levels is required for fault-tolerant systems and at some key points for basic recovery. To aid recovery, at a minimum, the medium must have redundancy. Medium redundancy allows for the recovery of the database in the case of storage subsystem failures, but it does not necessarily result in the ability for transaction recovery. For transaction recovery we must provide redundancy within the transaction subsystem. Transaction redundancy comes in the form of transaction actions. A *log* file is maintained in stable storage and contains all transaction operations that could affect the database's consistency and correctness. The information stored in the log may include a transaction before images (initial reads and initial data states on writes), after images (new database state information), and the specific actions required to get from the before image to the after image. In addition, to aid in the recovery, the database recovery manager may periodically create a copy of the database, called a checkpoint or snapshot. This represents a consistent correct copy of the database, which can be used for recovery if needed.

The recovery manager uses these pieces of information to aid in the recovery of transactions. The redo protocol uses the logs after images to restore a committed transaction's state to the persistent database. The undo protocol uses the before images of the database to restore the database to a pretransaction consistent state by removing any inadvertently written data items from the database. For the undo and redo protocols to operate correctly necessitates that the log be safe and persistent itself. For the log to be safe and persistent the database recovery manager must have the ability to force the flushing of the active log to the stable storage system. In addition, this flush function must be an atomic action. For redo the *commit rule* applies, which requires that the committed database changes be flushed to stable storage. For undo uses the write ahead log protocol applies, which requires that the before images for this transaction be written to the stable storage.

4.9.1 Undo/Redo

The undo/redo algorithm (Figure 4.21) is the simplest and least costly of the recovery algorithms at run time, but is the most expensive on recovery. This protocol accumulates actions and changes in the program data area and periodically writes these and other information out to the log file. There is no attempt to install changes on commit or otherwise directly to the database. The updates are handled periodically by the database system commit processing. The problem lies in the operating system's paging algorithm, which may propagate changes not ready for commit to the database. Under this protocol, on a failure, we require both undo and redo. The undo requires the use of the before images to remove changes that may have propagated to the persistent store inadvertently by the operating system's actions. The before images are written over any changes that have been installed. The redo protocol uses the after images stored in the log file to write data items that were committed by completed transactions whose results had not been installed to the persistent primary database copy. The idea behind this combined protocol is that some changes that may not be from committed transactions may have propagated to the per-

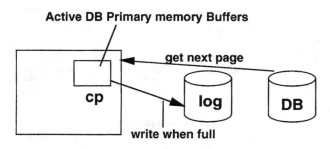

Figure 4.21   Transaction data flow for undo/redo

sistent storage and some from committed transactions may not have made it yet to the persistent storage before the failure. To correct this the database must either remove the bad changes or install the good ones to the persistent database storage.

4.9.2 No Undo and Redo

The no undo and redo protocol looks to simplify the recovery process and its cost by moving some of the work to the run-time processes. The protocol requires the holding of any active transaction change pages in primary memory. These pages cannot be allowed to be paged out of the memory inadvertently by the operating system's page replacement protocols (Figure 4.22). On the other hand, completed transactions that have committed can have their pages written out to either the persistent database or the log file or both. This protocol requires that *only* the after images be written to the persistent storage. The cost of this protocol is the added requirement of controlling where and when the writing of changes to the database will get installed. The benefit is seen at recovery time. Since no undo is required recovery will be faster, but the cost for blocking page writes of active pages will impact run time.

4.9.3 Undo and No Redo

To limit recovery to only requiring undo, we must perform some of the run-time database management tasks differently. Recall that the redo was needed when transactions that had committed had not yet installed their changes to the persistent database. To not require redo we must guarantee that a committed transaction's changes are installed into the persistent database and nowhere else. The protocol still forces before images of transactions into the database log and allows active transactions to be recorded. Upon a transaction's com-

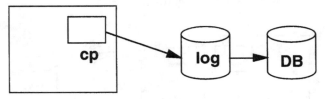

**No active pages written to DB
commit pages allowed to propagate**

Figure 4.22   Transaction data flow for no undo and redo

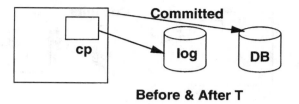

Before & After T

Figure 4.23 Transaction data flow for undo and no redo

mit, however, this information should be removed from the log and the transaction's changes written to the database's persistent storage (Figure 4.23). Since all the committed transactions' database changes have been written to the database, then only uncommitted transactions' effects must be removed. The undo protocol provides the means to perform this function. The cost of this protocol is the need to immediately and atomically flush committed transactions' changes to the persistent database at run time. The benefit is that on a failure the cost of recovery is limited to only the cost of resetting any active transactions' database-affected pages back to their before images.

4.9.4 No Undo and No Redo

If we wish recovery to be trivial, we can combine the previous two protocols into a single protocol that will require no undo and no redo on failures (Figure 4.24). The cost will be added processing at run time, but the advantage is a lower cost recovery. This may be an appropriate protocol where failures occur often and recovery is important to guarantee continuous service, although it is not without cost. The no undo and no redo protocols require that the database immediately write committed data to the persistent database and not allow the writing of any noncommitted database change pages to the persistent database. There is a greater run-time overhead in managing transaction change pages, but the benefit at recovery is substantial. This protocol, and many of the others discussed, can only work if the database can have control over how and when database change pages and transaction database active space are removed from the primary memory and returned to secondary storage.

4.9.5 Recovery Improvements

To improve overall recovery, both from the volume of transactions to recover and the cost associated with recovery, the recovery manager can utilize database checkpoints. A checkpoint is a copy of the data-

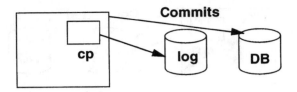

Figure 4.24   Transaction data flow for no undo and no redo

base at some point in time when the database is considered consistent. The question is when to perform a checkpoint and what granularity of checkpoint we should enforce—for example, a worst-case scenario is if a checkpoint on every read or write action must be performed immediately. No useful database work could be performed with this level of checkpointing in place. A more convenient point may be at the beginning of a transaction or subtransaction. In an ad hoc environment the beginning of a session may be appropriate; other environments indicate that the initial access to a major database structure, such as a relation or object, may be an appropriate point for a checkpoint operation. The decision on when to perform the checkpoint will be based on the system's need to recover and the time allocated to the recovery process. If recovery must be fine-grained and be performed quickly, then a fine-grained checkpoint at the object or transaction level may be appropriate. If run-time cost is more important, then a periodic checkpoint may be acceptable.

Other improvements in recovery can be delivered by simplifying the logging process and mechanisms. The difference between a physical log, where all change pages are recorded, and a logical log, where only the changed data items are stored, is fairly significant. If only one data item per page gets changed, the physical log would be required to maintain a copy of each total page, whereas the logical log would only be required to maintain a copy of the one data item per page changed and its location in the page. For low change volume the logical page log is a better approach. When there is a large percentage of page changes the physical log is an improvement. The tradeoff is storage cost against possible additional processing costs.

4.9.6 Forward Recovery

The previous discussions were directed at conventional recovery, which attempts to restore database operations by moving the database state back to some previously correct and consistent state that existed before the failure. For most database systems this is an acceptable approach. But for some new applications of database systems, such as real time, multimedia, and medical monitoring to name a few, this is not an acceptable approach. Something matched more to the needs of the applications is required. Forward recovery requires the knowledge of the *semantic* intent of a transaction's execution. The semantic information can be used to aid in the determination of which path of recovery the recovery manager should take given multiple options. Forward recovery requires that transactions be designed so that they can operate correctly on data that may be altered later in the execution.

Forward recovery may require that all data released for further use by other transactions be *safe* and *recoverable*. Safe data imply that the released information state does not depend on any uncommitted data. Recoverable data imply that the data can be modified to move them forward to a future state. Forward recovery can take on many different forms—for example, in a real-time database system recovery may be to simply do nothing. Waiting for the next scheduled update of a periodically changing data item may be more appropriate than computing an interim state, if the period is within correct ranges. Another form of forward recovery is to extrapolate data from known last valid points to a *best guess* future data point and use this as the restart point for a transaction. Conventional undo and redo is also acceptable for some applications. A more readily understandable form of recovery is to perform a compensating action to counteract the effects of a failure.

A form of forward recovery receiving a great deal of interest is the technique of user-directed recovery using condition-handling mechanisms. Condition handling is similar to exception handling in programming languages. The system can a priori define condition handlers for some known number of error or failure conditions. When one of these conditions occurs, the condition handler invokes the appropriate handler to fix the error or failure condition. For errors that are user generated, or that can be best understood by the application's environment, we can use user-supplied conditions and condition handlers. These would be the type of handlers for forward recovery within an application's sphere of knowledge—for example, an air traffic control system would know that if an error occurred in a track file the most likely place for the lost contact to be found would be the last known data point extrapolating to a new point using the last known speed and heading information. This type of recovery is best specified and constructed by the users who write the transactions.

Forward recovery is becoming an important function in modern databases that are being applied to nontraditional data sources—for example, real-time, multimedia databases must not be undone and redone; they must be reset to a future point and continued.

4.10 INTEGRITY MANAGEMENT

An important aspect of a database management system is the management of the correctness and the validity of data in the database. Integrity management deals with the specification, management, and maintenance of the database's correctness and validity. Integrity of the database is defined through a set of integrity constraints on the database and the active interpretation of these constraints and management of alterations when necessary. Active integrity management has three parts: the integrity check trigger, the constraint checker, and the response processor to the checker's return values. Constraints can take on many forms. The most common are the type constraints and the domain of value constraints—for example, a data item can have a constraint that indicates it can only take on the value of a character. Even if someone fed it an integer, it would be interpreted as a character, since the data type was to not be violated. The system may check the base types that are attempting to be written to an item and refuse to allow the action if there is a type incompatibility. Domain of value constraints specify all possible values that a data item may possess. This can be done explicitly via a set description method, or implicitly via a specified boundary value if the constraint fits such a model—for example, a constraint on the data item "sex" could be that it only can take on the value of male or female. The age of a person can be specified to be an integer between the value of 0 and 150, indicating that we do not think anyone will live beyond the age of 150 years. If this occurs then our database is not valid, since it no longer reflects the real-world entities it was designed to model.

The constraints can specify numerous data items as composites—for example, the data item "date" can only have the components day, month, and year. In addition, the day can only take on values from 1 to 31, the month must come from the set of calendar months (January, February, March, April, May, June, July, August, September, October, November, December), and the year must be greater than A.D. 1990. Integrity constraints can specify that a certain ordering be adhered to—for example, in the day component the day must go from 1 to 31 maximum in steps of one in increasing order. This implies a strict ordering and counting constraint on the data item. A transaction trying to change this data item outside of this constraint range of acceptable boundaries and conditions would fail and be rejected.

Constraints can be specified across data items and even entity boundaries—for example, we can specify that the number of students cannot exceed the number of professors multiplied by some reference value. These types of constraints are required when more complex relationships between entities are needed to model the real-world situation. Constraints can be aggregates, which specify that the set of all data items within a relation or entity must have some relationship between them—for example, we may specify a constraint that indicates the sum of all discrete accounts at a bank cannot exceed the total value of the bank's funds on hand.

Semantic constraints driven by the needs of transaction applications can be specified—for example, temporal constraints indicating the range of time that a data item is valid. Some application-driven constraints can have an effect on the underlying system—for example, environmental constraints that fix the storage location and permanency of the constrained data item(s). Performance-limiting or -enhancing constraints dependent on your view can be specified—for example, we may wish to fix the size of a relation in terms of number of tuples to bound worst-case search time. The shape and operational characteristics of a data item can be constrained—for example, the operations of a queue data structure or circular relation.

Operational constraints are necessary to specify the active nature of specified constraints—for example, constraints should be checked on updates of a data item, on reads of a data item, on an internal or external event in the system, and/or on a real-time click setting. The constraints could take on more semantic meanings if the user could better specify what is to be checked and when it is to be checked.

4.11 SECURITY CONSIDERATIONS

We will only say a bit about security here, as it is covered in greater detail in Chapter 13. Database security management has as its basic function to protect the database and its contents from unauthorized disclosure, alteration, and destruction. There are many aspects to security beyond the obvious ones. Security has legal, social, and ethical dimensions, which relate to the rights of someone to access information and the perception of others about these rights. Security conjures up the view of a physical room with locks and guards. This is a way to guarantee at least physical security in the sense of allowing only those who are perceived to have a need to access a system. A more important aspect is the policy of security. How does an organization decide that security is needed? How does it decide who gets authorization and access rights? These questions can possibly be answered by applying a need-to-know basis, or a more elaborate scheme. There are a variety of operational considerations. Once a policy is selected how does one go about implementing it; how is the desired effect guaranteed? To develop a secure database system we must begin with what is provided on the platform. Is the hardware secure? Do we have a privileged mode of operations, hardware keys, encryption, and secure lockable hardware elements built in? The operating system plays a big role in the ability to realize a secure database system. The operating system should provide the ability to check authorizations, validate users, verify their intentions, monitor their actions, and manage privileges to operating system–supported resources. The granularity of control plays a large role in the complexity and cost of the security subsystem. The database may need to provide security on the data item, record, tuple, table, file, database, and operations levels. Each level demands different requirements for supporting and implementing security.

4.11.1 Identification and Authorization

The first level of defense in a security system is the point of entry, whether it be a bank, office, house, computer system, or database system. The entry point should have at least the same controls as these systems. Before you can withdraw money from a bank, for example, you must first provide identification that indicates you have an account there. Second, to allow you to take money from the named account the bank will typically ask for some further identification to authenticate who you are. A database system or computer system is no different. Before someone is allowed to enter the system the user must first identify to the system who he or she is. The system then can check a list of authorized users and indicate that entry is allowed. This is the first level of defense: identification of a user's name. The second level of defense deals with determining if the user is who he or she claims to be. This authentication can take on many forms. In the simplest form, the system may require an additional password, known only to the system and the user. In more elaborate cases the authentication may include eye retina scans, fingerprints, key-card inputs, voice recognition, or some other complex form of identification.

As a secondary use of these two features, we can extend the identification and authorization policies and mechanisms to lower levels of the database. We could associate an access sentry with files, objects, relations, operations, or any other component of the database system. The tradeoff is the cost involved in constructing a system such as this, the cost in maintaining such a system, and the loss of performance that will result from the added overhead.

4.11.2 Authorization

Once a user is allowed in the system, do we allow him or her to have unlimited access? In your mainframe machine you would not like it if someone could get in and view your e-mail or a new product proposal. You would like to see further restrictions put on users so that they could only view and use is deemed fit for them to access. Authorization is the means through which we limit a user's view or operations within a system. The authorization policies and mechanisms are used to determine and set the level of access, the granularity of access, and the relationship of allowed access. Authorization mechanisms include capabilities, which are like tickets with a specific seat and quality of access, or access control lists of tables, which indicate elements of the database or users of the database and their access and execution rights on the database items.

The level of access restriction can span from no access to full unrestricted access and operational rights. Something in-between is more normal. The system may give read-only access to some users and restricted read access to others. Some may have write-only access, since they only produce data and have no reason to view any internal data other than their own. Some may get read and write access to a database item or area, while others may get specific operational access. The authorization mechanism must provide the means to specify who gets what level of access, and it must be able to guarantee the adherence to these restrictions. The granularity of access deals with what *view* of the database and its contents an authorized user gets. We may wish to give some users only a view of a piece of a relation or object instead of the entire object. We may wish to limit access to a subset of the database. The means to implement this is typically through a view mechanism, which allows a specific user only to know about specific subtypes or subelements of the database and nothing else.

Finally, even with these restrictions, the database security subsystem must deal with the true subversive person, who wishes to obtain information about the database through fraudulent means. Controls on this type of access must take into account the relationships of access and the duration and span of an access, and should include a set of inference rules to be checked when trying to detect an individual attempting a back-door approach to subverting the database. To thwart such individuals the database may be required to place limitations on retrievals—for example, the database may send erroneous or partial data to a subversive user in order to conceal classified information. The issue becomes that of the complexity of managing multiple variants of a data item strictly for security purposes. The security system may need to view collaborative information in a variety of ways in order to limit and detect when someone is attempting to combine unclassified information in ways that can allow the derivation of restricted or classified information. The last additional overhead to be discussed here is browsing. An important feature to bona fide users, but a powerful tool to the security offender, is a browsing mechanism. A browser can look at a variety of data at his or her level equal to or lower than the allowable security level, possibly collecting enough unrelated information to deduce something important—for example, if you ever want to know when something big is going on in the Pentagon, just examine the information on pizza deliveries. If there is a significant increase over a short period of time and for all hours of the day, a major operation is underway or being planned. The issue of the Trojan Horse and back-door methods to circumvent a security system are not trivial and will be addressed in later chapters.

Security is an important issue within the database community, although its use and implementation are driven by the tradeoff between the need to limit access and the cost associated with limiting access. The cost can be both one-time, involving the initial construction and population of the database, or it can be recurring. Recurring costs are driven by on-line checking of rights and testing for possible hidden agendas on accesses.

4.12 APPLICATIONS INTERFACES

The applications interface can take on many forms. The most common is a textual interface, where the user inputs a query in an interactive mode and the database returns text in the form of tuples, records, or some other program-related form. A second interface is a program interface, where queries are generated from within an application's program and responses are returned to the application in an application-usable form. The interface in this case is invisible to the end user. The end user sees the same applications interface as before. Whatever the interface is for the application, that is what the end-user's vision of the database is.

An interface can be more elaborate and include some further functionality. In some databases the interface is through a form, such as an order form or job application form. The database presents a form to the user, and the user fills it in. If the user is looking for some specific information, he or she can simply fill in a few of the entries on the form and indicate through a form entry to look for matches to the request. Multiple responses would be formed into a set of form pages, which the user can scroll through to retrieve the requested information.

Even more elaborate applications interfaces have been developed. Some are based on visual icons. The database may be a map with icons on it. These icons can be selected, and a variety of information extracted from them, by zooming in on the icon.

As databases find their way into even more systems, the applications interface will change to fit the needs of the applications the database is supporting. This has been the case with the object database system. The database interfaces to the applications in application-usable data formats. The database is no longer an isolated entity with its own rules and regulations; it is now becoming a member of a larger system, responding to and living within the system and its applications' rules and regulations.

5

Database Design Models

Paul Fortier

This chapter introduces and defines generic concepts used to design databases, such as requirements analysis, data definition, data constraints definition, normal forms, data usage patterns, data timing constraints, data associations, data diagrams, and storage requirements. These concepts are used in the design of information systems and database systems.

The information system or database management system has a wide range of realizations based on the real-world entity they are trying to model—for example, in a business manufacturing organization we may attempt to model all aspects of the enterprise, such as the engineering, manufacturing, sales, shipping and receiving, supply, and personnel departments, including all elements of each department (personnel, equipment, raw materials, finished products, and processes performed). In specialized applications, such as energy management, we focus on a limited aspect of the entire system. We may wish to focus only on the collection of sensor information and statistical information. In each case a different approach to database modeling and design may be necessary to realize an effective design and implementation.

5.1 INTRODUCTION

What is information or database specification modeling all about? Database specification models provide a means to describe real-world entities in a computer-processible form (Figure 5.1). Database specification models also present a process for abstracting real-world entities into composite representations. They give us methods to capture the static and dynamic nature of real-world entities—for example, how can we model or capture the identity of a person in a computer form? We could scan the person's picture into the computer; scan fingerprints; scan retina images; or capture static textual information about the person, such as first name, middle name, last name, street address, city of residence, county, state, country, zip code, Social Security number, age, telephone number, educational background, marital status, sex, language spoken, place of birth, parents' names, and so on.

The question becomes: How much data or information about an entity must be extracted and represented in the computer for it to be meaningful and accurate? What form of the available information best matches the intended application's needs? The answers have many dimensions and require us to more fully understand the meaning of information and the intended use of information's stored representation within the computer system. Once an understanding of the use of information within the real-world enterprise is determined, we can then determine how much and in what format this information should be represented in computer-usable form. During the determination of an application's information requirements it will become apparent which data are essential for the application, which data are nonessential, and what data entities represent information redundancies.

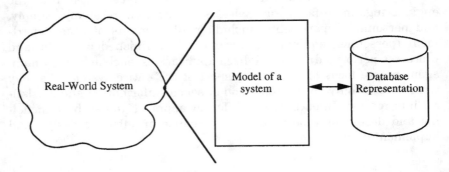

Figure 5.1   Database model specification

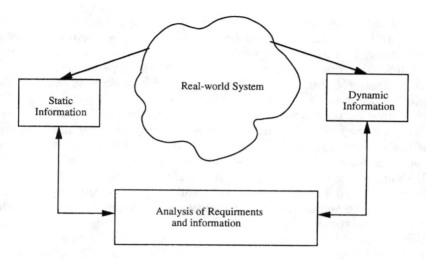

Figure 5.2   Data management model information requirement

The determination of what database model and database system to use for an application requires the collection and analysis of all static and dynamic information available about an enterprise (Figure 5.2). Why do we wish to use a particular data model or any model at all? Why not just develop the database directly? Direct design is not used, since it lacks the ability to provide traceability and various quality controls. Data models are used because they deliver a variety of benefits, such as:

- Providing a means to represent real-world objects or entities in computer-usable composite forms

- Capturing and representing associations or relationships among the real-world objects, allowing us to capture the dynamic nature of the real-world enterprise's activities

- Defining in logical terms how the objects interrelate

- Allowing the database designer to capture the static and dynamic organization and flow of information within a modeled enterprise

- Allowing modelers and users of the computer system to better understand the static and dynamic behavior of the system being modeled

- Aiding in the maintenance and changeability of the system over its lifetime

The determination of requirements for an application, as well as informational needs, will aid in the selection of an actual database structural data model for specification and design—for example, if our application requires scanning of a single attribute, such as a person's identification number or employer, across a collection of such attributes in order to find some similarity (such as which people work for company Y), then possibly a relational structure with attributes ordered on the search pattern key employer, may be optimal. Similarly, if the search is for a time sequence of data entities, such as a track sequence for an airplane ordered on a time tag, then possibly the CODASYL record-oriented data structure formed into a time-ordered ring or linked list of track files would best serve the application's needs. On the other hand, if the application's needs are to access abstract data structures, such as video and radar images, with operations mapped to the structure, such as select a location on a video map and coordinate the overlay of real-time radar, then the object-oriented data model would be a better choice. This implies that in order to determine the correct model we must determine the intended application requirements from both an informational and information processing perspective. It may not, however, be sufficient to just determine the application requirements for information classes (e.g., video, textual, graphical), for processing patterns (e.g., simply sweep over all information items), and for the application's intended use. It is essential to perform a detailed requirements analysis to define all possible attributes of the enterprise before we try to map these to a specific database system and data model.

5.2 REQUIREMENTS ANALYSIS

To determine how to construct the database management system for an application, the database design team must first determine the scope of the problem requiring a database system. Requirements analysis techniques are used to bound and define the scope and requirements of an application's domain. Requirements analysis examines the entire scope of the problem domain and includes:

- Defining human and user factors of an application
- Defining and bounding an application's functionality
- Defining all information managed and used by the application
- Determining from or to where all interfaces to an application derive
- Delineating all resources including computer hardware and software as well as physical systems

- Determining and bounding security requirements of an application's domain
- Determining the scope and impact of the application from environmental conditions
- Determining the quality, reliability, and operational aspects of an application
- Defining the type and requirements for documentation of an application

5.2.1 User Requirements

The users of an application define the scope of what the computer system and therefore the database management system must do—for example, if the application we are examining is a bank teller system, we must look at what type of users will use the bank's information assets. Human tellers, for example, will interact with the system to extract information about various accounts and perform tasks to alter accounts based on customer needs. These users require an interactive, but limited set of possible functions to perform. On the other hand, the bank can also have automated teller machines that interact with the database to extract customer data and perform yet an even more limited set of functions.

Requirements analysis at this level must determine who the users are of the application's system. How many of these users will there be in terms of minimums and maximums? What is the skill level of the users of the application's system? Finally, what type of user (human or computer) interacts with the application's system? Defining who the users of the intended application's system will be will aid in eliminating nonessential information during the other phases of requirements analysis.

5.2.2 Application Functionality

An important component of requirements analysis is the determination of application functionality. Application functionality is concerned with the definition of what the application being examined is expected to do. This definition includes a description of what the application is—for example, a bank teller system; and what the application is to perform—for example, the teller system is to allow finding, viewing, and altering consumer bank accounts. How often and when will the application perform? Again, for our bank teller example, the system is to perform on demand. The applications present and intended speed, response, and throughput also are included in this definition. With this information we can define the dynamic behavior of the application.

As an example we expand the bank teller application to include the operations that the tellers are required to perform. Through a process of examining the current application's processes and by interviewing users of the present system, we discover what type of operations the teller system performs. We find that the bank tellers perform the following functions:

- Request the status of a customer's account
- Cash a check drawn on a customer's account
- Deposit a check or cash into a customer's account
- Transfer funds from one of a customer's accounts into another account
- Compute and add interest to a customer's NOW account or passbook savings account
- Order new checks for a customer and charge his or her account
- Check the date of cancellation of a particular check

This set of functions represents those that the application's designers want to automate using a database system. In addition to these basic functions, the requirements analyst may also want to determine what number of account transactions per unit time is expected from the system based on the load seen in the paper version. The analyst may also want to determine the possibility of expanding the application's uses to allow for growth and change in the application's functions—for example, we may want to add credit card information for a customer's account or other banking functions beyond basic checking and savings.

5.2.3 Information Requirements

The information that is presently used by an application, as well as the representation of objects involved in the application, must also be defined during requirements analysis. The definition of the information and system objects includes the name or identifier for the object or information item, the information or object's relationship with other information items or objects, the organization of the information and the objects, the precision requirements for their representation, the accuracy requirements, the frequency of alterations, the lifetime of the information or object, and the diversity of their uses. Each requirement, when defined for all information items and objects within the system, will aid in database design, completeness, complexity, validity, and maintainability.

As an example of the type of information that should be collected and collated in the requirements analysis information phase, we again examine the bank teller application. If we look at the bank teller application, we can quickly define some of the major items of interest.

Information and objects within the bank teller application include the tellers, customers, account information, checks, cash, interest rates, account classifications, account owner information, check ledgers for all customers, and transaction classifications. Each of these objects has distinct attributes that can be recovered through examination of the application domain—for example, the tellers within our example are first classified as people with distinct attributes that define this general class of object.

```
PERSON
  ( name:        Character(30);
    address:     Character(30);
    ss number:   Integer(9);
    sex:         Male,Female;
  )
```

Second, they are also employees of the bank, which defines them as a specialized class of person called bank employee.

```
BANK-EMPLOYEE
  ( name:        Character(30);
    emp-ID:      Integer(3);
    ss number:   Integer(9);
    position:    Character(30);
  )
```

Likewise, we could classify customer by name, address, account identifiers, and phone number. To determine if this information is adequate to fully describe the object's information content, we must ask questions. How is this piece of information to be used? Is this representation accurate and correct? Is this definition complete? If these and other questions pertaining to the validity and correctness of this data can be answered affirmatively, then our representation is complete. In reality this is an iterative process that continues over the full requirements analysis time frame and into database design as we will see in later chapters.

5.2.4 Application Interfaces

Requirements analysis strives to define the entire environment in which the analyzed application resides. Included in this analysis is a determination of the information sources, information sinks, and information formats as used in the application. Information interfaces include all sources and destinations of information collected by, used by, or produced by the application under analysis—for example, sources of information can come from paper resources in the present system, or from sensors, computers, input/output terminals, and so forth. Sinks for information can also come from a variety of places and from numerous types of objects. Likewise, due to the numerous source and sink types, there will also be a variety of information formats. The definition of all sources, sinks of information, and their desired formats will help in refining the database's definition, organization, and implementation.

In the bank teller example the sources and destinations of information are complementary to each other. The tellers use information provided by the customers, and the customers use information provided by the tellers. What do these parties expect in terms of the format of the information passed between them? The typical bank teller expects the customer to come forward and provide one of the following forms of information: a check to be cashed, a check to deposit into an account, a passbook for a cash or check deposit, cash to deposit into an account, or a draft to transfer funds from one account into another account. The format of the information is in dollars with additional data available on the check to identify the payee and payer, the bank the check is drawn on, and the amount of the check. If cash is tendered there is an additional slip of paper with identifying information as to the account the cash is to be deposited to. The format of most of the data beyond the dollar amount is typically in character form. The only information not in character form is the check's number, the bank number, the account number, and the check writer's phone number.

5.2.5 Application Resources

All resources when taken together make up the platform upon which an application operates. Resources to consider when performing a resource requirements analysis include the physical platform the application is to operate upon, the computer hardware to be utilized in the database design, the timetable of the implementation, the number of sites involved, and the amount of money available to perform the implementation. The determination of resources is important to aid in the selection of a database system to apply to the application—for example, if the application has resources spread over a geographic area, it may be necessary to consider a distributed database system. On the other hand, if these distributed sites already have databases of their own and we wish to integrate them into a unified enterprisewide database management system, then we may opt for a heterogeneous database system model. In any case the determination of resource classes plays an important role in actual database implementation and complexity.

In our banking application there are a variety of resources to consider. First,where is the physical location or locations for the application? Are we developing a database to support a single bank site or multiple bank sites? If a single banking site, are there to be multiple processors, a single database server, or a mainframe handling the application? If there are multiple servers or processors, how are they presently configured or planned to be configured? How many end-teller terminals or workstations are to be supported? What type of peripheral devices are also supported—for example, are we supporting automated teller machines, electronic fund transfer, and/or secondary source access to customer accounts (e.g., ATM network)? These types of peripheral resources will indicate additional functionality required—for example, the above conditions may indicate the need for a secure modem or direct network link to a metropolitan or wide area network. Each of these will affect our ultimate database design and implementation. More will be said on this topic when we discuss database design and implementation later in the text.

5.2.6 Application Security Requirements

In defining the application requirements an important, often overlooked area during initial design is security. The security needs of an application directly impact the selection of a database system and the complexity of that system. System security can have multiple dimensions: It could include only access controls, such as login and password controls (authorization and authentication); or it could include physical isolation—very elaborate procedures to detect inference break-ins and other complex intrusions of security. The requirements analysis phase should determine what degree of security is needed within an application's domain and what the implications of such requirements are.

In our banking example there are obvious security measures required. The first is physical security for the bank and its contents. This form of security does not directly affect our application under study, but it does play a role. Security in a bank has many facets: First there are the locks on the doors and the security alarm system; internally there are surveillance equipment and physical barriers such as doors and partitions; and tellers have locks on their money drawers and on any other important documentation dealing with customers and finances. This leads us to realize that our information management system at the minimum will require authentication to determine who is trying to get into the information bank, as well as authorization to make sure that this person does have the right to look at this data. In addition to this level we also see that the tellers only have access to a limited set of the bank's data; therefore, we must also provide security barriers to limit the scope of their view into the database. The means to do this may come from limiting the view of the database the tellers can access as well as adding additional security points to recheck authorization rights to individual information items. We will see in later chapters dealing with secure databases and with security that there are numerous other issues and solutions.

5.2.7 Application Quality and Reliability Requirements

Another important aspect of requirements analysis is the quality and reliability requirements that will be levied upon the system. It is typical in most applications that excessive faults or failures cannot be tolerated—for example, if a teller continues to make entry errors to a point that the transactions at that station drop to an intolerable level, then corrective actions must be taken. Either we can send the teller out for additional training or fire the teller and replace him or her with a more efficient individual. In the same frame of thought the database system that will ultimately support the tellers' transactions must not have a high rate of faults or failures or it too will be sent out for repairs or be replaced altogether. If these faults or failures are of the hardware or intermittent software class, then they can be quantified into a measure of system quality. Typically this is measured as a mean time between failures. It can be quantified with or without added maintenance or improvements.

The second type of quality measure looks at the system's ability to continue operation in the face of faults and failures of a less severe class. This may even include the ability to recover from transaction aborts not caused by internal resource contention. Fault tolerance may be a highly desirable quality for our banking database system to possess. Other quality-based requirements that must be analyzed and quantified during requirements analysis include maintainability of the system, expandability of the system, availability, and recoverability. The main emphasis is to capture the application's software requirements or desirable qualities so that these can be addressed in the actual database system's design and development.

5.2.8 Application Documentation Needs

The last area of requirements analysis is documentation requirements. This may seem like a trivial area to consider, but it is not trivial in the eyes of the application's users. They will ultimately depend on these documents to get them through their normal operations as well as through sporadic faults and failures with the system. In addition, documentation may aid in future upgrades and ease of implementation as well as in maintenance. The typical documentation that application users want to see is user manuals. Once the application has been developed, they want a step-by-step walkthrough of the functions for future reference and for training new users. The application users may wish to have documentation on the composition and operation of the database system to aid in troubleshooting problems and for completeness. In addition, they may wish to have maintenance manuals and database administration manuals to aid in system maintenance and improvements.

5.2.9 Characteristics of the Requirements

For all of these requirements the requirements analyst must examine the data collected and determine how useful they are. In particular the information must be analyzed with regard to the following criteria.

Correctness—Does the information correctly represent the real world that it is modeling—for example, if we are modeling the information based on our bank tellers, have we adequately captured the definition of the teller entity?

Consistent—Do the data adequately capture the constraints of a real-world entity? Once an entity has been defined, we must be certain that the definition covers the entire range of possible values that the entity may take.

Complete—Does the represented real-world entity have any missing attributes? Are all the pertinent components of the real-world entity present in the modeled form?

Realistic Representation—Does the representation of the real-world entity make sense? Does the requirement make sense? Does it have a basis in some realistic entity?

Need—Does the requirement defined have a place in the application being modeled? Is the requirement some outside nonparticipant? Is the requirement useful or even used within the application?

Veracity—Is the requirement testable? Is there a way to determine if the requirement is correct, complete, or consistent in a quantifiable way? How can we determine if the requirement has meaning?

Traceability—Does the requirement fall into the domain of the application? Is the requirement traceable back to others? Does a feedback or feed-forward path exist that indicates that this requirement is connected to the application in a meaningful way?

Once the collection and analysis of an application's requirements have been performed, we should be able to begin the specification of the database schema using a database model. The requirements analysis will allow us to extract static and dynamic descriptions of the application's information content and operations. The static description of requirements will yield information items and information attributes. The dynamic description of the information requirements will yield a specification of temporal and activity constraints on information. These in turn will aid in the database's relationship definitions as well as for access constraints and patterns. The result of these views is an informational requirement for the application and information processing needs of the analyzed application. With this information the database designer can determine the optimum mapping of the database model and database system that will best support the application under design.

5.3 INFORMATION MODELING

The information modeling goal is to identify the major entities fundamental in an application and model them in a target database schema model—for example, in our teller application we have major entities for bank employees, tellers, officers, customers, and accounts. Since we are interested in the manipulation of customer accounts and not with other activities at the bank, we can ignore all other bank employees other than the tellers. We must define a teller and a customer along with the customer's accounts. We do this by using the information collected during requirements analysis and initial database design. This information will provide us with the essential information that will fully and correctly define the major entities to be modeled in the bank teller database—for example, a customer can be identified by a customer identifier, a name, an address, and phone number. We could likewise define customer accounts using account numbers and owner identifier number and account balance. These qualifiers that *define* an entity are grouped together in some fashion, based on the data model used, and stored for future reference. The following definitions hold for all of the database design models discussed later in this text with some modifications to meet model restrictions.

5.3.1 Data Entities

The fundamental item in our generic database model review is the entity. An entity is viewed as an atomic real-world item—for example, a person. A person is an atomic entity or item since he or she cannot be broken down into smaller pieces and still represent the same real-world item. This is not to say though that the entity cannot be further described. As shown in the previous introduction, a person has additional qualities that describe the entity. These will be discussed in the next subsection. An entity named person contains enough information to uniquely define a person. Each reference to the person entity refers to a singular representation of a person. There may be numerous occurrences of persons in the real world and thus in the database, but in naming a general class of real-world entities we use the singular form. Thus, the entity describing all persons is called and named PERSON, rather than persons.

A data entity represents a model of a real-world *thing* specified for storage and reference in computer-readable form. The specification of a data entity is always uniquely defined in the database model of an application environment and is represented in uppercase letters—for example, the person entity is specified as PERSON in the computer representation. The physical realization of the entity in the computer is dependent on the specification of the composite elements of the entity and the medium, language, and computer being utilized.

Examples of data entities within our bank teller example would be EMPLOYEE, TELLER, CUSTOMER, ACCOUNT, CHECK, LEDGER, and so forth. Each of these represents an atomic real-world item in our computer-usable representation of the bank teller application environment.

5.3.2 Data Attributes

As mentioned in the previous subsection, an entity is composed of additional descriptive information. This descriptive information uniquely defines what an entity is composed of. The components of an entity are called attributes or data items of the entity. An attribute is a single atomic unit of information that describes something about its named entity—for example, attributes of the entity PERSON may be *name, address, phone number, sex, age, identifying marks,* and *person identifier.* These attributes provide additional information about the PERSON entity. The additional information provides the means to uniquely define a person within the machine-usable form of the entity. In most database modeling languages an attribute is singularly named and is represented in lowercase characters—for example, the person entity would be represented as:

```
PERSON(name, address, phone number, sex, age, identifying
marks, person identifier)
```

This representation is termed the logical description of the entity, since it does not include the machine format for the entity and its attributes.

A data attribute represents a computer-usable model for the components of an entity. The physical representation of an entity and its attributes is typically defined using the concept of a named file and a file's physical record structure. The named entity can equate to the named file, and the attributes of the entity can equate to the records of the file. Each record will have the same physical description and take up the same amount of physical storage. The elements (data fields) of the records map directly to the attributes of the named entity.

Attributes can have the same name if in separate entities. No attribute within an entity specification can have a duplicate name. The differentiation of attributes of the same name from separate entities is accomplished through the association of entity name and attribute name—for example, we could have the PERSON entity with the attribute name and another entity EMPLOYEE, also with the attribute name. When referring to one or the other attribute we use the combination of entity name and attribute name to distinguish between them. In this example we would use employee_name and person_name when referencing the same attribute in both entities.

5.3.3 Data Associations

The above definitions only capture the static meaning of real-world entities. In the real world, items have relationships to each other—for example, an employee works for a particular company; a person is a spouse of one person and possibly the child of another person. The association that exists between the entities relates the data items to each other in a meaningful way. This information relationship must be captured by our database schema model if our resulting database is to be a reasonable approximation of the real-world entities that it models—for example, if we have two entities, one PERSON with the identifier person_identifier and a second entity CHILD with the identifier parent_identifier such that a person is the child of another person, then the parent_identifier in CHILD will match the person_identifier in PERSON. Likewise, a PERSON can find out who their children are by looking in CHILD and matching parent_identifier with person_identifier. It is through this form of data modeling technique that we can capture these relationships between entities in the database.

The existence of data associations defines that a relationship exists between two or more entities. Relationship and association are often used interchangeably to define this condition. In most database models the relationship between two or more entities is captured through the use of an intermediary linkage or linkages. These linkages can be formed using tables of relationship qualifiers, through logical pointer structures, or through active functions. The most common way to represent the relationship between entities is to use an additional entity called a relationship entity. In our bank teller example, CUSTOMER entities deposit funds into the ACCOUNT entity. To represent this relationship we form a relationship entity called DEPOSIT. The DEPOSIT entity has the attributes for the customer and the account to which he or she wishes to deposit. In addition, the relationship entity could have attributes associated with it that only are used in the relationship—for example, the deposits could have some limit attribute or some condition attribute that must be checked when the relationship is referenced. Relationships are used to aid the database in constructing how data are to be used and bound within the database.

Using the basic data model structures of entities, attributes, and relationships allows us to define real-world information in a computer-representable and -processable form. The combination of these elements provides the means to organize information into a cohesive and coherent grouping or map. This mapping of the information into entities, attributes, and relationships forms the data model. The data model provides the common view or map of an application that an enterprise can use in information management and processing.

5.3.4 Entity List

The database model uses the entities and their attributes and relationships to construct a representation of the modeled enterprise. The data model that results is in one or both of the following forms: an entity list or a data map. An entity list is a compilation of data entities and their attributes in some easily readable form. The typical

form is to list entities in uppercase letters and their attributes in lowercase letters enclosed in parentheses—for example, the CUSTOMER
entity from the bank could have the following representation:

```
CUSTOMER(customer_id, name, address, date-opened)
```

The entity list establishes the logical names to be used in the database design and use. The list alone, however, will not capture all of
the pertinent information needed for database implementation and
organization. The intended use for each entity and, more importantly,
the data relationships' definition and their intended use in the database must also be captured. To do this it may be necessary to use
additional methods. One candidate method is to use ideas from structured design techniques. In particular, the use of behavioral diagrams
and descriptions can aid in the capture of this information.

5.3.5 Data Schema Map

Another means of capturing the data and their organization is the
data schema map. The data schema map captures and documents a
database design's entities, the entities' attributes, and the relationships among the entities. The data schema map visually represents
the interrelationships of the schema. This approach provides for further refinements of the database design through the use of visual refinements. This is due to people's ability to better detect flaws from
visual rather than from textual queues.

The major components of the data schema map are the entities,
attributes, relationships, and cardinality of the association (Figure
5.3). The entities are represented by a rectangular box with the name
of the entity enclosed within the box—for example, the PERSON entity would be represented by a rectangular box with the word PER-
SON in the center, as shown in Figure 5.4. The attributes of an entity
are shown as ovals, with their attribute name enclosed in the oval.
The attribute names are written in lowercase letters, as shown in Figure 5.4. Relationships are indicated in the data schema map by using
connected lines. Lines are directed depending on the type of relationship—for example, the CHILD entity defined previously is related to
the PERSON entity by a simple relationship called *ISA*. An ISA relationship implies that the subtype must have a matching supertype to
exist. In our example the CHILD entity must be defined in the PER-
SON entity before it can exist as a CHILD.

These relationships are depicted in the data schema map using connected lines with added information to describe the cardinality of the

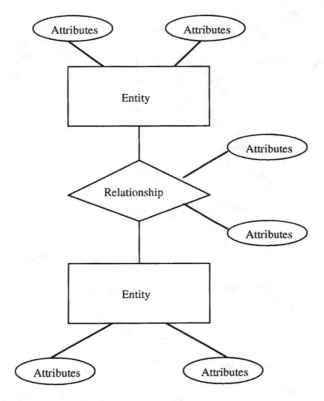

Figure 5.3   Components of the data schema map

relationship. For a one-to-one relationship a line connects the two entities. As an example of a simple relationship refer to Figure 5.5. In this example we have defined two entities: an EMPLOYEE entity and a TELLER entity. The EMPLOYEE entity consists of an *employee-ID*, *name, address, job,* and *salary* attributes. The TELLER entity consists of an *employee-ID, shift-number,* and *teller-training-level*. The relationship between EMPLOYEE and TELLER is a simple one-to-one relationship of the special type called ISA, as defined previously. The simple one-to-one relationship implies that one entity is related to only one occurrence of another entity. This relationship is also sometimes shown by a line with an arrow on both ends.

A second type of relationship is the one-to-many relationship. The one-to-many relationship is represented by the data schema map shown in Figure 5.6. In this example, we show a one-to-many relationship between the DEPARTMENT entity and the TELLER entity. We see that a department can have many tellers, but the tellers only be-

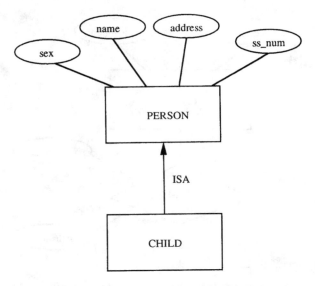

Figure 5.4   An entity's representation within a data schema map

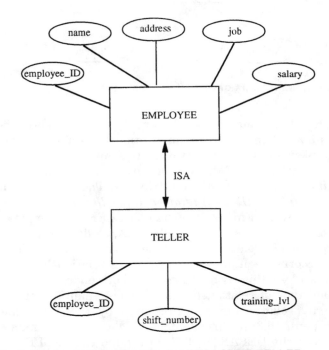

Figure 5.5   A one-to-one relationship for EMPLOYEE-TELLER

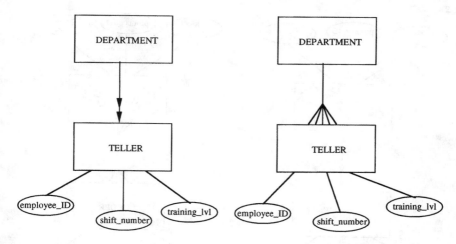

Figure 5.6   A one-to-many relationship for DEPARTMENT-TELLER

long to one department. The bank can have many departments, but the tellers only belong to one. In the data schema map shown in Figure 5.6, we represent this relationship in two ways. The first method uses double arrows at the end of the line from the DEPARTMENT entity to the TELLER entity. The double arrows indicate the direction of the one-to-many form of the relationship. The second form of representation for the relationship is shown in the second part of Figure 5.6. In this method a line from the DEPARTMENT entity to the TELLER entity is modified on the teller side with multiple lines fanning out toward the TELLER entity. The first method is more representative of the entity-relationship model described in the next chapter. The latter form is more common to general information engineering methodologies rather than a particular database schema model.

A third type of relationship is the many-to-many relationship. The many-to-many relationship is represented by the data schema map shown in Figure 5.7. In this form of multidimensional relationship, the related entities have a mutual correspondence with each other. In Figure 5.7 we show two related entities: an entity called PRODUCT and another called ORDER. In this example, the following many-to-many relationship is represented: an ORDER is for *many* PRODUCTS, but a PRODUCT can also be ordered in *many* ORDERS. To depict this relationship in a data schema map one of two conventions is typically used. The first convention uses double arrows on both ends of the line to indicate the many-to-many relationship. This graphical form is typical of the entity-relationship model. The second form de-

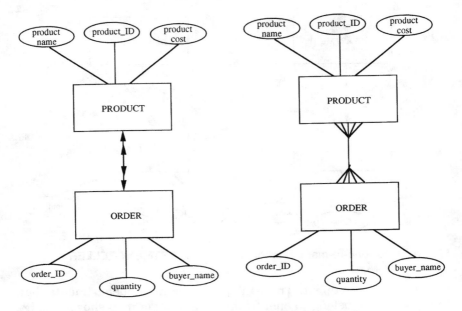

Figure 5.7   A many-to-many relationship for PRODUCT-ORDER

picting the many-to-many relationship uses a line that fans out on both ends, as shown in Figure 5.7.

To completely specify the intentions and constraints on the model we need some additional features—for example, we may need to indicate that a relationship is mandatory or that it is optional. A mandatory relationship indicates that the dependent entity cannot exist without the related OWNER entity—for example, in the ISA relationship between the EMPLOYEE entity and the TELLER entity, the teller cannot exist without the employee, but the employee can exist without the teller. This would be indicated in a graphical representation of this relationship with a line, or it can be indicated by a special symbol such as an *m*. For optional relationships a similar convention is used, as shown in Figure 5.8.

5.3.6 Logical Data Model Key Structures

To determine any instance of an entity uniquely requires the use of some form of addressing or recognition scheme that will uniquely identify the needed entity. The concept of a key or unique identifier has been used in the various database models that have been developed. A key is an attribute of an entity or object that enables the

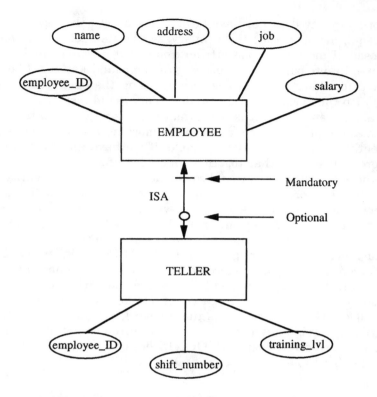

Figure 5.8   Mandatory and optional relationships

database system to uniquely reference the item. There are a variety of key types based on the required use within the database system.

The main type of key is the primary key. A primary key is used as the means to uniquely address and access one instance of an entity within an entity set—for example, in our bank teller entity, a primary key can be the employee's name, if this is unique within the entity, or the employee number. The primary requirement is that the chosen attribute values be unique for all entities within an entity set. If there is more than one attribute that matches the definition above, then all of the possible attributes that can uniquely define the entities within the set represent *candidate keys*. Candidate keys are all those that meet the criteria for being the primary key. The system, however, wishes to have only one attribute from all the attributes that represent the key. The selected candidate key is marked as the primary key. In the data schema map the primary key is typically shown by underlining the primary key's name.

A primary key does not have to be made up of only one attribute. The requirement is that the primary key be unique. A key that is composed of more than one attribute is called a *compound key*—for example, in our bank teller database, a compound key could be constructed for the EMPLOYEE entity by using the employee number along with the Social Security number. This would result in a unique key value, even though it is more than what is required to represent the teller uniquely. Compound keys are more useful in the context of interentity relationships—for example, if we have an order number and product number that together uniquely define quantity ordered, then these two attributes would constitute the key for this entity.

Another form of key useful for database design and modeling is the concept of a foreign key. A foreign key is represented as a subset of the primary keys from one entity set that is used as a pointer into the entity set from another entity set—for example, in the banking model our customers have a foreign key into the ACCOUNTS entity, using their account numbers. The foreign key allows them to have access to the account information without replicating the entire account information for every customer. The account number attribute in the CUSTOMER entity is referred to as the foreign key for the CUSTOMER entity. This foreign key is then used to acquire any details about the account referred to by the ACCOUNTS entity's match with the customer foreign key.

5.3.7 Logical Data Model Constraint Definition

Database systems are designed to represent a subset of a real-world enterprise's information. The database system requires additional limitations on the possible values that modeled data can possess in order to remain within the range of a real-world item's possible states. To provide these limits database systems use the concept of constraints. Database constraints come in numerous forms: They can limit the shape of a database's structures, as in the relational model; they can limit the functionality of a model, as in the record-oriented operations in the network model; or they can be limitations on the contents of data items. In the following subsections we address some of the possible constraints that can be specified on a database system's contents.

Structural Constraints   The structure of information within the database conveys a great deal of information about the entities that it represents—for example, if the structure of entities is flat files, such as the relational system, it can be best applied to simple data representation, such as the student database or teller database we have presented previously. On the other hand, if the structure of data is more complex, such as terrain vector data or composite video data, it can be formed into objects within the object model to allow more optimized management and manipulation of the stored information.

Structural constraints are specified to force the placement of information into structures that better match their applications' use. Data can be constrained to reside in fixed circular data structures for the purpose of automatic aging out of old data, or in a stack structure based on the need to push data into the structure and to pull them back out in a last in, first out manner. The important modeling concept to extract from this discussion is the need to specify in a logical fashion the structural requirements of an application's information so that an appropriate data model can be chosen to implement its storage and manipulation management. Other structural constraints can be specified to limit the size of a set of entities or to limit the number of instances of a particular object's class.

These types of constraints are becoming more relevant as database systems are being applied to a wider range of information processing applications. Multimedia systems and real-time systems have in particular driven a need to specify the structure of data beyond simple entities and attributes.

Type Constraints A common form of information constraint is the type constraint. This type of constraint limits the application to only one representation of information for an entity's attribute—for example, we may wish to limit the attribute name to just a character string of fixed length, or an address attribute to four substrings of type character. Type constraints allow a limitation of the range of information representations that an attribute can have. The typical constraints found within this category include characters, integers, reals, Boolean, and strings. These simple constraints can then be used to construct and further constrain more complex abstract data types—for example, we can represent a person's name as a first name of type character string, middle name as just a single character, and last name as a character string. A more complex data type may be an object of type person that can then take on all of the constrained characteristics of its subtypes or composite types.

Range Constraints Another class of database constraints refers to the possible values that a particular data item may possess. Such database constraints are used to limit the range of possible values that a data item can take on. The range of values for a data item can span some possible set of representations or contain some specific sequence of possible values—for example, in our bank teller database we may restrict the employee identifier to span values from 0 to 1,000. This type of constraint limits the range of values that the teller identifiers in our database can take from a low of 0 to a high of 1,000. Any values outside of this range would be erroneous and cause a violation on access.

Range constraints can be more specific and represent deeper semantic meanings of database-modeled information—for example, the meaning of the date information in a data item called DATE. The date is composed of a day attribute that is constrained to have only the values between 1 and 31, and further constrained by the month having to be as low as 28 days. The month attribute must span between January and December, taking on one of the values from the list of possible values. The year attribute can have a variety of range constraints. We may wish to only represent years from the present year forward, or from only some limited prevalues such as 1900, or we may wish to represent all years from the death of Christ onward. There are two classes of constraints represented in this example: The first is an ordering constraint, which constrains data to span a specific order and no other; the second type of constraint is a composite constraint. A composite constraint is one that spans multiple attributes with some related constraints. In the example a date is constrained to be represented by a day, month, and year. In addition, these attributes are constrained by ordering constraints to span specific values.

Relationship Constraints   Relationship constraints represent relationships on values between entities. Generally such constraints name two or more entities with some relationship constraint between them that must be met—for example, an entity for boss may have a constraint on salary stating that the salary of the boss cannot be greater than five times that of any subordinate employee. If the BOSS entity is separate from the SUBORDINATE entity, then this represents an interentity or interdomain constraint over the two entities.

Further relationship constraints can be constructed that use various logical relationships between data items in one entity with those in another entity. The major modeling concept to derive from this relationship is that constraints can and do span entities. Real-world objects have relationships between other objects that constrain the possible states they can be in. Likewise, the database system must also be able to represent these interobject constraints so that the database will accurately represent the real-world system being modeled within the database.

Temporal Constraints   Some information in the real world typically has some time frame of validity on its use. Data in such environments are created and are valid for only a specific time period. As an example the data derived from a radar tracking of an airplane for an air traffic control system are examined. When a track is derived from the radar, the displayed value for speed direction and position are only valid for a fixed period of time if the data are to have any valid meaning to air traffic management software using these data. The track is good only until the time that the next track is due. If this time is violated, any reads of the position, as well as speed and direction values, must be marked as invalid, or dirty. These values do not represent the reality of the modeled system, nor do they accurately reflect the actual information intended to be captured by this entity. Temporal constraints on data items are used as a means to specify the time frame of validity for a modeled piece of information. The constraints may be specific periods of time, time frames from an event, time frames from a specific real time, or some referenced time frame. The major concept is that data can have constraints that specify time as a means to determine the validity of a data item. More will be said about this kind of constraint in Chapter 11, which deals with real-time databases.

Location Constraints   The final class of constraint discussed in this section is related to the location of information in the database. This form of constraint is required for advanced database applications such as real-time or multimedia database systems. These classes of database systems require specific response from the database in terms of transaction deadline on execution or transaction synchronization with other transactions. To deliver these types of service, the database system is required to have more control over the way in which data are stored and accessed within the database. An example of this form of constraint would be found in real-time databases, which may require predictable response to specific data being managed by the database. The real-time database may wish to store specific *high-interest* data items in main memory to minimize the time delay in accessing this information. Likewise, in a multimedia database guaranteeing that specific transactions can share information and synchronize actions can require that specific information must be located in a specific place in memory for the purpose of sharing the information in a timely manner. More will be said about this type of constraint when we discuss multimedia databases later in the book.

5.4 DATA PARTITIONING MODELS

Database systems are not always going to exist in one computer. They typically consist of large collections of information that are stored over a wide geographic area in numerous computer systems. To support this model of an enterprise's information and information management requirements, our modeling capabilities must also be able to address data distribution and partitioning. To specify data distribution and partitioning at our data-modeling level requires the use of additional constraints. These classes of constraints must deal with how data are to be broken up over various sites and how these decomposed data can be unified for use. Specific uses of these types of constraints, as well as examples within actual systems, will be shown in later chapters.

5.4.1 Location Constraints

Location constraints deal with the location specification of data. These constraints can be at a logical site level versus a specific location. The main emphasis of location constraints is to place data at a computer system where they are needed. An example of such a constraint follows. An enterprise has a personnel office, a manufacturing office, and an engineering office. Each of these offices has a different set of information about the enterprise that it must maintain. To facilitate the maintenance and use of data at the most appropriate site requires that the proper information be placed at the site that needs it most. To do this the database modeler requires additional constraints on the data. In the example we would need to mark the personnel data with a personnel site computer system designation, the manufacturing data with manufacturing's computer site, and engineering data with engineering's computer system designation.

The constraints could be as simple as naming the site followed by the entities to be stored there. Conversely, the location constraints may need to name each instance of an entity if this level of granularity is needed. An additional problem comes when fragmentation of entity sets is allowed. If fragmentation is allowed we must add additional semantics to capture the extent of the fragmentation as well as the sites where the fragmented pieces are to be located. This also complicates access, as will be seen in Chapter 10.

5.4.2 Relationship Constraints

In addition to the constraints that indicate where a data item or entity is to be stored, additional constraints are needed to specify relationships between the partitioned or distributed entities—for example, an entity that is fragmented may still have an aggregate constraint that must be satisfied when updates to data items are being done. This constraint must be placed on the entities and specified in such a way that it is checked and adhered to when updating the data. To specify such a constraint requires two parts: First, a constraint must be specified on when to perform the constraint check, and second, it must be specified how to perform the constraint check—for example, the following constraint indicates a time and a constraint to be checked on the named entity.

```
ON UPDATE EMPLOYEE.* CHECK C1 on P1 and C1 on P2;
```

Such a check places a condition on partitions P1 and P2 to have constraint C1 checked and validated on the update operation on any attribute of the EMPLOYEE entity.

Further relationship constraints can be written to perform checks on database information stored in separate sites on application events, time boundaries, queries, database updates, or on a variety of other database conditions. An important issue that arises from these discussions is that of when to perform such constraint checks and how to use the results of these checks. There is still much controversy within the database community on this topic.

5.5 FUNCTIONAL DEPENDENCIES

To further refine the database model one needs to examine the relationships that exist among data of an entity. An initial design of an entity may still require refinement if it exhibits certain characteristics. The reason for looking toward further refinements is to limit possible problems with the final design. Some of these design problems are enumerated below using the following example entity for clarification.

```
SUPPLIER(Sname, Saddr, Item, Price)
```

In the example we will be using there is a SUPPLIER entity, which consists of four attributes: a supplier name (Sname), a supplier address (Saddr), an item identifier (Item), and a price for the item supplied (Price).

There are a number of problems with this entity it is presently specified. The first problem deals with data redundancy. With the entity as specified we will have the supplier name and supplier address repeated for each item we place in the database. This redundancy leads to problems with database maintenance and complexity. The second problem with this entity's specification deals with potential inconsistencies that may arise due to this added redundancy—for example, if we change the address of a supplier, it must be changed in all locations where this supplier supplies some part. If we miss one or input any part of a change erroneously, our database is now inconsistent. The third problem with this specification is concerned with insertion anomalies. We have a problem with recording information about a supplier without having an item, or recording information about an item without having a supplier. In this scenario if we want to insert information about a new supplier that presently supplies no items, we could not do this, since the item and price fields have no meaning. Likewise, if we want to insert some new items into the database, but at present have no supplier for these items, we could not perform this either, since the supplier name and address have no meaning. A fourth related problem deals with deletion anomalies. In the above example we could not delete a supplier without deleting all the items supplied by the supplier. Likewise, we could not delete some items without deleting the supplier that supplies them. These problems would result in a database maintenance nightmare.

A solution to these and other problems deals with entities' attribute relationships and semantics with each other. The attributes of an entity should support each other's meaning and not lead to redundant information or anomalies as discussed above. In our example a better structure would consist of the following three entities.

```
SUPPLIER(Sname, Saddr);

SUPPLIER-PARTS(Sname, Item);

PARTS(Item, Price);
```

In this structure the supplier information and the item information are decomposed into separate entities. By doing this insertion and deletion anomalies disappear. We can now represent a supplier that supplies no items, as well as items that are not supplied by any supplier at this time. To capture the additional semantic information about which supplier supplies which items, we need a third entity. This entity captures the dynamic supplier-item relationship intended in the original entity. With this structure we can easily add suppliers for items and items to suppliers without adding further redundant information and therefore reducing possible inconsistencies.

5.5.1 Functional Dependencies

The problems discussed in the previous section were due to problematic functional dependencies between attributes. A functional dependency exists between two or more attributes of an entity when one attribute is derived from or depends on the other for part of its semantic definition. The key attribute of an entity forms such a dependency. A key K *functionally* defines or determines the values for attribute X, a part of its entity by definition. A key uniquely defines each instance of an entity. This functional dependency is indicted by the following form, K -> X, and is read as K functionally defines X.

Functional dependencies come in many forms with a variety of rules to apply in order to have well-formed entities. Before we discuss further the rules for functional dependencies, we must first address some basic properties of functional dependencies. Given the following attributes and dependencies some basic properties will be defined.

$$A \rightarrow B, B \rightarrow C, DE \rightarrow F, W \rightarrow X, A \rightarrow C, AB \rightarrow C$$

Two basic properties of functional dependencies are equivalence and redundancy. Two sets of functional dependencies, $S1$ and $S2$, are *equivalent* if they are identical, yielding the same restrictions over the entire state space. For the two sets $S1$ and $S2$ if $S1$ = {A -> B, B -> C, A -> C} and $S2$ = {A -> B, B -> C}, then $S1$ is equal to $S2$ using the transitive property of functional dependencies. Using the transitive property of functional dependencies, if a set has functional dependencies A -> B, B -> C, then we can deduce that since A functionally defines B and B functionally defines C, there also exists the dependency A -> C, through the transitive relationship of A with C through B. Given this property we can then state that $S1 \equiv S2$, since all functional dependencies of $S1$ are represented in $S2$ and likewise.

Functional dependencies of a set are redundant if their semantics imply the same relationship. Likewise, they are redundant if the dropping of one dependency does not omit any valid states for the entity. In the example above the relationship A -> C is redundant in set $S1$, since the dependency is easily represented through the two other remaining functional dependencies. The same can hold between separate sets. In the example above $S1$ is redundant, since $S2$ represents all the functional dependencies within $S1$. In addition, $S2$ is a minimum set, since it also omits the redundant functional dependency A -> C that is in $S1$.

A third property of functional dependencies is *augmentation*. Using the set of functional dependencies above, if we take the relationships A -> C and W -> X, we can combine these through augmentation and have a new extended functional dependency AW -> CX. This property provides for the combination of constraints to form more complex constraints over attributes. An example might be when we combine our teller ID and functionally define JOB, with Social Security number defining Name, to get a new constrained relationship indicating that teller ID and Social Security number functionally define Name and Job classification. It may not be a pretty constraint, but it is one that could be needed by an enterprise.

These basic functional dependencies are fundamentally one-to-one relationships—that is, one key functionally defines one unique attribute or set of attributes. The basic design rule for such dependencies is to group dependencies that can be combined from a unique base attribute or key into a single entity. As will be seen, other design rules will tend to remove attributes from an entity or decompose attributes from one entity into separate entities.

One form of functional dependency to be avoided in database modeling and design is the derived dependency. A derived dependency exists when one dependency functionally defines the other and, in addition, is one where one attribute can, through a function, *derive* the other. An example of such a dependency is found in the PERSON entity. If there are two attributes, one date of birth and another age, then date of birth functionally defines age; yet, in addition, date of birth also can derive age simply by subtracting the present date from the date of birth. What age represents is redundant data that can be removed with no loss of information within the database. A second design rule, therefore, is to remove any derived dependencies from an entity, since these simply represent redundant information within the database.

Of more concern when designing the model of an enterprise's information database is the concept of multivalued dependencies. A multivalued dependency is a functional dependency of the form one to many. This type of dependency must be avoided in an entity if there exist additional interrelationships among attributes. An example of a multivalued dependency is illustrated with our TELLER entity. A teller can have many skills, indicating that an individual teller can have a multivalued dependency defining skills. Likewise, another example of a multivalued dependency between tellers exists when a teller has many children. These represent one-to-many relationships among the attributes of the proposed TELLER entity. The relationship between multivalued functional dependencies is depicted below.

```
EMP ->> SKILLS
```

This depicts the multivalued functional dependency between the teller as an employee and the skills attribute.

There are a variety of rules that should be used when reducing entities to well-formed database units. The first deals with multiple multivalued dependencies within an entity having dependencies between them. In the example below the employee's multivalued dependency defines skills as well as children.

```
EMP ->> SKILLS

EMP ->> CHILD
```

This relationship implies that for every employee there may be multiple skills defined and multiple children defined. The problem is how to maintain these data. Do we repeat each child for each skill or do we do the reverse? In either case we end up having a great deal of redundant information. The design rule that results from this tells us to split the two multivalued functional dependencies into two separate entities. One includes the employee, children, and the other includes the employee, skills.

The second design rule dealing with multivalued functional dependencies tries to remove the problem that arises when there exist two one-to-many relationships in one entity, both functionally defining the same attribute. As an example we are given an EMPLOYEE entity having an employee attribute with a multivalued functional dependency defining skills possessed and another attribute, job, that also has a multivalued dependency defining skills.

```
EMP ->> SKILLS <<- JOB
```

This entity would have problems in representing an employee that had a skill not needed for a present job, or a job that requires skills no present employee possesses. The design rule to apply here is that if a mutual functional dependency exists among attributes of an entity, the attributes should be decomposed over multiple entities.

The last design rule dealing with multivalued functional dependencies involves transitive multivalued functional dependencies. The problem with this type of dependency again deals with insertion, deletion anomalies, and added redundancies caused by the relationships. An example of such a dependency might be an employee from our teller model, who has multiple children, with each child covered by possibly one or more separate insurance policies. These functional dependencies are shown as:

```
EMP ->> CHILD ->> POLICY
```

In the example we could not represent the removal of a policy without also removing the child, not a desirable occurrence. To rectify this problem the design rule recommends splitting the two multivalued functional dependencies into two separate entities. This allows us to have a child represented without a policy.

More will be said about functional dependencies when we discuss the relational model in Chapter 8. The relational database model uses functional dependencies to discuss the normal forms of relational database design. The normal forms of relational database design deal with the shape of relations, the uniqueness of keys, and functional dependencies among attributes of a relation. These rules apply to all relational database designs and imply a degree of logical separation that aids in database maintenance, consistency, and use.

Semantic Modeling and the Entity-Relationship Model

Joan Peckham
Bonnie MacKellar

6.1 INTRODUCTION

Semantic databases were introduced in the late 1970s to augment the flat, but easily analyzed and normalized, relational tables. The primary goal was to develop data modeling constructs for the specification of data structures, and in some cases behaviors, that are closer to their "real-world" counterparts. One of the primary vehicles for the semantic enhancement of data models is the relationship, used to represent interconnections among data objects (we'll refer to data objects or instances as *objects* or *entities* from now on). This is somewhat reminiscent of the interconnections in the hierarchical and network databases. There is a major difference, however; the semantic relationships are used for the high-level modeling of the data. The semantic specifications are mapped to existing relational or other (such as object-oriented) implementations, and thus do not necessarily represent the physical structure of the data. This preserves *data independence*—the desired separation between the data as conceptualized by the end user and the data as they are actually stored and accessed on the lowest levels of the system.

A semantic model operates at a higher level than a physical model or even the relational model. This allows a designer to specify the interrelationships among data objects at a level closer to that of the everyday language of the domain, thus capturing and recording semantics that are important for the understanding and maintenance of the database. Although closer to the native language or conceptual currency of the "real world," the semantic model is a restricted set of well-understood constructs, which permits a uniform mapping to the underlying database. The end result is a clear set of database semantics, which provides documentation of the data for maintenance and understanding of the database once it is populated. Further, a set of semantic specifications provides a sound basis for the automated analysis and implementation of the application.

To illustrate, we utilize an example database application needed for the support of a building design system. This database must represent objects such as walls, doors, fastening hardware (e.g., doorknobs and latches), and windows, as well as the relationships among them. We model such objects with characteristics such as cost, material, and geometry. In addition, it is convenient to *explicitly* model interobject relationships among these objects—for example, a door assembly is the collection of objects that fills a door opening in a wall. We use a part relationship to model the explicit associations between each door assembly and its component doors, where each door assembly might have one or more doors associated with it. However, the semantics of each part relationship might be different—for example, a floor is part of a room, but a room can have at most one floor.

In Figure 6.1 we depict a relationship between objects of type DoorAssembly and objects of type Door. The semantics of the schema fragment include the following assertions about data objects and the relationships among them.

- There are DoorAssembly and Door objects that coincide with "real-world" door assembly and door objects from the application. These are indicated by the rectangular boxes. We say that these are objects of type DoorAssembly and Door, respectively.

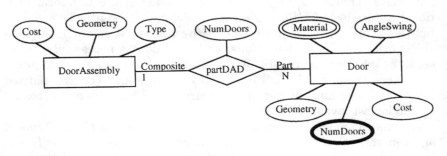

Figure 6.1   Sample relationship

- It is possible to associate pairs of DoorAssembly and Door objects via instances of a relationship named 'part_da_d'. This is indicated by the diamond around the relationship name.

- Objects of type DoorAssembly and Door, and instances of 'part_da_d' are structured with the attributes named by the circled items. Double circles indicate multivalued attributes. Bold circles indicate class attributes (explained next).

- There is a record of the total number of doors used in the whole building design (the class attribute, NumDoors).

- The direction of the part relationship is from DoorAssembly to Door. Thus, the DoorAssembly type plays the role of composite type, and the Door type plays the role of part type in the relationship. It is important to distinguish the roles of the participating relationships with which higher-order semantics are to be associated. An example is the case in which the semantics of all part relationships in a given database include an active rule, which states that a part object is deleted whenever the composite object is deleted.

  Roles are also important in defining recursive relationships—for example, a Door type might be able to serve both in the role of composite *and* in the role of part type in a part relationship. In this case, when connecting pairs of objects, it is important to identify which is the composite and which is the part.

- The cardinality of the relationship is 1:N, meaning that every DoorAssembly object may be connected to zero, one, or more Door objects, and every Door object can be connected to at most one DoorAssembly object.

- The relationship is binary, meaning that it connects pairs of objects of the two types DoorAssembly and Door. It is also possible to define ternary and other high-order relationships.

- Each relationship instance records how many Door objects are connected to each DoorAssembly object (the NumDoors attribute of 'part_da_d').

- If a Door object is deleted, and it is connected to a DoorAssembly object with no other connected Door objects, then the DoorAssembly object also must be deleted. We are assuming that these semantics are included in all part relationships by default. This may vary, however, depending upon the model or tool used for schema design.

The DoorAssembly and Door definitions are types in the sense that they represent templates for instances in the database—for example, Door is an entity or object type, a template for potentially many instances of Door in the database, each having the same characteristics (Cost, Geometry, Material, etc.), and the potential for connection to DoorAssembly objects via the appropriate 'part_da_d' connections. Similarly, the relationship type 'part_da_d' represents several instances of connections between pairs of DoorAssembly and Door entities.

We have discussed semantics that are of two general types: *static* and *dynamic*. Static semantics, or constraints, specify the correct structure and permissible states of the data. The first eight semantics in the preceding list are static. Dynamic semantics specify the correct means by which the database is to change states and at the same time maintain its constraints. The last semantic specification in the list is an example of dynamic semantics. In some cases the static semantics or constraints are also overloaded with the dynamic semantics. Thus, on some systems, if we specify a part relationship between WallSection (composite) and DoorVoid (part of a wall section representing the location of a door), this implies that if a WallSection object is deleted, then all DoorVoid objects must also be deleted. This might be carried out automatically by the database management system (DBMS) (see Chapter 19 regarding active systems), or it might be interpreted as documentation for the end user, who is expected to carry out the deletion of the DoorVoid objects whenever an associated WallSection object is deleted.

There are several problems with the semantic overloading of static semantics with dynamic semantics. First, the implementation of the dynamic semantics is not straightforward. Second, the actions to be taken when a static constraint is violated are not unique. In a building supply database, an object may be interpreted as a description of a kind of part, of which there is an unlimited supply, to be used in many parts of the design. Thus, removing a door object from the design (meaning that the door is no longer made or is not available) does not require the removal of all associated objects (openers, frames, etc.) from the database. The system must only delete the instance of the relationship connecting the door and opener objects.

In another interpretation of building design objects, part objects might always be representative of unique objects in the real world and must be associated with their owning objects. They are not capable of existing without their owners—for example, in Figure 6.1, suppose that DoorAssembly objects cannot exist without at least one associated Door object. In one implementation, the removal of the last connected Door object might trigger a simple error message to the end user. The building design system ArchE, which is currently under development at the University of Karlsruhe in Germany, uses this interpretation of design parts. In another implementation, the removal of the last door object might trigger the automatic removal of the DoorAssembly object. The implementaton of the ArchObjects architectural design system uses this interpretation.

Due to these and other complications, the development of techniques for the specification and implementation of dynamic semantics is still ongoing and is not usually found in existing commercial systems. For the remainder of this chapter, we will focus primarily upon static database semantics and the vehicles for their specification.

Ideally, it is the goal of semantic data models to provide constructs for the expression of the database semantics. The constructs must satisfy the following criteria.

1. Permit easy specification of the database application semantics.

2. Provide primitives that can capture the semantics of applications requiring hierarchies of interconnected and complex objects.

3. Provide semantics that are well described and understood so that it is possible to automatically compile the specifications to the database implementation, including the data types and operations needed to maintain correct database states.

4. Provide semantics that are well described and understood so that it is possible to automatically derive and/or construct correct and efficient internal database system structures and techniques, such as indexes, physical data organizations, and query optimization strategies.

There have been several proposals for the implementation of these models in the research community. These ideas continue to be used as a framework for development of other advanced techniques. However, the model that is most commonly used and integrated into commercial systems is the Entity-Relationship (ER) Model. The ER model is most often used as a design front end to commercial relational systems. Some examples include Salsa (Wall Data), S-Designer (Sybase), and ERWIN (Chen and Associates). The design is carried out on paper or on line using ER modeling constructs. Well-defined guidelines are then used to map these constructs to the database implementation.

Some current relational DBMSs provide automated mapping mechanisms from the on-line ER design to its implementation on a relational system—for example, ORACLE Forms and IEF (Texas Instruments) provide such capability. However, some generate data dictionary entries from the ER design and then the database construction is done by hand using the data dictionary and the data definition tools. Due to the increased use of commercial object-oriented databases to support increasingly complicated applications, well-developed strategies for mapping ER designs to object-oriented models have also been developed.

The primary modeling constructs of the ER model are *entity type* and *relationship type*. These model the objects of the database enterprise and the relationships among them. The entity types roughly correspond to the tables of the relational model. The relationships roughly correspond to the associations among tables that are established using foreign key references. The exact mapping between these two models will be shown in a later section.

The remainder of the ER modeling constructs can be viewed as constraints upon the entity and relationship types. The following list illustrates commonly needed and used constraint types and develops a vocabulary with which to discuss the ER model in the next section.

- Identification constraints: These constraints are used to specify the unique identification of entities, or collections of entities. An example from the relational model is the key constraint, which specifies that the key of a relation must uniquely identify its tuples.

- Existence (participation) constraints: These constraints specify the conditions under which specific entities can exist in the database—for example, stating that a Room object cannot exist unless it is connected to a Ceiling object via a part relationship.

- Cardinality constraints: These specify correct ways in which entities can be connected via a given relationship. The 1:N relationship between DoorAssembly and Door in Figure 6.1 is an example of a cardinality constraint. Notice that cardinality and existence constraints together define the allowable structure of the database. Each entity type participating in a relationship is constrained by both to determine the maximum (cardinality constraint) and minimum (existence constraint) extent to which its entities can participate in the relationship. These taken together are sometimes called structural constraints.

- Grouping constraints: These permit the specification of named groups of database objects—for example, a door might be composed of more than one type of material. Thus, we need to have a multivalued attribute, Material, within Door to store a listing of these materials. Also needed is the ability to name sets of objects of a given type—for example, instead of having a 1:N relationship between DoorAssembly and Door (see Figure 6.1), we might prefer a separate grouping type, DoorSet, between DoorAssembly and Door (see Figure 6.2), especially if there is to be separate information stored with respect to a set of door openings.

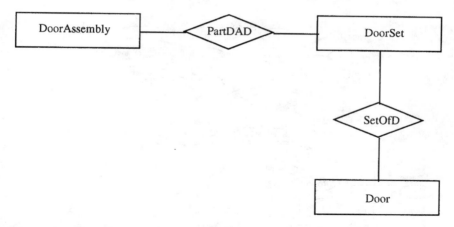

Figure 6.2   A grouping relationship

- Derivation constraints: These are used to specify information that is derived from other information in the database. The canonical example is an Age attribute that is derived from some other attribute stating the time of birth or creation of the object. A function is used to state the correct means of calculation of the derived attribute. In some systems this attribute is not stored, but derived at the time of access.

6.2 THE ER MODEL

Figure 6.3 shows a partial building design specification using the ER model. Entities (instances) represent real-world objects and are modeled using entity types (rectangular boxes) (e.g., Wall, Building, Ceiling, and Room Void). Relationships among entities are modeled with relationship types (diamond-shaped boxes)—for example, instances of 'part_b_bf' connect Building entities and BldgFloor entities, and instances of 'connect_ws_f' connect Floor and WallSection entities.

Both entities and relationships can have attributes, represented with round boxes (e.g., Geometry, Length, and ELType of WallSection; and NumDoors of 'part_da_d'). Multivalued attributes are permitted and represented with double-round boxes (e.g., the Material attribute of Fastener, DoorFrame, and Floor). Entity keys express identity constraints and are specified by underlining attribute names. It is permissible to have more than one key for an entity type, but if the design is implemented using the relational model, a primary key will eventually have to be chosen.

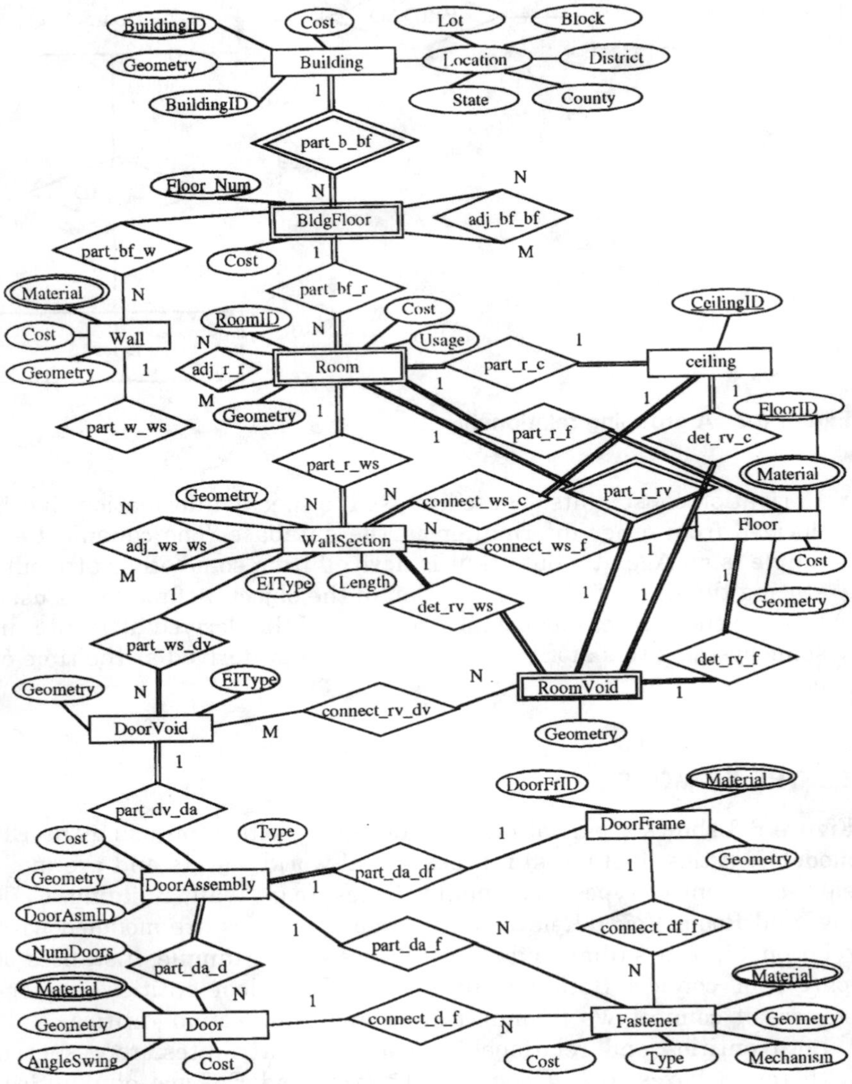

Figure 6.3 ER diagram for part of the building design database

In the example schema, part identifiers are the keys. This is a rather artificial key attribute, especially for assemblies, and illustrates one problem that the ER model shares with the relational model, namely that entity identifiers are based upon the entity's state (see Chapter 9 for a discussion of the means by which the object-oriented models overcome this problem). In the building design schema, BuildingID is shown as the key of Building; however, the keys of some attributes have been left out to reduce the complexity of the diagram.

Derivation constraints are handled as *derived* attributes—for example, attribute Cost is a derived attribute (indicated with the dotted circle around the attribute name). This attribute is derived from the building components' Cost attributes. The derivation function is specified in another phase of the schema design (mentioned later).

Composite attributes are offered to model collections of attributes that together form a higher-order attribute of an entity type—for example, Location is a composite attribute of Building consisting of Lot, Block, District, County, and State.

In the ER model it is possible to define entity types that do not have key attributes. These are called *weak entity types*. They represent sets of entities that are identified through a relationship with an owning type—for example, BldgFloor is a weak entity type without a key, but it gets its unique identification via its relationship with Building; Building is the *identifying owner*. The weak entity type is indicated with a double rectangle. Since types can participate in more than one relationship, the identifying relationship is also represented with a double diamond ('part_b_bf').

Weak entity types do not have to be distinct within their own type. Their association with an owning type uniquely identifies them as long as there are not two indistinct weak entities connected to the same owning entity. To maintain this constraint, weak entities are given a partial key, indicated by underlining the attributes of the partial key with a dotted or dashed line.

Roles can be expressed by placing the role names on the relationship connectors, as in Figure 6.1.

Cardinality constraints are expressed using annotations on the relationships—for example, the relationship 'connect_ws_f' between WallSection and Floor is N:1, meaning that for every WallSection entity, there is at most one Floor entity; and for every Floor entity, there are at most N-related WallSection entities.

Existence constraints are expressed with double lines between entity types and relationships whenever participation in a relationship is required by each entity of the type. The double lines between the entity type DoorVoid and 'part_ws_dv' indicate that the relationship is *total*, meaning that every DoorVoid entity must be connected to a WallSection entity via a 'part_ws_dv' relationship.

Although the ER model does not permit the specification of relationship types to be reused throughout large and complex schemata (such as the use of the part and connect relationships throughout this example), it is possible to specify each part relationship individually with varying cardinality and existence constraints—for example, the part relationship between WallSection and DoorVoid is 1:N; however, the part relationship between DoorVoid and DoorAssembly is 1:1.

Although many applications can be adequately modeled using only binary relationships, there are some situations in which ternary and higher-order (n-ary) relationships are necessary—for example, consider a travel agency database in which there are Hotel, Transportation, CarRental, Customer, and Agent entity types, recording information about real-world objects of each type (see Figure 6.4). A higher-order reservation relationship of degree five (five participating entity types) can be used to connect collections of entities of these types (Figure 6.4a). However, information will be lost if this association is incorrectly decomposed into several binary relationships (Figures 6.4b and 6.4c)—for example, if customer Fred Hong is connected to the Easy Sleep Hotel in Sedona, Illinois, and the car rental company, Smooth Riders of Dayton, Ohio, for the purposes of a business trip arranged by agent Bart Simmons, information about this four-way association might be lost if we use the four binary associations shown in Figure 6.4b. This could be corrected by including an identifier of the trip within each of the binary associations, but this fragments information and may compromise the advantages of the high-level semantic model as a vehicle for representing structures in a way that is very close to the human view of the application.

Choosing a cycle of binary relationship connections, as shown in Figure 6.4c, does not help. We may still confuse Fred Hong's hotel and mode of travel to Sedona with information about his other trips. The problem here is that the relationships are M:N. Fred Hong can be associated with one hotel for a trip to Providence and another for a trip to Sedona; thus, care must be taken to assure that the correct hotel is associated with the correct car rental and the correct agent.

In general it is wise to reconsider any cyclic structures for modification to n-ary relationships—for example, there is a cycle of relationship connections involving the DoorAssembly, DoorFrame, Fastener, and Door entity types in Figure 6.3. We choose not to model this as a 4-ary relationship because we need the connect relationships to be explicit. This is safe because of the cardinality of the involved part relationships. DoorAssembly objects cannot be accidentally confused with fasteners that are actually meant to be associated with other frames and assemblies. There will be only one DoorAssembly entity and one DoorFrame entity involved with each Fastener and Door entity.

The ER model also captures the domains of the attributes. This information is not usually included in the high-level ER dia-

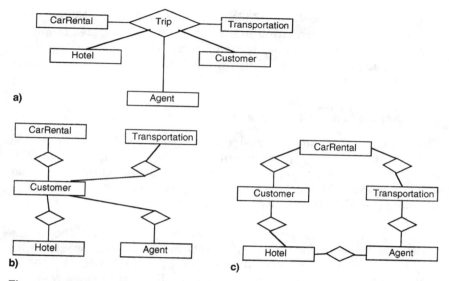

Figure 6.4   Possible configurations for the travel schema

grams—for example, if tools for the construction of an ER schema are provided via a graphical interface, then entities, relationships, and attributes are specified on one level, and pop-up menus or tables are used to specify attribute domains. Another example concerns the specification of derived attributes. The high-level graphical specification will simply identify an attribute as derived with the established ER diagrammatic syntax (dashed circle). The designer must then select the attribute to reach a table in which the formula for derivation of the attribute is written in a system-defined syntax.

6.3 MAPPING TO THE IMPLEMENTATION MODEL

The entity-relationship model is usually thought of as the high-level schema specification mechanism. Once the schema is defined using the ER model, there must be a well-defined mapping to the database implementation. In most industrial settings with standard applications, these mappings are to the relational, hierarchical, or network model. With the rapid growth of object-oriented systems, there are also techniques evolving for mapping to these systems.

Because the ER model is widely used in commercial design tools, and as a set of constructs for research into semantic modeling issues, there are many variations and extensions of the model. One example is a refinement of the structural constraints that permit the specification of a range of participation values (min,max) to be placed upon each entity type participating in a relationship. This states the minimum and maximum number of times each entity may participate in the relationship. The EER (Enhanced-ER) model consists of a collection of extensions to the core ER model.

6.3.1 Mapping to the Relational Model

The mapping from the ER design to the relational implementation proceeds in general by mapping entity and relationship types to relations, and attributes to relational attributes, but this varies somewhat to accommodate the weak entity type and multivalued attributes. The mapping proceeds as outlined in the following list.

- Map entity types to relations. For nonweak entity types, choose one ER key to serve as the primary relational key. For weak entity types, use the partial key (if any), augmented with the key of its owning type as the primary key. The attributes that came from the owning type will serve as a foreign key into the owning type. Each simple (single-valued) component of an ER entity type serves as a relational attribute. This includes simple composite attributes—for example, in the building design schema, we implement the Building entity type with attributes Type, Geometry, BuildingID (primary key), Lot, Block, District, County, State, and Cost (if this derived attribute is to be stored).

- For each binary 1:1 relationship, identify one of the relations that corresponds to an entity type participating in the relationship as primary, and the other as secondary. Include the key attribute(s) of the secondary relation in the primary relation as a foreign key into the secondary one. Attributes of the relationship are included in the primary relation. It is usually better to choose a relation that corresponds to an entity type that is total in the relationship as primary, thus avoiding the problem of null values in the relationship attributes and foreign key whenever an entity of the primary type is not involved in the relationship.

    When the participation of both entity types in the relationship is total, the two entity types can be merged into one relation if desired. This is safe because the relationship is 1:1 (no redundancy will be introduced) and participation is total (there is no need for separate representation of either entity)—for example, map DoorAssembly to the relation DoorAssembly (*DoorAsmID, Door FrameID*, Geometry, Type, Cost), and DoorFrame to the relation DoorFrame (*DoorFrameID*, Geometry). Room and Floor can be similarly mapped to two separate relations, or one relation containing all of their simple attributes. In this application, it is probably better to maintain separate Room and Floor relations due to the known access patterns of the database (rooms and floors are frequently accessed and designed separately).

- Each nonweak binary 1:N relationship type can be mapped by identifying the relation on the N side of the relationship as primary and the other relation as secondary. Augment the primary relation with a foreign key into the secondary relation. Single-valued attributes of the relationship are included as attributes of the primary relation.

- Create a new relation to implement each binary N:M relationship. Single-valued attributes of the relationship and foreign keys into the participating relations are included. The primary key of this new relation is the combination of the two foreign keys. This option can be used for 1:1 relationships and 1:N relationships whenever participation of the entity types in the relationship is sparse, thus avoiding the frequent use of null values in a primary relation (see above).

- Map each multivalued attribute to a new relation that combines it with the key of the relation to which it was attached. If the attribute is additionally composite, include all of its components. The primary key of the new relation is all of the attributes of the newly formed relation—for example, map the Material attribute of Floor to the relation FloorMaterial (*FloorID, Material*).

- Each N-ary, nonbinary relationship type is mapped in a way similar to the N:M binary relationships. One relation is formed from the key attributes of each of the participating relations, each of which forms a foreign key. All single-valued composite and noncomposite attributes of the relationship are included. The primary key is formed from the foreign keys, or use the key of a participating relation of which instances participate exactly once in the relationship.

6.3.2 Mapping to the Object-Oriented Models

There are two general ways to map binary 1:1, 1:N, and N:1 relationships to object classes. In both approaches, nonweak entity types are mapped to object classes.

The first approach uses the reference attributes of the object classes to support relationships. Most early mapping strategies utilized this idea, as do many commercial systems such as ONTOS. This is analogous to the "ER-to-relational" mapping for these relationships. However, many researchers advocate an alternative mapping in which relationship types are implemented as object types. This is analogous to the N:M relationship mapping to relational tables. Implementing relationships as objects is considered better because the design is better modularized. Including information in object classes about relationships in which the class will participate distracts from the design and understanding of the individual object types. Once the types are defined, the relationships in which they participate can be separately specified. Even in environments where the ER design is automatically mapped to the object-oriented implementation, schema evolution is easier whenever objects are specified separately from the relationships in which they participate.

There may be some environments in which performance is affected adversely by mapping relationships to objects. Reference attributes provide direct pointers among related objects. Thus, if the schema and access patterns of the database are expected to be somewhat stable, the schema is not expected to evolve, and the direction of access among object types is known, then the mapping of relationships to reference attributes might be the best choice. Automation of the mapping might make this an especially attractive alternative.

The following list outlines the techniques and is an integration of the "relationship-to-reference" attribute mapping and the relationship to object class mapping used in a prototype implementation.

- Map each entity type to an object class. Attributes are implemented with tuple constructors. Multivalued attributes are declared as set, bag (if duplicates are permitted), or list (if there is an ordering of the values) constructors. Composite attributes are mapped into tuple constructors.

- Define methods for each class. Utilize the subtyping (ISA) construct in the object-oriented language to define superclasses in which operations that are reused for all object classes are defined. Examples are methods that insert, delete, and modify objects, and those that instantiate and remove relationship instances. These methods must be defined for all classes—thus they can be generalized to a common superclass. Methods that might be coded for individual classes include the checking of constraints when objects are inserted and functions for computing the values of derived attributes.

- Weak entity types not participating in any relationship except their identifying relationship can be modeled as composite multivalued attributes of the owner object type.

- Reference attributes can be used for each binary relationship. The reference can be uni- or bidirectional. The reference in the 1:1 or N:1 direction must be single-valued. In the 1:N or N:M direction the reference must be set or list valued.

- Each n-ary relationship (where n > 2) is mapped to a separate object class, with reference attributes to the participating object classes. This option is also a good design alternative for all binary relationships, as discussed above.

6.4 SUMMARY

Semantic models provide a powerful mechanism for the specification of database schema. The semantic model is used primarily for the high-level conceptual design of databases. Currently commercial systems provide graphical tools for the construction of relational schemata using the ER model. Similar tools are evolving for object-oriented systems as well. Future research and development is needed in the area of semantic techniques to automate the implementation of the database from the semantic design.

Also of interest is the ability to capture information about various database subsystems. This includes security, performance, active and indexing characteristics, and optimization techniques. The high-level semantic information about associations among data objects, and the frequently traversed paths among them via these associations, provides a powerful tool for the construction of safe, correct, and efficient databases.

7

The CODASYL or Network Database Structuring Model

Paul Fortier

The CODASYL (Conference On DAtabase SYstems Languages) DBTG (DataBase Task Group), or network database model, has been around for a long time. This model was used as the reference model and blueprint for numerous early data management systems. No full implementations of the CODASYL standard exist, although many implementations have partial support. This chapter will outline the history of this database structuring model and the basic structure and operation of it, as well as future potential uses.

7.1 HISTORY OF CODASYL

The network database model represented the first de facto model to be embraced by a wide range of vendors to implement some of the first computer-based databases in the late 1960s to early 1970s. These early database systems were developed using the COBOL programming language as the native or host language for applications. These first database system concepts and designs were examined in detail by a study group (DBTG) of CODASYL in the late 1960s. The study was heavily influenced by the IDS system developed by Charles Bachman of IBM. The result of this study, published in 1971, was the first database standard specification, called the DBTG report. This report was the foundation upon which the ANSI X3H2 DML for the network database language standard evolved.

The database management specifications, as published by the CO-DASYL DBTG, were not initially greeted with extreme fanfare or universal acceptance. The initial report was put forth to ANSI in 1971 as a proposed standard, but it did not make it out of committee. The committee could not come to a consensus on the specification as it initially stood. This resulted in the CODASYL committee forming a permanent subgroup, called the Data Description Language Committee (DDLC), in 1972 to refine the specification and acquire acceptance by the greater database community at large. An important contribution of the DDLC was to revise the 1971 report to include data definition language and data manipulation sections. This was a break from tradition in that the same committee was handling both aspects of the language, whereas in the past this was accomplished by separate committees. An updated report, which included DDL and DML specifications, was completed in 1973. This updated report, however, still had problems that needed to be addressed. These problems dealt with language conflicts between the COBOL language and the CODASYL specification.

The result of this early groundwork was the development of numerous products by vendors who saw the potential for a standard database language and wanted to get an early jump on the competition. The problem was that none of the vendors implemented complete products; instead they chose subsets of the language and implemented to these. Just as is happening today with the object-oriented databases, the CODASYL database products did not possess enough common features to be interoperable or portable. This may have been the beginning of the end for the network database as a true standard.

In 1978 the CODASYL committee sent an updated and clarified version of its data definition language to ANSI X3H2 to consider as a standard. The X3H2 committee reviewed the submission, but did not accept it as a standard as it existed. The committee felt there were too many references to physical formats in the specification that would render the standard useless in the area of portability. The issue was that a standard should not specify implementation details, but functional and logical details. ANSI X3H2 used the baseline specified by the CODASYL DDLC committee and refined this into a draft ANSI standard. The ANSI draft version of the CODASYL DDL standard was published in 1981. The standard was not adopted since it lacked numerous elements. The major flaw was seen in the lack of a language-independent DML (data manipulation language). The original CODASYL DML was not proposed as a standard, since it was too closely tied to the COBOL programming language.

The X3H2 committee continued work on the CODASYL DML in a language-independent form, resulting in a draft report in 1984. The draft went through numerous refinements with the final standard being voted on and adopted by ANSI as a database standard in 1986. There has been no further work on the CODASYL database model and standard since that time. In fact there is no active component within ANSI or X3H2 that is working on this standard. Lately, there has been talk within the standards community that the standard will no longer be supported or maintained by ANSI in the near future.

7.2 DBTG ARCHITECTURE

The architecture of a database management system based on the CODASYL model resembles that of the ANSI/SPARC three-layered schema model. In this model there are three levels of abstraction supported: the lowest being the physical layer (internal schema), the middle being the global conceptual schema layer, and the top level being the user or group view layer (also referred to as the external schema).

Similar to the ANSI/SPARC model, the CODASYL database model supports three layers of data abstraction (Figure 7.1). The lowest layer is the data structure description, which provides the mapping of the schema records, fields, and relationships to physical storage repositories. The function of this layer is to isolate the physical data structures from the logical data structures of the database. This layer provides a map of the logical schema records, fields, and relationships to physical storage. By providing all bindings to physical storage in

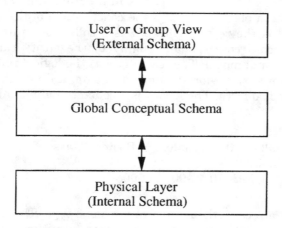

Figure 7.1   Architecture of a CODASYL DBTG database system

one layer the database designers have isolated changes to this single layer—for example, if a different linked list structure would benefit the processing done in the database, this can be reflected in the physical map without changing anything else in the database. The global conceptual schema represents the complete *logical* view of the database. All relationships, records, and fields are logically defined in this layer. The schema represents a description about the logical structure of the data, not the physical realization of the data. The top layer or external schema describes a user view into the logical database. This view may be only a partial description of the database; have different names for records, fields, and relationships; and have them ordered in a different way. Another variation may be the actual base type of a field. The subschema may view a data item from a different base view—for example, a character instead of an integer. Many of the CODASYL database implementations have some degree of these layers present in their designs, but do not adhere to any unifying method.

7.3 BASIC ELEMENTS

The most fundamental or lowest datum represented in the network database is the data-item, or *field*. A field corresponds to an attribute in the entity-relationship or relational models. Fields have nonchanging identifiers and base data types or formats. Examples of data-items are Name, Address, Phone number, and so forth. Like the other models these basic data-items have a field name and a field data type, which specify the values the field can have. The difference is that the CODYSYL model limits the values to a specific domain of values, instead of looking at base data types as in programming languages.

The basic data element used in the construction of the network database model is the record. A *record* is a collection of data-items, or fields. The record corresponds roughly to the entity class or tuple within a relational model. The *record type* is the logical representation of related information—for example, a Person, a Pilot, an Airplane, a Customer, and so forth. The *record* is a concrete individual entity—for example,

John Doe, 000-00-0000, male, 35, Boston, Mass
Boeing, 747, sr347747
John Smith, GMC, 10-14-90, 25,000

all represent a record, though not of the same type. The first item can be from the general person type, the second from the plane type, and the third from the car customer type.

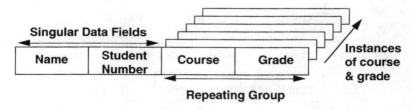

Figure 7.2   CODASYL DBTG records

The network data model allows these record types to have extended attributes; that is, an attribute or field of a record can have multiple instances of the field within the same record (Figure 7.2). This type of field is called a repeating group. In the example shown in Figure 7.2, the student record has two singular data fields (name and student number) and two fields that make up a repeating group (course name, grade), representing the courses and grades that an individual student has taken and received, respectively.

Repeating groups can be nested also; that is, a repeating group can itself have a repeating group (Figure 7.3). In Figure 7.3 an adviser has a name and an assigned department, but the adviser can advise multiple students who themselves can have taken multiple courses and earned multiple grades. Even though these are allowed in this model it is not highly recommended for maintenance and efficiency.

The basic collection type in the network model is the *set of records*. The set of records is similar to the entity set in the ER model and the relation in the relational model. The sets have relationships among them. The relationship between sets has *owners* and *members*. The owner of a set is the parent record type, and the members are the children of the parent type (Figure 7.4). This figure is also referred to

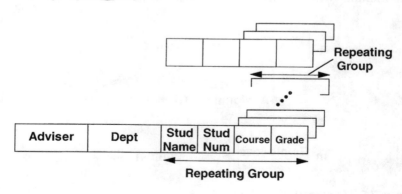

Figure 7.3   CODASYL DBTG records with repeating groups

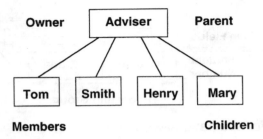

Figure 7.4 Set relationships

as a Bachman diagram and has been widely used to describe network database logical data structuring. In the example we have an adviser record type as the parent or owner and a set of members (students) of the set. The relationship between these two basic entity sets or record types is referred to as a *relationship*.

This relationship declaration is called a *set type*—for example, a department record has a 1:m relationship between employees, called assigned-to (Figure 7.5). In the example shown in Figure 7.4, the adviser *advises* students. The set type is advised of the relationship that exists between the two record types. Using this concept the repeating groups described previously can be broken down into records with set type declarations between them—for example, the student can have a 1:m relationship with course and grade. This can be represented by the logical Bachman diagram shown in Figure 7.6.

The network model has specific policies for set definition. Sets can only have one type of record as the owner, although more than one record type can be a member of a set—for example, we could represent the members of the academic community as a set with the relationship member where a professor, student, or support person is a mem-

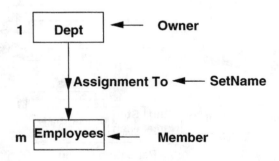

Figure 7.5 Assigned to set type

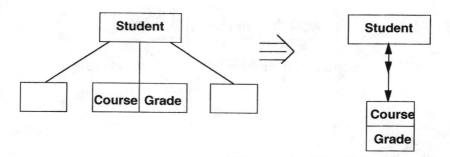

Figure 7.6   Student course grade relationship diagram

ber of the university (Figure 7.7). A second rule indicates that a member cannot belong to more than one record instance from a set—for example, we could not have a professor belong to two university instances from the same set. This limitation may force the modeler to select another representation to model such a condition. Even though the member cannot belong to more than one record instance from the parent set, a member could have multiple owners from *separate* sets—for example, the professor from Figure 7.7 could not belong to another university from the set of universities, but the professor could belong to some other organizations that are represented in other sets.

In Figure 7.8 a professor is a member of the university, and the professor can also be a member of the Association of Computing Machinery (ACM) or belong to the Institute of Electrical and Electronics Engineers (IEEE). In this example the ACM, IEEE, and University sets are the *parents* of the Professor set. The Professor set is a member of the ACM, IEEE, and University sets.

This type of multiple parent, single member relationship provides the means to represent some of the multivalued relationships discussed in Chapter 5—for example, if we have the Part, Supplier, and

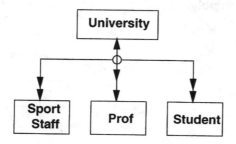

Figure 7.7   Multimember set type

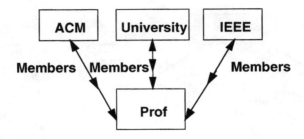

Figure 7.8   Multiparent, single member set type

Customer entities and we wish to relate these together by a relationship SPC (supplier, part, customer), we could represent this by a set type where the parent types are the Part, Customer, and Supplier sets, and the member of these sets is the SPC set, which includes a reference to the instance of Supplier, Part, and Customer that needs to be related (Figure 7.9).

A problem with the logical network model rules is that they cannot support the many-to-many relationships in a straightforward fashion—for example, if we wish to represent the relationship between three record sets, Professor, Student, and Courses, with the following relationships, Professor *teaches* Courses, Professor *advises* Students, *many* Students *in* Courses, and *Many* Courses *have* Students, we would have problems (Figure 7.10). To rectify the problem that multiple student instances cannot be parent records to a single course

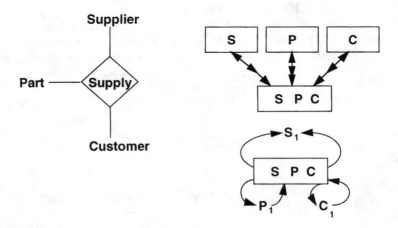

Figure 7.9   Multivalued relationships

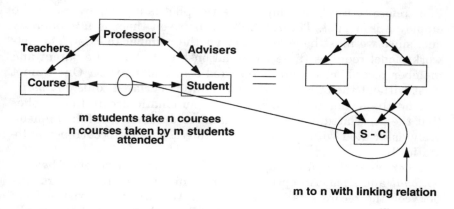

Figure 7.10   Many-to-many relationship

member and multiple course instances cannot be parents to a single student member requires a little sleight-of-hand.

To coerce the logical network to support the many-to-many relationship we need to add a *linking* relationship to change the many-to-many relationship between the Student and Course record sets into two one-to-many relationships, as seen in Figure 7.11. The new structure supports the many-to-many relationship through the link relationship. This linking relationship allows the relationships to be altered to simple one-to-many relationships.

The ISA relationship is a simple relationship, which has a mandatory member and parent element to it—for example, an employee ISA

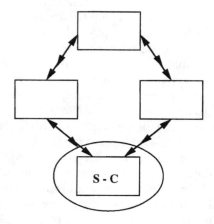

Figure 7.11   Many-to-many with linking relationship

Pilot refers to a relationship where the pilot is an employee and the employee is a pilot. The relationship between them is a *mandatory* one, since we must have an owner for the member to exist. The network model requires these ISA relationships to have the parent and member record set instances inserted at the same time. One cannot exist without the other. The membership is declared to be *automatic* to bind the owner to the member. An automatic declaration implies that the associated member, also declared automatic, will be immediately associated with its owner, creating a new set occurrence automatically.

Other types of relationships can be defined on record sets: They are *optional* and *fixed*. An optional relationship implies that a hard link between the record sets is not required. An Owner can exist without the member and a member can exist without the owner—for example, if we have two record sets, a set of customer records and a set of order records, we may want to be able to still store a customer record without a related order. This would occur when a customer at this point in time does not have an order pending, but is still nevertheless a customer. Likewise, an order does not need a customer to exist.

A fixed relationship is one that requires a link between record set owners and members. But it allows for the association of the records at run time using the connect and disconnect commands. This is a form of dynamic binding—for example, if we have an employee record set and a project record set, it would be desirable to be able to connect an employee to a project as needed and to disconnect the employee when finished.

A set relationship can be declared to be a combination of these types—for example, if we have the Customer record set and an Order record set, we may wish, when first ordering an item, to have the Order record automatically linked to a Customer record. Once the Order is settled the link becomes Optional. In this way we can still maintain the Customer record without a linked Order record.

Using these basic constructs and the linking relationship, the network model can be used to construct a variety of information schemata, from simple interconnects up to complex networks. To illustrate how it can be used to represent a more complex model we describe an airline reservation system (Figure 7.12). In this example we describe an airline that has planes, employees, parts, flights, departures, and passengers. The network describes the relationship between a flight and its scheduled departure—for example, Flight 231 is a round trip between Boston and Grand Cayman Island in the British West Indies. But it does not exist until it is assigned a departure time, gate, and date. Therefore, we require a relationship of the ISA type to define a flight as a departure. In addition, for a flight to depart it must have

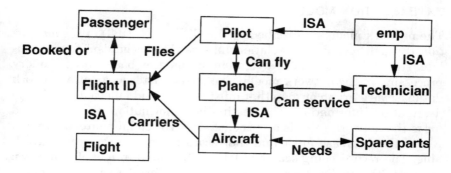

Figure 7.12   Airline reservation system

passengers. Passengers who wish to fly from Boston to Grand Cayman Island are *Booked on* Flight 231 on the departure date and time as specified. For the departure to be complete we require that an aircraft be assigned to the flight and a pilot to fly the airplane. To accomplish this the Pilot record has a relationship *flies* with the assigned departure record. The aircraft record set has a relationship *carries* between it and the departure record set. The model is now complete (the left side of Figure 7.12), and we can fly to Grand Cayman Island.

To make the airline schema complete we can further refine the definitions for Pilot and Aircraft. An Aircraft is a particular serial number on a particular plane. To determine if a pilot can fly a particular plane we need to know if the aircraft assigned to a departure is of the same type that the pilot can fly. To model these relationships we create a new record, plane, to maintain a list of the types of planes. A relationship *can fly* is created between pilot and plane, as well as a relationship ISA between plane and aircraft to capture the remainder of the desired relationship. Our airline would not be complete if we did not model mechanics and spare parts to fix the planes. We create three additional record sets, Employee, Mechanic, and Spare parts. The Employee record set is related to both the pilot and the mechanic record sets by an ISA relationship, since both pilots and mechanics are employees. The mechanic record set is related to Plane by a relationship *can service*. Finally, the Aircraft Record set is related to the Spare parts by the relationship *Needs*.

One can see from the complete Bachman diagram for this schema that the network model can readily be used to describe a required informational model of an enterprise. The problem with this model is that it does not leave room for ad hoc alteration of access paths or relationships, since they are cast in stone at schema specification time.

7.4 EXECUTION MODEL

The network model as specified by the CODASYL DBTG uses *navigation* through records and relationships as the mechanism to manipulate stored information. Navigation forms the basis for all query processing in the network model. The query writer looks at a network database as a graph or map that must be read and followed to *find* the destination information. The destination information being searched for is the network records and their fields. To read, update, or write a record the database must find the record and make the record available. The record being searched for can be found in one of two ways: the first form is *direct* access and the second form of access is *sequential*. Records accessed directly use the *physical* address of the record to access it. Records accessed sequentially are found by using their positioning within the network database and searching a record at a time (navigated) for the requested record beginning at some marker point.

The network database requires that records be part of only one record type and that each relationship between two records be of only one set type. This stipulation deals with requiring uniqueness of a datum facilitating access recovery. This property makes the data unique and therefore findable within the data, similar to the reasons for keys in the ER and relational model and unique identifiers in the object database model. One aspect of uniqueness is the key. The network database requires that the record type at least provides a unique key for entry access to a record set. The key is used as an *entry* marker for a set type, or it can be used as a basis point from which to relatively determine the location of a member.

The network database is organized as logical *files*, which can be organized in a variety of ways. The network model refers to these organization schemes as *location modes*. The model supports three location modes, DIRECT, CALC, and VIA SET. The DIRECT mode refers to physical addresses. Records that are organized by this mode are identified (uniquely) through their address within the file system. This address is a physical address uniquely defined in the storage system. It is referred to as its *database key*, defined by the system at the time the record is inserted into the database. This key remains invariant during the lifetime of the record and is also sometimes referred to as the *cursor*—for example, FIND Customer BY database key CID.

The CALC mode determines the address of a record through a computation using predefined attributes of the record that were declared as the primary key(s). The result of this function can then be used directly as the address of the requested record—for example, FIND Customer BY CALC (CID).

The VIA SET mode is used to access records that are *members* of the set type being looked for. A record within the record type being accessed can be found by traversing the set occurences in the set—for example, FIND Customer within set type USING CID.

The network model includes a construct that allows for the naming and allocation of a continuous area of secondary memory that has been allocated a portion of the database. This named continuous space is called a *realm*, or sometimes *storage area*. The realm storage area is created during database definition. A realm typically is used to group logical records and set types related by use or information content. This structure aids the database designer in organizing data based on definition and use patterns.

7.4.1 CODASYL Verbs

The network database is queried through the use of action *verbs*, which are embedded in a host language. The host language uses the database's data manipulation commands to access and pull in information required of the application and return information back to the database. The network database model works through three phases of operation in answering a query. The first phase is used to *find* stored records in the database. The second phase of operation extracts a found record into the user working area of primary memory for application processing. The third phase of operation follows an application processing on a recovered piece of information and involves returning the recovered information to secondary storage. The three main types of commands or verbs used for these phases of operation are FIND, GET, and STORE. These instructions either work on the stored records, or they operate on the recovered information in the user work area. To operate on the information in the work area the database user needs to keep track of the areas (physical) in the database where the application is working. The area that keeps track of pointers into the stored database records, files, and so on being operated on is called the *currency table*. The currency table keeps pointers the application code needs to execute on the stored database (Figure 7.13).

The currency pointers contain the physical addresses for the most recently accessed information. There is a currency pointer for each set type used in an application, for each named record type, for each realm accessed, and for the program itself. There are four major classes of currency pointers. They are Current Record of Record type

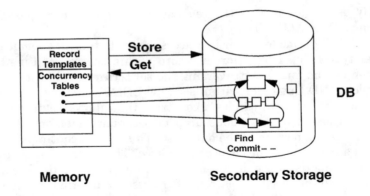

Memory   **Secondary Storage**

Figure 7.13   Phases of operation, pointers, and mapping

(CRR), Current Record of Set type (CRS), Current Record of Area (CRA), and Current record of Run Unit (CRU). The current record of record type is a pointer to the most recently accessed record over a record type used—for example, if we have issued a FIND on the Customer record for customer CID = 100, the CRR would point to the address for customer 100 once it is found. In this example, if the customer has a relationship set type named *orders*, the current record of set type would be set to the Customer address location determined by the find, since we are accessing the customer set type instance within the relationship. The current record of area would be set in this example to the record for customer 100, since this is the most recent record accessed within this area or realm (this assumes that there is only one area in this example; if there were multiple areas each would be set to the most recently accessed record within that specific area). The final currency pointer is the current record of run unit. In this example the pointer would be set to customer 100's address. On additional access commands, such as GET NEXT, this pointer would get updated to the most recent record being pointed to. The other pointers stay static until other record sets or areas are accessed. The current record of record type is set on the initial FIND to the beginning of the record set and stays static afterwards. These currency pointers become very important from a programmer's perspective for navigating through the networks stored in the database.

7.4.2 Network Navigation

To manipulate a CODASYL network database requires the use of keys and specifics of data structures that were set up at database design and installation time. To access a database directly requires the use of a database key or the CALC key. For a Customer record set stored in the database with the following structure, Customer (CID, Cname, Caddr, Cpno), it is up to the user or programmer to specify what access scheme is to be used and the portions of the database used for the access (keys, CALC attributes)—for example, if CID is specified as the KEY in the user auxilliary area of a program and C denotes an auxiliary area for storing records of type Customer, then the following query can be used to retrieve the address for a specific customer and to copy the record into the user working space.

```
C.CID:= 'C100';
FIND Customer BY CALC KEY;
```

followed by

```
GET Customer; Cname
```

This query finds the customer record using the key 'C100' to discover the address, possibly using a hash function. This address is then used by the 'GET' verb to retrieve and copy the customer's name into the variable C.Cname.

If instead we wished to use a direct access path, then a database key (absolute address) for the location of the customer record with the CID equal to 'C100' must exist. This key value is determined from the current record of record Customer. The pointer must be stored in a user-executable variable in user program space to be processed within the user program. The syntax of the query is much like it was for the CALC addressing scheme and is shown below.

```
C := CRR-Customer;
FIND Customer BY DATABASE KEY X;
```

followed by

```
GET Customer;
```

This query finds the customer record using the database address for customer stored in the CRR. This address is then used by the 'GET' verb to retrieve and copy the customer's record into user working space.

By using direct access mechanisms we can also search for multiple instantiations of a key value. This would be desirable in our example if we were looking for multiple orders from a single customer. To perform such a query the search must first locate the set occurrence for the Customer of interest, followed by a sequential search through the members looking for occurrences of the customer identifier within the relationship Orders.

```
C-O.CID := 'C100';
FIND C-O WITHIN Orders USING C-O.CID;
```

followed by

```
WHILE NOT EOF DO
BEGIN
    GET C-O; Onumber;
    FIND DUPLICATE C-O WITHIN Orders USING C-O.CID;
END;
```

This first command sets the search attribute to be used in the search. The first FIND command locates the record that matches the search field. The GET command returns the value of the customer order number pointed to. The second FIND locates another instance of the 'C100' identifier in the string of orders in the Order relationship. On the continuation through the WHILE loop the GET is encountered and the next order number retrieved. In this way all of the orders for this customer can be retrieved.

To perform a query using the sequential searching capabilities of the network model requires a bit more work on the programmer's part—for example, to find a number of customers in a record set of customers (Figure 7.14) requires first the setup of the initial pointer into the appropriate data structure, the Customer record set, followed by a scan through the set looking for the next occurrence, and retrieval of each occurrence separately. This is illustrated below.

```
FIND FIRST Customer;
WHILE NOT EOF DO
BEGIN
    GET Customer; Cname;
    FIND NEXT Customer;
END;
```

This query operates by initially setting up the search and retrieval through the first FIND command. The FIND is augmented by the verb FIRST indicating that the first pointer in the Customer record set is to be returned. With this pointer the sequential retrieval and search can proceed. The WHILE loop operates by returning the current record pointed to by CRR using the GET command. The value

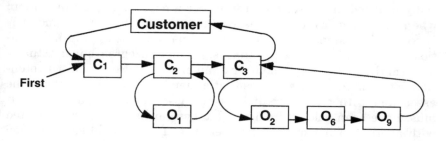

Figure 7.14   Customer record structure

returned is the customer name. After the value is returned the next customer record pointer in the chain is retrieved using the FIND NEXT command. The WHILE loop then continues getting the value within the current record and finding the next record until all of the customer records within the set have been examined and found.

The network database manipulation verb FIND can be used in conjunction with a variety of selection criteria to retrieve data based on known information—for example, you can find a record directly using the database key (form: FIND something BY DATABASE KEY), using an attribute through the CALC function (form: FIND something BY CALC KEY), by scanning a file of records to locate specific records or groups of records that meet some key values (form: FIND NEXT optionally [USING], or FIND DUPLICATE something WITHIN), search a relationship set for members that meet some condition (e.g., FIND FIRST or FIND NEXT WITHIN CURRENT), find all members of a set occurrence (e.g., FIND FIRST or FIND NEXT something WITHIN CURRENT something else USING a third something), find an owner of a record in a set occurrence, (FIND OWNER of something), or find the current record within a set type (FIND CURRENT something).

A database manipulation language would not be complete if it did not allow for the update, insertion, and deletion of records and fields within records. The network database manipulation language is no different. An update to the database in the network model may include the alteration of physical structures and hidden actions based on the schema and relationships between records in the database. Recall from our earlier discussion the set relationships between records, in particular the automatic, manual, mandatory, optional, and fixed modifiers that are tacked onto the relationships within the schema. These modifications result in specific required database actions when a related record is affected in an appropriate manner.

For the automatic connection option, when a new owner record is inserted in the database a corresponding member record is automatically inserted into a set occurrence. For a manual connection option, when a new owner record is inserted into the database a new member is required to be inserted at the same time with the appropriate relationships specified explicitly; that is, the user program must actually perform the insert of the member or an error will occur. The set retention option mandatory specifies that a member record must always be associated with an owner. If it is not associated with an owner, it must have been deleted from the database or have been reassociated with another owner of the same set type. The optional set retention option indicates that the member does not have to be tied to an owner to exist in the database. It can be represented on its own, separate from the owner. An example would be when we wish to maintain a customer record even when the customer has no outstanding orders pending in an order customer relationship. The final optional set retention qualifier is the fixed option. The fixed option indicates that the owner and member cannot be split and reallocated to another member or owner. The relationship is fixed and cannot be broken. The member occurrence must stay related to the same owner occurrence throughout its existence.

Beyond these specific structures that cause hidden or implied actions for insertion and deletion there are explicit operators to insert, delete, and modify data in the network database. These operators are STORE, ERASE, and MODIFY. To insert a new record into a network database the STORE operator is used—for example, to insert a new Customer record into the Customer set, one first populates the fields of the customer record with the new data in the user work area and then executes the STORE operation to insert it into the database.

```
C.cname :=  'Central';
C.CID := 'C400';
C.Caddr := 'Boston';
C.Cpno := 'p25';
STORE Customer;
```

This simple example would insert the record (C400, Central, Boston, P25) into the Customer record set at the present location of the current record pointer. Like the GET command the STORE can use the various addressing schemes to determine where to insert the record into the database.

The ERASE command is used to delete a record from the database. The record deleted is the present record pointed to by the current record of run unit. This command deletes all references to this record even in set occurrences (relationships) of which this record is a part. It is important to note that this command will also be affected by the optional binding conditions set on the relationships of which this record is a part, as specified in the description of automatic, manual, mandatory, optional, and fixed options.

The last command that can affect the contents of stored data is the MODIFY command. This command is used when an alteration to the contents of an existing record is required, without replacing the entire record. The MODIFY command allows the programmer to select specific fields within a record, alter them, and store them back into the database—for example, in the previous Customer record, if the stored record instance (C400, Central, Boston, P25) were erroneously inserted with the company name Central when it should have been Centile, the MODIFY command could be used to change the one field instead of removing an entire record and replacing it. To perform the alteration one first has to find the appropriate record that is to be modified and set the current record of run unit to this pointer. The operation then goes on to set the appropriate field and replace the field as follows.

```
C.Cnum := 'C400';
FIND Customer BY CALC KEY;
C.cname :=  'Centile';
MODIFY Customer;
```

In this example we first set the key for the CALC function to the appropriate attribute, the customer number. This is then used by the FIND command to set the pointer to the appropriate record. The customer name field is then reset in the user work space and placed into the appropriate field designator. Finally, the value is placed into the record, replacing the old value.

7.5 PROS AND CONS OF THE CODASYL MODEL

The strength of the CODASYL model is in its close fit to the underlying storage structures. If data structures remain stable, the model and implementations can meet high-performance requirements. The network database model requires the database modeler to form all information into *networks* of interrelated data structures. These networks then become the only means through which these data can be accessed. New relationships among the data cannot be readily created or implied through the use or view taken by the users of the database. It is specifically due to this inflexibility that this model has lost ground over the years to the relational object database models.

The network database systems, however, do have a place in the information management world. They and their hierarchical relationship account for an enormous volume of legacy information management systems, encompassing a huge volume of stored information. Due to this investment in the past these systems will be around for quite some time to come, although their impact will become less and less prominent as time goes on. Present systems, which must use these legacy databases, try to isolate them through the use of encasement in object wrappers or within specific interface programs written to allow extraction of the stored information.

Companies are finding, however, that to maintain their competitive edge they must replace these systems and upgrade to modern paradigms if they are to survive in the new information world. Information is the largest and most important commodity in most modern businesses and will continue to be so as more people come on line. The growth of the personal computer and workstation platforms and their movement away from this traditional model will ultimately lead to its demise. As more information from these legacy systems is requested and needed in these new machines, the owners and maintainers of these information banks will feel the need to bring them into the twenty-first century. This will ultimately seal the fate of these antiquated systems.

8

The Relational Data Structuring Model

Paul Fortier

8.1 INTRODUCTION

The relational database model has been with us for almost 25 years, although actual production-quality systems have only been readily available off the shelf for about 10 to 15 years. This model has proven itself as a strong environment for database design and database-user support. The simplicity of the database structure, using relations (tables), and the richness of data manipulation, using relational calculus operations, have produced a flexible environment for designers and users of such systems. The relational database management system and relational database model's roots are explained in a series of papers published by E. F. Codd in the early 1970s. Since then the relational database concept has been extensively researched and developed, and the concept has been described in numerous textbooks. It has been expanded from its earlier, strict foundation to now include objects in its latest transformation in the SQL-3 language. In this chapter we examine the fundamentals of the relational database model. We will examine its basic structure, data storage mechanisms, operations, use in database management systems, and its potential for the future.

8.2 BASIC FEATURES OF RELATIONS

The most fundamental property of the relational database model is that all information entities are represented as two-dimensional arrays of data items, called relations. These data structures are not randomly ordered or loosely organized. The structure and the definition of a relation forces numerous properties to be applied to the encased data items. The relations are structured in the form of named tables consisting of columns and rows. A table's name represents the relation's name within the database. The name of a relation placed into a database is a time-invariant specification. Thus, the name of this relation cannot be changed, duplicated, or altered in this database over its lifetime. The columns of the table represent the attributes or components that make up a relation's entries—for example, an employee relation can be comprised of these attributes: employee-identifier, employee-name, employee-age, job-title, department, and salary. These attributes form the definition for entity instances that are represented within this relation. The names of attributes defined for a relation are also time invariant. Thus, their name and specification cannot be altered, changed, or duplicated within this relation. In addition, the specification of a relation includes the specification of the set of possible values that each attribute can possess. Formally, this is described as follows:

> Given sets $S1, S2, S3, \ldots, Sn$, where for each Si there exists a domain of values DOM(i) = {Si} such that for any attribute i, its set of all possible values is derived from DOM(i). The domains of the various sets do not necessarily have to be distinct.

The rows of the table represent an ordered set of value attributes from the domain of values for each attribute. These rows are called tuples and are formally described as follows:

> Given sets $S1, S2, S3, \ldots, Sn$, an element of a relation is an n-tuple, represented as a set where the first element is taken from $S1$, the second from $S2$, and so on up to element n being taken from set Sn.

A relation is comprised of a set of such n-tuples, as defined above. In addition, a relation has a property that declares there can be no duplicate tuples within the relation's set of tuples—for example, for all tuples of a relation R, for all pairs of tuples $ti, tj, ti \neq tj$.

As an example we define an employee relation (as shown below) to be composed of six attributes and six tuples with the following definitions for the domain of values for each attribute.

```
CREATE TABLE Employee
   (emp_ID ( INT (4), NONULL)
```

```
name ( CHAR (20)),
age ( INT (3)),
job ( CHAR (5)),
dept ( CHAR (5)),
salary ( INT (6))  )
```

The above definition uses some features from the relational Structured Query Language (SQL) to define the format of the relation and to bound the domain of values for the attributes. In this example the employee relation consists of six attributes, where their domains of possible values are chosen from the sets of characters (CHAR) or integers (INT) limited to some number of characters or integer size based on the descriptor for the data type. In addition, one attribute, emp_ID, has an additional constraint: It must always have a value; it cannot be undefined or unambiguous. We will see why later. Graphically this relation is shown in Table 8.1.

In the example relation shown in Table 8.1 the following properties hold.

- The relation is named EMPLOYEE.
- The relation EMPLOYEE has six attributes or columns (emp_ID, name, age, job, dept, salary).
- Each row in the relation is composed of the same attributes shown above and in the same order.
- Each attribute of EMPLOYEE has the definitional constraints depicted in the CREATE TABLE specification.

Table 8.1 Employee Relation Example

Emp-ID	Name	age	job	dept	salary
100	Adams	60	Admin	Prsnl	50,000
200	Jones	30	Mangr	Prod	40,000
300	Smith	35	Weldr	Prod	25,000
400	Doe	28	Cuter	Prod	22,500
500	Kent	25	Asmby	Prod	15,750
600	Wilson	32	Suply	Ship	17,500

- To uniquely define any row in the EMPLOYEE relation the relational model requires that a KEY exist as part of the relation. In this relation the unique identifier is emp_ID, which is, therefore, the primary KEY for EMPLOYEE.

- The number of rows in the relation is referred to as the *cardinality* of the relation. The EMPLOYEE relation above has a cardinality of six.

- The number of attributes or columns in the relation is referred to as the *degree* of the relation. The EMPLOYEE relation above has a degree of five.

- There are no duplicate tuples in the EMPLOYEE relation.

- No implied ordering is required within the relational model, although the EMPLOYEE relation does have the employee tuples ordered by the employee identifier.

The names of attributes within a relation are required to be unique in order to be able to differentiate between attributes within a relation, although the name used to describe an attribute in one relation can be reused within another relation in the same database—for example, referring to the EMPLOYEE relation previously defined, we could have another relation in the database, PERSON, that also includes the attribute's name and age. Even though these attributes have the same definition, the elements themselves are still unique and can therefore be differentiated from each other, since they are from separate relations. Addressing them as separate attributes is as easy as referring to the two relations and their attributes using a dot notation. This form of addressing is shown as

```
cname := EMPLOYEE.name;
```

or

```
cname := PERSON.name;
```

The name of a relation in the database, however, cannot be reused within the specification of the entire database. In our example, this means that we could not have another relation in our database that has the name EMPLOYEE or PERSON.

The specification of the attributes within a relation must be separate from the specification for an attribute's domain of values. In our example, the attribute name is specified first followed by the domain of values for the employee name attribute. The domain of values is specified as a character string that consists of up to 20 characters. The employee's age is specified first by an attribute name or identifier, called *age*, followed by a specification for the domain of possible values that age can take on to be positive integers with a range of three integers. This would allow the representation of a person's age from 0 up to 999.

To guarantee that the tuples within a relation can be differentiated from each other, we must specify a unique identifier. In the EMPLOYEE relation the employee identifier is specified as a nonnull value with a range of four integer locations. This gives us a range of 0 to 9,999 employee identifiers. In addition, we may need to specify that this is the key for the relation to limit its representation further. As a key the attribute is further constrained to require that each occurrence of a data item of this type be unique across all such data items within this relation only. What this means is that no two employee identifiers can have the same value.

There can be numerous types of key attributes in a relation. The first and most important is the primary key. A primary key is the attribute within a relation that uniquely defines any tuple within the relation. A primary key also has a property declaring that it cannot possess the null value. A key can also be constructed from multiple attributes—for example, if we had a parts database where the parts identifiers were not unique, a primary key could be constructed by combining the part identifier with a vendor identifier.

```
PART(part-id, vendor-id, partname, unit-cost);
```

The combination of the two attributes, if they provide a unique value, would represent the primary key for the relation. A key constructed in this manner is called a compound key. Compound keys are common in relational databases for use as relationship implementers—for example, the simple PART relation described previously could be used as the relationship construct to link suppliers (VENDORS) with parts (PARTS). In this way we could represent a relationship where a particular part is available from multiple vendors or a relationship where a vendor supplies multiple parts.

There also can be times when a relation has numerous attributes that could qualify as a primary key—for example, in the EMPLOYEE relation if we add an additional attribute called Social Security number (ss#), there now exists a second attribute, which, by definition, has a unique representation for each person represented in the company. Both of the attributes could therefore act as the key for this relation. They are then both called *candidate keys*. Candidate keys can be used in many ways—as the primary index into a relation, as a secondary index into a relation, or as a means to provide a path for the combination of relations during relational operations.

The fourth form of key found in the relational model is the foreign key. A foreign key is an attribute in one relation that has a matching attribute in another relation, where the match is to a primary key in the foreign relation. From this definition, if attribute A from relation R is a foreign key in relation S, then there must be elements in S indicating that for each value of A in R there is a match to a primary key value in S. An example is shown in the three following relations.

```
VENDOR( Vendor-No, Vendor-id, Vendor-name, Vendor-city)

SUPPLY( Vendor-No, Part-No, Qty)

PART( Part-No, Part-name)
```

If Part-No is a foreign key in SUPPLY, according to the previous definition, there must exist a matching value in PART for Part-No, which is the primary key in the PART relation.

8.3 DATA TYPES SUPPORTED

The relational model supports all of the common data types that would be found in most modern programming languages. The basic data types supported include characters and character strings, real numbers, integer numbers, Boolean values, and a special type called a null type. Complex representations for data can also be represented—for example. if we wished to limit the possible values for an attribute Sex in the PERSON relation to either Male or Female, we could specify that Sex is of type character string and that the only valid character sets are the letters Male and Female in these specific orders. To do this, additional metainformation is required from the database to restrict the domain of possible values that an attribute can take on. These will be discussed further later in this section. The special data type NULL is required by the relational model to represent attributes that have no value in relation to their specification—for example, in our EMPLOYEE relation if we added an attribute for phone number

```
EMPLOYEE( emp_ID, name, age, job, dept, salary, phone-no)
```

and wished to have the ability to represent an employee who did not own a phone, we could not represent this possibility with the relational model without the use of a null value. This is due to the relational model's requirement that all elements of a relation have meaning and cannot be empty. The NULL value is a way to indicate to the relational model that there is no value for the attribute that has the NULL value present.

The NULL value itself can also have a deeper meaning. NULL does not simply need to be an identifier for an unknown or missing value. NULL identifiers can themselves come from a domain of possible NULL values. In the previous example, an employee can have a phone number, but may wish it to stay unknown to everyone except the head of the company's personnel department. A NULL value with a deeper meaning can be used for this purpose. The NULL value used could be an encoded form of the phone number, with the head of personnel being the only individual capable of decoding the number if it were required for use. The EMPLOYEE relation has some tuples populated with data, some of which are nulls, as shown in Table 8.2.

The NULL values are of two types: The first is an encoded null for employee Adams, and the second is a normal NULL indicating the empty value for employee Wilson.

The relational model does not, however, at present support complex data types directly—for example, if we wanted to represent an object, such as a bag or a queue with operations to insert items and take out items of different types as an attribute within a relation, we could not represent this in the basic relational model. Relations only support flat data structures or tables, where the attributes are one-dimensional type representations. More complex representations would take much more effort within the relational model to support. We will see later on in the text how some ongoing efforts by the X3H2 Committee of the American National Standards Institute (ANSI) is working toward the solution to this problem. This committee is working on extensions to the SQL language to include objects (abstract data types) as a basic feature of the database.

Relations and the attributes within them have data and relationship dependencies that are applied to them. These data dependencies are semantic conditions that are applied to data in the relation and that must be satisfied if the relation's contents are to be valid—for example, the simple constraints on the range of values within an attribute specified by the size qualifier within an attribute's specification. For the EMPLOYEE relation the number of employees is limited to 1,000, from 0 to 999, the size of the integer field for the attribute. Likewise, the sex attribute is further constrained to take on only one of two values, either male or female. These represent simple constraints or restrictions on the possible values that an attribute can possess.

Table 8.2 Employee Relation Example with NULL Values Used

Emp-ID	Name	age	job	dept	salary	tele_num
100	Adams	60	Admin	Prsnl	50,000	6171234567
200	Jones	30	Mangr	Prod	40,000	4018413666
300	Smith	35	Weldr	Prod	25,000	5089999991
400	Doe	28	Cuter	Prod	22,500	4016836835
500	Kent	25	Asmby	Prod	15,750	5083219877
600	Wilson	32	Suply	Ship	17,500	NULL

A key dependency is also a restriction on the possible values that a key can possess. In addition, this restriction encompasses all tuples of the relation in its restriction—for example, if we had a relation that maintained information about books in a library, the relation could look as follows.

```
BOOKS(call-No, Title, Author, Publ-Date, Publisher,
Address)
```

The Call-No is the key and would need to be further constrained as follows.

```
Call-No = DOM { Values } where for all
    Ci ∈ Call_No, Ci is unique and NOT NULL
```

A relation is said to be *well formed* if for all tuples of a relation, each tuple represents a *unique collection* of attributes that are functionally defined by a primary key value.

The data dependencies defined for relational databases can be placed into one of two classes. The first class is referred to as static dependencies. Static dependencies are constraints that must be satisfied for all states of the database—for example, time-invariant dependencies such as key dependencies. The second class of dependency is referred to as dynamic dependencies. Dynamic data dependencies are those that must be satisfied during the transition from one database state to another database state—for example, in the EM-PLOYEE relation we could specify a constraint on the salaries attribute to indicate that salaries can only increase; they cannot decrease.

```
ON transition DO
    CHECK NEW EMPLOYEE.salary ≤ OLD EMPLOYEE.salary
```

In this constraint the condition is checked whenever the named transition occurs—for example, we can indicate that this should be done on all reads, writes, or updates to the database. The transition also can be events in the database—for example, the transition could be a transaction commit, initiation, abortion, or some other transition that can be marked in the database.

A relational database **D** is considered correct and consistent if, and only if, all relations **R** of the database **D** at any time **t** satisfy all consistency constraints **C**. This is shown as

$$\textbf{Dt} = \text{SAT } (\textbf{D,C}) \text{ -> CONSISTENT database}$$

Simple consistency as discussed up to this point is called pointwise consistency. A database is pointwise consistent if all of the consistency constraints on each data item are met.

A second, more encompassing constraint, is referred to as Interrelational Dependency, or IND constraints. An interrelational dependency is a constraint that spans multiple relations—for example, using our previous EMPLOYEE relation along with a new relation called PILOT, shown in Figure 8.1, the following must hold. The employee identifier in EMPLOYEE must have a related entry in the PILOT relation. In addition, the relationship further indicates that there is one pilot in the PILOT relation that relates to one employee in the EMPLOYEE relation. A further example of interrelational dependencies can be derived from relationships described in Chapter 5. Relationships represent specific interrelational dependencies.

Given the three relations in Figure 8.2, the following must hold for the PARTS, SUPPLIER, and SUPPLY relations. The SUPPLY relation contains a foreign key for the PARTS relation and a foreign key for the SUPPLIER relation. These two foreign keys are used to relate a part in the PARTS relation with a supplier in the SUPPLIER relation. No supplier can have an entry in the SUPPLY relation unless there is a corresponding part in the PART relation.

A database is said to be *valid* if it maintains the following qualities.

1. The database is pointwise consistent.
2. The database satisfies all interrelational dependencies.

Emp-ID	Name	age	job	dept	salary
100	Adams	60	Admin	Prsnl	50,000
200	Jones	30	Mangr	Prod	40,000
300	Smith	35	Weldr	Prod	25,000

EMPLOYEE

Pilot-ID	Name	Flt-hours	Certify
130	Adams	6000	B-737
240	James	300	C-121
360	Scully	3500	Md-38

PILOT

Emp-ID	Pilot-ID	Assigned to
100	130	B-737-3335547
400	360	Md-38-144278
700	240	C-121-1332

EMPLOYEE-PILOT

Figure 8.1   Interrelational dependency

Interrelational dependencies need not be based only on relationships between relations based on key values. The interrelational dependencies can also encompass relationships that require one relation to exist; that is, the dependent relation cannot exist without the par-

Part-ID	Name	U- cost	Qty
100	screw	.10	1000
200	bolt	.25	2000
300	flange	.57	500

PARTS

Sup-ID	Name	Address	Certify
130	Adams	SanFr	B-737
240	James	Bostn	C-121
360	Scully	NewYk	Md-38

Supplier

Part-ID	Sup-ID	Order Qty
100	130	B-737-3335547
400	360	Md-38-144278
700	240	C-121-1332

PARTS-SUPPLIER

Figure 8.2   PARTS-SUPPLIER interrelational dependency

ent. Inclusion dependencies are best explained by using the ISA relationship described in Chapter 5. Going back to the PILOT and EMPLOYEE relations previously described, we can see that the ISA relationship is defined within this relationship through the PILOT employee identifier and the EMPLOYEE employee identifier. This relationship is meant to indicate that in the ISA relationship a pilot is an employee. In this example the dependent key, employee identifier, in the EMPLOYEE relation is a foreign key in the PILOT dependent relation. The foreign key can be the dependent relation's primary key or a secondary key.

Foreign key as primary key:

```
PILOT(employee-id, planes)
```

or foreign key as secondary key:

```
PILOT(Pilot-id, employee-id, planes)
```

8.3.1 Functional Dependencies

Functional dependencies are used to design well-formed relations and to guarantee that they meet the properties necessary for relational data manipulation. A functional dependency defines how one attribute of a relation relates to another from the same relation. Functional dependencies are used to define what information should be included in the same relation and what information should be removed. There are basic rules for the grouping and partitioning of information, as we will see shortly. Data items are functionally related if one defines the other—for example, a person's name defines his or her age, or a person's name defines his or her sex. A simple notation is used to describe these relationships—for example, if an attribute A functionally defines an attribute B, this relationship is shown as **A --> B**. This notation is used throughout the remainder of this section. A data item defines another when it physically is related to and derives or defines the context of the other attribute—for example, if we have a relation PERSON with the attribute's name, birth date, and weight, these attributes are functionally defined by the person they represent or are related to. A person by definition defines a birth date and a weight. A particular person must have a date of birth and, if he or she exists, also a weight. These functional relationships can be shown graphically using the following relationship descriptors.

Given that A represents a person's name, B represents the person's birth date, and C represents the person's weight, we can define the functional dependencies as name functionally defines birth date, and name functionally defines weight. These are shown as

$$A \dashrightarrow B$$

and

$$A \dashrightarrow C$$

These examples represent simple one-to-one relationships, as in the ER model. One attribute functionally defines another in a one-way direction. Functional dependencies of this type can be used to aid in relation design and normalization.

Functional dependencies can be more complex than the simple ones previously illustrated. A functional dependency can be defined on augmented attributes (groups). As an example, assume there exist two attribute fields defined as zip_state and city_state. The zip is augmented by state in one attribute, and in the other the city is augmented by the same modifier state. In this relationship the zip functionally defines the city as the basis dependency, **ZIP --> CITY**. This dependency is then *augmented* on both sides of the relationship by the modifier state **ZIP-state --> CITY-state**. This augmentation does not alter the functional dependency in any way. This is shown as the following generic functional dependency property dealing with augmentation.

If

$$A \dashrightarrow B$$

and we augment A and B by X, giving us AX and BX as augmented attributes, then

$$AX \dashrightarrow BX$$

A third property of functional dependencies is transitivity. Transitivity implies that one attribute can be transitively related to another through some intermediary. As an example, if we have the basic functional dependencies **STATE-ZIP --> CITY-STATE** and **CITY-STATE --> CITY-STATE-ZIP**, through the property of transitivity, since STATE-ZIP functionally defines CITY-STATE and CITY-STATE functionally defines CITY-STATE-ZIP, STATE-ZIP functionally defines CITY-STATE-ZIP. This is shown graphically as

$$\textbf{STATE-ZIP} \dashrightarrow \textbf{CITY-STATE}$$

and

$$\textbf{CITY-STATE} \dashrightarrow \textbf{CITY-STATE-ZIP}$$

then by transitivity

STATE-ZIP --> CITY-STATE-ZIP

In general, if there exist functional dependencies **A** --> **B** and **B** --> **C**, then by the transitivity property **A** --> **C** holds. A transitive dependency can be used to decide which attribute is best suited to be the key of a relation.

A fourth form of functional dependency is the derived dependency. A derived dependency exists when one attribute can be used to *derive* the value of another attribute—for example, in the PERSON relation, if we have the attributes **name**, **date-of-birth**, and **age**, we readily recognize the functional dependency between name and date-of-birth and name and age. In addition, we may recognize that the attribute age can be computed quite readily from the date-of-birth attribute. This can be accomplished quite easily by creating a function that uses today's date and subtracts the date of birth to find the age of a person. This dependency is shown as **date-of-birth** *derives* --> **age**. One can see that the age attribute is a redundant piece of data and does not need to be included in the database. The rule to apply on derived dependencies is to avoid them within a relation. Redundant data must be maintained in common and by having such data around we open up the problem of update synchronization and accuracy.

A fifth form of functional dependency is the multivalued functional dependencies. A multivalued functional dependency exists when one attribute defines many instances of another attribute—for example, in a relation for employees we may have fields for employee name, skills possessed, children's names, and many others. In such a relation for each employee many tuples may be required to show all the job skills, and many tuples may be needed for representing an employee's children. To represent all information at any time would require that we repeat the same skill for every child represented and vice versa. This results in a relation with many redundant fields and problems with update anomalies and insertion anomalies. As an example, the employee relation is shown in Table 8.3.

You can readily see from Table 8.3 that there are problems with this approach. If Adams has another child or acquires a new skill, we would be required to add additional tuples to represent this. Every tuple must have all the nonchanging data as well as the new data. This added redundancy becomes more of a problem for maintenance of the database. This type of dependency is to be minimized in a relation to limit the redundancy that results. In general a multivalued dependency should exist alone in a relation; there should not be several multivalued dependencies within a single relation.

Table 8.3 Employee Relation Example with NULL Values Used

Emp-ID	Name	Child	age	job	dept	salary	tele_num
100	Adams	John	60	Admin	Prsnl	50,000	6171234567
100	Adams	Mary	60	Admin	Prsnl	50,000	6171234567
100	Adams	John	59	Markt	Prsnl	55,000	6171234567
100	Adams	Mary	59	Markt	Prsnl	55,000	6171234567
200	Jones	Tom	30	Mangr	Prod	40,000	4018413666
200	Jones	Tom	33	Tec_W	Prod	45,000	4018413666
300	Smith	June	35	Weldr	Prod	25,000	5089999991
400	Doe	Greg	28	Cuter	Prod	22,500	4016836835
500	Kent	NULL	25	Asmby	Prod	15,750	5083219877
600	Wilson	Jane	32	Suply	Ship	17,500	NULL

A multivalued dependency is depicted as follows. A multivalued defines B as

$$A \dashrightarrow B$$

There are many types of multivalued functional dependencies that can occur. The first is when a single attribute multivalued defines two others. A multivalued defines B and A multivalued defines C as

$$A \dashrightarrow B$$

and

$$A \dashrightarrow C$$

This dependency is described in the previous example where employee multivalue defines skill and employee multivalue defines children.

A second form of multivalued functional dependency exists when two attributes functionally define a third attribute—for example, a multivalued dependency exists when A multivalued defines C and B multivalued defines C as

$$A \dashrightarrow C$$

and

$$B \text{ -->> } C$$

An example of such a dependency is found when we wish to represent an employee who possesses multiple skills and also define a job that requires multiple skills to perform.

$$\text{Employee -->> Skill <<-- Job}$$

In this example we could not add an employee with a skill not needed for a present job or add a job that has no employees with the correct skill level.

A third form of multivalued functional dependency is the transitive multivalued dependency. A transitive multivalued dependency can be viewed as a nested relationship—for example, if an attribute A multivalued functionally defines an attribute B and then attribute B multivalued functionally defines C, we have a transitive multivalued dependency.

$$A \text{ -->> } B$$

and

$$B \text{ -->> } C$$

An example of such a relationship would exist if we have our employee relation with the following attributes and relationships. An employee multivalued defines children of the employee and the children multivalued define doctors.

$$\text{Employee -->> Children -->> Doctors}$$

In this example we could not remove a doctor's name without removing the child, due to the dependency.

The basic design rule for relational databases dealing with multivalued functional dependencies is to split the dependencies into separate relations. The previous example with employee, children, and doctors should be broken up into two relations: one with the employee and children and a second with the children and their doctors. In this way the insertion and update anomalies that result from these groupings can be minimized.

8.4 DATA RELATIONSHIPS SUPPORTED

The relational model makes no distinction between entities and relationships, as was the case with the generic database design model and the ER model. The relational model uses relations to describe entities and relations with foreign keys to represent relationships. For one relation to be related to another requires the ability to represent one attribute or multiple attributes in one relation with others in the related relation—for example, if we have two relations, one for employees and their children and the second for children and their doctors, relating them would require us to use the children field in the employee relation as a secondary key to the children field in the children and their doctors relation. Through the operation of relational calculus operations on the data, the relationships can be actively discovered. In the ER model these relations were defined in a relationship entity. The relational model can represent relationships in a similar way by using an intermediary relation that names the related fields' keys together—for example, in the previous employee child and child doctor relations we could add identifiers for the employee (employee-ID) and the children (children-ID) to provide a unique address into the relations. These in turn can be used in a relationship called, for example, Employee-Child, with attributes employee-ID and children-ID only. The pairs can now be used to group any employee with any child. In such a way the relational model can easily be configured to support all of the relationships defined in the generic database design model and in the entity-relationship model.

8.5 EXECUTION MODEL

The most fundamental property of the relational database system is that data are presented to the user as tables. All actions performed on relations within the database result in new relations with a cardinality and degree derived from the combination of the relations being operated on and the relational operator being applied. To access the new data produced, a user must place the results of a relational operation into a user program data structure. The relational data manipulation model provides a variety of relational operators to examine and restructure stored relations for users' purposes. There are two types of operations: unary and binary. The unary operations are used to access singular attributes or tuples, multiple values of a single attribute, or tuples within a single relation. The binary operators are used to combine multiple relations in a variety of forms and results are placed into a new relation. The unary operators are the select operator and the projection operator. The binary operators include the join, union, intersect, difference, and Cartesian product. These operators will each be addressed in the following subsections.

8.5.1 Select

The *select* operator is one of the most basic of the relational unary operations. The select operator is used to choose one row or some sub-

Table 8.4 Employee Relation Example

Emp-ID	Name	age	job	dept	salary	tele_num
100	Adams	60	Admin	Prsnl	50,000	6171234567
200	Jones	30	Mangr	Prod	40,000	4018413666
300	Smith	35	Weldr	Prod	25,000	5089999991
400	Doe	28	Cuter	Prod	22,500	4016836835
500	Kent	25	Asmby	Prod	15,750	5083219877
600	Wilson	32	Suply	Ship	17,500	NULL

set of rows from a named relation based on given selection criteria. Selected tuples are used to construct a new relation. The selection criteria may be based on the specific value of one or more attributes of a tuple or specify a range of values for attributes of a tuple. (See Table 8.4.)

To select the row with employee Adams we could write a variety of queries that use unique values within this tuple—for example,

```
SELECT emp_ID, name, age, job, dept, salary
    FROM Employee WHERE name = 'Adams'
```

or

```
SELECT emp_ID, name, age, job, dept, salary
    FROM Employee WHERE age = '60'
```

or

```
SELECT emp_ID, name, age, job, dept, salary
    FROM Employee WHERE salary = '50,000'
```

The result in all three cases would be to retrieve the tuple from employee with Adams' information into a temporary relation.

In all cases the select statement results in some subset of the total tuples in the database being retrieved (Figure 8.3). The select operator is the most frequently used operator in the relational database

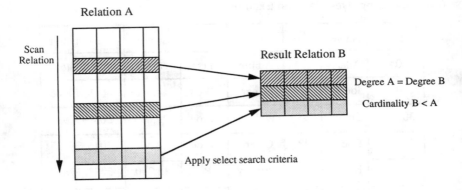

Figure 8.3 Select operation

manipulation language's repertoire. The basic operation is a comparison on a row by row basis looking for matches to the selection criteria. If a tuple does not match, it is eliminated from incorporation in the resultant table. If the tuple matches, it is copied into the resultant tempory relation. For a full select of all attributes, the degree of the resulting table will be the same, but the cardinality will be equal to or less than the cardinality of the relations being queried.

If we issued the following query

```
SELECT emp_ID, name, age, job, dept, salary
   FROM Employee WHERE salary > '25,000'
```

the resulting relation would have three tuples within it, as shown in Table 8.5. In such a way the select operator can be used to restrict retrieval to specific tuples only, or it can be used as a tool to browse through the tuples of a relation within the database.

The selection criteria can have numerous attributes to search and match on, as well as to support a variety of comparison operations—for example, we could write a query that searches for matches on one attribute only or that searches on all of the attributes for a specific match as

```
SELECT emp_ID, name, age, job, dept, salary
   FROM Employee WHERE emp_ID ='100' AND name ='Adams'
      AND age = '50' AND job = 'Admin' AND dept = 'Prsnl'
      AND salary = '25,000' AND phone-no = '6171234567'
```

In reality most queries will fall somewhere between these two extremes. Also, the user typically does not know specifically what he or

Table 8.5 Resultant Relation from Select Example

Emp-ID	Name	age	job	dept	salary	tele_num
100	Adams	60	Admin	Prsnl	50,000	6171234567
200	Jones	30	Mangr	Prod	40,000	4018413666
300	Smith	35	Weldr	Prod	25,000	5089999991

she is looking for; only some criteria about the boundaries being searched are known. The connecting operations of **AND, OR**, and **NOT** are supported to connect search conditions. The comparison operations do not need to be only equal (=). The search operations can be less than (<), greater than (>), not equal to (≠), less than or equal to (≤), and greater than or equal to (≥).

In addition, one could set the select conditions to be specific values that an attribute could possess—for example, we could write a query on the employee database to look for employees who perform specific jobs such as welding and assembly.

```
SELECT emp_ID, name, age, job, dept, salary
    FROM Employee WHERE job IN [ 'Weldr' 'Asmbl']
```

This query would result in a relation with two tuples, as seen in Table 8.6.

Selections that request a range of values also can be easily written—for example, to select the employees who make a salary between $10,000 and $30,000 would require a query that uses a range restriction with the AND operation.

```
SELECT emp_ID, name, age, job, dept, salary
    FROM Employee WHERE salary ≥ '10,000' AND salary ≤
'30,000'
```

The result of this query, Table 8.7, is a new table with four tuples, where each of the tuples has its salary field between the search boundaries. If we had set the boundary as salary > '17,500' **AND** salary < '25,000', the resulting table would have only one entry for employee 400, whose salary is the only one within the range. Even though employee 300 makes $25,000 and employee 600 makes

Table 8.6   Selection Operation Result on Employee Relation

Emp-ID	Name	age	job	dept	salary	tele_num
300	Smith	35	Weldr	Prod	25,000	5089999991
500	Kent	25	Asmb	Prod	15,750	5083219877

$17,500, the operations do not include equality; therefore, these tuples are not matched.

8.5.2 Projection Operator

The second unary operator is the *projection* operator. The projection operator is used to select specific columns and eliminate other columns from the resulting table (Figure 8.4). The resulting table may have some rows that will have duplicate fields. If this occurs, the duplicates are removed from the resulting table in order to maintain the relational property that all tuples must be unique.

If we have our employee database, as shown in Table 8.8, and we write a projection query that projects the age and department attributes, the resulting table will initially have duplicate entries that must be removed.

PROJECT age, dept **FROM** Employee

The PROJECT operator is not actually found in the relational standard language SQL, but is inferred by the removal of some of the select attributes in the list after the key word SELECT. However, for clarity of presentation we use the key word PROJECT to differentiate between the two.

Table 8.7   Employee Relation Example with NULL Values Used

Emp-ID	Name	age	job	dept	salary	tele_num
300	Smith	35	Weldr	Prod	25,000	5089999991
400	Doe	28	Cuter	Prod	22,500	4016836835
500	Kent	25	Asmby	Prod	15,750	5083219877
600	Wilson	32	Suply	Ship	17,500	NULL

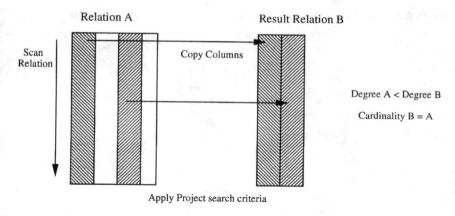

Figure 8.4   Projection operation

In Table 8.9 we see that the result has two tuples that are duplicates. To keep the relation in proper form one of the duplicates must be removed. The resulting final relation has five tuples with no duplicates, as shown in Table 8.10.

Similar to the select operation, the projection operation can have restriction clauses associated with it to allow for removal of tuples from the resultant relation. However, this is not the meaning or intended use of the initial projection operation.

It is more common to group the selection and projection operators into the same query when this form is applied. In this form a query would be able to project only the listed attributes from the relation in the select operation into the list after the keyword SELECT; the re-

Table 8.8   Employee Relation Example with NULL Values Used

Emp-ID	Name	age	job	dept	salary	tele_num
100	Adams	60	Admin	Prsnl	50,000	6171234567
200	Jones	30	Mangr	Prod	40,000	4018413666
300	Smith	25	Weldr	Prod	25,000	5089999991
400	Doe	28	Cuter	Prod	22,500	4016836835
500	Kent	25	Asmby	Prod	15,750	5083219877
600	Wilson	32	Suply	Ship	17,500	NULL

Table 8.9　Initial Projection Result Relation for Employee Example

age	dept
60	Prsnl
30	Prod
25	Prod
28	Prod
25	Prod
32	Ship

mainder of the select would be as previously indicated in Section 8.5.1. As an example, if we wished to project only the names and ages of all employees who make between $15,000 and $30,000, we could write the following query.

```
SELECT name, age FROM Employee
    WHERE salary >= '15,000' AND salary <= '30,000'
```

This query would result in a table similar to Table 8.11, with four tuples and two attributes. It can be seen from this example that the

Table 8.10　Final Projection Result Relation for Employee Example

age	dept
60	Prsnl
30	Prod
25	Prod
28	Prod
32	Ship

Table 8.11 Selection and Projection Applied to Employee Relation

Name	age
Smith	25
Doe	28
Kent	25
Wilson	32

combination of the select and the projection operators gives us the ability to isolate even single data items from a large relation. The select operator allows access to only the required tuples, and the projection operator allows us to retrieve only the needed attributes from the reduced table.

8.5.3 Union Operator

The *union* operator is a binary relational operation that acts on two relations and forms a third relation with all the elements from the other two, excluding any duplicates (Figure 8.5). The union operator can only be applied to relations that have the same identical degree (number of attributes) and that are from the same domain (characteristics of the attributes match). The resulting relation will have a cardinality that is equal to or less than the sum of the cardinalities (magnitude equal to the number of tuples in the relation) of the relations being unioned. For the following examples we use three relations. The first relation (Table 8.12) represents a list of vendors for a company.

The second relation (Table 8.13) represents a list of companies and their addresses. This relation has the same degree and matching domains of the first relation, the vendor relation.

The third relation (Table 8.14) represents a list of vendors that supply a particular part and have some quantity of that part on hand.

The union operation can be applied to these relations, resulting in new combinations of the data in them—for example, if we wish to take the union of the Vendor and the Company relations, **Vendor UNION**

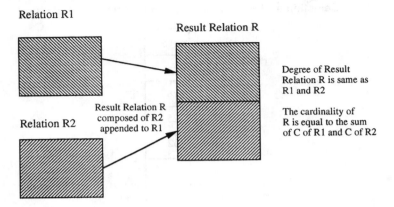

Figure 8.5   Union operation

Company, the operation will be to check if the degree of the relations match and if the domains of the attributes in the same columns of the two relations match. Since they do match in this case (Vendor number, Vendor name, Vendor city are the same in both relations), then the union operation can proceed. The union operation executes by first taking all the elements in one relation, copying them into the result relation, and then one by one inserting tuples from the second relation if they have no exact match in the resultant relation.

By using the relations previously described, the resultant relation (Table 8.15), will have six tuples: four contributed from the first relation and two tuples from the second relation. In addition, you should notice that two tuples from the second relation (V100, Smith, Boston) and (V300, Brown, Houston) have been eliminated from the final relation, since they represent redundant tuples in the unioned relation.

Table 8.12   Vendor Relation

Vendor number	Vendor name	Vendor city
V100	Smith	Boston
V200	Jones	Chicago
V300	Brown	Houston
V400	Franklin	Las Vegas

Table 8.13 Company Relation

Vendor number	Vendor name	Vendor city
V100	Smith	Boston
V500	O'Beirne	Lowell
V600	Jezak	Lenox
V300	Brown	Houston

Table 8.14 Supply Relation

Vendor number	Part number	Quantity
V100	P25	12
V200	P31	5
V300	P35	10
V100	P1	32

Table 8.15 Resultant Vendor-Company Unioned Relation

Vendor number	Vendor name	Vendor city
V100	Smith	Boston
V200	Jones	Chicago
V300	Brown	Houston
V400	Franklin	Las Vegas
V500	O'Beirne	Lowell
V600	Jezak	Lenox

If we attempted to perform the union of the Vendor relation and the supply relation,

```
Vendor UNION Supply;
```

we would find that the operation cannot occur. An error condition would be sent back to the user or the program issuing the query. The error occurs because the relations are not *UNIONable*. This is due to not meeting one of the requirements for the union operation. The two relations do have the same degree, but the individual attributes' domains are not consistent. The first attribute in each match, so this is not the error. The second position attributes and the third position attributes from the two separate relations, however, do not match. This mismatch error causes the union operation request to be denied. The result therefore is no new relation.

8.5.4 Difference Operator

The *difference* binary operator, like the union operator, executes on two relations, forming another relation based on the relational difference operation. In this operation the two relations must have the same degree (number of attributes), and the attributes of the two relations must match in terms of the domain of values for the attributes (in the same relative position in the relations) from the separate relations. The two relations are compared tuple by tuple to determine what is in one relation, but not in the other; that is, we are trying to determine how the two relations differ—what one has that the other does not. The cardinality (number of resulting tuples) is equal to or less than the cardinality of the first relation in the binary operations list.

In the previous example, if we first try to determine the difference from the Vendor relation with the Company relation (Vendor **DIFFERENCE** Company), the following operation must be performed. First the Vendor table structure and component types are compared to the Company relation structure and types to see if the operation is even possible. In this example, the degree of the Vendor relation matches the degree of the Company relation. The second check looks at the individual attributes of the two relations to see if they match in terms of data type. In the example, the first attribute of the Vendor relation matches the first attribute of the Company relation. The check succeeds and goes on to the second attribute in Vendor and Company. These too are found to match in terms of data type. The final match is to check the third attribute from the two relations. These are also found to match in terms of data types. In addition, not

Table 8.16   Vendor Relation

Vendor number	Vendor name	Vendor city
V100	Smith	Boston
V200	Jones	Chicago
V300	Brown	Houston
V400	Franklin	Las Vegas

only do these relations and their attribute data types match, but they are even given the same names. This does not have to be the case for the relations to be unionable or dissimilar. They must only match in terms of degree and attribute base types, not by the names the fields are given—for example, if the Company name is called company name instead of name, the two fields will still match. There is no problem with mismatched attribute names, only with the types of the attribute data fields. The operation is then released for execution to the underlying difference operator.

The difference operation performs its function by examining the first tuple in the Vendor relation (V100, Smith, Boston) (Table 8.16) and comparing this tuple with each tuple of the Company relation, one tuple at a time. If tuple (V100, Smith, Boston) is not found in the Company relation, it is placed in the result relation for the difference operation. Since it is in the Company relation, the operation goes on to the second tuple of the Vendor relation, having copied no tuples into the result relation.

The second tuple from the Vendor relation (V200, Jones, Chicago) is removed and compared to each of the tuples in the Company relation (Table 8.17). Since the Company has no tuple that matches this tuple, it is placed into the resultant relation.

This selection of a tuple from the Vendor relation and comparison of this tuple to all tuples in the Company relation continues until all of the tuples in the vendor relation have been examined in this way.

The resultant relation (Table 8.18) has only two tuples in it: tuple (V200, Jones, Chicago) and tuple (V400, Franklin, Las Vegas). All other tuples of the Vendor relation have matches in the Company relation and therefore are not reflected in the resultant relation.

Table 8.17 Vendor-Company Relation

Vendor number	Vendor name	Vendor city
V100	Smith	Boston
V300	Brown	Houston
V500	Jezak	Lenox
V600	O'Beirne	Lowell

If the operation is reversed—that is, we perform the operation Company **DIFFERENCE** Vendor—a different resultant relation may occur. This is due to the method of operation. We are comparing the *first* relation with the *second* relation, looking to see what tuples are in the *first* relation *but not* in the *second* relation. In this binary relational operation we see that there are again only two tuples that are in the Company relation, but are not in the Vendor relation (Table 8.19). These tuples are (V500, O'Beirne, Lowell) and (V600, Jezak, Lenox).

8.5.5 Intersect Operator

The third binary operation is the *intersect* operator. The intersect operation is used to find the tuples that are common in the two relations operated on. The operation is performed by taking one tuple at a time from the *first* relation and comparing it to each tuple in the *second* relation, looking for a match. If a match is found, the matched tuple is copied into the resultant relation. If no match is found, the comparison continues with the second tuple of the *first* relation and so on until all tuples of the *first* relation have been compared to all tuples of the *second* relation.

For our example relations introduced earlier, the Vendor and Company, the binary intersect operator executes in a manner similar to

Table 8.18 Resultant Vendor-Company Difference Relation

Vendor number	Vendor name	Vendor city
V200	Jones	Chicago
V200	Franklin	Las Vegas

Table 8.19   Resultant Company-Vendor Difference Relation

Vendor number	Vendor name	Vendor city
V500	O'Beirne	Lowell
V200	Jezak	Lenox

the union and difference operators. The first step in the execution is to check if the two relations' degree is the same. If not, the intersect operation is aborted. If the degrees do match, the second check determines if the attributes of the two relations match in terms of base types. If they match, the operation of the intersect is allowed to continue.

The intersect operation follows that of the union and difference operations. The test is to see what tuples in the *first* relation are also in the *second* relation. In this example the binary operation being performed is Vendor **INTERSECT** Company. The operation executes by taking the first tuple from the Vendor relation (V100, Smith, Boston) and comparing this tuple to each of the tuples in the Company relation, one at a time. If the comparison finds that the tuple (V100, Smith, Boston) is in the Company relation (which it is), then the tuple is copied into the resultant relation. The operation continues by taking the second tuple from the Vendor relation (V200, Jones, Chicago) and comparing this to each tuple in the Company relation. Since the tuple (V200, Jones, Chicago) has no match in the Company relation, it is not copied into the resultant relation. This selection of the next tuple in the Vendor relation and comparison to each tuple in the Company relation continues until we have exhausted all tuples within the Vendor relation. The resultant relation (Table 8.20) has two tuples (V100, Smith, Boston) and (V300, Brown, Houston).

The intersect operation's execution is such that reversing the order of the relations does not have an effect on the outcome. This is due to the nature of the operation. The intersect operation compares the two

Table 8.20   Vendor Intersect Company Resultant Relation

Vendor number	Vendor name	Vendor city
V100	Smith	Boston
V300	Brown	Houston

relations, looking for all tuples that are in both of them. Therefore, whether we place Company first or Vendor first, we are still looking for all matches, not differences as in the difference operation, and all tuples, including the matches, as in the union operation.

8.5.6 Cartesian Product Operator

The Cartesian product is used to combine relations of separate forms (differing degrees and domains) into larger relations that include the tuples from both relations in a new relation. The operation is to take each tuple from the *first* relation and create a new tuple in the resultant relation by combining this tuple individually with *each* tuple from the *second* relation. The result of a Cartesian product operation will have a degree less than or equal to the sum of the degrees of the relations being operated on (Figure 8.6); that is, the resultant relation will have as many attributes as the two relations involved combined. The cardinality of the resultant relation will be equal to the product of the magnitude of the cardinalities of the two relations—for example, if two relations, R1 and R2, are being operated on by the binary Cartesian product, and the cardinality of R1 is 5 and the cardinality of R2 is 10, then the cardinality of the resultant relation will be equal to $|R1| * |R2|$, which is $5 * 10 = 50$. This implies that the resultant relation is comprised of *all possible pairs*! The problem with this op-

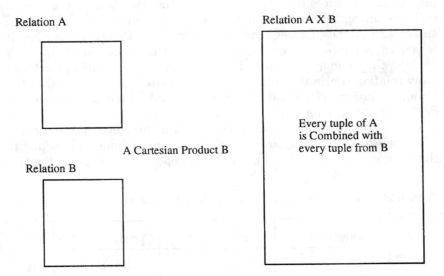

Figure 8.6   Cartesian product operation

eration is that many of the combinations have no meaning; they do not relate to any meaningful representation of any real-world entity. The Cartesian product and its meaning can be better described by an example. First, the Cartesian product operation is indicated by an X. If we perform the following operation, Vendor X Company, the result is computed by combining all tuples of the vendor relation with all tuples of the company relation. The operation does not require us to check the degree or the domains of the relations or attributes, respectively, before we perform the operation. The Cartesian product operation executes by taking the first tuple from the Vendor relation and concatenating the first tuple from the Company relation, finally placing this new, *larger* tuple into the resultant relation. The result of this first operation is shown as

```
(V100, Smith, Boston) X (V100, Smith, Boston) --> V100,
Smith, Boston,V100, Smith, Boston.
```

Selecting a tuple from the Company relation and concatenating it with the Vendor relation's first tuple continues until we have concatenated all of the Company's tuples to the Vendor's first tuple (Table 8.21).

We then continue this operation by taking the second tuple from the Vendor relation and concatenating each tuple from the Company relation until we get through the entire Company relation. This operation is repeated again and again until the entire Vendor relation has been run through, with each tuple of the Vendor relation being concatenated with each tuple of the Company relation until all combinations of each relation have been generated (Table 8.22).

You can see from Table 8.22 that there are numerous meaningless combinations generated in this way—for example, V100, Smith, Boston, V500, O'Beirne, Lowell, is not telling us anything about the two vendors in terms of any meaningful relationship. In addition, while

Table 8.21 Vendor-Company Cartesian Product Partial Resultant Relation

Vendor number	Vendor name	Vendor city	Vendor number	Vendor name	Vendor city
V100	Smith	Boston	V100	Smith	Boston
V100	Smith	Boston	V500	O'Beirne	Lowell
V100	Smith	Boston	V600	Jezak	Lenox
V100	Smith	Boston	V300	Brown	Houston

Table 8.22   Vendor-Company Cartesian Product Resultant Relation

Vendor number	Vendor name	Vendor city	Vendor number	Vendor name	Vendor city
V100	Smith	Boston	V100	Smith	Boston
V100	Smith	Boston	V500	O'Beirne	Lowell
V100	Smith	Boston	V600	Jezak	Lenox
V100	Smith	Boston	V300	Brown	Houston
V200	Jones	Chicago	V100	Smith	Boston
V200	Jones	Chicago	V500	O'Beirne	Lowell
V200	Jones	Chicago	V600	Jezak	Lenox
V200	Jones	Chicago	V300	Brown	Houston
V300	Brown	Houston	V100	Smith	Boston
V300	Brown	Houston	V500	O'Beirne	Lowell
V300	Brown	Houston	V600	Jezak	Lenox
V300	Brown	Houston	V300	Brown	Houston
V400	Franklin	Las Vegas	V100	Smith	Boston
V400	Franklin	Las Vegas	V500	O'Beirne	Lowell
V400	Franklin	Las Vegas	V600	Jezak	Lenox
V400	Franklin	Las Vegas	V300	Brown	Houston

there are some relationships that make sense, we see that there are also added redundancies. Performing the Cartesian product of these two relations may not have any relationship with real-world meaning.

It may make more sense to join items that have some correspondence to each other—for example, if we perform the Cartesian product of the Vendor relation with the Supply relation, we can at least see some resultant tuples that may be telling us something useful (Table 8.23). This Cartesian product can at least give us some potential information about which company supplies what part in what quantity and where this company is located. But you will still notice that there are many tuples that have no correspondence with reality. The only tuples that are useful are those where one of the attributes in one relation are equivalent to one in the other relation—for example, tuple one (V100, Smith, Boston, V100, P25, 12) has attribute one equal to attribute four, indicating that vendor 100, whose name is Smith, is located in Boston, supplies part number 25, and has 12 of these parts

Table 8.23   Vendor-Supply Cartesian Product Resultant Relation

Vendor number	Vendor name	Vendor city	Vendor number	Part-number	Quantity
V100	Smith	Boston	V100	P25	12
V100	Smith	Boston	V200	P31	5
V100	Smith	Boston	V300	P35	10
V100	Smith	Boston	V100	P1	32
V200	Jones	Chicago	V100	P25	12
V200	Jones	Chicago	V200	P31	5
V200	Jones	Chicago	V300	P35	10
V200	Jones	Chicago	V100	P1	32
V300	Brown	Houston	V100	P25	12
V300	Brown	Houston	V200	P31	5
V300	Brown	Houston	V300	P35	10
V300	Brown	Houston	V100	P1	32
V400	Franklin	Las Vegas	V100	P25	12
V400	Franklin	Las Vegas	V200	P31	5
V400	Franklin	Las Vegas	V300	P35	10
V400	Franklin	Las Vegas	V100	P1	32

on hand. However, if we look at tuple two in Table 8.23, we see that there is no meaning to this tuple since it tells us two unrelated pieces of information. Tuple two tells us there is a vendor whose number is 100, has the name Smith, and is located in Boston, and that a vendor whose number is 200 supplies part number 31 and has five on hand. These are unrelated and do not convey any meaningful *relationships*, which is the intent of the relational model. We will see in the following section how this problem is corrected by the more refined *equijoin* binary relational operator.

8.5.7   Join Operator

The *join* is a more useful form of the binary Cartesian product. The binary relational join operator merges two relations, based on the matching of values from one attribute in each relation (Figure 8.7). The two relations are said to be *joined* over the two attributes. The

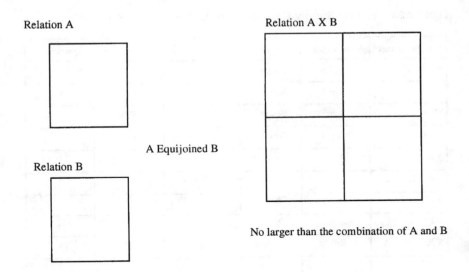

Figure 8.7   Equijoin operation

join condition or test can be viewed as the *selection criterion* over the two relations—for example, we may wish to join the Vendor relation and the Supply relation together to find vendors that supply parts and in what quantities. The select criterion for this join would be that the Vendor's *Vnum is equal to the Supply Vnum*. This query is shown as

```
DOMAIN of V IS Vendor;
DOMAIN of S IS SUPPLY;
Vendor JOIN Supply WHERE V.Vnum = S.Vnum;
```

The result of the *equijoin* operation is a new relation with the degree of magnitude of the sum of the Vendor and the Supply relations minus one. The reason there is one less attribute is that the attribute used in the selection criterion need not be repeated. It would represent a redundant data item and can therefore be discarded. The cardinality of the result will lie between zero and the cardinality of the product of the two relations.

The join operation conceptually works much like the Cartesian product. Before the join operation can begin, the two relations *match* attributes are checked to see that they are of the equivalent base types and that their domain of values is within ranges that would allow a join to proceed. The join operation then begins by taking the first tuple of the *first* relation and, using the *match* attribute in relation one, looking for a matching *value* in the selected match attribute of the second relation. If no match is found, the second relation's next tuple is selected and compared, looking for the same match. This selection and checking continues until a match is found. When a match of the two values in the match attributes from both relations is found, the two tuples are merged together into a single new tuple and placed in the resultant relation. The search then continues using the same tuple from the first relation until all tuples of the second relation are exhausted. When this occurs the join operation then selects the second tuple of the first relation and repeats the above selection, comparison, matching, and creation of new tuples until all of the tuples in the first relation have been compared to all of those in the second relation. This search and comparison requires that the second relation be searched as many times as there are tuples in the first relation; in other words, given that R1 is the cardinality of the first relation and R2 is the cardinality of the second relation, we perform R1 * R2 selections and comparisons to join the two relations.

As an example, we can join the Vendor relation (Table 8.24) and the Supply relation (Table 8.25) by searching and matching the vendor number from the Vendor relation with the vendor number from the Supply relation. To perform the join we first must be sure that the join is possible by checking that the join match attributes have the same base type and come from a compatible domain of values. In the example, since the two attributes represent the same values (that of vendor numbers), and the numbers are constructed alphanumerically followed by three-digit integers in both relations, the join can proceed. The join begins by selecting tuple one (V100, Smith, Boston) from the Vendor relation, placing the value of the match attribute (Vendor number) into a match register. This value is then used as the value to *look* for a match with the value in the Supply relation's first attribute (the Vendor number). In the example, the first tuple in the Supply relation matches the vendor numbers. The tuple (V100, Smith, Boston) from Vendor is merged with tuple (V100, P25, 12) from the Sup-

Table 8.24 Vendor Relation

Vendor number	Vendor name	Vendor city
V100	Smith	Boston
V200	Jones	Chicago
V300	Brown	Houston
V400	Franklin	Las Vegas

Table 8.25   Supply Relation

Vendor number	Part number	Quantity
V100	P25	12
V200	P31	5
V300	P35	10
V100	P1	32

ply relation, forming a new tuple (V100, Smith, Boston, P25, 12), which is placed in the resultant relation (Table 8.26). The search continues comparing tuple (V100, Smith, Boston) to tuples two and three in the Supply relation, but finding no match. In the comparison with tuple four (V100, P1, 32) from the Supply relation we find another match. The tuple (V100, Smith, Boston) is once again merged with the new matched tuple from the Supply relation (V100, P1, 32), forming a new tuple (V100, Smith, Boston, P1, 32), which is then stored in the resultant relation. After this match we are at the end of the Supply relation. The join operation then continues by selecting the second tuple from the Vendor relation (V200, Jones, Chicago) and performing the same selection and comparison of each tuple in the Supply relation against this new search tuple.

This scan of the second relation finds one match with tuple (V200, P31, 5). This match results in a new merged tuple, which is created and placed in the resultant relation (Table 8.27). The search continues until all of the tuples in the Vendor relation have been compared and attempts have been made to match them with all tuples from the Supply relation. The resulting final relation is shown in Table 8.28.

Table 8.26   Partial Resultant Joined Vendor and Supply Relation

Vendor number	Vendor name	Vendor city	Part number	Quantity
V100	Smith	Boston	P25	12
V100	Smith	Boston	P1	32

Table 8.27   Partial Resultant Joined Vendor and Supply Relation

Vendor number	Vendor name	Vendor city	Part number	Quantity
V100	Smith	Boston	P25	12
V100	Smith	Boston	P1	32
V200	Jones	Chicago	P31	5

The join operation is a powerful operator when used in conjunction with the other unary and binary relational operators. A database user can create and perform very powerful searches on a relational database using these operators—for example, we could add an additional relation called Part (Table 8.29) and ask questions of our database, such as: *Give the names of Vendors who supply more than two nuts and the quantities supplied.*

This query could be generated as follows.

- JOIN Vendor and Supply and Part on V.Vnum equal to S.Vnum and on S.Pnum equal to P.Pnum.
- SELECT those tuples in the resulantt relation where Part name is equal to Nuts.
- PROJECT vendor name and quantity from the reduced joined relation.

With our previous relations this query would result in an answer with only one tuple (V100, Smith, Boston, P1, 32, Nuts) meeting the query restrictions. The final answer would return only the vendor's name (Smith) and the quantity of nuts (32) as the final answer.

Table 8.28   Resultant Joined Vendor and Supply Relation

Vendor number	Vendor name	Vendor city	Part number	Quantity
V100	Smith	Boston	P25	12
V100	Smith	Boston	P1	32
V200	Jones	Chicago	P31	5
V300	Brown	Houston	P35	10

Table 8.29   Part Relation

Part number	Part name
P2	nut
P1	bolt
P3	Screw

8.6 SUMMARY

The relational model has proven itself over the last 25 years to be a highly flexible and easy-to-use database model. The relational model has been implemented in a variety of systems, from simple personal computers to massive back-end database servers with many end-user stations. The simplicity of the model and its ability to be understood and used by the nondatabase professional have resulted in its extended use and acceptance. It has proven over time to be superior to the hierarchical and network database models and the systems that preceded them.

The relational model appears to still have a future in today's expanding database and information management marketplace. The model is being researched for expansion into a mixed relational and object-based model to further enhance its usefulness to a wider range of users and applications beyond the simple table operations originally envisioned for it. Research into how to include abstract data types, methods, and a variety of other features for multimedia, temporal, and real-time support are being developed. More will be said on the expansion of this model and its languages in later chapters dealing with specific classes of database systems and database management system definition and language standards.

9

The Object-Oriented
Data Structuring Model

Paul Fortier

The object-oriented database model is relatively new. It has no single accepted standard or de facto implementation. We will introduce the basic structure of this model in terms of data representation and data manipulation, and follow with a discussion about the future of this model as an implemented database management system.

9.1 INTRODUCTION

Database systems must manage large quantities of persistent reliable shared information. As was shown in previous chapters, there are a variety of approaches to organizing, storing, and managing large volumes of structured data. The first model for database design was the network and hierarchical database designs, followed by the more popular relational model. All three of these models were best suited to data that had simple structures and exhibited access regularity. These models are best represented by applications such as the management of personnel records, inventory control, end-user sales, and business records. Applications such as these have fairly simple data structures, relationships, and data usage patterns.

```
Class Map
    ( Quadrant    Map type,
      Lat_lon     location type,
```

```
    Topology    Contour type,
    River       directed water type,
    Mountain    elevate contour type,
    Roads       segment type,
    Towns       population cntr type
    etc.
  );
```

More recent trends have attempted to apply these three models to more advanced applications, where data are not represented by simple record-like structures and do not exhibit simple access and manipulation behavior. These applications require more complex abstract data types, such as pictures, audio, icons, bags, lists, queues, and maps, which all have unique operations defined and used on these data types by supported applications—for example, a map object can be defined by the longitude, latitude, and time dimension for location; by contour lines running from point to point to define topography; and by icons representing major embedded objects, which themselves may be objects. In addition to these definitions, the object may have hidden data associated with sectors of the map. We could represent population densities, animal densities, vegetation, water, buildings and classifications (e.g., single family, high rise, industrial, residential), pollution concentrations, and other information, all encoded using natural abstract data types derived from an application's typical use (Figure 9.1).

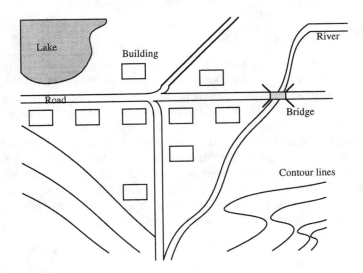

Figure 9.1   Map abstract data type

The conventional models would be forced to define these data in rather coarse ways, such as BLOBs (binary large objects), with no added information associated with the BLOBs other than an identity. The traditional database models lack the expressiveness to define such objects easily or completely, and they do not possess the ability to define complex operations on data structures. Conventional database models lack even rudimentary support to define operations on stored data, since these data models are computationally incomplete.

To rectify these deficiencies and to provide the benefits of database technology to nontraditional application domains, database researchers and vendors looked to combine evolving object-oriented programming languages with database technology. We are not quite sure if this revolution was brought on by the object-oriented programming language people or by the database management community looking for more robust data storage and manipulation facilities.

Object-oriented databases have evolved to fill a need for sharing of persistent complex information using the application of known successful techniques. Before object-oriented databases existed, applications created and owned their own set of data files, each with its own unique format and structure. Data in such applications were often stored redundantly due to multiple applications' uses and were difficult to maintain consistently and correctly. Each application acting on a data file would typically have its own version of the data file, which might not even have any relationship to any other copy of the data file. Creation of new applications requiring the same data would often need to go through painful data extraction procedures and preprocessing of the data before the information could be deemed reliable enough for use. Once designed, applications were dependent on the stored structures, making these structures difficult to change or improve.

Enter databases, which improved this picture drastically. Databases provide a single uniform view of stored information expressed in storage structure independent terms. The decoupling of logical and physical data structure, along with controlled sharing and maintenance of data correctness, integrity, and consistency, has facilitated improved application development, maintenance, and life-cycle costs. Management of data by one set of optimized routines results in more uniform performance and further optimization.

Even with these generic advantages of databases, they were slow to become acceptable within specialized information processing environments. This was due to the limitation of conventional databases in relation to complex data storage and manipulation. High-performance computing platforms offered the venue through which complex data-intensive applications, such as computer-aided design (CAD), computer-aided software engineering (CASE), and office information systems (OIS), evolved.

CAD systems represent an application domain that was the impetus for the development of object technology both in the programming language and database system design areas. CAD systems typically require complex object representations, such as transistors, resistors, and their layouts within a circuit. These data structures require complex abstract data representation and possess nonclassical data manipulation requirements. CAD data users need to alter the size and shape of circuit structures, overlay patterns on top of each other, and test if the altered topology will operate as designed. Such operations require not only the ability to model the circuit structures in the database, but also the operational behavior of these structures.

Two major problems associated with the application of a conventional database to support such advanced applications are the data impedance mismatch and operational impedance mismatch. The data impedance mismatch exists between a database and supported applications when it is necessary to translate the application's data into a suitable database storage structure or to translate database structures to application structures on accesses. An example will help illustrate this problem. Using the map abstract data type (ADT) (Figure 9.2), data impedance mismatch occurs when the storage system is a relational database, and we try to store the definitions of map icons as a tuple or a set of tuples. It would be difficult to specify a road, elevation line, or river adequately using records. The map abstract data type does not readily lend itself to the regular structure of the rela-

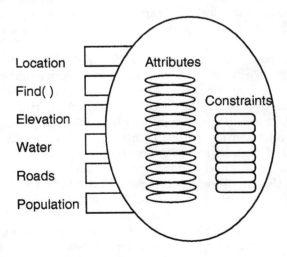

Figure 9.2 Map abstract data type

tion. It would be much easier to structure the map as a composition of other abstract data item types, such as roads, intersections, rivers, bridges, hills, mountains, meadows, and other structures. These structures should be defined in the best native characterization from the application domain, instead of a collection of flat files and simple record types, as available from relations.

The second impedance mismatch is found between the database language and the application's host language—for example, the difference between a declarative language such as SQL and a programming language such as C. There is a possibility of a loss of information between the languages due to the inability to directly represent program data structures such as objects and persistent storage structures such as relations. The problem lies in the programming languages' lack of specific database management system features for persistence, security, schema, concurrency control, and recovery. On the other hand, the database definition and manipulation language lacks the computational completeness of the general-purpose programming language to allow full specification of an application's functionality and its information management.

9.2 BASIC CONCEPTS

Object-oriented database management systems are based on a more computationally complete model. Object-oriented databases possess the natural features of a programming languages, such as SmallTalk or C++, along with extensions to support database specification and maintenance. For an object-oriented programming language and system to be considered a database language and system, the following basic features must be present. A database consists of a schema, which is a nontrivial description of data structure and meaning. The database structuring policies and mechanisms should provide for forming of data items into meaningful elements, such as records or objects, and grouping these structures into more complex data structures, such as lists, relations, sets, bags, and trees. Basic operations must be provided to create, modify, and delete data structures. Means to access the stored information using powerful query mechanisms typically also are a major part of a database management system.

An important component of a database's data structuring is the representation of relationships between data items or data structures within the database's schema. Relationships are named structures, which can themselves have valued components. Relationships provide the means to link normally unrelated data items or structures to model more advanced data semantics. In addition to relationships, a database provides persistence and storage for these persistent data items. Persistence, a fundamental requirement of a database management system, implies that data have a lifetime beyond the process that created them. Data are created and persistently stored into the database so that they can be *shared* by more than the process that created them, in a simultaneous manner (concurrency). Other features of data within a database and of a database management system include data integrity constraints, used to define ranges of correct states for data items and their relationships in the database; database security; database query processing; semantic and restricted views of the database; and data administration concepts. Security provides for access authorization and authentication as well as access control. Query processing is a facility of databases that provides for the specification of what action on the database is required without specifying how it is to be performed. Without these and other fundamental features of database systems, the object-oriented paradigm cannot be brought into the database paradigm.

9.2.1 Objects, Methods, and Messages

The fundamental concept in an object-oriented database system and the object-oriented database model is the object (Figure 9.3). An object is an abstract representation of a real-world entity stored in a computer system. An object consists of two parts: a state, which defines the meaning of the object at a point in time, and an interface, representing the only means through which the state of the object can be referenced. The maintenance of the privacy of an object's state is crucial to the fundamental concept. Objects encapsulate their private parts (state) and reveal their public parts (interface) only. The interface to an object consists of a set of operations that returns values for the state of an object (e.g., the object's encapsulated attributes) or simply performs some hidden operation on the encapsulated state. Operations on objects are invoked through the sending of a request or message (operation and parameters) to the named object, which contains the requested operation and stored state. As long as the types of the message parameters match the interface types, the operation requested can be performed. If they do not match, an error occurs. The operations act on the stored state, based on the defined operation and input parameters, just like a procedure call or function call in contemporary programming languages. An object's operations are implemented by methods, which are pieces of code that perform the desired operations on the encapsulated object's state. Methods have privileges not available to users of the object. A method can access the *private* encapsulated state (memory) of the referenced object.

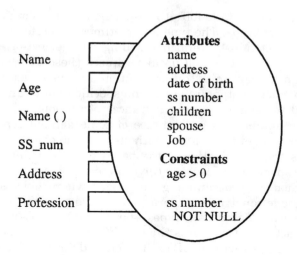

Figure 9.3 A person object

Object methods can have their names *overloaded* with many possible method implementations for the same named method—for example, we could specify a method ADDER, which takes as parameters two data items, which must be of the same type.

```
ADDER (TypeA: parameter one, Type A: parameter two)
```

The ADDER method adds the two provided parameters together, returning the result in the same type as the parameters. This method could then be used to add two integers, two reals, two complex numbers, two binary numbers, or two characters, if that is the intent. The underlying object would be required to have a separate implementation for each of the different parameter types possible. The object-oriented system contains rules that are used to determine the correct implementation to use at run time. This process, called dynamic binding, is performed at run time using the dispatching policies and mechanisms of the base object management system.

9.2.2 Types, Classes, and Encapsulation

A *type* describes a set of objects with the same characteristics—for example, a person can be described by a simple set of attributes, such as name, age, sex, address, and Social Security number. The type allows us to describe a collection of different objects based on their similarities, leaving out details for either specific instances of an object or for a modifying subtype. The type is sometimes also referred to as the *class* of an object. Most literature dealing with object-oriented programming and object-oriented databases uses these two terms interchangeably, although some differentiation has been used in some reports; in particular, type refers to the specification of an object and class is used to refer to current instances of an object. Every object stored in the database is an instance of some defined type or class. The specific class defines all the methods that the object will respond to as well as the specification of the behavior to be exhibited by the method in response to a message (invocation).

In most modern programming languages where objects are supported, language constructs are provided to allow for the specification of abstract encapsulated data types—for example, in C++ the definition of abstract data types uses the CLASS specification to aid in the specification of user-defined ADTs. The class definition allows for the definition of PUBLIC and PRIVATE parts of an object as well as for the definition of the method implementation and interface.

A class or type is not, and most likely will not be, constructed as a self-contained entity. The object model provides for the construction of more complex types using predefined types called superclasses. Using these predefined classes, a new object, which is composed of instances of other objects, can be specified. A person class can be defined using the supertype's name, address, and date of birth as follows.

```
CLASS person {
        Name nm;
        Addr addr;
        DOB dateob;
        PUBLIC:
            Name     name();
            Addr     address();
            DOB      dob();
        };

    CLASS name {
        PRIVATE
            VARCHAR(15)  fname
            VARCHAR(15)  mname
            VARCHAR(15)  lname
        PUBLIC:
            name ()
            {

            RETURN   fname, mname, lname;
```

```
CLASS addr {
    PRIVATE
        VARCHAR(15) street
        VARCHAR(15) city
        VARCHAR(15) state
    PUBLIC:
        name ()
        {
    RETURN  street, city, state;
```

where class person is composed of class name, class address, and class dob, which were defined previously. Each of these is a superclass, and person is a subtype composed of these classes. In the context of these inherited classes, the subclass not only inherits the state of a superclass, but also the behavior defined by the superclass. The combination of all these superclasses and any additional behavior and state variables defined in the subclass constitutes its definition.

By using these concepts, we can construct very complex objects composed of a variety of other objects and their functions. Objects are constructed using the instances of objects defined previously. This is not to say that an instance of an object must belong to only one other object. In the previous example, the address for one person can be the address for another person in real life (e.g., a husband, wife, and children all live at the same address); therefore it is desirable for the data modeling facility to support the same capabilities for data *inheritance*. Such a data modeling facility would be highly desirable from a database management perspective. We could, for example, move a family by simply changing their address instance. Without inheritance we would be required to have a copy of the address in each instance of a family member, and would be required to change all of these *copies* of the address. This is not a desirable feature from a database management and maintenance view.

9.2.3 Encapsulation and Types

A goal of any data modeling facility is to be extensible. It is important to the applications supported by a modeling language that existing modeled entities be allowed to change and grow with the applications they support.

The existing facility must be flexible enough to allow for the specification of future possibly complex structures (Figure 9.4). This is a primary reason for the demise of the early network and hierarchical data models and for the limitations seen with the relational data model. The original data models were not expressive enough to sup-

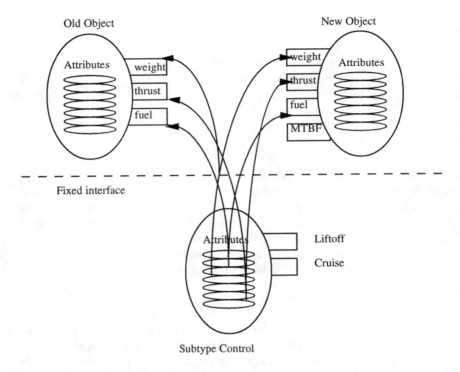

Figure 9.4   Encapsulation concepts

port complex data structures, such as maps, video, images, and sound, seen in modern computing system application domains. One method for providing extensibility is through a language's ability to define new data types beyond the basic built-in data types. A data type checking mechanism is embedded as a component of a data type definition mechanism. The ability to extend data types requires the means to verify the existence of the new type. Paramount to the definition of new types is the concept of abstract data type. Abstract data types encapsulate their implementation within their specification. Using the concept of ADT new types can readily be constructed. The new types, through encapsulation, allow only their interface definition to be accessible. This interface is rigidly defined and typed. By fixing the interface to objects, it allows the methods implementing objects to be altered or replaced as long as the interface remains consistent. Encapsulation allows for the independent specification and implementation of the internals of objects separate from all others.

In the example of Figure 9.4, the encapsulation of the engine abstract data type allows for the replacement of the old type definition and implementation with an improved or extended version of the same object, which maintains all of the existing functionality (with the interface definition remaining consistent), and also provides extensibility by adding new operations to the interface as needed. The advantage is that all of the old objects referencing operations from the engine object need not be altered when the new type is defined and placed into the existing system. The new operations are also available for new objects to use as needed.

9.2.4 Object Identity

Unlike any other data model discussed up to this point, the object model provides a mechanism by which any object within the system is uniquely defined. Each instantiated object within an object-oriented environment is assigned a unique identifier, referred to as an object's identity. An object's identity is an invariant value across all possible modifications to an object. The identity of an object is like a pointer to an item in memory.

The pointer and the object are fixed and cannot change if the item is to remain identifiable using the assigned pointer. When using such a concept, it is important to represent the identifier using an immuta-

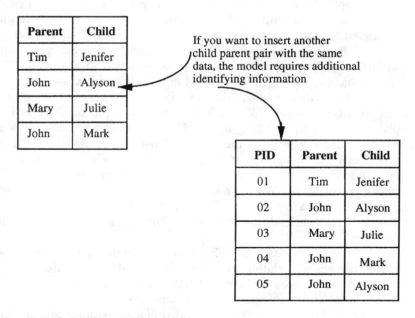

Figure 9.5   Relation model identifiers

ble (unchangeable) form of data structure. This property implies that there is no operation that can alter the correspondence between an object and its identifier. By using the identifier feature of objects, it becomes possible to distinguish between two objects—for example, by using object identity we could determine whether two objects were equal (have the same values for their attributes) or are identical (are the same object). In a conventional database model such as the relational model, having two tuples in the relation with the same values would be impossible, even if they were representing different real-world entities. To fix such a problem in the relational model we are required to add a key field, which is unique for all unique entries (Figure 9.5). To include two tuples with the same value we would be required to insert two unique identifiers for these tuples, typically represented by unique keys in the relational system. On the other hand, with the object model and with object identifiers, when each person instance (a tuple of the relation in Figure 9.5) is created, each is assigned a unique unchangeable identifier, which cannot be changed. When the second repeated *values* JOHN and ALYSON are repeated, they are created (instantiated) as a new object with its own unique identifier. To determine if the two are the same, we can simply compare their object identifiers. If they have the same identifier, they are the same object; if not, they are unique.

This concept of object identifier can be used to provide even further refinement of storage and access efficiency. In the previous example, if we wished to add Mark's mother, Joan, to the relational structure shown in Figure 9.5, we would still be required to have an additional redundant record attribute for Mark. This is shown in Figure 9.6. By using the object model with its concept of identity and inheritance, we can simply instantiate both Mary and John—with each having a pointer to the instance of Mark. Mark does not need to be repeated, simply referenced by the two objects Mary and John using functions defining children to detect and locate Mark. Likewise, it would be relatively easy to determine if Mark is the same child in the object model, since the object identifiers would need to be identical for the objects to be the same. This is not the case with the relational model. Without added linking relationship records, it could not be readily determined if Mark, the son of Mary, is the same person who is the son of John.

A problem exists with the inheritance concept within the object model. If we wish to delete an object in the object-oriented model, there may be references to the object that will be left dangling; that is, they will point to a nonexisting object and must be somehow taken care of. The problem comes from the nature of inheritance and the use of this hierarchical construction and access feature in constructing

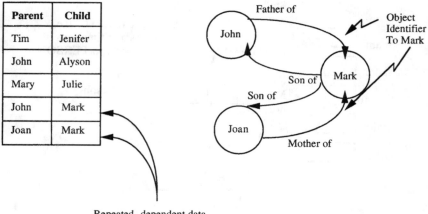

Parent	Child
Tim	Jenifer
John	Alyson
Mary	Julie
John	Mark
Joan	Mark

Repeated, dependent data

Figure 9.6   Object identity

and using objects. Through inheritance, we use object types or instances defined or instantiated in the further definition or use of subtypes. This dynamic referencing results in a database architecture that cannot predetermine all links and therefore make deletion straightforward. Instead, in the object model we must use concepts to collect objects that are awaiting deletion into a region of storage, where objects can be maintained until no references remain on the objects. At that point, when no references remain on an object, the object's space can be reclaimed and reused. This technique, used in numerous object-oriented programming languages, is similar to operating system garbage collection techniques used for memory management.

9.2.5 Inheritance

We have already introduced the concept of inheritance in our discussion of object identity and type specifications. Inheritance is a feature of object-oriented models and systems that allows for the reuse of basic and constructed types to be used in the further definition of more complex data types—for example, if we define a type person composed of attributes for name, address, and Social Security number, with functions to construct an instance of the type and to access the instance variables name, address, and Social Security number.

This definition (Figure 9.7) could then be used to specify a type for a special class or refined class of person such as an employee or a student. It would be desirable for the employee or student subtype to

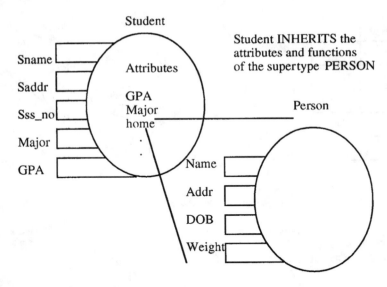

Figure 9.7   Object inheritance

inherit the properties (attributes) and operations from the person supertype to avoid the need to repeat the properties and their associated
operations in each of the subtypes. The new types, student and employee, would each have their own added attributes and operations,
but both would also have all or a subpart of the person type and its
operations available—for example, a student instance could use an
inherited person instance to derive the address and name of the student as well as the student's Social Security number. This allows the
student subtype or the employee subtype to use the attributes and
operations defined within the person type without needing to rewrite
the methods or the type definition for the person type within the subtypes. This form of construction allows for a concise definition of new
attributes and methods within an object without the added complexity
of any inherited information cluttering up the definition or being repeated as part of the basic definition.

In a system that does not support inheritance, such as a relational
system, the attributes for person would need to be linked into the
relations for employee and student. This could be accomplished by
having a reference relation that has a tuple for each student in the
student relation that has a reference to one person in the person relation. To extract the names and addresses of students, we would need
to join the student relation with the person relation, and then output
the names and addresses from the resultant joined table. This process
could become very expensive if the class types are complex and have

detailed method implementations. Each method would require a mapped application program on the relational side to perform the operation provided by the methods embedded within an object's structure.

Inheritance can be extremely powerful if used correctly—for example, within an object-oriented database system each object could inherit the type *persistent object,* which would provide features for persistent storage of an object and its maintenance in the database. Likewise, objects could inherit transaction features, concurrency control features, security features, constraints, triggers, and many other extended capabilities through the inheritance concept without repeating or reproducing code and data. Global features inherited by all objects that are to be part of the database facilitate the construction and cooperative operations of an object-oriented database system. It will be seen later in this text how some object-oriented databases have used this facility to define basic database management properties as global object classes.

9.2.6 Overloading and Late Binding

Inheritance supports the concept of reusing the same definitions and operations of a supertype within the body of a related subtype, as was shown in the previous example of person and student types. This does not, however, give us the ability to use the same name or operation for different types—for example, we cannot use gps from student to determine gpa for a different grading system. A unique aspect of object-oriented languages is the ability to overload method names by providing separate implementations of a given name for each type specified and a path to the various implementations. Overloading of function names is also referred to as polymorphism. As an example, we could define a basic type such as an arithmetic object, which is used to perform basic addition and subtraction functions. What would make this different, would be if we also wished to use the same object operation name for a variety of additions and subtractions of different data types. This would require that the object be defined with a variety of implementations for the add and subtract operations—one for each type to be operated on. The implementations redefine the operation of the add or subtract for the various types passed into the method. In this example, if we wish to have the ability to add integers, reals, binary, complex, or characters, we would need five separate implementations of the add operation and five separate implementations of the subtract operation. Each implementation is for use by one of the named type parameters, using the same name to perform the named operation, providing different input parameter types. This redefinition of the

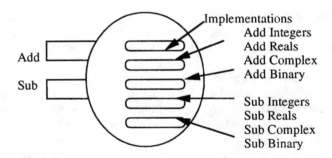

Figure 9.8   Object overloading and late binding

name for an operation based on the input parameter type is referred to as overloading. The overloaded name must be bound to the appropriate implementation at run time. This run-time binding of operation to implementation is called late binding (Figure 9.8).

Late binding requires that the run-time system has the ability to rectify the difference between input parameter types to a named operation at run time and can find an appropriate implementation to support execution. The concept of *dispatching* is used to rectify a name to an implementation. The typical means to implement dispatching is to form the various implementations into a type lattice (Figure 9.9), where the types of the expected parameters to the implementations are used as the means to select which implementation to use. The dispatcher traverses the structure to find a match between the type parameters provided in the method call and the types in the lattice. The search continues down the type lattice to the lowest-level

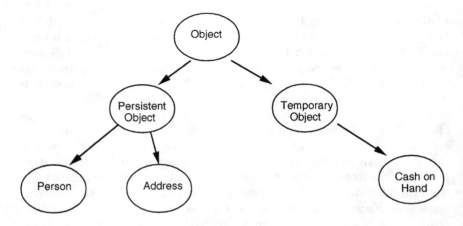

Figure 9.9   Object type lattice

subtype matching the requester's types. A variety of data organizations can be used to make the search more efficient. The search space can be formed into a tree, with the leaves as the outer subtypes and the root as the base supertype, or it could be organized as a directed acyclic graph or hash buckets. By organizing into such data structures, the search space can be further reduced and perhaps more optimally organized at compile time.

9.3 OBJECT-ORIENTED DATABASE MODEL

The object-oriented database systems extend basic features of object-oriented programming languages. The most significant change from object-oriented programming languages is the property of persistence. Persistence in an object-oriented database must be explicitly defined and is an extension from the basic programming language supporting object orientation. It is not as simple as just indicating that an object is persistent or not. An object can have a lifetime of persistence that is bounded by an event or through various definitions. Persistence of an object can first be defined at different times in an object's life and possibly can be redefined at a later time. An object can become persistent at object creation through explicit definition—for example, create persistent people or create temporary people would create one type class as persistent and one as temporary. Objects can become persistent when they encounter another persistent database structure such as a root data type—for example, a root data type persistent object can be used to define all other subtypes as persistent. By using this scheme, an object could become persistent at any time by becoming connected to a subtype of the root object through assignment. Alternatively, an object can become persistent when it is assigned to specific persistent storage classes. As long as objects stay assigned to the persistent storage class, they are persistent. Objects can be coerced into persistence by an envoker requesting the object to be persistent, or an object can be designated as persistent when instantiated from a persistent type. If an object is not persistent, then it must be temporary or transitory and follow the rules of the object-oriented programming language through which it is supported.

9.3.1 Database Fundamentals

Many researchers and authors have indicated some fundamental features of object-oriented databases that must be present if the model is to be complete and provide the functionality expected from commercial databases. First, the object's state variables must be encapsulated and protected from direct access. Second, objects in the database should be persistently defined by a root type and therefore reachable through this root type. Third, object instances should know about their type, possibly through a basic inherited feature of database objects that provides a method to return object type if queried. Fourth, polymorphism of object operations must be a supported feature and will require dynamic binding of types for implementation. Fifth, collection types to group objects are fundamental to database structuring and for support of queries. Sixth, relationships between objects should be supported as fundamental components of database structure. Finally, the object model should support query facilities and versioning. In the following sections we will review a few of these features and illustrate them with examples.

9.3.2 Object Representation

Each definition of an object defines a logical *representation* used to store and manage the state of its instances. This representation consists of a data structure that is only available to the methods that operate on the data on behalf of the applications. The data structure consists of attributes (Figure 9.10), which may be valued attributes or

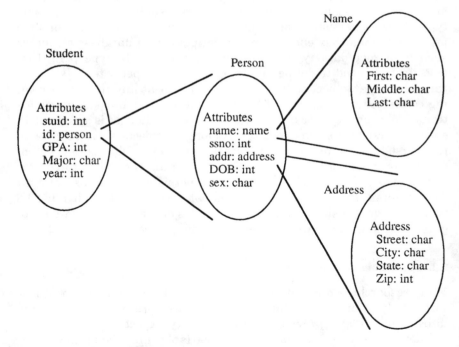

Figure 9.10 Object representation

references to other objects (inherited types). These inherited types are distinct identifiable objects, which have their own attributes and identity and may even be referenced from other objects. For example, in Figure 9.10 the object student has a simple data structure represented as a set of attibutes, stuid, ID, gpa, major, and year. The attributes are represented by four valued types and one reference to another separate object, person. Similarly, the person object is defined as a data structure with its own valued attributes: ssnumber, date of birth (dob), and sex. Person also uses references to further object instances to complete its structure, referring to object type name and address.

These referenced objects complete the description of the object, but are not physically part of the object. Attribute values are bound to a specific object's structures and representations, whereas objects are not bound totally to an object's attributes. An object can be referenced and connected to any object, based on access and context, whereas the values are bound to individual objects and are private to the bound object. Representations for objects in a database are further supported by collection types, such as sets, bags, tuples, arrays, lists, and multisets. These type constructors provide the means to group objects of the same, related, or similar type into extended structures that can be readily queried and/or optimized for storage—for example, to create an object that resembles the structure of a relation we could create a type row, which is an object consisting of a linear list of data items where each field of the row is unique. With the row we can further define a subtype as a multiset of rows (Figure 9.11). This multiset of row objects could be further refined to have methods for relational manipulation of the multiset of rows. This would allow the abstract

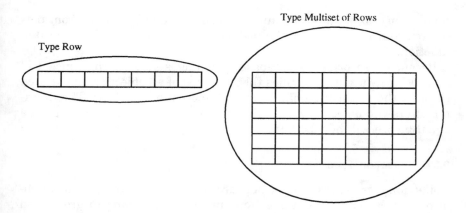

Figure 9.11   Multiset of row objects

data type multiset of rows to be manipulated as if it were a relation in a relational database.

9.3.3 Type Hierarchy

As was presented earlier, the property of objects for type inheritance is a powerful concept, which allows objects to be constructed from other objects. Type inheritance also provides for code reuse, since, through inheritance, the code generated for a type's method implementation is available for use by any subtype that uses this type for a portion of its definition and operation. Through type hierarchies and the properties inherited, subtypes can specify their own operations, using inherited type operations as components of their own operations. This property is referred to as substitutability, which indicates that when a type T is a subtype of another type t, then operations or values of t are substituted for those in T's references—for example, for the student type described above, if student is declared as type person, then functions on person, such as name, are also available by objects of type student, as shown in the following code frgaments.

```
student is a subtype of person
```

and

```
define name(nm : person)
```

and

```
declare sp : student
```

then name(sp) is allowable and will use the function name from person to acquire the name of the instance of student using this inherited function.

Recent object-oriented database lanaguages support the concept of *mutability*. Mutability implies that the type of an object can be altered through the application of a mutator function on the type. The mutator alters the object's type so that two instances of a type that were equal before will now be different.

9.3.4 Collection Type

Collections, as referred to earlier, are an important component of object-oriented databases. Collections provide the means to group and organize objects that possess some form of relationship between them.

The grouping of related objects implies that these collected objects are now some new type and must have their own set of properties and operations. Collections are themselves objects and can have their own properties and operations defined on the objects they group—for example, we could have a type set and apply this to a group of student instances or supplier instances. What this implies is that we now have two distinct collections, a set of students and a set of suppliers, which each have their own embedded operations and share some common operations inherited by the supertype set. Objects that are grouped in collections must match the allowable types supported by the operations defined on the group. This implies that we could not have objects of different types in the same collection, if these objects must coordinate actions based on the type of the collection and its supported operations.

The generic supertype collection supports the properties of cardinality, empty, and ordered, and allows duplicates. Cardinality indicates the number of objects in the collection, empty indicates that the collection has no objects in it, ordered indicates whether the collection is structured or unstructured, and allows duplicates indicates that the collection can hold duplicate objects. The abstract type collection supports operations on all collection types constructed from it to create, delete, or insert an object in a collection; remove an object or replace an object in a collection; retrieve an object from a collection; select an element from a collection given some selection predicate; determine if an element from an object exists or if a particular object contains a particular element; and create an iterative pointer to allow spanning an entire collection.

With the basic abstract collection type specification more specific collections can be created. Supported by numerous object-oriented databases are the collection types set, bag, list, and array. The set is an unordered collection that does not allow duplicates (Figure 9.12). A set can use all the collection operations described previously, and can exhibit the properties of the collection type. In addition, the set supports the creation of the set of a specific type and the insertion of elements into the set (without allowing duplicates). Set operations include Union, Intersect, Difference, Copy, Subset determination, Proper Subset determination, Superset determination, and Proper Superset determination. By using these operations we could, for example, take two sets of employees and perform the union on them to get a new set that has all the elements from both of the sets with no duplicates.

The bag is an unordered collection type, which is allowed to have duplicates (Figure 9.13). The bag supports the union, intersection, and difference operators on compatible sets. We could form a collection of all the children of the faculty with the bag abstract data type. This

SET {  }

Figure 9.12 Set collection type

collection could have duplicates if two faculty members are married. Their children could be repeated within the bag, but this may be a desired effect by the creator of this collection.

The list collection type is an ordered group of objects that allows duplicates (Figure 9.14). The ordering of the objects within the list is determined by the order of insertions into the collection, not by any particular index or sorting. Orderings of any type or form can be constructed by the programmer through the use of operations that allow for the insertion, removal, and replacement of objects in the list using a location in the list as the means of determining where the operation will be applied—for example, in the list shown in Figure 9.14, if a new object is to be inserted in the list after Ben, but before John, using the available operations we could specify

```
insert_element_after(child, 2)
```

Likewise, we could use modifiers to insert a new object before a location or to replace an element at a location in the list, where location is a relative position, such as a count (first, last, second, etc.).

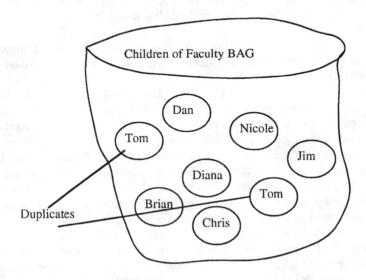

Figure 9.13 Bag collection type

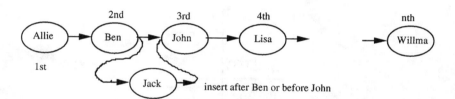

Figure 9.14 List collection type

The last collection type typically found in object-oriented database models and systems is the array collection type (Figure 9.15). Arrays are a collection type of one dimension with a varying length. Array size can be initialized or changed as the array is populated or accessed. The array collection type allows objects to be organized and accessed as if they were placed in an indexed list. Operations exist to insert, remove, replace, or retrieve objects at a given location in the array collection. Such operations and data structure allow the database system to construct structures where index values are reserved for specific object instances or, if populated, can be used as indexes into the collection of objects. An array object collection can be scanned in order one at a time using the position index as the access pointer.

9.3.5 Object Relationships

A data relationship is an identifiable, named correspondence between objects and/or their attributes or operations. Relationships among data items in a database are recognized as an important component in object-oriented design, although few object-oriented database systems directly support information relationships—such support is left to the individual object implementations. By leaving the specification, design, and implementation of relationships to individual object implementers, flexibility and regularity of support is lost, as is the possible benefit of encapsulation and inheritance, since the implementation of relationships is specialized for each object instance. Relationships in other database models are one of the most fundamental components of their data models.

Relationships in the object model can be represented as separate objects that name the involved object instances, any specific attributes private to the relationship, and constraints on internal attributes and objects involved in the relationship (Figure 9.16). A relationship is described through two parts: The subject of the relationship is the relationship object itself, pointed to by the tail of the directed arrow,

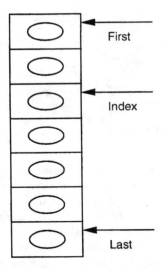

Figure 9.15 **Array collection type**

and the members of the relationship are the objects at the head of the arrow, as shown in Figure 9.16.

In this example, the student object is related to the faculty object through the relationship advisers. The relationship is a one-to-many

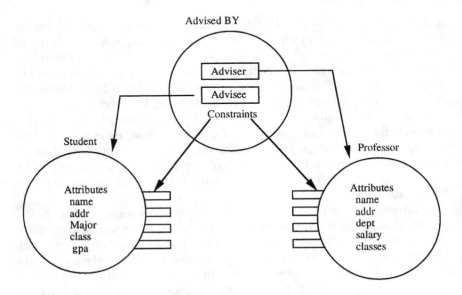

Figure 9.16 **Object relationship**

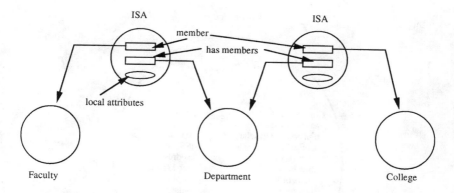

Figure 9.17   ISA relationship

relationship, where one faculty member could have multiple advisees. The relationship has no local attributes, but has a constraint of the classes taken by the student and the classes taught by the adviser. The example shows a simple relationship, although many relationships will have attributes of their own and constraints on these and their related objects.

The simplest relationship is the one-to-one relationship between two object instances—for example, the simple ISA relationship described in Chapter 8 is such a relationship. An example is that a faculty member is a member of a department and only one department, and the department is an element of a college (Figure 9.17). In this example the faculty object is related to the department object through the ISA relationship. The faculty object is a member of the department through the ISA relationship and the object pointers to the involved instances. Likewise, the department is a member of the college, and the college has a member department. In addition to the simple relationship, the ISA object could have its own attributes and values for them—for example, the ISA relationship object could have local private attributes for the number of faculty in the department or the budget for the faculty in the department (Figure 9.17).

Relationships can be one way, symmetric, or multivalued. A single-valued relationship or one-way relationship involves two objects, where one object points to the other, but there is not a relationship in the other direction—for example, in Figure 9.18 the agent is in the office, but the office is not in the agent. We can determine the office from the agent, but not the other way around. To get the reverse relationship, indicating which agents are in which offices, we would need an inverse relation on the office—for example a relation that indicates the office *has agents*. By including an inverse relationship, we can

Employee

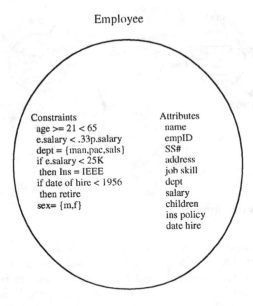

Constraints	Attributes
age >= 21 < 65	name
e.salary < .33p.salary	empID
dept = {man,pac,sals}	SS#
if e.salary < 25K	address
then Ins = IEEE	job skill
if date of hire < 1956	dept
then retire	salary
sex= {m,f}	children
	ins policy
	date hire

Figure 9.18   Single-valued relationship

have the effect on one object in the relationship cause a corresponding effect on the other member of the relationship—for example, if the office is changed for the agent, then this fact would be reflected in the relationship and would cause the agent to now show up in a different office object.

Relationships can be symmetrical, implying that they naturally have a corresponding bidirectional relationship — for example, spouse_of can be applied to either side of a relationship and would return the other. In some object-oriented systems bidirectional relationships are the true relationships, and all others are referred to as properties.

Multivalued relationships are the more common relationships in the data modeling world—for example, a course has multiple students; a faculty member advises multiple students. Multivalued relationships are relationships where a collection of object instances all have the same relationship to one another—possibly a singular object instance. In general relationships can have combinations of these categories and typically do.

If relationships are considered as objects themselves, then they should be able to possess all of the attributes and properties inherent to an object—for example, a relationship should be able to possess attributes and values; it should be able to have operations defined on these attributes with constraints on their values and operations. Relationships, however, are not your ordinary objects. A relationship cannot exist without the object or objects it combines through the named relationship. This implies that a relationship cannot be instantiated apart from the objects it is attached to—for example, we cannot have the advisers relationship without the student and the faculty that the relationship names and provides the linkage to. The subject and the members of the relationship must exist. They represent a unique identity for the relationship, like a key to the relationship. In a sense they represent the same meaning as a key, since you could only have one instance of a named relationship and connected object.

Relationships can be implemented in a variety of ways: We could maintain the relationships as a set or as an extent table, where an extent table represents a list of pointers to objects collected into a similar type structure. We could, for example, have an extent table that maintains a list of all instances of the student abstract data type. This table would keep references to all instances of the student objects, making it easier to access and manipulate these objects. We could use this structure to keep the references to the related objects and the data associated with them. The intent of these implementations and the relationships themselves is to enable the navigation of a relationship from one end to another. As an example, you could search a family tree of relationships by initiating a traversal of a relationship on persons that includes a relationship called parent of. By beginning with you, you could successively search for parent of; when you get an answer, you could again search the relationship parent of to find the parents of the parents and so on until the tree comes to an end at the last known link of the relationship chain.

9.3.6 Object Constraints

Constraints are used to aid in the maintenance of database integrity, correctness, and validity. Constraints provide for additional correctness checking of a database's contents beyond the conventional programming language concept of type correctness. These database correctness conditions are predicates written on the correctness of the state of values and the relationship of these database items' values against each other. Constraints can be complex and can be arbitrary-application specific; that is, a constraint can be specific to the support of an application's correctness, as well as for the database's correctness. These constraints are written against class definitions, where all elements of the class must meet the specified conditions to be considered correct.

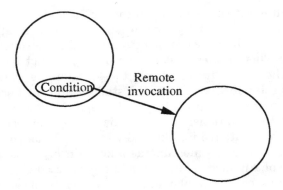

Figure 9.19   Object constraints

Typical constraints are written to check that the type of a data item matches the type of the data item's specification, or that the data item is within some indicated range of values (Figure 9.18). Constraints can be specific to a type—for example, the department attribute of Figure 9.18 can only take on the values manufacturing, personnel, or sales. The same form of restricted set constraint holds for the attribute sex, which only can take on either male or female.

Some constraints can be more complex: Instead of being defined to maintain a domain of correct possible values for a data item, they may be set up to restrict the value in one object based on a reference value from another object. These are referred to as referential constraints. In Figure 9.18, the constraints that set the salary maximum of an employee at one-third the salary of the supervisor is such a referential constraint, since the value for the supervisor must be retrieved from the instance object for the supervisor and then used as the value to determine the validity of the constraint.

Constraints can be written to restrict the values or boundaries on a collection of objects—for example, for the employee object in Figure 9.18, we may wish to maintain an upper boundary on the sum of the salary for all employees. This constraint could not be written easily into the object in Figure 9.18; it would necessitate the existence of an upper-level object (a relationship possibly) that has access to all of the composite objects of the collection (Figure 9.19). Another alternative is to have a handler object, which is bound to all instances of the employee object and catches and checks all updates to the salary attribute before they are allowed to be executed by the object instance's methods. This form of constraint consists of the constraint predicate and a constraint action part, sometimes referred to as a handler. The action is performed if the constraint is true, similar to an IF statement in modern programming languages.

A problem with constraints in object-oriented systems is when to check the constraints. It may be necessary to indicate explicitly when a constraint is to be checked so that it is not checked in-between the coordinated alteration of constrained objects—for example, if the employees in the employee object have a constraint on the sum of the values of the salaries, it would not be desirable to check this constraint on the update of each object, especially if all the salaries are being modified, as it is the value of the sum *after* all of the employee salaries have been adjusted. This would be the case when a cost of living adjustment is being applied to all employees, thus increasing the ceiling value for the sum by the same percentage.

In some object-oriented database systems constraints are explicitly defined as a component of the objects, while in others they are defined as stand-alone objects that refer to other objects when performing their operations (constraint checking)—for example, stand-alone constraints can be defined using a keyword, Constraint:, followed by a constraint specification (definition of the predicate to be checked) and a handler to correct the constraint violation if one is detected during the predicate's evaluation. Constraints defined in this way would require the calling of operations from named objects to acquire the values to be used in the predicate's checking. Likewise, there would have to be operations on the involved objects to correct the effect of a found constraint violation. As an example, in our employee object, a constraint specification would require an operation on employee salary to read the salary value, and another operation to set the salary value by a handler if a violation is detected.

Other constraints are directly embedded in an object's specification. As part of a class definition, the values of an attribute or a relationship between multiple attributes of an object can be checked directly as part of an operation's specification or as a stand-alone operation unto itself. In our employee object, we could have the constraint on the value of the sex of an employee checked using the constraint

```
Class Employee {

    Name string(20);

    ...


Constraint:
    sex == 'male' || sex == 'female';

    ...


};
```

The constraint can be checked whenever the attribute is accessed, only when it is updated, or based on some specified event. Constraints can be a powerful tool in the maintenance and operation of a database if they are correctly specified. Constraints can be active, such as triggers in database systems, or they can be passive. Active constraints can check their bound objects when events, time, or some other condition is satisfied, whereas passive constraints are only checked when they are encountered in an operation. Passive constraints must be embedded in an object's operations code, whereas active constraints need not be, although they would still operate even if they were embedded in an object's operations code.

9.3.7 Query Processing

Relational and network database models have specific data manipulation operations available to them. Any extended functionality within the relational or network database manipulation language must come from user-appended application code, which extracts database information from the database and performs the intended extension service. This limitation results from the structure and fundamental design of these languages, as well as their underlying theoretical data storage and manipulation models.

The object-oriented database management system's languages, on the other hand, support an unbounded range of possible data manipulation primitives, which are defined based on how data are to be used and represented within the system and to applications. In addition, these methods can be changed in the future through object modifications and recompilations and would then become the basic operations in the database management system. This is not the case in the relational or network models, where the fundamental operations cannot be changed or altered.

Query processing in the object-oriented database model requires some additional structuring within the database to increase the efficiency of query processing. In object-oriented databases, data are accessed by acquiring object identifiers (pointers) and using these pointers to move through the database. Without the means to cluster objects, object-oriented databases can drop back in time to emulate *navigation* as the means for answering queries, as in the network database systems. By supporting the clustering or grouping of objects into collections, sets, bags, lists, and arrays, the object model has allowed for the construction of high-powered query processing operations similar to those found in the relational model. Without these structures the object-oriented database model is no better than a

pointer-chasing method and may need to traverse numerous unrelated objects to find those objects of interest.

With these structures it would then become quite easy to write queries of the form

```
Select (Object2 : SET(T), FROM Object1: SET(T) WHERE P:
Predicate);
```

Such an operation would iterate over the set of objects in Object1's
set, and those that meet the conditions set in the predicate P would be
placed in the second set, Object2. It may not be as simple as it seems,
since writing a predicate for such a query can itself be complex. With
object properties such as inheritance and polymorphism it may be extremely difficult to write code that would be optimimal for these structures. On the other hand, if the structures are specified such that
ordering or grouping based on object state values may be possible,
then more optimal query processing and even query optimization is
possible.

The object query language (OQL) of the object data management
group (ODMG) is formatted after that of the SQL relational query
language. The object data manipulation begins with SQL structure
and adds components to this object to increase the flexibility of the
possible manipulations—for example, if we wished to query the cluster of person objects defined earlier to find all persons who have the
name Ollie, we could generate the following code.

```
Select distinct struct (p.name, p.address
    from p in employee
    where p.name = "Ollie")
```

This query builds a new unnamed structure, which contains all the
employees with the name Ollie and their addresses. The object model,
however, delivers additional capabilities not found in the relational
data model. By using some of the basic features of the object model,
we can construct unnamed structures, such as a set of names and
phone numbers, by using the struct operator in the set structure.

```
set(
    struct(name: "Abagail", phone: 555-999-5511),
    struct(name: "Gail", phone: 617-668-1234),
    struct(name: "Kathy", phone: 508-999-8541)
)
```

This set could then be used in an application or as an element of a database item by making the set persistent. The set can then be queried to find elements (object instances) within the set. The same data object could be formed into a list by applying the list structure as

```
list(
    struct(name: "Abagail", phone: 555-999-5511),
    struct(name: "Gail", phone: 617-668-1234),
    struct(name: "Kathy", phone: 508-999-8541)
)
```

or as a bag by

```
bag(
    struct(name: "Abagail", phone: 555-999-5511),
    struct(name: "Gail", phone: 617-668-1234),
    struct(name: "Kathy", phone: 508-999-8541)
)
```

or as an array

```
array(
    struct(name: "Abagail", phone: 555-999-5511),
    struct(name: "Gail", phone: 617-668-1234),
    struct(name: "Kathy", phone: 508-999-8541)
)
```

Each of these structures has built-in functions, as was discussed earlier in this chapter—for example, we could ask the question, Is Kathy a member of the list?, by simply using the exists operator with the set of names and numbers

```
exists p in Kathy.name : person.name = "Kathy"
```

we could also simply test for membership in the structure by asking

```
Kathy in SET<T>
```

Other operations exist to determine how many objects are in a collection and if the collection is ordered and what the order is, as well as operations to perform simple manipulations and comparisons on the contents of the structures. Such an operator is the Max operator, which returns the maximum valued object based on the qualifier (predicate) provided. The OQL language calls for support of the tradi-

tional SELECT ... FROM ... WHERE structure—for example, given
the objects student and professor and the relationship takes and inverse taught by, to find all the students who take a course with Professor Einstein we could write

```
groups : bag

Select   groups(student: S.name)
From S in Students
    T in S.takes
    P in T.taught_by
Where P.name = "Einstein"
```

The result of this query will be a bag of name groups, which will
contain all the names of students who took a course taught by Professor Einstein.

The object model supports the concept of sorted collections to aid in
query processing. The sort operator takes a collection of objects and
sorts them in lexicographic order based on the given expression—for
example, to sort the list of students we recovered from the previous
example we could simply write

```
Sort S in Students by S.name
```

This sorts the bag of students on their name and returns the result in
a bag.

Operations to group objects from a collection or from a free search
into collections based on predicates is provided—for example, if the
collection of professors had attributes on classification as an associate,
assistant, and full professor, we could group them all into their respective classifications by

```
Group P in Professors

By ( entry: P.classify ="assistant",
    middle: P.classify = "associate",
    terminal: P.classify = "full")
```

This gives a set of three elements; each of these elements has a
property called a partition, which contains the set of professors that
enters that category. The type of the result is a set structure with the
headings entry, middle, and terminal—all of type Boolean and a partition of type set of professors.

These collections can be indexed to allow for indexed access. This operation will operate on the list or array structures to return the value of the object in a list or array based on the given index value—for example, given the list of student names as

```
list( Andrew, Bob, John, Thomas, Victor)
```

and if the third item in the list were wanted, we would simply append [2] to the end of the specified list. This would return the name John.

```
list( Andrew, Bob, John, Thomas, Victor) [2].
```

The reason this returns John is that the list is numbered from zero on up so the third item would be 0, 1, 2, or the item with the index 2. To extract a sublist simply list the elements wanted—for example, to get Bob and John would require

```
list( Andrew, Bob, John, Thomas, Victor) [1:2],
```

which returns the items indexed from 1 to 2. If a greater range were wanted, a larger index list is inserted. Operators exist to retrieve the first or last element from a list, allowing, for example, for the easy extraction of boundary conditions.

Relational query capabilities can be performed on collections through the application of the binary set expressions—for example, the except operation returns the objects from a collection that are not named in the except condition. Professors except full, returns all the professors who are not full professors. The union operation takes two collections and creates a new collection, which includes all the objects from both the collections. The intersect operator takes two collections of objects and returns the objects that are in both the collections.

Many of the existing object-oriented languages offer other facilities to iterate over collections—for example, the regular iteration operators, such as the for loop and the while loops, are retrofitted with extended functionality to allow for their application to queries over collections of objects. The for loop, for example, could be applied as

```
For I in collection type [suchthat-clause] [by-clause]
statement
```

In this form the body of the loop, the statement, is executed once for each element of the specified collection; the loop variable, I, is assigned the object values in turn. As an example, if we apply the for loop construct to the searching of the professors' object to see what the names of the children of faculty members with full professorships are, we could generate the following

```
For P in professor
    For C in P->children such that (P->classify == "full")
        struct(p->name, C->name)
```

This results in a structure where the professors' names and their children form an object in the structure.

Query processing in the object-oriented database model is in its earliest stages, but it is expected that great improvement in performance will be forthcoming.

9.3.8 Versions

Versions are typically thought of in the context of configuration management. A typical application is in the management of multiple versions of a program, or the historical maintenance of some data that change over time, but whose past state is just as important as the present state. Object-oriented databases have evolved with this as a primary concern in their support. Object-oriented systems began to support design applications where versions of a design are imperative. Versions are a means to record the history of an object. Versions can be organized in an object model as a collection of objects, where each of the objects can have almost all of the same values as the other objects, differing only in the time the values were recorded—for example, we could have a history of temperatures from a sensor. Each reading for some period of time may be the same value—the only difference would be in the value of the time at which the version of the temperature was taken.

```
time 1: value 100
time 2: value 100
time 3: value 100
time 4: value 100
time 5: value 100
time 6: value 100
    .
    .
    .
time n: value 100
```

In the example, the only difference is in the time tag on the data object; all other parameters and instance variables are the same. The object model, however, must treat these as separate distinct objects, related by a relationship indicating that they are a history of the named object.

A versioning system must support the ability to query the collection based on position or the values of the given temporal component. In addition, a versioning support element must possess the ability to configure a collection of collections to group items that may have relationships between them into a larger version. An example of this feature is a programming environment where there are multiple modules for a program, and each of the modules has a separate version of the designs. It may be desirable to collect the most recent of all these composite collections into a single collection, which would represent the state of the entire program at this point in time.

9.3.9 Active Objects

Conventional database systems are passive, implying that data do not react to conditions surrounding the database or to values within the database. Data and the database's state can only be altered, viewed, and manipulated by data manipulation primitives executed within the context of a data manipulation language. Databases are being required to become a more integral and proactive component of an application's environment.

To turn a passive database into an active database requires two elements: an active constraint checking and a triggering facility. The constraint facility must have the ability to actively check the predicates assigned to it, based on timing boundaries or event conditions. When a constraint is violated, the trigger facility is used to handle the condition encountered, based on some predefined actions.

In conventional database systems, the database must check object states and initiate actions if the appropriate conditions are met. Constraint primitives that check the database state automatically as a basic part of the database's specification and definition must exist. By defining the database to take care of its own corrective actions, this burden can be removed from the applications, thus relieving the applications' designers from performing database maintenance operations. Triggers are a central and essential component of an active database. Triggers can be aperiodic or periodic, and can be based on time intervals, time boundaries, or events. Triggers consist of condition predicates and triggered actions. The difference between triggers and

Transaction

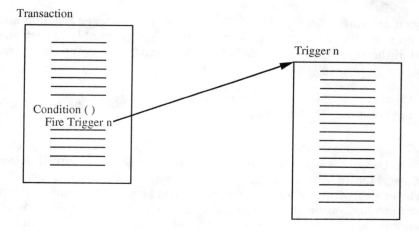

Figure 9.20   Example trigger action

constraints is that constraints must maintain database integrity before a commit, whereas triggers need not. A trigger actively checks the constraint it has been defined to control and maintain; a constraint does not actively check conditions. The trigger condition that results in the firing of the trigger action is treated as a separate transaction's remote call, and the triggered action is treated as a separate transaction (Figure 9.20). If a trigger, for example, is defined on the value of a temperature data item's value, the temperature, after rising to a level that triggers a handler, could fall below the trigger condition's threshold temperature before the response handler can complete. This implies that a trigger, even when invoked by an appropriate condition state, must still check the condition again before continuing the handler process to guarantee the correct action is taken.

Triggers and their conditions typically are associated with real-time data and events—for example, if the temperature sensor must synchronize its read with a pressure sensor, the condition predicate must access both sensor readings from the database within some small time frame, and with the same relative time of data creation or update, for the information to be used reliably, correctly, and with confidence.

Triggers are typically designed to be one shot or perpetual (aperiodic or periodic). Aperiodic or one-shot triggers, once activated, are fired when conditions are satisfied and once completed are deactivated. A one-shot trigger, once deactivated, must be explicitly reactivated if the designed condition is to be examined and fired on once again. Conversely, a perpetual or periodic trigger is a trigger that, when activated (fired), will perform the designed trigger function and then reset itself (i.e., it resets to a state where it is able to test and catch the same constraints as before). The general trigger mechanism is

```
time expression, trigger_condition => trigger_action,
time expression.
```

Triggers are associated with objects and are activated explicitly when the object is created (instantiated). A trigger is a named object, whose identified function is activated by the call. Once activated a trigger's constraint checkers become active, based on the mode of constraint checking in place (e.g., passive checks performed on updates, commits, or an active constraint checker that uses a timer mechanism). Once a trigger is activated, it can only be removed by either being fired and suspended through its own actions, or by being explicitly removed using something similar to

```
deactivate (trigger_ID)
```

The trigger, once deactivated, remains idle until reactivated through an explicit action. Triggers can be removed from the system through deletion of the object instance that represents the trigger.

Triggers can be used for a variety of purposes—for example, to signal to a client or server database when a specific condition has been met, to test database states to detect threshold conditions, and to simply issue transactions on fixed temporal boundaries. Triggers, as well as their timing constraints, can be written across object boundaries to link object activities based on interobject referential or relationship information. Triggers are a powerful mechanism in the construction of active databases and in the further evolution of object-oriented databases into a larger variety of application domains.

9.3.10 Transactions in Object-Oriented Databases

Transactions are the mechanism within database management systems that provide enforcement of the ACID properties. In an object-oriented database system, transactions are used for enforcing these transaction properties and extending them in a more flexible way. Object-oriented databases were developed to support nontraditional applications, such as computer-aided design and control-oriented environments, where transactions can be long lived and require syn-

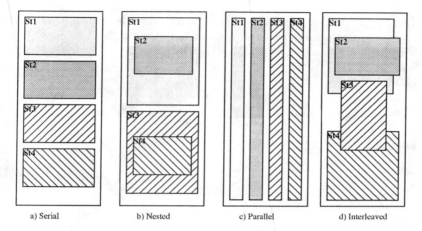

a) Serial   b) Nested   c) Parallel   d) Interleaved

Figure 9.21   Extended transaction model examples

chronous operation and cooperative executions. Just as in the conventional transaction model, the object-oriented transaction model supports primitives to begin transactions, prepare transactions for commitment, commit transactions, and abort transactions. In addition, to provide for more flexible and semantic use of transactions, numerous object-oriented databases and prototypes support enhanced transaction facilities, such as partitioned commit, partitioned recovery, semantic concurrency control, and other features aimed at loosening the rigidity of the ACID properties that control transaction correctness and consistency.

A variety of extended transaction models have been proposed. These models attempt to provide extended transaction functionality by restructuring the execution model and correctness criteria for transactions—for example, nested transactions, serial transactions, parallel transactions, and interleaved transactions (Figure 9.21). Each of these models attempts to extend the concept of transaction to encapsulate other transactions in more flexible ways. The concept of all these models, however, is to allow some of the components of a transaction to commit, and therefore become visible to the outside elements, before the parent transaction is committed. To construct extended transactions, additional primitives are required to bind database actions to a transaction's scope, to control and coordinate early commit and release of resources of some partition or subpart of a transaction, or to provide semantic recovery for these components to guarantee correct and consistent execution.

The basis of all transactions is the concept of bounding the execution space of composite database operations using the transaction begin and the transaction end primitives as shown.

```
BEGIN_T ( )
    ...
    database access code;
    ...
PREPARE_TO_TCOMMIT ( )
    ...
COMMIT_T ( )
    or
ABORT_T ( );
```

By using these classical transaction control primitives, the object-oriented database transaction also binds all accesses, modifications, creations, and deletions of objects and their encapsulated components into an atomic unit of execution. Accesses are kept isolated from other transaction executions and database constraints. A transaction in this model will include the begin and end delimiters, object operations and user application code, constraint operations, and commit code.

```
BEGIN_T ( )
    ...
    OP_ID (OID);
    ...
    OP_ID (OID);
    ...
PREPARE_TO_COMMIT ( )
    ...
COMMIT ( )
    or
ABORT ( );
```

The extended transaction model adds operations to begin embedded transactions, called subtransactions, to this set of transaction primitives. To construct a nested transaction model would require the embedding of subtransaction begin and end primitives within the parent transaction's boundaries.

```
BEGIN_T ( )
    ...
    OP_ID (OID)
    ...
```

```
BEGIN_SUB_T ( )
...
OP_ID (OID);
...
OP_ID (OID);
...
PREPARE_TO_COMMIT_SUB_T ( )
   ...
COMMIT_SUB_T ( )
   ...
OP_ID (OID)
   ...
PREPARE_TO_COMMIT ( )
...
COMMIT ( )
```

To coordinate the initiation of subtransactions based on synchronizing or coordinating actions with outside events or timing conditions, the model requires the addition of extended constraint specifications for pre- and postconditions on transaction or subtransaction execution. Preconditions are represented by a set of predicates that must be satisfied before the transaction or subtransaction can begin execution. Likewise, to commit a subtransaction or transaction similar predicates, called postconditions, must be satisfied if the commit is to be allowed. This constraint must be checked during the "PREPARE TO COMMIT" phase of a transaction or subtransaction. As an example, we could set a transaction $T2$ not to begin execution before a dependent transaction $T1$ had begun, by setting a precondition that checks this predicate. We could additionally make this transaction a nested transaction where the child subtransaction must be sure that it begins after $T2$ has begun and that $T0$ has also begun. This guarantees that $T3$ is a child of $T2$ and that $T3$ has the needed information from $T0$ when needed. For postconditions we set the child subtransaction to be serializable and the parent to be dependent on the comit of $T3$, $T1$, and $T0$ by specifying these conditions in the postconditions for the parent transaction $T2$.

```
BEGIN_T2 ( )
   PRE_CONDITION_T ( NOT BEFORE T1 )
   ...
   OP_ID (OID)
   ...
   BEGIN_SUB_T ( )
      ...
```

```
   PRE_CONDITION_SUB_T3 ( AFTER T2 and T0 BEGIN)
      . . .
   OP_ID (OID);
   . . .
   OP_ID (OID);
   . . .
 PREPARE_TO_COMMIT_SUB_T ( )

   POST_CONDITION_SUB_T ( SERIALIZABLE T3)
      . . .
 COMMIT_SUB_T ( )
 . . .
 OP_ID (OID)
 . . .
PREPARE_TO_COMMIT ( )
   . . .
   POST_CONDITION_T ( T3 COMMIT AND T2 AND T0 COMMIT )
   . . .
COMMIT ( )
```

Additional primitives are added to the model to allow the setting of conditions and procedures for recovery of transactions or subtransactions, for the isolation level of the transaction or subtransaction, for synchronization dependencies with other transactions, for access mode restrictions, and for commit dependencies.

```
SET TRANSACTION <transaction-name>
   [PRECONDITION <boolean-exp>]
   [POSTCONDITION <boolean-exp>]
   [[RECOVER ON <condition>]
       [AUTO | SEMI <transaction-name> | MANUAL]]
   [CRITICALITY LEVEL <criticality-level>]
   [ISOLATION LEVEL <isolation-level>]
   [ACCESS MODE <access-mode>]
   [DIAGNOSTIC SIZE <value-spec>]
```

For enhanced synchronization with external real-world events and for support of advanced user applications, time control over execution is also proposed for advanced object-oriented database management systems by many authors. For these temporal primitives, transactions are supplied with operations to initiate transactions synchronously, asynchronously, to begin execution before or after some specified time, to complete a transaction or subtransaction before or after some specified time, and to create a periodic trigger to initiate this transaction every time period specified until some completion time.

```
BEGIN TRANSACTION <transaction-name> (<input-parameters>)
    [SYNC | ASYNC]
    [START BEFORE <datetime-value-exp>]
    [START AFTER <datetime-value-exp>]
    [COMPLETE BEFORE <datetime-value-exp>]
    [COMPLETE AFTER <datetime-value-exp>]
    [PERIOD <interval-value-exp>]
        [START AT <time-exp>]
        [UNTIL <boolean-exp>]


<datetime-value-exp>
    CURRENT_DATE | CURRENT\_TIME [<time-precision>] |
    CURRENT_TIMESTAMP [<timestamp-precision>]
    EINITIATE (<tid>) | ESTART(<tid>) | ECOMPLETE (<tid>) |
    ECOMMIT (<tid>) | EABORT (<tid>)
```

When the BEGIN TRANSACTION statement is executed, the information contained in the input arguments is passed to the named transaction to start its execution. Part of this process involves checking the precondition of the transaction and, if the precondition evaluates to true, returning a transaction identifier (tid), which can be used to refer to that transaction execution. If the precondition does not evaluate to true, or the system is unable to execute the transaction, the transaction identifier returned will be NULL. The use of exceptions and other mechanisms to help the transaction writer react to such occurrences must still be examined within this transaction concept.

The first clause of the BEGIN TRANSACTION statement specifies whether the transaction is to run synchronously or asynchronously. If left unspecified, the default is synchronous. The BEGIN TRANSACTION statement also allows the specification of timing constraints on the transaction execution. In SQL2, date-time valued expressions have been defined, and can include references to date-time value functions. We have extended the available date-time value functions to include EINITIATE, ESTART, ECOMPLETE, ECOMMIT, and EABORT. EINITIATE returns the time the transaction was initiated by a user or another transaction. ESTART returns the time the transaction started execution in the system. ECOMMIT returns the time that the transaction committed. EABORT returns the time that the transaction aborted. ECOMPLETE returns the time that the transaction either committed or aborted. If the event has not yet occurred, the functions will return an infinite time value called UNDEFINED. Date-time valued expressions and interval expressions would need to be extended to accommodate this value appropriately. The SYNC or ASYNC statements are used to provide for the synchronous or asynchronous execution of the named transaction. Asynchronous transactions are executed based on an event condition derived from the period Boolean expression.

Present database languages such as SQL2 do not support the cooperative execution of transactions or their statements. Transaction synchronization can be specified through the use of the pre- and postconditions on transaction execution. Likewise, subtransactions can be synchronized with each other or other transactions using the pre- and postconditions. To synchronize at a finer level of granularity (e.g., an SQL statement or an object operation) requires an additional constraint on statements. The SYNC and ASYNC statements could also be applied to single statements along with conditions to block and wait for response, suspend execution until an external event completes, wait for a time signal, or suspend until a rendezvous message is received. The SYNC or ASYNC statements are associated with the select statements or transaction initiation statement as specified previously.

The time specified can be absolute, relative, or based on event-initiated time. The main concept to derive from this discussion is the added flexibility possible through the object-oriented database model and through the use of endemic properties of objects that can allow partitioned commit and control of objects in isolation from each other.

9.4 OBJECT ORIENTATION AND THE CLIENT/SERVER MODEL

Just as there are multiple CORBA-based database management architectures, there are many ways to construct and operate a client/server-based object-oriented database management system. Object-oriented database managers have numerous alternatives on how objects can be stored and how they can be executed to improve performance. There are basically two modes of database object storage in such architectures: the passive object storage approach and the active object storage approach. These object storage approaches differ in how they maintain the storage of the state and the methods for objects in the database. Three major architectural improvements have been postulated and implemented within existing object-oriented database management system products. These architectures optimize where object management occurs and how object storage is organized and managed. The three techniques are the object/server, the page/server, and the file/server architectures.

9.4.1 Passive Object Storage

In the first object storage approach, objects are decomposed into two separate components: object state and object method. The persistent database storage maintains the object state, or values of objects within the database, while the object's methods are placed at the sites that will be using them. The object methods can be replicated into each site and potentially all applications, and the object state (the values) is stored within the database repository (persistent storage medium).

There are obvious advantages to this approach. For compiled systems, all method code required by an application can be located where needed. The replicated code can be placed in a single repository (object manager) on each of the sites that will be using the objects, or the method code can be in-line expanded in each application code. The object method approach keeps the interface between application and objects consistent, but it requires the applications to go out of their process execution space to acquire information from another process, the application site's object manager. The second method, in-line expansion, requires no added external access for method code, but it still requires interaction with some form of management software to coordinate object state access.

By locating object method code where it will be used, the volume of data transfers between the client and the server can be greatly reduced. Instead of requiring the entire object (state and methods) to be transferred between the persistent storage medium and the application process, only the object state needs to flow over the communications channel. The movement of the methods from under the direct control of the database management system to the client sites results in some database management services being required on the application sites to guarantee correct and consistent object management—for example, services such as object management, transaction management, object-level concurrency control, and copy synchronization can be provided on the application site.

Moving object methods from the server to the application site, relieves the server of an additional processing load. Since object methods are not colocated with the objects' state, the server cannot perform method executions. Releasing the server of this processing load frees up the server to support an increased number of clients. Additionally, the server can be freed up for the performance of database manage-

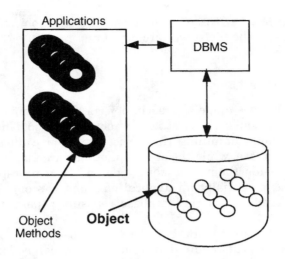

Figure 9.22   Passive object/server architecture

ment functions—for example, lock management, recovery management, integrity management, constraint enforcement, condition handling, database security enforcement, transaction management,
redundancy maintenance, and synchronization, which all require
more total database state semantics to perform.

Figure 9.22 depicts the passive data storage architecture. The main
drawback with this architecture is the loss of control over object
method execution given up by the server (persistent storage medium)
process. Without adequate distributed cooperative controls, the client
applications could access the stored data (especially if object state
data are passed to a client and held for later use).

9.4.2 Active Object Storage

In the second object storage alternative approach, object state and
methods are stored together in the database's persistent storage repository. The interface between the server and the client transmits
object method execution request messages, object method results, or
possibly entire objects (state and methods). The server (persistent
storage location and storage management process) can operate as a
central processing site, only allowing messages for method executions
to be received, leaving performance of all method requests to be performed on the objects' storage site and transmittal of method results
to the requesters. This data processing model may result in a lessening of transmissions over the data channel between the requester and

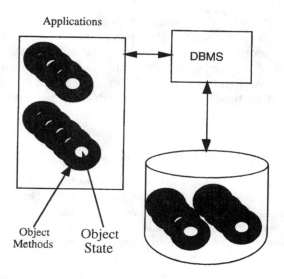

Figure 9.23   Active object/server architecture

server, but may result in the server performing all method executions. Due to increased processing loads, the server would not be able to support as many clients (applications), and this possibly would result in reducing the server's performance. The server in this scenario becomes the processing bottleneck, limiting the throughput of object method execution and the number of applications that can be concurrently supported.

The active database/server architecture approach is shown in Figure 9.23. In this approach there is no need to determine where object methods are to be stored. Only one copy of the objects' operations exists, and their safety is ensured through the centralization of storage and execution.

An alternative to storing and managing the state and methods on the centralized server, and to reduce the load on the server, is to allow objects (state and methods) to be transmitted to the application's working space for execution. In this alternative policy, the server acts as a distribution point, receiving requests for object method execution, determining the validity and correctness of the requests (concurrency control, access authorization, etc.), and, if successful, transmitting entire objects (state and methods) to the application's working space for execution. The advantage of this policy is the offloading of data processing (method execution) from the server to the applications, and the added processing power (cycles) gained by distributed processing (multiple methods executed can be executed concurrently in multiple applications). An advantage of this approach is in added client/server communications to transmit both object state and methods and possibly increased coordination processing and communications to maintain correct and consistent database processing within a distributed processing environment. Another advantage is the maintenance of object (state and methods) allocation and deallocation by the database storage server.

9.4.3 Object/Server Architecture Alternatives

The object model implementation for a client/server architecture offers additional possibilities for decomposition and distribution of database processing. The client and server can each have some portion of the database management system's software resident. The major difference in this approach, as compared to the relational model's architecture, is that the communications data transfer volume between the client and the server is increased and the data processing load on the client increases while at the same time it is reduced on the server. The reason this form of architecture prevails in object-oriented database systems is due to the active nature of objects (method executions) and their data encapsulation properties (added security and processing options), which make distribution easier than in the monolithic relational model. Guaranteeing the ACID properties required of executing objects embedded within transactions requires that more of the management decisions be brought closer to the applications executing the methods. In addition, since generally complex object-oriented database systems utilize pointer chasing through complex network-like structures during execution, it makes more sense to locate the objects as close to the applications as possible for performance considerations. Object-oriented systems tend to interleave database processing and application processing due to the tight coupling between the application language and the database language's data types, thus enhancing performance. If the database objects and data management are colocated with the application software, performance can be further enhanced. An advantage of the object-oriented client/server data processing approach over the relational approach is the reduction in the data processing load on the server through the offloading of portions of the data processing and data management processing to the clients. Offloading processing allows for the possibility of supporting a greater volume of clients per server site. One disadvantage over the relational/server intensive data processing approach is the probable increase in data transfer traffic within the system caused by servers shipping objects to client sites and the transmission of objects back to the server upon client completion.

This does not mean that the object-oriented model implementations must follow the approach of storing an entire object (methods and state) on the server and the transmission of the entire object upon client request. As a secondary tradeoff, the object model can look at data storage and data management software storage differently than the relational-based model. Communications costs can be reduced in several ways. First, by storing replicas of an object's methods on sites using the object, requiring object's state flow across the communications medium. Second, by moving the storage management from an object-based to a page-based scheme, possibly resulting in less replicated communications costs due to fine-grained versus coarse-grained transmission and control over database objects and groups of objects within pages. Again, there is a tradeoff to consider when dealing with balancing reduced communications costs, processing costs, and the resulting reduction in data availability. In addition, the movement of objects and pages to client sites from server sites can cause ripple effects, where client sites may be required to perform additional services and coordination activities dealing with concurrency control, recovery, query processing, and transaction management, which otherwise the sites would not be required to perform.

9.4.4 Object/Server Approach

In the object/server architecture, the majority of database management services still reside in the server sites. Services include the transaction manager, recovery manager (including log management), lock (concurrency control) manager, the object manager, file and index manager, page manager and physical storage management, and I/O management. The primary transfers between the client and the server are objects, requiring the client and the server to possess object management software to allow the manipulation of unique objects. This approach requires that the client and the server maintain caches for most recently used objects. To access an object a client initially searches its local cache. If the object is found in local space, it can be used; if not found, the client sends a request to the server to locate the object. The server looks in the server's local object cache first, followed by searching the page cache and then the file space on persistent storage to find the object.

Once the object is located it is copied into the server cache and the client cache for future reference based on object-caching policies in place. An advantage of this architecture (particularly when precompilation of applications and transactions is provided) is the ability to store methods for objects at all sites of use. The database system, however, would be required to perform some optimization to deter-

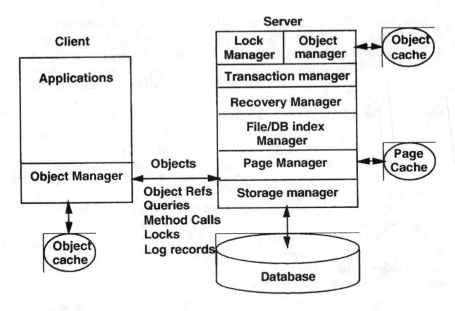

Figure 9.24   Client/server, object/server model

mine when it is advantageous to perform the query on the server or on the client based on the volume of data present. Another advantage is concurrency control: Since all database service actions other than method invocations are performed at the server, it becomes relatively simple to provide a lock management service on the server to maintain correct execution sequences on the server objects and the client copies. The architecture of the object/server model is shown in Figure 9.24.

The object/server architecture is not without its drawbacks. A worst-case scenario may require a remote object transfer request to the server on each object reference, if the local cache cannot satisfy requests. The problem is compounded when objects are composed of other objects. If the client does not possess a service to determine object clustering, then it must request objects as encountered, which would result in more time waiting for objects than executing objects (not a good option for a real-time system). Another problem with client object management is due to replication of objects across multiple clients and servers. On execution of an object's method in the object cache, the object managers must also cause the same action to occur on other copies of the object, if objects are to remain consistent. The overhead related to maintaining cache consistency may erase the benefit of distributing the object management to the clients. The distribution of object management also increases the complexity of the servers. Instead of a centralized design for all data management services, such as concurrency control and recovery, the servers must now support distribution and cooperative services across the sites.

9.4.5 Page/Server Approach

In the second server architectural approach, the interface between the client and the server is changed from a single object to storage allocation pages. The major theme of this object-based client/server architecture is to offload more services to the client, keeping the server as a simpler storage manager. The architecture moves the page and file manager, along with the object manager, to the clients and removes some of the problems and complexity of the object manager–based client/server approach. In the paged client/server architecture, the server site has most of the applications required for the interactive support components of the database removed and placed on the client. The server maintains the physical storage manager, a copy of the page manager, page cache manager, log manager, lock manager (concurrency control), recovery manager, and transaction manager. The interface between the server and the clients is page references, lock manipulation requests, log records, and disk data pages. By using this architecture, the client can be optimized to store objects only, pages only, or both, based on application requirements.

The page/server approach, shown in Figure 9.25, further distributes the database management processing load to the application processes. The advantage is that clients (applications) can still use object caching for references requiring only a single object or a small number of objects from a page. However, if client applications require a larger portion of a disk page, the page manager can pull in the entire page, allowing for decreased access time. This approach also takes care of the problem with complex or deeply connected objects. Complex objects can be stored on one page or on a number of pages in the client, reducing repeated requests for individual objects from the server, as was the case with the object/server architecture. Since most of the object processing load is performed on the client, the servers are freed up to support potentially more clients concurrently, hopefully improving performance. A disadvantage is that the lock management and recovery are still centralized as are the storage management services. In addition, the advantages may disappear from this approach if objects frequently used together are not clustered on a page or group of pages. Performance could degrade to requiring a reference to the server on every access, if there is not adequate clustering on pages. A

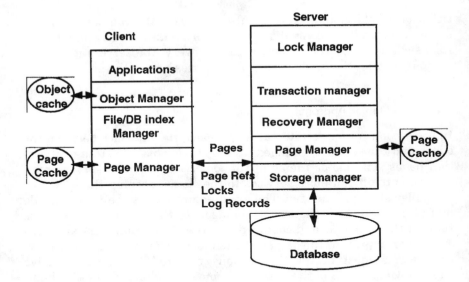

Figure 9.25   Client/server, page/server model

concern with the page/server approach is based on its advantage. Releasing control of disk pages to client sites removes central control over page accuracy, consistency, and correctness. A distributed update synchronization and concurrency control protocol must be used if copies are to be maintained. The advantages of the paged and the object/server methods can only be realized if applications using these methods are structured to fully use the partitioning. A tradeoff must be considered if specialized hardware is needed for processing queries. If many clients need such capabilities, it may be more advantageous to place them on the server. Added hardware, however, would alter the architecture and possibly make it more complex.

9.4.6 File/Server Architecture Approach

The third approach moves storage management services and database management services out to client nodes. The major theme within this architecture is to move all but essential database management synchronization functions out to the clients. The resulting system is much closer to a distributed processing architecture than a client/server architecture.

The file/server architecture is shown in Figure 9.26. The third client/server architecture is referred to as the file manager architecture.

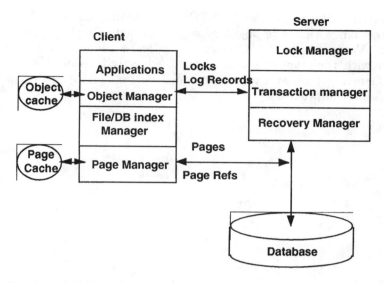

Figure 9.26   Client/server, file/server model

In this architecture most of the object management services are moved to the clients, but also the storage manager's I/O processing capabilities are moved to the clients. This allows clients to directly read and write database pages through a system-supplied service. Sun's Network File System (NFS) remote file service provides such a feature. The file/server architecture has the advantage of removing a layer of operating system–induced overhead from the data processing chain. Since the I/O service runs within the operating system, no user context switching is needed. To maintain database correctness and consistency, the lock manager and log manager are maintained in the server. The problem is that since the I/O service is a direct operating system function, the clients would be required to send additional initial request lock messages before a read or write could be executed. Improvements can be made if we use some form of semantic concurrency control or an optimistic scheme that can be performed on the clients. This would, however, require that objects individually maintain their own consistency and accuracy, which is counter to the policies in place in most commercial database products.

Examples of object-oriented databases include Versant, ONTOS, O2, Objectivity, ObjectStore, Itasca, and Gemstone. These database systems, however, do not implement the same client/server architectures. Itasca, O2, and Gemstone store objects within the database using the active database storage approach, whereas Versant,

Objectivity, ObjectStore, and ONTOS chose to implement object data storage using a passive object storage approach. On the other hand, Itasca, Versant, and ONTOS use the object/server architecture combined with their object storage policy. Objectivity, ObjectStore, O2, and Gemstone, as well as an extended version of ONTOS, use the page/server approach.

10

Distributed Database Management Systems

Paul Fortier

10.1 INTRODUCTION

Distributed database systems combine technology from two different areas: databases and communications. Databases have evolved from simple uniprocessor environments to multiprocessing systems and recently to collections of database systems that wish to share resources. Communications systems have evolved from the simple I/O subsystems to master-slave cooperative computer systems to collections of loosely connected computer systems to tightly coupled collections of resources unified into a *single* virtual system. The evolution of centralized databases into distributed databases resulted from a need derived from the applications using database systems. Most enterprises' data storage and use have moved from a centralized posture to one where shared information is required at all points within an enterprise if it is to operate efficiently and competitively. Past enterprise systems consisted of remote islands of data, which were not interconnected or available for remote access among the sites of an enterprise. The development of communications networks provided the stimulus to develop means to access an enterprise's information remotely, without initially integrating it into a singular database. This early use of remote information led to additional developments aimed at integrating these remote islands of data into a single, seamless, and virtual database system, accessible from all sites as if any selected piece of information were stored at the site of query origin.

Distributed computing and distributed system are terms often misused within computing literature. The term has been used to describe collections of loosely organized, nonhomogeneous computers; for describing collections of computers interconnected via a shared memory; and even simply communications networks. Before we can discuss what a distributed database is, we must first establish our definition of what distributed processing is. It is not that easy to describe what uniquely defines a distributed computer system. A distributed computer system is described along a few dimensions. A distributed computer system must have multiple remotely located computers. These computers must be interconnected via some form of communications medium. The computers act as independent participants in a global, singularly unified entity. The cohesiveness by which these remote computers synchronize actions defines the coupling and true unification of the distributed system. In the literature all of these elements have been used to define what a distributed computer system is, although they use a sliding scale where each of these dimensions can span some domain of possible values. This implies that there is not, as of yet, one distinct definition of what constitutes and defines a distributed system. Some properties, however, stand out clearer than others: These properties include distribution of computing resources, distribution of data, and distribution of control. The fundamental concept in a distributed system is that the elements that define and control the conventional uniprocessor system are all themselves distributed. The amount of distribution of resources, data, and control defines whether a system is a distributed system, a multiprocessing system, or some other form of system architecture.

The reasons for distribution are as important, if not more so, as the distribution itself. Computing power was distributed in order to better handle the needs of an enterprise's computing tasks, and to provide a platform to solve larger, more complex computing problems. One problem solved by distributed processing was that of placing computing power where needed, while not isolating the processing engines and their applications. The second problem addressed by distributed processing looked at breaking up a task into component elements that could be executed in parallel at a variety of sites. Both problems, however, look at divide-and-conquer approaches to problem solving. One is loosely coupled, looking to share data and results; the other is tightly synchronized, performing unified tasks in multiple segments, yet synchronizing the return of results. From these simple examples we can see that distributed processing is chosen as a solution to a

general need for increased information access and increased processing capacity.

10.2 DISTRIBUTED DATABASES

A distributed database is based on and constructed from a homogeneous database system model, with the data and management software
partitioned over multiple computing sites, constructed on top of a distributed computing system foundation (Figure 10.1). The sites of the
system are connected via some form of communications infrastructure. The communications medium is typically a low-speed local area
network with data rates ranging from tens of kilobytes per second up
to a hundred megabytes per second or more, but it is not a high-speed
backplane. The communications subsystem acts as the conduit
through which the data flow between disjoint database systems
spread throughout the distributed system. The databases that reside
on the nodes of the communications system are logically related by a
unifying global database schema based on a unified singular database
model. The database distribution is transparent to the users of the
database at any site. Their view of the database is a single, locally
accessible database management system. All details of the communications and data distribution are hidden from the end user in a fully
distributed database system.

Data within the distributed database can be distributed in a variety
of ways. The data can be partitioned across all the sites, or the data

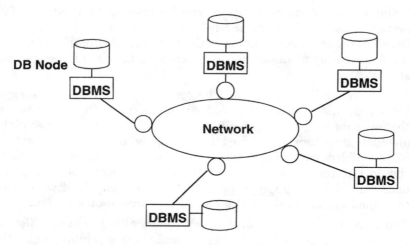

Figure 10.1   Distributed database system

can be replicated on each site. The decision on how to partition and replicate information is based on the needs of applications and the ability of the systems to support added storage and processing associated with such policies. Not all sites in the system need be identical. Some may have added storage assets, while others may have enhanced processing resources. In addition, not all of the sites need to have secondary storage locally available. All sites, however, must have the ability to manipulate data anywhere within the distributed database system in a transparent fashion.

10.2.1 Advantages of Distribution

There are some obvious advantages to distributed databases that result from the distribution of data, control, and resources. These advantages include the following.

* Information can be stored at the location where it is most frequently used. This differs from the centralized databases, where all data were located in one place, and all users had to remotely connect into the database for access to information. This centralized approach added additional communications cost, greater load on the single computing platform, and reduced throughput.

* Improved performance can be realized through distribution of the workload over several computing sites. True parallelism can be achieved in a distributed architecture. There are lower overhead costs due to reduced contention for a single resource.

* Reduced cost of communications can be realized by locating information where it is most needed. Instead of remote users being forced to request needed information at a central site, they can have the data readily available on their local site, increasing the speed of access.

* Greater reliability is possible. The very nature of a distributed system—replicated, loosely coupled complete computing systems—is the basis for constructing fault-tolerant and reliable systems. If the distributed system is designed appropriately, it can take advantage of the added distributed resources that aid in system recovery, should failures of hardware and/or software occur—for example, a node failure may simply require the reallocation of software from the failed system to some other site in the distributed system.

* Expandability is enhanced. If the current configuration of a distributed system exceeds its capacity or performance requirements, the system can be easily upgraded by adding a new node to the system. Ease of expansion is an important attribute of a distributed system.

- Higher data availability, integration of an entire enterprise's information assets, and increased ability to share information and processing enhance applications support. Data can be kept where they are produced, yet still be accessible from any area within a fully connected enterprise. This results in improved use of a corporation's most valuable asset—its information. Data need not be kept in one location, thereby increasing the volume of data that can be accessed simultaneously by a factor equal to the number of database sites.

- Local autonomy is maintained, while not sacrificing sharing of information. Sites in the distributed database can exhibit local control over the storage, maintenance, and use of data created and stored locally, while at the same time not limiting the enterprise's integration of this information into a virtual entity. Local autonomy allows information to be optimally managed by the creators of the data, while maintaining global usability without compromising any local security, maintainability, and/or access policies.

10.2.2 Disadvantages of Distribution

A distributed database, as you can see, has numerous advantages. These advantages, however, are sometimes also disadvantages. Distribution of data, control, and resources aids in data processing, but comes at a price. Distributed database systems are still not well understood or uniform in functionality. A distributed database will be much more complicated across a wide range of functions than an equivalent centralized database system. The control of a distributed database is itself distributed, leading to further complications and possible loss of performance. As discussed in Chapter 4, there is a need for security in database systems, likewise in distributed databases. Security in such environments can be even harder to realize due to the vulnerability of the communications medium. Some disadvantages and complications of distribution include the following.

- Database design will be much more complicated in a distributed database. Designing the logical structure will be basically the same in a distributed homogeneous system, although schema mapping to physical storage takes on a new meaning with distribution. Where to place data and how to partition data across sites becomes a new cost in the design process.

- Distributed query processing offers a benefit in that additional parallel processing of subqueries is possible. The distribution, however, also increases the number of possible processing strategies to examine before a query is initiated.

- Database directory management becomes a global problem. If all sites are to know the physical location of data within the system, then each must have a complete directory that provides this information. These directories now themselves become a distributed replicated database, which must be maintained consistently and be kept up to date. Replication implies that any change to an item within the directory on any site must be immediately reflected accurately on all other sites before regular processing can continue. This may require the use of a large portion of the added processing cycles if schema changes are frequent.

- Transaction processing and concurrency control must also deal with the distribution of the database. A transaction on one site may trigger actions or require actions from numerous other database storage sites to perform a designed function. The transaction processing will require cooperation and coordination with other sites' transaction managers to correctly perform a transaction and to guarantee transaction ACID execution. A portion of this processing deals with distributed concurrency control processing. Concurrency control must now coordinate and schedule the execution of data manipulation requests from distributed transactions, with possibly limited information about global activities.

- Related to distributed concurrency control and transaction processing is distributed deadlock detection. If locking is used in a system, then deadlock is possible, and therefore the condition of deadlock must be checked for. In a distributed system deadlock can occur within a single site, as in a centralized uniprocessor system, as well as across remote sites. The detection of deadlock across sites will require the construction of a global waits for graph (the existence of a cycle within the graph indicates that deadlock exists). The construction of such a graph will be costly and will require that additional resources be applied to this task at all sites.

- Recovery in a distributed system can become both easier and harder at the same time. Greater redundancy enhances recoverability if it is used properly. On the other hand, greater redundancy also increases run-time complexity. To maintain redundant data's consistency requires that we make all updates to any data on any site atomic on all sites unanimously. To do this requires additional synchronization processing and communications. The update must be distributed to all sites; each site must acknowledge its receipt and install the new information. A failure at any of the sites makes the database inaccurate.

- When integrating remote legacy (old databases already in use) database systems into a single distributed system, we have some additional problems to deal with. The databases may not have the same data model (relational, object, network), may not have the same version of a product, and may have numerous other inconsistencies. These may lead us down the path of heterogeneous database systems rather than true homogeneous distributed systems.

10.3 DISTRIBUTED DATABASE ARCHITECTURE

A distributed database system does not need to be of one uniform structure, with each node a mirror of all others. Distributed database architectures have evolved from their supporting distributed processing system's framework and structure. Distributed database management systems constructed to this point typically follow one of three main architectural themes: They are either local database systems that are extended by a global component (Figure 10.2); uniform distributed databases, where all sites have all or some elements that, when taken together, form the fully distributed database system (Figure 10.3); or the client/server architecture (Figure 10.4).

In the first architecture, a distributed database is formed by distribution extensions to local autonomous database systems on each site. The local database managers act as independent database systems, but can have queries or updates generated either locally or remotely. It becomes the function of the global database servers to provide for the transparency of data distribution and remote data accesses. The local databases act as they would if they were each isolated singular databases. The local databases perform transaction processing, recov-

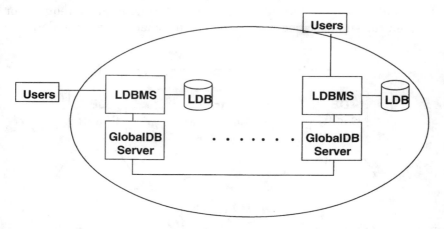

Figure 10.2 Distributed database system architecture using local databases

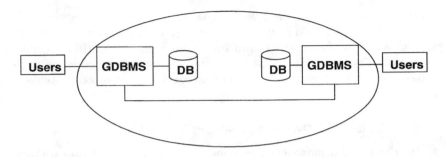

Figure 10.3   Global complete distributed database system

ery management, security management, concurrency control, storage management, user-interface management, and catalog management as isolated individuals. The global database server handles the distribution element of the database. The global element manages the global conceptual schema, which maintains a global data map for the entire database as a single logical entity. This function of the global database server provides for the transparency of all data within the database. Transparency managed by the global database server includes data, network, replication, fragmentation, and database partition transparency. The goal is to provide each local site with a virtual single database, stored locally, consisting of the concatenation of all the local databases within the system. Any local database has access to all data within the system through its interface to its copy of the global schema.

To access data anywhere within the distributed database system, a local database must formulate and issue a remote query request for data on the site specified within the global schema, or, if the data are

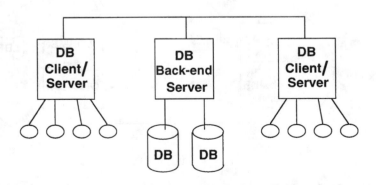

Figure 10.4   Client/server distributed database system

stored locally, the database generates a local query. Any locally generated query that cannot be handled at the local site is handed over to the global database server. The global database server locates the site where the data are stored, using the local database's copy of the global data catalog. By using the global data catalog information, the global database server forms the remote query into a message and sends this message to the database site containing the data. The remote database site accepts the message, unbundles the query, and inserts the query into the local database system's transaction processing stream, where it is treated like any other locally generated query. When the query is answered, the response is bundled back into a response message and sent to the database site that originated the query. On reception, the response is removed from the message packet and forwarded to the local database system as if it were a response to a local query. The local database returns the reponse to the application that originated the query to close the loop.

The important architectural point to notice in this discussion is how local sites act as independent databases. There is no concept of synchronization of remote accesses or coordination of remote transactions. Each database on each site performs its own recovery, concurrency control, security, buffer management, and transaction processing. The global database element has the job of adding in and coordinating the distribution of data and transactions. Dependent on the level of integration provided by the global database server, this coordination can be very loose or can require tighter interaction from the local databases. If loose coordination is used, the global database server may be used only as a means to locate remote data, retrieve remote data, and format and route remote requests. On the other hand, if the degree of coordination is high, then the global database server may also coordinate global transactions, global concurrency control, global recovery, and other management functions on all sites.

The second architecture, the fully distributed database system, has a higher degree of cohesiveness among the sites of the database system. This cohesiveness is a result of the design's basic approach, which is to have the entire system operate as a unified whole. There are two types of architectures represented by this form of distributed database: One is a totally distributed, fully replicated database system; the other is a fully distributed partitioned database system. In the first form of database system, each database site has a complete set of database/server functions, although each of these is constructed as a fully distributed cognizant component. These elements are constructed with distribution built in, instead of as an add-on as in the first architecture. Transaction processing is a global function, which must take into account the state of data and transactions on other sites to determine the correct operation to perform next in order to guarantee global transaction ACID properties. In the fully replicated approach each site cooperates with all others in making global decisions on issues such as commit processing and update synchronization. The advantage of this approach is in its reliability. Since every site has a copy of all database software, recovery from a site failure becomes relatively simple. The added cost with this architecture is in synchronization and cooperation for all management decisions within the database system. The cost, however, is well worth it if increased performance and reliability are achieved.

In this architectural approach to a fully distributed database, functions of the database are partitioned to separate sites within the system—for example, the distributed catalog manager may be at one site, requiring that any changes to the schema be performed on this site. The distributed transaction manager may be at another site, the query processing software at another, and recovery software at yet another site. By partitioning the software of the system, the processing load is partitioned to separate sites also. To perform a particular database management service task, a global system manager residing at each site would be invoked to request the required service function on the database site of storage. Once a service is requested, the global database requester service would wait for the service response, indicating the status of the requested action. However, in actuality, this is not very practical.

One advantage of this approach is that the decision-making process is located at only one site and therefore no added communication is necessary to make decisions on management issues. The advantage, however, also becomes a problem. By having the various functions located throughout the system, each database service request must be sent through a service message for each major database function to the site where the service is located. This could result in bottlenecks for functions that are heavily utilized. In addition, if a site goes down, the function located on the failed site is also lost to the system. This could result in the system being halted by the failure of one site. This possibility makes one of the advantages of distributed processing not too effective in this case. Due to the limitations of this approach a more complete approach is typically taken.

In both of these architectures the decisions to be made deal with what to distribute and how to coordinate actions across distributed hardware and software. The three elements that can be distributed are the components of the system, the functions of the database system, or the data within the database. Components include the database repositories (disk drives) and the processing engines (query processing, reliability processing, transaction processing, etc.). Functions that can be distributed include transaction management, query management, security management, and concurrency control management. Finally, data could be distributed (fully replicated, partitioned, or factored). When designing a system from scratch all of these design decisions will be encountered and must be examined and traded off against each other for cost, reliability, and performance.

The third architecture is not a true distributed database system, but is included here due to its importance from a vendor and client perspective. The client/server architecture is a hybrid architecture, where each site has some partial elements of the database management system, but only a few sites possess all the elements, including most of the database itself. The client machines possess the ability to initiate queries and coordinate the responses for applications running on their platform. In addition, these nodes may have the ability to store some portion of the distributed database and manage these assets in support of the global database. The client nodes form queries that cannot be answered locally into bundled complete queries to the server nodes in the network. The server machine(s) services the remote requests for numerous client nodes. In addition, these service nodes provide for all the necessary management and maintenance of the data on their site. These nodes provide for recovery, security, cooperative processing across multiple servers, transaction processing, concurrency control, query processing, and storage management.

10.4 DISTRIBUTED DATABASE DESIGN

The design of a distributed database system requires the determination of how data in the database are to be stored across the sites within the system. This assumes that the database management software and distributed computing system are already designed. The distribution of data in the database must take into account the degree to which information is to be shared among the nodes of the network, the behavior of the access to data if they are shared, and the ability to predict the stability of the access pattern. The degree of sharing is important when determining where to place a piece of information and whether or not this piece of information should be further partitioned or even replicated. If a piece of information is not shared, then it can be placed at the site of use with no further analysis required. Data that are used by more than one site should be analyzed to determine which site uses the information most frequently and with the greatest volume. The site determined by such an analysis should be assigned the data to minimize overhead and delay for the frequent user. If, on the other hand, a piece of data is highly utilized by numerous sites, it may become necessary to create copies of these data at a number of sites to ensure availability. These decisions about where to place data must not be determined simply based on usage patterns. The secondary consideration for data placement is based on the way in which the data are used. If the pattern of data use is constantly changing, then determining a site for permanent storage of data may be optimal today and dismal tomorrow. If the usage pattern is static or nearly so, in the sense that the data are used by the same sites with the same relative frequency and with few sporadic alterations, then these data can be stored at the site of highest data utilization and available data storage volume, which will result in good performance. The problem is that the truth in usage patterns is somewhere in-between the two end points. Data usage will change over time as applications are added or deleted from the system and as the present applications are altered or change their usage of data. This may result in a database mapping that may need to be altered periodically if efficiency is to be maintained.

To develop a plan (site map or global distributed schema) for the placement of data in the database the designers must first develop a set of requirements for the database system and collect all pertinent data to be managed and stored within the database (Figure 10.5), as in the case with the centralized database models. By using this initial collection of data and requirements, the development of initial relations (entities, objects, or files) and relationships between them can proceed as in the centralized database design process described in Chapter 6. This results in an initial global conceptual schema for the entire database. The development of the conceptual schema can also result in the development of individual user or application views of the database as part of the process. Once an initial database design has been developed, a distribution plan can be devised. To develop the distribution plan the applications that will be initially executing within the database must be reexamined as to their access patterns and sites of allocation within the intended distributed system. This initial analysis of applications will then lead to an analysis of the loading of both programs, data and processing, that will be realized at each site. This analysis may possibly result in further reallocations of application software to other sites to balance the loading and proposed data flow among them. This process of analyzing the allocations and loadings continues until an initial system load is developed. With this plan the database analysis can continue.

Data placement is initiated by analyzing the data requirements for each application, as well as the usage pattern of the required data each of these applications has. This information is composed into initial composite data loads and usage patterns for all sites within the database. To determine a final load these initial loads must be ana-

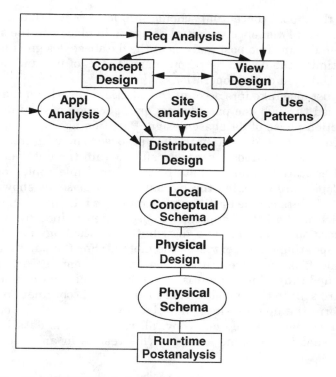

Figure 10.5 Distributed database design process

lyzed as to the resulting data and control flows across the network, based on this initial loading as a starting point. This analysis must include what effect the added cost of replication, partitioning, or fragmentation will have on the normal functioning of the database. It is not an optimal distribution plan to simply place all data at the sites where they are used, without concern for the implications of added run-time costs—for example, if a piece of data is used at all sites, and we initially assign it to all sites to make the reading of this information optimal, we will pay a heavy price for any updates to this information. A write to any piece of these data will result in a write being generated to all sites of the database. In addition, it is not actually this simple, since the write must be atomic, possibly requiring all sites to become unaccessible while the write occurs (commit processing). What this illustrates is one added cost that must be taken into account when a data item is to be replicated. Replication improves access time, but it increases update time drastically. Once an optimal or near-optimal logical map is determined, physical database design can be undertaken. The result of this phase is a logical-to-physical mapping of the global conceptual schema into local conceptual and physical schemata. Even once an initial design is in place and the system is operational, run-time postanalysis of the database design is necessary to reoptimize the design based on the statistics of use and access dynamics collected during operations.

We must also take into account the additional overhead that may be introduced through the partitioning or replication of data during the distribution phase of database design. Partitioning implies that there is one copy of each data item in the database. The data items get cut up and are distributed to separate sites within the database (Figure 10.6). Replication implies that there are multiple copies of a data item. Copies are allocated throughout the database, as shown in Figure 10.6. If data can be partitioned or replicated, the process for choosing which is the better approach to use is determined by trading off the access speed gained by a distribution method against the added cost of updating data created by the method. For the partitioned case, the tradeoff is the added cost to read a data item against the lower cost of updating. Since there is only one copy of a data item, all updates are sent to the one site. There is no added coordination required to perform the update, since there is only one copy of the data item. Also, since there is only one copy, all reads for this data item must also be sent to the same location. This results in an added cost for

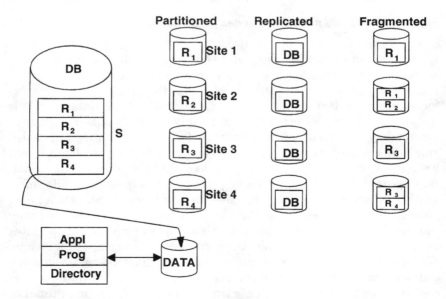

Figure 10.6   Distributed database schemes

reading. All reads must suffer the cost of transmitting a request and receiving a response.

For the replicated data item case, the tradeoff is again between access speed and update cost, although the costs are different. Since there are multiple copies of a data item available, reads can be directed to any copy of the data item. This should on average result in a reduced access cost for the replicated database, especially in the fully replicated case where there is a copy of all data items on all sites of the database. The costs will be at least reduced by two transfers over the network: One for the request and one for the response can now be removed. The costs for updates, however, are not quite as good. For updates, the replicated database requires the added costs involved in replicating the update operation at all sites in the system. This will require not only the added communications costs, but possibly added synchronization costs to coordinate the update to ensure atomicity and correctness of the update at all sites. We can see from this discussion that the decision to replicate or partition is not an easy one. A general rule to follow based on the costs discussed above is to replicate when reads are more frequent than updates and to partition when updates are more frequent than reads. It may not be quite as simple as this and may require some simulation or analysis to get a more thorough answer. The method to prove your design will be based on the size of the design and the cost associated with change once the system is installed and operational. It will be easier to justify on-line changes for a system with low maintenance costs than for one where the cost of maintenance is substantial.

The previous discussion looked at two costs in determining how to distribute data in the database; however, there are others. If there is insufficient storage space on a node, transmission costs are too expensive, or processing costs are too expensive, then an additional decomposition of the data items may be necessary, or some additional partitioning may be required—for example, if partitioning cannot be done cleanly due to space limitations or processing limitations, the initial partition may need to be fragmented (Figure 10.6). Fragmentation can be done on the tuple level or on the attribute level of a relation. This may result in added costs in processing queries that request information over the full range of a relation's tuples and attributes, although this could also be an advantage if the fragmentation is done based on usage patterns. If we have two queries that each use only half a relation, then the relation can be fragmented over two sites, allowing for parallel access and processing of the queries. Fragmentation is not typically used in distributed systems, but can be considered in specialized circumstances such as those just described.

If there is limited storage space available on a site for all of the relations that optimally should be stored on the site, based on the analysis of use and access patterns, then some alternatives must be addressed. Distributed design must look at alternatives when the primary, optimal solution is not viable. In this case we may choose the next best site available from the same analysis, but with the primary site removed. In this way we have removed the site that is overloaded and have considered other, *near-optimal* alternatives. Likewise, if we find that sites have inadequate processing resources available for query processing or database processing needs, we may look to alternative allocations based on next best fit with adequate free resources. If communications is the resource that is to be reduced, we may look to replication to minimize communications required for queries. This, again, is adequate when an excessive volume of updates is not expected. If updates are more frequent, we may be forced to pay the price of increased communications. Decisions should be made based on balancing the costs associated with access, updates further refined by storage, processing, and communications. The optimal solution will be based on the costs most justifiable to the applications being supported.

A further issue with data distribution deals with the management of the database's metadata. The database directory or catalog is itself possibly distributed. This then becomes another distributed database that must be designed and supported in the final architecture. The directory is used by the database management system for all aspects of data management. It is used for query processing, transaction processing, concurrency control, security, recovery, and many other management functions. Like the initial database design the directory supports the directory's design, and its location must be evaluated based on the applications (database management functions) that use it. We can see that the distributed database design problem is not a simple one to solve.

10.5 DISTRIBUTED QUERY PROCESSING

An issue with centralized conventional databases and with distributed databases is how to efficiently acquire and process information based on a user's request. Database manipulation languages typically indicate what data are being looked for, not how to find and retrieve data. This leaves it up to the underlying database query processing software to determine how to retrieve the requested information. In the centralized case the query processing problem looked at minimizing the cost of accessing information using metrics based on the size of involved relations. Query processing takes as input an initial query in the host language and transforms this into a low-level execution plan to retrieve the wanted information. The transformed query should return a correct response in an efficient manner. The goal is to reduce the consumption of computing resources in processing the requested query. The strategy for realizing this reduction in the transformed query is typically to reallocate where and when selections and projections are performed, as well as the order in which relations are joined or operated on by other binary relational operations. The basic idea is to reduce the number of tuples to be passed on to the next stage within a query processing execution plan. By reducing the number of tuples to be operated on, the cost is proportionately reduced for all following stages.

As an example, if we have an initial database with two relations, Employee(Eno, Ename, Address, Title) and Project(Eno, Pid, Responsibility, Assig-time), we can generate a query to find the names of all employees working on project Rtsorac. The initial query may look like

```
RANGE of E IS Employee
RANGE of P IS Project
        SELECT   Ename
          FROM   E, P WHERE E.Eno = P.Eno
           AND   P.Pid = "Rtsorac"
```

This SQL query can be represented in an equivalent relational algebra query, which will be easier to optimize and demonstrates the methods applied in the optimization.

$$\Pi Ename(\sigma\ Pid = "Rtsorac"\ AND\ E.Eno = P.Eno\ (E \times P))$$

It can be readily seen that this query is not optimized, since it includes the Cartesian product as the basis operations from which to initiate the remainder of the selections and projections (Figure 10.7). This query can be optimized by pushing down the selections and projections as low as possible on the tree to minimize the information passed to the next stage in the tree. In this example we wish to push the selection of P.Pid = "Rtsorac" down the query tree to just after the relation P.

In addition to pushing down the selection of the project identifier to the project relations access, we need to push the selection of E.Eno = P.Eno down to the Cartesian product to transform the Cartesian product operation into an equijoin. We also want to project up to the equijoin only the information needed in the join and final result. We can see that to perform the equijoin we need only pass up the employees' names and identifiers from the two relations, as shown in Figure 10.8.

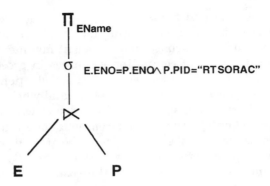

Figure 10.7 Initial query tree

The final operation is to project the employees' names from the relation resulting from the equijoin of the employee and project relations.

It can be seen that the cost for a given query can be readily reduced through the application of some simple principles. Further cost reductions can be realized through the manipulation of join orderings when multiple joins are to be performed within a query or through reordering of other binary operations. These optimizations require a computation of cost functions for each ordering and then choosing one that matches the minimal cost function chosen for the optimization criteria. Many well-known algorithms exist to perform this cost function and selection; they are based on the use of heuristics to reduce the possible search space.

In a distributed database system the optimization process is even more complicated. It will not be sufficient to simply decide the optimization based on pushing down selections and projections, and ordering

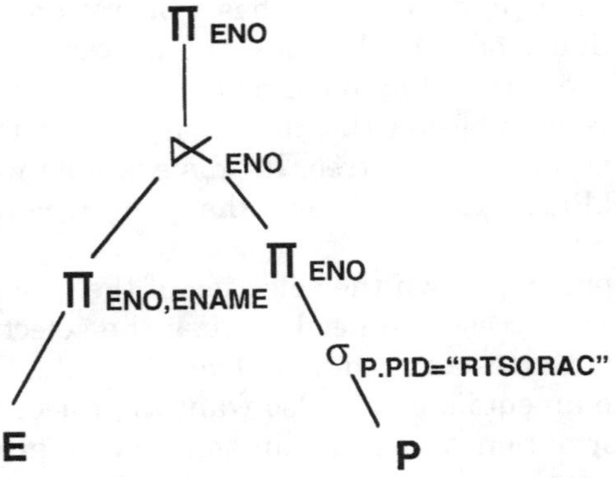

Figure 10.8 Optimized query tree

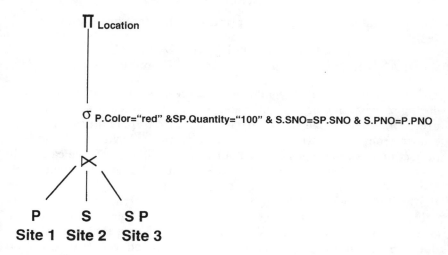

Π Location

σ P.Color="red" &SP.Quantity="100" & S.SNO=SP.SNO & S.PNO=P.PNO

$\bowtie$

P S S P
Site 1 Site 2 Site 3

Figure 10.9 Initial distributed query tree

the executions. There is an added cost to consider in the distributed case due to the distribution of relations and communications. The communications costs come into play when relations involved in a query are distributed over several sites. The optimization must now also select the best site to process data and determine in what order the processing should be performed across the distributed sites. This added cost increases the solution space that must be searched for in determining an optimal execution plan for a given query. The goals of the optimization are similar: We want to maximize the concurrency of queries, minimize the local processing cost, and in addition minimize the communications cost, all while selecting an appropriate site for the query's answer and intermediate processing results.

As an example, we could have a database with three relations on three sites: on site one, relation Part (Pno, Pname, Color); on site two, relation Supply (Sno, Sname, Location); and on site three, Sup-Part (Sno, Pno, Quantity). We could then ask in what cities suppliers that supply red parts in quantities greater than 100 units are located. The structured query language representation for this query could be

```
RANGE of P IS Part
RANGE of S IS Supplier
RANGE of SP IS Sup-Part
     SELECT   Location
        FROM   P, S, SP   WHERE   P.Pno = S.Pno
        AND   S.Sno = SP.Sno   AND   SP.Quantity > "100"
        AND   P.Color = "red"
```

This translates to an initial unoptimized relational algebra query

Πlocation (σ Color = "red" AND ~Quantity = "100"
AND E.Eno = P.Eno AND S.Sno = SP.Sno (P × S × SP))

The initial query tree would not include any differentiation on ordering of execution or any optimizations, as discussed previously (Figure 10.9). To optimize this query we would first apply all the methods known from the centralized databases to push down selections and projections as low as possible. In our example this means we can push down the selection σ Color = "red" to just after the node for relation P. We can also push down the selection σ Quantity = "100" to just after the node for relation SP. In addition, we can further reduce the involved relations by applying some early projections on the reduced results from the selections. We can project Sno and Pno from the reduced SP relation; project only Pno from the reduced P relation; or project only Sno and Location from S, since these are the only attributes needed for the joins and the final result. Under the assumption that the cardinalities of the three relations are such that after the reductions, but before the joins, the cardinality of SP is less than that of S and that S is less than P and ($|SP| = 10 < |S| = 100 < |P| = 500$), the optimization of the communications cost and the order of execution have the following options and costs, assuming the cost of communications is C and the result must be on the site of P.

1. Move P to site of SP at a cost of 500C; move result of P joined with SP to site of S at a cost less than or equal to 10C; move this result back to site of P at a cost of less than or equal to 10C, for a total cost of approximately 520C.

2. Move S to site of SP at a cost of 100C; move result of S joined with SP to site of P at a cost less than or equal to 10C, for a total cost of 110C.

3. Move SP to site of S at a cost of 10C; move result of SP joined with S to site of P at a cost less than or equal to 10C, for a total cost of 20C.

4. Move SP to site of P at a cost of 10C; move result of SP joined with P to S at a cost less than or equal to 10C; move this result back to site of P at a cost of less than or equal to 10C, for a total cost of 30C.

5. Move SP and P to site of S at a cost of 510C; move result of SP joined with S and P back to site of P at a cost less than or equal to 10C, for a total cost of 520C.

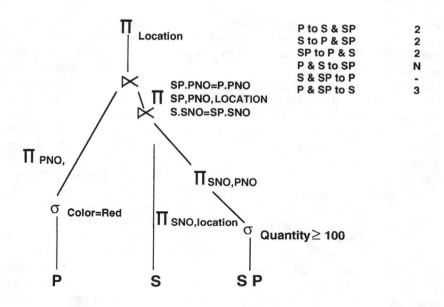

P to S & SP	2
S to P & SP	2
SP to P & S	2
P & S to SP	N
S & SP to P	-
P & SP to S	3

Assume Cardinality SP <S < P
Move result of SP & Select & Project to S
Move joined result of S & SP to P Final result on P

Figure 10.10   Optimized distributed query tree

6. Move SP and S to site of P at a cost of 110C—no cost to move result since it is already at site of P, resulting in a total cost of 110C.

7. Move S and P to site of SP at a cost of 600C; move result of SP joined with S and P back to site of P at a cost less than or equal to 10C, for a total cost of 610C.

8. Move P to site of S at a cost of 500C; move both relations, since no reduction is possible, to site of SP at a cost of 600C; move this result back to site of P at a cost of less than or equal to 10C, for a total cost of 1,010C.

9. Move S to site of P at a cost of 100C; move both relations, since no reduction is possible, to site of SP at a cost of 600C; move this result back to site of P at a cost of less than or equal to 10C, for a total cost of 710C.

It can be seen from the nine options above that there is a wide range of possible communications costs to consider, as well as order of execution costs, when deciding which of these options makes the most optimal sequence to choose. Two options to discard immediately are options 8 and 9, since the initial moves result in no reductions, making these worst-case options. Options 1, 5, and 7 also have a very high communications cost. This is caused by the movement of relation P, the largest over the network. It should be the goal to move only the smaller relations or smaller results. Options 2 and 6 have much better costs, but still are more expensive than options 3 and 4. Of these two options (3 or 4), option 3 has the least cost, since it does not need to return the final result back to the origination site P. The optimized query tree that results from this process is shown in Figure 10.10.

The optimization process must take into account the costs of communications and the cost of the binary operations with reductions in order to compute the costs of various options. To perform this cost computation may require the maintenance of historical information or relational statistical information about the cardinality of relation fragments based on a variety of selection criteria. If this information is not available, then the rough sizes of the relations alone can be used as the criteria for selection. This may not result in the most optimal execution ordering, but it is a best-guess estimate based on the available information. In addition, this approach may be more cost effective to implement due to the need for minimal statistics. Another consideration to take into account is the size of the possible optimization options in performing the cost computation. For a relatively small number of relations this execution plan space can get very large and must be reduced using a variety of heuristics. Some of the heuristics may include choosing only the closest nodes or neighbors of a node for movement options, or even grouping nodes into clusters that can then be costed together.

10.6 DISTRIBUTED TRANSACTION PROCESSING

Transactions, like other database services, can be distributed. The cost of distributed transaction processing is manifested at the points in a transaction's execution where coordination is required to guarantee the ACID properties of executing transactions on the database. Transactions are defined as the unit of execution within a database system and the unit of work upon which the ACID properties are applied. The functions of transactions in a distributed system do not change. Transactions are still required for all access and manipulation of data stored within the database. They are expected to maintain database correctness and consistency while delivering high performance. Distributed transactions, on first view, appear to offer the possibility of increasing the performance of application access to the database. If there were no additional control and coordination involved, this would be the case. By adding additional transaction processing engines to the transaction processing resources, one would expect to have an increase in the transaction throughput of the system. This thinking is, however, a bit misleading. The addition of more processing engines does increase the available cycles for transaction work, but not in a linear manner. The added transaction processing resources also require additional coordination policies and mechanisms to continue to deliver the intended properties of transactions in a database system.

Transactions within a distributed database system operate in a cooperative manner (Figure 10.11). Transactions issue requests (messages) for services to other database managers within the system. During the execution of transactions within the distributed database system, the remote database managers, along with the initial data manager of the executing transaction, collect and maintain the state of the executing transaction to aid in coordination and correct execution of the transaction. As a transaction executes, it requests locks or some other means to gain exclusive access to read or write database items, and it develops a list of affected database items.

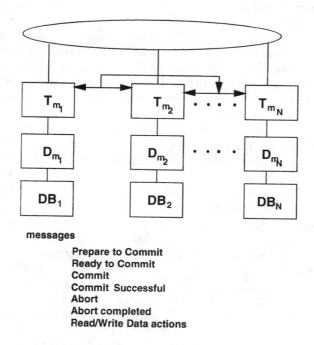

messages

    Prepare to Commit
    Ready to Commit
    Commit
    Commit Successful
    Abort
    Abort completed
    Read/Write Data actions

Figure 10.11 Distributed transaction processing

When the executing transaction has completed its operations (reads, writes, and computations) and is ready to commit, the transaction must issue a prepare to commit message to all database management sites where data items were acquired for use during the transaction's execution, as well as any other sites possessing replicated data items that were written during this transaction's execution. As sites that have been issued the prepare to commit message are ready to commit, they return their status to the coordinating site (the site where the transaction initiated): either ready to commit or not prepared (aborted). The coordinating transaction must then determine, based on the responses received, if all the participants are prepared to commit, or at least a majority if this is an allowable form of commit policy. Once the coordinator has determined that the transaction has enough of the participants in a state that is deemed safe to commit, the coordinator can issue a commit message. After the commit message has been issued, the coordinator waits and collects the commit responses from the participants. Once all the responses have been returned, the coordinator can complete the transaction's processing by cleaning up the active transaction control block and data structures and issuing a commit complete message to the participants.

On the other hand, if the executing transaction, for some reason, fails or aborts during execution or during commit processing and coordination, the coordinator must issue commands to coordinate the abortion of all participants with this transaction. An abort sequence is required if the coordinator determines it must abort, or if the participants cannot complete the requested processing for the coordinating transaction. If abort is required, the coordinator must issue an abort message to each of the participants and wait to be signaled through response messages as to the ability of the participants to abort the active transaction. Once all of the abort commands have been issued and the responses returned, the coordinator can issue the final message indicating that the abort is completed.

The basic addition to conventional centralized transaction processing is an added sequence of steps or phases to guarantee that the distributed participants are in an appropriate state. The added step is a coordination step, which requires that a sequence of messages flows back and forth among the participants and the coordinator of the transaction. The added step has resulted in this process being referred to as the three-phase commit protocol. The added cost with this protocol includes the additional coordination messages and the control protocol, which must determine if the majority rules or if the actions must be unanimous. More will be said on these voting protocols when we look at update synchronization protocols.

10.7 UPDATE SYNCHRONIZATION

When replicated data items exist in the distributed database repositories on the database system, they result in increased data item availability, but they also introduce a problem in maintaining the concurrency between the replicas in the database system. There are a variety of protocols that have been developed for the maintenance of distributed replicas. These protocols all deal with the coordination of updates in the database to keep the copies in a relatively consistent state. Numerous techniques exist for coordinating updates in a distributed database system, including the following.

- Centralized locking
- Primary copy update
- Distributed cooperative views
- Unanimous agreement
- Moving primary

The centralized locking protocol is one of the simplest to implement, but also is one of the most costly. In this update synchronization protocol, all lock requests on data items are presented to a centralized lock manager located on one node in the distributed system (Figure 10.12a). The centralized lock manager in turn then issues the same lock to all requested copies of the data item to be write locked for update. Once all of the update locks on the named data item are collected throughout the database system, the update can proceed. The central lock manager can then allow the requester to perform its in-

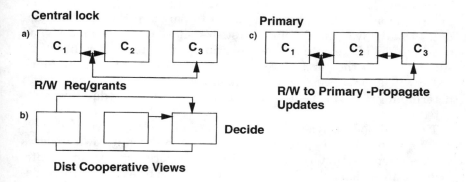

Figure 10.12   Update synchronization protocols

tended update once the locks have all been acquired. A problem with the centralized approach is the overhead involved in having all lock request messages flowing into one site and all lock commands flowing out of the same site. This form of locking will result in an excessive load on the central lock site. The lock manager must also handle the lock requests for reads, making this expensive even for a read-only or read-mostly database system.

The primary copy update protocol improves on this slightly by assigning a single site as the primary site for updates of data items. All updates are directed to this site, where they are coordinated to guarantee correct update of the database's data items. Once the update is accepted by the primary, the primary then propagates the update to the other sites in the system. The result is a database system where there is one node that is 100 percent accurate at all times; all the other nodes represent some past historical shadow of the primary. The other nodes in the system are constantly catching up with the primary node. A problem with this protocol, similar to centralized locking, is the loading that will occur on the primary site. If updates exceed reads by a large margin, the system will come to a halt trying to handle the volume of updates, making this a poor choice for systems with such a loading. The advantage of this technique, however, may be in its ability to offload the cost of update to only one site, and to allow for unrestricted reads to nonprimary copies of the data. If the reading transactions do not require fully consistent and up-to-date data, they can find any free replica and use this for their data (Figure 10.12c).

An improvement to this protocol can be found by examining the weakness and making a slight alteration. By allowing the primary update site to be rotated to the transaction requesting the update, or by allowing for some number of primaries, the update service can be greatly improved. One technique looks to partition the database updates evenly over the database system's sites. Each site is assigned some portion of the database as the primary update site for that data. All updates for the particular data items are directed to the appropriate site. The only issue with this approach is the added overhead in determining on which site the particular primary updater was located.

The third update synchronization scheme is called distributed cooperative views. In this protocol each site coordinates its own updates for transactions that run on its site as the primary execution site. These transactions use the local site update facilities as the coordinator of the system update. The coordinator uses a scheme whereby the updates are issued to all sites and the sites respond with the outcome of the update (Figure 10.12b). If the outcome meets the criteria of the decision protocol, then the update is deemed correct and the synchronization protocol completes its processing, releasing any resources used in the update's processing. The key to this protocol is to come up with a decision protocol that will ensure adequate correctness without excessive overhead. A few schemes have been postulated and constructed around the concept of majority voting. In these schemes, to either read or write a data item, transactions must collect answers from several of sites. If the response exceeds some given *majority*, the read or write is then accepted as accurate.

The last update synchronization scheme is referred to as the unanimous agreement policy. In this protocol an update is performed by issuing the update from the coordination site to all the other sites in the database. The participant sites accept the request and must determine if they can perform the update correctly. If the update can be performed, the participants issue a prepare to update vote to the coordinator. If the coordinator collects the prepared to update from all the participants, then the update can be performed; if not, the update must be rejected and cannot be performed anywhere. This represents an all-or-nothing protocol, which guarantees that the copies of all data in the database are totally accurate and up to date.

10.8 DISTRIBUTED RECOVERY

Recovery is required by database systems to guarantee the survival and correctness of the database in the event of failures. Distributed database systems require the same features. Database recovery must provide policies and mechanisms to recover from media failures, processing platform failures, and transaction failures. Failures for distributed databases include those in the conventional case, but also include partial failure of the processing platform, since now it is composed of numerous processors, and both partial and total communications failures.

Under normal database operational conditions, maintaining the correctness and consistency of the database is the task of the transaction processing facilities. The recovery manager is an important part of these facilities and has the function of preserving database correctness, consistency, and transaction ACID properties in the event of a system failure. This requires that the recovery manager be tightly woven into the fabric of the remaining data management functions.

The problem of recovery is well understood within the conventional nondistributed database realm. In distributed databases the problem is much more complex due to the possibility of multiple site failures, communication media failures, and network partitioning due to partial network failures. Traditional solution methods will not operate correctly within this environment due to the added variables that must be considered.

Recovery in a distributed environment begins with the infrastructure. Due to the fundamental construction of distributed computer systems, recovery is readily supported. A distributed system fundamentally supports redundancy in hardware and can support redundancy in software. Recovery requires that the *state* of the transactions and the database be preserved so that they can be restored upon the detection of a failure. To recover from site failures requires the logging of transaction operations by more than one site and the maintenance of applications and support software for a site on more than one machine. By maintaining a hot spare, the failure of a site will have little effect on overall operations. An alternative to a hot spare requires additional support services and logging facilities. These would be used to determine the status of other resources in the system and whether they could suppport the failed software to get it back into service.

Distributed recovery requires a system service that can maintain a mapping of the resources in the system and maintain the condition they are in at any point in time. The system application and support software must be loadable from multiple sites in the system and must be configurable on any of a number of sites in the system. The recovery manager must be able to configure around network failures or reallocate software such that a partitioned network can continue operations as two separate systems until they are brought back on line (Figure 10.13). Once brought together the partitioned sites must be able to extract the logs from each other and reapply these to the other partition to bring the entire system ultimately to a consistent state.

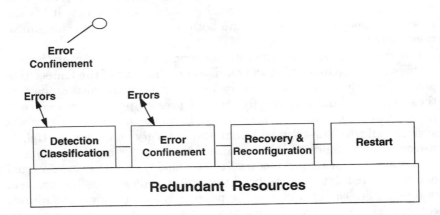

Figure 10.13 Recovery manager components

The main emphasis in recovery, from a database perspective, is that the redundant resources improve the capabilities of the system to readily and easily recover from failures. The distribution adds some additional concerns but none that require very elaborate workarounds. The only added software is configuration management software and redundancy management software to maintain a system's resource map and to maintain replicas to aid in the recovery process. Just as in the conventional case, logging of network actions will aid in the ability to recover the database in the event of a communications media failure.

11

Real-Time Database Systems

Victor Fay Wolfe
Lisa Cingiser DiPippo

11.1 INTRODUCTION

Real-time databases manage time-constrained data and time-constrained transactions. They are useful in systems such as automated manufacturing, avionics, military command, control and communication, and programmed stock trading. In each of these applications, a computer system uses environmental data as input and must produce output to control its environment. Since data in the system represent the "current" state of the environment, these data are constrained to have been recorded recently enough to be considered valid; that is, "current" sensor readings or "current" stock prices may be constrained to be no more than a few seconds old. Since environmental control must often be performed within a certain time interval to be correct, the transactions that operate on the data are also time-constrained; that is, a military vehicle's evasive action, determined based on a transaction retrieving environmental data from the real-time database, may have to be performed by a certain deadline to be correct. This chapter describes the issues, research, and actual implementations of real-time database management systems.

A real-time database is a component of a *real-time system*. A real-time system is one in which timing constraints, such as start times, deadlines, and periods, must be met for the application to be correct. There has been a great deal of work in real-time systems that influences real-time database design. We summarize this work in Section 11.2.

The presence of real-time requirements adds requirements to real-time database management. Typical database management systems enforce logical consistency constraints only, whereas real-time databases have *temporal consistency constraints*, such as validity intervals for data and time constraints for transaction execution, that must also be enforced. In Section 11.3, we describe the additional dimension of temporal consistency constraints and the requirements these constraints impose on the real-time database management system.

To rationalize and express these constraints, several models have been proposed for real-time database systems. These models incorporate various aspects of traditional database models and various aspects of temporal consistency requirements. We describe two relational models and one object-oriented real-time database model in Section 11.4.

In the rest of the chapter, Section 11.5 describes two existing commercial real-time database management systems, one academic prototyping effort, and the Real-Time SQL standardization efforts. Section 11.6 summarizes current research in real-time database systems, focusing mostly on transaction scheduling and concurrency control. Section 11.7 summarizes what real-time database technology is available and discusses open questions in real-time database design.

11.2 REAL-TIME SYSTEMS

In a real-time system, timing constraints must be met for the application to be correct. This requirement typically comes from the system interacting with the physical environment. The environment produces stimuli, which must be accepted by the real-time system within timing constraints. The environment further requires control output, which must be produced within timing constraints.

One of the main misconceptions about real-time computing is that it is equivalent to fast computing. This myth can be challenged by arguing that computing speed is often measured in average-case performance, whereas, to guarantee timing behavior, in many real-time systems worst-case performance should be used; that is, in a delicate application, such as a nuclear reactor or avionics control, where timing constraints *must* be met, worst-case performance must be used when designing and analyzing the system. Thus, although speed is often a necessary component of a real-time system, it is often not sufficient. Instead, *predictably meeting timing constraints* is sufficient in real-time system design.

This section describes the characteristics and requirements of real-time systems. It also describes work in real-time operating system scheduling, which is important when considering how real-time database temporal consistency can be enforced.

11.2.1 Real-Time System Requirements

Real-time systems require that timing constraints be expressed and enforced, and their violations handled. The unit of time-constrained execution is called a *task*. In a real-time database, time-constrained transactions are considered tasks. Timing constraint expression can take the form of start times, deadlines, and periods for tasks. Timing constraint enforcement requires predictable bounds on task behavior. The handling of timing constraint violations depends on the tasks' requirements: whether they are *hard, firm,* or *soft* real time. We now examine each of these aspects of timing constraints.

Expressing Timing Constraints Most real-time systems specify a subset of the following constraints.

- An *earliest start time* constraint specifies an absolute time before which the task may not start; that is, the task must wait for the specified time before it may start.

- A *latest start time* constraint specifies an absolute time before which the task must start; that is, if the task has not started by the specified time, an error has occurred. Latest start times are useful to detect potential violations of planned schedules or eventual deadline violations before they actually occur.

- A *deadline* specifies an absolute time before which the task must complete.

Frequently, timing constraints will appear as *periodic execution constraints*. A periodic constraint specifies earliest start times and deadlines at regular time intervals for repeated instances of a task. Typically, a *period frame* is established for each instance of the (repeated) task. As shown in Figure 11.1, period frame i specifies the default earliest start time and deadline for the ith instance of the task. When periodic execution is originally started, the first frame is established, at time S in Figure 11.1. For periodic execution with period p, the ith frame starts at time $s + (i - 1)p$ and completes at time $s + (i)p$. As this indicates, the end of frame i is the beginning of frame $i + 1$. Each instance of a task may execute anywhere within its period frame.

Figure 11.1 Periodic executions

Modes of Real Time Real-time constraints are classified as hard, firm, or soft, depending on the consequences of the constraint being violated.

A task with a *hard* real-time constraint has disastrous consequences if its constraint is violated. This characteristic is depicted in Figure 11.2a, where the task causes a large negative value to the system if its deadline is missed. Many constraints in life-critical systems, such as nuclear reactor control and military vehicle control, are hard real-time constraints.

A task with a *firm* real-time constraint has no value to the system if its constraint is violated. This characteristic is depicted in Figure 11.2b, where the task's value goes to zero after its deadline. Many financial applications have firm constraints with no value if a deadline is missed.

A task with a *soft* real-time constraint has decreasing, but usually nonnegative, value to the system if its constraint is violated. This characteristic is depicted in Figure 11.2c, where the task's value decreases after its deadline. For most applications, most tasks have soft real-time constraints. Graphic display updates are one of the many examples of tasks with soft real-time constraints.

In some systems the mode of real time is captured in a task's *importance* level. In these systems task importance is categorized according to the mode of its timing constraint (hard, firm, soft). In other systems, importance is more general and tasks can be assigned importance relative to each other over a wider granularity of levels. Note

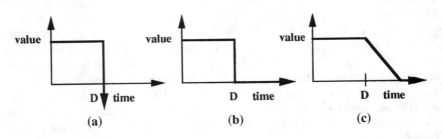

Figure 11.2 Modes of real time

that importance is not the same as *priority*. Priority, which is discussed in more detail in Section 11.2.2, is a relative value used to make scheduling decisions. Often priority is a function of importance, but it also can depend on timing constraints, or some combination of these, or other task traits.

Predictability: In order to predictably meet timing constraints, it must be possible to accurately analyze timing behavior. To analyze timing behavior, the scheduling algorithm for each resource and the amount of time that tasks use each resource must be known. To fully guarantee this timing behavior, these resource utilizations should be worst-case values, although some soft real-time systems can tolerate average-case values that offer no strong guarantee.

Determining the resource usage time of tasks is often difficult. Results that can be obtained are often pessimistic worst cases with very low probability of occurring. Consider CPU utilization, which is one of the easier utilizations to determine. To establish a worst-case CPU utilization, all conditional branches in the task must be assumed to take their worst path, and all loops and recursion must be assumed to have some bounded number of instances. Also, other task behavior, such as whether the task can be preempted from the CPU while waiting for other system resources, must be considered; that is, if a task requires dynamic memory allocation, is it swapped off the CPU awaiting the memory allocation? CPU utilization is only one factor in a task's resource requirements. A task also needs resources such as main memory, disk accesses, network buffers, network bandwidth, I/O devices, and so forth. Furthermore, the use of these resources is interrelated and thus cannot be computed in isolation. The problem worsens in database systems where "logical" resources, such as locks on data structures and database buffers, are additional resources to be considered. There has been work in determining worst-case execution times, but in general this work makes limiting assumptions and/or produces very pessimistic results. Still, in order to guarantee, or at least analyze, the adherence to real-time constraints, resource utilizations of tasks must be known, so these rough estimates are used.

Assuming that worst-case resource utilizations are known, analyzing timing behavior for predictability depends on the scheduling algorithms used. In the next subsection we discuss several real-time scheduling techniques and the forms of analysis that these techniques facilitate.

Imprecision: The introduction of timing constraints adds another dimension to real-time computing: It may need to be *imprecise*; that is, due to time "running out," the results produced by a task or set of tasks may not be exactly correct. In systems where timely but less accurate results are better than late exact results, imprecision may be tolerated; that is, an air traffic control system may need a quick approximate position of an incoming aircraft rather than a late exact answer. Often the imprecision that is allowed must be within a specified bound; that is, the position data might have to be accurate within a few meters. More accurate data are desirable, but can be sacrificed if timing constraints do not permit it.

11.2.2 Scheduling

Real-time scheduling essentially maps to a *bin-packing problem*, where tasks with known resource utilizations are the boxes, and the timing constraints establish the size of the bin; that is, each task can be considered a "box," whose size is its utilization of the resource being scheduled. The start times and deadlines of the tasks establish the boundaries of a "bin," or collection of bins, in which the boxes must be packed. The bin-packing problem is NP-hard, so optimal real-time scheduling, in general, is an NP-hard problem. However, heuristics have been developed that yield optimal schedules under some strong assumptions, or near-optimal results under less-restrictive assumptions.

There are many scheduling algorithms. Typically, a scheduling algorithm assigns *priorities* to tasks. The priority assignment establishes a partial ordering among tasks. Whenever a scheduling decision is made, the scheduler selects the task(s) with highest priority to use the resource. There are several characteristics that differentiate scheduling algorithms.

- *Preemptive versus nonpreemptive:* If the algorithm is preemptive, the task currently using the resource can be replaced by another task (typically of higher priority).

- *Hard versus soft real time:* To be useful in systems with hard real-time constraints, the real-time scheduling technique should allow analysis of the hard timing constraints to determine if the constraints will be predictably met. For firm and soft real time, predictability is desirable, but often a scheduling technique that can demonstrate a best-effort, near-optimal performance, is acceptable.

- *Dynamic versus static:* In static scheduling algorithms, all tasks and their characteristics are known before scheduling decisions are made. Typically, task priorities are assigned before run time and are not changed. Dynamic scheduling algorithms allow task sets to change and usually allow for task priorities to change. Dynamic scheduling decisions are made at run time.

- *Single versus multiple resources*: Single-resource scheduling manages one resource in isolation. In many well-known scheduling algorithms, this resource is a single CPU. Multiple-resource scheduling algorithms recognize that most tasks need multiple resources and schedule several resources. End-to-end schedulers schedule all resources required by the tasks.

Rate-Monotonic and Earliest-Deadline-First Scheduling For a set of independent, periodic tasks with known execution times, it has been proven that *rate-monotonic* CPU scheduling is optimal. Here optimal means that if any scheduling algorithm can cause all of the tasks in a set to meet their deadlines, then rate-monotonic can too. Rate-monotonic scheduling is preemptive, static, single-resource scheduling that can be used for hard real time. Priority is assigned according to the rate at which a periodic task needs to execute: The higher the rate, which also means the shorter the period, the higher the priority. A supplemental result facilitates real-time analysis by proving that if the CPU utilization is less than approximately 69 percent, then the task set will always meet its deadlines. For *dynamic* priority assignment that is also preemptive and single resource, earliest-deadline-first scheduling is optimal, and any task set using it with a utilization less than 100 percent will meet all deadlines.

Such results come with strong assumptions. Among these assumptions is one that requires tasks to be independent. Subsequent work has relaxed many of these assumptions. It has been shown that task sets where the tasks can coordinate via mechanisms such as semaphores can still be analyzed if they use *priority-inheritance* protocols. In these protocols, a lower-priority task that blocks a higher-priority task (e.g., by holding a semaphore) inherits the priority of the higher-priority task during the blocking. With priority-inheritance techniques, *priority inversion*, which is the time that a higher-priority task is blocked by lower-priority tasks, can be bounded and factored into the worst-case execution time of each task. Utilization analysis can then be used to determine if timing constraints will be met. Nonperiodic tasks can also be accommodated using a *sporadic server*, which periodically handles nonperiodic tasks. Real-Time Mach is a real-time operating system that employs many of these techniques.

POSIX Scheduling The POSIX real-time operating system standards offer rudimentary real-time scheduling support in UNIX-like systems. The POSIX standard mandates that the CPU scheduling be preemptive and priority-based, with a minimum of 32 priorities (see Figure 11.3). Individual implementations may offer more priorities, but the

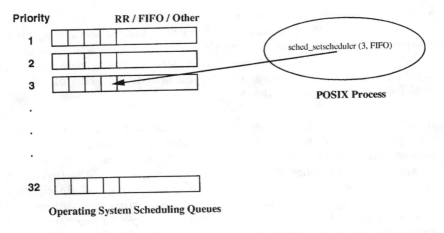

Figure 11.3 Real-time scheduling in POSIX operating systems

minimum is 32. The scheduling algorithm is simple: The highest-priority ready task executes, possibly preempting a lower-priority task. Tasks can dynamically change their own priority level or, in some cases, the priority level of other tasks. Within a priority level, tasks may be scheduled round-robin (with a system-determined time quantum), or first-in-first-out (which is essentially round-robin with an infinite time quantum). This intrapriority scheduling is an unfortunate choice for real-time systems, since it is not cognizant of timing constraints. Despite this limitation, rate-monotonic and earliest-deadline-first real-time schedulers have been built on real-time POSIX-compliant operating systems.

Resource Reservations Real-time scheduling techniques have been developed that dynamically can handle arriving tasks using multiple resources. These techniques are based on resource reservations where each task attempts to reserve a time slot for itself during which it is guaranteed use of all resources that it requires. Tasks are allowed to make resource reservation requests based on a priority; the highest priority makes the request first. Priority is a weighted function of the task's deadline, execution time, and resource use. These techniques also allow for limited backtracking, so that if allowing a task to make reservations before another task would cause deadlines to be missed, another pattern of reservations may be tried. These techniques achieve near-optimal results. Note that although these reservation techniques are not optimal, they have much less stringent assumptions than other reservation techniques. The Spring kernel is based on these scheduling techniques.

Scheduling Imprecise Computation Several algorithms have been proposed for scheduling tasks that allow imprecise computation. In these algorithms, tasks are decomposed into a *mandatory* part and an *optional* part. The mandatory part is considered hard; the optional part is considered soft. These algorithms attempt to schedule all mandatory parts of tasks and to schedule optional parts to minimize some error metric. The error metric indicates the consequences of not executing an optional part. There are several error metrics, each with a different scheduling algorithm that minimizes it; that is, in systems with task-importance levels, error might be weighted by each task's importance. The accompanying algorithm schedules optional parts of higher-importance tasks whenever possible. Although this is a good first step toward managing the imprecision in real-time systems, further research is needed to guarantee that resulting imprecision is within system limits.

11.3 REAL-TIME DATABASE REQUIREMENTS

Real-time databases have all of the requirements of traditional databases, such as managing access to structured, shared, permanent data, but they can also require management of *time-constrained data* and *time-constrained transactions*. Furthermore, to facilitate analysis of timing behavior, certain real-time database functions may need to exhibit predictable timing behavior.

11.3.1 Temporal Consistency

Many requirements in a traditional database come from the desire to preserve the logical consistency of data and transactions—for example, typical database management systems strive to maintain logical consistency by enforcing serializability of transactions and operations on each data value. A real-time database additionally requires enforcement of *temporal consistency* constraints. In a real-time database there are four forms of consistency constraints (summarized in Table 11.1): transaction logical consistency, data logical consistency, transaction temporal consistency, and data temporal consistency.

Transaction Logical Consistency Transaction logical consistency constrains the values of results produced by transactions. It is supported in most traditional database management systems—for example, *serializability* is a traditional transaction logical consistency correctness criterion. It requires that the results of transaction execution be equivalent to the results of some serial execution of the transactions. Techniques such as two-phase locking are designed to preserve seri-

Table 11.1   Forms of Consistency for a Real-Time Database

	Temporal Consistency	Logical Consistency
Transaction	e.g., Start, Deadline, Period requirement	e.g., Serializability
Data	e.g., Absolute validity interval	e.g., Serializable operations

alizability and, therefore, transaction logical consistency. In a real-time database, traditional transaction logical consistency may be "relaxed" to allow bounded imprecision, as will be discussed in Section 11.3.2.

Data Logical Consistency   Data logical consistency is supported by most traditional database management systems. Range constraints, such as one constraining certain data values to be nonnegative, are examples of data logical consistency constraints. Some consistency constraints are preserved by requiring that basic read and write operations on data be serializable. This can be done by typical read/write locking. Like transaction logical consistency, in a real-time database, data logical consistency may be "relaxed."

Transaction Temporal Consistency   Transaction temporal consistency constraints require that transactions be treated as real-time tasks (see Section 11.2) with timing constraints such as deadlines, start times, and periods. The constraints may be hard, firm, or soft. Violations of the timing constraints should be treated as a consistency violation by the database management system and appropriately recovered from.

Data Temporal Consistency   Data temporal consistency constrains how old a data item may be and still be considered valid. These constraints come from the fact that data used by time-critical applications often must closely reflect the current state of the application environment. Data are collected at discrete intervals and hence represent an approximation of reality. As time passes, this approximation becomes less accurate, until it reaches a point where the value is no longer reflective of the state of the environment. It is at this point in time that we say the data value is no longer temporally consistent. There are two forms of data temporal consistency constraints.

- *Absolute Temporal Consistency*—where a data item's age must be within a certain interval of the current time—for example, a sensor value might have to have been recorded within two seconds of the current time to be considered absolutely temporally consistent.

- *Relative Temporal Consistency*—where several data values must have been recorded with the same time interval; that is, if a sensor data value representing the speed of a radar track and another representing the last measured position of the track are used to derive the new position, they may have to have been recorded within one second of each other for the derivation to be valid. This is a relative temporal consistency constraint between the speed and the last measured position data items.

11.3.2 Bounded Imprecision

As discussed in Section 11.2, real-time constraints may make precise computation impossible. In a database, a value is imprecise if it differs from the corresponding value resulting from each possible serializable schedule of the same transactions. In many applications, some imprecision is tolerated; that is, it may be sufficient for the position of a radar track to be within a few meters of its exact value. Although imprecision may be allowed, it must always be bounded. Thus, database logical consistency constraints for many real-time applications do not require the exact logical consistency that typical non-real-time databases do. Instead, the real-time database logical consistency constraints can allow bounded imprecision.

Imprecision can result from data management itself due to inherent conflicts between temporal and logical constraints. These conflicts make it difficult for a database management system to maintain all four forms of consistency constraints that are present in a real-time database (see Table 11.1 in Section 11.3.1)—for example, in order to maintain precise transaction logical consistency (e.g., serializability), a transaction t_{update} that updates a piece of data x may be blocked by another transaction t_{read} that is reading x. If x is getting "old," it would be in the interest of its temporal consistency to allow t_{update} to execute. However, this execution could violate the precise data logical consistency of x or the precise transaction logical consistency of t_{read}. Thus, there is a tradeoff between maintaining temporal consistency and maintaining logical consistency. If logical consistency is chosen, then there is the possibility that a piece of data may become old or that a transaction may violate a timing constraint. If, on the other hand, temporal consistency is chosen, the consistency of the data or of the transactions involved may be compromised.

Priority inversion, mentioned in Section 11.2, is another example of the conflict between logical and temporal consistency. Priority inversion occurs because a lower-priority task/transaction is not preempted from a resource when a higher-priority task/transaction needs the resource. Optimal scheduling results (which support temporal consistency) require such a preemption. Thus, priority inversion is the result of choosing precise logical consistency over a potential violation of temporal consistency.

A consequence of relaxing logical consistency, such as allowing nonserializable schedules or sequences of data operations, is that logical imprecision may accumulate in the data in the database and in the transactions' views of the data. Recall the example described earlier in which an update transaction t_{update} wishes to preempt a reading transaction t_{read}, in order to maintain the temporal consistency of the data. If this preemption is allowed, t_{read} may get an imprecise view of the data, because it may read the value written by an uncommitted update transaction. The imprecision of a data item may be local to the view of a single transaction, such as when one transaction reads data written by another uncommitted transaction. A data item may also be imprecise with respect to future transactions that access it, such as when two transactions that write to the data item interleave.

Since imprecision may be inevitable in a real-time database, the database management system is required to manage the imprecision and bound it.

11.3.3 Predictability

As discussed in Section 11.2, predictable execution may be important in certain real-time applications. As a component of such systems, the real-time database may need to exhibit predictable behavior. This characteristic may generate several requirements for the database management system.

- Bounded worst-case execution times of all database primitive commands
- Bounded sizes of tables and data structures
- Bounded use of memory
- Bounded waits for database buffers
- Bounded waits for secondary storage retrievals
- Bounded blocking due to concurrency control
- Bounded numbers and lengths of transaction aborts
- Bounded indexing for locating data items
- Use of real-time transaction scheduling that facilitates predictability

As in all real-time applications, achieving such predictability often requires either making pessimistic worst-case assumptions, using drastically simplified subsystems, or both.

11.3.4 Transactions

There are three types of transactions in a real-time database: *sensor* transactions, *update* transactions, and *read-only* transactions. All of these transactions can have temporal consistency requirements. Sensor transactions are write-only transactions that obtain the state of the environment and write the sensed data to the database. Sensor transactions are typically periodic. Update transactions can both read from and write to the database either periodically or aperiodically. Update transactions can be used to write values derived from computations or user input. Read-only transactions, such as some user queries, read data from the database and can also be either periodic or aperiodic.

Conventional transactions are structured to enforce the ACID properties. These properties differentiate transactions from other tasks by facilitating reasoning about the logical consistency of transactions and data. However, the ACID properties ignore the temporal consistency requirements found in real-time databases.

To better support real-time applications, real-time databases redefine the ACID requirements to allow better support for temporal consistency while maintaining support for logical consistency. These definitions utilize semantic information to determine to what degree the ACID properties must be enforced. The redefinition of ACID properties for real-time transactions includes the following.

- *Atomic*—An atomic transaction implies all-or-nothing execution of the transaction. For real-time transactions, atomic execution is selectively applied to those pieces of the transaction that have a critical need for totally consistent data, instead of the transaction as a whole. Also, due to allowed logical imprecision, a "rollback" of a transaction in the "nothing" alternative of all-or-nothing may not roll back to the original state. Instead, the transaction may be allowed to end in an inconsistent state as long as the resulting imprecision is bounded.

- *Consistent*—As discussed earlier, the consistency that typical ACID transactions seek to maintain is precise logical consistency. Real-time transactions must support a tradeoff between temporal consistency and logical consistency. This tradeoff can introduce bounded temporal or logical imprecision.

- *Isolated*—Conventional transactions are required to have the property of appearing to have isolated execution. This implies that there be no dependencies in execution between transactions. In real-time databases, transactions may need to communicate and synchronize with other transactions to perform control functions. Transactions may need to synchronize on external time boundaries, system events, another transaction's results or end conditions, or they may need to perform some integrated set of tasks for an application that requires sharing of system state knowledge.

- *Durable*—The durability property of transactions implies that the results of a transaction are persistent and permanent. In a real-time database system, data must still be persistent, but not necessarily permanent. Temporal consistency constraints may indicate that some data are invalid and thus no longer needed. Another example is a circular queue data structure, which is commonly used in real-time databases to bound memory usage. This structure requires deletion of the oldest item when the queue is full and a new item is added. Durability of data must be specified semantically by the constraints and structure of the data, not by an implicit feature of a database or by a transaction's execution.

11.3.5 Summary of Real-Time Database Requirements

Most of the requirements discussed in this section are also specified in the Navy's Next-Generation Computer Resources Database Standards Requirements Document and in the specification for Real-Time SQL (see Section 11.5.4). To summarize, we list the requirements for real-time databases (which are assumed to be in addition to the requirements of non-real-time databases).

1. *Modes of Real Time*—A real-time database management system may support hard real-time, firm real-time, soft real-time, and/or non-real-time modes of operation.

2. *Real-Time Transactions*—A real-time database management system requires the ability to allow users to issue real-time transactions, where selected ACID properties are applied to parts of the transaction (note that ACID properties are not required on an entire transaction), and start events, deadlines, periods, and importance of the real-time transactions are enforced.

3. *Data Temporal Consistency*—A real-time database management system requires the enforcement of absolute and relative data temporal consistency constraints.

4. *Real-Time Scheduling*—A real-time database management system requires real-time transaction and operation scheduling for all resources allocated in the database system. The scheduling algorithm(s) should attempt to maximize meeting timing constraints and criticality (or some synthesis of these two attributes) of transactions, as well as attempting to maintain both logical and temporal consistency of data. Scheduling for hard real time requires support for analysis of predictable timing behavior.

5. *Bounded Imprecision*—A real-time database management system may allow logical and temporal imprecision of data. It must provide the capability to constrain these imprecisions.

6. *Timing Constraint Violation Recovery*—A real-time database management system requires support for recovering from timing constraint violations of transactions and violations of temporal consistency of data.

7. *Predictability*—A real-time database management system is required to specify the probabilistic and worst-case utilization amount and time for all resources (e.g., CPU time, memory, devices, data objects) of every DBMS function that can be used in hard real-time operation.

11.4 REAL-TIME DATABASE MODELS

Several models have been developed to express the characteristics of real-time databases. We review two general models and one object-oriented real-time database model in this section.

11.4.1 Ramamritham Model

Ramamritham presents a model of a real-time database in which both absolute and relative timing constraints are expressed on data. Transactions are characterized by the types and implications of their timing constraints.

Real-Time Data A data object in the Ramamritham model is represented by $d{:}(value,avi,timestamp)$, where d_{value} represents the real-world data value, d_{avi} is the absolute validity interval of the data item, and $d_{timestamp}$ is the time at which d_{avi} begins. Absolute temporal consistency of a data object d is maintained at a time t if $\mid t - d_{timestamp} \mid \le d_{avi}$.

A set of data objects used to derive another data object is stored in a relative consistency set, R. R_{rvi} is the relative validity interval of the set. Relative temporal consistency is maintained as long as the timestamps of each data object in R are within R_{rvi} of each other. In other words, $\forall \; d, \; d' \in R \mid d_{timestamp} - d'_{timestamp} \mid \leq R_{rvi}$. The timestamp of derived data is a function of the timestamps of the data used to derive it.

Consider the following example: Let $temperature_{avi} = 5$, $pressure_{avi} = 10$, $R = \{temperature, pressure\}$, and $R_{rvi} = 2$. If $current\_time = 100$, then $temperature = (347, 5, 95)$ and $pressure = (50, 10, 97)$ are temporally consistent. However, $temperature = (347, 5, 95)$ and $pressure = (50, 10, 92)$ are not temporally consistent, because even though the absolute consistency requirements are met, R's relative consistency is violated.

Real-Time Transactions   Transactions in the Ramamritham model are characterized along three dimensions: the way in which the data are used by a transaction, the nature of the timing constraints, and the implication of a missed deadline.

Real-time transactions can use data in one of three ways. *Write-only transactions* write to the database. Sensor transactions are generally write-only. *Update transactions* derive data by reading and performing calculations and store these data in the database. *Read-only transactions* read data from the database.

Timing constraints on transactions come from temporal consistency requirements of the data or from requirements imposed on system reaction time—for example, an update transaction may be required to execute every five seconds because the data that it writes have an absolute validity interval of five seconds. On the other hand, another transaction may need to be performed within a certain amount of time to satisfy external requirements—for example, the constraint:

If *temperature* > 1,000,
then *within* 10 *secs* add coolant to reactor

requires that the transaction to add coolant be executed within ten seconds. The effect of missing a deadline is the third way of characterizing transactions. The model uses *hard, firm*, and *soft*, as previously described, as values of this characteristic.

11.4.2 Kim/Son Model

Kim and Son present a model of real-time databases that draws some of its concepts from the Ramamritham model. The model has been broadened to include non-real-time data and to classify transactions based upon the type of application in which they may be used.

Real-Time Data Objects The Kim/Son model divides data objects into two types: *continuous* and *discrete*. Continuous objects are objects whose value can become invalid with time. Such objects can be obtained directly from a sensor (*image object*) or computed from the values of other objects (*derived object*). Discrete data objects are non-real-time objects in that their values do not become obsolete with time.

Each continuous data object has associated with it a *timestamp*, which tells when the current value of the data object was obtained. The *absolute validity duration* of a continuous data object is the length of time during which the value of the object is considered valid. A *relative validity duration* is associated with a set of data objects Σ_y used to derive a new data object y. A set Σ_y is relatively temporally consistent if the *temporal distance* between y and any data object in Σ_y is not greater than the relative validity duration rvd_y.

Real-Time Transactions Real-time transactions in the Kim/Son model are characterized by: the implication of missing a deadline (hard, critical [firm], soft real time); arrival pattern (periodic, sporadic, or aperiodic); data access pattern (write-only, read-only, update, or random); data requirement (known or unknown); run-time requirement (known or unknown); and accessed data type (continuous, discrete, or both).

Given the types of data objects described above and the characterization of real-time transactions, there are hundreds of possible transaction classes. However, only some of these classes are feasible in a real-time database; that is, it does not make sense to have a hard real-time transaction with random arrival pattern, random data access set, and unknown execution time. The Kim/Son model classifies transactions based upon how an application may use them. Table 11.2 summarizes the transaction classes.

Class I transactions are hard real-time periodic transactions. Such transactions have all data and run-time requirements available in advance. They represent the only writing source for continuous data objects, and thus it is feasible to guarantee their hard timing constraints. This class of transactions can be further broken down into subclasses.

- Class IA transactions maintain the temporal consistency of continuous data objects. They are write-only, and, since each such transaction is the only writer to a continuous data object, there are no conflicts between Class IA transactions.

- Class IB transactions are update transactions. They read some data objects, compute new values, and write to derived data objects. They do not conflict with other Class I transactions because each data object has only one writer.

- Class IC transactions periodically retrieve data values from the database. They are read-only transactions with hard deadlines.

Class II transactions are read-only transactions with some critical timing constraints. These timing constraints come from system response time requirements and not from data temporal consistency requirements. Because Class II transactions can access both discrete data objects (which require serializable access) and continuous data objects, timing constraints cannot always be met. However, since the only source of unpredictability in Class II transactions is the data requirement, the transaction execution time is a function of only one variable.

All transactions not belonging to any of the other classes can be categorized as Class III transactions. They have either soft or firm deadlines, their data and run-time requirements are not always known, and they access both continuous and discrete data objects.

Most real-time applications have transactions in each of the above classes. Consider a medical information system, for example. Class IA transactions are those that update the dynamic physical status of a critical patient from the sensor devices, such as blood pressure, heart rate, and body temperature. Transactions that write derived information from the raw data are Class IB transactions. Transactions monitoring the physical status of the patient can be categorized as Class IC transactions. A Class II transaction in this example might be a decision-making transaction during a critical operation on a patient. Such a transaction may access not only the patient's current physical status, but also his or her medical history. Class III transactions in this example include record-keeping transactions, such as retrieving weight or height.

11.4.3 RTSORAC Model

The RTSORAC model incorporates features that support the requirements of a real-time database into an extended object-oriented model. It has three components that model the properties of a real-time object-oriented database: *objects*, *relationships*, and *transactions*.

Objects Objects represent database entities. Each *object* consists of five components $\langle N, A, M, C, CF \rangle$, where N is a unique name or identifier, A is a set of attributes, M is a set of methods, C is a set of constraints, and CF is a compatibility function. Figure 11.4 illustrates an example of a **Train** object for storing information about a train control system in a database.

Table 11.2 Classification of Kim/Son Real-Time Transactions

	Class I			Class II	Class III
Property	A	B	C		
Timing Constraints	Hard			Critical	Soft or Firm
Arrival Pattern	Periodic			Sporadic	Aperiodic
Data access Pattern	Write-only	Update	Read-only	Read-only	No restriction
Data requirement	Known			Unknown	Unknown
Run-time requirement	Known			Unknown	Unknown
Update data type	Image	Derived	N / A	N / A	Discrete
Correctness criteria	Temporal Consistency			Both	Logical Consistency
Transaction schedule	Nonserializable			Both	Serializable
Performance goal	100% guarantee			Statistical	No Guarantee, but best-effort

Each attribute of an RTSORAC object is characterized by $\langle Na, V, T, I \rangle$. Na is the name of the attribute. The V field is used to store the value of the attribute, and can be of some abstract data type. The T field is used to store the time at which the value was recorded. The I field of an attribute is used to store the amount of imprecision associated with the attribute, and is of the same type as the value field V.

Each method of an object is of the form $\langle Nm, Arg, Exc, Op, OC \rangle$. Nm is the name of the method. Arg is a set of arguments for the method, where each argument has the same components as an attribute, and is used to pass information in and/or out of the method. Exc is a set of exceptions that may be raised by the method to signal that the method has terminated abnormally. Op is a set of operations that represents the actions of the method. These operations include statements for conditional branching, looping, I/O, and reads and writes to an attribute's value, time, and imprecision fields.

The OC characteristic of a method is a set of operation constraints. An operation constraint is of the form $\langle Noc, OpSet, Pred, ER \rangle$, where Noc is the name of the operation constraint, $OpSet$ is a subset of the

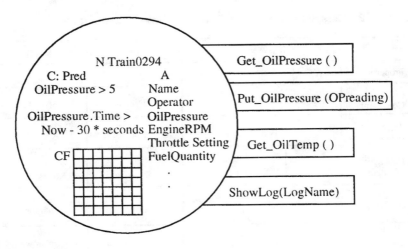

Figure 11.4   Example of Train object

operations in *Op*, *Pred* is a predicate (Boolean expression), and *ER* is an enforcement rule. The predicate is specified over *OpSet* to express precedence constraints, execution constraints, and timing constraints. The enforcement rule is used to express the action to take if the predicate evaluates to false. A more complete description of an enforcement rule can be found in the following paragraphs describing constraints.

Here is an example of an operation constraint predicate in the **Train** object.

```
Pred: complete(Put_OilPressure) < NOW + 5*seconds
```

A deadline of NOW + 5*seconds is specified for the completion of the Put_OilPressure method.

The constraints of an object permit the specification of correct object state. Each constraint is of the form ⟨*Nc, AttrSet, Pred, ER*⟩. *Nc* is the name of the constraint. *AttrSet* is a subset of attributes of the object. *Pred* is a predicate that is specified using attributes from the *AttrSet*. The predicate can be used to express the logical consistency requirements by using value fields of the attributes. It can express temporal consistency requirements by using the time fields of attributes. It can express imprecision limits by using the imprecision fields of attributes.

The enforcement rule (*ER*) is executed when the predicate evaluates to false, and is of the form ⟨*Exc, Op, OC*⟩. *Exc* is a set of exceptions that the enforcement rule may signal, *Op* is a set of operations that represents the implementation of the enforcement rule, and *OC* is a set of operation constraints on the execution of the enforcement rule.

As an example of a temporal consistency constraint, consider the following. As mentioned earlier, the **Train** object has an oil pressure attribute that is updated with the latest sensor reading every 30 seconds. To maintain the temporal consistency of this attribute, the following constraint is defined.

```
N:          OilPressure_avi
AttrSet:       { OilPressure}
Pred:       OilPressure.time > Now - 30*seconds
ER:         if Missed <= 2 then
                OilPressure.time = Now
                Missed = Missed + 1
                signal OilPressure_Warning
            else signal OilPressure_Alert
```

The enforcement rule specifies that if only one or two of the readings have been missed, a counter is incremented indicating that a reading has been missed and a warning is signaled using the exception OilPressure_Warning. If more than two readings have been missed, then an exception OilPressure_Alert is signaled, which might lead to a message being sent to the train operator. The counter Missed is reset to zero whenever a new sensor reading is written to the OilPressure attribute.

The compatibility function of an object expresses the semantics of allowable concurrent execution of each ordered pair of methods in the object. For each ordered pair of methods (m_i, m_j), a Boolean expression $(BE_{i,j})$ is defined. $BE_{i,j}$ can be evaluated to determine whether or not m_i and m_j can execute concurrently. Based on the semantics of the application, the compatibility function may allow method interleavings that introduce imprecision into the attributes and method arguments. Therefore, in addition to specifying compatibility between two method invocations, the compatibility function expresses information about the potential imprecision that could be introduced by interleaving method invocations. There are three potential sources of imprecision when method invocations m_i and m_j are interleaved: imprecision in the value of an attribute that is written by both m_i and m_j, imprecision in the value of the return arguments of m_i when m_i reads attributes written by m_j, and imprecision in the value of the return arguments of m_j when m_j reads attributes written by m_i.

Figure 11.5 demonstrates several examples of the compatibility function and its associated imprecision accumulation for the **Train**

Compatibility	Imprecision Accumulation
A: CF (Put_OilPressure ( ), Put_OilTemp ( ) = TRUE	No Imprecision
B: CF (Get_OilPressure(P1), Put_OilPressure (P2)) = (OilPressure.time <= Now - 30 * seconds) AND (	OilPressure.value - P2.value	<= (P1.implimit - P1.ImpAmt)	Increment P1.ImpAmt by	OilPressure.value - P2.value	

Figure 11.5 Compatibility function examples

object shown in Figure 11.4. In example A of Figure 11.5, the compatibility function is used to specify that the methods Put_OilPressure and Put_OilTemp can always run concurrently. This is appropriate because these two methods access different attributes. No imprecision is introduced in this case. Example B demonstrates trading off logical consistency for temporal consistency. If the temporal consistency constraint on the OilPressure attribute has been violated (*OilPressure.time <= Now – 30*seconds*), then the compatibility function specifies that the Put_OilPressure method invocation can execute concurrently with an active Get_OilPressure method, presumably to restore the temporal consistency of the OilPressure attribute. The *CF* restricts this interleaving to occur only if the amount of imprecision in the argument *P1* of the Get_OilPressure method invocation does not exceed the limit specified by the invoking transaction (*P1.implimit*). The amount of imprecision to add to *P1* in this case is also specified by the compatibility function. Note that although we use only simple methods (essentially reads and writes) in this example, the compatibility function can specify imprecision accumulation for general object methods.

Note how the RTSORAC model supports the tradeoff of logical consistency for temporal consistency found in real-time databases. Object designers can semantically express their preferences toward logical or temporal consistency in certain situations by using the RTSORAC compatibility functions. The imprecision field of each attribute allows accumulation of the imprecision that could result from the tradeoff. The model can use constraints on imprecision fields to express limits on the allowed amount of imprecision.

Relationships Each relationship in the RTSORAC model represents an aggregation of two or more objects and consists of ⟨*N, A, M, C, CF, P, IC*⟩. The first five components of a relationship are identical to the same components in the definition of an object. In addition, objects that can participate in the relationship are specified in the participant set *P*, and a set of interobject constraints is specified in *IC*.

Figure 11.6 illustrates an example of an energy management relationship for relating a **Train** object with a **Track** object. The **Track** object stores information, such as track profile and grade, speed limits, maximum load, and power available. The energy management relationship uses both train and track information to determine control algorithm parameters, such as fuel-efficient throttle and brake settings.

Each participant in a relationship is of the form ⟨*Np, OT, Card*⟩. *Np* is the name of the participant. *OT* is the type of the object participating in the relationship. *Card* is the cardinality of the participant, which is either *single* or *multi*. Constraints can be used to express cardinality requirements of the relationship, such as minimum and maximum cardinality of the participants. In Figure 11.6, train and track are single cardinality participants.

The interobject constraints placed on objects in the participant set are of the form ⟨*Nic, PartSet, Pred, ER*⟩. *Nic, Pred,* and *ER* are as in object constraints, and *PartSet* is a subset of the relationship's participant set *P*.

The predicate is expressed using objects from the *PartSet*, allowing the constraint to be specified over multiple objects participating in the relationship. Enforcement rules are defined as before by ⟨*Exc, Op,*

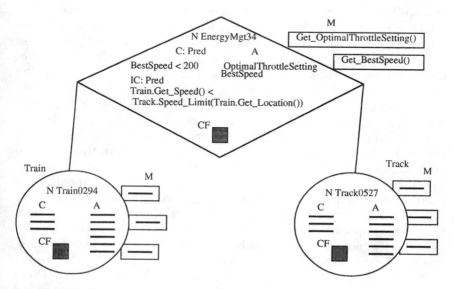

Figure 11.6   Example of energy management relationship

$OC\rangle$; however, the operations in Op can now include invocations of methods of the objects participating in the relationship.

As an example of an interobject constraint, consider the energy management relationship in Figure 11.6. A **Train** object will be on one specific segment of track, represented by the **Track** object participating in the relationship. The train should obey the speed limits set on the track segment, so the following interobject constraint predicate could be specified.

```
Pred: Train.Get_Speed() < Track.Speed_Limit
(Train.Get_Location())
```

If the speed of the train exceeds the speed limit posted at the train's location on the track, then the corresponding enforcement rule signals SpeedLimitExceeded.

Transactions An RTSORAC *transaction* has six components $\langle Nt, O, OC, PreCond, PostCond, Result\rangle$, where Nt is a unique name or identifier, O is a set of operations, OC is a set of operation constraints, *PreCond* is a precondition, *PostCond* is a postcondition, and *Result* is the result of the transaction. Each of these components is briefly described in the following text.

The operations in O represent the actions of the transaction. They include statements of the language in which the transaction is written and method invocations on database objects (MI). Method invocations (MI) are of the form $\langle MN, ArgInfo\rangle$, where MN is the method name (prepended with the appropriate object identifier), and $ArgInfo$ is a set of tuples containing argument information. Each argument tuple is of the form $\langle aa, maximp, tcr\rangle$, where aa is the actual argument to the method, $maximp$ is the maximum allowable imprecision of the argument, and tcr is the temporal consistency requirement of the argument. The fields $maximp$ and tcr are specified only for arguments that are used to return information to the transaction. These fields allow the transaction to specify requirements that differ from those defined on the data in the objects—for example, the transaction might be willing to accept a value whose temporal consistency requirements have been violated in order to meet other timing constraints. The data may still be useful to the transaction because of other available information (e.g., it may be able to do some extrapolation). A transaction may also specify that data returned by a method invocation must be precise ($maximp$ is zero).

OC is a set of constraints on operations of the transaction. These constraints are of the same form as the operation constraints specified for methods $\langle Nc, OpSet, Pred, ER\rangle$. They can be used to express precedence constraints, execution constraints, and timing constraints—for example, a transaction may require that a sensor reading be returned within two seconds.

PreCond represents preconditions that must be satisfied before a transaction is made ready for execution—for example, it may be appropriate for a transaction to execute only if some specified event has occurred. The event may be the successful termination of another transaction or a given clock time. *PostCond* represents postconditions that must be satisfied upon completion of the operations of the transaction. The postconditions can be used to specify the semantics of what constitutes a *commit* of a transaction containing subtransactions. *Result* represents information that is returned by the transaction. This may include values read from objects, as well as values computed by the transaction.

11.5 REAL-TIME DATABASE SYSTEMS AND STANDARDS

This section reviews several real-time database development efforts. It first examines the only two commercial products to advertise themselves as "real-time databases": Zip RTDBMS for DBx, and EagleSpeed RTDBMS from Martin Marietta. It also presents an academic prototype real-time oject-oriented database based on Texas Instrument's Open Object-Oriented Database system. Finally, it reviews the proposed Real-Time SQL standard. These reviews are done using the requirements for real-time databases that were presented in Section 11.3.

11.5.1 The Zip Real-Time Database System

Zip RTDBMS from DBx, Inc. is proclaimed to be a memory-resident, high-speed, real-time database management system. Version 1.2 currently runs on the LynxOS 2.2 operating system, which is consistent with the POSIX 1003.4 real-time operating systems standards. Implementations of Zip for other platforms are also under development. Zip provides bounded response time, static definition and evaluation of schemata and data access behavior, and a priori query optimization before run time. It features preallocation of system resources at database creation time, as well as fixed-time attribute and index resolution at run time.

The bounded response time is designed for atomic operations, such as insertion, deletion, and so forth, performed directly on the data. Some response times collected from Zip average-case timing sweeps are shown in the Table 11.3.

Table 11.3   Zip RTDBMS Average-Case Timing under LynxOS 2.2 i486/50

Function	Timing
createDB	1 sec
connectDB	90 ms
insertDB	520 us
deleteDB	820 us
destroyDB	40 ms
disconnectDB	50 ms

In Zip, all tables and queries are defined statically in a user-created data definition language (DDL) file. The DDL has some similarities to standard languages, such as SQL, but it is Zip-specific. The DDL file is parsed by a Zip utility and converted into a schema binary file, used by both the client and the database server. The schema file contains database specifications, table, and index definitions. An example of a data definition file, simplified for demonstration, is presented in Figure 11.7.

```
1:  define database db_name      ("sampleZipDB");
2:  define database db_dir_path  ("/local/db");
3:  define database db_phys_addr (0x0);
4:  define database db_size      (393216);
5:  define database db_grants    (0777);

6:  create table calibrate_parameters (
7:  unit_id     byte2     not null, unique
8:  cal_value   byte8f    not null,
9:  tolerance   byte8f,
10: descript    string[4],
11: cal_cycle   byte2,
12: cal_date    date      not null,
13: timestamp   tstamp );

14: define table calibrate_parameters   (STATIC, 10000);
15: define index unit_id_idx on calibrate_parameters (unit_id)
16: ideal,
17: load (100%),
18: distinct (10000);
```

Figure 11.7   Example Zip DDL

In the example, the database specifications are defined in lines 1–5, along with one table at lines 6–13, and an index at lines 15–18. The table contains a sequence of variables (columns) of various data types. Zip supports a total of 12 types plus the string data type. One distinguished variable in the table is timestamp, which is not implemented, but proposed for the next release of Zip. The timestamp supports the determination of temporal consistency of data.

After a table has been declared in Zip's DDL, it must now be set to a particular type and size. In Figure 11.7 the table type is \verb+ STATIC+, and its size is 10,000. Three types of data relation (table types) are supported by Zip. STATIC relations deal with records of fixed size and a relatively stable content. Only SELECT and IPDATE operations can be used with these tables. BOUNDED relations are of fixed maximum size, but with time-varying content. All operations are allowed on these tables. ROLLING relations resemble a fixed size queue, where the new insertions force the old data down the queue until eventually there is no more "room" for these data and they are lost, hence simulating "aging" of data. The last type is important in many real-time environments where the value of the data changes with time, and fixed-sized resources are necessary.

The last statement in the example DDL file is a declaration of the table index. It identifies the *key variable*, the load factor, which is the percent of free spaces, and the number of distinct keys that are used to compute optimal hashing methods for the table. Although any query could be generated, only the queries created with the indexes in mind are efficient.

Since the schema file is available before the creation of the database, most of the system allocation is done during the creation. Once running, the server can be accessed by multiple clients via a multitude of connections, each according to the specifications defined in the schema file. It is worth noting that the version of Zip we review here does not have any user-friendly interface for generation of the DDL files, but DBx claims plans for SQL compatibility in the future versions. Along with all other components of the DDL, file queries must be created by hand in the client program itself (see Figure11.7).

Figure 11.8 shows a simple query that selects all tuples from a table called stock, which contains two columns: id and price. The table is assumed to have been declared earlier. The bindDBvariable function specifies to the database what columns to work with while processing a query. The function's parameters contain a database handle, column name, and type information. In the example query the columns in lines 2 and 3 are bound, and then a selection is performed in line 4 with the selectDB function. This function accepts the database handle and error function as parameters. The return value tids is a pointer to

```
1:   declareDBrelation(DBhandle, "stock")
2:   bindDBvariable(DBhandle, id_name,  &id,  &id_type)
3:   bindDBvariable(DBhandle, price_name, price, price_type)
4:   tids = selectDB(DBhandle,DEFAULT_FUNC)
```

Figure 11.8 Example of Zip query

an array of tuples that was selected. Once selected, these tuples can be traversed with the nextDBtuple function (not shown) and accessed individually.

The Zip RTDBMS claims quick execution times, because the system is relieved of much of the traditional database functionality, such as query parsing, relation and attribute resolution, and index selection. In addition, the whole database resides in a shared memory special file with every access calculated as a base plus an offset pair. The implementation is multithreaded and optimized for the underlying real-time operating system environments.

Although the features described previously pertain in part to those found in a real-time database, Zip RTDBMS clearly lacks some of the major components. This is because Zip was designed for hard real time, which requires the elimination of many features in order to preserve predictability. Most of the characteristics of real-time transactions mentioned previously are not supported, nor is dynamic real-time scheduling. Data temporal consistency, both absolute and relative, is not supported; however, functions such as get_earliest_timestamp, get_latest_timestamp, and testDBtimestamp are proposed and would be available for client applications to implement. Zip does not perform any logical or temporal imprecision data management; hence, bounded imprecision support cannot be claimed. Time constraint violation recovery is nonexistent, since neither transactions nor data temporal consistency violations can be detected. Concurrency control for clashing requests is not real time; instead, Zip chooses standard locking in all cases. Predictability is one issue that Zip supports well by providing bounded response time on all database calls, although at the sacrifice of unlimited storage capability. Overall, Zip RTDBMS is perhaps better considered a real-time data store, rather than a real-time database. It claims only one of the real-time database features discussed in Section 11.3.

11.5.2 The EagleSpeed Real-Time Database System

The EagleSpeed real-time database management system is the commercial release of a database designed for a submarine command system. It is based on the ANSI CODASYL (network) data model. It is designed to support hard real-time applications. The stated goals of EagleSpeed are

- To synchronize with environmental processes that must be controlled
- To support a priori determination of system schedulability
- To provide predictability and punctuality of transaction access
- To provide speed, determinism, and minimalism

It has achieved the predictable execution time required by hard real time in several ways. First, EagleSpeed implements only a subset of database management functionality. The removal of database system functionality places more burden on the application writer. It only provides a subset of the CODASYL verbs, requiring the applications writer to define other functionality. Second, by utilizing the network data model's ability to fix logical data structures in advance, it fixes access time to the data. Third, it uses one single-layer schema, which minimizes overhead due to mapping levels and due to maintaining metadata. Fourth, the physical location of data objects can be fixed to facilitate retrieval.

Transactions are Ada programs with ACID properties. They are invoked via messages sent to their site of storage. In addition, the system allows direct access to the transaction manager and the operating system to facilitate real-time performance. Timing constraints on transactions are not supported, since it is assumed that a priori analysis will determine if all transactions meet timing constraints. Transactions are given priorities and scheduled by the underlying operating system. Concurrency control is handled by strict two-phase locking with no imprecision allowed. Like Zip, EagleSpeed is a fast, predictable real-time data store, but it lacks some features of a full real-time database.

11.5.3 Real-Time Extensions to the Open Object-Oriented Database System

A prototype object-oriented real-time database system has been designed at the University of Rhode Island. It implements the RTSORAC model, described in Section 11.4.3, by extending the Open Object-Oriented Database System (Open OODB). The Open OODB system was initiated by the U.S. Advanced Research Projects Agency (ARPA). The original goal of Open OODB was to establish a common, modular, modifiable, object-oriented database system suitable to be used by a wide range of researchers and developers. Open OODB is designed so that features such as transaction management, query interface, persistence, and so forth are modules that can be individually "unplugged" and replaced by other modules.

The basic conceptual system architecture of Open OODB is shown in Figure 11.9 (along with the real-time extensions). The *support managers* are modules that are currently implemented as library routines that get linked into the user's C++ program to (transparently) provide the extended database capabilities. *Policy managers* (PMs) provide extenders to the behavior of programs by coordinating the support managers—for example, the *Persistence Policy Manager* provides applications with an interface through which they can create, access, and manipulate persistent objects in various address spaces. The *Transaction Policy Manager* enables concurrent access to persistent and transient data; its implementation in the current alpha release is

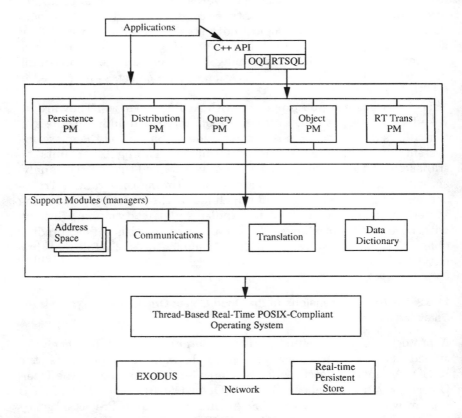

Figure 11.9 Open OODB architecture with real-time extensions

a trivial mapping to Exodus write locks on all objects. Other policy managers include those for distribution, change management, indexing, and query processing. The query interface is in two forms: an extended version of C++ and an SQL-like language called OQL, which must be embedded in C++ code.

Real-Time Extensions   The RTSORAC extensions to the Open OODB architecture are designed within Open OODB's original framework, as shown in Figure 11.9.

There are two changes to the system's underlying architecture: implementation of extensions using a real-time POSIX operating system; and incorporation of a real-time persistent storage subsystem, which is the Zip RTDBMS described in Section 11.5.1. Additionally, two policy managers have been added: One for real-time transaction management, and one for real-time object management.

The interface to the real-time Open OODB prototype is an extension to OQL, based on the real-time SQL language, which is described in Section 11.5.4. The prototype real-time extensions provide the capability to create arbitrary real-time attribute classes by using the type of the value field as an argument to a C++ template that provides time and imprecision capabilities.

Transactions in the real-time Open OODB are C++ programs that include the schema file of object type declarations. Each transaction is a real-time SQL program (see Section 11.5.4), which is compiled into a POSIX process. Each process maps all database objects that reside in shared memory into their own address space. The process uses calls to the semantic concurrency control mechanism to lock objects while using them. These calls are provided by the Open OODB policy manager code. Once an object is locked, the transaction calls the object's methods as if the object were in the transaction's own address space. A transaction process uses calls to the underlying operating system to set its priority and to set alarms for start times and deadlines.

The real-time transaction scheduling performed by the Transaction Policy Manager is essentially a mapping of timing constraints expressed in RTSORAC transactions into real-time POSIX priorities for transaction processes. This mapping is designed so that the transaction process priorities realize earliest-deadline-first (EDF) scheduling.

Although the real-time extension to Open OODB is an academic prototype, it does address many of the requirements of a full real-time database. The use of the RTSORAC model is instrumental in the real-time extension's support of the requirements discussed in Section 11.3. The RTSORAC model expresses logical consistency, temporal consistency, and imprecision constraints, as well as their tradeoffs for both data objects and transactions. It also supports expression of complex data types and associations among data items. The prototype uses main-memory objects with semantic real-time concurrency control to achieve fast access that observes the semantics of the logical, temporal, and imprecision constraints.

11.5.4 Real-Time SQL

For the past three years organizations including the University of Rhode Island, the University of Massachusetts—Dartmouth, the U.S Department of Defense's Next-Generation Computer Resources (NGCR), Database Interface Standard Working Group (DISWG), and the American National Standards Institute's (ANSI) Predictable Real-Time Information Management Task Group (PRIS-TG) have been working to define real-time database extensions to SQL. These extensions involve timing constraints on data (in SQL data definition), timing constraints on SQL data manipulation, recovery from timing constraint violations, support for predictability, and flexible transaction structure.

Currently, SQL (called SQL2) supports the definition, manipulation, and control of data in a relational database system. However, the current SQL standard (SQL2) has no provisions for real-time database support. The standard does have mechanisms for constraint expression, support for expression of time, and rudimentary transaction structure—all of which provide a basis for developing real-time database extensions.

SQL2 Time Specification SQL2 provides sufficient syntax and semantics for specification of timing expressions. There are three *date-time* data types: DATE, TIME, and TIMESTAMP. These data types can be used to express absolute time, such as 9:00 A.M. There is also an *interval* data type, called INTERVAL, that can be used to express a period of time, such as five minutes. SQL also supports three *date-time* valued functions: CURRENT_DATE returns the current date, CURRENT_TIME returns the current time, and CURRENT_TIMESTAMP returns the current date concatenated with the current time.

The arithmetic operators, +, −, *, and /, and the usual comparison operators (=, <>, <, <=, >, >=) have been defined over date-time data types and *interval* data types. Temporal SQL2 has proposed a precise definition for representation of time within the database. This definition includes the concept that time has a discrete representation, and that the smallest unit of time is called a chronon.

Data Temporal Consistency Constraints in SQL2 are mechanisms for specifying the logical consistency requirements of data. They can be specified on columns, tables, and as stand-alone entities (called assertions) within the database—for example, a constraint can be used to specify a range of values for a data-item, or to make sure that a foreign key in one table corresponds to a primary key in another.

Specification of Data Temporal Consistency Constraints In RTSQL, data constraint definitions are extended to allow for specification of temporal consistency requirements of the data. These requirements are usually expressed by indicating the maximum acceptable age for a data-item. Computation of the age of a data-item requires that the system record the time that the data value was determined (perhaps it is the time the value was generated by a sensor, or the time that the value was written). Since it would not be necessary to determine the age of every data-item in the database, the following RTSQL clause can be specified during definition of a data-item to specify that a timestamp will be required.

```
<data timestamp clause> ::=
    [WITH TIMESTAMP <datetime type>]
```

Note that <datetime type> is a type provided by SQL2. Access to this timestamp value is through a function on the data-item called TIMESTAMP—for example, the timestamp value on the data-item temp_reading would be accessed as TIMESTAMP(temp_reading). Also note that SQL2 provides a function that returns the current time, called CURRENT_TIMESTAMP. SQL2 provides syntax for constraint specification that can be used to specify temporal consistency requirements when used in conjunction with CURRENT_TIMESTAMP and the TIMESTAMP function—for example, the following constraint, temp_reading_avi, specifies that for the data-item temp_reading to be absolutely temporally consistent, it must be less than ten seconds old:

```
CONSTRAINT temp_reading_avi
    CHECK (CURRENT_TIMESTAMP - TIMESTAMP(temp_reading))
            DAY to SECOND
            < INTERVAL '10' SECOND
```

Here, the SQL2 CHECK clause contains a Boolean expression, which computes the age of temp_reading and determines whether it is less than ten seconds old. SQL2 does not allow constraint specifications to include references to any of the functions that return dates and times (such as CURRENT_TIMESTAMP). From the example shown, it is obvious that this restriction must be relaxed in RTSQL.

Relative temporal consistency among data-items can be expressed by comparing their timestamps—for example, the following constraint speed_bearing_rvi specifies the relative temporal consistency requirements of speed and bearing.

```
CONSTRAINT speed_bearing_rvi
    CHECK TIMESTAMP(speed) BETWEEN
        TIMESTAMP(bearing) - INTERVAL '2' SECOND
        AND TIMESTAMP(bearing) + INTERVAL '2' SECOND
```

Here, the speed timestamp is checked to see if it is within two seconds of the bearing timestamp.

Constraints themselves may be valid only for a given period of time. The following RTSQL clauses can be specified as part of a constraint specification to indicate when a constraint is active.

```
<constraint validity interval clause> ::=
    [AFTER <datetime value expression>]
    [BEFORE <datetime value expression>]
```

The previous speed_bearing_rvi constraint is specified to be active only after CONTACT_MADE, where CONTACT_MADE is of a *datetime* data type.

```
CONSTRAINT speed_bearing_rvi
    CHECK TIMESTAMP(speed) BETWEEN
        TIMESTAMP(bearing) - INTERVAL '2' SECOND
        AND TIMESTAMP(bearing) + INTERVAL '2' SECOND
    AFTER CONTACT_MADE
```

Note that the <constraint validity interval clause> may be applied to any constraint specification.

Data Temporal Consistency Violations One of the SQL working groups, SQL2/PSM, is developing support for *condition handling*. Condition handling allows a more active response to the completion of an SQL statement. When a statement is executed, it will either raise an *exception* condition or a *completion* condition.

Data temporal consistency constraint violations in RTSQL are detected when a data value is read. This means that the exception will be raised by a statement that may have a corresponding exception handler available. Such a constraint violation could occur if the sensor supplying the data malfunctions or the transaction responsible for the update misses its deadline. An exception handler could attempt to update the data value or it could simply signal the user that a sensor check should be performed.

Timing Constraints on Execution   SQL2 does not provide any mechanisms for placing timing constraints on statements or transactions. RTSQL specifies time-constrained execution by placing timing constraints on individual data manipulation statements or, as appears in SQL2/PSM, a block of statements.

Specification of Execution Timing Constraints   Specification of execution timing constraints uses the following clauses.

```
<timing constraint clause> ::=
    [START BEFORE <datetime value expression>]
    [START AFTER  <datetime value expression>]
    [COMPLETE BEFORE <datetime value expression>]
    [COMPLETE AFTER  <datetime value expression>]
    [PERIOD <interval value expression>
      [START AT <time expression>]
      [UNTIL <boolean expression>]]

  <datetime value function> ::=
    CURRENT_DATE | CURRENT_TIME[<time precision>] |
    CURRENT_TIMESTAMP[<timestamp precision>]
```

The START BEFORE and COMPLETE BEFORE clauses are used to express the latest start time and latest finish time for the execution of the statement. The START AFTER and COMPLETE AFTER clauses are used to express the earliest start time and earliest finish time for the execution of the statement. The PERIOD clause allows for the establishment of a periodic execution of a statement. The START AT portion of the PERIOD clause establishes the period frame. The UNTIL portion of the clause allows for the specification of the conditions that must be met before periodic execution can terminate.

Recall that in SQL2, *date-time* valued expressions have been defined, and they can include references to *date-time* value functions. In RTSQL, if such functions are included in an expression, they are all evaluated before the statement begins execution. Further, all of the occurrences of the *date-time* value functions in a statement will appear to have been evaluated at the same instance of time. This holds true for nested statements, where a compound statement may contain statements or other compound statements. Suppose we have the following:

```
X:BEGIN
    SELECT price FROM stocks WHERE name="Acme"
        COMPLETE BEFORE CURRENT_TIMESTAMP + INTERVAL '30' SECOND;
    -- other computations
END X COMPLETE BEFORE CURRENT_TIMESTAMP + INTERVAL '1' MINUTE;
```

The execution timing constraint on the SELECT statement specifies that it must complete execution within 30 seconds. The timing constraint on the compound statement specifies that it must complete execution within one minute. Note that the value of CURRENT_TIMESTAMP will be the same for both timing constraints (since they appear in the same compound statement).

Detecting an execution timing constraint violation can be done through the use of timers. When a statement is encountered, the timing constraints are evaluated, and timers are set for the various types of timing constraints.

Predictability Support   In order to support the predictability requirement of real-time databases, RTSQL introduces a concept called a *directive*. Directives provide information to the database system to facilitate maintenance of the constraints and predictability. Directives differ from constraints in that constraints address the logical and temporal consistency requirements for data and operations. The applications that utilize the database system determine these consistency requirements, which in turn are mapped to constraints. Directives provide additional information to the database system to facilitate maintenance of the constraints and predictable access time to data. As such, directives may involve hardware characteristics. Real-time SQL supports the following directives.

- *Data Storage Location*—The RTSQL storage directives are used to allow programmers the ability to specify where and how a data-item or table is to be stored. The following clause, part of a table definition, is used to specify storage requirements

```
<storage clause> ::=
    [STORE IN <storage type> [AT <location>]
```

where the domains of <storage type> and <location> are architecture-dependent—for example, STORE IN main_memory could be used in a SQL table definition to specify that the table be stored only in main memory. The AT <location> clause could be used to store the table at a particular location in main memory. Fixing the location of the data-item can facilitate ensuring predictable access time to it.

- *Data Storage Size*—To allow determination of an upper bound on the time it takes to access a table, the following RTSQL directive clause can be specified during the definition of a table

```
<table size clause> ::=
    [SIZE UPPER LIMIT <integer>]
```

indicating that this is the maximum number of data-items that can be in this table.

- *Relative Importance Level*—This directive allows for the specification of the relative importance of an action. A scheduling algorithm may use relative importance of tasks as a parameter in determining scheduling priority of the tasks. Not all systems will utilize this directive, and, as such, these systems would be free to ignore this directive upon notification. Also, the semantics of the various levels can vary in different systems; hence, the portability of this directive is limited. The importance directive clause is as follows.

```
<importance clause> ::=
    IMPORTANCE LEVEL <importance level>
```

- *Asynchronous Execution*— In real-time applications, it may be useful to notify the system that some actions can be done asynchronously. Specification of asynchronous execution of a statement in SQL3 is done using the following clause.

```
[ ASYNC ( <async statement identifier> ) ]
```

If left unspecified, the default is synchronous. SQL3 also provides a statement for testing the completion of an asynchronous statement.

```
<test completion statement> ::=
    { TEST | WAIT }
    { ALL | ANY | <async statement identifier list> }
COMPLETION
```

The TEST alternative is used to check to see if asynchronous statements have completed execution. If they have not, an exception condition is raised. The WAIT alternative is used to wait for the asynchronous statements to complete execution. If the asynchronous statements have already completed execution when the WAIT statement is executed, an exception condition will be raised.

- *Worst-Case Execution Time*—This directive specifies the worst-case execution time (*wcet*) of a statement. This value is made available to the system by the user, who has determined this value through analysis.

11.6 REAL-TIME DATABASE RESEARCH

The vast majority of research in the field of real-time databases has focused on concurrency control and transaction scheduling. Scheduling transactions in a real-time database involves determining which transactions execute when. Similar to tasks in other real-time systems, real-time transactions have priority and must be scheduled accordingly in order to meet specified timing constraints. However, unlike most other real-time processes, real-time transactions access shared data. Therefore, real-time transaction scheduling must take into account the logical consistency of the data and transactions as well as temporal consistency; that is, concurrency control must be considered when scheduling real-time transactions.

A real-time transaction scheduling algorithm has two components: a policy for assigning priorities and a concurrency control mechanism. This section is broken down to describe recent research in real-time database priority assignment policies and in real-time database concurrency control.

11.6.1 Priority Assignment Policies

There has been a great deal of research toward applying real-time scheduling policies to real-time database transaction scheduling. Two factors are used in scheduling real-time transactions: criticality and deadline. A scheduling policy in which each transaction is assigned a priority at the time of arrival is based on the factor of *relative deadline* divided by *criticalness*, where relative deadline is the difference between the transaction deadline and its arrival time. A performance evaluation compares the combined scheduling protocol with two others that use only deadline (earliest-deadline-first) or only criticality (most-critical-first) for assigning priority. The results of these tests indicate that transactions that are scheduled using both deadline and criticality miss fewer deadlines and abort fewer transactions than those scheduled using only one of the two factors.

There are two real-time transaction scheduling protocols that are based on the earliest-deadline-first (EDF) priority assignment policy. The adaptive earliest deadline (AED) protocol is based on the fact that

EDF works best when all or most of the transactions can be scheduled. In the AED protocol, transactions are divided into two groups: *HIT* and *MISS*. The size of the *HIT* group is determined by a dynamic control variable called *HITcapacity*. When a transaction arrives in the system, it is assigned a random key value. It is then inserted into a key-ordered list of the transactions currently in the system. If the transaction's position in the list is less than or equal to *HITcapacity*, it is assigned to the *HIT* group; otherwise, it is assigned to the *MISS* group. Within the *HIT* group, the priority ordering is by earliest-deadline. The priority ordering in the *MISS* group is random.

The goal of the AED algorithm is to collect the largest set of transactions that can be completed before their deadlines in the *HIT* group. Then the transactions in the *HIT* group can be optimally scheduled using the earliest-deadline priority assignment. In order to reach this goal, the *HITcapacity* control variable must accurately predict the size of the *HIT* group. The value of *HITcapacity* is dynamically updated through a feedback process that examines the hit ratio of the transactions in the *HIT* group versus the hit ratio of all of the transactions.

A second protocol further enhances the AED protocol to allow a transaction's value to be taken into account. The goal is to maximize the sum of the values of those transactions that commit by their deadlines. The new protocol, called hierarchical earliest deadline (HED), groups transactions, based on their values, into a hierarchy of prioritized buckets. It then uses a protocol similar to AED within each bucket to determine the relative priority of the transactions in the bucket. The transactions within a bucket are ordered based on transaction value. As in AED, the priority ordering within the *HIT* group in each bucket is earliest-deadline, but unlike AED the priority ordering within the *MISS* group is highest value rather than random.

11.6.2 Concurrency Control Mechanisms

Most concurrency control mechanisms for real-time databases adapt non-real-time techniques to take time into account. Both pessimistic (lock-based) and optimistic real-time concurrency control techniques have been proposed. In these techniques, serializability is the chosen correctness criterion. Some researchers have recognized that relaxing the serializability requirement can benefit real time. By using application-specific knowledge, semantic concurrency control techniques can provide increased concurrency. Some of the semantic concurrency control techniques described in the following text benefit real-time implicitly with the added concurrency that is available. Others explicitly take temporal consistency into account to further enhance the benefit of using semantics.

Lock-Based Concurrency Control   Many of the lock-based real-time concurrency control techniques are based on the traditional two-phase locking technique. The techniques combine two-phase locking with the priority ceiling real-time scheduling algorithm to handle the priority inversion problem. One technique assumes that all transactions are periodic. The scheduling algorithm assigns higher priority to transactions with shorter periods. In this version of the protocol, all locks are exclusive. The priority ceiling of a data object is the priority of the highest-priority transaction that can lock the object. When a transaction T requests a lock on object O, if the priority of T is not higher than the priority of the data object with the highest-priority ceiling of all data objects currently locked by transactions other than T, then the lock is denied. Otherwise, the lock is granted. If a transaction blocks a higher-priority transaction, it inherits the higher priority while the blocking occurs. When this protocol is combined with a two-phase locking scheme, the resulting concurrency control mechanism bounds blocking to at most one lower-priority transaction.

Another protocol is modified to produce the *Read/Write Priority Ceiling Protocol*. The new protocol allows read/write locking and defines three parameters for each data object in the database. The *write priority ceiling* of a data object is the priority of the highest-priority task that can write to the object. The *absolute priority ceiling* of a data object is the priority of the highest-priority task that can read or write to the data object. The *r/w priority ceiling* of a data object is set dynamically. A task cannot read/write-lock a data object unless its priority is higher than the highest r/w priority ceiling of data objects locked by tasks other than itself. Since the highest r/w priority ceiling of the locked data objects represents the highest-priority level at which the currently active transactions can execute, the protocol ensures that a transaction executes at a priority level higher than all preempted transactions.

It has been pointed out that the priority ceiling protocol requires prior knowledge about the data objects to be accessed by each transaction. This requirement is too restrictive, and a new protocol, which uses priority inheritance combined with priority abort for transaction scheduling, has been presented. In the new protocol, called conditional priority inheritance, when a priority inversion is detected, if the lower-priority transaction is near completion, it inherits the priority of the high-priority transaction. This avoids wasting the resources that would result in aborting the nearly complete transaction. If the low-priority transaction is not near completion, it is aborted, avoiding the long blocking time for the high-priority transaction.

The key to the conditional priority inheritance algorithm is determining when a transaction is nearly complete. A threshold value h is derived so that if the amount of work left to be done by a transaction is less than h, priority inheritance is applied; otherwise priority abort is applied. The sensitivity of h on performance was studied through experiments, and the results indicate that with respect to deadline miss ratio, the algorithm performs best for $1 < h < 3$.

In the *2PL-HP* (two-phase locking with high priority) protocol, conflicts are resolved by aborting lower-priority transactions. If a transaction requesting access to shared data has a higher priority than all other transactions holding locks on the data, the lock holders abort and the requester gets the lock. Otherwise, the requester waits for the holder to release the lock.

Another variation of the priority abort idea is called *H2PL* (hybrid two-phase locking). In this technique certain conditions, such as transaction workload, are checked to avoid unnecessary aborts. Also, whenever a lower-priority transaction that is blocking a higher-priority transaction aborts and therefore has to be restarted, its priority is raised to that of the higher transaction to prevent priority inversion (priority inheritance). In H2PL, when a transaction requests a lock and a conflict is detected, if the two transactions have the same priority, the requesting transaction is aborted and restarted. In the case where the requesting transaction has higher priority than the transaction holding the conflicting lock, if either the waiting requester or a restart of the holder would miss its deadline, then one of them must be aborted. If the holder is being blocked, it will be aborted; otherwise, the transaction that is further from completion is selected for abortion. Whenever a lower-priority transaction is restarted, its priority is raised to that of the higher priority requesting transaction in order to avoid priority inversion. If the requesting transaction has lower priority than the holding transaction, the transaction that is further from completion is aborted and restarted.

The results of performance tests indicate that H2PL performs well for different types of transactions, because it is capable of giving preference to higher-priority transactions while minimizing the impact on lower-priority transactions.

It has been recognized that the serialization order produced by a concurrency control algorithm should reflect the priority of the transactions. A protocol in which the serialization order of active transactions is adjusted dynamically, making it possible for transactions with higher priority to be executed first, has been presented. Thus, higher-priority transactions are never blocked by uncommitted lower-priority transactions, while lower-priority transactions may not have to be aborted due to conflicts.

Each transaction is assigned a priority based on its deadline and its start timestamp. The execution of each transaction is divided into

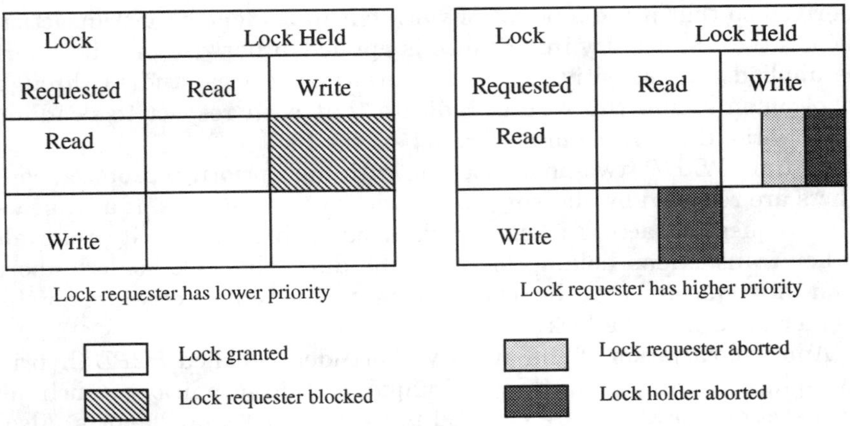

Lock	Lock Held		Lock	Lock Held	
Requested	Read	Write	Requested	Read	Write
Read		▨▨▨	Read		░ ▓
Write			Write	▓	

Lock requester has lower priority   Lock requester has higher priority

☐ Lock granted   ▨ Lock requester blocked   ░ Lock requester aborted   ▓ Lock holder aborted

Figure 11.10   Lin/Son lock compatibility table

three phases: the *read phase*, the *wait phase*, and the *write phase*. In the read phase, the transaction acquires read locks on data-items and performs prewrites in its own local workspace. The locking protocol is based on the principle that higher-priority transactions should complete before lower-priority transactions. Figure 11.10 shows the lock compatibility tables for this protocol. The compatibility depends on the priority of the transactions in question, as well as the types of locks. The wait phase of a transaction allows it to wait until it is allowed to commit. A transaction can commit only if all transactions with higher priority that must precede it in the serialization order are either committed or aborted. A transaction in the wait phase is aborted if it conflicts with a lock request by a higher-priority transaction, or if a higher-priority transaction that must precede it in the serialization order has already committed. At the end of the wait phase, if the transaction has not aborted, it is assigned a final timestamp and is committed. In the write phase, a transaction writes all of its changes permanently to the database. The data manager receives write requests for each data object in ascending timestamp order.

Optimistic Concurrency Control   A study of real-time concurrency control techniques indicates that in systems in which late transactions are discarded, a real-time optimistic concurrency control mechanism outperforms the pessimistic technique. A real-time optimistic concurrency protocol called WAIT-50 has been presented. In this protocol, a lower-priority transaction waits at validation time for any conflicting higher-priority transactions to give the higher-priority transactions a chance to meet their deadlines first. A wait control mechanism monitors transaction conflict states and dynamically decides when and how long a low-priority transaction should wait for its conflicting higher-priority transactions.

A real-time optimistic concurrency control technique called OCC-TI uses timestamp intervals to detect conflicts. Every transaction is assigned an initial timestamp interval of $(0, \infty)$. The interval is adjusted to represent serialization-order dependencies. A final timestamp is assigned from the interval at the end of the validation phase. The validation of a transaction consists of adjusting timestamp intervals of concurrent transactions and restarting conflicting transactions whose intervals cannot be adjusted. This technique uses the concept of dynamic adjustment of serialization order.

Semantic Concurrency Control A semantic concurrency control mechanism utilizes application-specific knowledge to increase concurrency, sometimes defining less-restrictive correctness criteria than serializability. In some cases, these correctness criteria are somewhat ad hoc, in that they are based completely on the specific semantics of the application. When serializability is relaxed, imprecision can result in the data and in the transactions. Several correctness criteria have been proposed that formalize how to use application semantics and how to manage the resulting imprecision.

Most work in semantic concurrency control can be divided into two categories: *transaction-based semantic concurrency control* and *object-based semantic concurrency control*. Transaction-based semantic concurrency control capitalizes on the semantics of the known transactions in the system to allow interleavings that might not be allowed in a traditional scheme. Object-based semantic concurrency control manages access to each object in the system based on the semantics of the operations defined on the object. Some of the semantic concurrency control techniques described in the following text benefit real-time databases through the added concurrency they provide. Others take a more active role in real time by using the temporal requirements of the data and transactions as part of the application semantics.

Correctness Criteria Transaction-based semantic concurrency control with a formal method for determining correct schedules has been presented. An *atomic unit* of a transaction T_i relative to another transaction T_j is defined to be a sequence of consecutive operations of T_i such that no operations of T_j are allowed to be executed within this sequence. *Atomicity* (T_i, T_j) refers to the ordered sequence of atomic units of T_i relative to T_j. A schedule of transactions is a *relatively* *atomic schedule* if, for all transactions T_i and T_j, no operation of T_i is interleaved with an atomic unit of T_j relative to T_i.

In general, relative atomicity specifications tend to be conservative because not all potential conflicts occur. The class of relatively atomic schedules can include interleavings of operations that do not have any dependencies between them. An operation o_2 directly depends on an operation o_1 if o_1 precedes o_2 and either both operations are in the same transaction or o_1 conflicts with o_2. A *relatively serial schedule* is defined to be analogous to the concept of serial schedules in the serializability theory. A schedule is relatively serial if, for all transactions T_i and T_j, an operation o of T_i is interleaved with an atomic unit U of T_j relative to T_i, and o does not depend on any operation p in U, then any other operation q in U does not depend on o. A schedule is *relatively serializable* if it is conflict equivalent to some relatively serial schedule. This definition provides a formal correctness criterion for transaction-based concurrency control. It also presents a method for determining if a given schedule is relatively serial by testing for acyclicity of a directed graph.

The use of imprecision in databases and in real-time systems is synthesized and formalized through the concept of *similarity*. New correctness criteria, less restrictive than serializability, are based on the idea that data values that are sufficiently close may be interchanged as input to a transaction without undue adverse effects.

Similarity of a data object is defined by the user based on the semantics of the data. Two views of a transaction are similar if, and only if, every read event in both views uses similar values with respect to the transaction. Two database states are similar if the corresponding values of every data object in the two states are similar. These definitions are used to extend the traditional correctness criteria, final-state serializability, view serializability, and conflict serializability to new criteria based on similarity.

Epsilon serializability (ESR) is a correctness criterion that generalizes serializability by allowing bounded imprecision in transaction processing. ESR assumes that serializable schedules of transactions using precise data always result in precise data in the database and in precise return values from transactions.

A transaction t specifies limits on the amount of imprecision that it can import ($import\_limit_{t,x}$) and export ($export\_limit\_{t,x}$) with respect to a particular data-item, x. For every data-item x in the database, a data ε-specification ($data\_\varepsilon_x$) expresses a limit on the amount of imprecision that can be written to x.

The amount of imprecision imported and exported by a transaction t with respect to data-item x, as well as the imprecision written to x, is accumulated during the transaction's execution through *import_imprecision$_{t,x}$*, *export_imprecision$_{t,x}$*, and *data_imprecision$_x$*, respectively.

ESR defines *safety* as a set of conditions that specifies boundaries for the amount of imprecision permitted in transactions and data. Safety is divided into two parts: transaction safety and data safety. Safety for transaction t with respect to data item x is defined as follows.

$$TR\text{-}Safety_{t,x} \equiv \begin{cases} import\_imprecision_{t,x} \leq import\_limit_{t,x} \\ export\_imprecision_{t,x} \leq export\_limit_{t,x} \end{cases}$$

Data safety can be formalized for data-item x as follows.

$$Data\text{-}Safety_x \equiv data\_imprecision_x \leq data\_\varepsilon_x$$

Therefore, ESR is guaranteed if, and only if, *TR-Safety$_{t,x}$* and *Data-Safety$_x$* are invariant for every transaction t and every data-item x.

Object-Oriented Epsilon Serializability (OESR) takes the general ESR correctness criterion and specializes it for the RTSORAC real-time object-oriented database model.

Data in the RTSORAC model are represented by objects. Safety for an object o is defined as follows.

$$Object\text{-}Safety_o \equiv \forall\, a \in o_A\ (a.ImpAmt \leq data\_\varepsilon_a)$$

where o_A is the set of attributes of o; that is, if every attribute in an object meets its specified imprecision constraints, then the object is safe.

Transactions in the RTSORAC model operate on objects through the methods of the object. Data values are obtained through the return arguments of the methods and are passed to the objects through the input arguments of methods. Let t_{MI} be the set of method invocations in a transaction t, and let o_M be the set of methods in an object o. The method invocations on o invoked by t are denoted as $t_{MI} \neg o_M$. Safety of a transaction (OT) t with respect to an object o is defined as follows:

$$OT\text{-}Safety_{t,o} \equiv \\ \begin{cases} \forall_m \in (t_{MI} \neg o_M)\ \forall_r \in ReturnArgs(m)\ (r.ImpAmt \leq import\_limit_r) \\ \forall_m \in (t_{MI} \neg o_M)\ \forall_r \in InputArgs(m)\ (i.ImpAmt \leq export\_limit_i) \end{cases}$$

that is, as long as the arguments of the method invocations on object o invoked by OT t are within their imprecision limits, then t is safe with respect to o.

Thus, object-oriented epsilon serializability (OESR) is guaranteed if, and only if, $OT\text{-}Safety_{t,o}$ and $Object\text{-}Safety_o$ are invariant for every object transaction t and every object o.

Transaction-Based Semantic Concurrency Control   A *semantically consistent schedule* is defined as a schedule that transforms the database into a consistent state. Transactions are classified into semantic types based on what they do in the database. For each type, a *compatibility set* is defined to identify which other types are compatible with (i.e., may interleave with) the given type. The user divides a transaction type into *atomic steps*, where a step represents some indivisible, real-world action. Any interleaving that is allowed is between these user-defined steps. When a transaction requires access to a data object, it requests a lock. If no other locks are held on the object, the request is granted and the object keeps track of the compatibility set of the type of transaction holding the lock. If another transaction attempts to lock the same object, the transaction processing mechanism checks to see if the type of the requesting transaction is in the compatibility set of the transaction already holding the lock. If so, the lock is granted; if not, the transaction must wait to gain access to the object. In this technique, serializability is replaced as a correctness criterion by *semantic consistency*.

In a similar approach each transaction has a different set of breakpoints with respect to each different transaction type. This approach allows varying levels of concurrency among different types of transactions. Transactions are grouped into *nested classes*. As the classes become more refined, the level of atomicity becomes finer. For each class, breakpoints inserted in a transaction define where other transactions of the same class can interleave. The breakpoints of higher-level classes are carried down to the lower-level classes. Therefore, for each transaction t, the set of breakpoints where another transaction t' can interrupt is determined by the lowest class containing both t and t'. The levels of atomicity produced by this technique form a hierarchy of allowable interleavings among transactions.

Another transaction-based semantic concurrency control mechanism creates fewer restrictions on allowable interleavings. Nested classes are not used, and therefore the interleavings are not required to be hierarchical. Transactions are classified by types and are divided by placing breakpoints between operations where certain interleavings are allowed. Each breakpoint has associated with it a set, called the *interleaving set*, containing the types of transactions that are permitted to interrupt at that point. Four kinds of locks are used in the concurrency control technique described: *shared, exclusive, relatively shared*, and *relatively exclusive*. A shared lock or exclusive lock is

Table 11.4 Lock Compatibility Table

Lock			Lock Held	
Requested	S	E	RS	RE
S	Yes	No	YES	COND
E	No	No	COND	COND

granted in the traditional way for read access or write access, respectively. Relatively shared and relatively exclusive locks are used to produce nonserializable interleavings. At a breakpoint, the lock can change depending on the actions taken before that point. A shared lock becomes a relatively shared lock at a breakpoint if there is no update before it; otherwise, it becomes an exclusive lock. An exclusive lock always becomes a relatively exclusive lock at a breakpoint. A compatibility table (Table 11.4) is given for these four locks and while some of the entries are simply YES or NO, others, labeled COND, depend on whether or not the type of the transaction requesting the lock is in the interleaving set of the type of the transaction holding the lock. Locks are released after termination of the transaction.

The similarity stack protocol (SSP) defines similarity of data, based on the time at which the data are written. Two data-items are considered to be similar if their timestamps are within a specified bound. Transactions are placed on a scheduling stack according to their priorities. Read/write events of different transactions may swap positions on the stack as long as they are similar.

Several concurrency control techniques have been designed to maintain epsilon serializability. Concurrency control techniques in which read-only transactions need not be serializable with other update transactions, but update transactions must be serializable among themselves, have been described in the literature. The techniques are variations of two-phase locking, timestamp ordering, and optimistic concurrency control. Several concurrency control protocols extend the concept of epsilon serializability to distributed databases. They allow divergence from consistency among database sites as long as their differences remain within specified limits.

Object-Based Semantic Concurrency Control The techniques described in this section take advantage, to varying degrees, of the opportunity for increased concurrency provided by the object-oriented paradigm.

An object-based semantic concurrency control technique can be used in a system that allows nested data objects (i.e., objects containing other objects). A hierarchical structure, called a *granularity graph*, is used to represent the nesting. The outermost object is represented at the root of the graph, and the children of the root represent the objects nested inside. For each operation defined on the object, an *affected set* is computed, containing all nodes in the graph that are affected by the operation. Concurrency is controlled by avoiding conflicts among the operations on the object. A conflict occurs between two operations if they do not *commute*, that is, if the order in which they are performed affects the results returned by the operations or the resulting state of the object. The approach to determining compatibilities between operations is divided into two steps. First, the semantics of the operations are analyzed to determine if they are always compatible, never compatible, or conditionally compatible. The second step is performed dynamically when the operations are requested, to determine the value of a conditional compatibility. This value is determined by computing the intersection of the affected sets of the two operations in question. If this intersection is empty, then the operations commute and therefore are compatible.

Another object-based mechanism uses commutativity as the definition of compatibility. Two slightly different versions of commutativity are defined: *forward commutativity* and *backward commutativity*. The difference between these criteria is subtle, but they are both necessary because each one is used with different recovery mechanisms. Forward commutativity is designed to work with intentions lists, while backward commutativity works with recovery using undo logs. One of the major results of this is that concurrency control and recovery are closely linked and must be considered together. When compatibility between operations is in question, commutativity is computed dynamically.

In another, more recent technique compatibility between operations is based on *recoverability* and not on commutativity. An operation, $o1$, is recoverable relative to another operation, $o2$, if the outcome of performing $o2$ is the same whether or not $o1$ executed immediately before $o2$. Recoverable operations are allowed to execute concurrently but must commit in the order in which they were invoked.

The three object-based semantic concurrency control techniques previously described add concurrency to a database by exploiting the semantics of the object's operations, but each technique ultimately requires serializability as a correctness criterion. Concurrency can be increased even further by relaxing the serializability constraint. The database designer defines the compatibility between operations on an object. This user-defined compatibility may or may not preserve serializability. Consistency constraints are determined by the designer and implemented through the compatibility relations.

RTC, a language to control real-time concurrency, has been presented. Objects called resources have actions defined on them. The *compatibility relation* C_r is a nonsymmetric relation on these actions that determines if two actions are compatible, that is, if the actions can be overlapped to result in a consistent state of the resource. The designer of the system must ensure the correctness of the compatibility relation with respect to the semantics of the resource being defined.

In another technique the user is responsible for defining compatibilities. The user defines all possible dependencies among the operations of an object, possibly involving values of parameters. Some of these dependencies are characterized as insignificant, because cycles formed by them do not affect data consistency. Rather than using serializability as the correctness criterion, a schedule is considered correct if it can be ordered with respect to a relation formed by combining all of the significant dependencies in the objects involved.

Another concept uses a type-specific locking protocol. The locks that a transaction requests should be held only as long as the semantics of the application suggest. Therefore, each application will use a type-specific locking protocol to determine when locks should be released.

Another concurrency control protocol allows bounded inconsistency. The protocol works on an object-based model. In this model, a transaction invokes an operation on an object and the object has a set of possible actions, called the resolution set, from which to execute the operation. The state of an object is defined by the sequence of resolutions that has been performed in response to invoked operations. Two resolution sequences are considered equivalent if the resulting object states are the same.

The object designer determines compatibility of object operations based on the concept of commutativity with bounded inconsistency. For every resolution sequence $o_p.o_q$ of the operation sequence $p.q$, the designer defines a *forward resolution set dilating function* (f_{pq}) and a *backward resolution set dilating function* (b_{pq}). These functions are defined such that for every state s, if there is a resolution sequence $o_p.o_q$ of the operation sequence $p.q$ with o_p in the resolution set of p $(rs(p))$ and o_q in the resolution set of q $(rs(q))$, then there exists a resolution sequence $o_{q'}.o_{p'}$, which is equivalent to $o_p.o_q$ for the operation sequence $q.p$ with $o_{p'}$ in $f_{pq}(rs(p))$ and $o_{q'}$ in $b_{pq}(rs(q))$.

The resolution set dilating functions are placed in a compatibility table. When a transaction invokes an operation on an object, the concurrency control mechanism looks in the table and evaluates the resolution set dilating functions to determine if the invoked operation is compatible with all concurrent operations in the object. If the operations are found to be compatible, the resolution sets of the corresponding operations are updated to take into account any inconsistency that may have been allowed by the interleaving of operations. The object designer specifies inconsistency limits for each operation and the protocol ensures that the limits are not violated.

Another concurrency control technique is based on the RTSORAC model (described in Section 11.4.3). It uses *semantic locks* to determine which transactions may invoke methods on an object. The semantic locking mechanism uses a set of preconditions and the object's compatibility function to determine if a requested semantic lock should be granted.

The compatibility function is a run-time function that evaluates a Boolean expression and is defined on every ordered pair of methods of the object. The Boolean expression is used to determine if the pair of methods involved can execute concurrently. It may contain predicates involving characteristics of the object or of the system in general, such as affected sets of methods, temporal consistency and/or imprecision of the data involved, and values of method arguments.

In the semantic locking mechanism, there are two possible outcomes to a semantic lock request: either the semantic lock becomes active and the associated method invocation is executed, or the request is placed on a priority queue to be granted later. Figure 11.11 illustrates the steps of the semantic locking mechanism.

The first phase of the semantic locking mechanism computes the potential amount of imprecision that the requested method will introduce into the attributes that it writes and into its return arguments. The next phase of the semantic locking mechanism tests preconditions that determine if granting the lock would violate temporal consistency or imprecision constraints. If any precondition fails, then the semantic locking mechanism places the request on the priority queue to be retried when another lock is released. If the preconditions hold, the semantic locking mechanism updates the imprecision amounts of the data that will be affected by execution of the requested method. Upon successful passing of the preconditions, the semantic locking mechanism checks the compatibility function to make sure that the requested method is compatible with all of the currently active method invocations, as well as all requested method invocations on the queue with higher priority. For each compatibility function test that succeeds, the mechanism accumulates the imprecision that could be introduced by the corresponding interleaving. If all tests succeed, the semantic locking mechanism grants the semantic lock, places it in the active lock set, and makes the requested method ready for execution. If any test fails, the mechanism restores the original values of any changed imprecision amounts and places the request in the priority queue to be retried when another lock is released.

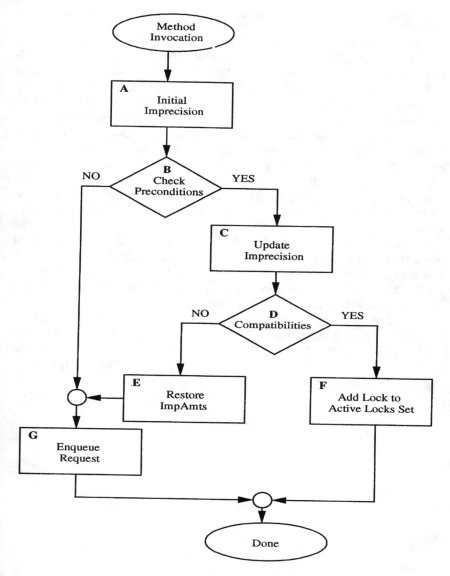

Figure 11.11   Semantic locking mechanism

This concurrency control technique allows for the expression of the tradeoff between temporal and logical consistency, through the user-defined compatibility function. It has been shown to maintain OESR under certain restrictions, and thus can bound imprecision while making an active effort to meet data and transaction timing constraints.

11.7 SUMMARY

The added dimension of temporal consistency requirements to the requirements of a traditional database complicates the design of real-time databases. Furthermore, the predictability concern of hard real-time applications often requires simplification of database techniques. This paradox has caused real-time database development to lag behind that of non-real-time databases. For this reason the only two commercial real-time databases that we know of, Zip and EagleSpeed, are still far from meeting most real-time database requirements. Recent research in modeling, scheduling, and concurrency control has started to pave the way for better-suited real-time database systems. The potential market for real-time databases in control applications is large. Standardization efforts, such as RTSQL, should help further the development efforts.

Despite the recent research and development efforts, there remains a great deal of work to be done to make real-time databases fully meet the requirements outlined in Section 11.3. Some these questions include: What architecture and operating system support is necessary? How is recovery performed? How can inconsistency be managed and used? How do these requirements impact *active database* design efforts? How does distribution affect real-time requirements? Can such real-time database systems actually be built and used? Can their interfaces be standardized? The next five years should be important ones in answering some of these questions.

12

Interoperating and Integrating the Multidatabase and Systems

David K. Hsiao

This chapter is based on a featured speech with the same title delivered at ACM CSC '95. I would like to thank Professor T. Y. Lin of California State University at San Jose and Dr. Richard Brice of MCC Corporation for inviting me to deliver the speech on which this chapter is developed.*

12.1 INTRODUCTION

Heterogeneous and multidatabase systems have evolved due to a real need of the information management community. Data are a valued commodity in most modern organizations. The goal of modern business is to collect and maintain the most up-to-date information on business issues of relevance to an organization in order to aid in the decision-making process within the organization. Companies have realized that the holder of the most up-to-date and complete information that describes a problem space or competitive marketplace will be in the best position to make the optimal business decision. We all know that the company making the best decisions typically becomes the wealthiest company. So information is power in this context. The problem is that not all needed or desired information is derived from

---

* Dr. Hsiao is Professor of Computer Science, Computer Science Department, Naval Postgraduate School, Monterey, CA 93943

a single, nor is it in a uniform, easy-to-use format. This poses a problem to the information seeker who wishes to extract the most important information from many diverse sources. That is where multidatabase systems and heterogeneous computing systems come into play. As we will see, there are a variety of solutions for solving the heterogeneous and multidatabase information management problem.

12.2 THE DATABASE PROBLEM

What is the database problem that requires the interoperable and/or integration solution? The central issue to deal with is the stored information's data structure—its representation and the access schemes in place to extract and use the information. It would be a wonderful world if there were but one database information model and but one access method. This would allow anyone to enter a database, browse through the stored information, extract what looks interesting, and/or store information required for future use—all without any added burdens. However, this is not the state of the world today: Simply look at the pages of the Internet—at the volume of database products and the number of vendors that have shown up on this medium. There are, of course, relational database products, which may or may not implement the full relational database standards specified within the American National Standards Institute's (ANSI) Structured Query Language (SQL). There are also network database systems, but none that adheres to the NDL standard for full conformance. There are numerous object-oriented database system products. They do not, however, have a standard database model or language as of this writing, but are moving forward toward an acceptable consortium standard. Then there are the mixed models, in particular the relational and object models that have been proliferating lately. This simple overview of the world of standards does not even begin to touch the myriad data format standards that exist in the common business community, the medical community, the industrial community, the engineering community, and so on. All of these organizations and factions want to see and store their data and information in very diverse forms. So how is this cornucopia of information and dialects to be pulled together? Does it make sense to try? Is the database problem real and prevailing? In other words, we do not want to work on fictitious or frivolous problems.

12.2.1 The Database Problem versus the Large Organization

The database problem only occurs in large and established organizations in the United States, such as the Department of Defense (DoD), auto manufacturers, national retailers, and telecommunication companies. This problem occurs in few large and established organizations outside the United States. However, such foreign companies will, in due course, have the same database problem facing our domestic companies; in other words, the database problem we will discuss here is rooted in large and established organizations. These organizations must overcome the problem in order to be competitive in the Information Age.

12.2.2 Two Factors Causing the Problem

Let us review two basic factors that have caused the database problem in the United States. The first factor is the characteristics of classical and modern databases and database systems. The factor is the organizational needs and requirements of all databases and database systems.

Factor One: The Characteristics of Databases   The first factor causing the database problem is the characteristics of classical and modern databases and systems. There are three characteristics of every classical or modern database and its database system: The first is its specialization in a distinct class of database applications; the second is the permanency of its database; and the third is the regularity of its database transactions. These three characteristics can be abbreviated as application specificity, database permanency, and transaction regularity. We elaborate on them in the following paragraphs.

Application Specificity: Regardless of what the manufacturer of a database system (DBMS) may claim, the database and its DBMS are developed for supporting a specific class of database applications. As an example, we look at the hierarchical database system.

Example one: Hierarchical databases and hierarchical database management systems are intended for product assemblies. Hierarchical databases were first developed to support applications where the nature of the problem could be broken down into composite pieces. They were first introduced in the 1960s by IBM to support an aircraft parts database and the information management system that supported the database. An aircraft is a superassembly of several major assemblies: the fuselage, landing gears, engines, avionics, and others. Each major assembly consists of several subassemblies: for the fuselage, for example, there are wings, tails, the interior, the exterior, and others. Each major subassembly consists of several sub-subassemblies. At the bottom of the superassembly, there are individual records of individual parts. This is called the multilevel, one-to-many correspondence of data. The entire hierarchical database of the aircraft assembly is maintained by the database. Thus, the hierarchical database and hierarchical database management systems (HDBMSs) are

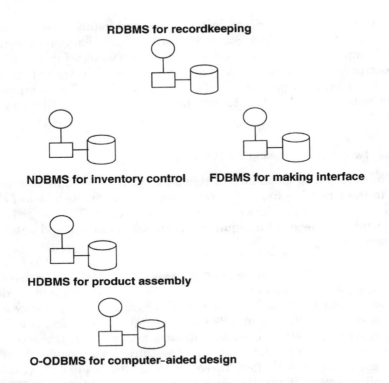

Figure 12.1   Automobile hierarchical assembly

specialized in the application to problems such as product assemblies—for example, a hierarchical database that could be built to support an automobile assembly (Figure 12.1) would consist of a hierarchical breakdown of the components of the vehicle.

Example two: The network database and the network database management system (NDBMS) are specialized in the application for inventory control. Retailers are not manufacturing products; therefore, they are not interested in product assemblies themselves. Instead, as retailers of products, they are mostly concerned with supplies of products and the whereabouts of suppliers. We note that one supplier may supply several products and one product may be supplied by several suppliers. (This is called the many-to-many correspondence.)

The U.S. Department of Defense (DoD) is a heavy user of the network database and its network database management system (NDBMS). The network database system was developed by the DoD to keep track of its inherently interrelated database entities—for example, weapon systems, troop relationships to weapon systems, and other information with hard-wired relationships. Even though the DoD does not make conventional weapons, it must, nevertheless, keep track of all the parts of each weapon and the suppliers of all these parts and weapons. (It is not surprising that the first call for the network database and its NDBMS in the 1970s was issued by a committee, CODASYL, dominated by DoD database users. All the major computer companies in the 1970s, except IBM, manufactured NDBMSs.)

Example three: The relational database and relational database management system (RDBMS) are specialized in the application of recordkeeping. The popularity of Ingres, ORACLE, and IBM-DB2, introduced in the late 1970s and early 1980s, is primarily due to the fact that any organization, large or small, must keep records. There are payroll records, personnel records, asset records, and many others. There is always the one-to-one correspondence between individuals (persons or items) and records kept for these individuals.

Example four: The functional database and functional database management system (FDBMS) are specialized in the application of making inferences. The introduction of Daplex by CCA in the 1980s was due to its functional database management system. The functional database can have millions of facts and thousands of rules for making inferences. The functional database management system manages all the stored facts and rules. The application of rules to stored facts and to inferred facts is mathematically equivalent to the application of functions on one or more variables—thus, they are termed functional.

Examples five and six: The object-oriented database and object-oriented database management system (O-ODBMS) are specialized in the application of either inheritance hierarchies of records, the covering of two or more inheritance hierarchies of records, or both. These are the database and database system of the 1990s.

Because object-oriented database management systems are appearing in this decade and are instigated from many sources, they are too new to settle on a "standard" concept of object-oriented database management. Most of the object-oriented databases and object-oriented database systems have the first of the following two capabilities.

1. Inheritance hierarchies of records: Records of a hierarchy are termed objects. The object-oriented hierarchy is different from the arbitrary hierarchy employed in the hierarchical database and hierarchical database management system. It is based on its inheritance, where objects at a lower level of the hierarchy are required to have (inherit) some of the attributes and operations of the objects at a higher level in the hierarchy. The object-oriented data-

base and object-oriented database management systems, although intended for computer-aided design (CAD) applications, are, therefore, good for product assembly applications as well.

2. The covering of hierarchies: Objects of an object class in one inheritance hierarchy may each associate with (cover) some subset of objects of an object class in another inheritance hierarchy. From inheritable same objects, this association (covering) creates for each of them a network of objects inherently different from it. The object-oriented network is different from the arbitrary network in the network database and network database management system, since the association (covering) criterion must be defined by the database creator in terms of properties of both object classes. Therefore, the object-oriented database and object-oriented database management system, although intended for aggregation applications, are also good for inventory control applications.

Our concluding remarks on application specificity are that, from the previous six examples, we have learned that classical and modern databases and their database systems are application-specific; that is, all specialize in certain kinds of applications, although object-oriented databases and database management systems have broader applications (i.e., application-general).

It would be overkill to use an object-oriented database and its O-ODBMS for recordkeeping, since the relational database and its RDBMS have been doing a superb job with recordkeeping since the 1980s. Also, a relational database and its RDBMS should not be used for making inferences. Although we can store facts as tuples (i.e., records) in the relational database, we cannot store inference rules as tuples in the same database.

Database Permanency: Unlike files of an operating system that can come and go, the database of a database management system is permanent. Although updates of a database are done regularly, the database created for the organization tends to stay with (or survive) the organization permanently. Do not confuse the term permanency with the term archives. Good operating systems periodically create a copy of all the files on the tape as archives—so do database management systems, which routinely create all the updates on the disk for back-up and recovery purposes, and periodically create a copy of all new and updated data in the database for archival purposes. Tape archives are needed in certain systems. However, for backing up updates, there is an additional need for a disk, not tape, system in a database management system.

Our concluding remark on database permanency is that database permanency requires its DBMS to maintain the database during the lifetime of the organization.

Transaction Regularity: Transactions and programs are different. A contrast of their differences may increase our understanding of the transaction. A program is written in some programming language and compiled by the language compiler into computer instructions for execution. During the program's execution, the program reads some input data from an input medium, performs some computations, and writes some output data into an output medium. Most programs are computation bound, since the amount of time spent on computations is much larger than the amount of time spent on reading and writing data. A program has a short lifetime, since we tend to change the computation often, which means either writing a new program or modifying the old program.

A transaction is written in some data manipulation language and partly interpreted by the language compiler/monitor into database management system calls for execution. During the transaction's execution, the transaction retrieves some data from the database, performs some updates, and stores updated data into the same database. Most transactions are I/O bound, since the amount of time spent on the storage and retreival of data is insignificant compared to the time spent on updates. A transaction has a very long lifetime, since we tend to update data in the database without changing the computation of these data.

Consider a payroll transaction for a biweekly payroll. The transaction must be executed biweekly against all the biweekly payroll records in the database. The number of biweekly payroll records is equal to the number of biweekly salaried employees.

For each biweekly employee, the transaction must do three operations: retrieve the biweekly payroll record for each employee, update a small number of figures in the record to reflect the number and the amount of pay rendered, and store the updated record into the same database. The retrieval, update, and storage transactions are I/O bound, since the retrieval and storage of hundreds and thousands of records are extensive I/O operations, which can overlap with the small amount of computations needed to recalculate these figures for each record.

The last storage operation is complex, since it cannot simply store updated figures over original figures. Three auxiliary I/O operations must be accomplished with the storage operation: store the original data and updates to a backup-and-recovery disk for a possible transaction and/or system failure, store the original data on a tape for archival purposes, and send the updated record to the printer for a hard copy.

Our concluding remarks on transaction regularity are that transactions have a long lifetime, transactions must be run on the DBMS against data coming from the database regularly over the entire lifetime of the organization, and transactions involve large amounts of I/O and small amounts of computations.

In summary, three characteristics of the database and its DBMS causing the database problem in a large organization are application specificity, database permanency, and transaction regularity.

Factor Two: The Organizational Needs   The second factor causing the database problem is the organizational needs and requirements of all the databases and database systems used in an organization. These can be divided into three categories: application multiplicity, data sharing, and resource consolidation. We examine each of these categories in the following paragraphs.

Application Multiplicity: A large company must keep records; control inventories; manage parts, components, and assemblies of all the products; come up with new designs; work out new regulatory compliances; and maintain the organizational hierarchy or hierarchies of the company. As an established company, the organization may have been using, over the years, first the hierarchical database and hierarchical database management system for product assembly; next the network database and network database management system for inventory control; the relational database and relational database management system for recordkeeping; the functional database and functional database management system for making inferences on market surveys and regulatory compliances; and finally the object-oriented database and object-oriented database management system for the computer-aided design of new products and for the organizational management of units, subunits, and human and physical resources of all the units.

The above scenario of a large and established company indicates that due to its large size and its long establishment, the organization always has multiple database applications—for example, in recordkeeping, product assembly, inventory control, design automation, regulatory compliances, and organizational maintenance. To support multiple and diverse applications, many heterogeneous databases and their database management systems have been introduced into the organization over the years. The heterogeneity of these databases and database management systems is directly proportional to the multiplicity of these diverse database applications. In Figure 12.2, we depict five distinct database platforms, that is, that the application

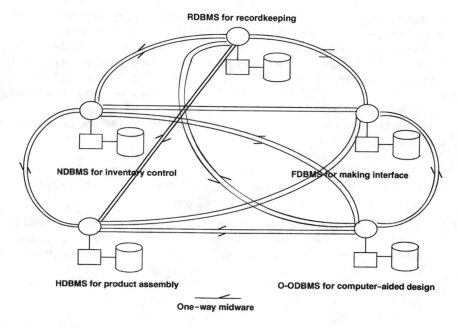

Figure 12.2   Complexity of data sharing in a heterogeneous DBMS

multiplicity and database heterogeneity of the organization are both equal to five.

Data Sharing: The corporate memory and assets are mostly recorded in various heterogeneous databases in the corporation. In order for the corporation to access them periodically for the purpose of devising a new business strategy, a new regulatory compliance, a better understanding of corporate assets, or a better appreciation of corporate practices, the sharing of data among all the heterogeneous databases and database management systems must be facilitated. Therefore, data sharing among all the in-house databases and database management systems is a necessary requirement for a modern corporation to be competitive in the Information Age. The effective use of information collected in various heterogeneous databases and efficient processing of information by any database management system are the modern organizational requirements for databases and database management systems.

The complexity of data sharing among heterogeneous databases and database management systems increases multiplicatively over the heterogeneity of these databases and database management systems—for example, if there are n heterogeneous databases and database management systems in a corporation, then the maximal data sharing is achieved if we allow n * (n − 1) one-way, system-to-system or database-to-database accesses. n * (n − 1) means that n multiplies (n − 1); the product is close to n squared. The complexity of data sharing among heterogeneous databases and database management systems is therefore on the order of n squared. See Figure 12.2 for a maximal complexity of five heterogeneous databases and database management systems in a corporation.

Resource Consolidation: The following three factors prompted the need for resource consolidation.

1. Due to the database permanency and transaction regularity, every database and its DBMS must be maintained within the organization for the entire lifetime of the organization.

2. Due to the application specificity of each database and its DBMS and the application multiplicity of a large and established organization, the organization must use a number of heterogeneous databases and their respective database systems. The heterogeneity of the databases and systems means the heterogeneity and multiplicity of database applications. Thus, the organization must have several teams of professionals, each supporting a database and its DBMS and writing transactions for the application.

3. With a number of heterogeneous databases and systems in the organization, data sharing among all the databases and their database systems requires new software, new hardware, and additional professionals for solving the data-sharing complexity. The number of professional teams in the organization is one greater than the heterogeneity of databases and systems or the multiplicity of database applications.

The consequence of the previous three factors is important: With the multiplicity of databases, database management systems software, database management systems hardware, and support personnel, the cost of sustaining heterogeneous database applications in an organization is high. In addition, the organization needs data sharing among heterogeneous databases and database management systems if it is to operate effectively. The cost of data sharing will be additional, regardless of the method or methods used for data sharing. Therefore, from the viewpoint of an organization, there is an acute need within the organization for the consolidation of these resources for the purpose of reducing the overall cost to the organization. Resources to be consolidated are, of course, heterogeneous databases, heterogeneous database management systems software, data-sharing software, heterogeneous database management systems hardware, data-sharing hardware, and various teams of the support personnel.

12.3 SOLUTIONS FOR SOLVING THE DATABASE PROBLEM

In order to accentuate the database problem in a large and established organization, we introduce the following new terminology. All the heterogeneous databases in the organization are said to form a multidatabase. Depending upon a specific solution, the multidatabase can be considered as any one of the following three.

1. Logically one and physically one
2. Logically many and physically many
3. Logically many and physically one

There is no solution for a multidatabase that can be logically one and physically many (we'll elaborate on this in paragraphs dealing with individual solutions). We need an interoperable solution for data sharing in a multidatabase environment. We need an integration solution to consolidate all the data of the multidatabase, all the software for both data sharing and database management system operations, all the hardware, and all the support personnel.

12.3.1 Solution One: The Massive Many-to-One Conversion

This solution is deceptively simple. It calls for the selection of a "standard" data model, a "standard" data language, and a "standard" database management system, so that

1. All the data in the multidatabase are converted into a database based on the standard data model.

2. All the existing transactions written in various data languages are rewritten in the standard data language.

3. All the existing heterogeneous database systems, their computers and storage devices, and various teams of support personnel are to be retired.

4. There is only one standard database management system on one computer (albeit a database supercomputer) and its new storage devices, with the support of only one new team of support professionals.

In this solution, both requirements of data sharing and resource consolidation have been met. Although physically there were many heterogeneous databases, transactions, and database management systems before the conversion, none of the original data models, data languages, or database systems is supported (logically) in the new data model, data language, or database management system. The only exception would be found if one of the original databases were the same model as the new database system. Both logically and physically, there is only one new consolidated database, with its new database management system, its new hardware, and one new team of support personnel.

This solution is called the *logically one and physically one* solution. In the logically one and physically one solution, there is no need for any interheterogeneous database and database management system communication. Every user employs the same data model to view data, the same language to write transactions, and the same database to store and retrieve data. The entire multidatabase and multidatabase management systems are converted into a homogeneous database and database management system. We know homogeneous users do not have interoperable issues. Meanwhile, all the heterogeneities are integrated into a homogeneous entity. There is no integration issue any more. The massive many-to-one conversion seems to solve both our interoperable and integration problems.

There are many problems with this solution. The first one is the choice of the target (i.e., standard) data model, target (standard) data language, and target (standard) database management system for the conversion. There seems to be two likely targets for this conversion: either a simple and classical one, such as the relational data model, structured query language (SQL), and relational database management system (RDBMS); or a complex and modern one, such as the object-oriented data model, object-oriented data language (O-ODL), and object-oriented database management system (O-ODBMS).

Missing the Database Conversion Target We may want to convert a heterogeneous database into an equivalent and new relational database. There are many limitations, as the following text indicates.

The limitations of primary and foreign keys—We can use the foreign key of the relational data model to simulate the parent-to-child hierarchy in the hierarchical database—for example, the foreign key can be used to "relate" a tuple in the parent relation to another tuple in the child relation. However, the foreign key, as well as the primary key, is a one-for-one key; that is, one key value identifies one tuple. It is not a one-for-many key. If the parent tuple is related to many distinct child tuples of the other relation, then we have a problem with using the foreign key. It takes some clever designs on the part of the conversion expert to use a number of one-to-one keys to "simulate" a one-to-many key. In real-world nondatabase applications, as well as in hierarchical, network, and object-oriented database applications, the need for one-for-many keys is great—for example, we use a master key to open several distinct locks. The master key is a one-for-many key.

The limitation of composite keys—The primary or foreign key of a parent relation can be composed of several primary keys of other child relations, thereby allowing the parent relation to be related to several child relations. This use of composite keys simulates effectively a parent-to-children relationship, that is, a parent-to-children hierarchy. However, this use of either the primary key or the foreign key restricts a single tuple from each child relation to be related to the parent tuple. In hierarchical and network databases, it is possible for two or more child records (tuples) of the same record type (of the same relation) to be related to a parent record (tuple). Again, it takes some clever designs on the part of the conversion expert to use a number of one-to-one primary or foreign keys to "simulate" the relationship of one tuple of a parent relation for many tuples of each child relation and many child relations.

Keys and schemata are no substitution for data diagrams—The use of either foreign keys, primary keys, or both to simulate hierarchies and networks is at best tedious and at worst confusing. The clear and elegant hierarchical and network data diagrams of their respective databases have become a collection of relation schemata with spiderweb-like pointers coming from these key-carrying relations.

Violation of the referential integrity—Child tuples may be deleted without knowing that they have been referenced by foreign keys in some other (parent) relations. Thus, we discover at a later time that these foreign keys refer to no child tuples. We then have dangling foreign keys! They are said to violate the referential integrity of the relational database. One way to avoid such violations is not to delete tuples referenced by foreign keys. However, at the deletion time the tuples to be deleted are identified by their primary keys, not by their (parent) foreign keys. How would the deletion operation know the whereabouts of foreign keys referencing these tuples?

Manual versus automatic invocation of referential and integrity safeguards—In either the hierarchical or network database, its database management system always leads the child record to its parent or owner record by way of the built-in pointers. However, in the relational database, when a tuple is referenced by a foreign key, no lead from the tuple can be obtained on the whereabouts of the tuple containing the referencing foreign key. In addition, the network database management system has elaborate and built-in retention (i.e., no deletion) and insertion options (i.e., constraints), which are invoked by the network database management system automatically to prevent possible violation of referential and other integrities. In the relational database management system, data integrity must be asserted and invoked by the user through actions within a relational transaction.

The limitation of fixed-length records—All the nonrelational databases accommodate variable-length records. The relational database does not. Thus, when converting all the heterogeneous databases into a relational database, all the variable-length records become fixed-length tuples with padded null values. Problems of a null value are many.

- It is not a value; therefore, it cannot be computed upon.

- All the algorithms must be rewritten in order to identify null values and avoid null values in their computations.

- It is a placeholder; therefore, it takes up storage space.

- A placeholder does not indicate whether the value is temporarily absent or permanently prohibited.

The limitation of possible realization of some constructs in other, more recent and more advanced data models—Neither the functional database nor the object-oriented database can be readily converted to an equivalent relational database. For a functional example, the multivalued function, Indicator, may produce one or more indicative values, depending on the malfunction number of the function used. In the functional notation, we write the above as

$$\text{Indicator (malfunction } i) = \{v_1, v_2, \ldots, v_{ni}\}$$

We note that ni's may be different for different i's. How to represent this multivalued function as a number of relations (since by definition a relation is a single-valued function) is a major conversion problem.

The limitation on encapsulating operations with data—The concept of embedded operations (also called methods or actions) in an object class cannot be readily converted into embedded operations in a relation. In fact, in the relational data model, only attributes are included in the relational schema of a relation. No operations are included in any relational schema of a relation. Relational operations are embedded in the relational data language, such as SQL and Ingres. Transactions written in either relational data language can be applied to any relation.

In the object-oriented transaction, all the operations of the transaction on a given object class must be those named operations embedded in the object class. In other words, it is not possible to have an object-oriented transaction to operate on objects of an object class with operations unnamed and not included in the object class.

The relational data model enforces the attribute inheritance on all the tuples in a given relation. The object-oriented data model enforces, in addition to the attribute inheritance, the operational inheritance on all the objects in a given object class. How to enforce operational inheritance in a relational database is another conversion issue.

The limitation of rewritten transactions for existing applications—The application specificity and transaction regularity require the rewritten transactions to apply specifically to each ongoing application on a regular basis. How can we be sure that the new transaction has captured the intent and extent of the established and ongoing applications? Neither the relational professionals nor the nonrelational professionals are versed in two or more data models and data manipulation languages. We must hire a large number of bilingual specialists who know extremely well at least two data models and two data languages with one being the source (i.e., one of the heterogeneous ones minus the relational) and the other being the target (i.e., the relational).

Where and how could we recruit so many bilinguists, assuming we have plenty of funds for hiring? Even if we can hire many bilinguists with great expense for the database and transaction conversion, there are still issues of the viability and quality of the database and transaction conversion. There may be one or more heterogeneous databases, and one or more transactions cannot be converted into the relational standard effectively and efficiently, regardless of the profound expertise of these linguists.

Overkilling the Conversion Target   In target two, we use the latest data model, data language, and database management system as the conversion target. Thus, the object-oriented data model, data language, and database management system are the targets. However, this may be overkill. Since most of the classical and modern data models can be subsumed in the object-oriented data model, most of the classical and modern data languages can also be subsumed in the object-oriented data languages. Finally, as we will see in the following paragraphs, object-oriented database management systems are known to be complex and, at present, slow, and they would probably require more hardware and software than any of the other database management systems.

More complex and slower database systems—After the database and transaction conversion, O-ODBMS will be more complex and slower with these subsumptions.

Application-general and its negative impact on all the specific applications—One of the main reasons we use the application-specific data model, data language, and database management system is that for the application the model, language, and database management system are effective and efficient. It is not surprising that almost all the recordkeeping applications have been taken over by the relational databases and their relational database management systems; all the product assembly applications have been taken over by the hierarchical databases and their hierarchical database management systems; all the inventory control applications have been taken over by the network databases and their network database management systems; and all the inference-making applications have been taken over by the functional database and the functional database management system.

Now, the object-oriented data model, O-ODL, and the O-ODBMS are application-general, since they subsume all the data models, data languages, and database systems, as well as their applications. The problem with the application-general O-ODBMS is that it is less effective and less efficient for each specific application.

The Logically One and Physically One Solution In solution one, both the logical multidatabase and the physical multidatabase are the same. The user sees what the multidatabase has stored. Thus, we convert a set of heterogeneous databases into a single homogeneous database. All the heterogeneous database users become homogeneous; that is, they all learn the same standard model, language, and DBMS.

12.3.2 Solution Two: The Two-Way Midware

This solution is aimed at resolving the data-sharing problem among heterogeneous data of the multidatabase of the organization. Referring to Figure 12.2 again, we need

$$2 * \binom{n}{2} = 2 * \frac{n(n-1)}{2} = n(n-1)$$

one-way midware. For $n = 5$, there are 20 one-way midware. The one-way midware for any pair of heterogeneous databases and database systems operates as described in the following subsections.

Providing a Homogeneous Database Schema for Heterogeneous Data

Based on the data model of the first database system, one-way midware provides a homogeneous database schema for heterogeneous data of the database in the second database system. The effect is that the heterogeneous data are homogeneous to users of the first database system—for example, the relational-to-hierarchical midware may create a relational schema for a hierarchical database for the purpose of allowing relational users to view and access a hierarchical database relationally (e.g., with SQL). More precisely, we call this the relational (à la hierarchical) schema.

Translating a Transaction into an Equivalent One in the Other Data Language Based on grammars of data languages of the first and second database systems, respectively, the midware translates transactions written in the data language of the first database system into equivalent transactions in the data language of the second database system. The one-way midware then forwards each equivalent transaction to the second database system for processing. The syntactical and semantic equivalence of data and language constructs in the first pair of data model and data language and those in the second pair of data model and data language is known to and built into the one-way midware. Evidently, the writer of the midware is a bilinguist.

If a relational transaction, for example, written in SQL, is sent through the relational to hierarchical midware, then the midware translates the SQL transaction into an equivalent hierarchical transaction such as DL/I. Further, the midware forwards the DL/I transaction to the hierarchical database management system, say, IMS, for processing. IMS manages the hierarchical database, since DL/I is the hierarchical data language of IMS.

Converting Heterogeneous Results into a Homogeneous Equivalent Once the equivalent transaction is executed in the second database system, it may produce results that are in the data-model format of the second database system. The resulting data are forwarded to the midware. On the basis of the database schema created earlier, the midware then transforms the resulting data into the data-model format of the first database system and forwards the newly formatted data to the user of the transaction in the first database system.

If we continue with the previous example, then the DL/I transaction can generate some results (i.e., hierarchical data). These hierarchical data are forwarded to the relational-to-hierarchical midware. In consultation with the relational (hierarchical) schema, the midware transforms these data into equivalent relational data such as tuples and relations. The midware then routes them to the appropriate waiting SQL transaction.

Concluding Remarks on the Midware **On the possibility of two-way midware**—Since the one-way midware knows the semantic equivalence of data-model and data-language constructs of two database systems, it can be extended into a two-way or both-way midware—for example, the relational-to-hierarchical midware can be extended to hierarchical-to-relational midware as well. Thus, we have relational-to-and-from-hierarchical midware. This two-way or both-way midware is termed relational-hierarchical midware for short.

On the multiplicative number of two-way midware—The number is exactly the following binomial coefficient.

$$\binom{n}{2} = \frac{n\,(n-1)}{2}$$

We see that this number is still multiplicatively large, if the heterogeneity of the multidatabase and systems in the organization is large—for example, for seven heterogeneous databases and systems, we need 21 two-way midware packages.

On the lack of quality control of all the midware—Each two-way midware is developed by a bilinguist. It is seldom the case that the same bilinguist develops different two-way midware. Using the previous example, for only a heterogeneity of seven, we need 21 bilinguists for 21 different midware. Where can we find 21 first-rate bilinguists to develop our own two-way midware? Or, where can we find 21 companies that can supply 21 first-rate, two-way midware packages?

On the absence of any solution for resource consolidation—It is this shortcoming that renders the midware solution incomplete and transient. Large and established organizations are all downsizing. The multiplicative addition of midware packages, although facilitating data sharing, has increased the cost of sustaining the multidatabase and its database systems, without eliminating or replacing any heterogeneous database or system.

The Logically Many and Physically Many Solution In solution two, despite the presence of a great deal of midware, users of the multidatabase are heterogeneous. Thus, the multidatabase is both logically many and, since there is no physical consolidation of data, physically many.

12.3.3 Solution Three: The Some-Conversion and Some-Midware Solution

So far, we have reviewed solution one (massive many-to-one conversion) and solution two (the two-way midware). Both have severe limitations. Nevertheless, both are practical to certain extents. Solution three is to take up their practical extents, in order to approximate the data-sharing and resource-consolidation requirement of the organization.

Many-to-Some Conversion Instead of Many-to-One In our discussion of the many-to-one conversion, we have pointed out the following: On the one hand, RDBMS is application-specific for recordkeeping. On the other hand, O-ODBMS is application-general. However, to support the recordkeeping application on O-ODBMS is overkill.

The many-to-two conversion solution is many-to-some—The many-to-two (or m-to-2) conversion solution suggests that the organization is to have only two heterogeneous databases and two heterogeneous database systems—for example, the relational database of all the records is managed by the relational database management system, run on its own computer and storage devices, and supported by a team of relational professionals. All the other heterogeneous databases for other applications (e.g., in product assemblies, inventory control, and inference making) are converted into an equivalent object-oriented database. Further, all the other transactions (written in nonrelational data languages) for other applications are rewritten in the object-oriented database language. They are object-oriented transactions for object-oriented database management systems. There is a need for computer and storage devices dedicated to the object-oriented database management system. Additionally, there is a need for a support team of object-oriented database professionals.

The conversion effort may require a large number of bilinguists. However, once the conversion process is completed, their presence and effort will no longer be needed.

The m-to-2 conversion consolidates resources into two sites—Because this conversion integrates all the heterogeneous data into two heterogeneous databases and two separate database systems, there is still the intersystem data-sharing issue.

Interoperating two heterogeneous databases and their systems—In this multidatabase, the heterogeneity n is 2. Thus, $n * (n - 1) = 2$. In other words, we need only two one-way midware packages or one two-way midware package. They are the relational-to-object-oriented midware and the object-oriented-to-relational midware. Collectively, these are called the relational object-oriented midware.

Comments on the Many-to-Some Conversion **Pros of using the solution**—This practical solution has reduced some problems associated with the many-to-one conversion—for instance, instead of being a massive effort, it becomes less massive with fewer conversions. It also reduces the number of midware packages used in the new environment. However, it does not eliminate any of the problems associated with conversion and midware; it only mitigates these issues.

Cons of using the solution—This solution locks the database user to the existing data models, languages, and database systems. If a new data model, language, and database system appear in the future for a new database application, then the only ways to support the new application are: (1) converting its data into either one of existing heterogeneous databases and (2) translating its transactions into equivalent transactions written in either one of the existing data languages.

More cons of not using the solution—If we do not convert the new application and new database technology into the existing multidatabase and systems, then we can start a new database, write a new set of transactions, and run a new DBMS. In this way we return to our root of the database problem where all the databases, transactions, and systems are scattered in the organization with no data sharing and resource consolidation.

12.3.4 Solution Four: The Multiple-Interface and Single-Kernel DBMS

By combining the practicality of solutions one and two, we have found a compromise in solution three (the some-conversion and some-midware solution). Nevertheless, solution three has some of the short-term limitations and long-term problems exhibited in solutions one and two. Now, we review a new solution, solution four, in the following paragraphs. Solution four is still experimental, although it may turn out to be the most promising solution in providing interoperable and integration solutions to the multidatabase and its database management systems.

The Two-Layer Architecture of the New DBMS In Figure 12.3, we depict an example of the two-layer architecture of the new database management system. The bottom layer is the system layer on the hardware, called the kernel database management system, or, for short, the kernel. As a database management system, it has its own data model, language, and database management system operations. They are known as the attribute-based data model (ABDM), the attribute-based data language (ABDL), and the primary operations of the attribute-

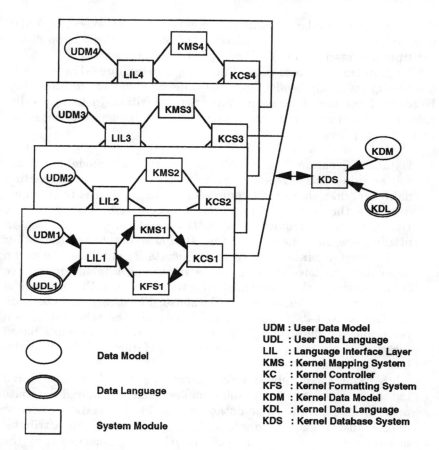

UDM : User Data Model
UDL : User Data Language
LIL : Language Interface Layer
KMS : Kernel Mapping System
KC : Kernel Controller
KFS : Kernel Formatting System
KDM : Kernel Data Model
KDL : Kernel Data Language
KDS : Kernel Database System

Data Model

Data Language

System Module

Figure 12.3 Attribute-based database management system architecture

based database management system (ABDBMS). As a singly modeled and monolingual database management system, ABDBMS supports only the attribute-based database. Thus, the kernel is a homogeneous database management system. On the other hand, the top layer is the system layer interacting with the user. This layer consists of all the model/language interfaces. A particular model/language interface is named after a well-known pair of data model and data language for which interaction and interface took place between the user and the database—for example, there is the relational/SQL interface.

The role of the kernel—The kernel allows the attribute-based user to create an attribute-based database in the kernel. For this database, an attribute-based schema for the attribute-based database is created by the kernel. Briefly, we call it the attribute-based schema.

With the attribute-based schema, the kernel also executes ABDL transactions over the attribute-based database. This role is no different from any stand-alone DBMS of the past and present.

The function of each model/language interface—The software complexity of each model/language interface varies considerably. Here, we forgo any discussion of their complexities. Instead, we discuss their common functions. Each model/language interface has three distinct functions.

1. Database Creation: The interface knows the data model of the database into which raw data are to be entered. If it is an existing database, then there exists a database schema. If it is to be a new database, then a new database schema is created for the database. Except for the attribute-based ABDL interface, which creates an attribute-based schema for the attribute database, the other model/language interfaces create schemata for databases based on other data models—for example, a relational database may have been created by the relational/SQL interface due to the presence of the schema for the relational database. Physically, it is still an attribute-based database. Logically (i.e., via the schema), it is a relational database. For this reason, we call the attribute-based schema for the relational database the relational (à la attribute-based) schema.

   In ABDM, the database is seen exactly as the (physically) stored database. However, in the relational schema, the stored database is different from the same database seen by the relational user or SQL transaction. The stored database is actually an attribute-based database equivalent to the relational database seen by the relational user or SQL transaction. Thus, logically there are many heterogeneous databases via their corresponding schemata. Physically, there are only attribute-based databases.

2. Query Execution or Transaction Processing: This function of each interface is similar to a real-time compiler/monitor. Whenever a query or transaction is submitted to an interface, the interface does the following.

   - Retrieves the appropriate schema for its own use

   - Translates all the statements in the user query or transaction into an equivalent ABDL query or ABDL transaction

   - Forwards the ABDL query or transaction to the kernel for execution or processing

   - Monitors the execution or processing

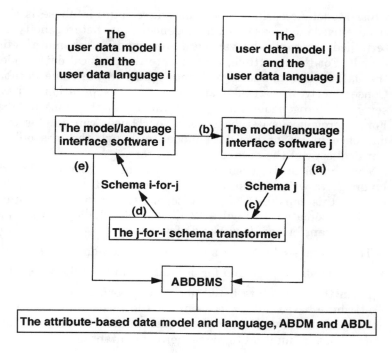

Figure 12.4   The j-for-i schema translation

- Converts all the attribute-based results into the data-model form of the user on the basis of the schema on hand

- Forwards the results to the user query or transaction

The relational user, for example, may submit a SQL transaction to the relational/SQL interface. The interface immediately does the following.

- Retrieves the relational schema for its own use

- Translates all the SQL statements in the transaction into an equivalent ABDL transaction

- Forwards the ABDL transaction to the kernel for execution

- Monitors the execution

- Converts all the attribute-based results into the relational form on the basis of the schema on hand

- Forwards relational results to the user or the SQL transaction

3. Cross-Model Accessing: Since the entire multidatabase is an attribute-based database (i.e., homogeneous), its heterogeneity is determined externally by various heterogeneous schemata defined over it. For the first time, we separate the physical data model of the database from the logical data model of the same database. Consequently, we can take advantage of this separation by having several heterogeneous schemata defined over the same database. For heterogeneous database users, each user can see his or her database in his or her data model, although there is only one physical copy of the database for all users.

More importantly, each user can use his or her familiar data language to write transactions for processing the same database. In fact, this capability of many schemata for the same database can be automated. In Figure 12.4, we depict the logic of the j-for-i schema transformer. It works as follows.

- There is an i-schema for a database in the i data model.

- There is also a j-schema for a database in the j data model.

- From the two points listed above, we learn that there are two attribute-based databases—one for the i user and the other for the j user. Now, what if the i user wanted to use the j user's database in addition to his or her own database?

- The j-for-i schema transformer accepts as input the j-schema of the j user's database and the semantic equivalence of the i data model and the j data model.

- The j-for-i schema transformer produces an i-for-j schema (for short, the i-schema) for the database in the j data model.

- By now, the i user has two i-schemata: one for his or her own database based in the i data model and the other for someone else's database based in the j data model. The i user can now cross-access heterogeneous data in another database as if these data were homogeneous data in the local database.

In Figure 12.5, we depict an experimental multiple-interface and single-kernel DBMS, known as the multimodel, multilingual, and multiple back end DBMS with cross-model accessing capabilities (for short, M3DBMS with CMAC).

We note in Figure 12.5 that there are three relational database schemata for the same relational/SQL interface.

1. The middle relational schema is created by the relational/SQL interface in the database of the relational user.

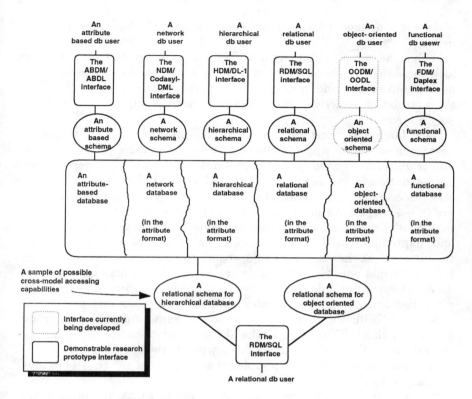

Figure 12.5   Data sharing in M3DBMS with CMAC

2. The left relational schema is produced by the hierarchical-for-relational schema transformer for the database created by the hierarchical user.

3. The right relational database schema is produced by the object-oriented-for-relational schema transformer for the database created by the object-oriented user.

Effectively, the same relational user is accessing three heterogeneous databases relationally, that is, with SQL transactions.

Complexities of Language Interfaces and Schemata versus One-Way Midware Packages   If the heterogeneity of the multidatabase is n, then there are (n − 1) language interfaces. There is no need for the kernel language interface, since this is the native mode. Further, each of the (n − 1) language interfaces requires up to (n − 2) schemata. The complexity of language interfaces and their schemata is therefore (n − 1) * (n − 2).

Is this the same complexity of n * (n − 1) one-way midware? Let us look into each language interface and its schemata more closely. The multiple-interface and multiple-schema approach has the following characteristics, which are not found in either the one-way or the two-way midware.

Each language interface and all its (n − 2) schemata are mapping heterogeneous data and transactions into the same equivalent data and transactions based on the kernel data model and language of the kernel database management system (KDBMS). This is the (n − 2) other-to-one kernel mapping (i.e., many-to-one mapping). Since there are (n − 2) schemata for each of (n − 1) interfaces, there are (n − 1) * (n − 2) others to the same kernel mapping (i.e., still a set of many-to-one mappings). On the other hand, in the midware approach, for all the other (n − 1) heterogeneous databases to be interoperable with one heterogeneous database, the midware approach requires (n − 1) one-way midware. For this one database, there is the many-to-one mapping. However, there are n heterogeneous databases and there is a need for n different many-to-one (not the same ones, but different ones) mappings. Thus, this is the set of many-to-many mappings of the midware. From the complexity viewpoint, the set of (n − 1) * (n − 2) many-to-one mappings is simpler than the set of n * (n − 1) many-to-many mappings.

Further, there is the quality-control issue of these mappings. The professionals who support the kernel data model, data language, and KDBMS can exercise software quality control on all the (n − 1) * (n − 2) language interfaces and schemata being mapped into KDBMS, whereas n teams of professionals scattered at n different sites are likely to have uneven quality control of their respective n * (n − 1) midware packages.

In conclusion, the multiple-interface and multiple-schema approach is simpler and more methodical than the midware approach.

Is the interface and schema complexity the same as the midware complexity? We have asked this question once in a previous paragraph. The answer was that even if they have approximately the same complexity number, the interface and schema software is simpler to implement and easier to control than the one-way and two-way midware software. Here, we return again to the simplicity and control issues. Only the complexity of language interfaces matches the complexity of the one-way midware of (n − 1) * (n − 2) software modules. There are only (n − 1) language interfaces whose complexity is close to the complexity of n one-way midware packages. Since n and (n − 1) are close, we square off the complexity n with the complexity (n − 1).

The remaining (n – 2) schemata for each language interface should not be used to square off the remaining (n – 1) one-way midware packages, although (n – 2) and (n – 1) are close. This is because each schema is just a data definition of kernel data in terms of data semantics of a heterogeneous data model. There is little software complexity in the schema itself, except the definitional information. Further, the production of these heterogeneous schemata for the same kernel has been taken over by the schema transformer. By using the compiler-transformer technique and feeding the transformer with semantic equivalences of different models with the kernel, it is possible to generate a specific schema transformer for a language interface. Therefore, the complexity of (n – 2) schemata and their schema transformers is smaller than the complexity of the additional (n – 1) one-way midware packages.

Kernel Approach versus Conversion of Heterogeneous Databases

The kernel approach looks superficially like the conversion approach, where all the heterogeneous databases are converted into homogeneous databases—for example, relational. All the heterogeneous transactions are converted into homogeneous transactions written in a common data language—for example, SQL. Thus, both the database and transactions are supported by a homogeneous DBMS such as RDBMS. Now, let us examine the difference of using the kernel in lieu of the conversion.

The kernel is based on the attribute-based data model, language, and ABDBMS. First, we discuss ABDM. The attribute-based data model (ABDM) has a number of characteristics that are not found in contemporary data models.

1. The database is modeled in two parts—the base data and metadata. Base data consist of records; metadata consist of data about records.

2. Records can be variable length as well as fixed length; no use of null values as fillers.

3. Metadata include two kinds of keys—the value range keys and discrete value keys. Further, they allow the real-world concept of master keys to be realized in the ABDM. (A master key in the real world opens several door locks.) In ADBM, a key can be one-for-many (i.e., one record referring to several records).

4. The number of keys per record is unlimited; no use of address-dependent pointers in a record.

5. Key attribute types, discrete key values, and key value ranges are kept in metadata. Further, an equivalence relation (ER) is developed automatically for base data on the basis of metadata.

6. The ER is used to partition the database into mutually exclusive subsets of the base data, known as clusters. Cluster IDs are also kept in metadata.

7. Cluster base data are distributed over parallel database stores using a one track per store algorithm.

8. Metadata stores and base data stores are on separate sets of disks for concurrent processing.

Next, we discuss ABDL. The attribute-based data language (ABDL) consists of a small number of metadata operations, as well as a small number of base data operations. Of the base operations, all but one are set-oriented operations (i.e., operating on one set of records at a time). To refer to the record set, the operations use one or more Boolean expressions of predicates. Directly, an ABDL transaction can be sent to ABDBMS for execution. This is known as the native mode. However, and more likely, the ABDL transaction is an output of a model/language interface, where the user has written a transaction in a data language different from ABDL—for example, consider the relational model/language interface. The relational user may have been interacting with the interface and since written a SQL transaction on the interface. The interface translates the SQL transaction to an equivalent ABDL transaction and routes the equivalent transaction to an ABDBMS for execution. All the resulting data for this transaction will be forwarded to the interface by the ABDBMS. The interface then converts these data to relational format in real time with the relational schema on hand. Thus, the interface is a real-time compiler/converter/monitor.

Finally, we discuss ABDBMS. There is no commercial ABDBMS. Thus, the software architecture is not fixed and may be subject to further research and experimentation. Nevertheless, due to its clustering capability of base data and its separation of meta- and base data, ABDBMS can best be implemented on a supercomputer with parallel database processors and their corresponding parallel database stores.

The architecture of parallel database processors and parallel database stores is known as the multiple back end architecture. The database supercomputer with the multiple back end architecture is depicted in Figure 12.6. In M3DBMS with CMAC, the three Ms stand for multiple back end, multimodel, and multilingual. CMAC stands for cross-model accessing capabilities.

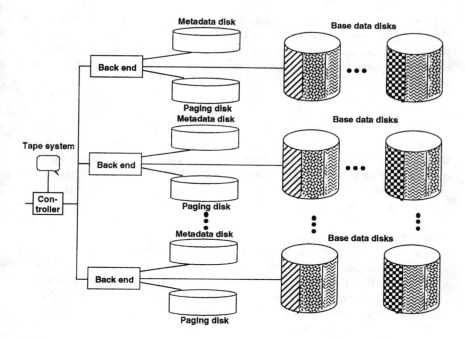

Figure 12.6   The architecture of the multiple back end supercomputer

In conclusion, the kernel solution is better than the conversion solution. The former is focused on a new and parallel architecture. The latter is based on a conventional computer architecture.

12.4 SUMMARY

In solution one, massive and brute-force conversions of both transactions and databases are not simple, but simple-minded. Nevertheless, if achievable, the converted database and target system is homogeneous and there is no interoperable issue (i.e., no data-sharing problem). As a single database supported on a single database system, it is the ultimate integration (i.e., resource consolidation). The bottom line is that all-for-one conversion is not achievable with contemporary database technology.

In solution two, the interoperability (data sharing) among n heterogeneous databases and systems is achieved through n * (n − 1) one-way midware. However, no integration (no resource consolidation) takes place. Further, the control of all these midware also poses a new problem.

In solution three, conversions to two databases and their respective DBMSs can occur. The midware for the interoperable two may be developed. Thus, some integration and some interoperability have become reality. However, this solution is a temporary and compromised solution.

Finally, in solution four there is a new two-layer DBMS architecture. The model/language interfaces and their cross-model accessing schemata provide the total interoperability. The kernel DBMS provides the total integration, although all the heterogeneous databases must be converted into the kernel form. The user's transaction requires no conversion. It still views the user's database through the schema based on the user's data model. In other words, the user and user's transaction do not see the database conversion effect. More importantly, there is no conversion of any transaction written in a heterogeneous data language.

The kernel integration without massive conversion of transactions is a better integration solution. The many-models/languages-to-one-kernel interfaces and their cross-model accessing schemata are better interoperating solutions than two-way midware. However, solution four is an ongoing research and experimentation project. It has not, as of this writing, found its way into the commercial sector.

13

Multilevel Database Security: Milestonesand Issues

David Rasikan*
Sang H. Son*
Bhavani Thuraisingham†

Multilevel security for database systems has been a topic of active research, with the Bell-LaPadula security properties being the basis for ensuring multilevel security of a system. In this chapter, various approaches for supporting database security, including problems encountered, important milestones, and open issues, are discussed. The problems involved in building secure relational databases (with special reference to the SeaView model), including inference problems, secure object-oriented database systems, secure distributed databases, secure concurrency control mechanisms, interaction among security requirements, real-time requirements, and correctness requirements of a database, are also discussed.

13.1 INTRODUCTION

The concept of security in computer systems has its roots in operating systems for controlling the access of programs, processes, or users to the resources defined in a computer system. The model of protection has usually been an access matrix, where the rows of the matrix rep-

---

* Department of Computer Science, University of Virginia, Charlottesville, VA 22903
The work of Rasikan and Son was supported by ONR, DoE, and IBM.
† The Mitre Corporation, Burlington Road, Bedford, MA 01730.

resent the user or process and the columns represent resources or objects. Each entry (i, j) of the matrix consists of a set of access rights, which defines the set of operations that a process, i, could invoke on an object, y. This form of access control is called discretionary access control, since it is only adequate for preventing unauthorized access to "honest" users, while unauthorized access by malicious users cannot be prevented.

Most secure database systems use a mandatory access control mechanism based on the Bell-LaPadula model. This model is stated in terms of subjects and objects. An object is understood to be a data file, record, or a field within a record. A subject is an active process that requests access to objects. Every object is assigned a classification and every subject is assigned a clearance. Classifications and clearances are collectively referred to as security classes (or levels) and they are partially ordered. The Bell-LaPadula model imposes the following restrictions on all data accesses.

1. Simple Security Property: A subject is allowed read access to an object only if the former's clearance is identical to or higher (in the partial order) than the latter's classification.

2. The *-Property: A subject is allowed write access to an object only if the former's clearance is identical to or lower than the latter's classification.

The above two restrictions are intended to ensure that there is no flow of information from higher-level objects to lower-level subjects. Since the above restrictions are mandatory and enforced automatically, the system checks the security classes of all reads and writes.

Secure database systems having the Bell-LaPadula conditions for security are called multilevel secure databases (MLSDBMS) or trusted database management systems (TDBMS), since each entity in the database can be at a different level, as shown in Table 13.1. Here, each element can take one of three possible levels: U (Unclassified), S (Secret), or TS (Top Secret).

The basic issues involved in the design of a multilevel secure database system include the following.

1. Classification Granularity: What is the smallest entity in the database for which a level can be assigned? In the earlier secure relational models it was an attribute or a tuple. In the case of secure object-oriented databases, the smallest entity could be an object or the attributes/methods of an object.

Table 13.1 View of a Multilevel Relation

A1	C1	A2	C2	A3	C3
mad	S	17	S	x	TS
foo	U	34	U	w	S
ark	TS	72	TS	z	TS

2. Consistency and Completeness: Classification constraints are rules for assigning levels to data when they are entered into the database. In order that a given set of constraints specifies meaningful classes, the constraints should be consistent (i.e., they should not define conflicting classes for the same data) and complete (i.e., they should assign a class to all data).

3. Inference Control: The inference control problem concerns preventing inference of unauthorized information—for example, in a [STUDENT, GRADE1, GRADE2, GPA] relation, if attributes STUDENT, GRADE1, and GRADE2 are UNCLASSIFIED and GPA is CLASSIFIED, then an UNCLASSIFIED user can derive the GPA from a knowledge of GRADE1 and GRADE2.

4. Aggregation: Aggregation problems arise when a collection of up to N items of a given type are not sensitive, but a collection of greater than N items is sensitive—for example, a single attribute value of GRADE1 is not sensitive, but the values of GRADE1 for all the students in the class are sensitive, since the grade distribution curve can be derived from this information. This problem is closely related to inference and the same techniques are used to solve both problems.

5. Covert Channels: The Bell-LaPadula conditions protect against direct unauthorized disclosure of data, but they cannot guard against indirect means by which subjects at higher access classes can pass information to subjects at lower access classes. Covert channels will be discussed in greater detail later in the chapter.

6. Polyinstantiation: Polyinstantiation refers to the simultaneous existence of multiple data objects with the same name, where the multiple instances are distinguished by their access class. Polyinstantiation arises when a tuple, T_I, exists at level C_I, and a subject at level $C_2 < C_I$ tries to create a new tuple, T_2, with the same primary key as in T_I. If the database system prevents the subject

from creating the tuple, the lower-level subject can infer that the same tuple is present at a higher level, based on the denial of service. To avoid this, the tuple is polyinstantiated. This leads to more complex semantics for the model, but it is an unavoidable overhead.

7. Concurrency Control: The correctness requirements for a database system conflict with the security requirements of the database. Active research is ongoing regarding the development of secure concurrency control algorithms that are free from covert channels and that also yield acceptable performance.

Some of the early efforts regarding trusted database management systems include the design of the Hinke/Schaefer model, which supports classification at the attribute level; the I. P. Sharp model, which supports classification at the tuple level; and the Navy Surveillance Model. An interesting approach to building a trusted database management system (TDBMS) was the Integrity Lock approach, where a trusted filter was designed to mediate access to data in an untrusted DBMS. The filter associates each entry in the database with a security classification. Whenever an access request is received by the filter, the classification of the request is checked against the classification of the requested entry and, depending on the result, access is granted or denied. Note that the security check on a request is done only by the filter and and no modifications need to be made to the database management system itself. This approach was shown to be susceptible to Trojan Horse attacks, and future research concentrated on building security into the database management system.

The various architectural approaches proposed for designing secure database systems, as well as the recent developments in topics such as secure concurrency control and polyinstantiation, have resulted in the development of commercial multilevel secure database management system products. Most of the major database management system vendors are now marketing multilevel secure database management system products. Some of these products have been evaluated against the Trusted Database Interpretation.

This chapter focuses on some of the recent developments in multilevel database system research and discusses important issues. Section 13.2 deals with multilevel relational models with special mention of the SeaView model. Section 13.3 discusses current research in inference control systems, and Section 13.4 discusses secure object-oriented data models. Section 13.5 deals with secure distributed database systems. In Section 13.6, the focus is on the interaction among security, concurrency control, real-time requirements, and the correctness conditions that must be satisfied by a secure scheduler.

The summary points to the limitations of existing systems and discusses topics for future research.

13.2 SECURE RELATIONAL DATA MODELS

The first successful multilevel secure relational data model was the SeaView model, which provided a focal point for research in database security. It addressed important issues such as element-level classification, polyinstantiation, and decomposition of relations. Some of the shortcomings of the model have been studied, and alternate proposals have been made. The components of the SeaView model and the alternate proposals are described in the following subsections.

13.2.1 Multilevel Relations

To deal with multilevel data, the SeaView formal model extended the concept of a relation to include classification labels at the element level. Specifically, a multilevel relation, R, is any relation where there exist classification attributes, C_i, for each data attribute, A_i. It is represented as the schema $R(A_1, C_1, \ldots, A_n, C_n)$. Treating classification labels as attributes in a schema has the advantage of providing a simple means for formulating selections based on classification in a relational query language. An example of a multilevel relation is given in Table 13.1. Authorization to access relation, R, does not give a subject, S, access to all data in the relation instance. The relation is filtered such that the only data seen by S are those that are dominated by readclass(S). The effect of this is that all multilevel relations are actually views parameterized by an access class, as illustrated in Table 13.2. Therefore, a multilevel relation, R, can also be viewed as a collection of state-dependent relation instances, R_c—one for each access class c. These multiple instances are intended to represent the version of reality appropriate for each access class.

13.2.2 Multilevel Relational Integrity Rules

Since filtering gives subjects at different access classes different views of the database, the integrity rules of the relational model—namely, entity integrity and referential integrity—must be extended to ensure consistency of the data visible at each class. The integrity rules are thus restated, as discussed in the following subsections.

Multilevel Entity Integrity Single-level entity integrity states that no tuples in a relation can have null values for any primary key. This is

Table 13.2   Secret View of the Multilevel Relation in Table 13.1

A1	CI	A2	C2	A3	C3
mad	S	17	S	null	S
foo	U	34	U	w	S

because the primary key uniquely identifies a particular tuple. If this constraint is to be satisfied with respect to the data visible at each access class, then, in a given tuple, all the elements forming the primary key must be uniformly classified—that is, they must all have the same access class. Otherwise, a subject whose access class is lower than that of the highest key element would see null values for some of the elements forming the key. In addition, the access class for the primary key must be dominated by the access classes of all other elements in the tuple. The reason for this requirement is that the primary key is needed to uniquely select a tuple and corresponding element. If the primary key class were not dominated by the access class of some element in the tuple, then that element could not be uniquely selected by a subject operating at the element's access class. The integrity constraint can be formally stated as: Multilevel Entity Integrity—let AK be the set of attributes forming the primary key of a relation, R. All classification attributes, C_i, corresponding to data attributes A_i in AK have the same value within any given tuple of R, and this class is dominated by the value of each classification attribute, C_j, whose data attribute, A_j, is not in AK. No tuple in an instance of R can have null values for any of the primary key attributes.

Multilevel Referential Integrity Multilevel referential integrity states that every foreign key must reference a tuple that exists in some other relation where the key is primary. In a multilevel database this means that a foreign key element cannot reference a tuple with a higher access class, because the referenced tuple would appear to be nonexistent at the access class of the foreign key element.

Multilevel Referential Integrity—for each foreign key in a relation, there exists one, and only one, primary key in the referenced relation. Within a tuple, the access class of each element comprising a foreign key must be the same (i.e., the foreign key attributes must be uniformly classified) and must dominate the access class of the primary key element(s) in the referenced tuple.

13.2.3 Polyinstantiation

Overview An important contribution of the SeaView project was the formulation of polyinstantiation as a fundamental property of multi-level relations. As discussed in the introduction, polyinstantiation is necessary as a means for closing covert channels. Polyinstantiation in SeaView can arise in the following instances.

1. Subject clearance dominated by access class of data: This refers to a case where a lower-level subject attempts to insert new data into the relation where data already exist (invisibly) with the same name at a higher access class. Polyinstantiation is done by inserting the new data, which are distinguishable from the existing data by their classification. Table 13.3 shows the effect of a SECRET user inserting a tuple with AI being "ark," as well as updating A3 for Ai being "mad" to "q." The tuple with primary key "ark" and the tuple with primary key "mad" are polyinstantiated.

2. Subject clearance dominates access class of data: If a subject attempts to insert a tuple that has the same primary key as that of an existing tuple with a lower access class, the operation can be denied and the subject notified of the conflict without opening a covert channel. This is because a covert channel is established only when information flows from a higher-level subject to a lower-level subject. In this case, however, such an information flow is not enacted, since the access class of the subject is higher than that of the already existing tuple. However, it has been argued that this is needlessly restrictive and that this form of optional polyinstantiation should also be allowed. This point is illustrated by the relation shown in Table 13.4. Assume that only

Table 13.3 Polyinstantiated View

AI	CI	A2	C2	A3	C3
mad	S	17	S	x	TS
mad	S	17	S	q	S
foo	U	34	U	w	S
ark	S	54	S	z	S
ark	TS	72	TS	z	TS

Table 13.4   Violation of Multivalued Dependency

Starship		Objective		Destination	
Enterprise	U	Exploration	U	Talos	U
Enterprise	U	Spying	S	Talos	U
Enterprise	U	Spying	S	Rigd	S

the first tuple is present in the relation, where a starship Enterprise has an exploration mission to planet Talos. Now a SECRET subject may want to use this as a cover story to hide a SECRET spying mission to Talos (i.e., the subject may need to insert the second tuple). If optional polyinstantiation were not allowed, the insertion of the second tuple would be prohibited.

Modeling Polyinstantiated Tuples and Elements   The   effect   of   polyinstantiation is formalized by the following integrity constraint. Polyinstantiation integrity: For a relation, R, let AK denote the subset of data attributes designated as the primary key; let CK denote the access class of AK; and let CR denote the subset of remaining classification attributes; that is, each C_i in CR corresponds to some attribute, A_i, that is not part of the primary key. Then, FK = AK U CK U CR is defined as the full primary key for R. Thus, each tuple is uniquely determined by its primary key, primary key class, and all classification levels for remaining attributes. Stated formally: Given a relation, R, with primary key AK and key class CK, the following functional dependency holds for each attribute, A_i, in AK:

$$AK, CK, C_i \longrightarrow A_i$$

That is, each element of a nonkey attribute, A_i, is distinguished by its access class, C_i. If multiple tuples contain the same values for AK, CK, and C_i, then they contain the same value for A_i (i.e., an element cannot be polyinstantiated within the same access class).

13.2.4 Decomposition into Standard Relations

Another important contribution of SeaView was the decomposition of a multilevel relation into single-level relations. Further, each single-level standard relation, in turn, is mapped onto one or more single-level storage objects, which are protected by a reference monitor that enforces mandatory security. Therefore, a subject, S, will be unable to access any data in an underlying relation unless level(S) dominates

Table 13.5   Relation RS

AI	CI	A2	C2	A3	C3
mad	S	17	S	null	TS
foo	U	34	U	w	S

the level of the storage object that contains the data. This decomposition serves two important purposes. First, it considerably reduces the disclosure risk to classified data, because all multilevel data are partitioned by access class for storage. Second, the decomposition provides an automatic and secure means for deriving filtered views of a relation at the different access classes.

In the next two subsections, we will look at two approaches to decomposition. We begin by defining a filter function, which maps a multilevel relation to different instances, one for each descending access class.

The c-instance, R_c, of a multilevel relational database is the view of the database as seen by a subject at level c. Given the c-instance, R_c, of a multilevel relation, the filter function, f, produces the c' instance $R_c = f(R_c, c')$ for $c' < c$. A tuple, t', is an element of R_c, if, and only if, t' can be derived from some t in R_c as follows: $t'[AK, C_{AK}] = t[AK, C_{AK}]$ where the level of elements of $C_{AK} < = c'$ and for A_i not in AK $t'[A_i, C_i] = t[A_i, C_i]$ if $t[C_i] <= c' = <$null, $t[C_{AK}]>$ otherwise. The S-instance R_s of Table 13.1 is given in Table 13.5.

We will now discuss two proposed decomposition methods.

Replicated Decomposition   Replicated decomposition is a highly redundant method of decomposition where a stored relation at access class c has data for all access classes dominated by c. Decomposition and storage are done after a straightforward application of the filter function. Recovery of the entire relation is not a problem, because R_h, where h is the highest access class in the relation, is nothing but the entire relation. There are two problems associated with this decomposition: The first problem is the amount of redundant data stored; the second problem is that when an update is made to an attribute in a particular instance, R_c, it must be propagated to all instances $R_{c'}$, where $c' > c$.

Nonredundant Decomposition   Let [L, H] be the range of access levels for all attributes in the relation, R, to be decomposed. The two groups of relations are constructed as follows.

1. Primary Key Group Relations—Construct $R_{1,c}$ (A_1, C_1, C_2, ... C_n) for c in [L, H] as follows: For every tuple t in R, if either $t[C_1] = c$ or $t[C_1] < c$ and there exists i, $t[C_i] = c$, then insert t' in $R_{1,c}$ such that $t'[A_1,C_1] = t[A_1,C_1]$, $t'[C_i] = t[C_i]$ if $t[C_i] <= c$, $t[C_1]$ otherwise.

2. Attribute Group Relations—Construct $R_{i,c}$ (A_1, C_1, A_i, C_i) for $1 < i <= n$ and c in [L, H] as follows: For every tuple t in R such that either $t[C_1] = c$ or $t[C_1] < c$ and $t[C_i] = c$, insert t' in $R_{i,c}$, such that $t'[A_1, C_1] = t[A_1, C_1]$, $t'[A_i, C_i] = t[A_i, C_i]$ if $t[C_i] = c$, $t'[A_i, C_i] = $ <null $t[C_i]$> f $t[C_i] > c$.

The instance R_c is recovered from the decomposition as follows.

$$P_{i,c} = \text{UNION}_{c'} <= c \ R_{i,c'}$$
$$R_c = P_{1,c} \times P_{2,c} \times \ldots \times P_{n,c'}$$

13.2.5 Update Semantics for Multilevel Relations

Formal operational semantics for the three primitive multilevel relational operators INSERT, UPDATE, and DELETE have been developed. The motivating principles in developing the update semantics were to make sure that the update operations were as close to standard SQL as possible. In defining the relational operator, a restricted form of the *-property is assumed where a subject has write access to an object if, and only if, the subject is at the same access class as the object (i.e., an UNCLASSIFIED subject can insert or update only an UNCLASSIFIED tuple, not a SECRET tuple).

The INSERT Statement The INSERT statement executed by a subject at level c has the following general form

$$\text{INSERT}$$
$$\text{INTO } R_c \ [(A_i[,A_j] \ldots)]$$
$$\text{VALUES } [(a_i[,a_j] \ldots)]$$

The INSERT statement works in a straightforward manner. A subject at access class c can insert a tuple, t, in R_c if R_c does not already have a tuple with the same primary key value and key class as t. In the inserted tuple, the access classes of all data attributes as well as the tuple class are set to c.

The UPDATE Statement The general form of the UPDATE statement is given by

$$\text{UPDATE } R_c$$
$$\text{SET}$$
$$A_i = s_i \ [,A_j = s_j] \ldots$$
$$[\text{WHERE } p]$$

For each attribute, A_k, specified in the SET clause, the intent of the UPDATE operation is to modify $t[A_k]$ to s_k for all tuples, t, in R that satisfy the predicate, p. However, in multilevel relations this operation has to be implemented a little differently to prevent illegal information flows. The two cases that need to be considered are the following.

1. Effect of an UPDATE at the user's access class—There are two components to the effect of this operation. First, all tuples, t, that satisfy the predicate, p, are replaced by t′, which is identical to t except for those data attributes that are assigned new values in the SET clause. Second, if there is some attribute, A_k, in the SET clause with $t[C_k] < c$, then the unmodified tuple is also kept (i.e., polyinstantiation takes place).

2. Effect of an UPDATE above the user's access class—Consider a tuple, t, in R_c. Let A_k be an attribute in the SET clause such that (i) $t[C_k] = c$ and (ii) $t[A_k] = x$, where x is nonnull. There may be many tuples, u, in $R_{c'} > c$ that have the same primary key as tuple t. To maintain polyinstantiation integrity, the effect of the update has to be propagated to all such tuples, u.

The DELETE Statement   The DELETE statement has the following general form: DELETE FROM R_c [WHERE p]. Here, p is the predicate expression that helps identify those tuples in R_c that are to be deleted. Only those tuples, t, in R_c that satisfy p and for which $t[TC] = c$ are deleted from R_c. In addition, polyinstantiated tuples in $R_{c'} > c$ that satisfy p are also deleted.

13.3 INFERENCE CONTROL

13.3.1 Overview

It is possible for users of any database management system to draw inferences from the information that they obtain from the databases. The inferred knowledge could depend only on the data obtained from the database system or it could depend on some prior knowledge possessed by the user in addition to the data obtained from the database system. The inference process can be harmful if the inferred knowledge is something that the user is not authorized to acquire—that is, a user acquiring information that he or she is not authorized to have access to has come to be known as the inference problem in database security.

Of particular interest is the inference problem that occurs in a multilevel operating environment. In such an environment, the users are cleared at different security levels and they access a multilevel database, where the data are classified at different sensitivity levels. A multilevel secure database management system manages a multilevel database, where its users cannot access data to which they are not authorized. However, providing a solution to the inference problem, where users issue multiple requests and consequently gain access to unauthorized information, is beyond the capability of currently available multilevel secure database management systems.

Early approaches to handling the inference problem have been reported. Since then, several other efforts have also been reported. One set of approaches focused on handling the problem during query processing. The assumption here is that it is as a result of querying the database that users acquire information to which they are not authorized. Another set of approaches, which has been the major focus, handles the inference problem by designing the multilevel database in such a way that certain security violations are prevented. With this approach the security constraints, which are rules that assign security levels to the data, are processed during multilevel database design and subsequently the schemata are assigned appropriate security levels. More recently, there have been proposals to develop solutions to handle the inference problem that can result from data mining. Data mining technology is advancing rapidly and tools are now available for users to extract information from the database. However, this type of extraction could result in security violations.

It has been demonstrated that the inference problem was in general unlovable. Therefore, it is impossible to find a complete solution to handle this problem. Nevertheless, the approaches that are being developed can handle certain types of inferences and prevent/detect security violations. The current challenge is to develope viable operational products based on the prototype tools and systems. Furthermore, research should focus on developing techniques to handle the inference problem that could result from data mining. The remainder of this section provides an overview of constraints processing during query, update, and database design to handle the inference problem.

13.3.2 Constraint Processing

To prevent unauthorized acquisition of information by a user, a powerful and dynamic approach to assigning and reclassifying security levels is needed. There have been proposals for an integrated approach to processing security constraints, where some security constraints are assigned/changed during query processing, some during update processing, and some during database design.

Security constraints are rules that assign security levels to data. Various types of security constraints include the following.

- Constraints that classify a database, relation, or attribute. These constraints are simple constraints.

- Content-based constraints, which classify any part of the database depending on the value of some data.

- Event-based constraints, which classify any part of the database depending on the occurrence of some real-world event.

- Association-based constraints, which classify associations between data.

- Release-based constraints, which classify any part of the database, depending on the information that has been previously released.

In the rest of this section, we will see how inference is prevented at each stage of constraint processing.

13.3.3 Inference Control during Query Processing

An extended security policy to handle inference violations has been presented. This policy is stated below.

- Given a security level L, E(L) is the knowledge base associated with L—that is, E(L) will consist of all responses that have been released at security level L over a certain time period as well as the real-world information at security level L.

- Let a subject at level L pose a query. The response, R, to the query will be released only if the following condition is satisfied: For all security levels, L*, where L* dominates L, if (E[L*] Union R) => X, then L* dominates level(X).

The policy states that whenever a response is released to a user at level L, it must be ensured that any user at level L* > L cannot infer information classified at a level L+ > L from the response, together with the knowledge acquired. In the design of the query processor, the technique is to modify the query depending on the security constraints, the relevant previous responses released, and real-world information. In addition to query modification, some further processing of the response, such as response sanitization, may need to be performed. The query constraint processor examines the response, the security constraints, and the data already in the release database and determines whether all of the response should be delivered to the user.

13.3.4 Constraint Processing during Database Design

In a proposed model, the classification of all attributes or collections of attributes without any dependency on data values is handled during database design. As a result, all association-based and simple constraints are decided during the database design phase itself. In the algorithm for handling association-based constraints, the input is a set of association-based constraints and a set of attributes. The output of this algorithm is a set of clusters for each security level. Each cluster for a security level L will have a collection of attributes that can be safely classified together at level L.

13.3.5 Update Constraint Processor

When an update request is submitted, the security level of the data item being updated might have to be reassigned depending on its new data value. This is because a content-based constraint may be present on that data item. In addition, a new security level may have to be assigned to some data already in the database. The update constraint processor utilizes simple and content-based security constraints as guidance in determining the security level of the data to be reclassified.

An architecture for an update constraint processor has been developed. It consists of a constraint manager, which manages the security constraints on the data items, and a security-level computer, which communicates with the constraint manager to obtain the relevant constraints and computes the new security level for the data to be reclassified. Once the correct levels of the data are determined, the information is passed to the level upgrader, which is responsible for actually upgrading the data.

13.4 SECURE OBJECT-ORIENTED DATABASES

Object-oriented database management systems are gaining popularity due to their inherent ability to represent conceptual entities as objects, paralleling the way humans view the world. However, these systems, by themselves, do not provide adequate support for secure operation. Consequently, multilevel object-oriented database management systems are needed to ensure mandatory security. A security model that does not limit the power and flexibility of expression (e.g., by limiting the allowable levels of related portions of the schema) of an object-oriented database system is desirable.

Since OODBMSs provide a richer model of data and processing and use different implementation techniques than RDBMSs, new problems arise, over and above those addressed for secure RDBMSs. In RDBMSs, the primary unit of activity is the tuple, whereas in OODBMSs it is the object. An object consists of a set of attributes (name-value pairs or another object), a set of methods (operations applicable to the object), and object identifiers (OIDs) that uniquely identify an object. An association is the link between an object instance, an attribute, and the attribute's value. Association could also represent membership of the object in a collection of other related objects. There are several areas where secure OODBMSs are not comparable to RDBMSs.

- Values versus identifiers: Relational databases have only data values; they have no identifiers or explicit links.

- Methods: Relational databases have no methods. In the relational world we are dealing only with passive data, where information flow is possible only through reads and writes. This is called the passive object/active subject paradigm. However, in the object-oriented model, the properties of a passive information repository, represented by attributes and their values, are combined with the properties of an active agent, represented by methods and their invocation. Information flow is not only through reads and writes on attributes, but also through objects sending messages among themselves. At an interobject level, objects are communicating with each other via asynchronous message passing. At the intraobject level, methods read and write instance variables. Mechanisms must be incorporated into secure OODBMSs to control a method's access to database objects.

- Inheritance: Flexibility in inheritance can be inconsistent with having protection only at a coarse granularity.

- Implementation styles: The goals differ substantially between relational and object-oriented systems, with the latter often placing a higher value on integration with a programming language and speed in support of programs, and less value on data protection or transaction management. RDBMSs mediate every access to data, and this narrow interface lends itself to security; in OODBMSs, method code can be invoked directly at run time without mediation. These differences in requirements and emphasis can complicate the task of retrofitting security into existing OODBMS designs.

The first problem that needs to be considered in a security model for object-oriented databases is the granularity of classification: Which entities in the database need to be assigned an access level? A very fine-grained labeling scheme would likely prove confusing and could lead to increased overhead, since every single access to an attribute would have to be verified for conformance to the security properties. On the other hand, labeling only a single kind of coarse granule (e.g., object) creates problems—for example, a major advantage of an object model is that a single object can gather diverse information about something in the real world. Such an object is unlikely to exist at a uniform security level, so coarse granules may not mirror its security needs.

Let us survey some of the previous work on developing secure OODB models. One model is called SODA. SODA supports three of the entities that are basic to the object-oriented paradigm: classes, objects, and methods. A labeling constraint for an object consists of a set of label ranges, one for each labeled entity within the object. Methods are conceptually labeled with two security classifications: the classification of the originating method and a current operating classification. It is the intent of the SODA model to have the current classification level of a method activation represent the greatest lower bound of the classifications of all data that the method has read or has been granted access to. This means that method activations will always have their classification raised to the level of the data read by or visible to them. However, this information read is prevented from being passed back to an originating method operating at a lower classification. A method activation can modify or create an object of a particular classification if the method's current classification equals that of the object in question, the method's current classification is dominated by the upper bound of the classification range of the object, and the lower bound of the classification range is dominated by the user's access class. If these rules are not satisfied, then a write/create operation fails. Therefore, if a method attempts to update an object, then the failure of the attempt would be due to the method's current classification not being equal to the level of the object. Reporting this to the user allows the user to infer the existence of an object at a higher level, creating a covert channel. To remedy this situation, SODA introduces polyinstantiation for instance variables. Polyinstantiation requires, for each labeled instance variable, that objects be instantiated at each security level within the security level range set by the constraint. This action produces a set of objects for each instance variable. When an instance variable is modified at a given access class, the appropriate member within the set is replaced or a new object is added in the case where no member of the set formerly existed.

There are two problems with the SODA approach: First, its ability to raise a method's current classification to that of any object read could result in an undesirable upward cascade of current classification levels for a method execution. Second, the TCB must be invoked each time a method's classification has to be raised, resulting in a major overhead.

A set of constraints for the classification of entities in the model has been proposed. A fine-grained classification is adopted, with an attribute being the smallest entity that can be assigned a classification. In this model, access classes are associated with classes, objects, members (attributes), and methods of an object. The properties that were defined are as follows.

Hierarchy Property: level(O2) >= level(O1) for all O1 and O2 such that O1 is a superclass of O2. Since a subclass derives its definition from the parent class, this definition is quite intuitive. The same property applies between a class and an object of that class—that is, level(O1) >= level(Cl) where O1 is an object of class C_1.

Facet Property: level(V) >= level(O) for all V and O such that V is an attribute of object O. This is another way of saying that if an object name is sensitive, the attributes of the object are at least as sensitive.

Inheritance Property: Attribute V_2 that an object O2 inherits from O1 is classified at least as high as the corresponding facet V_I of O1. This is a corollary from the Hierarchy Property, since, just as a subclass must be at least as sensitive as its superclass, its attributes must be at least as sensitive as those of its superclass. This property is valid only when the subclass is derived from one, and only one, parent class. In the case where a class has more than one parent class, the Multiple Inheritance Property applies.

Multiple Inheritance Property: If a class inherits an attribute from two or more parent classes, the class inherits the attribute with the lowest classification—for example, suppose class WALKING-SHOE belongs to two classes: ATHLETICSHOE and ORTHOPEDIC-SHOE. Suppose also that ATHLETIC-SHOE has an UNCLASS-IFIED attribute, SIZE, and ORTHOPEDIC-SHOE has a SECRET attribute, SIZE. Then, WALKING-SHOE must inherit the UN-

CLASSIFIED SIZE attribute from ATHLETIC-SHOE. Otherwise, an UNCLASSIFIED user, knowing that WALKING-SHOE is a subclass of both ATHLETIC-SHOE and ORTHOPEDIC-SHOE, by observing that WALKING-SHOE has no SIZE attribute, could infer that WALKING-SHOE, and thus also ORTHOPEDIC-SHOE, has a SECRET SIZE attribute.

As can be seen from the properties defined above, this is only a beginning toward modeling a multilevel object-oriented system. It deals only with the "passive" aspects of the object model and has not considered control of information flow.

Messages between objects are considered to be the only instrument of information flow. Information transfer among objects can take place either when a message is passed from one object to another or when a new object is created. In the first case, information can flow in both directions: from the sender to the receiver and back. The forward flow is carried through the list of parameters contained in the message and the backward flow is through the return value. In the second case, information flows only in the forward direction: from the creating object to the created one (e.g., by means of supplying attribute values for the new object). A transfer of information does not have to occur every time a message is passed. An object acquires information by changing the values of some of its attributes. Thus, if no such changes occur as a result of a method invocation in response to a message, no information flow has been enacted. We say that the forward flow has been ineffective. Similarly, if the return value of a message is null, the backward flow has been ineffective. The two types of flows discussed are direct flows. An indirect flow occurs when object O1 sends a message to object O2 and O2 does not change its internal state as a result of receiving the message, but sends a message to O3 and O3 changes its state. Both direct and indirect illegal flows should be prevented if the system is to be secure. In a security model developed by S. Jajodia and B. Kogan, a simplifying assumption is made with respect to the nature of methods. All methods are said to belong to one of four types: read methods, which just read the value of an attribute; write methods, which modify the value of an attribute; invoke methods, which invoke another method via the sending of a message; and create methods, which create a new object. The model places restrictions on the allowable activity for each method type and contains a filtering algorithm, which enforces these restrictions on each message.

The single most important advantage of the Jajodia/Kogan model is its conceptual simplicity. The rules that protect against violations of policy are encoded inside the message passer, and this placement contributes to the possible existence of a small TCB. The main problem with the Jajodia/Kogan model is the assumption that all complex methods can be broken down into sequences of the four simple methods previously mentioned. No formal argument supporting this assumption has been made. Also, methods would have to be statically classified by their basic function (read, write, create, invoke), or they would have to be examined at run time in order for the message-filtering algorithm to work correctly. The former requirement is difficult to ensure and the latter requirement would result in extra overhead.

Since the field of object-oriented databases is relatively new, security for object-oriented databases is also still in its preliminary stages. The ideas that have been discussed provide useful starting points, the problems to focus on, and the solutions to some of them.

13.5 SECURE DISTRIBUTED DATABASES

The key issues involved in distributed multilevel database management are the following.

1. Distributed system architecture
2. Strategies for distributing data and for keeping track of data distribution globally
3. Optimal execution strategies for queries

An important issue in distributed database management is the architecture of the system: the number of sites, the underlying network software, and so forth. The underlying network has to be trusted in order for the distributed database to be trusted. Another important design choice concerns the assignment of access classes to sites. As the assignment becomes less and less homogeneous, the software for keeping track of information globally becomes increasingly complicated and performance declines.

A distributed secure database system has been described, where the system consists of several nodes, each node capable of handling multilevel data (i.e., each node has a trusted DBMS). The database at each node is represented by a multilevel relational data model. The global view of the distributed database uses the same multilevel relational data model used by the local system. In addition to a local TDBMS, each node also has a distributed processing component, which manages the global schemata and is also responsible for distributed query execution. The local TDBMS manages the local multilevel database. The distributed query processor is responsible for keeping track of and managing the data distribution.

Two possible approaches can be used to distribute relations.

1. The relation can be fragmented according to some selection criteria and each fragment can be stored at a particular node.
2. The relation is fragmented by security level. When a tuple is entered into the relation, it is entered into the fragment corresponding to its security level. As more and more tuples are entered into a particular fragment, further fragmentation may take place at the same security level.

Each TDBMS is capable of creating a view of a relation at the security level of the querying object. The distributed processing components merge the various views created by the individual TDBMSs in order to obtain a single global view at the security level of the querying object. Relations and tuples of the relation can be assigned a classification in this model. Tuples can also be polyinstantiated. Polyinstantiation is also allowed across sites, which introduces increased complexity into the query processing algorithm.

In a heterogeneous distributed environment, secure operation is in general much more complex than in a homogeneous environment. Handling different security accreditation ranges is one such problem. At each site, a scheme has to be developed to interpret the security access class of a subject that submitted a transaction at a remote site with a different classification range. Other types of heterogeneity include different concurrency control techniques and data models. Resolving these issues in a secure manner is still an open issue.

13.6 MULTILEVEL SECURE DATABASE CONCURRENCY CONTROL

The two components necessary to maintain the correctness of data in a database are concurrency control and recovery. In multilevel systems, there is the additional problem of maintaining correctness without violating security requirements. In the following section, the interaction between the security requirements of a database and concurrency control is discussed.

13.6.1 Secure Concurrency Control

The central issue in secure concurrency control is covert channel analysis—for example, consider the access requests of two transactions as presented to the scheduler.

T1(S):   R(x,U)   W(x,U)
T2(U):   W(x,U)

The scheduler, to maintain serializability, might reorder the transactions as shown.

T1(S): R(x,U)   W(x,U)
T2(U):   W(x,U)

The write by the UNCLASSIFIED transaction, T2, is delayed due to the actions of a SECRET transaction, T1. This constitutes a covert timing channel, because a high-level user may signal information to a low-level user by modulating the delay in processing its transaction. Thus, for the scheduler to be secure, the equivalent serial schedule, as apparent to a low-level subject, should not be affected by high-level subjects. This is an intuitive definition of noninterference.

Conditions for Correctness of a Secure Scheduler Covert channel analysis and removal is the single most important issue in multilevel secure concurrency control. The notion of noninterference has been proposed as a simple and intuitively satisfying definition of what it means for a system to be secure. The property of noninterference states that the output as seen by a user must be unaffected by the input of another user at a higher access class. This means that a user at a lower access class should not be able to distinguish between the output from the system in response to an input sequence, including actions from a higher-level user, and an input sequence in which all input at a higher access class has been removed.

An extensive analysis of the possible covert channels in a secure concurrency control mechanism and the necessary and sufficient conditions for a secure, interference-free scheduler have been presented by T. E. Keefe, W. T. Tsal, and J. Srivastava (see the Bibliography). Three basic multilevels of correctness are discussed. For the following definitions, given a schedule, s, and an access level 1, purge(s, 1) is the schedule with all actions at a level > 1 removed from s.

1. Value Security: A scheduler satisfies this property if values read by a subject are not affected by actions with higher subject classification levels. Stated formally, for an input schedule, p, the output schedule, s, is said to be value-secure if purge(s, 1) is view-equivalent to the output schedule produced for purge(p, 1).

2. Delay Security: This property ensures that the delay experienced by an action is not affected by the actions of a subject at a higher classification level. An action, a_1, is said to be delayed with respect to another action, a_2, if, and only if,

    • The action a_1 appears before a_2 in the input schedule
    • The action a_1 follows a_2 in the output schedule

- The action a_2 is the last action in the input schedule for which the first two conditions are satisfied

For an input schedule, p, and an output schedule, s, a scheduler is delay-secure if, for all levels 1 in p, each of the actions a_1 in purge(p, 1) is delayed with respect to a_2 in the output schedule produced for purge(p, l) and is delayed with respect to a_2 in purge(s, l).

3. Recovery Security: A set of transactions is in a deadlock state when every transaction in the set is waiting for an event that can only be caused by another transaction in the set (such as release of a lock). Deadlock is a problem unique to locking protocols and is not an issue in timestamp schedulers and optimistic concurrency control. However, even these schedulers can reach a state from which they cannot continue without aborting one or more transactions. For simplicity, these two conditions are lumped together and are called a deadlock.

When a deadlock is detected, some of the actions in the schedule must be aborted, allowing the others to proceed. If resolving the deadlock can allow a high-level transaction to modify the values read by a low-level transaction or can affect the delay a low-level transaction experiences, a covert channel can arise. When a deadlock occurs, other channels are available for signaling in addition to those protected by value security and delay security. The following condition takes care of these channels: A scheduler is recovery-secure for all schedules, p, if, on the arrival of an action, A_x, for scheduling one of the following conditions occurs.

1. If a deadlock occurs, resulting in a set of actions, D, being rolled back, then for all subject classification levels 1 in p, which dominate one of those in D, a deadlock also occurs in response to the schedule purge(l, p) on the arrival of the action, A_x, with the actions purge(l, D) being rolled back.

2. If no deadlock occurs on the arrival of A_x, then for all subject classification levels l in p, it does not occur on the arrival of A_x in the input schedule purge(l, p).

Recovery security ensures that the occurrence of a deadlock appears the same to a low-level subject, independent of whether higher-level actions are in the schedule or not. The actions taken to recover from deadlock are also not affected by the presence of higher-level transactions.

Approaches to Secure Concurrency Control   In this section, we discuss some of the existing concurrency control algorithms and see why they fail or yield unacceptable performance for secure databases.

Locking and Timestamp Ordering   Locking will fail in a secure database because the security properties prevent actions in a transaction, T1, at a higher access class from delaying actions in a transaction, T2, at a lower access class (e.g., when T2 requests a conflicting lock on a data item on which T1 holds a lock). Timestamp ordering fails for similar reasons, with timestamps taking the role of locks, since a transaction at a higher access class cannot cause the abortion of another transaction at a lower access class.

Optimistic Concurrency Control   Optimistic concurrency control for a secure database can be made to work by ensuring that whenever a conflict is detected between a transaction, Th, at a higher access class in its validation phase and a transaction, T, at a lower access class, the transaction at the higher access class is aborted, while the transaction at the lower access class is not affected. A major problem with using optimistic concurrency control is the possible starvation of higher-level transactions—for example, consider a long-running transaction, Th, that must read several lower-level data items before the validation stage. In this case, there is a high probability of conflict and, as a result, Th may have to be rolled back and restarted an indefinite number of times.

Multiversion Timestamp Ordering   A secure version of the multiversion timestamp ordering (MVTO) scheduler has been presented. The difference between basic MVTO and secure MVTO is that secure MVTO will sometimes assign a new transaction a timestamp that is earlier than the current timestamp. This effectively moves the transaction into the past with respect to active transactions. To be more precise, when a transaction begins, it is assigned a timestamp that precedes the timestamps of all transactions active at strictly dominated access classes and that follows the timestamps of all transactions at its own access class. This approach to timestamp assignment is what makes it impossible for a transaction to invalidate a read from a higher access class. This method has one drawback: Transactions at a higher access class are forced to read arbitrarily old values from the database due to the timestamp assignment. This problem can be especially serious if most of the lower-level transactions are long-running transactions.

Replicated Database Architectures   A concurrency control mechanism for secure databases using a replicated architecture has been discussed. This approach does not suffer from the problem associated with the secure optimistic concurrency control protocol, but it has the same problem as the secure multiversion timestamp ordering scheduler. Consider a long-running unclassified transaction that starts off by writing to a data item, X. In order for the effect of this write to be visible at the databases of higher security levels, the transaction, T, has to complete and the update has to be propagated one by one until it reaches the site of the highest access class. This might take an unacceptably long time and until then, transactions at higher security levels have to read an old value of X.

Recent Work   Recently, there have been several significant efforts to improve the performance of secure concurrency control algorithms. A secure version of the two-phase locking protocol has been presented. This version introduces the concept of a virtual lock. A virtual lock on a data item, x, is granted to an action in a lower-level transaction when a conflicting lock is held by a higher-level transaction. The lower-level transaction is then allowed to proceed with its execution without blocking. An interesting solution to the starvation problem for higher-level transactions has been discussed. Two copies of the database are maintained: One is a snapshot—a complete and consistent copy of the database from which data values can be read, but to which updates are not made. Higher-level transactions access snapshots of low-level data. Periodically, new snapshots are taken and higher-level transactions are methodically given access to the new snapshots. The problems of when and how to take the snapshots and how to grant access to the snapshots have also been discussed. This approach precludes the existence of long-running transactions. This is because, before a snapshot is taken, transactions that have read values from the old snapshot must be allowed to either commit or abort. If transactions are allowed to run indefinitely, this waiting time before a new snapshot is taken would be unbounded. A static analysis of the read and write sets of transactions is performed, and, based on this analysis, the order of submission of the transactions to the scheduler is controlled in such a way that serializability is maintained. The scheduler that is used is the *Trusted ORACLE* scheduler (product of Oracle Corporation), which maintains levelwise serializability. This approach, however, totally ignores the problem of starvation of higher-level transactions.

It is easy to see that the problems with any concurrency control mechanism are present because a higher-level transaction cannot interfere with a lower-level transaction. This makes the mechanism unfair, because higher-level transactions are starved for service. A transaction at a higher access class *cannot* perform the following procedures.

1. Preempt a transaction at a lower access class: If it is allowed to do so, it is possible that it can control the number of times a lower-level transaction is preempted, thereby opening a covert channel.

2. Conflict with a transaction at a lower access class: If such a conflict does occur, the higher-level transaction has to be aborted, not the lower-level transaction.

3. Grant priority of execution over a transaction at a lower level: That would be a violation of delay security. The longer a transaction, the greater the probability of conflict with a transaction at a different access class and, therefore, the greater the starvation.

13.6.2 Security, Concurrency Control, and Real-Time Databases

Real-time database systems are systems in which time is a key factor, and the correctness of the system depends not only on the results produced, but also on the time within which the results are produced. There are two important problems associated with real-time databases: maximizing the number of transactions that meet their deadline and ensuring predictability. Conventional databases cannot be used in real-time applications due to the inadequacies of poor performance and lack of predictability. New techniques have been developed to manage the consistency of a real-time database and to take into account the timing constraints of transactions through priority scheduling schemes. Another property unique to real-time databases is the temporal consistency of data. Most of the data items in the database have associated with them a validity interval—the length of time for which the data item is considered to have a useful value.

Let us discuss the applicability of concurrency control algorithms to a real-time database. Of the existing concurrency control approaches for conventional databases, only optimistic concurrency control can be used to provide serializability for a single-version secure database. This approach, however, was shown to result in starvation for higher-level transactions. The application of this approach to real-time databases would be disastrous, because almost all higher-level transactions would invariably miss their deadlines. It is also very difficult to predict beforehand how many times a transaction would be aborted and restarted before completing execution (i.e., predictability is low). The MVTO scheduler, previously discussed, had the drawback that higher-level transactions were forced to read arbitrarily old values from the database. This method is also not suitable for real-time databases, because transactions would be reading temporally inconsistent values from the database if they read arbitrarily old values.

There are two approaches that can be explored to yield time-cognizant concurrency control algorithms for secure real-time databases.

1. Improvements to existing concurrency control algorithms for secure databases could be effected to make them time-cognizant.

2. Correctness criteria that are weaker than serializability would result in increased concurrency.

Several publications relating to real-time databases have explored these approaches with respect to conventional databases. The problem arises when these approaches are applied to secure databases, because covert channels can be introduced by priority-based scheduling. All existing real-time systems schedule transactions based on some priority scheme. The priority usually reflects how close the transaction is to missing its deadline. Priority-based scheduling of real-time transactions, however, interacts with the property of noninterference, which has to be satisfied by secure schedulers. Consider the sequence of transactions input to a scheduler.

T_1 (SECRET):	R(X)
T_2 (UNCLASSIFIED):	W(X)
T_3 (UNCLASSIFIED):	W(X)
T_4 (UNCLASSIFIED):	R(X)

Assume that T_1, T_2, and T_3 have priorities 5, 7, and 10, respectively, and the priority assignment scheme is such that if priority(T_2) > priority(T_1), then T_2 has greater criticalness and has to be scheduled ahead of T_1. In the above example, T_2 and T_3 are initially blocked by T_1 when they arrive. When T_1 completes execution, T_3 is scheduled ahead of T_2, since it has a greater priority than T_2, and the transaction execution order would be T_1, T_3, T_2, T_4. However, if the transaction T_1 is removed, the execution order would be T_2, T_3, T_4, because T_2 would have been scheduled as soon as it had arrived. The presence of the SECRET transaction T_1 thus changes the value read by the UNCLASSIFIED transaction T_4, which is a violation of value security. For the same reason delay security is also violated, because the presence of T_1 delays T_2 with respect to T_3. The only solution to this problem appears to be the weakening of the security requirements or to somehow introduce a certain amount of randomness into the system so that it can be guaranteed that a higher-level transaction cannot directly influence the execution of a lower-level transaction in a deterministic fashion (i.e., even though a covert channel can be created, its effective bandwidth is very low).

A database state is said to be correct if a collection of integrity constraints is satisfied for the contents of the database. Each transaction is assumed to be correctly written so that its execution will maintain the integrity constraints. By induction, the serial execution of a collection of transactions will preserve the correctness of the database. The big advantage of serializability is that it is easy to produce serializable histories. However, researchers have realized that serializability is unnecessarily strong for many applications and can significantly increase transaction response time. An approach to increasing concurrency of transaction execution using the semantic information available about the transactions has been proposed. The main idea is to divide each transaction into a sequence of (atomic) steps so that interleaving may be permitted at various points inside the transaction. In other words, instead of requiring that the execution of these transactions be serializable, we may allow any concurrent execution of these transactions in which their steps occur atomically. This approach is not directly applicable to secure databases, however, because a higher-level transaction cannot be interleaved with the execution of a lower-level transaction at its breakpoint. A new model of multilevel atomicity, which defines three different degrees of atomicity that can be requested for a transaction's execution depending on the needs of the application, has been introduced. This model is based on the fact that lower-level security operations in a transaction must be able to commit or abort independently of higher security–level operations. A taxonomy of various correctness criteria that focus on database consistency requirements and transaction correctness properties has been presented. Development of alternate correctness criteria for secure databases is worth investigating, because of the basic asymmetry of read and write operations in a secure database. Taking the restricted *-property (where a transaction, 25, is allowed to write a data element, x, if, and only if, level[x] = level[Tj]), the only conflict that can occur between a transaction, T_1, at a low access class and a transaction, T_2, at a higher access class is a read in T_1 with a write in T_2. This seems to suggest that serializability is necessary only for transactions within the same access class, and for transactions in different access classes, weaker correctness criteria would suffice.

13.7 SUMMARY

The previous sections have studied approaches to multilevel security in different database models. However, there are still a number of open issues.

1. Secure Object-Oriented Models: As explained previously, the current findings are preliminary in nature and further work needs to be done before a complete secure design can be implemented.

2. Security Policies: Throughout this chapter, the Bell-LaPadula model has been taken to be the only requirement for all existing secure database systems, mainly because of the DoD-mandated criteria. This model is acceptable for a military database, but doubts have been raised about its applicability to commercial systems. It has been contended that the DoD criteria are concerned only with secrecy, whereas commercial enterprises are also concerned with data integrity (illegal data modification); that is, the system must also protect itself from fraud by an authorized user. Two additional properties for security have been proposed: well-formed transactions and separation of duties. The concept of a well-formed transaction is that a user should not manipulate data arbitrarily, but only in constrained ways that preserve the integrity of data. A good example of a well-formed transaction is double-entry bookkeeping in accounting systems. If an entry in the book is not recorded properly, it can be detected by an independent test (balancing the books). It is thus possible to detect frauds, such as the issuance of unauthorized checks. Well-formed transactions alone are not sufficient to ensure integrity of data, since, if a single user is responsible for each independent test in the well-formed transaction, fudging the data associated with each test can be done by the user. The separation of duty ensures that each part of a well-formed transaction is performed by a different user.

D. D. Clark and D. R. Wilson (see the Bibliography) explain the operations that can be performed on the commercial database, whereas the Chinese Wall security policy deals with the security of data in the system. The Chinese Wall security policy can be easily visualized as the code of practice that must be followed by a market analyst working for a financial institution providing corporate business services. Such an analyst must have access only to data about companies that are not in direct competition with each other. In the model, data are grouped into "conflict of interest classes" and, by mandatory ruling, all users are allowed access to at most one data class. These properties cannot be modeled by the

Bell-LaPadula model. Incorporation of these properties into the mandatory security model discussed thus far is no easy task.

3. Secure Concurrency Control: The interaction among the security requirements, the correctness requirements, and real-time requirements of a database management system were previously discussed. The existing secure concurrency control mechanisms were shown to yield unsatisfactory performance, especially for higher-level transactions. Further research needs to be done to develop an integrated approach that handles all three conflicting requirements.

4. Inference Problem: As stated previously, several developments have been reported concerning approaches to handle the inference problem. The current challenge is to develop viable commercial and/or operational products based on the existing prototype tools and systems. Also, research should focus on developing techniques to handle the inference problem that could result from data mining.

5. Secure Distributed Database Management: The current challenge concerns the interoperability of trusted database management systems. In particular, the different security policies have to interoperate. Other issues include schema integration and transaction processing in secure heterogeneous environments.

14

Fault-Tolerant Database Systems

Paul Fortier

14.1 INTRODUCTION

Fault tolerance is a property of computer systems that defines how they respond and recover from failures. A fault-tolerant computer system must be able to allow faults, failures, or errors to enter the system's boundaries; be able to detect the fault, failure, or error; and execute some corrective action to restore system operations to the state that existed before the failure. The measurable effect of fault tolerance is the availability of system resources for applications' use. A fault-tolerant system will have a very high system availability factor, whereas a non-fault-tolerant system will have a low availability factor.

14.2 BASIC PROBABILITY

To qualify the availability measure and to further define what constitutes a fault-tolerant database system, we first need to look at some basics of probability and reliability engineering. The basics of probability attempt to define the possibility of some event occurring, given some other conditions over some period of time, denoted P (event). Probability is defined as a fraction that takes on the values from zero to one, where zero indicates that the event never occurs, and one indicates that the event always occurs, with all the values in-between these extremes indicating that the event occurs between never and definitely—for example, given the probability of an event E is $P(E) = .5$, then the event E is just as likely to occur as it is not likely to occur. What this means is that on the average the event occurs half of the time.

Given the probability of an event occurring as P (event), then the probability that the event may not occur is simply the probability of the event always occurring minus the probability of the event occurring, or

$$1 - P \text{ (event)} = \text{probability of event not occurring}$$

For events that are independent (an assumption made often in probability computations), the performance of one event, $E1$, does not affect the possibility or probability of the second event, $E2$, from occurring; therefore, the probability $P(E1)$ does not affect the probability $P(E2)$ and vice versa in independent events—for example, the probability of a CPU failing is not dependent on the probability of a disk failing.

Given two independent events with probabilities, $P(E1)$ and $P(E2)$, representing the probability of a CPU failure and the probability of a disk failure, several possible conditions can be looked at—for example, what would be the probability of the CPU and the disk failing at the same time, or what is the probability of either the CPU or the disk failing, but not both in the same time frame? For both the CPU and the disk to fail at the same time, the probabilities of each occurring are combined as a product of the two as

$$P \text{ (CPU and Disk)} = P \text{ (CPU)} * P \text{ (Disk)}$$

That is, the probability of both events occurring is equivalent to the product of their individual probabilities. So if the probability of a CPU failing over some period of time is .25, and the probability of the disk failing is .5, then the probability of both the disk and the CPU failing over the same period of time is

$$P \text{ (CPU and Disk)} = .25 * .5 = .125$$

This implies that there is a 12.5 percent chance over the specified time period that both the disk and the CPU will fail.

Likewise, we could attempt to determine what the probability is that one would fail but not the other. This probability is defined as P (1st or 2nd), which for small probabilities equates to the P (1st) + P (2nd), and for larger probabilities equates to P (1st) + P (2nd) * $2P$ (1st) * P (2nd). For the above probabilities for the CPU and disk, we use the second form, since any probability above 10 percent is considered large. For the CPU and disk the formula then becomes

P(CPU) + P(Disk) * 2P(CPU) * P(Disk) = .25 + .5 * 2(.25) * .5 = .375

for the probability that the CPU fails and the disk does not, or as

P(Disk) + P(CPU) * 2P(Disk) * P(CPU) = .5 + .25 * 2(.5) * .25 = .5625

for the probability that the disk fails and the CPU does not. These formulas indicate that there is an increased chance that one of the two will fail, but not both.

Probabilities, since they are independent, imply that the probability of an event occurring in some period of time is not related to the probability of the same event occurring in some different period of time. This is referred to as the memoryless property of independent probabilities. The practical effect of this is that for some given component, for instance the CPU, the likelihood of the CPU failing today or tomorrow is not related and can be treated as independent, unrelated probabilities—for example, for the disk drives in the previous examples, if their probability of failure on any given day is .5, then the probability of the disk failing today or tomorrow is

P(Disk_today) + P(Disk_tomorrow) * 2P(Disk_today) *
P(Disk_tomorrow) = .5 + .5 * 2(.5) * .5 = .75

which implies that there is a 75 percent chance that the disk will fail either today or tomorrow, given that the independent daily probability of failure is 50 percent.

An important measure for reliability derived from probabilities is the mean time to an event, referred to as MT (event). It has been shown that for probabilities much less than one and for memoryless events the mean time to an event is related to the reciprocal of the event's probability, or

MT (event) = 1/P (event)

If we had, for example, a probability of failure for the CPU of .02 and a probability of failure for the disk of .04, then the mean time for failure for the CPU is

MT(CPU) = 1/.02 = 50 days

and the mean time for failure for the disk is equivalent to

MT (Disk) = 1/.04 = 25 days

which is simply the reciprocal of the probability of failure for either device. To determine what the mean time to fail for either of the devices is, we use the reciprocal of their combined probabilities. Since the values for the probabilities are small, we can use the formula

$$P \text{ (CPU or Disk)} = P \text{ (CPU)} + P \text{ (Disk)} = .02 + .04 = .06$$

From this combined probability we can easily find the mean time to failure for either of the devices when combined as the reciprocal of this probability, or

$$MT \text{ (CPU or Disk)} = 1/P \text{ (CPU or Disk)} = 1/.06 = 16.66 \text{ days}$$

By using these simple notations many of the required failure rates and probabilities can be determined.

14.3 FAULT TOLERANCE

In modern computer systems, and particularly database systems, failure cannot be tolerated. Downtime of the computer system means a loss of information and its availability. A loss of information availability can mean the loss of a competitive edge in today's business sector, which is so reliant on up-to-date information for decision making. Due to this requirement for highly available data, database systems must by definition be fault tolerant, or at least quickly recoverable. Early systems simply looked at increasing data availability, by ensuring data recoverability. This is sufficient when periods of data inaccessibility are tolerable. For most database systems this is a tolerable condition; however, for an ever-growing sector of database applications, this is not the case. On-line transaction processing systems, real-time systems, monitoring systems, and advanced information processing systems cannot tolerate downtime. Fatal flaws in system design may be discovered if downtime is allowed. Fault-tolerant database systems were designed to support this niche market within the information management community. The goal of fault tolerance is to maintain the availability of the system at its highest design potential.

14.3.1 Fault-Tolerance Basics

A database system can be viewed as a single element consisting of successively more finer-grained elements. Each element itself has possibly additional subelements (Figure 14.1). Fault tolerance must be defined from the smallest discernible (replaceable or reconfigurable unit) element up to the entire system in order to deliver required reliability and level of service.

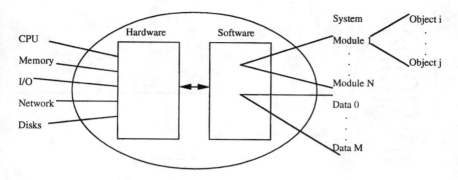

Figure 14.1   Hierarchical structure of fault tolerance

Each element of the system has a specified behavior and an observed behavior—for example, an ALU of a CPU takes two numbers as operands and adds them together, returning a single result of the same number of bits in the resultant word as in each of the operand words (Figure 14.2). For all classes of inputs, a specific output is specified—for example, adding the operands 1 and 2 results in 3, and nothing else. This specified behavior is the expected correct result for this operation. If the result returned is anything but 3, an error has occurred. The detection of this erroneous result is called the observed erroneous behavior. Observed behavior can be both correct and erroneous. It is the determination whether this observed behavior is erroneous or correct that defines the function of detection.

There are a variety of classifications or definitions for what constitutes a wrong condition in a system. A random error condition is a

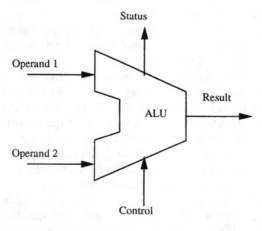

Figure 14.2   Single element and behavior

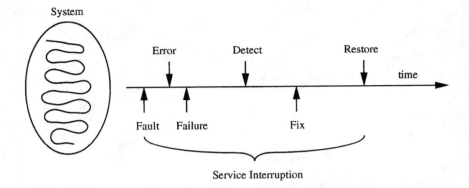

Figure 14.3   Time line for error occurrence and restoration

fault and may not be repeatable. A repeatable or detectable and trace-able error condition is an error. Errors that cause service interruptions or that are not readily recoverable are failures—for example, a failure of a program may be due to a divide by zero error, which may have been due to a design fault induced by a programmer's mistake. The time between when such an error occurred and when the failure resulted is called the error's latency. The actual failure is an effective error, whereas before the error manifested itself it was a latent error.

The major goal is to maximize the mean time between failures and to minimize the mean time to repair and restore system operations once an error is manifested. Figure 14.3 shows the processes required in the initial detection of a latent error and the restoration of service. When a fault occurs, it does not necessarily result in an immediate error. Faults may need to be repeated a number of times until a threshold value is reached, where an actual error occurs and can no longer be masked out. In addition, single errors may not result in a detectable fault, but may manifest themselves at a point down the road in the form of a propagated error. The propagation of an error can go on for some time before the condition that originally caused the error results in some noticeable faulty execution or value.

Only after a fault causes some loss in system functionality, does it become detectable. Detection, however, can take on multiple proactive forms. First, to detect a true fault, detection software can simply collect results of some computation and periodically run some form of diagnostic software test on the collection of data items to detect if errors in the computation may have occurred. Second, detection can be more active by periodically having detection software run to "test" the health of hardware and software and seek out faults before they manifest themselves as operational faults. This test software must

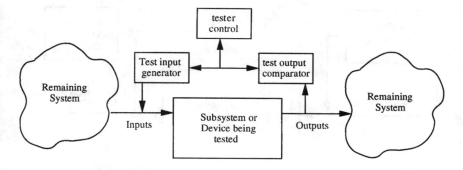

Figure 14.4   Hardware tester architecture

feed the hardware and software to be tested with known "stimuli." Based on the provided stimuli, predetermined output results are then looked for. If the expected results are not returned and detected, then a fault condition has been found. A third approach is to collect status from software and hardware self-checks and initiate further high-level tests when fluctuations from the normal ranges are seen. These techniques are referred to as fault detection and program monitoring tests for the hardware and software, respectively.

For hardware fault detection one typically requires additional hardware to "test" the hardware subsystem. The test hardware is designed to "feed" the tested device with a fixed known test pattern or sequence designed to flex all the components that comprise the monitored device (Figure 14.4). The test hardware is designed to sense when the device to be tested is in an idle state and to use this knowledge to trigger a test sequence. The test sequence may be required to save any volatile state information of a device for restoration once the test is completed. The test device then stimulates the tested system device with a set sequence of data and control signals (e.g., input operands and operation instructions for an ALU) and monitors the results. Results can be input to some additional hardware device, such as a pattern recognition device or comparator, to determine the validity of the test.

To detect errors in software a similar approach can be taken. Program monitoring can be applied to software to collect statistics about the operation of a software element (e.g., a subroutine, function, or module) for use in later operational analysis. Program monitoring is nonintrusive and simply logs the actions of a piece of software. This logged data can later (e.g., during a downtime of the system or low utilization period) be checked for inconsistencies or other telltale signs of faults. A variety of pattern recognition techniques have been devel-

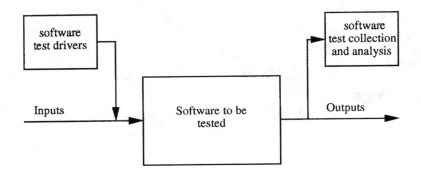

Figure 14.5   Software testing architecture

oped to examine logs of results for some specific types of data processing software. A more common approach is to monitor software results and compare the observed outputs to known outputs for the same input data forms. When observed results do not match expected results, a potential fault has been identified. To be sure of an error, the test should then trigger some more formal test software that will further examine the degree and scope of a fault.

The test software (Figure 14.5) can be periodically given control over the application software to be tested and can run the software through some known sequence of tests, which examine the various paths through the tested software. The goal of test software is to examine the correctness of all the paths through the software in order to ensure it is fault free. This is not, however, practical, since software testing has been shown to be an NP complete problem, which does not have a known efficient solution. The problem is that software will have many more paths than hardware, since bad addresses and other changes in data and program control are possible in software, but not in hardware.

These schemes, however, only result in the sensing of some error in the tested component. The component can be fairly high level (e.g., a processor, entire memory, input/output controller, etc.) and may not actually indicate to an acceptable granularity which piece of software or hardware is the culprit. To determine which element is the source of a fault requires more intrusive testing, referred to as fault localization and fault isolation testing. Fault localization attempts to determine from where the detected error is emanating. The localization may be to the specific component (i.e., an integrated circuit or software block of code) or at a higher level of abstraction—for example, to a replaceable unit such as a plug-in circuit board or downloadable software module. The goal of fault isolation testing is to locate the fault and remove the ability of the fault to propagate beyond the detected faulty item. Fault isolation and detection techniques operate by working from the point (typically an output) where the fault was detected inward through all connected, interrelated components until the source of the fault is located. The process of localization uses techniques, as previously defined, to test the correctness of a stage and, if it tests correctly, remove it from further examination. In this way items are tested, validated, and removed from the test path one at a time until the path leads to the error-generation point. Once the error-generation point is found, the item is shut down, or has data routed around it to isolate and remove the erroneous item before it affects any other elements in the system. If this cannot be performed, the system may require further corrective procedures to restore correct system operations.

Once an error has been detected, located, and isolated, restoration must be performed. Restoration can be as simple as resetting an element or as complex as reconfiguration of hardware and software components to work around an error condition that cannot respond to simple actions. All of these affect the availability of the system as a measurable quantity. The availability commonly is defined as the measured ratio of the mean time to failure divided by the mean time to failure added to the mean time to repair a failure, where mean time to repair includes detection, localization, isolation, and restoration processes.

$$\text{Availability} = \text{MTTF/MTTF} + \text{MTTR}$$

Fault tolerance and reliability go hand in hand. Higher reliability of components will result in longer mean time to failure, which results in higher system availability and, therefore, a more fault-tolerant system. The system is fault tolerant in the sense that fewer faults will occur, and those that do occur will have a smaller effect on overall system performance. However, any fault will result in a loss of performance, even if only during fault recovery. From this perspective, even minor faults that occur infrequently will still result in a less fault-tolerant system, if the fault results in any loss in performance even when it is isolated.

14.3.2 Fault Avoidance

A more appropriate means for constructing a fault-tolerant system is to reduce the possibility of a failure, or of a failure affecting system availability. Failure probability can be reduced by introducing additional design steps that are aimed at catching design flaws and to design in error-correction techniques to remove the effect of an error on the overall design. Design correction through increased hardware and software testing can reduce the volume of latent errors that is allowed to pass through to the final design. Error correction uses techniques that involve redundancy to remove an error from propagating from the input to a stage at the output—for example, if a bit is being corrupted in a memory word, cyclic redundancy checks with multiple parity bits, along with coding techniques for the data, can provide bit-error detection and correction for such simple errors. Additional error-correction techniques use more complex techniques, which use forms of redundancy and result reconstruction to detect and correct errors.

14.3.3 Recovery and Restoration

It is not always possible to simply correct an error and continue processing using the same components. Often it is the case that the erroneous component will fail again, resulting in the need for another correction. This approach works fine as long as the class of error continues to be one that is correctable. If the error is deemed a hard error (i.e., one that is not recoverable), then further mechanisms and policies must be in place to effect recovery and restoration of services. First, it becomes apparent that a protocol must be in place to detect the continued appearance of the same error and to trigger a more robust corrective action when this condition is detected. Typically this involves some form of logging, which keeps a count of the number of times an error occurs and the degree and reach of the failure. As a failure reoccurs, and it becomes apparent that it is not being effectively resolved using simple corrective techniques, a triggering of further, more encompassing corrective actions is needed. One such technique uses reconfiguration of resources to restore correct service. Reconfiguration is a concept whereby resources are pooled and reallocated to applications based on some reasonableness of fit. The goal of reconfiguration is to reallocate resources in such a way that minimizes the effect on running applications, yet results in full restoration of the failed application detected through error-detection methods. For reconfiguration to be possible, the system must maintain a dynamic map of system resources and their respective processing loads. In addition, these resources must be quantified in such a way that captures the envelope of supportable activities, so that an additional software component can match application processing and resource needs with available resources that can provide adequate service to the failed activities. If an application running a sensor data reduction software application detects unrecoverable errors and must be reconfigured, it is necessary that the hardware to which it will be moved also supports

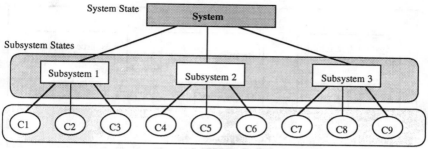

Figure 14.6 System availability manager

the connectivity necessary to extract the sensor data and provides the appropriate processing assets.

Reconfiguration consists of three major functions or elements: a system availability manager, a resource manager, and a reallocation manager. The system availability manager is a hierarchical process that collects status on individual components and combines this collected element data into a composite subsystem status, which ultimately is used to create a systemwide map of system component status (Figure 14.6). The goal of the collection and recombination of the status data is to construct and maintain a dynamic map of the health of the system and its composite pieces. The system availability manager uses low-level program monitoring and fault-detection tests to perform self-health tests. In addition, tests for self-health are explicitly provided and are called diagnostic tests. These tests specifically look at the complete health of the components.

The system resource manager maintains a map of the applications and their resource needs for all applications within the system—for example, if the same temperature control software requires two types of sensor data and a specific operating system, this information would be logged into the resource manager application's load time. The resource map, along with the system's resource availability map, is used by the reconfiguration software to determine possible reallocations of software to available hardware based on failed components, software needing to be reallocated, and resource loadings. Numerous allocation and reconfiguration schemes have been devised—for example, one of the simplest schemes uses a first-fit approach, which attempts to find system elements with the appropriate resources available and with enough spare capacity to fit the software needing relocation. This scheme does not attempt to optimize overall system performance, or to minimize the loading on any resources. It only finds the first avail-

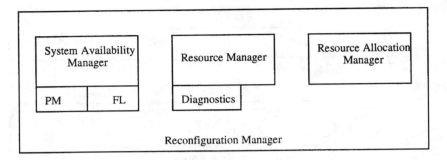

Figure 14.7 Reconfiguration software architecture

able system and grabs the resources. It may bring the failed software back on line quickly, but it ignores possible loading and contention problems due to this allocation. If, for example, the existing software has high input and output loading and the software to be reallocated also has significant input and output loading, then, even though enough capacity exists on the basic resources to support the processing demands, there may still be a slowdown in overall system performance, because of added wait time and input and output processing due to additional contention and service times associated with these devices. (See Figure 14.7.)

Other reconfiguration schemes attempt to do the exact opposite and try to find an optimal resource fit; that is, they try to find the least loaded device with the least demand on its input and output channels that can support the reallocation and still have spare capacity. This is referred to as a worst-fit scheme. Other schemes for resource reallocation attempt to balance the load evenly on all devices. Such a reallocation scheme would possibly require the examination of all active software and would look at the reallocation of all this software so that each node or resource element is equally loaded and equally shares input and output burdens. It is apparent that the first two reconfiguration policies may require minimal time to execute in finding a new load, but may result in less than optimal long-term support. The latter reconfiguration approach would result in more optimal long-term performance, but may cause too much disturbance on run-time software to be realistically considered. Whichever reallocation scheme is chosen, however, will result in restoration of services once the affected software and/or hardware components are removed, and their input and output streams are routed to the new allocated resources where the software now operates.

Detection and correction, along with reconfiguration, maintain the viability of the system; however, it still results in some elements of the system being unavailable for repair time. Repair time is the time it takes to assess damage, determine a reallocation, perform the reallocation, and restart the affected application. This actually results in a fault-tolerant system, but one with lower availability due to the reconfiguration policies and mechanisms. There are also other techniques, which involve more up-front design work and cost more in terms of hardware and software complexity and software volume.

14.4 HARDWARE REDUNDANCY AS AN APPROACH TO FAULT TOLERANCE

The basic idea applied to achieve fault tolerance is to provide some form of redundant computation engine to check the results of an application or a piece of hardware resource for errors. This concept extends beyond what is traditionally thought of as redundancy in database systems. Typically in database systems, redundancy is thought of as simply requiring the maintenance of a copy of the data to provide a backup if something should go wrong with the main database due to a transaction-induced error. This form of redundancy is used for recovery, not for fault tolerance.

In a fault-tolerant design, redundancy is used as a means to detect and stop execution immediately before execution is allowed to proceed and propagate an error beyond the present boundaries. Redundancy is not used simply as a means for maintaining a copy of some entity, but for an actual executing twin, which can be readily placed in service for the primary version if a failure occurs, or can be used to immediately detect when the twin is acting erroneously. This approach to fault tolerance results in a "fail-fast" module. The module can then be quickly switched to a redundant spare once an error is detected, using all hardware elements for detection and switching (Figure 14.8). In Figure 14.8, each module is redundant internally, with a comparator used to test if the outputs of each device agree. If the output is good, the comparator issues a logical Boolean signal to the selector hardware (e.g., an AND gate), which selects between module one or two as the output to use. If module one is executing correctly, module two is never used. If, on the other hand, module one should develop an error, such that the result of m-1 does not match the result of m1-2, then the comparator will return a logical false output state, resulting in module two's output being selected as the correct output, and module one is removed from further execution. This form of redundancy for fault tolerance is sufficient if the mean time to failure of the modules is quite high, and if repair is allowed once a hard fault is found in module one. If this is not the case, then module two now becomes the sole computation engine for the designed application, and, if it should fail,

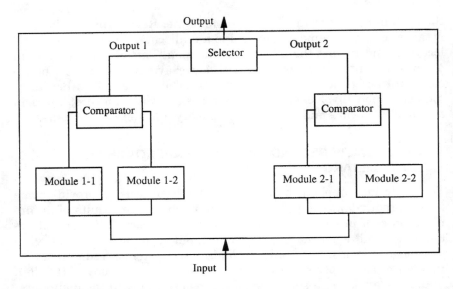

Figure 14.8   Redundant modular system architecture

the system will also fail, requiring further recovery actions such as reconfiguration.

The reliability of such a design can be computed using the probabilities defined earlier. If the probability of a single module's failure is $P = .25$, then the probability of them both failing is $P * P = .25 * 25 = .0625$, indicating that the probability of them both failing is one-quarter as large as either failing singularly. In addition, since the probability of failure went down, the mean time to failure increased, since they are reciprocally related to MTTF $= 1/.0625 = 16$ days.

A solution to this weakness in design is to add additional modules to the architecture, as shown in Figure 14.9. In this architectural approach to fault tolerance, the number of modules is increased to three. The output of each module is compared to that of the other two modules; if a match is found between either of the compared pairings of elements, or with all three pairs, then that output is used as the valid result for this application module. If no match is found, then the entire module is suspect, and reconfiguration is again needed.

The probability of the three-element module is increasingly more reliable, and again can be quantitatively determined by the probabilities. If the probability of failure for any of the elements is $P = .25$, then the probability that they all fail is the product of all their probabilities, or $P * P * P = .25 * .25 * .25 = .015625$, indicating that the probability of them all failing is one-sixteenth the probability of any one failing. Likewise, this implies that the mean time between failure

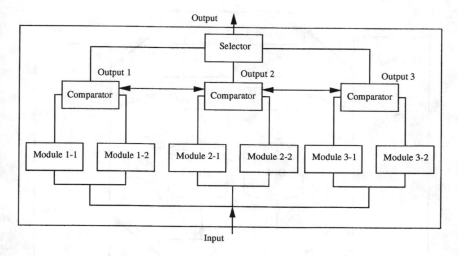

Figure 14.9   Tri-modular redundancy

also goes up drastically to MTTF = $1/.015625$ = 64 days, or four times longer than the mean time to failure for the dual modular unit.

This approach can be further improved on by increasing the redundancy of a module element from three to some maximum number N. By increasing the number of modules, the probability of success goes up, as does the complexity of the design. The tradeoff to consider is higher fault tolerance at an increased cost in complexity and design. Modules can be organized into hierarchies or network structures to further reduce the probability of failure and to speed up the computation of the results through the various layers of comparisons and selections.

Hardware fault tolerance can be relatively easily obtained using such techniques as redundancy and recombination policies and mechanisms that reduce the probability of failure. This form of fault-tolerant design can be applied quite easily to the hardware that supports a database system. Redundant disks with redundant cross-strap connections, disk controllers, main memory, processors, and interconnection for all of these elements can be provided.

Figure 14.10 represents a minimal fault-tolerant architecture for a database management system. With this architecture, any hardware failure can be quickly recovered from and worked around by switching from the failed component to its redundant pair. Through the analysis of the reliability of each device, the degree of redundancy (e.g., dual, tri, quad, etc.) can be increased for less reliable items and can be lessened for more reliable components. In this way any single error, and possibly combinations of single errors (failures), will not cause the en-

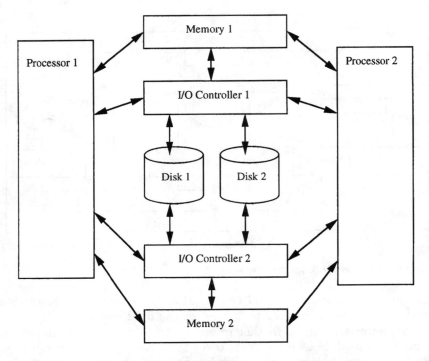

Figure 14.10   Redundant database management system module

tire database management system hardware to fail. The general operational mode required to guarantee quick and painless switching on a failure requires maintaining the spare as a "hot," ready-to-go device. A hot spare is one kept 100 percent redundant in hardware and the hardware state so that on a failure execution can immediately switch over to the hot spare.

14.5 SOFTWARE REDUNDANCY AS AN APPROACH TO FAULT TOLERANCE

With adequate interconnectivity and switching circuits, hardware failures can be almost completely masked out using N modular redundancy techniques, resulting in a highly available system and a highly fault-tolerant system. The real problem, however, lies in the software that runs on the hardware, and is therefore the major concern in the design of fault-tolerant database management systems. Hardware fault-tolerance design techniques and defect-testing techniques follow specific procedures. Hardware can be relatively completely tested for correctness and accuracy. Software, on the other hand, does not possess the same "provably correct" paradigms. Software testing and software reliability follow more ad hoc techniques. Software is typically run through some tests for some "bake-in" time, which is meant to "prove" that the software will at least last for the period of time of the test run before some unforeseen or untested error or fault appears. The problem is that software is more susceptible to faults, resulting in failures becoming manifested quickly. In addition, it becomes increasingly difficult, as software becomes more complex, to trace, detect, and isolate software errors. Also due to general-purpose computers, which are more reliant on software, the volume and complexity of computer software will increase. All of this results in more possibilities for software errors to creep in and reduce system reliability and availability.

Modern programming techniques have helped to reduce the volume of errors that still exist in an application, but they have not removed them totally. Structured programming, code walkthroughs, code inspections, regression testing, and alpha and beta testing of software has increased quality, but a few bugs per thousand lines of final code are still common in most applications. Software can be improved, but this will require time and money, which are not typically available to any real project.

Some techniques do exist, however, that try to remove or isolate the effects of probable latent errors in software. One approach, similar to that used in hardware fault tolerance, is to create multiple unique versions of a program and group them together into a single module with a single input and a single output (Figure 14.11). The idea is not to replicate the software, since each copy would still have the same latent errors, but to construct N unique versions of the software to solve the same problem. Each version is written by a separate software design team, which may use separate algorithmic solution techniques. Each of the unique versions is then carefully tested in isolation and improved upon, as in the single software case. The N versions of the same program are then integrated into a single module, which solves the single problem they were all designed for. The N versions operate in parallel, with the final result from the N versions chosen by taking the majority correlated response from the N versions as the correct result. This approach should, but it is not guaranteed, mask out many separate errors in the different versions.

A second approach uses modular programming concepts, breaking up each definable element of the software into one module, each with a definable state input and a state output. A set of constraints on the inputs and the outputs is then designed, which can check the correctness of the inputs and the outputs based on the designed time and state descriptions. If the constraints are not validated, the module fails and corrective actions begin. The problem with this and the pre-

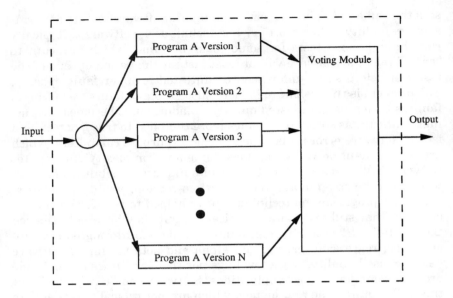

Figure 14.11   Software redundancy through versions

vious approach is in the added complexity and possibly the added overhead caused by applications implemented in these ways. What is to be done when an error is found within these architectures? Testing is not trivial, since each software package or module is coded separately and will not have the same internal or intermediate states. It may be more advantageous to construct "steel" software the first time, and add some additional checking software to monitor the software's activities. This is actually more desirable, since numerous software errors are transient, caused by data corruption or instruction corruption due to external forces such as a hardware fault or bad input data.

The desirable mode for providing fault tolerance uses correction, detection, and restoration for database systems and involves the use of redundant data, logging, shadow execution, and correctness checking, as well as monitoring and conventional recovery. For fault tolerance the shadow database system must be prepared to take over for the primary database with little or no delay. This requires that the databases be removed from direct contact with applications (see Figure 14.12). Instead, interaction with the databases is through messages, which can be routed to both or either redundant database site depending on the fault recovery policy in place. The approach is for all database operation requests, such as transaction initiation, transaction commit, transaction abort, data item reads or writes, and so forth to be sent as messages to both copies of the database management sys-

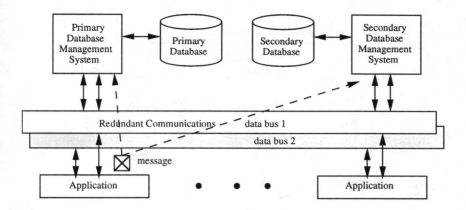

Figure 14.12   Redundant database systems

tem. All operations at all levels of the database management system must be checkpointed and logged to nonvolatile storage to allow postanalysis and monitoring of correct executions, as well as to provide quick recovery and restart from any intermediate state errors. This process will require additional primitives at various levels within the database management system software. The tradeoffs with this policy are high data availability and minimal downtime on restoration from detected errors against possible additional run-time overhead to maintain the redundant copies in such a high state of readiness.

By analysis of executing database systems, a model of the execution paths, both critical and noncritical, through the database management system software can be quantified. With this information additional recovery and fault-tolerance policies and mechanisms can be constructed to improve the software's overall quality and reliability. The client/server approach can be improved through further redundancy policies for software execution shadowing. Such approaches would allow the restoration of services upon a failure to numerous checkpoint positions within the stream of system execution.

The process of commit can be improved by using multiple copies of the database software (as discussed earlier), issuing all requests to all N versions of the database, and using the commit points of transactions as the coordination points upon which to validate the correctness of transaction operations on all of the databases. The N versions send their copy of the result to be committed to each other; if the versions are acceptable, each of the N-1 versions would issue a prepare to commit message. If they all agree, a commit is issued and they all respond as committed. If not accepted by a majority, the commit would be failed and the commit processing for the transaction would not com-

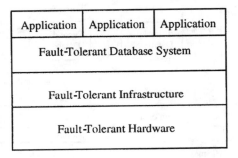

Figure 14.13 Fault-tolerant system architecture

plete. The transaction would be aborted and removed from all of the sites.

It can be seen from this overview of fault tolerance, that fault tolerance in software is difficult to achieve and is expensive to realize, both in time and complexity. If the application requires such fault tolerance and correctness of results, then the cost and delay may be acceptable (Figure 14.13).

14.6 SUMMARY

For database fault tolerance, we must begin with a fault-tolerant hardware architecture, followed by a fault-tolerant software system infrastructure, which includes a fault-tolerant operating system and fault-tolerant network communication service. This platform can then be used to construct a fault-tolerant database management system. The fault-tolerant database management system must begin with redundancy of the database information, the database metadata, and all database-related software and management information.

The database software must be designed using sound fault-tolerant and software engineering principles to remove, limit the reach of, or mask most errors from bringing the system down. Some form of N-version programming, with mutually exclusive parallel executions that are validated against each other, must be used. Overhead can be minimized by keeping the most intrusive and time-consuming coordination activities to critical points in database processing, such as at commit time. By using these techniques, fault-tolerant database management systems are possible, but at a cost.

Multimedia Database Management Systems

Bhavani Thuraisingham*
Son K. Dao†

15.1 INTRODUCTION

A multimedia database management system (MMDBMS) provides for the efficient storage and manipulation of data represented as text, images, voice, graphics, and video. In addition, users can also periodically update the multimedia database so that information contained in it accurately reflects the real world. Some MMDBMSs are being extended to provide the capability of linking the various types of data in order to enable users to have access to large amounts of related information within a short space of time either by browsing or querying the system. It has been found that such systems are useful for a variety of applications, including C4I, CAD/CAM, and air traffic control. Although multimedia information systems have received a great deal of attention recently, methodologies for designing applications that utilize such systems have received little attention.

Recently, much research has been carried out on designing and developing MMDBMSs, and, as a result, prototypes and some commercial products are now available. However, there are several areas that need further work. Research on developing an appropriate data model to support data types such as video is needed. Some have proposed

---

* The Mitre Corporation, Burlington Road, Bedford, MA 01730
† Hughes Research Laboratories Inc., Malibu, CA 90265.

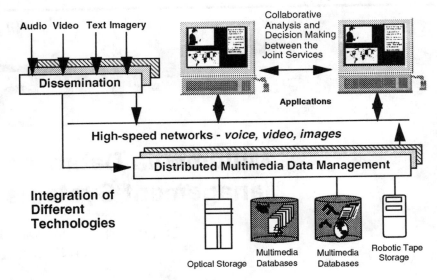

Figure 15.1   Future information systems

object-oriented database management systems (OODBMSs) for storing and managing multimedia data, since they have been found to be more suitable for handling large objects and multimedia data, such as sound and video, that consume considerable storage space. Although such systems show some promise, they are not sufficient to capture all of the requirements of multimedia applications.

A vision for future information systems is illustrated in Figure 15.1. The ultimate goal is to provide for the seamless access and fusion of massive amounts of data, information, and knowledge in a heterogeneous and real-time environment in order to carry out the functions of an enterprise without diminishing resources. To achieve this vision, massive, multimedia, and heterogeneous databases have to be integrated so that analysts and decision makers can effectively query and obtain relevant information as well as update the information in a timely manner.

In addition to integration problems, there are other outstanding problems in each technology area. Figure 15.2 illustrates the issues that need further investigation in various data management technologies—for example, in the case of heterogeneous database integration, handling semantic heterogeneity is a major problem. Appropriate transaction models, as well as security policies, are also needed. For multimedia database management, the challenges include synchronizing different data types such as voice and video. While there are numerous issues that need to be resolved, this chapter focuses on the

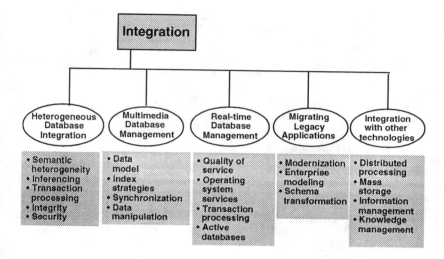

Figure 15.2 Outstanding problems

developments and challenges in a specific data management technology area—multimedia database management systems.

15.2 ARCHITECTURES FOR AN MMDBMS

This section describes various architectures for an MMDBMS. As illustrated in Figure 15.3, an MMDBMS could be designed based on a loosely coupled architecture; that is, the database management system (DBMS) is used to manage the metadata information while a file manager manages the multimedia files. An integration module is responsible for integrating the DBMS with the multimedia file manager. An advantage with this architecture is that we could use multimedia file management technology with DBMS technology to produce an MMDBMS. A disadvantage is that the DBMS is not utilized to manage the multimedia database. Therefore, features such as concurrency control, recovery, query facility, integrity, and security, which are the functions of a DBMS, may not be applied to the multimedia database. However, commercial products based on this approach are available.

Figure 15.4 illustrates a tightly coupled architecture between the DBMS and the multimedia file manager; that is, the DBMS manages the multimedia database. The advantage of this approach is that the traditional features provided by the DBMS are applied to the multimedia database. However, with this approach, a new kind of DBMS is

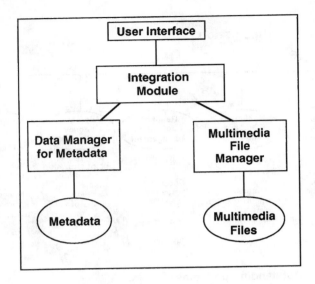

Figure 15.3 Loosely coupled architecture

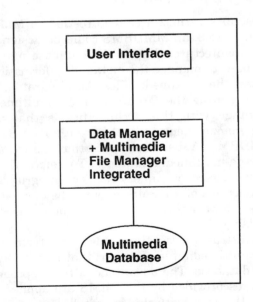

Figure 15.4 Tightly coupled architecture

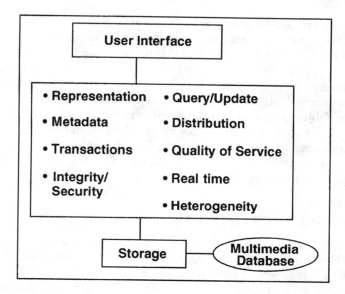

Figure 15.5 Functional architecture

needed. A great deal of the research in multimedia database management is focusing on this approach.

A functional architecture for an MMDBMS, which is based on the tightly coupled approach, is illustrated in Figure 15.5. As shown, the functions include data representation, query/update service, data distribution, metadata management, transaction processing, quality of service, real-time processing, integrity/security, and handling hetero-

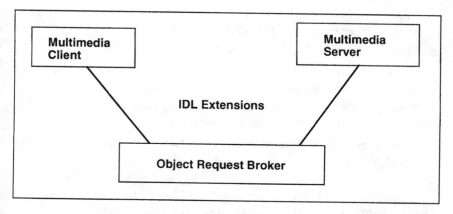

Figure 15.6 An architecture for interoperability

geneity. Users access the MMDBMS through a variety of interfaces that support text, images, voice, and video. The storage manager is responsible for accessing the multimedia database.

Figure 15.6 illustrates an architecture that supports distributed and heterogeneous multimedia applications. It utilizes an Object Request Broker (which may be based on the Object Management Group's Common Object Request Broker Architecture [CORBA]) for interoperability. As shown, a multimedia client object communicates with a multimedia server object through an Object Request Broker. The client, as well as the server, could be based on legacy code or developed specifically for multimedia information management.

15.3 FUNCTIONS OF AN MMDBMS

There are several issues that need to be addressed to develop an MMDBMS. They include issues about data representation, data manipulation, transaction processing, metadata management, data distribution, storage management, quality of service, maintaining data integrity and security, user interface, heterogeneity, and real-time processing. We discuss these issues, with examples, in the following subsections.

15.3.1 Data Representation

The following is a list of issues for data representation.

1. The support for dynamic classes and class hierarchies is needed as new kinds of information may be arriving periodically.

2. The concept of an object needs to be determined—for example, an object could be as small as a frame or could be as large as a set of frames describing a meaningful scenario.

3. The object attributes have to be defined.

4. Temporal aspects of objects, such as the dates when the corresponding scenarios occurred, have to be represented.

5. Time duration of objects, such as the length of time it will take to display the object, has to be represented.

6. The objects may continue to evolve as new information is obtained about an object.

7. The relationships between the objects need to be represented—for example, objects with associated time intervals that overlap may inherit properties from one another. The relationships also include statements such as "an object, A, has to be synchronized (such as

played with, before, or after) with object B" and "objects A and B describe the same scenario."

8. In many cases, the relationships between the objects may not be precise. In this case the imprecise relationships have to be represented, possibly with fuzzy values. These include statements such as "objects A and B describe similar scenarios" and "the value of the attribute B of object A has a fuzzy value of 0.5."

9. In addition to one-dimensional objects, support for two- and three-dimensional objects, such as maps and solids, may need to be provided.

10. Other features provided by object-oriented data models, such as composite objects, versioning, and so forth, need to be supported.

11. Mappings between the global representation and local representations have to be provided if the local data representations are different.

Figure 15.7 illustrates data representation. In this example, a collection of frames is represented as an object. Each object has an annotation, which displays the time sequence for that object—for example, object A consists of 1,000 frames and occurs between 6/93 and 8/93 while object B consists of 1,200 frames and occurs between 7/93 and 9/93. The metadata (or schema) for the objects may be dynamic. Addi-

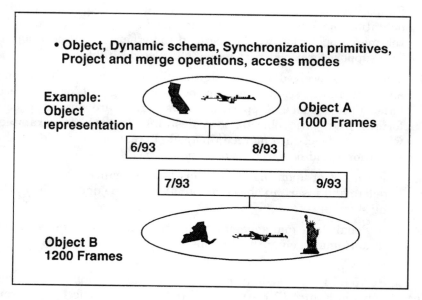

Figure 15.7   Data representation

tional information may also be stored in the metadata, such as access modes and synchronization primitives (played before, after, or together). Operations supported may include project, where an object is projected over a time interval, or merging, where two objects are merged depending on some time intervals.

15.3.2 Data Manipulation

The following is a list of issues for data manipulation.

1. Support for operations such as query, browsing, and filtering of objects as well as updating objects needs to be provided. The typical modes of display would include display object, play forward, play backward, and synchronize objects A and B. Extensions to languages such as SQL could also be used for certain operations. These include "select * from object A, where value of attribute B is XXX" and "select objects A and B, where A and B describe the same scenario."

2. Support for editing objects, including operations for merging, overlapping, aggregating, and disaggregating objects, needs to be provided—for example, objects A and B could be merged over overlapping time intervals, or an object, C, could be projected onto some time interval to form smaller objects.

3. Support for update operations needs to be provided. This includes operations such as create, delete, and modify objects—for example, the merge operation would result in the creation of a new object. The support for concurrent updates is also desirable.

4. Views have received a lot of attention in relational database management. More recently they are being investigated for object-oriented data models. Supporting views, which are virtual objects formed from base objects, is a desirable feature—for example, when two objects are merged, instead of creating new objects, the operation could be specified as a view.

5. The concept of updating objects has to be specified. Does it mean to delete and insert an object, or can an object be updated by modifying some parts?

6. The global data management techniques have to work with the local data management techniques.

Figure 15.8 illustrates data manipulation—for example, the two objects shown in Figure 15.7 are merged to form a new object over interval 7/1/93 and 7/31/93. When merging two objects, some of the

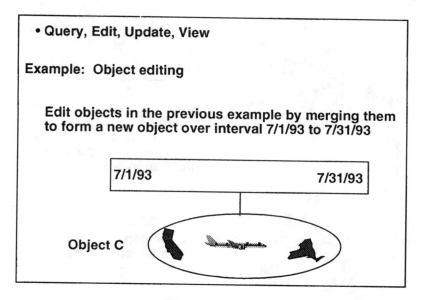

- **Query, Edit, Update, View**

Example: Object editing

Edit objects in the previous example by merging them to form a new object over interval 7/1/93 to 7/31/93

7/1/93   7/31/93

Object C

Figure 15.8   Data manipulation

information in each of the objects may have to be deleted. The result, which is object C, is also an object.

15.3.3 Transaction Processing

Concurrency control and recovery are major issues in transaction processing. The main concern for multimedia databases is whether special mechanisms will be needed—for example, are there transaction processing algorithms specific to multimedia database management? Research on this topic is just beginning.

Figure 15.9 illustrates transaction processing, where a transaction updates a multimedia object as well as the annotation for the multimedia object; that is, the two operations are atomic—either both are performed or none of the two are performed.

15.3.4 Metadata Management

Metadata describes the data in the database. For a multimedia database, much of the information for video and audio data may be stored in the metadatabase—for example, information about the frames, the events that they represent, and so forth may be part of the metadata. Figure 15.10 illustrates a database that consists of the map of the world and the associated metadatabase that describes the map.

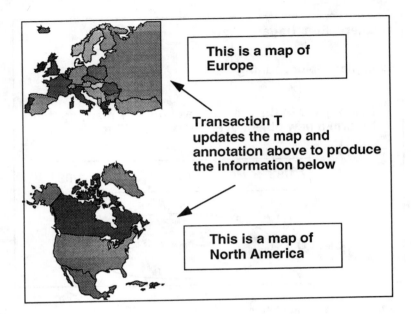

Figure 15.9   Transaction processing

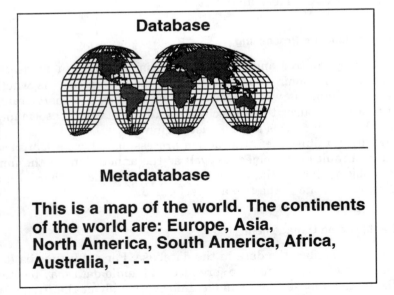

Figure 15.10   Metadata management

Metadata management functions are similar to the DBMS functions, such as querying and updating the metadata. One of the major challenges for multimedia databases is managing large metadatabases. This is because a large amount of information may be needed to describe multimedia databases such as video and audio databases.

15.3.5 Data Distribution

The usual issues with data distribution include: How should the objects be distributed? How should fragmentation and replication be supported? Is the cost of transmission the major factor in determining the optimization strategies? Are there special considerations for multimedia data?

Figure 15.11 illustrates a distributed multimedia database. Database 1 consists of a map object, database 2 consists of a vehicle object, and database 3 consists of a landmark object. The union of databases 1 and 2 is also displayed. The result of this union consists of both map and vehicle objects.

15.3.6 Storage Management

The following is a list of issues for storage management.

1. What techniques should be used for caching objects? When demand for new objects arises, which of the following objects should be moved: least frequently used, least recently used, oldest, or the one with the least critical value?

2. Should objects be created as a result of operations, such as merge, or should they be specified as views? If they are created, where should they be stored?

3. Is a hierarchical storage mechanism needed? Are there special index strategies and access methods?

A great deal of research has been carried out with regard to developing appropriate access methods and index strategies for traditional database systems. Current research is focusing on developing such mechanisms for next-generation systems, such as object-oriented database systems. The challenges are on developing appropriate access methods and index strategies for multimedia database systems—for example, for multimedia data, indexing could be done not only by content but by type, language, context (i.e., where, how, when the data

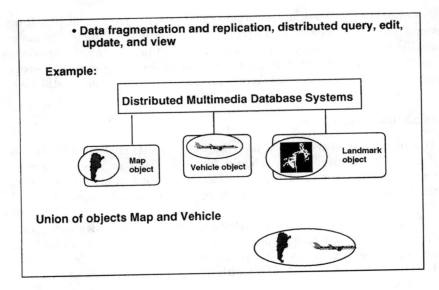

Figure 15.11 Data distribution

were collected), author (i.e., for documents), and speaker (i.e., for voice). The challenge is how to index and provide improved mechanisms for extracting the information used for indexing—for example, the ability to automatically index via voice is desired. Additionally, the ability to index voice and video (with associate voice) with their transcriptions (i.e., time alignment) is necessary.

Figure 15.12 illustrates the use of index files to access a database. In this example, an index file is maintained to access the key XXXXX. By using an indexing mechanism, the query processing algorithms may not have to search the entire database. Instead, the data to be retrieved could be accessed directly. Consequently, the retrieval algorithms are more efficient.

15.3.7 Quality of Service

The quality of service primitives determines the service to be provided to the users and will depend on the application—for example, is some information, although imprecise, better than no information? Will low-resolution images be sufficient for certain cases?

Figure 15.13 illustrates quality of service, where during a crisis mode, we need a complete picture, while during normal operation an incomplete picture could suffice.

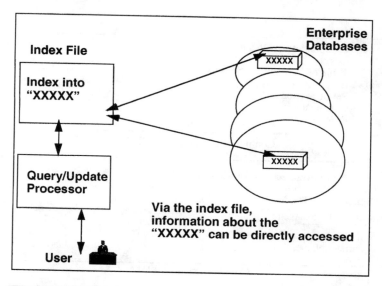

Figure 15.12   Indexing

15.3.8 Maintaining Data Integrity and Security

Maintaining data integrity will include support for data quality, integrity constraint processing, concurrency control and recovery for multiuser updates, and accuracy of the data on output. Security mechanisms include supporting access rights and authorization. Multilevel security is also needed for certain multimedia applications.

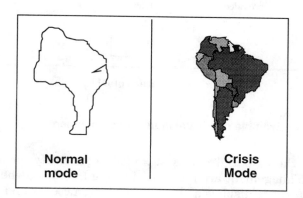

Figure 15.13   Quality of service

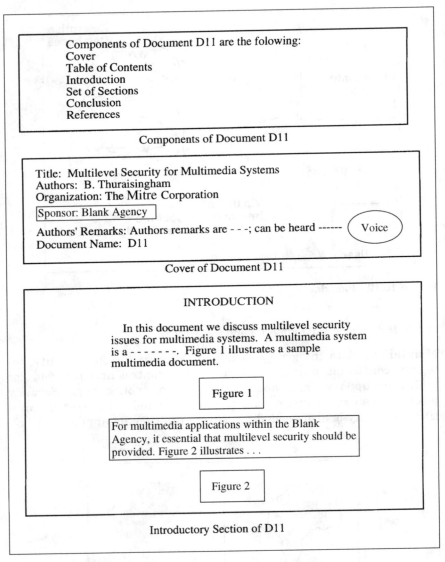

Figure 15.14 Example multilevel multimedia document

Some of the essential points of multilevel security for multimedia database management are illustrated in Figure 15.14, where a multilevel document is displayed. The darkened structures and text represent Secret information, while the plain structures and text represent Unclassified information. The intent is for users to acquire only data at or below their level. So, if a user cleared at the Unclassified level

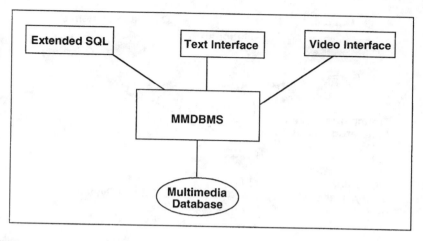

Figure 15.15   User interface

queries the database, then the darkened portions of the multimedia data are not displayed to him or her.

15.3.9 User Interface

Research has somewhat separated user interface issues with data management issues. Some expect the two fields to merge in order to provide support for intelligence multimedia data management capability. Supporting extensions to SQL, which has been the main concern of data management researchers, is one aspect of user interface. Other aspects include graphical interfaces for object manipulation and tools for operations such as browsing. Figure 15.15 illustrates multiple user interfaces for an MMDBMS.

15.3.10 Heterogeneity

Figure 15.16 illustrates an example of interoperability between heterogeneous database systems. In this example, a relational database system, a legacy database system such as a hierarchical database system, and an object-oriented database system are connected through a network. The goal is to provide transparent access, both for users and application programs, for querying and executing transactions.

There are several technical issues that need to be resolved for the successful interoperability between these diverse database systems. Heterogeneity could be utilized with respect to different data models, schemata, query processing techniques, query languages, transaction management techniques, semantics, integrity, and security. Further-

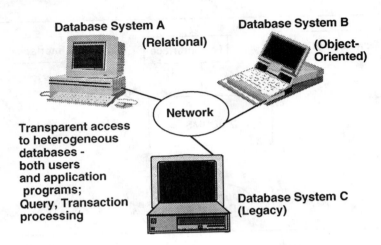

Database System A
(Relational)

Database System B

(Object-Oriented)

Network

Transparent access to heterogeneous databases - both users and application programs; Query, Transaction processing

Database System C (Legacy)

Figure 15.16   Interoperability of heterogeneous database systems

more, for multimedia applications, heterogeneity could be utilized with respect to different data types.

There are two approaches to interoperability. One is the client/server approach where the goal is for multiple clients to communicate with multiple servers in a transparent manner; the other is the feder-

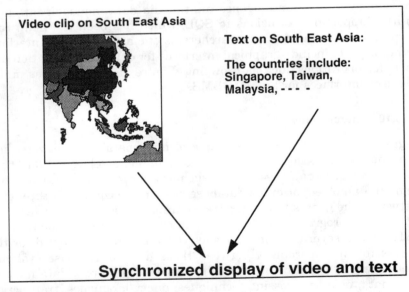

Video clip on South East Asia

Text on South East Asia:

The countries include: Singapore, Taiwan, Malaysia, - - - -

Synchronized display of video and text

Figure 15.17   Real-time multimedia processing

ated database management approach, where a collection of cooperating, autonomous, and possibly heterogeneous component database management systems, each belonging to one or more federations, communicate with each other.

15.3.11 Real-Time Processing

A real-time database management system is a DBMS in which the queries and transactions have to meet timing constraints—that is, predictable execution is desired. Much of the research in real-time DBMSs has focused on transaction processing. In many cases, multimedia applications have to meet real-time constraints—for example, the audio and video databases may have to be synchronized for smooth display. While there have been many recent discussions on integrating real-time and multimedia data management technologies, there is still much research to be done. Figure 15.17 illustrates the synchronization of text and video data.

16

Database Machines

Paul Fortier

16.1 INTRODUCTION

Database systems have always pushed the envelope where performance is involved. This is even more true in recent database systems when applied to computer systems dealing with advanced applications such as computer-aided design, command and control, multimedia, and high-transaction throughput systems. Advanced applications such as these require preprocessing of data and specialized data processing to operate effectively. Conventional mainframe-resident databases, or those operating on a conventional general-purpose computer system, cannot support efficiently the data processing needs of applications and the extended data processing and access requirements of the supporting database management system—for example, if an application requires a small portion of a large collection of data on a disk, the complete information must be brought into the memory for reduction processing (possibly not all at once, either) in a conventional database system. The data are reduced and then sent forward to the application for use. Such reduction processing is quite common in relational and advanced database systems, where query processing must locate a specific combination of information from a large search space. The processing involved in scanning numerous large relations could cripple performance on even a large processor.

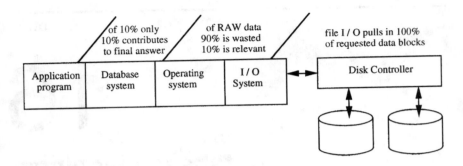

Figure 16.1   Ninety-ten rule

The problem that occurs when an application only requires a small portion of the actual data requested is called the ninety-ten rule (Figure 16.1). The ninety-ten rule depicts a general problem that has been encountered with numerous database processing systems up to this point in time. The problem is best described by an example. Given an initial database with just three relations—**Student, Courses**, and **Enrollment**—the following query could be generated on the student database to find all the students who took Database Systems II in spring 1996.

```
SELECT Students FROM Student WHERE Student.SID= (Select
SID FROM Enrollment WHERE Enrollment.CID= (Select CID
FROM Course WHERE Course.title="Database Systems II") and
Enrollment.date = "Spring 1996");
```

The above query would require reading the entire three relations from the disk, processing each tuple in each relation to perform the requested search (possibly a join over all three relations), and passing forward the result to the next stage of the query processing stream (the user interface). The end result would be the names of those students who took the course in spring 1996. The end result may represent just a small portion of the original data. Statistics have indicated that this procedure typically reduces the initial data read to less than 1 percent in most general queries on conventional database systems.

The result of this ninety-ten rule problem is that 99 percent of the data pulled from the disk are not typically useful to the application generating the query. In our example, if 100,000 students are searched over 1,000 courses and one million enrollment records, this rule can result in over one million additional data items read that will not be used by the application in the end. That's an enormous amount of added processing, which could be performed in a more optimal fashion elsewhere.

The manner in which the ninety-ten rule generally applies to a database system is shown in Figure 16.1. In this figure, a query results in an initial access and retrieval from the disk. This initial access pulls in 100 percent of all data that must be processed to answer a query. In our example this would include the **Student, Courses,** and **Enrollment** relations. These data flow from the disk and through the input/output system, possibly under direct control of the operating system (this implies that all data need to be handled in some way by system service functions). The initial database reductions will typically remove 90 percent of these data in answering the query. Of these reduced data the final application typically uses only 10 percent of this information to perform the actual application processing the query was intended to support. This rule has led to the demise of many a database system, especially a poorly designed or poorly operated database system.

To alleviate the problems exhibited by the ninety-ten rule, numerous concepts have emerged, including replacement processors, elaborate architectures (multiprocessors, distributed processors), dedicated machines, intelligent storage devices, and specialized exotic hardware devices. Each of these solutions has merits based on the increased performance returned against the added cost and complexity to realize the added performance. The problems these solutions attempt to solve are varied. There are basically three classes of problems dealt with in these solutions to the ninety-ten rule. The first solution class deals with the data storage and retrieval problem and the flow of information. The second solution class deals with the data processing problem to reduce the raw data extracted from storage into a form readily usable by the database system. The third solution class deals with the data flow or control problem associated with optimizing data reduction operations and storage data flow reductions. The information processing problems of moving data from secondary storage, reducing data to usable forms, and coordinating data processing to optimize reductions places a burden on conventional database systems due to lower supportable database load levels (volume of transactions per second supportable) and general database system performance (average- and worst-case transaction turnaround times) lags.

The concept of fixing the performance problems of a database management system through solutions aimed at altering the data processing path's structure is not new. Database machines or specialized solutions for database processing performance issues have been researched, developed, and added to database products for over 20 years. As long as databases have existed, there has been research on specialized means to improve performance. Some have been successful, while others have proven to be poor performers or, more often than not, too expensive to become part of a commercial product.

16.2 THE CONVENTIONAL HARDWARE SOLUTION

Hardware solutions looked at the problem resulting from the ninety-ten rule as one solvable through brute-force methods. If an application did not have the processing capacity to support its needs, then somehow the capacity must be increased. This was the basic philosophy for solving most processing problems in early computer systems, and this carried through to early database systems. The approach was to analyze the performance of the database system, discover what element or elements were the root of the performance degradation, and increase the capacity of the poorly performing elements to fix the problem.

As shown in Figure 16.2, the main solution technique is simply to increase the size of the element causing the problem—for example, if the CPU only supports one million instructions per second, and the analysis of the database system's performance points to the database management system as being CPU bound, the database requires ten million instructions per second to minimally meet design goals. The problem is that not enough instructions per second can be processed to meet the needs of the database processing in the present system. To fix the problem we can look up processors in the local computer system's hardware manual and find one that can support ten million instructions per second. This processor is then used to replace the present processor in the computer system, effectively increasing performance by tenfold from one million instructions per second to ten million instructions per second. One can easily see the relative short-sightedness of this approach. Adding more hardware only increases the ability of the monolithic central processing unit to perform the present function. This leaves no room for growth and misses the point that the central CPU is still the primary bottleneck. Data still flow through the CPU in the same fashion. No alterations of any data flow sequences have occurred.

In addition, by adding more CPU capacity to solve one performance problem we may have uncovered or created other performance problems. The added CPU may not scale up to the performance indicated by the analysis. The cause of this less than linear performance gain is mainly due to the effects of interactive elements of the database system—for example, the added CPU capacity can result in some other

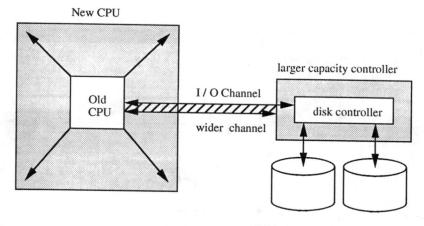

Figure 16.2   Conventional hardware solutions

database element not operating up to snuff. Adding CPU capacity can result in the disk becoming the new bottleneck, or the data channel between the disk and memory becoming the new bottleneck. The memory itself can become the limiting factor. Increasing the speed of the CPU will have no result if the data and instructions cannot get from the memory to the CPU in a timely fashion. What can result is a system that must have all elements increased in size and within performance parameters that are consistent with the domain of the initial bottleneck device to realize the required performance increase.

An alternative solution to simply increasing the size (throughput) of the individual elements within the database is to increase capacity through the addition of added equivalent devices. In the example above, to get ten million instructions per second to support the processing needs, we may opt to add ten equivalent processors to the one already in the system, connected to the same memory and input and output bus. The resulting architecture is referred to as a multiprocessor (Figure 16.3). The processors are configured such that the operating system can allocate one physical processor to each software process. Each of these processes can be one section of a partitioned query, which can then be performed in parallel as separate chunks, followed by the coordination of results with other processors to complete the processing.

An issue to consider before taking this approach over simply purchasing a single larger CPU involves added software and hardware complexity and added cost. If each of the added processor's cost is one-tenth or less of the price for a new, single high-performance CPU (with everything else considered equal), then from a cost comparison

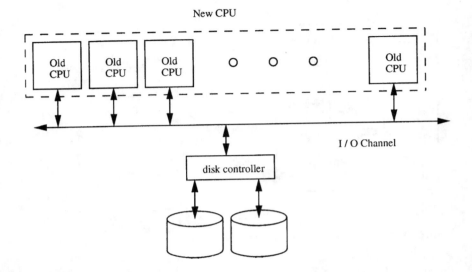

Figure 16.3   Multiple CPU architecture

the multiprocessor configuration may be a better buy. On the other hand, if the ten processors cost more than or are equal to the cost of a comparable single, large mainframe CPU, then replacement by the single larger CPU may be more cost effective. This is especially true when processor software and hardware coordination and overhead costs are taken into account. The multiple processors will require added synchronization and control policies and mechanisms, if the functionality of the user's software is to remain unchanged. Control software to partition the data processing workload over the processors would be required, as would software to control data (memory) partitioning between processors. Operating system software would require updating to include control blocks for the multiple processors processing load management, memory data partitioning, allocation, and access management, in addition to coordination control requirements. The operating system may not be expandable to handle the multiple processors. In this case, a new multiprocessing operating system would be required. The new multiprocessing operating system may not work with all of the remaining software, including the application code, requiring all of these software elements to be recoded or, at a minimum, recompiled and rebuilt into the new environment. We may then find after all this that the new system does not perform up to the level expected with the addition of ten processors. The performance loss is mainly due to added process synchronization and result reformation.

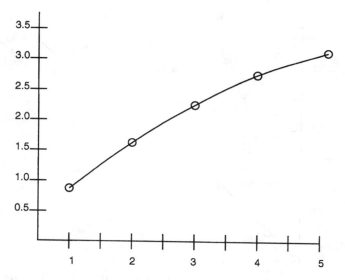

Figure 16.4 Multiprocessor performance

Findings from many studies indicate that the overhead may not be at all trivial. In fact, numerous cases have been publicized where the cost of adding processing capacity through redundant CPUs can result in less than 20 or 30 percent of the new processors' processing cycles being available to perform application processing. This becomes more apparent as more processors are added (Figure 16.4).

Not all multiprocessing configurations are this bad. It depends on the degree of coupling and the tightness of control needed over the multiple processors. An improvement in performance can be realized through looser coupling of the processors and the central memory. If each processor is given some local memory and a fixed location (block) in the shared global memory for its own dedicated use, performance can be improved. Off-line code optimization can better decouple data processing and data storage with this architecture, so that cleaner partitions, requiring less control and synchronization interaction, can be achieved. This results in more of the added processing capacity being available for use in application processing (Figure 16.5). The best result would be a linear improvement in performance achieved through the linear addition of processors. Linear improvement is, however, only a goal and cannot be achieved with such an architecture, since some coordination is still required.

This decoupling can be taken a step further by decomposing the database hardware into distinct CPU memory clusters, combined over a communications channel. This channel can be a backplane (Figure

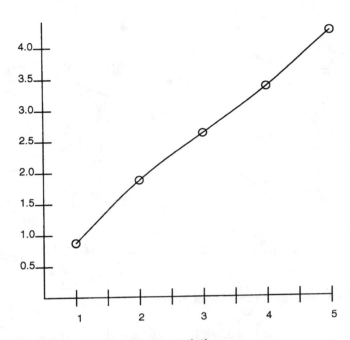

Figure 16.5 Improved performance statistics

16.6), or a shared local area network. The CPUs are allocated either separate chunks of an application's database query or their own database query stream to process in isolation from all of the other clusters. In the first case, the queries must be analyzed and decomposed such that the distribution of subqueries is effectively performed as disjoint subqueries—for example, perform all disjoint subqueries in separate processors, perform joins in other processors, coordinate subqueries in yet another processor, and so on. This approach has the same burden

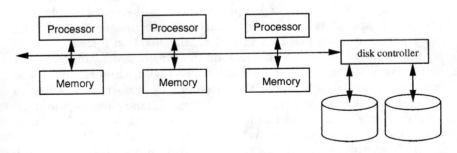

Figure 16.6 Decoupled multiple processor memory pairs

as the multiprocessor, in that the queries must be optimized to limit the need for interdevice control and synchronization. If interaction cannot be minimized, then the performance realized will not be optimal.

The second database configuration approach does not attempt to perform single queries faster, but looks to perform more queries on more processors in parallel. The second approach requires some system-level control that knows about processor loads. When a new job enters the system, it is routed to a processor that has the least load. The added cost would be borne at both compile time and run time. At compile time the added cost would be in determining loading requirements (how much time and space is required for this query) for a query, and at run time the added cost would be in finding a site suitable for execution. In addition, the location of a processor memory cluster can depend on the proximity to stored information required by the query. If a previous job used needed data, it may be desirable to allocate this processor memory cluster to the new job in order to minimize the need to access secondary storage.

This approach, however, does not relieve the basic problem of secondary storage overhead and delays. Each processor in both approaches would still be required to page in and out data from disk storage as needed. In addition, since the disk(s) is not intelligent (cannot parse requests to determine an optimum execution order), the processors must take turns accessing the disk. If only one disk and controller are available, then the CPU will spend more time waiting on input and output than performing useful work, which, of course, is not the effect desired.

A further refinement is to provide each of the processors with its own disk. By providing these assets, each processor can request data as needed from its local disk storage, as long as the entire database is stored at all sites. The redundant databases stored on the distributed disks would be required to have the copies maintained in a synchronous manner. An update on one processor must be reflected on all others before any additional processing is allowed. This may be an unrealistic and costly addition to provide. Remember, the original intent was to get a tenfold increase in processing to meet the demands of applications. The addition of ten processors with ten primary memory banks and ten additional disk drives (Figure 16.7) may not represent a cost-effective means to increase the required performance. It may cost more than envisioned and even result in less performance gains if not correctly configured. Adding the disks with redundancy requires adding additional database management system software to maintain the correctness and validity of the databases—for example,

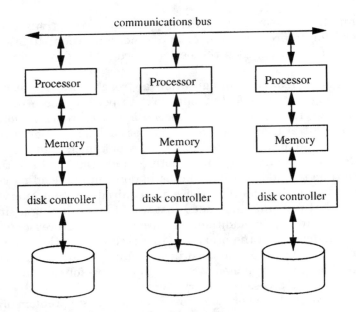

Figure 16.7 Multiple complete processors

with full redundancy an update on one site must be performed on all sites atomically if the databases' consistency and correctness are to be maintained. Such global updates can require the access and locking of all copies of the data-item on all the sites until the update is completed at every site. Update synchronization such as this can easily defeat the purpose and any potential benefits of the additional hardware. Devices not involved in the access of a particular data-item, but which are bound to the same lock granule, would be blocked from accessing the disks and therefore effectively blocked from doing any further data processing. Even those queries not accessing the involved page or lock granule would be impacted. The time associated with accepting a remote update, performing the required lock actions, processing the update, releasing the locks, and cleaning up memory would be forced on all processors, requiring blocking of any local actions until the remote updates are incorporated. The time used for disk access, memory access, and CPU processing by this process is lost to local queries for use in performing local database work.

Issues brought up by this approach have been discussed Chapter 10. It was shown that distribution can be used effectively to increase performance, but is best applied to applications that lend themselves to distribution, as well as to data that can be effectively partitioned without dependencies between the data partitions.

16.3 BACK-END DATABASE MACHINE

A second major solution does not simply look at throwing more of the same hardware at the problem, or merely increasing the capacity of the computing platform by increasing the number or volume of general computations per second that can be performed. Simply increasing the number of processors, the size of the memory, or the number of disks will not result in a long-term improvement in performance. We have to look at the fundamental mismatch in device speed and performance and at the overall flow of data and control to determine the true problem areas and to devise improved solutions. The same bottlenecks caused by the ninety-ten rule still exist. More data are being drawn into the application's engine than is needed for the application's use. The problem is not that data are flowing into the application's processor—it is that inappropriate data, along with essential information, are being drawn in. The solution therefore is to remove the spurious, nonessential information from the accessed data stream before it is transferred to the application's engine from the data repository. This can be accomplished in a number of ways, as we shall see.

The most obvious solution is to place some form of data reduction engine or data filter between the data repository and the application's data processor (Figure 16.8). This filter can have many forms—for example, it could be a specialized piece of software that exists on the same physical processor as the application's engine. The filter could be a simple piece of hardware that is set to intercept items from a data stream and pull out elements that either meet a search condition or do not meet a search condition. Both of these alternatives, however, are not performing the intended function in a general way that would lessen the load on the application's processor. Placing the reduction software in the same processor as the applications would result in a reduction of data that flow into the application, but it would not reduce the volume of data that would flow from the secondary storage to the application's processor. The same delay in processing and reducing the data flowing from the secondary data repository to the application's processor would still be present. In addition, there would be an added overhead in transferring the request from the application to the database to the filter and then to the secondary storage device, along with added synchronization and control information that would be required to flow between the reduction software, the database software, and the application software. The hardware-only reduction element would only be useful for some predefined set of data reduction requests and operations—for example, if we knew the type of reductions that would occur, we could provide a hardware comparator to

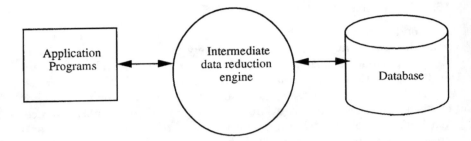

Figure 16.8   Database filter data reduction solution

detect the required data as they flow by and return these data to the database for further reduction. It would not be possible to construct a device that could handle all possible requests, unless the reduction hardware device itself became a general-purpose programmable device. In this case it no longer is a hardware-only reduction device.

A more general-purpose solution, and one more viable and possibly less costly, uses a separate processor as the reduction engine (Figure 16.9). The process of reducing queries from the raw data form into a refined answer, which transfers only the needed 1 percent of data to the applications, must be developed and coded as a general-purpose piece of software on the machine. What is preferable about this mode of reduction is that it can use the existing database query processing software and simply move it to the new processor. This can be handled easily if the processor in the host and the processor in the reduction engine are the same. By using a general-purpose processor for the reduction engine, we can further offload database functionality to the separate database processor. Database query processing code, as well as secondary storage input and output routines, can be reallocated from the application's host platform to the reduction engine.

We could further this movement even more by transferring all but application interface routines, which support application interface to the database management system to the reduction engine. The application device simply issues queries to the reduction engine, which processes these queries and returns an answer to the requesting application. The reduction engine has become a bit more encompassing in this scenario, and it has become known as a back-end database machine. The back-end database is populated with all the database management system software and all the secondary storage management software. By offloading from the host processor the database management system software and the storage management software, there is less contention for host resources, leaving more computing cycles for application code. This movement of software alone will im-

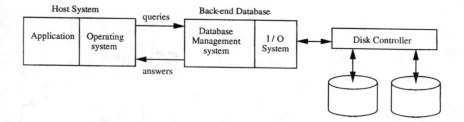

Figure 16.9 Back-end database machine

prove performance by freeing up more cycles for application software and by reducing the contention for resources.

The problem with this line of thought, however, is that it is not 100 percent accurate. Even though we have reduced the load on the host computer, we have not truly removed the ninety-ten rule from the path of the applications. We have simply moved a portion of the cost over to another machine, but the total cost still lies in the way of the application's data access. The back-end database machine, however, will be less loaded (only database software and some operating system software, no applications software), than the original machine and should therefore be a bit more responsive. The added performance will come from lower contention for system resources and through the ability to reduce extracted data on the back end before sending these data to the applications. Unfortunately, we still have the same problem exhibited in the centralized uniprocessor case, but now this problem is on the back-end machine; that is, the back-end computer must now contend with the same secondary retrieval problems as the original system. There is still only one secondary storage controller, only one input and output path, and only one database processor. The same problem of accessing the needed file or files on the secondary storage exists, as does the transfer of the accessed file or files to the memory on the database processor. In addition, the same problem of extracting the needed information from the raw transferred data still exists. This solution simply moved the problem further from the application domain, but it did not in any way change the nature of the problem or the solution applied. For any true advantage to be found with this approach, we must look at some additional reallocation or rearchitecting of the solution space.

One refinement of this solution is to increase the capacity of the back-end database system. However, instead of simply exchanging one processor with another, which would still have the same problem, we add additional back-end databases and secondary storage devices.

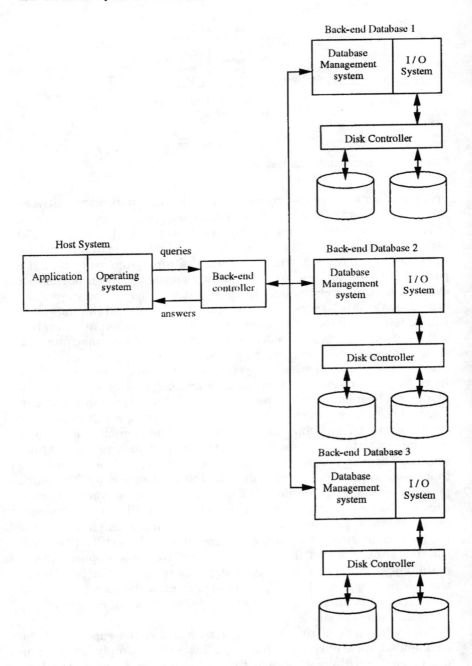

Figure 16.10 Multiple back-end databases

In this configuration (Figure 16.10), we take the same back-end database machine defined above, with a single CPU and stand-alone input and output controller and replicate these. This alone will not increase the performance drastically. We will still have the problem of a single disk controller acting as the only conduit for raw data transfers from the disk to the back ends' memory. The back ends would have the capacity to process a greatly increased load of raw data, but instead of using this added capacity to process more information, the machines would be wasting these cycles waiting for input from the single shared resource, the disk controller. With additional effort the back ends could be kept busy by pipelining output from the disk controller at its optimal speed to all the back ends concurrently. This approach would allow the back ends to be partitioned or configured such that they can perform requested queries in a distributed manner. To perform a query in this manner requires additional control and coordination software. One approach for providing this uses a single back-end controller, which is used to accept application queries, partition the query into parallel chunks, and issue the commands to the multiple back-end engines to perform the requested actions. Finally, this control processor recombines the answers into the final response to be sent to the requester. The bottleneck in this approach is the single back-end storage subsystem.

The bottleneck can be reduced by providing a secondary storage bank for each of the back-end database machines. The secondary storage devices can be fully replicated or partitioned, depending on the flexibility required and the overhead the designers are willing to incur. If the secondary storage is replicated, then updates become a problem. All nodes would be required to synchronize updates in order to maintain the consistency and correctness of the database and the copies. If the back-end system is updated more often than it is read, this approach may be too costly to provide. On the other hand, if the query pattern is read mostly, then this is a very strong approach, with positive benefits. By having data fully redundant any query can be directed to any back end. The controller simply would be required to keep track of which processor is free and route requests to the first free processor, or to the lightest-loaded processor. The solution gets a bit tricky once the ratio of reads to writes approaches 70 percent. Once we see that 30 percent of the operations are writes, the replication must be reconsidered. In this case the database may be better served by partitioning the database over the available secondary storage banks. With the data partitioned over the sites, query processing must be performed so that only the portion of a query that uses data on a specific device is forwarded to that device. To effectively perform query processing in this way requires additional processing capacity and overhead on the back-end controller to interpret incoming queries, decompose them into subqueries on the appropriate database partition, issue the subqueries, and coordinate and assemble the final response to forward to the requesting application.

This second approach is also not without its flaws; if the query pattern is such that one partition of the database receives much more traffic than any other, this node becomes the system's new bottleneck. The most heavily loaded, and therefore the slowest back end in the group, becomes the limiting element in the system's performance. To increase performance in this situation requires a compromise design. The most heavily utilized data are replicated, while the remainder of the database is partitioned in such a way as to permit sharing the processing load as equally as possible. The replicated nodes would be required to synchronize updates and coordinate actions; other nodes, not maintaining replicas, could operate in isolation. The tradeoff examines the cost versus performance considerations of full replication against partitioning and against a mixed approach in terms of the added hardware and software costs in relation to the added performance gained. In this type of design data placement and replica minimization become important considerations in determining performance.

These solutions, however, still suffer from the secondary storage and retrieval problems caused by the ninety-ten rule. Raw unprocessed data are transferred to the back-end database machine or machines, and are processed, reduced, reformatted, and sent on to the application's processors. The input/output delays and associated waiting time have not been improved, nor has the time it takes to find and extract the raw information from the secondary storage. The only advantage gained by all of the above architectures is the decoupling of database and application processing. No improvement in processing algorithms or access has been realized—only more general-purpose hardware and software have been dedicated to the processing job.

16.4 DATABASE STORAGE ENGINE SOLUTION

A solution to reduce the effect of the ninety-ten rule on the database management system and the applications it supports utilizes added hardware and software attached at the site of data storage.

Hardware dedicated to the database management system's storage management and to raw data access preprocessing and reduction can be much simpler than the previous section's general-purpose computer system (Figure 16.11). Such support can greatly reduce the flow of data across the interface from the storage management subsystem and the database management system. If even a simple microprocessor is embedded in the disk controller, along with added software to

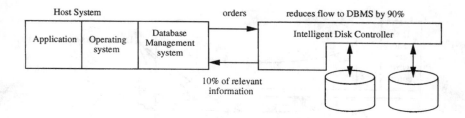

Figure 16.11   Intelligent disk controller architecture

organize and provide faster paths for data retrieval, some of the over-head can be removed from the database and applications on the attached host. This architecture approach only would result in a small reduction of embedded software on the host, but in a section of software where most delays related to waiting and transferring data occur. If the microprocessor has full control of disk allocation and retrieval, the disk could have data structured and stored in such a way as to optimize access for some specific subclass of queries. Another alternative is to give the microcontroller more ability in terms of actual disk head control. With knowledge of the disk's storage structures and data maps, along with control over disk head movements and access, the controller could process multiple requests in parallel and determine which request to retrieve next based on minimizing head movement and disk rotation. In this way the basic speed of the data access and transfer can be increased dramatically. This approach will result in some improvement in performance, but there still is a limit on the volume of information that can be transferred and processed by a single disk head, moving from track to track, and a single processor extracting and reducing information.

To improve the capabilities of this concept and architecture we must consider some additional dedicated hardware. The bottleneck still appears to be at the disk data access, manipulation, and transfer points. One way to try to fix this problem is to throw hardware at the problem. The particular kind of hardware must be chosen so that it delivers a substantial improvement in relation to the cost associated with this added hardware. With the advent of cheaper disk drives and drive technology improvements there are many options available. One option is to add additional drive read/write heads to the disk unit. In particular, instead of a moving head disk controller, the optimal improvement is to go with a separate read/write head for each track of the disk drive (Figure 16.12). In this disk architecture configuration of each track of the disk platter surface has an individual read/write head positioned statically above the track. To access information on a

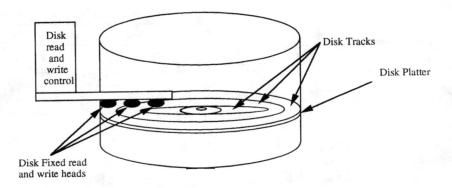

Figure 16.12   Multiple read/write head disk architecture

specific track on the disk, the controller addresses the appropriate disk head directly, then reads data from the track as the track spins by. In the best case the data are right at the site where the head is when reading is initiated, and these data can be directly read out. In the worst case the data have just passed the heads and must be extracted on the next rotation of the disk. On average any piece of information required can be extracted within one-half of a disk rotation. The total cost to get a piece of data is one instruction to address a specific head, plus one-half the rotation time of the disk plus transfer time. This fares quite well against the typical time on a conventional disk with one read/write head and a movable disk read/write arm. The conventional disk requires added time to seek the appropriate track on the disk. Seek time is not trivial and typically represents the major cost of disk access delay. The moving arm is a physical delay caused by manual motion, which is much slower than moving electrical signals.

Using this scheme data can be extracted more quickly from the disk; however, these data are still simply accessed and read into a memory space on the controller for further processing. The controller must still deal with the entire raw data read in from the disk. No filtering is performed—simply a faster extraction of the raw information. This still leaves us with the ninety-ten rule: giving us 90 percent of data to process and search through faster. To improve this situation another alternative, which uses the same intelligent disk with one read/write head per track, as well as a processor memory combination with each read/write head, is possible (Figure 16.13). The separate processors can be programmed to search for a particular piece, pattern, or range within the raw data being accessed, or the processor

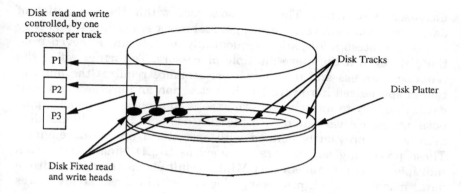

Disk read and write
controlled, by one
processor per track

P1

P2

P3

Disk Tracks

Disk Platter

Disk Fixed read
and write heads

Figure 16.13   Dedicated read/write heads and processor per track

can be set up to scan data as they flow past, pulling out information that meets a given search pattern. Data not meeting this pattern are simply discarded. In this manner the processors on each track could concurrently search for data on all the tracks, speeding up the access by a factor equal to the number of tracks. The processor set up to coordinate the actions of the numerous track processors can act as a clearinghouse for all data found that meet search criteria, or it can act as the combinatorial processor, which recombines or further reduces retrieved data based on higher-order data processing queries.

The retrieved information will answer an entire query passed to the back end from the coordinating database back end. The back end would then be required to possibly perform some additional postprocessing to finalize the response to the service's host application and to perform additional data management functions, such as security checking, transaction processing, concurrency control synchronization, and recovery processing. The back end still functions as the main database management system—it merely uses the intelligent disk controller to reduce information required for processing a given query. The intelligent disk should reduce the data to the 10 percent of the ninety-ten rule, if the disk map and configuration are optimal and the processors on each head are adequately coordinated. This is the approach that has been used in numerous early database machine research as well as in some early commercial database machines.

16.5 SMART MEMORIES

As shown previously, speeding up the data path from the disk to the database management system and providing data reduction services increases performance. The processors used within the application of data reduction, however, are still general-purpose machines, and they can only process information sequentially as data are removed from the disk, even if there are multiple processors. To further refine the reduction process and to improve performance requires the application of specialized hardware for the extraction and processing of raw data. One way to improve performance is to replace the general-purpose processors associated with the disk heads in the intelligent disk architecture previously defined with specialized processing engines. These processing engines are designed as SIMD (single instruction multiple data) machines or as MIMD (multiple instruction multiple data) machines. Each processing element within these architectures contains specialized processing elements and data storage elements, which allow the comparison of data streams, as they flow past or through the processor, against preloaded search parameters.

The architecture of such a machine can look like that in Figure 16.14, where each processing engine consists of a simple arithmetic logic unit, match registers to hold data patterns being searched for, and data storage paths and storage arrays to store found strings. The devices can be constructed such that either a relational tuple is ex-

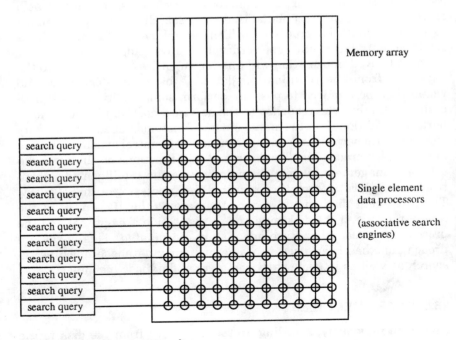

Figure 16.14   Smart memories

tracted from a data stream on a match, or an object (abstract data type state information) is extracted on a match. In either case the device simply needs to maintain a value indicating the size of the item to extract upon a match and where within the object or tuple the match data-item is located.

Typical special-purpose architectures applied to this problem operate in multiple cycles. Typical cycles include a read cycle, a compare cycle, and a write cycle, each of which may be performed multiple times. The first operation locates raw data on the secondary storage medium. By locating information of interest on the disk, we could use the multiple head disk unit to access any piece of information within one-half a disk rotation, using a simple search and transfer protocol. The second operation transfers some known quantity of the located raw data into a high-speed cache memory, sized for the attached disk (e.g., sector size). The transferred data can be processed as they are being transferred or once they are stored. Raw data in the cache are scanned for matches and partial matches to detect needed information. The match is done on only the specific field or fields within the full width of a tuple. The Boolean comparisons can be, for example, equality, greater than, less than, similar to (search for some subset of a word), or not equal to. Data that meet the search or selection criteria are latched and transferred to a secondary storage pool for result holding. With a wide enough data path the search could compare two relations on two processing engines simultaneously, in essence performing a join operation.

The combination of having specific dedicated read and write heads per disk track and a processing engine per track can greatly speed up selection of tuples from a relation. The speedup may be great enough so that we can reduce the raw data by the initial 90 percent. This does not, however, result in completed, nested, or complex queries, which may require additional processing of acquired and reduced raw data to answer a specific request. To rectify this may require the cascading of multiple database processing engine stages, each of which further refines data access and processing towards the end goal of answering the query.

The cascading of the engines provides a means to make multiple passes over a stream of data, allowing for the performance of complex operations, such as a join or union operation, over some relations. In Figure 16.15, the first stage of the database engines extracts the needed relations, filtering out all information except what is needed to perform the complex operation and to answer the requested query. Given that there are two relations, Employee and Student (Figure 16.16), and a query is asked to determine which students are also

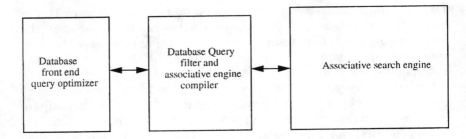

Figure 16.15 Cascaded database processing engines

employees, what their jobs are, what their salaries are, and what departments they work for, the following query could be written.

```
Range of E is Employee
Range of S is Student
Select E.name, E.job, E.salary, S.dept
     From Employee and Student
     Where E.ssno = S.ssno;
```

The query could be answered in a few different ways. We could first select all the employees and all the students from the secondary storage, without reduction, and then scan through the employees for each entry in the student relation. We could then select only the columns needed from the resulting search. This approach does not seem to use

EID	Dept	Job	Salary	SSno	Name
E01	CS	Prof	50K	0357	John
E02	EE	Prof	50K	0158	Sally
E03	MS	Inst	40K	0256	Tom
E04	AR	Sec	20K	1234	Tim
E05	EG	Tech	25K	5678	Joan
E06	ME	Prof	35K	9108	Jane
E07	CS	Aid	10K	0001	Bill
E08	EE	Aid	10K	0102	Judy
E09	MS	Aid	10K	0115	Jack

SID	SSno	Addr	Degree_prog	GPA
S01	0102	Pitt	CS	3.0
S02	0115	Bost	CS	3.5
S03	1113	Hart	EE	4.0
S04	0833	NewY	MS	3.2
S05	1518	SanD	AR	3.1
S06	1122	SanF	EE	2.8
S07	0001	Chic	BI	3.0
S08	0707	Sprg	EE	2.25
S09	0078	Miam	LA	3.25

Figure 16.16 Employee and student relations

the capabilities of the reduction engines very well. An alternative is to select only the required attributes from each tuple into a temporary memory using the first stage of the reduction engines. This would result in two reduced relations, with one having five attributes—name, department, salary, job, and ssno—and the second having only one, ssno. These two results could then be used to further process the query in the second stage of processors. The subresult with just ssno can be used to set up the search conditions for the database search engines in the second stage. If there are enough processors, then a single item per processor could be set up. If there are not enough engines to set up the problem this way, then the load would be split between the engines, and the search would be performed for separate student data-item ssno settings over each employee tuple until all students have been matched against the database. This form of processing could additionally reduce the search time and computation time for the query, further improving performance and reducing the effect of the ninety-ten rule.

This solution is not, however, general enough to be readily applicable to more complex databases, such as object-oriented databases. The above techniques are best suited for regular database storage structures and conventional value-oriented data processing requests. The computational speed of such a database system is still dependent on the platform upon which the database is constructed. The conventional von Neumann (stored program and data) computer is primarily limited by the data paths between the central processing unit and the data storage repositories, as are the database engine architectures listed above. The concept is still to extract information from the secondary storage device and perform the intended operations on the data once they are placed into another machine's storage subsystem. Database back ends will only become more commonplace when the specialized hardware necessary for their improved performance can be more readily constructed and their performance becomes more general purpose. Present architectures are too specialized and difficult to mass produce, which further limits their applicability to a wider range of database application domains.

16.6 DATABASE MACHINES

A more exotic approach to solving the ninety-ten rule is to construct specific hardware components that each do some portion of the database's data processing operations—for example, we may have a specialized application-specific integrated circuit that implements a pattern recognition application, or one that implements a specific data search algorithm, such as a binary search or a bucket hash algorithm.

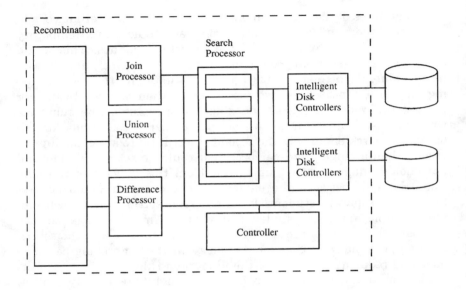

Figure 16.17   Application-specific devices

These devices each perform a specific function for the database system, but do it in a general manner; that is, they can have their specific flow of processing altered based on input data and control signals, much like any general-purpose computer. The difference is that the functions or operations available to these machines are not general in the sense of normal computers; they are general in relation to database operations—for example, the storage manager application-specific integrated circuit would have instructions to allocate space on the disk; locate files, records, and items on the disk; delete items, records, or files; and update items, records, or files. The storage manager ASIC could possess all of the attributes of the intelligent disk and the smart memories rolled up into one specialized computing device tuned to the management of stored binary information. A separate storage manager could be designed and developed tuned to the underlying data model—for example, a record-oriented versus an object-oriented storage manager.

The concept of a database machine is to take the ideas that were applied to disk management and improve the disk data processing path by applying these same concepts to the remainder of the database processing functions. The fundamental concept is to turn the software processing algorithms of the database management system into hardware computing elements that implement the same functionality (Figure 16.17). This can be done in a number of ways. The software components can be directly converted into a hardware state machine, which simply converts the software to a mix of hardware and firmware. This approach will improve performance, but it is not the most optimal way to convert the software system into a hardware system.

A better approach is to analyze the functionality delivered by each element of a database and determine what essential operations are required: which of these can be performed in special-purpose hardware and which must be performed in general-purpose hardware. From this determination the database machine can be designed and constructed. The ultimate goal is to remove all remnants of the ninety-ten rule from the data path of the application's processor. Applications simply request information operations and receive answers. The interface is kept to only usable information; all intermediate data and data reduction and processing are handled within the database machine.

The implication with the above proposal is that *all* database processing and database management operations would be done within some form of specialized hardware or firmware elements. This would include concurrency control, query processing, transaction processing, recovery management, and interface processing. Each of these operations would be analyzed for its fundamental operations. These would then be implemented within a specialized hardware device—for example, for the transaction processor, we would, at a minimum, require operations to begin, end, commit, and abort transactions. Each of these operations would be analyzed as to the functions required by each operation and an implementation for each would be chosen, which would then be implemented within the hardware—for example, the begin transaction operations must create a tag in the lock manager to maintain the list of held resources by this transaction, and a log entry for this transaction in the recovery manager would be initiated, as would the generation of a checkpoint marker to maintain a checkpoint of any item used by this transaction. On transaction end, transaction entries within all tables must be checked to determine if this transaction can move toward commit or abort. If commit is chosen, the hardware must write all intermediate data in an atomic action (instruction operation). If the transaction cannot commit, then recovery actions must be initiated. This may require issuing a command to the recovery processing engine on this site to perform required actions.

A specialized processor would be required for all functions within a conventional database management system. A concurrency control processor implementing one of the favorite protocols, such as locking or timestamp ordering, would be required for all sites where data

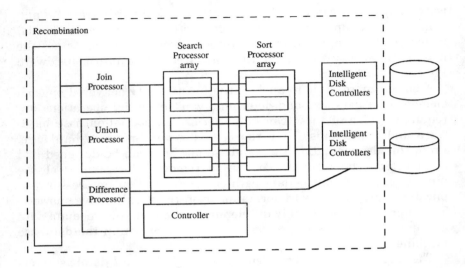

Figure 16.18 Pipelined application-specific sorting and searching devices

would be hosted and where alterations are possible. Likewise, a recovery processor must also be resident on all sites where database processing can be executed. The recovery processor would require hardware to implement checkpointing operations, to construct an execution log, and to perform a variety of recovery operations—for example, we may need checkpoint instructions to perform a checkpoint on a transaction initiation, subtransaction initiation, or on some fixed point in time or a point based on an event.

Instructions for aborting a transaction would then initiate undo and redo hardware. The redo hardware would use the checkpoints with stored intermediate information to restore the state of transactions completed but not as yet installed into the permanent store, and the undo hardware would use the checkpointed data to restore these data to a correct previous state. The hardware can actually store two copies of data and use pointers to indicate which version is the primary copy and which is a secondary or active copy.

Much of the hardware for a database machine would be related to searching and organizing data to aid in a search. Typical processing engines would be sorters and search hardware. The sorter can be used to preallocate and store data to prepare for an upcoming query. The search hardware can use data specially stored to hasten a data search, but can also use added hardware to aid in a search—for example, using associative or content-addressable memories for indexes or for primary keys in tables. Using multiple sorted attribute strings all linked into the appropriate storage can hasten a search from many or even all attributes simultaneously (Figure 16.18). These devices can be configured in a variety of architectural configurations, which can further aid performance—for example, we could form the sorting and searching devices into a data processing pipeline, which extracts information; sorts the raw data into ordered records on a chosen attribute or attributes; passes these data to a reduction engine, which selects only tuples having meaning to the query, or to the search engine to locate specific entries. This in turn could then be piped into additional processors, such as join processors or union processors.

Join processors would be organized and specialized to provide parallel searching of two files for records that have fields of equivalent form and match on the value of their contents. These in turn would be gated into a join processor, which would form a new record with a size (number of attributes) equal to the sum of the attributes of both records minus one. The lost attribute representing the join field from the two records would, by definition, be the same and can therefore be discarded.

Likewise, a similar processor to form a union could be constructed as a string comparator (Figure 16.19). The processor consists of two wide word registers, which each can hold a single tuple from a relation or some subset of a tuple, and a wide yet simple ALU, which can either subtract two values supplied or add the contents of one register with another complement and set a result register if all outputs are zero (could use an OR gate connected to all output bits to detect zero). The processor would take the two strings of equal length and compare them. If string one is found to be equal to the string provided in string two, then string two is discarded and the next string of the same length from file two is gated into string two's register. If, upon examining all entries in file two, string one does not match any string part of the second file (i.e., it is found to be unique), string one would be appended to string two already in the result file. Once all entries from file one have been compared in the same way with all entries from file two, the result file will contain the union of the two files.

To perform an intersect of the two files, the same hardware could be used. The comparison for intersect is interested in whether a string in file one is equal to a string in file two. If the two strings are found to be equal, then append the string to the result file; if they are not equal, then discard the string held constant. The two string files must be searched so that all strings in file one are compared to all strings in file two. The result file should be no greater than the size of the smallest file. The difference between the first hardware is only in the test element after the comparison. In the union case an OR gate could be used to examine all the output bits together—if any were one, then

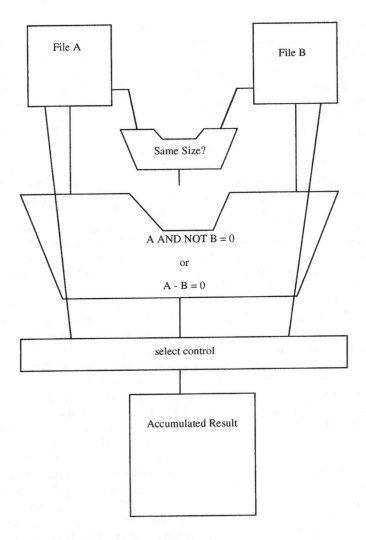

Figure 16.19 Union and intersect processor

the two strings were different and could be included in the result string. For the intersect, we are only interested if they are equal, so an AND gate could be used to determine when they are all ones or all zeros. Some additional logic to control when to gate and when to gate results would be required. The important concept to gather from this discussion is that appropriate hardware can be constructed to perform the required operations. The database management system software can be eliminated and totally replaced by hardware. This results in a hardware device that has a very high level language associated with it. A user query would be required to be configured as a sequence of high-order relational operations, which would be interpreted by the hardware to perform the intended operations.

The resulting application-specific processing device can perform database functions in parallel or serial, depending on the needs of the operations being requested. Much like the control unit in a conventional central processing unit, the database control unit would be required to interpret incoming database commands and compute an optimum execution plan. There are, however, problems with this hardware-only database machine. The complexity of developing such a device can be prohibitive. In addition, if there is not a large enough market for a specialized device, it can become too expensive. An example of this problem was seen by Ferranti's DY-4 database accelerator. The machine was constructed as a dual card insert for a Sun workstation or Digital Equipment VAX workstation. The cost of the cards was about $85,000 for the pair. The performance was about 500 to 1,000 simple transactions per second to 250 complex transactions per second. For a specific class of database storage (relational) and specific workloads, this was a very high performance implementation that provided a true benefit. The problem, however, was that the processor performed almost all database operations in hardware and left very little flexibility for performing other operations. In addition, the interface language chosen was not based on a standard database language. The cards required specialized input control streams, meaning that applications already in existence would require recoding, which was not a viable alternative for large applications that could benefit from such performance and could also afford the cost. The result was that only a few of these machines (exactly three) were sold in the United States, resulting in a commercial failure. The ideas used in this machine, however, were solid contributions to the science of database processing. They helped develop hardware search engines, intelligent storage elements, and specialized relational operation engines—all within a well-architected package. The lesson here is that flexibility and adherence to standards may be more important than high performance gained through divergence from interface standards.

The Ferranti machine may have been overdesigned for a specialized subset of database applications or for a perceived applications area, which never materialized. To stay away from such black holes, the database machine designer must make design decisions based on sound market demands. It makes market sense to speed up the general access of information from a disk drive. It may make market sense to colocate processors and memory assets on the same card as the disk controller. But it may not make sense to add specialized hardware, since the controller now becomes incompatible with other nondatabase users of the disk, thereby lowering its market scope.

It appears that the combination of intelligent disk drives and separation of application processing from database processing makes the most economical sense. The worst elements of the ninety-ten rule can be removed, or at least isolated, so they can be better controlled. Successful database machines, such as the early Britton-Lee IDM machine, used this approach. This machine combined general-purpose disk banks with enhanced database processing in general-purpose processors colocated on the same backplane as the disk controllers. This in essence provided a platform on which special-purpose software could reside. They also added an additional processor to handle database management processing and command interpretation. This device coordinated actions of other general-purpose processors and dedicated database software to perform database actions in a parallel manner. The added resources available on the application processors for application code and on the database processors made up for loss of optimal design and provided a cost-effective alternative to expensive database hardware. The final choice of what architecture is appropriate will be driven by the application's demands. It has been shown in more recent work that many more gains in performance can be realized by improved operating systems and database systems that respond to the *dynamic* needs of applications, instead of the policy of average execution that was previously the norm for operating system and database system design and development.

17

Advanced Database
System Concepts

Joan Peckham
Paul Fortier
Bonnie MacKellar

17.1 INTRODUCTION

Database management system uses have been expanding quickly as database technology catches up to application needs. In addition, applications are finding out that databases offer desirable features that they can utilize. This chapter will define some of these advanced database management systems and their application niches. We will focus on what makes these database application areas unique and what types of solutions are being proposed for these environments.

17.2 ACTIVE DATABASES

Relational database management systems are used for most traditional applications, such as airline reservations, business inventory, and business management applications. The object-oriented systems were developed to meet a growing demand for systems to support non-traditional applications such as Computer-Aided Design/Computer-Aided Manufacturing (CAD/CAM). However, neither the relational nor the object-oriented models adequately support these applications because they lack the following features.

- Active semantics: In a large complex database schema, the interactive update behavior of the data objects can be very complicated—for example, deleting a DoorFrame object in a building design database means that its associated DoorAssembly object (if there is one) should also be deleted. However, the DoorVoid (which represents the location in a wall where a door assembly should be placed) associated with the deleted DoorAssembly would not automatically be deleted. The database designer should be able to specify such behaviors and expect that the database will automatically carry out such specifications. This capability is not part of most existing database specification and management systems.

- Nonstandard transaction processing: The execution of one transaction in the system may trigger the initiation and execution of additional and related transactions. The relationships among these transactions are very different from the traditional model of independent concurrent transactions assumed in traditional systems. Alternative transaction processing strategies are required.

The following text discusses research directed toward the support of these features in active systems.

17.2.1 Active systems

Active systems were developed to support the specification and implementation of the automated propagation of actions needed in the database to maintain data constraints under changes due to database updates. Databases that have built-in features to support the specification and implementation of these actions are called *active databases*.

In order to specify an active database, constructs for active rule expression are necessary. Two well-known constructs are the Event-Condition-Action (ECA) rules of the HiPac project and the production rules developed by Widom and others. For convenience, we will use the ECA paradigm and vocabulary for the following discussion. The building example would appear as follows as an ECA rule.

```
event delete Door object
condition the associated DoorAssembly object has
    no associated Door objects
action delete DoorAssembly object
coupling Condition and action are executed together in a
separate transaction and in the deferred mode.
```

When the *event* is detected in the database, the *condition* is evaluated to determine if the *action* is to be initiated. The *coupling* indicates how the rules are executed in the context of the transaction processing system. Here we have specified that the rule is executed at the end of the parent transaction (the transaction that contains the event), within the body of a single child transaction, and executed while the parent transaction is suspended. Other alternatives for coupling will be discussed in Section 17.2.2.

While the constructs used for update rule enforcement seem relatively simple, many issues arise with respect to their implementation in any type of system. Here we discuss transaction processing, rule processing, and rule design. We also consider the application of active techniques to real-time databases as an example of an advanced active system.

17.2.2 Transaction Processing in an Active System

Traditional transaction processing models assume that transactions are independent, atomic, and isolated sequences of operations that are processed in a uniform manner to maintain data consistency in a concurrent environment. The active paradigm requires some alteration to this paradigm. When a transaction is submitted to the system (e.g., in transaction T in Figure 17.1), it may contain some actions that are events of a given active rule. This implies that in conjunction with transaction processing, some rule processing must also be done. Thus, the system must initiate one additional transaction, T', to process the rule condition, and another, T'', to carry out the action if the condition evaluates to true. Another alternative is to place both the condition evaluation and the action execution within one transaction. In any case, every time a database update action (within a transaction) that serves as an event in an update rule is executed on the system, one or two additional transactions may be initiated in response to it.

These transactions are not independent, since there must be some coordination among them for the processing of the rules. In the HiPac system, the coupling construct specifies the execution relationships between the transactions that perform the event and the condition evaluation, and also between the transactions that perform the condition evaluation and the action execution. Three modes are possible between the event and the condition evaluation; similarly, the same modes are possible between the condition evaluation and the action.

- Immediate: When the triggering event occurs, evaluate the condition immediately in the same transaction (preempt the transaction containing the event to evaluate the condition).

- Separate: When the triggering event occurs, evaluate the condition in a different (concurrent) transaction.

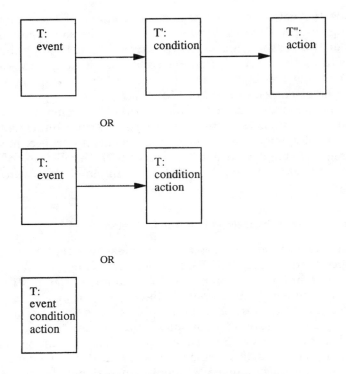

Figure 17.1 Possible rule processing within transactions

- Deferred: Evaluate the condition in the same transaction as the condition, but at the end of the transaction.

Thus, each system must decide the rule processing strategy relative to transaction processing. There can be a defined system default mode, or the rules designer can specify the proper mode. Either may require alteration of existing transaction processing features and/or additional rule constructs to capture end users' specifications.

17.2.3 Rule Processing Semantics

When an active rule is being executed, the system must first evaluate the condition to determine if the action should also be executed. The condition is an expression that evaluates to true or false, usually based upon the results of a query to the database. This means that the state of the database determines whether or not the the action must be executed. However, it is not clear which state of the database should be accessed. Two choices are the state of the database before the event is executed and the state of the database after the event is executed. Widom overcomes this problem by augmenting the query language constructs used in the statement of the condition to permit specification of the database image (before or after) that should be accessed when evaluating the rule.

Another problem is the development of correct algorithms for rule execution in an environment where a single event can possibly initiate the execution of several actions. Widom has also investigated this problem with a set of rule processing algorithms, which clearly specify the ordering of the execution of multiple rules.

17.2.4 Checking and Analysis Tools

Active rules are specified individually, but, due to their transitive nature, they can propagate throughout the database in unpredictable ways. It is very important to have a schema design tool that permits clear specification and analysis. Also needed is a schema checker to determine if there are cyclic, incomplete, or conflicting structures, and whether or not the order in which rules are executed will impact the end result. In the SORAC (Semantic Objects, Relationships, and Constraints) project at the University of Rhode Island, five different schema difficulties were identified.

- The rules must not be cyclic to guarantee termination of rule processing.

- Sets of rules with the same event must not transitively trigger the same action unless it is understood or specified whether the action is executed once for all paths, or once for each path.

- Paths that lead to denials need special treatment. A denial is an ECA rule in which the action is a rollback of the event, thus possibly denying the end user the ability to execute the event. These must be presented to the system designer, who should decide if transitively propagated denials are correct in the context of the application.

- Operations that always lead to denials must also be identified. In most environments, these are design errors.

- A set of rules in which the same event leads through different paths to conflicting or contradictory actions must also be identified for the rules designer.

Widom and others have looked at conditions in a set of rules that guarantees confluence and termination.

- Termination: If a set of rules is guaranteed to terminate, then we say that they satisfy termination (same as above).

- Confluence: If the order in which a set of rules is processed uniquely determines the final state of the database, then confluence is satisfied.

Other researchers have looked at correctness from the perspective of constraints (statements of correct database states) implying specific update rules. They express constraints using horn clauses and have developed a method for looking at the constraint expressions to determine if they are correct (*object-centered*). If the constraints are object-centered, then involved object types are guaranteed to be properly connected. This assures that the rules make sense in the context of the schema and have acceptable performance characteristics.

17.2.5 An Advanced Application (Active Real-Time Systems)

Most experiments with active systems have addressed applications in which events are database updates. However, in real-time environments, it is the progress of time that can trigger a rule—for example, consider a constraint that specifies that the age of a sensor-supplied attribute, Train.speed, must not be older than five seconds. This can be implemented with an active rule.

```
event   Train.speed.age > 5 * sec
condition true
action Signal (outside_speed_sensor_alarm)
coupling Condition and action are executed together in a
separate transaction and in the immediate mode
```

The implementation of these rules is somewhat different. In many active prototype systems, a monitor is implemented that detects the execution of a database update that is an event. However, in the real-time case, system alarm must be set every time the speed attribute is read from the sensor, or the speed attribute's age must be read periodically to determine if age exceeds the specified limit. Approaches to modeling and implementing constraints in the real-time environment have been addressed. The proper scheduling of active rules and transactions is an especially important issue in the real-time domain.

17.2.6 Conclusion

Researchers have many issues to clarify with regard to the specification, analysis, and implementation of rules in database systems. This explains the lack of commercial products that provide an integrated active database environment. Academic prototypes and active extensions of existing systems are now being developed that will most likely lead to fully integrated commercial implementations in the future.

17.3 FLEXIBLE TRANSACTION PROCESSING

17.3.1 Introduction

Real-time database management systems are needed if the goals of the national information infrastructure (NII) are to be met. Real-time databases will deliver data over the NII where needed, when needed, and in a timely manner. Applications of the NII include electronic commerce, digital libraries, crisis management, advanced manufacturing, education, environmental monitoring, health care, and public access to government information. Core components of the NII are a real-time persistent object store and information infrastructure services to support the definition and manipulation of NII information.

Real-time database management implies a model of data processing that is counter to the conventional mindset. Real-time information management must perform predictably, in a timely manner, and provide consistency and correctness of database access, while maintaining the highest degree of data availability possible. Conventional information management, where serializability and constraint enforcement are monolithically applied, run counter to these real-time needs.

A real-time database must maintain database consistency and transaction correctness, but must also handle time-constrained transactions, time-bounded data, and a variety of resource constraints that are not addressed in conventional environments—for example, in a hard real-time database system, transactions must execute in such a way that they meet deadlines, while not violating any temporal, spatial, data, storage, or access constraints defined on the transaction and database items. Various transaction, database structuring, scheduling, and concurrency control protocols have been researched and developed to meet these needs, although they have not, as of this writing, found their way into integrated production-level systems, nor have they been adopted as standards for database systems.

Numerous schemes have been developed to *schedule* transactions for real time, but they do not adequately address concurrency control as part of the equation. For real-time database systems to become a reality, time, as a resource and item to optimize upon, must be integrated into all elements of a computer system. Time must be used for CPU, I/O, and network, as well as for software scheduling. The ability to structure the database and transactions appropriate to an application's needs and to control execution based on timing, consistency, recovery, and availability needs of the application must be developed.

This section describes concepts for the Applications Programming Interface (API) layer for a real-time structured query language. We focus our discussion on the transaction model—its specification, implementation, and execution. The text describing the transaction model is broken down into related research, database and transaction model, real-time SQL language specification, and implementation.

17.3.2 Related Research

Related research for real-time database management spans many areas. These include database structure and specification, transaction structuring and specification, real-time scheduling, transaction recovery, concurrency control, and query language standardization. We examine these areas briefly below.

Database Structure and Specification The structure and specification of databases has traditionally been performed based on a monolithic view of the collection of data-items forming the database. Real-time databases require altered structures that support application needs, not database management needs. Time, as an integral part of the database and transaction structure definition and use, is required.

Transaction Structure and Specification Transactions have traditionally been viewed as the means by which consistency and correctness of the database are ensured through the ACID properties applied to transactions. The ACID properties include *Atomic, Consistent, Isolated,* and *Durable* execution of transactions on a monolithic database. Real-time systems require the redefinition of these terms for the support of real-time and application needs, not database need, for serializability. Real-time database research points out the need to alter the structure and use of transactions in order to increase concurrency, timeliness, and predictability of transactions to support real time.

Real-Time Scheduling Scheduling in a database system implies both transaction selection and concurrency control interleaving of operations. Scheduling of transactions and their operations is a more complicated problem than that of task scheduling in an operating system. A great deal of work has been done on integrating scheduling with concurrency control at the paper level, although little of this work has been implemented. Before we can have real-time transactions, we need to determine how to manage the selection and concurrent operation of conflicting transactions based on their temporal needs.

Transaction Recovery The conventional model of transaction recovery does not support the concept of real time. Recovery based on transaction saves points, and undo and redo lose sight of the dynamic forward motion of time in a real-time database. Time is a measure used for consistency and correctness in a real-time database—as such it must be used to aid in recovery. Recovery in real-time database management systems must take into account application needs when determining how and if to recover.

Concurrency Control Real-time transactions can only succeed in providing consistent, correct, timely, and predictable service to applications if concurrency control policies and mechanisms can deliver higher degrees of concurrent access, higher data availability, and lower blocking time. Concurrency control must take into account user application needs in determining how to perform interleaving of operations and how to optimize access.

Query Language Standardization Database query languages have been evolving slowly over the last few years. Practitioners have seen the merits of standards and are following the same path. The database language SQL has evolved from its initial form into the more mature SQL2 form. Beyond this, SQL is evolving into the object model via the SQL3 evolving standard and into real time via recommendations for an RT-SQL.

17.3.3 Database and Transaction Model

Real-time database management requires a new model for database and transaction structure and execution. The database cannot be viewed and operated as one monolithic structure nor can the database structure, storage, consistency, and correctness be determined without the aid of application users and system developers. Likewise, transactions cannot be viewed as static, nonchanging closed execution vehicles. Transactions must be capable of being tailored to the real-time needs of applications, yet they must also guarantee some form of ACID properties. The difference is in what constitutes the ACID properties and correct transaction execution. We will review these concepts in the following sections.

Real-Time Databases Real-time databases are different from conventional databases in several ways. First and foremost, a real-time database uses time as a component of data and as a measure for consistency and correctness determination. Second, a real-time database is structured to support the needs of real-time applications, not to support database maintenance and operations.

Database Structure—A real-time database must be able to support the needs of real-time applications. To provide this the database must be structured toward the application's requirements. Real-time applications require data to be available. One way to support such a need is to allow for a finer-grained partitioning of the database and to allow for looser application of constraints across the partitions. Our model of a database allows for the database to be partitioned into disjoint elements, whose consistency and correctness can be maintained in isolation from the monolithic whole. In addition, the application or database designer can specify how the database structures are to be stored and accessed—for example, data should be stored as a circular linked list or tree structure to facilitate the use of these data.

Database Constraints—A richer set of database constraints is needed to support real time. The database can have conventional constraints on the range of values and referential constraints, but in addition it must support other constraints, such as temporal, spatial, data dependency, storage, active, and access. These additional constraints allow application writers to define the semantic relationship between the data in the database, the system these data are operating in, and the users manipulating these data.

Database structuring and database constraints will be further examined when we look at language extensions that support real-time and flexible transactions.

17.3.4 Transaction Structure

A new transaction structure and execution paradigm based on the needs of real-time applications is needed. Transaction structure should model the processing needs of the application, not the database managers. A transaction consists of boundary markers encapsulating the upper and lower bounds on database access for this transaction. These boundaries are used to determine or define the execution envelope for the transaction. The transaction includes several parts, such as precondition, specification, body, postcondition, and recovery. The precondition part defines predicates that determine the conditions the

Transaction T

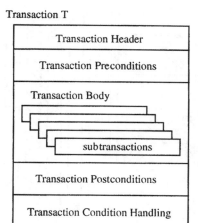

Figure 17.2   Flexible database transaction structure

transaction must satisfy in order to begin execution. The specification part is used to define data structures, timing requirements, resource limitations, data dependencies, transaction criticality, atomicity of the transaction, preemptability of the transaction, and execution dependencies.

The body of the transaction (Figure 17.2) includes database access code and transaction processing code. The internal structure of the body will be further described in the next paragraph. The postcondition contains predicates that define what constitutes the correct execution of this transaction. Following the postconditions is the transaction recovery part. The recovery part contains application-defined recovery mechanisms for defined errors. If this part is omitted, a default recovery can be chosen at database definition time.

The second major difference from the conventional model is the internal structure of the transaction body. To facilitate the modeling of numerous application execution models, our transaction model includes constructs for partitioning transactions into subtransactions. A subtransaction can have all the components defined for a transaction, and, in addition, it can include information on the type of subtransaction processing supported.

If we want the simple serial string of subtransactions shown in Figure 17.3a, we would model this by defining that the subtransaction boundaries do not overlap (the precondition is that the predecessor has completed) and that commit is allowed upon completion of a subtransaction. This models the transaction as a set of disjoint subtransactions that commit serially. Such a structure could also be used to

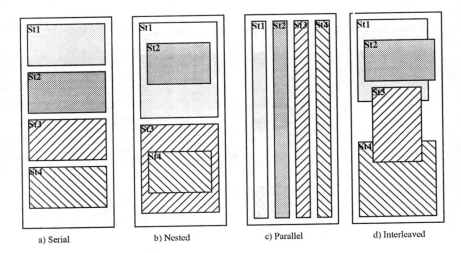

a) Serial   b) Nested   c) Parallel   d) Interleaved

Figure 17.3   Database subtransaction structure

model a long-duration transaction. Likewise, we could model concurrent or parallel executions (Figure 17.3b) as subtransactions having the precondition that all must begin at the same time. Conversely, we could model a set of disjoint parallel subtransactions as being commit related by specifying in the postconditions that they cannot commit until all are ready. By using a similar argument, we can also model multilevel nested transactions using placement of subtransaction boundaries and pre- and postconditions on execution (Figure 17.3c). To model a more complex interleaved model we place begins where needed, specify on what partition of the database this subtransaction is to operate, and then specify under what conditions the subtransaction can commit relative to interleaved siblings (Figure 17.3d).

What makes our subtransactions unique from past, rigid transaction partitioning schemes is our use of commit dependencies and data dependencies defined between subtransactions. These dependencies define how and when commit can occur. Control over these by the programmer allows for early commit or deferred commit along with increased concurrency. In conventional nested models, sequential models, and parallel models, siblings defer until the parent transaction determines it is commit time. In our model subtransactions can make this decision explicitly based on their semantic knowledge of the execution dependencies.

A flexible transaction structure, as described here, allows the transaction application writers to select the degree of consistency and correctness they need from the database. The job of the transaction processing subsystem is to guarantee that the database's consistency is not violated by these specifications and executions. This requires the use of the decomposed database defined using constraints and structures to bind data-items into units upon which consistency is ensured. Once the database is partitioned in such a way, the execution of the above transactions and subtransactions must be controlled so that they do not violate the consistency of the components. The correctness of such a scheme has been proven by numerous researchers in different environments. Our scheme allows application writers and the database designers to increase data availability and concurrency through early commit, thereby aiding real-time performance.

17.3.5 Transaction Constraints

In order to increase concurrency and data availability while meeting timing, predictability, and database correctness requirements, we need a richer set of constraints. To increase concurrency and data availability we need constraints to allow for database partitioning and disjoint constraint enforcement. For management of time we need temporal constraints on data and transactions. These allow for the determination of execution ordering. For predictability we need constraints on execution time, data-item size, physical storage structure, I/O logical and physical storage structure, bounded blocking time, and bounded recovery time. To meet the needs of correct execution of an application's transaction requires transaction correctness criteria derived from the application's needs.

With increased semantic information available, the system can make optimal decisions on execution sequences. With pre- and post-conditions on transactions, transaction writers can further control how transactions and subparts interact and relate to each other. The combination of pre- and postconditions, along with increased transaction constraints, results in transaction execution that can be tailored to support real-time applications.

17.3.6 Transaction Properties

The conventional database transaction processing model has no a priori knowledge about transaction execution or needs and therefore cannot make a priori ordering decisions. The real-time processing model wants all semantic information about transactions available before run time to optimize execution a priori. To realize this a real-time database needs a richer set of transaction semantics to aid in preordering of transaction operations. The real-time transaction correctness criteria and consistency constraints will determine what optimal execution implies. This statement implies weaker ACID properties for transactions defined by the users, not by the database designers. Transaction ACID properties need to be redefined in terms of correctness for real time. These properties are defined as follows.

- *Atomic:* An atomic transaction implies the all-or-nothing execution of the transaction. The concept of all or nothing applied to an entire transaction must be altered. Atomic execution should be selectively applied to pieces of a transaction that have a critical need for totally consistent data. The atomic property is applied to these pieces acting on disjoint pieces of the database to ensure consistency on the decomposed pieces in isolation.

- *Consistent:* Transactions given an initial consistent monolithic database state will transform the database to a new consistent state, where consistent is described by the evaluation of constraints defined on the database. Real-time databases have a different view: Consistency is defined by the set of consistency constraints and by the decomposition implied by these constraints or defined by database designers. Consistency of the database is determined by a *best-effort* approach and is managed on the partitioned pieces in isolation instead of as a monolithic whole. This allows for incremental checking and validating of consistency, thereby increasing data availability, potential concurrency, and lessening transaction failure due to constraint violations.

- *Isolated:* Transactions are required to have the property of independent execution in conventional databases. Independence implies that transactions act in isolation from all other transactions. There are no dependencies in executions between transactions. In real-time databases this property of transactions may not be true. Transactions may need to know about and interact with other transactions in order to perform an application's function. Transactions may need to synchronize on external time boundaries, system events, and/or another transaction's results or end condition—or they may need to perform some integrated set of tasks for an application that requires sharing of system state knowledge.

- *Durable:* The durability property of transactions implies that the results of a transaction are persistent and permanent. In a real-time database system this property may not hold uniformly. Time is an important aspect of all data-items and actions in a real-time system. Time is used to determine or define persistence. Data may be assigned a lifetime, after which they become nonpersistent, or a data-item may be part of a database structure that has events, at which time data-items disappear (e.g., circular queue). Durability of data must be described by the constraints defined on data and by the structure of data, not by a basic feature of a database or a transaction's execution.

- *Correct:* We add a fifth property that transactions should have: correctness. Correctness is defined by the results of evaluations of transaction pre- and postconditions and through the application of execution directives. Correctness on data is defined by a richer set of constraints and through directives applied to the data-items and their database structures.

17.3.7 Transaction Recovery

Conventional transaction recovery is based on recovering to a past state. In real time the past is gone—we need a forward-recovery technique that provides temporal consistency of the database based on loosened definitions. Recovery in real-time systems is in the eyes of the user, not the database. Since the users know how data are being used, recovery should be defined by the application's needs—for example, in a real-time system, applications may not need or want recovery back to a previous state. Instead, they wish recovery to be performed by delaying restart until the next update cycle. In a real-time system many data-items' lifetimes are short, so waiting is better than recovering. Recovery may require blocking others until a new update, or it may require forward recovery to move to a present consistent state. Recovery is best left to user applications. Transactions could all have recovery code as part of their structure. These routines would either cause a subtransaction to alter the database or to compute an interim value for this transaction to use.

17.3.8 Summary

In this section we examined concepts for flexible transactions for real-time database management applied to the standard SQL language. These concepts address two important needs of real-time system application programmers. The first deals with control over the structure and execution of databases and their manipulation. The second deals with the integration of time as a measure for data and transaction correctness and consistency. The described research and transaction structuring and processing model show that flexible transaction specification and execution can result in increased concurrency, facilitating more timely access and incremental data availability while still delivering the benefits of database management.

17.4 TEMPORAL DATABASES

The area of time in databases has been receiving a lot of press over the last five years. There are two camps on time use in database systems—the first is the real-time community and the second is the temporal community. The real-time database researchers look at time as a means to order and operate a database management system, whereas the temporal database researchers look at time as a means to historically collect and maintain "copies" of data-items based on their time of access or instantiation. Real time differs from temporal in the sense that time, in the real-time database, is used as a means to define the lifetime and usefulness of data and transactions within the database (see Chapter 12 for further details).

Temporal databases use time as a means to order and collect historical data. Data records, tuples, or objects in a temporal database have timestamps associated with them. These timestamps can then be used to order data-items in the database, to identify unique versions of a data-item in the database, or to provide a means to sequence through the data-items in the database. The timestamp in a temporal database can be used to encode the valid time of a data-item in the database or to encode the transaction time that is used to manage the execution of transactions on temporal data-items.

Temporal database research presently is aimed at incorporating the current TSQL model into the object-oriented database model and to expand the capabilities of temporal databases into nontraditional application domains—for example, in geographical systems time is used to model spatial relationships. In financial planning, medical treatment, and ecological information–monitoring systems, temporal data are essential to the correct execution of the applications, although little if any database system support exists for these applications at this time. Multimedia data pose both problems and interesting research topics for the temporal database community. Multimedia inherently include temporal properties—for example, video segments, audio segments, video documents, and multimedia documents all include time markings for synchronization as well as for access support. There is no reason why these applications should not or could not be supported by temporal databases with further extensions for synchronization of access and deadline-driven transactions.

The interested reader is directed to *The TSQL2 Temporal Database Language* (Kluwer Academic Publishers, 1995) for further information about the fundamental model for temporal database management systems and languages.

18

Database Standards

Donna Fisher
Janet Prichard

18.1 STANDARDS PROCESS

Standards have played a major role in the development and wider dissemination of database management systems and information managed in them. Standards for database management systems come in a variety of flavors. There are the true international standards, which have been accepted by a number of countries. There are national standards, which have been accepted in the United States. Finally, there are de facto standards, which have evolved due to the widespread use of a particular process or technique. Standards have evolved within all sectors of the economy to allow for more interchangeability of components from a wide variety of vendors. An example of the need for standards comes from the early days of the industrial revolution. The initiation of mass production required that components for a product be interchangeable; that is, they had a specification that was rigidly defined and rigidly manufactured to the specified tolerances. By following these techniques it was found that cars could be produced at a faster rate and were easier to maintain and cheaper to produce. The concept of a "standard" for specification and construction of an element is still the foundation of numerous markets today—for example, there are standards for televisions, power, computer languages, road composition, concrete composition, and many more everyday commodities. Without these standards the world as we know it would be quite different.

This chapter provides general information about national and international database standards. It discusses what, where, how, and why these standards were developed and by whom.

18.2 USEFUL ACRONYMS

The standards process uses numerous acronyms. There are several acronyms that will be helpful in understanding the standards described in the remainder of this chapter.

ANSI	American National Standards Institute
CCITT	International Telegraph and Telephone Consultative Committee
CD	Committee Draft
DIS	Draft International Standard
IEC	International Electrotechnical Commission
IEEE	Institute of Electrical and Electronics Engineers
IS	International Standard
ISO	International Organization for Standardization
JTC1	Joint Technical Committee 1
NIST	National Institute for Standards and Technologies
SC	Subcommittee
WG	Working Group
X3	Accredited Standards Committee

18.3 WHAT ARE STANDARDS?

Standards are documented agreements containing technical specifications or other criteria to be used as rules, guidelines, or definitions of characteristics, and to ensure that materials, products, processes, and services are adequate for their purpose. The economic players in a given industrial sector—suppliers, users, and often governments—agree on specifications and guidelines to be applied uniformly across materials, products, and services.

The format of the conventional credit card and phone card is derived from an ISO International Standard. When a card is developed in accordance with the standard, which defines such features as an optimal thickness (0.76 mm), it ensures that the card can be used worldwide. As you can see, standards have the capacity to increase the reliability and effectiveness of the goods and services we use. Standards can be determined through general practice and use within a market sector—for example, the disk operating system, or DOS, developed by Microsoft for IBM became an industry standard for operating systems through use. Such a product is referred to as a de facto or de jure standard. There are many such products in all sectors of the economy that have become standards in this way. Standards result in wider dissemination and use of products that adhere to them. Users of standard products and services have more confidence in products and services that conform to international standards. Assurance of conformity can be provided by manufacturers' declarations, or by audits carried out by independent bodies.

18.4 WHY STANDARDS?

Standards exist in such diverse fields as information processing, textiles, distribution of goods, energy production, and financial services. The current economic conditions foster a diversity in suppliers. Fair competition between these suppliers needs to be grounded in clearly defined common guidelines. Today's industries depend on the use of components, products, and services that have been developed in other sectors—for example, data management is used in almost all industry sectors from military to financial. Standards are an explicitly defined vehicle to encourage guidelines for competition and to foster the interchangeability of components between and within industry sectors. Without standards consumers could not purchase goods from multiple sources and integrate them into a cohesive package—for example, without power standards and power receptacle standards, we could not simply go out and purchase electronic goods from any source. We would be limited to the vendor that provided the power and the receptacles. Another example is in the consumer electronics sector. Without standards we could not mix and match audio and video components as we do. Think what the world would be like if you could only buy your audio equipment from a single vendor!

18.5 WHERE ARE STANDARDS DEVELOPED?

Standards can be and are developed and adopted by almost every organization. Standards development organizations include government (National Institute for Standards and Technology [NIST], the Department of Defense, and the Department of Energy); consortia groups, such as X/Open, OMG, and the SQL Access Group; and industry organizations (e.g., Microsoft's MS-DOS). The adoption of standards helps a given organization run more efficiently—for example, if a given word processing product is selected as the company standard, it ensures that documents can be passed among employees with little

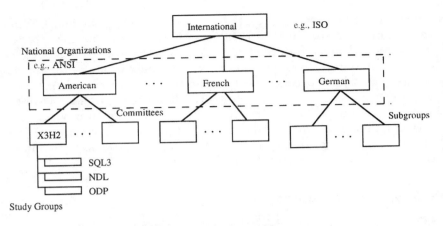

Figure 18.1   Standards organizations hierarchies

problem. Without a well-documented and long-term supported standard, this would only be a short-term solution. In cases where the supplier is continually changing a product, the company is required to make constant upgrades as previous versions quickly become obsolete and are often not supported. This is a definite reason for consumers to demand a standard. A standard may allow for product improvements, while still supporting the old version of the standard, without requiring changes to any user-developed applications or data files.

This section focuses on the nationally or internationally accredited standards development organizations that define and approve standards. These approved standards are developed at the national and international level in a forum where users and providers reach consensus concerning the detailed specification of a given technology area. Specifically, this section will look at the following accredited standards development organizations: International Organization for Standardization, American National Standards Institute, and X3.

18.5.1 International Organization for Standardization (ISO)

The International Organization for Standardization (ISO) is a worldwide federation of standards bodies from over 100 countries (one standards body from each country—for example, ANSI from the United States, AFNOR from France, and DIN from Germany) (Figure 18.1). It is a nongovernment organization established in 1947 (more information regarding the history of ISO can be found in the ISO home page). Its mission is to promote the development of standardization and related activities in the world with a view to facilitating the international exchange of goods and services, and to developing cooperation in the spheres of intellectual, scientific, technological, and economic activity. The results are international agreements published as International Standards (IS). ISO collaborates closely with its partner, the International Electrotechnical Commission (IEC). The IEC covers electrical and electronic engineering; ISO covers all other subject areas.

18.5.2 American National Standards Institute (ANSI)

In the United States, standards are developed under the authority of the American National Standards Institute (ANSI), which is the U.S. member body of ISO. ANSI, founded in 1918, is a private, not-for-profit membership organization, which coordinates the U.S. standards development bodies and approves American National Standards. It consists of approximately 1,300 national and international companies; 30 government agencies; 20 institutional members; and 250 professional, technical, trade, labor, and consumer organizations.

ANSI ensures that a consistent set of consensus-based standards is developed. ANSI's requirements for due process and consensus guarantee that American National Standards earn high levels of confidence and credibility and achieve broad acceptance. In addition, ANSI represents U.S. interests in international standardization. Through the ISO and IEC, the United States has the opportunity to effectively influence the outcome of the European Community's standards activities. There are a number of accredited standards committees under ANSI. These include the Institute of Electrical and Electronics Engineers (IEEE) and X3.

18.5.3 Accredited Standards Committee (X3)

X3, established in 1961, is accredited by ANSI to develop voluntary standards. X3 provides its over 3,000 members with countless opportunities to know and influence the key issues, activities, and people that drive national and international information technology standards in dynamic areas of commerce, technology, and society. X3 members have early and ready access to a wealth of technical information affecting the future of information technology on a global basis. Members actively participate in a deliberative consensus-building process that is both national and international in scope. X3 standardization efforts are in the field of information technology and encompass the storage, processing, transfer, display, management, organization, and retrieval of information. Figure 18.2 provides a view of the U.S. standards-making committees associated with the X3 organization.

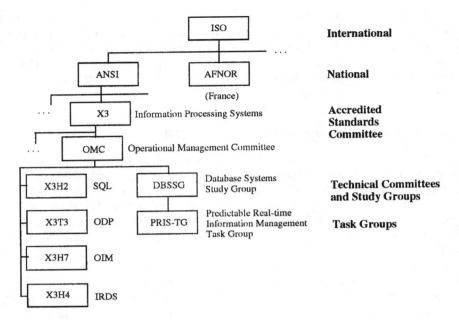

Figure 18.2   ANSI X3 standards committees

18.5.4 Database Standards Organizations

Numerous organizations are involved in developing database standards. Some database standards bodies are accredited by national and international bodies (e.g., ANSI and ISO), while others are industry consortia efforts (e.g., OMG and ODMG), reflecting the opinions of a number of highly interested companies and application developers. Past history has shown that enduring standards are typically developed within the context of accredited standards bodies, while at the same time some of the consortia-based endeavors have survived due to inertia by consumers and the volume of vendor product infusion. Within the context of database standards there is only one accredited standard, SQL, which is supported by a U.S. national body, ANSI, and an international body, ISO. The SQL standard has evolved from a strict relational model to a relational/object model, with recent efforts aimed at moving this model to a more general object/relational model.

Database standards are controlled by a few organizations worldwide. Membership in these organizations is open to any interested party, as is the right to vote. Organizations or individuals who wish to participate are required to indicate their intentions in a written format and back up the letter through attendance at a sequence of national and international meetings. Once an organization or individual

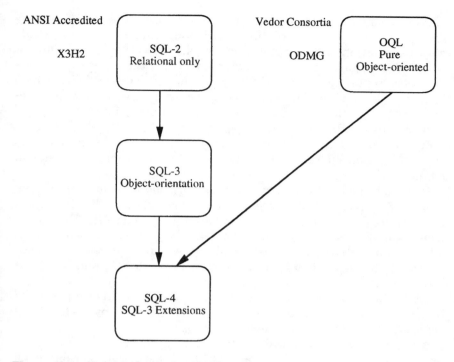

Figure 18.3   Database standards bodies

is accepted into a standards body as a voting member, voting rights are determined based on member attendance records and participation at standards meetings, as well as on standards ballot votes. Inaction by a member results in removal of voting rights and ultimately removal from committee membership. The present international and national committees are organized in a hierarchy (Figure 18.3) with ISO (international level) at the top of the hierarchy. Each country that is registered as a member of ISO has its own organization, determining that country's position on standards proposed for the international arena—for example, in the United States the standards body is ANSI, in France it is AFNOR, and in Germany it is DIN. Each of these organizations comes to the international platform with a single stand on topics of interest, as determined by their national body efforts between international standards meetings.

These national bodies in turn work on the establishment of national standards for topics of interest to their particular group. ANSI, for example, has working groups in most technology areas, such as engineering, computer languages, database systems, and manufacturing. Each of these national standards bodies is further broken down to specific technology committees, technical working groups, and study groups—for example, ANSI has a subgroup called X3, which deals with information processing systems. Under X3 is the OMC, or operational management committee, which oversees the efforts of accredited working groups. One working group under OMC is X3H2, which is responsible for the development and maintenance of the SQL database language. In support of this effort are numerous study groups, such as the DBSSG (database systems study group), which look at promising technologies, determine if they are ready for mainstream standardization efforts, and recommend if these technologies should be pursued.

One such X3H2 study task group had the job of examining the viability of real-time database management standards. The findings of this group indicated that X3H2 should pursue standardization of real-time extension to SQL3, since the technology had reached a point where standards would be beneficial and would move the technology forward. The result has been a proposal to ANSI, X3, and X3H2, as well as to ISO, with the intention of creating an additional extension to SQL3 to support real time. It is anticipated that this proposal will be accepted later in 1996 by ANSI and early in 1997 by ISO. At present both of these look like favorable projections.

A second form of standardization is not accredited by any national or international standards organizations, but has considerable clout due to market forces. This is consortia-based standards, as embodied by the OMG and their efforts. The OMG and OMDG have as their charter the goal of fostering the growth and use of object-oriented database management systems, and the consolidation of the object-oriented model into a single unified model. Toward these goals, the OMG and ODMG organizations have developed the object database model and the object query language. This effort has been published as the ODMG-93 report. The major results of this effort were a common object model, the object definition language, the object query language, and bindings to the C++ and SmallTalk languages. In addition to these models, the OMC also developed an interoperability model called the common object request broker architecture (CORBA). This model provides the services to glue multiple, possibly heterogeneous systems and objects together into a singular unified system.

18.6 DATABASE STANDARDS IN X3

The most prevalent and widely used database standards today are those defined in X3, namely the SQL standards. However, other standards exist that also merit mention due to their influence in the process.

18.6.1 Data Management

Data management refers to the language services required to define, use, and control access to data, independent of the application process. These services are generally provided by a Data Definition Language (DDL), a Data Manipulation Language (DML), and a Data Control Language (DCL).

The Network Database Language (NDL)   NDL, also known as Network Database Language, is a standard interface for database management systems based on the network data model (as opposed to relational, hierarchical, or object). Although clearly influenced by the CODASYL de facto standard, NDL is not CODASYL and must not be confused with CODASYL. The standard details the syntax and semantics of three database interfaces: (1) a schema interface, for the declaration of structures and integrity constraints of an NDL database; (2) a sub-schema interface, for the declaration of a user view of the database; and (3) a module and data manipulation interface, for the declaration of database procedures and executable statements of an application program.

The standard was approved by ANSI in 1986 and by ISO in 1987. The two documents do not recognize each other's existence, but they are word-for-word identical. No further standards development is planned. The intent was that CODASYL-conforming systems be able to claim conformance to NDL with minimum effort. However, none of the original CODASYL systems have done so. The primary reason for mentioning NDL here is that it has been one of several important influences on the real-time database interface standard work currently underway.

Remote Data Access (RDA)   X3H2 is responsible for the specification of a protocol that provides access to data stored at remote sites using a DDL. The RDA specification establishes a remote connection between an RDA client, acting on behalf of an application program, and an RDA server, interfacing to a process that controls data transfers to and from a database. The goal of the RDA standard is to provide interconnection of applications and database systems within heterogeneous environments. RDA provides such services as dialog management, association control, resource handling, and data language services between a single client and a single server. DDL statements are sent as character strings with a separate list of input parameters. Resulting data or exception conditions are returned. Transaction management services are also included for both one- and two-phase commit protocols. RDA does not consider multiple connections. Part 1, the generic definition, and Part 2, the SQL specialization for SQL 1989, are approved international standards. Work is currently in progress to revise Part 2 to include SQL 1992.

Of interesting note are the results of the remote database access protocols standardization. The standard was developed and some products were developed and fielded. The product, however, received little support from the technical community. The products developed and made available for purchase made little gains in the marketplace and have been overrun of late by emerging standards, such as those of the ODMG, and the common object request broker architecture (CORBA), which is receiving much interest from object-oriented and non-object-oriented remote database access camps. The RDA standards are an example of a technically viable solution, which has resulted in little industry support and therefore may possibly die due to inaction (similar to what happened to the NDL standard after it was published).

SQL Ada Module Extensions Description Language (SAMeDL)
ANSI X3.168-1989 specifies two approaches to standard language bindings to SQL: an embedded approach (which inserts SQL statements into the application program and requires the use of a preprocessor to generate the appropriate source code) and a module approach (which makes procedure calls on the SQL module). Another approach consists of the implementation of the SQL Ada Module Extensions (SAMe) methodology by the SQL Ada Module Extensions Description Language (SAMeDL). The SAMe approach is based on the SQL module language described in the ANSI standard. The advantage of SAMeDL is that it promotes portability by separating Ada code from SQL, thus avoiding the need for a preprocessor. The SAMeDL work is still under development and will be standardized by ISO Working Group 9. Currently, no standard compliant products are available for Embedded SQL in Ada (they are only available in proprietary products).

Structured Query Language (SQL) SQL is an English-like language used to access data in relational database management systems. ANSI SQL and ISO SQL are essentially word-for-word identical specifications. FIPS SQL adopts ANSI SQL for federal use and, in addition, specifies FIPS levels of conformance and several additional FIPS conformance requirements for each level. FIPS SQL specifies default "sizing" and "documentation" requirements that are not specified in the other standards. X3H2 is the technical committee responsible for development of ANSI SQL. ISO/IEC JTC1/SC21/WG3 is the international working group responsible for the development of ISO SQL.

Both groups cooperate with the intent of producing identical SQL standards.

Both ANSI and ISO SQL development groups are currently working on SQL3, the informal name for a major SQL enhancement anticipated to be published in several parts over the next three to five years. One part will be a call-level interface (SQL/CLI). Another part will be Persistent SQL Modules. A third part will specify object concepts in SQL3, including user-defined abstract data types, object identifiers, class hierarchies, and other features normally associated with object data management.

The SQL3 database standards efforts include extensions to the basic SQL2 language to include abstract data types and objects in the relational model. The ANSI SQL language was first standardized in 1986. The model has since been revised two times—in 1989 and again in 1992. The resulting specification became known as the SQL2 language. The major changes seen at this time were the inclusion of the client/server model, the set transaction statements, concept of domains, and the drop statement to alter a schema.

Since the SQL2 model was published, the ANSI committee has embarked on one of its most ambitious efforts: the alteration of the basic relational model and the development of a consistent extension, which became known as the SQL3 language. SQL3 represents a radical change from the traditional relational model. The SQL3 model introduced the concept of abstract data types (objects) embedded within tables (relations). The embedding can be within a simple one-column table, where the objects are basically viewed as a set or multiset of objects grouped together, up to objects introduced as an extended attribute within a relation (Figure 18.4).

The SQL3 database model introduced the concepts of abstract data type, object identifiers, object reference, encapsulation, methods, and functions as the only means to acquire and manipulate data within the database—as well as subtypes and inheritance, polymorphic functions, program flow of control, parameterized types, stored procedures (precompilation of database manipulation code callable by identifier in code), dynamic triggers, enhanced security, subtransaction savepoints, and much more. SQL3 is a computationally complete model, since it does not require a host programming language to exist as did the previous standard languages generated by the SQL committee.

Beyond the basics of SQL3 the ANSI committee has pursued additional extensions to the base database model, including SQL MM, SQL/temporal, and SQL/RT. A new ISO project has recently been proposed to develop a class library of application-specific objects. Its title will be SQL Multimedia (SQL/MM). It will include optional parts that can be specified separately for the following application areas: full

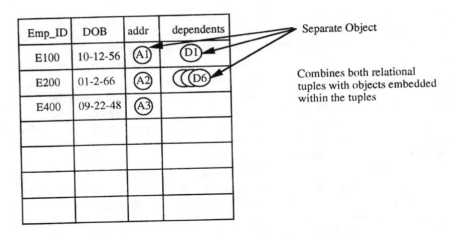

Figure 18.4   SQL3 relational/object model

text, graphics, images, geographic information systems, audio, video, spatial, and so forth. Completion of the initial SQL/MM parts are planned for the 1995–1996 time frame, with others to follow as appropriate thereafter. The SQL/MM, multimedia extension, looks at creating a multimedia class library for SQL3 databases to use in specifying and using multimedia objects within the SQL3 framework.

A new ANSI and ISO project has been formed during 1995, under the SQL3 groups, to develop extensions for temporal support within the SQL3 database language standard. Temporal features allow for the incorporation of time tags on the tuples of data in the database and the manipulation of data-items in the database using the time tags as access points or query components. SQL/temporal adds additional data types to the foundation SQL3 to handle historical data types and their manipulation. The new basic type is the period data type with the concepts of tuple timestamping. These basic additions are then used for valid time support of past and future time periods and for user-defined time support, such as instants, intervals, and spans.

The most recent proposed extension for SQL3 came from one of X3's study groups, DBSSG's predictable real-time information systems task group (PRIS-TG), and proposes extensions for real-time support for SQL3 databases. SQL3 real time includes concepts for time-constrained data, time-constrained transactions, predictable access, and loosened definition, as well as support for transaction ACID properties, forward and semantic recovery, and added transaction scheduling and synchronization primitives.

Some additional features aimed at infrastructure support include a group of extensions, referred to as directives. Directives give hints to the database management system for ways to aid in meeting the timing constraints (e.g., place data structure in primary memory, fix the maximum size of a data structure). At the present time there has been initial discussion of "real-time" data management requirements and their incorporation into the SQL standardization committee's SQL activities.

What the Future Holds: ODMG and SQL Merging into Alignment?   A series of joint meetings between members of the SQL3 committee and the ODMG committee were held in December 1994, April 1995, and again in July 1995 to discuss SQL3/OQL accommodation. The goals of these meetings were to determine what the status of the two data models and standard languages were, where the models differ, and how they can be brought into alignment. These discussions were fueled by a desire to merge the two standards into a single database query language in order to avoid fragmenting the marketplace and overloading vendors wishing to pursue both the extended relational and pure object-oriented database management systems.

The results of these meetings were that the languages can be brought more into alignment and possibly merge at some point in the future. For this to occur the ODMG must examine the inclusion of the following SQL3 features: adding of nulls to the ODMG data model, adding tables to the model, adopting SQL-compliant syntax to OQL (e.g., changing OQL's SELECT to SELECT_OBJECT), and pointing to SQL-92 to include SELECT_OBJECT. SQL's triggers, views, and constraints (possibly even assertions) must be added to the ODMG model. It must also include SQL's UPDATE, INSERT, and DELETE statements, as well as the dispatch function in the ODMG standard. Ensuring that SQL's OIDs can be "stored" in an OQL database is another consideration.

SQL can improve its posture in terms of OMG and ODMG's stance by including OQL's pure objects into the SQL3 language and the SELECT_OBJECT operator, replacing INSTANCE with extent tables, enhancing SQL's triggers to include ADT usage, adding "object views" to SQL, and specializing the dispatch function to allow the classical object model for method invocations inside ADTs. Finally, a radical means of conformance may include the OQL language being incorporated as part of the SQL standard. It appears from these discussions that the two organizations wish to merge, while keeping the best features of each independent model.

18.6.2 Security

Many database systems require secure, reliable, accountable access to a variety of heterogeneous DBMSs that are interoperable with multiple trusted operating systems and networks. Current standardization efforts include work on remote data access, SQL, transaction processing, remote procedure calls, and application program interfaces. POSIX IEEE P1003.6 defines security extensions for the POSIX ISO 9945-2 (1990) and FIPS 151 operating system interface standards. However, there is no de jure standard that presently meets security requirements of a trusted DBMS.

The trusted database interpretation (TDI) of the National Computer Security Center's "Rainbow Series" translates the evaluation criteria established in the Trusted Computer Security Evaluation Criteria (TCSEC, also known as the "Orange Book") for application to DBMSs.

Despite the lack of an industrywide standard pertaining to DBMS security, several vendors have released products that claim to be interoperable and that appear to satisfy much of the security. These products could create de facto standards for DBMS security, but will no doubt involve interoperability difficulties, which will need to be resolved.

18.6.3 Real-Time Data Management

Real-time database managers are database managers designed to provide services with deterministic costs. Further, those cost functions are provided with the interface for developers to compute and guarantee system response. Real-time database managers must provide both services with deterministic costs and cost functions available to system developers. Traditional or conventional database managers either provide probability cost functions or do not make the cost functions available to the system developers. To meet the need of real-time databases requires additional infrastructure support, such as real-time schedulers, priority schedulers, preemptive schedulers, flexible memory allocation schemes, and real-time communication schemes. Some of these deficiencies are presently being addressed through operating system extensions such as those provided and proposed under the POSIX real-time operating system.

POSIX Real-Time Extensions   The POSIX series of standards is being developed under the sponsorship of the Portable Applications Standards Committee (PASC) of the IEEE Computer Society. POSIX.1, which has been approved as an international standard (ISO/IEC 9945-1), defines an operating system interface and environment based on UNIX. It is intended to provide application portability at the source-code level. Numerous PASC working groups are defining extensions to POSIX.1, as well as profiles (i.e., suites of standards) for various application environments. In particular, Working Group 1003.4 is defining real-time extensions to POSIX.1 and a series of profiles for real-time application environments. The current products of Working Group 1003.4 are IEEE 1003.1b, P1003.1g, and P1003.13.

IEEE 1003.1b specifies interfaces for the following real-time facilities, which represent modifications and extensions to POSIX.1.

- High-resolution clocks and per-process timers
- Priority-based scheduling
- Memory locking
- Memory-mapped files and shared memory
- Counting semaphores
- Message-passing interprocess communication
- Real-time signals
- Asynchronous I/O
- Synchronized I/O

P1003.1g specifies a threads extension to POSIX.1. Threads are lightweight processes, which share an address space, and thus provide a low-overhead concurrency mechanism that is crucial for real-time applications. The specification of the threads extension introduces new synchronization primitives, namely mutexes and condition variables.

P1003.4b specifies interfaces for the following additional real-time facilities.

- Spawn (a new process-creation mechanism)
- Timeouts on blocking services
- Execution time monitoring
- Sporadic server scheduling
- Device control
- Interrupt control
- Advisory information on application program file and memory usage

P1003.13 specifies four real-time application environment profiles. The profiles range from a minimal real-time system to a general-purpose real-time system.

Predictable Real-Time Information Systems Task Group (PRIS-TG) The Predictable Real-Time Information Systems Task Group (PRIS-TG) is a task group of the X3 (Computers and Information Processing Committee) Database Systems Study Group (DBSSG). PRIS-TG's relationship to the X3 standards organization is described below. The purpose of the PRIS-TG is to determine if the technology for real-time systems in general and for real-time information management is sufficiently mature for standardization. The PRIS-TG was tasked to develop a predictable real-time information systems reference model, evaluate existing predictable real-time information systems technology, and determine the need for standardization in this area.

The objective of the PRIS-TG study was to establish a framework for future predictable real-time information management standards activities, both extensions to ongoing Structured Query Language (SQL), Information Resources Dictionary System (IRDS), Remote Data Access (RDA), Open Distributed Processing (ODP), Object Information Management (OIM), Portable Operating Systems Interface for Computer Environments (POSIX), Ada, and computer security development, as well as related future standards.

The task group reviewed and evaluated existing and developmental products claiming to be real-time information management systems, as well as real-time products with information management capabilities. The task group also reviewed and evaluated published literature and research activities concerning real-time information management technology worldwide.

Presently there is a trend in industry to develop products that conform to open systems standards. Database management systems are no exception, although standards in this technology area are relatively new and still evolving. Presently there are real-time database products available (DBx Inc., Martin Marietta, Westinghouse). These products do not yet address all the needs of real-time database applications, although they are a step in the right direction. However, they do not conform to real-time database standards, since none exist. These products have concepts for time-driven transactions, time constraints on data, and some architectural dependency considerations. Additionally, they interact with hardware systems through real-time open system operating systems standards such as POSIX 1003.4.

The Predictable Real-Time Information Systems Task Group (PRIS-TG) performed a study to determine the maturity and viability of real-time database management systems to include such technology in existing and emerging ANSI standards. The findings highlight the lack of support for real time in conventional database systems, the need for such support, the maturity of real-time database technology, and the availability of products and supporting standards.

Real-Time Database Systems Technology Nearly all existing database standards and existing products do not have support for real-time service to applications. Conventional SQL products are based on the model of a monolithic database (persistent storage) with serialization of transactions acting on the database as the correctness criterion. Conventional database recovery is based on the checkpointing of the database with the application of log actions to redo or undo the effects of transactions on the database at the time of a failure.

While conventional database management implementations support a wide range of application areas, it has been shown by numerous researchers, product developers, and vendors that this model limits the ability of databases to be applied to a wider array of computer-based information processing and management applications, such as those for real-time computing systems. Numerous examples of how real-time database management could improve performance within computer-aided design, computer-aided manufacturing, medical monitoring and diagnostics, Department of Defense mission-critical systems, on-line transaction processing systems, and other application areas have been defined in the literature.

Work has progressed beyond the research phase into testbed systems and currently into available off-the-shelf products that exhibit features necessary for the support of real time in the database environment. These products and research address the need to extend conventional database concepts to include time as a component for database consistency, correctness, and manipulation and to address the requirement for predictability of access. In the database specification area the move is to limit the flexibility of on-line alteration of database structures to deliver predictable access to the database while giving more control to the database designer to limit how the database can be used, where it will be stored, how it will be structured in storage, how the database is partitioned, and how constraints affect correctness and consistency.

Research, prototyping efforts, and product development address the need of the real-time programmer to exhibit more control over the specification, structure, access, manipulation, and recovery of the database and transactions. The focus of these efforts is on the loosening of the conventional ACID properties defined for a database's transactions and the development of more flexible transactions to increase concurrency and data availability, limit data blocking, prevent cascading aborts, and exhibit controlled recovery—all under transaction control.

Standards in other areas of the information infrastructure that support real time are also evolving. The IEEE has recently released a real-time extension (IEEE 1003.1b) to the POSIX operating system interface standard (IEEE 1003.1). This standard provides support for real-time scheduling of tasks, concurrent execution of tasks, and extended control over numerous elements of the computer system. Evolving SQL standards are looking into the support of concepts that will aid in the introduction of real time into the standard—for example, there are additions to the SQL3 standard for objects, triggers (the concept for triggers presently in SQL is sketchy at best), time reference, more refined constraint definitions, and enhanced database and transaction structuring.

When taken together these indicators demonstrate the need for real-time databases and the viability of the technology. Real-time database management systems will become commonplace in the computing arena in the next five to ten years. To ensure that the development of such systems results in interoperable, open products requires standardization of application interfaces. It is a recommendation of the PRIS Task Group that the technology is sufficiently mature (concepts are well understood) to permit standardization efforts to begin now.

PRIS-TG , under the auspices of X3/Operational Management Committee/Database Systems Study Group (DBSSG), established the need for real-time database standards. Industry and government have a need for real-time information management systems and, in the absence of any standards in this area, are developing proprietary products to meet real-time application needs. Real-time application developers lack a consistent methodology for developing the information management portion of their application. Standards in this area would facilitate application portability. The primary goal of this task group was to establish a framework for future standardization efforts in this area. The final report was published documenting the findings of this group.

The X3/OMC DBSSG PRIS-TG has found that real-time data management technology has a solid foundation for standardization. At the present time there are existing products that exhibit fundamental features for real-time data management. In addition, several government, industry, and academic research programs are developing further prototypes and refinements of the numerous areas mentioned in this report. The University of Massachusetts—Amherst has developed real-time concepts and prototypes for scheduling protocols, real-time transaction processing, and real-time recovery; the University of Rhode Island, University of Virginia, and Carnegie Mellon University have been researching real-time database management systems and constructing testbed systems; and the U.S. Air Force's FIRM (Functionally Integrated Resource Management) program and several other programs have established a solid foundation for real-time data management standards development.

The technology is at a point where many basic concepts have reached stability, as indicated by the increase in product developments. The further refinement of these basic features will enhance the stability of any developed standard. Some areas within this technology will require additional work to refine and stabilize the concepts to a point where a specific and lasting standard can be developed. In the time frame it will take to develop a standard, current and potential advances in the real-time database management area should have matured and stabilized.

18.7 NEED FOR STANDARDIZATION EFFORT FOR DATABASE MANAGEMENT

Industry, academia, individuals, and government have a need for information management systems and, in the absence of applicable standards, will develop proprietary, one-of-a-kind products to meet information processing application needs. The proliferation of one-of-a-kind solutions for evolving information management applications will only make interoperability more difficult later on. An information management system is one that provides information or response at a given time on demand, but generally not before. Requirements for advanced information management are found in many sectors, such as military, credit card validation, stock market trading and analysis, medical, airlines, computer-aided design, computer-aided manufacturing, and nuclear power control. Presently there is a large movement in the DoD and industry to capture legacy systems and to incorporate their information into on-line information infrastructures. Without having advanced database management system standards in place as soon as possible, capturing legacy system databases may not be possible, leaving their information unavailable until their systems can be rewritten in some new standard format.

18.8 FRAMEWORKS AND CONSORTIA

DARPA

The U.S. Department of Defense funding agency sponsoring work on knowledge representation standards initiative, Open OODB, and the NIST Persistent Object Testbed.

IEEE

1730 Massachusetts Avenue, N.W.
Washington, DC 20036-1903
Phone: (202) 371-0101

Object Management Group (OMG)

The OMG is a consortium established to promote object-oriented concepts and methods. The OMG architecture defines an interface called Object Request Broker (ORB). The Object Model Task Force is developing a description of a concrete object model.

Open Systems Foundations (OSF)

A consortium that, as part of its project, is defining a distributed management environment (DME) utilizing object concepts.

11 Cambridge Center
Cambridge, MA 02142

SQL Access Group

A consortium of users and vendors working to advance the RDA protocol and planning to work on a call-level interface to SQL systems.

c/o Robert Crutchfield
Fransen and Associates, Inc.
2171 Campus Drive, Suite 260
Irvine, CA 92715
Phone: (714) 752-5942

X/Open

A consortium of users and hardware and software vendors developing portability guides for languages, databases, and operating systems.

1750 Montgomery Street
San Francisco, CA 94111
Phone: (415) 323-7992

Other important information . . .

SQL, NDL, SAMeDL Point of Contact:

Dr. Leonard Gallagher
National Institute of Standards and Technology
Technology Building, Room A266
Gaithersburg, MD 20899
Phone: (301) 975-3251
E-mail: Lgallagher@nist.gov

POSIX Real-Time Point of Contact:

Bill Corwin, 1003.4 Chair
Intel Corporation HF3-64
5200 Elam Young Parkway
Hillsboro, OR 97124
E-mail: wmc@littlei.intel.com.

PRIS-TG Point of Contact:

Donna K. Fisher, former Chair DBSSG
NCCOSC RDTE DIV 412
49180 Transmitter Road, Room 2
San Diego, CA 92152-7341
Phone: (619) 553-4095
Fax: (619) 553-6288
E-mail: dfisher@cod.nosc.mil

19

Sample Database Management Systems Products

Paul Fortier
Anitha Basavaraj

In this chapter we will introduce example systems that have been implemented using the database design and operational models described in the previous chapters. This sampling is by no means exhaustive, nor is it complete. We merely attempt to describe some database products that are readily available and cover a wide spectrum of performance—from single-user personal computer–based products to sophisticated multiuser mainframe-supported products. We cover products that support the relational, network, object-oriented, and object relational database models.

19.1 NETWORK DATABASE MANAGEMENT SYSTEMS PRODUCTS

Martin Marietta Corporation has developed a real-time database management system based on the ANSI CODASYL network database model. Adherence to this model is not complete, because the product does not support the full standard; however, it does capture the intent of the network model in terms of the data storage structures and access schemes supported.

The EagleSpeed real-time database management system is the commercial release of a database designed for a submarine command system. It is based on the ANSI CODASYL (network) data model. It is designed to support hard real-time applications. The stated goals of EagleSpeed include the following.

- Synchronize with environmental processes that must be controlled
- Support a priori determination of system schedulability
- Provide predictability and punctuality of transaction access
- Provide speed, determinism, and minimalism

EagleSpeed has achieved the predictable execution time required by hard real-time applications in several ways. First, it implements only a subset of database management functionality. The removal of database system functionality places more burden on the applications writer. It only provides a subset of the CODASYL verbs, requiring the applications writer to define other functionality. Second, by utilizing the network data model's ability to fix logical data structures in advance, it fixes access time to the data. Third, it uses one single-layer schema, which minimizes overhead due to mapping levels and due to maintaining metadata. Fourth, the physical location of data objects can be fixed to facilitate retrieval.

Transactions are Ada programs with ACID properties. They are invoked via messages sent to their site of storage. In addition, the system allows direct access to the transaction manager and the operating system to facilitate real-time performance. Timing constraints on transactions are not supported, since it is assumed that a priori analysis will determine if all transactions meet timing constraints. Transactions are given priorities and scheduled by the underlying operating system. Concurrency control is handled by strict two-phase locking with no imprecision allowed. Like Zip, EagleSpeed is a fast, predictable real-time data store, but it lacks some features of a full real-time database.

19.2 RELATIONAL DATABASE MANAGEMENT SYSTEMS PRODUCTS

19.2.1 ORACLE

Products ORACLE provides the following products.

Personal ORACLE7—the Power ORACLE7, for Windows

ORACLE7 Workgroup Server—database for workgroups

Enterprise ORACLE7—the relational DBMS

ORACLE Text Server—tackles information overload by integrating textual and relational data

ORACLE RDB—a high-performance, high-capacity client/server relational database for Alpha AXP and VAX systems

ORACLE Gateways—facilitates enterprise-wide information management by providing access to the data, applications, and systems in today's diverse computing environment

ORACLE Networking—the network security software for client/server database environments

ORACLE Context—a natural language processing technology that identifies themes and content in English text

ORACLE Systems Management—database and network administration tools

The following paragraphs describe Enterprise ORACLE7, the relational DBMS.

Introduction ORACLE7 supports the full range of enterprise data management requirements for on-line transaction processing systems, data warehouses, and client/server and distributed database applications. ORACLE7 leverages investment in development, deployment, and maintenance to deliver the maximum benefits of open, relational systems across your enterprise, while minimizing the risks, complexity, and costs of moving to open systems. ORACLE7's integrated, dynamic parallel query technology enables open data warehouse applications while preserving compatibility with all server functionality.

Features

Data Model It has a relational data model. ORACLE7 provides extensive 8- and 16-bit character set support, including the Unicode variable-width UTF-2 encoding. ORACLE7 national language support (NLS) ensures that error messages, sort order, date format, and other conventions automatically adapt to the native language. Separate national calendars, including Japanese Imperial, ROC Official, Thai Buddha, Persian, and Arabic Hijrah, are supported. Arabic and Hebrew display character set support is also available. ORACLE7 supports deployment of heterogeneous client/server and distributed database configurations by automatically and transparently performing any necessary character set conversions.

Data Manipulation   SQL Implementation: 100-percent ANSI/ISO SQL 92 entry-level compliant—NIST tested; ANSI/ISO standard precompiler applications interface (API); robust SQL extensions including UNION, INTERSECT, MINUS, outer join, and tree-structured queries (CONNECT BY); and SQL3 in-line views (query in the FROM clause of another query).

Declarative Integrity Constraints: 100-percent ANSI/ISO standard declarative entity and referential integrity constraints; CHECK, DEFAULT, and not NULL constraints; PRIMARY, FOREIGN, and UNIQUE keys; and optional DELETE CASCADE.

It has a SQL optimizer, which provides cost-based, syntax-independent optimization; ANALYZE table statistics generation; nested-loop and sort-merge join selection; "Star" query algorithm support; and manual UNION ALL predicate push-down.

Distributed Queries and Transactions

Transparent remote and distributed query

Distributed, optimized joins

Location transparency, network transparency

Integrated distributed query architecture

Transparent, multisite distributed transactions

Distributed SQL updates and remote procedure calls (RPCs)

Commit transparency

Automatic failure detection and resolution

Transaction Processing

Multithreaded server architecture

Scalable SMP performance

Shared database buffer cache

Shared SQL cache (SQL statements, PL/SQL procedures, functions, packages, and triggers)

Shared dictionary cache, fast and group commits, deferred writes

ORACLE7 parallel server provides clustered, MPP, and hybrid parallel systems support

Multiple nodes share access to a single ORACLE7 database

Easy incremental expansion of processing resources

Linear scalable increases in performance

High-availability applications

Consolidated system administration

Transactional data access:

- B-tree single column and concatenated column indexes
- Clustered tables, hash clusters, application-specific hash functions
- ROWIDs
- Query results directly from index lookup

Concurrency and Recovery   Unrestricted row-level locking, no lock escalation, contention-free queries, unique sequence number generation, nonblocking, and multiversion read-consistent query results.

On-line backup by file, table space, or database; on-line recovery; parallel recovery; parallel backup/restore utility; read-only table spaces; mirrored multisegment log files; checksums on database and redo log file blocks; and dynamic resizing of database files.

Data Replication   Multiple, read-only snapshots (basic primary site replication):

Full transactional consistency and data integrity

Full and subset table replication

Incremental refresh of snapshot copies

Event- and demand-based refresh

Symmetric Replication

Updatable snapshots (both master and snapshot tables updatable)

Multiple master configurations (full table replication between master sites)

Hybrid configurations (combine snapshot and multiple master configurations)

Fail-over configuration support

Automatic conflict detection and resolution

Distributed schema management

Triggers

Procedural code executed automatically on INSERT, UPDATE, or DELETE

Triggers execute either BEFORE or AFTER operations

Triggers fire once per statement or once per row

Modeled after ANSI/ISO SQL3 specification

Data Security Choice of internal or external user authentication: External choices include the following.

Operating system

OS security package

Network operating system

Security service

Authentication device

Encrypted passwords

Full data stream encryption through DES and RSA RC4 encryption algorithms

Complete protocol support and application transparency

Fine-grained database privileges

Hierarchical role-based security for group-level access control

Site-customized DBA roles

Roles are basis for ANSI/ISO SQL3 security standard

Evaluated at US TCSEC C2, European ITSEC E3

Automatic auditing on per-session or per-object basis

Application-specific or context-sensitive auditing via PL/SQL stored procedures and database triggers

Open Gateways

Data source transparency

Transparent SQL gateways

Transparent procedural gateways

Distributed queries and update transactions

Compliant with XA standard for TP monitor coordinated two-phase commit

Application Development   SQL Implementation: 100-percent ANSI/ISO SQL 92 entry-level compliant—NIST tested; ANSI/ISO standard precompiler applications interface (API); robust SQL extensions including UNION, INTERSECT, MINUS, outer join, and tree-structured queries (CONNECT BY); and SQL3 in-line views (query in the FROM clause of another query).

Declarative Integrity Constraints: 100-percent ANSI/ISO standard declarative entity and referential integrity constraints; CHECK, DEFAULT, and not NULL constraints; PRIMARY, FOREIGN, and UNIQUE keys; and optional DELETE CASCADE.

Stored Procedures

PL/SQL procedural extension to ANSI/ISO standard SQL

- Strongly typed variable declarations (SQL datatypes)
- Block structure
- Flow control including FOR and WHILE loops, IF . . . THEN . . . ELSE
- SQL cursor support
- Static and dynamic SQL support
- Robust exception handling

Subprogram types: procedures, functions, and packages

Subprograms stored in shared, compiled form

Called from ORACLE and third-party tools, ORACLE Precompilers, ORACLE Call Interface, SQL Module, other stored procedures' database triggers

Remote procedure calls (RPCs) protected by transparent two-phase commit

User-defined PL/SQL functions in SQL

Cursor variables for easy retrieval of multirow result sets

Wrapper utility hiding PL/SQL application code in binary source format

Programmatic Interfaces

ORACLE Precompilers

- Embedded SQL and PL/SQL application development

- 100-percent entry-level ANSI/ISO X3.135-1992 compliant
- FIPS flagger meets FIPS 127-2 requirements

ORACLE Call Interface: procedure/function call interface

ORACLE SQL Module

- SQL Module language application development
- 100-percent entry-level ANSI/ISO X3.135-1992 compliant
- FIPS flagger meets FIPS 127-2 requirements

19.2.2 Microsoft

Overview   Microsoft is the provider of the following products: Microsoft BackOffice and Windows NT Workstation, Microsoft Office, Microsoft Windows 95, Visual FoxPro 3.0, Visual C++ 4.0, and Visual BASIC 4.0.

With Microsoft Visual FoxPro 3.0, developers can create applications to run on any Windows-based, 16- or 32-bit operating system, whether it is Windows 3.X, Windows NT, or Windows 95. Visual FoxPro complies with the Windows 95 logo requirements and gives users direct access to Microsoft BackOffice server components. It supports several features of object-oriented programming, such as inheritance, subclassing, encapsulation, and polymorphism.

The following paragraphs describe Microsoft Access, which belongs to the Microsoft Office family, a relational DBMS.

Introduction   Like all Microsoft Office family members, Microsoft Access is a 32-bit application for the Microsoft Windows 95 and Windows NT Workstation (version 3.51) operating systems. It takes full advantage of Windows 95 functionality, such as shortcuts to the desktop and briefcase replication to keep multiple copies of the database synchronized. Database Wizard automatically builds tables, queries, forms, and reports. New filtering options in Microsoft Access can use Filter By Form to filter information utilizing the same forms used to view and enter data.

Features

Data Model   It supports a relational data model. Data formats supported: directly imports, exports, and links to Btrieve, 1 dBASE III Plus, dBASE IV, dBASE 5.0, Microsoft Excel 3.0 to 7.0, Microsoft FoxPro 2.x, Microsoft SQL Server, 2 SYBASE SQL Server, 2 Paradox 3.0 to 5.0, and ORACLE RDBMS version 7, ASCII text, and any

ODBC-compliant databases; import and export: Lotus 1-2-3 and Visual FoxPro 3.0.

Managing and locating information: Intelligent tables—You can start a new table easily. Just start typing data as you would into a worksheet in Microsoft Excel. Intelligent tables identify the type of data entered and format new text as you type.

Import Wizard: You can start with your existing data in another database or spreadsheet. The Wizard steps you through the process of converting these data into native Microsoft Access format.

Table Analyzer Wizard: Use an existing flat-file list or spreadsheet and quickly transform these data into a powerful relational database in Microsoft Access.

Filter By Selection/Filter By Form: Once your data are stored in Microsoft Access, get answers with a mouse click with Filter By Selection.

Improved Form and Report Wizards: Regardless of the underlying tables or queries, you can create the exact view you require. After selecting the relevant data, choose from one of the suggested layouts for professional-quality forms and reports.

Multipage Print Preview: View several preview pages at once. You decide how many pages as well as how the pages are organized.

Answer Wizard: To get help, just type in a question, and the Answer Wizard gives you the information you need.

Breath new life into your data. Run an existing list, spreadsheet, or database through the Table Analyzer Wizard to transform it into linked Microsoft Access tables for more flexibility.

Share information with other applications: PivotTable Wizard—Use the analytical capabilities of Microsoft Excel pivot tables directly from within Microsoft Access to add new dimensions to data.

Microsoft Word Mail Merge Wizard: Automatically make mail merges.

Office Family Member: Use familiar tools and technology shared across the Microsoft Office family, such as AutoCorrect, spelling checker, and Format Painter. In addition, File Open, File New, and File Find menus based on the Windows 95 Explorer allow file management.

OfficeLinks with OLE: With this you can add spreadsheets from Microsoft Excel and documents from Word.

Data Manipulation Rushmore Technology makes query performance faster. Autoform and Autoreport let you create data entry forms with a single click of the mouse; Quick Sort speeds and simplifies data sorting; Form Wizard and Report Wizard help to create forms and reports; subqueries and SQL passthrough; transaction support.

Database engine capabilities include input masks, required field support, engine-level validation rules, referential integrity, cascading updates and deletes, group- and user-level security.

Tools   Microsoft Access has a full-featured development environment with an integrated debugger and the event-driven Access BASIC programming language. Referential integrity with cascading updates and deletes helps to manage integrity of the data. Engine-level validation helps guarantee the integrity of the data. Menu Builder gives graphical tools to build menus without writing code. Expression Builder simplifies creating expressions and calculations.

19.2.3 Sybase

Sybase offers a wide range of relational database products, such as relational database servers, client/server architectures, database design and operational tools, database management products, intermedia products, and packaged solutions.

Sybase's SQL server system is the backbone of their relational database products. This product supports the full ANSI/ISO SQL-89, FIPS 127-1; entry-level ANSI/ISO SQL-92; and C2 targeted full X/Open X/A distributed transaction support. Through adherence to these standards, Sybase's client/server back end can interoperably support user applications that are compliant with any of these standards. The main product within the Sybase server is a relational database management system. The Sybase SQL RDBMS runs on a variety of platforms from personal computers to minicomputers and workstations, to large multiprocessing systems that can support thousands of users.

The Sybase relational database management system and the SQL server support on-line backup and recovery, two-phase commit, referential and base type integrity management, and interface with any X/A-compliant transaction processing monitor. The Sybase server presently is configured to run on over 20 platforms that support a variety of infrastructure support services. The product supports up to 32,767 databases per physical server, with each database requiring a minimum of 48 Kbytes per user excluding database storage requirements. Each database theoretically can support two billion relational tables per database, 250 columns per relational table, 251 indexes per relation, and up to 30 characters per database item field name. The number of rows (tuples) in the database is limited only by the available disk space. Basic standard specified data types are supported.

Sybase additionaly supports products as follows:

- A replication server, which supports replicated databases that are geographically distributed.

- An enterprise client/server architecture, which supports distributed clients and multiple centralized servers that can be integrated into a unified database sytstem.

- A navigation server, which is a product that integrates a variety of Sybase servers into a singular powerful distributed query engine to support high throughput for large complex database management systems application requirements.

- A secure SQL server, which guarantees secure management of databases under this product's control.

- An OPEN client/open server architecture, which provides a call-level interface to the Sybase servers allowing heterogeneous access to Sybase databases.

This description is only a brief introduction to the numerous products provided by Sybase that support the relational database model and applications that are built upon this database. Further details on these and other products can be acquired from Sybase by sending them e-mail at webmaster@sybase.com or contacting the company directly.

19.3 OBJECT-ORIENTED DATABASE PRODUCTS

19.3.1 Borland

Company Overview   Borland is a provider of products and services targeted to software developers. Borland is known for its software development products such as Delphi, Borland C++, Paradox, dBASE, Borland Database Engine, and Interbase.

Visual dBASE 5.5 is a second-generation object-oriented xBASE product. It is based on Visual tools and a flexible programming language. A significant addition to Visual dBASE 5.5 is the Visual inheritance. This is the ability to visually create libraries of custom forms and controls that can be reused throughout a developer's application.

Delphi client/server, in addition to the native code compiler and Visual two-way tools, includes high-performance native drivers for development and deployment on remote servers; team development support for checking, checkout, and version management; Visual Query Builder for visually designing complex queries; Visual component library source code to more than 75 prebuilt objects; Reportsmith SQL edition for queries and reports on remote servers; and a local Interbase server deployment kit for stand-alone applications.

Paradox 5.0 for Windows delivers database users query speed, reporting speed, ease of use, superior integration with other applications, and a smooth transition to Windows 95. The graphical environment, independent debugger, data modeling tool, and over 200 new ObjectPAL commands help developers create new applications. Also, Paradox's object-oriented design allows code reusability.

Borland Database Engine 2.0 for Windows is an object-oriented database with features such as open, complete and transparent data access, native access to PC and SQL data, transparent connection to ODBC data sources, access to Paradox and dBASE, and it is designed for a heterogeneous environment.

dBASE 5.0 for Windows is an object-oriented database. It supports facilities to manage data and build database applications for Windows. The features of this product are described below.

Features

Data Model dBASE 5.0 is an object relational data model, which includes inheritance, encapsulation, and polymorphism. It supports predefined classes and new class creation, as well as user-defined data types. The binary field type enables storage of complex data types, including sound, graphics, and multimedia in database tables; and an OLE field stores OLE objects from other Windows applications inside dBASE applications. It employs automatic record and file locking and screen refresh. Event-driven transaction processing ensures data integrity, enabling users to roll back entire blocks of transactions at any time.

The following data types are supported.

Character: up to 32K characters per memory variable

Numeric: up to 20 digits

Float: up to 20 digits (19 significant)

Date, Logical

Memo, binary, OLE fields limited only to memory and storage capacity

Read and write Paradox data format

Read and write SQL data

It permits design of dBASE, Paradox, or SQL tables; set indexes; display, add, change, or delete data in browse; and form or columnar layout.

Data Manipulation

SpeedFilter technology for fastest results

Query dBASE, Paradox, and SQL data at once

Editable views

Select and order fields with mouse

Link tables visually

Include complex conditions and calculate fields

The dBASE language supports event-driven programs. The object model includes inheritance, encapsulation, polymorphism, support for OLE and DDE, support for VBX v1.0 controls, direct access to DLLs, and Windows API calls. It is extensible with C, C++, or Pascal, and supports multimedia applications, remote and local SQLEXEC() function, codeblocks and function pointers, local and static variables, multidimensional arrays, sparse arrays, arrays as objects, array functions, constraint and integrity relations, cascading deletes, and parameter passing.

Concurrency and Recovery   AUTO SAVE writes to disk automatically and provides data validation. It supports automatic file and record locking, automatic retry when record/file is locked, indication of which users have locks, change detection and screen refresh, and transaction processing with rollback.

Tools

Interface components: SpeedBars and SpeedMenus for quick access to common tasks

dBASE Navigator: view and access tables, queries, forms, reports, labels, programs, images, and sounds, launch designers from within Navigator

Catalog Manager: organize related files by dragging and dropping into separate catalogs, see relations visually

Modify any object with Object Inspector

Application development tools: two-way tools for queries, forms, and menus generate object-oriented source code; Form Designer; Crystal Reports for dBASE; debugger; powerful Expression Builder; built-in, C-style preprocessor and test coverage analysis

19.3.2 O2 Technology

Company and Product Information   O2 is an object database management system useful for developing large-scale client/server applications. It is a platform designed to meet business and technical application needs. It is suitable for software engineering, CAD/CAM, telecommunication, technical data management, and geographical information systems (GIS), as well as for financial, banking, and insurance applications. A brief description of the O2 system and its features is given in the following paragraphs.

O2 Engine is an object database engine combining all the standard database features with all the features of an object-oriented data model. O2 Engine manages complex and multimedia within a client/server architecture.

O2 Web provides a set of tools to develop a World Wide Web (WWW) server based on the O2 system.

Introduction   O2 is an object database system that complies with the Object Data Management Group (ODMG) standard. It has a development environment that includes a set of user interface tools. The O2 architecture follows the ODMG architecture. The functional architecture of the system is shown in Figure 19.1.

O2 Engine is the main part of the system. O2 Engine is built on top of the O2 store, a transactional file management system. O2 store is an independent module that builds persistence and database services

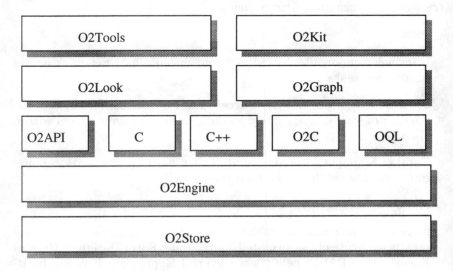

Figure 19.1   O2 functional architecture

for the software system. O2 store can be used directly through an application programming interface that supports the following features: collection of structured data and long record items, persistent records, client/server in page mode, data distribution, index management for collection, transaction, warm and cold recovery, administration, and security.

On top of O2 store, O2 Engine implements a full database management system with an ODMG-compliant object data model. O2 Engine can be used directly through an application programming interface that provides support for the ODMG object model, storage management and execution of methods, management of persistent and temporary objects, client/server both in page mode and object mode, version management, and schema management (support, evolution, and runtime updates).

Application developers can use O2 Engine through various language interfaces, such as a C++ seamless interface, a C interface, the ODMG OQL query language, an object fourth-generation language (4GL), and O2C. O2 Engine also has user interface tools such as O2Look and O2Graph.

Basic Features

Data Model O2 Engine supports the standard ODMG object data model. The basic types supported can be defined as being atomic—Boolean, string, character, integer, real, and bits—while the complex types can be defined as tuple, list, and set constructors. A list is an ordered collection whose elements are accessible by an index. A set is an unordered collection, and the constraint "unique" prevents duplicate elements in the collection.

O2 Engine can distinguish between "objects," which have an identity, and "values." The objects are considered as instances of classes and values are instances of types. The objects and values are physically represented in terms of O2 store records. A class is defined by its types and methods.

```
class City
    type tuple(name: string,
        map: Bitmap,
        hotels: set(Hotel))

    method how_many_vacancies(star: integer): integer,
        build_new_hotel(h: Hotel)
end;
```

```
class Hotel
    type tuple(name: string,
        read stars: integer,
        read free_rooms: integer)

    method reserve_room: boolean,
        check_out
end;
```

O2 provides encapsulation at three levels: class, schema, and database.

The method search in the O2 Engine is carried out at run time (late binding). Simple and multiple inheritance are supported in the O2 Engine: A new class can inherit, refine, or redefine the properties of one or more existing classes. You can execute methods in the O2 Engine even if the classes are not completely defined. Data definitions in the O2 Engine are grouped into logical entities called schemata. The data definitions from one schema can be imported into another, which in turn permits the creation of reusable libraries of classes.

Persistence Clustering and Schema Management   Persistence status of an object can be declared at creation time and persistence is an immutable property of the object. A transit object cannot become persistent. To enforce data integrity, it offers persistence by reachability; that is, when an object or value becomes persistent, so do all its components. Any object or value can be made persistent via the reachability mechanism. Unreferenced objects are garbage collected automatically. Persistence maintains object identity and referential integrity. Temporary and persistent data are uniformly viewed by programs, making persistence totally transparent. Persistence and typing are orthogonal.

When an object becomes persistent, it is promoted to the persistent space as near as possible to its parent. The DBA can control the clustering strategy. Clusters can be preloaded at the beginning of each such session, thus increasing overall performance. O2 Engine can manage versions of objects. It enables users to create new versions by deriving from an existing one, delete existing versions, or merge two versions. The version manager of O2 is viewed as an O2 class named Version, belonging to a predefined system schema.

The O2 schema manager is responsible for the creation, retrieval, update, and deletion of classes, types, methods, functions, applications, and global names. A base contains persistent roots and hence is associated to a particular schema. Several bases can be created using the same schema. Data belonging to a base can be exported and accessed in another base. The set of schemata and bases of the O2 system can reside on one or more O2 volumes distributed over the network.

Data Manipulation   O2 Engine manipulates data of different sizes and structures: complex objects, small and large collections, text, image, sound, and so forth. It allows users to store, retrieve, and manipulate complex objects through various programming interfaces, such as C, C++, OQL query language, and the fourth-generation language O2C.

C++ Interface   The C++ interface allows users to implement persistence in any existing or new C++ applications. It permits code reuse by importing classes from different schemata.

O2 enhances the standard C++ environment by providing the following features.

- Persistent pointers, which allow memory pointers to persist in a database after the end of an application. A persistent pointer to a C++ class Person, for example, is denoted Ref<Person>2.

- Generic collections, which implement array, list, set, and bag C++ classes—for example, a set of Person is denoted Set<Ref<Person>>.

- Persistence roots, which are named objects or values to which a C++ object can be attached directly or tentatively—for example, an O2 name "people" of type set of Person, can be accessed through the C++ variable, s, by declaring

```
Set<Ref<Person>> s("people")
```

or by using the "lookup" method defined on the class Database.

- Database system support, including transactions, indexing, and tools such as OQL and O2Look.

- Object identity is guaranteed in C++.

- Referential integrity is guaranteed.

- O2 inheritance model is compatible with C++; multiple inheritance is fully supported.

- Automatic management of dynamic memory.

The OQL Object Query Language   The OQL is an SQL-like query language extended to deal with complex values, complex objects, and methods. A query allows usersto extract information from the database and compute a result. Instances of possible queries include the following.

- A named value

```
Canadian_Cities
```

This query gives as a result a set of objects of type set(City).

- An attribute of a named object

```
Montreal.what_to_see
```

This query gives as a result a set of values of type set (garden city).

- A structure of tuple

```
struct(number_of_hotels: count:(Montreal.hotels),
      vacancies: Montreal>how_many_vacancies(3))
```

This query gives as a result a tuple with two attributes of type integer. The second one is computed by calling a method on the named object "Montreal."

- A set

To select information from a collection according a predicate, one can use the ternary operator.

```
select information (x)
from x in collection
where predicate (x)
```

Concurrency Control   Concurrency control is designed to be used in a multiuser environment. O2 Engine manages the access to objects using serializability as the correctness criterion for a concurrent execution of transactions.

O2 Engine is implemented with a two-phase locking mechanism on pages and/or files. When the concurrency control is disabled, a gain in performance is obtained for applications running alone or for read-only applications.

Two programming modes are available: read-only mode in which no modification of the database is allowed (data can be simultaneously modified by other users) and transaction mode or protected mode in which full concurrency control is enforced.

Rollback and Recovery   O2   Engine   guarantees   data   reliability: Changes made during transaction can be globally validated or discarded using Commit or Abort commands.

O2 Engine has a rollback facility: Changes are logged so that it is possible to restore a consistent state after a failure.

O2 Engine also implements recovery protocols for both workstation and server process crashes and provides save and restore tools.

Interface Tools   The O2 interface tools O2Look and O2Graph support the display and manipulation of large, complex and multimedia objects on the screen. These tools provide the following services.

- They allow the programmer to create simply and quickly high-quality graphical user interfaces by means of "ready-made" object presentations on the screen.

- "Ready-made" presentations can be customized to match the requirements of specific applications—for example, colors, fonts, and layouts can be redefined.

19.4 OBJECT RELATIONAL DATABASE MANAGEMENT SYSTEMS PRODUCTS

19.4.1 UniSQL

Company and Product Information   UniSQL is a provider of Object Relational Database Management Systems (ORDBMS). The UniSQL Server is a client/server object relational database system that provides support for large and complex data types, as well as transparent integration of data from multivendor databases such as ORACLE and Sybase SQL Server. The UniSQL Server consists of two components: UniSQL/M DBMS is a UniSQL Server's unified object relational database engine. UniSQL/M Multidatabase is a UniSQL Server's transparent access to existing relational, object-oriented, and prerelational databases and file systems.

Applications of UniSQL include computerized patient records, document management and publishing, satellite support systems, network management, complex financial analysis and trading, engineering, geographic information systems, defense systems, manufacturing, e-mail record system, and insurance systems.

Introduction   UniSQL is a unified relational and object-oriented system that extends the relational model with core object-oriented concepts found in object-oriented programming language concepts, such as encapsulation of data, object identity, multiple inheritance, arbi-

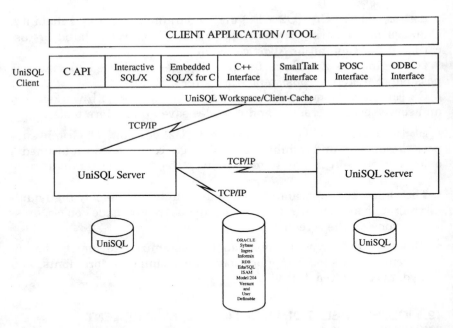

Figure 19.2   UniSQL architecture

trary data types, and nested objects. This OODB extends the ANSI SQL relational language and corresponding call-level interface to an object-oriented SQL and corresponding call-level interface. The OOPL interface layer underneath it is a persistent storage manager with full database features for the OOPL.

Figure 19.2 shows the UniSQL architecture. Application developers can access the UniSQL/X database via a call-level interface (UniSQL/X API), object-oriented SQL (SQL/X), UniSQL C++ interface, Microsoft Open Database Connectivity (ODBC) interface, the UniSQL family of graphical database interface tools (UniSQL/4GE), and the Oil and Gas exploration and production (E&P) Data Access Language.

UniSQL/X also has multimedia framework that provides a built-in class hierarchy of basic multimedia data types and operations. It also allows application developers to uniformly access unstructured multimedia data stored in the native UniSQL/X database and in operating system files.

Basic Features

Data Model   The UniSQL/X DBMS extends the relational model in three ways, reflecting object-oriented concepts. Hence the data model can be categorized as the object relational data model. The first extension reflects the basic concept of object-oriented systems—the value of an object is also an object—by allowing the value of a column of a tuple to be a tuple of any arbitrary user-defined table, rather than just an element of a system-defined data type number (number, string, etc.). Allowing a column of a table to hold a tuple of another table directly leads to nested tables. The second extension is the object-oriented concept of encapsulation: combining data and a program (procedure) to operate on the data. This is incorporated by allowing users to attach procedures to a table and have the procedures operate on the column values in each tuple. The third extension is the object-oriented concept of inheritance hierarchy. The UniSQL/X DBMS allows users to organize all tables in the database into a hierarchy such that between a pair of tables, P and C, P is made the parent of C, and C inherits all columns and procedures defined in P. The table hierarchy offers two advantages over the conventional relational model of a simple collection of largely independent tables. It allows the user to create a new table as a child table of one or more existing tables; the new table inherits all columns and procedures specified in the existing tables and their ancestor tables. It also makes it possible to enforce the ISA relationship between a pair of tables.

Relational terms are replaced by the object-oriented terms: "table" to "class," "tuple of a table" to "instance of a class," "column" to "attribute," "procedure" to "method," "table hierarchy" to "class hierarchy," "child table" to "subclass," and "parent table" to "superclass."

The UniSQL/X DBMS also extends a relational model; that is, it allows the row/column entry of a table to have a set of values rather than just a single value, and it also allows the set of values to be of more than one arbitrary data type. The restriction in the relational model stipulating that the row/column entry of a table can hold only a single value forces the users to create an extra table and/or duplicate tuples in one column of a table.

Data Manipulation UniSQL/X DBMS query language is a superset of ANSI SQL. If a set of classes is defined just as tables in conventional relational databases, the users of the UniSQL/X DBMS query language can issue all queries in ANSI SQL syntax, including joint and nested subqueries, queries that group and order the results, and queries against views. An example of queries on classes Person and Employee follows.

```
SELECT Job, Avg (Salary)
FROM Employee
```

```
WHERE  Salary > 50000 AND
       Age > 30
GROUP BY   Job;


SELECT Employee.Name
FROM Employee
WHERE Employee.Salary >
Employee.Manager.Salary;
```

The UniSQL/X DBMS query language also allows the formulation of four major additional types of queries. It allows path queries (queries against nested classes), queries that include methods as part of search conditions, queries against a set of classes in the class hierarchy, and queries that manipulate members of a set from a set-valued attribute in a class.

An example of a path query that retrieves nested objects is "Find the names of all employees and their managers for those employees who earn more than 50000 and whose hobby is tennis." This query is evaluated against the nested objects defined by the classes Employee and Activity. The query is formulated by associating the predicate Name= 'tennis' with the class Activity and the predicate Salary > 50000 with the class Employee. The query returns all attributes of Employee from the nested Employee objects that satisfy the query conditions.

```
SELECT *
FROM Employee
WHERE Salary > 50000 AND
              Hobby.Name = 'Tennis';
```

An example of a query on a class hierarchy would be to retrieve instances from a class and all its subclasses. In the following query, the keyword ALL causes the query to be evaluated against the class person and its subclass Employee.

```
SELECT Name, SSN
FROM ALL Person
where Age > 50;
```

An example of a query that manipulates numbers of a set in a set-valued attribute would be to retrieve the name and number of hobbies of each employee whose salary is greater than 50000.

```
SELECT   Name, (SELECT
                 Count (Col)
                 FROM TABLE
                 (Hobby) AS
                 Temp (Col))
FROM Person
WHERE Salary > 50000;
```

The SQL2 derived-table subquery includes the SELECT constructs and a temporary table (named Temp) with a single attribute of the Person Class and computes the number of "tuples" in the "table."

Workspace Management The UniSQL/X DBMS provides workspace management facilities to automatically manage a large number of objects in memory. It automatically converts the storage format of objects between the database format and the memory format, converts the OIDs stored in objects to memory pointers when the objects are loaded from the database into memory, and maintains such objects in the workspace. These facilities are essential for making the objects persistent and for supporting the performance requirements in object navigation for application programs written in OOPLs.

Multimedia Management UniSQL/X DBMS provides all the requirements of the multimedia data management, such as the following.

1. The ability to represent arbitrary data types and specification of procedures that interact with arbitrary data sources.

2. The ability to update, query, insert, and delete multimedia data.

3. The ability to specify and execute abstract operations on multimedia data—for example, to play, fast forward, and rewind one-dimensional data as audio and text and to display, expand, and condense such two-dimensional data as a bit-mapped image.

4. The ability to deal with heterogeneous data sources in a uniform manner.

UniSQL/X DBMS can be summarized as follows. It supports full ANSI-compliant SQL query capabilities, including joins of multiple tables, nested subqueries, aggregation functions, and grouping and ordering of query results.

The object-oriented SQL supported in the UniSQL/X DBMS also includes additional facilities to query complex nested data and class hierarchies, and queries that include methods in search conditions.

UniSQL/X DBMS provides automatic optimization and processing of queries of arbitrary complexity.

It supports view definitions, and queries and updates through views. View definitions are extended to account for object-oriented concepts; in particular, a view definition can include methods, views can be organized in an inheritance hierarchy, and a view can be the domain of an attribute of a view.

The UniSQL/X DBMS provides all common access methods for expediting query processing, such as B+ tree indexes, extendible hashing, external sorting, and clustering.

It supports transaction management to guarantee the serializability consistency criterion that RDBs ensure.

The UniSQL/X DBMS provides automatic concurrency control using the two-phase locking protocol. It supports share and exclusive lock modes, granularity locking, and intention mode locks. It supports physical locking at the page level, and logical locking at the object level and class level. Further, it supports automatic upgrading of locks; that is, it automatically converts locks on individual objects of a class to a single lock on the class. It supports locking on both user data and system control data, such as system catalogs and index pages.

The UniSQL/X DBMS provides automatic recovery using the write-ahead logging protocol to ensure database consistency in the face of system crashes. It maintains a log of both before and after images of data when the data are updated. Further, it performs periodic checkpointing of updates, and flushes updated objects in the workspace to the database at the end of each transaction. It supports recovery from both soft crashes (crashes that leave the disk intact) and hard crashes (crashes that destroy the disk).

Dynamic schema evolution is supported. As with RDBs, the user can dynamically add a new class, add a new attribute to an existing class, drop an attribute from a class, and drop an existing class. Also, consistent with support of the object-oriented data models, the user can designate an existing class as a superclass of another existing class, remove this designation, add a new method to an existing class, and drop a method from an existing class.

The UniSQL/X DBMS supports triggers to allow the user to tailor automatic enforcement of database consistency or automatic execution of prespecified actions when prespecified events occur. The user can specify a triggering event, conditions to evaluate upon triggering, and actions to take.

Finally, the UniSQL/X DBMS allows the database administrator to tune the performance and resource use by adjusting system parameters. It makes available a large number of tunable system parameters, such as the fill factor in a data page, the triggering point for garbage collecting the workspace, and so forth.

Tools UniSQL also provides a toolset called UniSQL/4GE, which includes an application development tool called ObjectMaster, a database administration tool called the Visual Editor, and a reporting tool called MediaMaster.

UniSQL provides C, C++, and SmallTalk interfaces, in addition to ODBC and UniSQL's own extended SQL interface called SQL/X.

19.4.2 Illustra

Illustra, from Illustra Information Technologies Inc., is a database server that was developed for advanced applications requiring support for alphanumeric, character, text, video, images, and documents within a single database management system. The fundamental concept in Illustra is to embed object-oriented data specifications and manipulation capabilities within the well-founded structure of the relational data model. The goal is to expand the data types of the relational database system through the integration of abstract data types within the product, and to improve the query capability of object-oriented databases through the use of the relational model's advanced query capabilities.

Illustra supports the relational database's flexible and powerful access through the standard SQL data manipulation language, limits the access to data within the database using standard security controls, supports full server-enforced data integrity, and supports the standard concept of transactions by managing their execution and recovery.

Illustra extends the fundamental features of the relational database model by incorporating features of the object-oriented database model. Illustra provides the ability to create any user-definable abstract data type. The products provide extended optimized access to the user-defined extended data types. Through the incorporation of object-oriented concepts database designers are provided with encapsulation, inheritance, and polymorphisim—all desirable facilities for developing nontraditional database management systems. Added performance enhancement comes through direct accessing of objects using object identifier pointers. In addition to these aspects of object-oriented and relational database models, Illustra also offers an event scheduling and notification system to allow for the construction of active database services based on the interpretation of events within the database.

Illustra offers an additional service that extends client data types into the server, allowing for further access optimization. These extensions place defined objects into libraries, which are then available for use by any client within the system. These are similar to the multimedia data libraries being developed under the SQL3 multimedia working group.

Further tools for application developers are provided as add-ons to the Illustra database system and product line. Illustra suppports both 3GL and 4GL environments. C, C++, and industry standard SQL are supported, as well as Visual BASIC and ODBC (open database connectivity) under Microsoft environments.

19.5 SUMMARY

In this chapter we attempted to provide an overview of several database products for each of the major database models presented in this text. We have not, however, provided specific examples of database products for each of the specialized database management systems described. Unfortunately, due to space limitations, the described systems have been covered only in a cursory manner. For more details the interested reader should contact the vendors and request further information on specific products, tools, or extensions.

Bibliography

Abbott, R., and H. Garcia-Molina. "Scheduling Real-Time Transactions." In *Proceedings of the ACM SIGMOD*, March 1988.

Agrawal, D. "Optimistic Concurrency Control Algorithms for Distributed Database Systems." Ph.D. Thesis, State University of New York at Stony Brook, 1987.

Agrawal, D., J. Bruno, A. E. Abbadi, and V. Krishnaswamy. "Relative Serializability: An Approach for Relaxing the Atomicity of Transactions." In *Proceedings of the 13th Symposium on Principles of Database Systems*, 1994, pp. 139–149.

Aksit, M., J. Bosch, W. Van der Sterren, and L. Bergmans. "Real-Time Specification Inheritance Anomalies and Real-Time Filters." In *Proceedings of the European Conference on Object-Oriented Programming*, 1994.

Albert, S., V. A. Ashby, and S. E. Hicks. "Reference Model for Data Management, Security, and Privacy." *ACM SIGMOD Security, Audit, and Control Review*, vol. 10, no. 2–3, Spring/Summer 1992.

Allcin, J., and M. McKendry. "Synchronization and Recovery of Actions." In *Proceedings of the 2nd Annual ACM Symposium on Principles of Distributed Computing*, August 1983.

Ammann, P., F. Jaeckle, and S. Jajodia. "A Two-Snapshot Algorithm for Concurrency Control in Multilevel Secure Databases," In *Proceedings of the 13th IEEE Symposium on Security and Privacy*, Oakland, CA, May 1992, pp. 204–215.

ANSI. "Portable Operating Systems Interface Standard." Technical Report. Washington, DC: ANSI, September 1993.

Aswatnarayan, R. "Performance Analysis of Concurrency Control Algorithms in Distributed Database Systems." Ph.D. Thesis, Drexel University, 1988.

Badrinath, B., and K. Ramamritham. "Semantics-Based Concurrency Control: Beyond Commutativity." *ACM Transactions on Database Systems*, vol. 17, March 1992, pp. 163–199.

———. "Synchronizing Transactions on Objects." *IEEE Transactions on Computers*, vol. 37, May 1988, pp. 541–547.

Baer, J. L. *Computer Systems Architecture*. Rockville, MD: Computer Science Press, 1980.

Bancilhon, F., C. Delobel, and P. Kanellakis. *Building an Object-Oriented Database System: The Story of O2*. San Mateo, CA: Morgan Kaufmann, 1992.

Baralis, E., and J. Widom. "An Algebraic Approach to Rule Analysis in Expert Database Systems." In *Proceedings of the 20th International Conference on Very Large Databases*. San Mateo, CA: Morgan Kaufmann, 1994.

Batini, C., S. Ceri, and S. Navathe. *Conceptual Database Design*. Redwood, CA: Benjamin-Cummings, 1992.

Bell, C., and A. Newell. *Computer Structures: Readings and Examples*. New York: McGraw-Hill, 1971.

Bell, D. E., and L. J. LaPadula. "Secure Computer Systems: Unified Exposition and Multics Interpretation." The Mitre Corp., March 1976.

Bernstein, P. A., V. Hadzilacos, and N. Goodman. *Concurrency Control and Recovery in Database Systems*. Reading, MA: Addison-Wesley, 1986.

Berra, B. et al. *IEEE Transactions on Knowledge and Data Engineering*. August 1993.

Bertino, E., and L. Martino. *Object-Oriented Database Systems: Concepts and Architectures*. Reading, MA: Addison-Wesley, 1993.

Bestavros, A. "Timeliness via Speculation for Real-Time Databases." In *Proceedings of the IEEE Real-Time Systems Symposium*, December 1994.

Biliris, A., S. Dar, N. Gehani, H. Jagadish, and K. Ramamrithham. "Asset: A System for Supporting Extended Transactions." In *Proceedings of the ACM SIGMOD*, March 1994.

Binns, L. "Inference through Secondary Path Analysis." In *Proceedings of the 6th IFIP Working Conference on Database Security*, Vancouver, British Columbia, August 1992.

Birman, K. "Implementing Fault-Tolerant Distributed Objects." *IEEE Transactions on Software Engineering*, vol. 11, June 1985.

Biyabani, S. "The Integration of Deadline and Criticalness in Hard Real-Time Scheduling." Master's Thesis, University of Massachusetts, 1988.

Blaustein, B. T., S. Jajodia, C. D. McCollum, and L. Notargiacomo. "A Model of Atomicity for Multilevel Transactions." In *Proceedings of the 14th IEEE Symposium on Security and Privacy*, Oakland, CA, May 1993, pp. 120–134.

Booch, G. "Object-Oriented Technology and Industrial-Strength Software Development." *Computer Science Syllabus*, vol. January/February, no. 5, 1993.

Brewer, D., and M. J. Nash. "The Chinese Wall Security Policy." In *Proceedings of the 11th IEEE Symposium on Security and Privacy*, Oakland, CA, April 1990, pp. 206–214.

Buchmann, A. et al. "Time-Critical Database Scheduling: A Framework for Integrating Real-Time Scheduling and Concurrency Control." In *Proceedings of the 5th IEEE Data Engineering Conference*, February 1989.

Bultzingsloewen, G., K. Dittrich, C. Iochpe, R. Liedtke, P. Lockemann, and M. Schryro. "Kardamon—A Dataflow Database Machine for Real-Time Application." *ACM SIGMOD Record* 17(1), March 1988.

Bundell, G., and G. Trivett. "Real, Real-Time Transactions." *Bulletin of the IEEE Technical Committee on Data Engineering* 17(1), March 1994.

Burns, A., and A. Wellings. *Real-Time Systems and Their Programming Languages*. Reading, MA: Addison-Wesley, 1990.

Burns, R. "A Conceptual Model for Multilevel Database Design." Paper presented at the *5th Rome Laboratory Database Security Workshop*, Fredonia, NY, October 1992.

Carey, M., M. Franklin, and M. Zaharioudakis. "Fine-Grained Sharing in a Page/Server OODBMS." In *Proceedings of the ACM SIGMOD International Conference on Management of Data. ACM SIGMOD Record*, vol. 23, no. 2, June 1994.

Cattell, R., ed. *The Object Database Standard: ODMG-93, Release 1.1.* San Mateo, CA: Morgan Kaufmann, 1994.

Chen, P. "The Entity-Relationship Model: Toward a Unified View of Data." *ACM TODS (Transactions on Database Systems)*, vol. 1, no. 1, March 1976, pp. 280–290.

Cingiser, L., L. C. DiPippo, and V. F. Wolfe. "Object-Based Semantic Real-Time Concurrency Control." In *Proceedings of the 14th Real-Time Systems Symposium*, December 1993.

Cingiser, L., P. Fortier, and J. Peckham. "What Is a Database?" In *Database Management System Interface Standards Working Group (DISWG)*, Ft. Lauderdale, FL, August 1993.

Clark, D. D., and D. R. Wilson. "A Comparison of Commercial and Military Computer Security Policies." In *Proceedings of the 8th IEEE Symposium on Security and Privacy*, Oakland, CA, April 1987, pp. 184–194.

CODASYL Committee. "CODASYL: Report of the Data Description Language Committee." *Information Systems* 3, 1978, pp. 247–320.

CODASYL Task Group. "CODASYL: ACM Conference on Data Systems Languages." CODASYL Data Base Task Group (DBTG) Report. New York: 1971.

Codd, E. F. "A Relational Model of Data for Large Shared Data Banks." In *Readings in Database Systems*, 2d ed. San Mateo, CA: Morgan Kaufmann, 1994.

———. *The Relational Model for Database Management, Version 2.* Reading, MA: Addison-Wesley, 1990.

———. "Extending the Database Relational Model to Capture More Meaning." *ACM Transactions on Database Systems*, December 1979.

Cook, P., S. Son, and A. Weaver. "The Starlite Project: Phototyping Real-Time Software Operating Systems, Communications Networks, and Database Systems." University of Virginia Technical Report: May 1988.

Cornhill, D., and L. Sha. "Priority Inversion in Ada." *ACM Ada Letters*, 1987.

Date, C. *An Introduction to Database Systems*, 5th ed. Reading, MA: Addison-Wesley, 1990.

David, R., and S. H. Son. "A Secure Two Phase Locking Protocol." In *Proceedings of the 12th Symposium on Reliable Distributed Systems,* October 1993.

Dayal, U., B. Blaustein, A. Buchman, U. Chakrauarthy, M. Hsu, R. Ladin, D. McCarthy, A. Sosenthal, and S. Sarin. "The Hipac Project: Combining Active Databases and Timing Constraints." *ACM SIG-MOD Record* 17(1), March 1988.

Deitel, H. *An Introduction to Operating Systems.* Reading, MA: Addison-Wesley, 1984.

Delcambre, L., B. Lim, and S. Urban. "Object-Centered Constraints." In *Proceedings of the IEEE 7th International Conference on Data Engineering,* 1991.

Denning, D. E. "Commutative Filters for Reducing Inference Threats in Multilevel Database Systems." In *Proceedings of the 6th IEEE Symposium on Security and Privacy,* Oakland, CA, April 1985, pp. 134–146.

Denning, D. E., and S. G. Aid. "Checking Classification Constraints for Consistency and Completeness." In *Proceedings of the 8th IEEE Symposium on Security and Privacy,* Oakland, CA, April 1987, pp. 196–201.

Denning, D. E., S. G. Aid, M. Morgenstern, and P. G. Neumann. "Views for Multilevel Database Security." In *Proceedings of the 7th IEEE Symposium on Security and Privacy,* Oakland, CA, April 1986, pp. 156–172.

Denning, D. E., T. E. Lunt, R. R. Schell, M. Heckman, and W. Shocldey. "A Multilevel Relational Data Model." In *Proceedings of the 8th IEEE Symposium on Security and Privacy,* Oakland CA, April 1987, pp. 220–234.

Dewitt, D., P. Futtersack, D. Maier, and F. Velez. "A Study of Three Alternative Workstation/Server Architectures for Object-Oriented Database Systems." In *Proceedings of the 16th VLDB Conference,* Brisbane, Australia, August 1990.

Diaz, O., and P. Gray. "Semantic-Rich User-Defined Relationships as a Main Constructor." In *Object-Oriented Databases: Analysis, Design, and Construction.* Edited by R. Meersman, W. Kent, and S. Khosla. Amsterdam: North-Holland, 1991, pp. 207–224.

Dijkstra, E. W. *Cooperating Sequential Processes.* Eidenhoven, Netherlands: Technical University, 1965.

DiPippo, L. C. "Object-Based Semantic Real-Time Concurrency Control." Ph.D. Thesis, University of Rhode Island, 1995.

DiPippo, L. C., and V. F. Wolfe. "Object-Based Semantic Real-Time Concurrency Control with Bounded Imprecision." *IEEE Transactions on Knowledge and Data Engineering.* In press.

Doherty, M., J. Peckham, and V. F. Wolfe. "Implementing Relationships and Constraints in an Object-Oriented Database Using Monitors." *RIDS93*, 1993, pp. 347–363.

Downing, A., I. Greenberg, and T. F. Lunt. "Issues in Distributed Database Security." In *Proceedings of the 5th Aerospace Computer Security Conference*, December 1989.

Drew, P., and C. Pu. "Asynchronous Consistency Restoration under Epsilon Serializability." Technical Report OGI-CSE-93-004, Department of Computer Science and Engineering, Oregon Graduate Institute, 1993.

Eisenberg, A. "A Brief Description of the SQL3 Data Model." Redwood City, CA: Oracle Corporation, February 1995.

Elmagarmid, A. K., ed. *Database Transaction Models for Advanced Applications*. San Mateo, CA: Morgan Kaufmann, 1992.

Elmasri, R., and S. Navathe. *Fundamentals of Database Systems*. Redwood, CA: Benjamin-Cummings, 1989.

Eswaran, K., J. Gray, R. Lorie, and I. Traiger. "The Notion of Consistency and Predicate Lock in a Database System." *Communications of the ACM* 19(11), 1976.

Farrag, A. A., and M. T. Ozsu. "Using Semantic Knowledge of Transactions to Increase Concurrency." *ACM Transactions on Database Systems*, vol. 14, December 1989, pp. 503–525.

Fekete, A. "Topics in Distributed Algorithms." Ph.D. Thesis, Harvard University, 1987.

Finkelstein, C. *An Introduction to Information Engineering*. Reading, MA: Addison-Wesley, 1989.

Fisher, D., P. Fortier, D. Hughes, and M. Roarke. "Final Report of the DBSSG Predictable Real-Time Information Systems Task Group." DBSSG Document Number PRISTG-95-1, February 1995.

Fortier, P. "DBSSG, PRIS-TG: Database Management Systems Reference Model." PRISTG95-01, Feburary 1995.

————, ed. *Handbook of Local Area Networks.* New York: McGraw-Hill, 1994.

————. "Data Management Concepts for Real-Time C3 Systems." In *Proceedings of the Joint Navy IR and IED Symposium,* June 1994.

————. "Early Commit." D.Sc. Thesis, University of Massachusetts, Lowell, 1993.

————. "Real-Time Transaction Processing." In *Proceedings of the 3rd Annual Research and Development Information Exchange Conference,* April 1992.

————. "Applications-Specific Architecture: A Concept for Real-Time C3 Systems." In *Proceedings of the 1st Joint Navy IR and IED Symposium,* June 1989.

Fortier, P., D. Pitts, and T. Wilkes. "Experiences with Data Management in Real-Time C3 Systems." In *Proceedings of the SEDEMS II Conference,* April 1993.

Fortier, P., and J. Prichard. "Concepts for a Real-Time Structured Database Query Language (RT-SQL)." In *Proceedings of the IFIP/IFAC Workshop on Real-Time Programming,* June 1994.

Fortier, P., J. Prichard, and V. F. Wolfe. "SQL/RT: Real-Time Database Extensions to the SQL Standard." *Standards and Interface Journal.* In press.

————. "Flexible Real-Time SQL Transactions." In *Proceedings of the Real-Time Systems Symposium,* December 1994.

Fortier, P., and J. Rumbut. "Issues and Concepts for a Real-Time Database Management." In *Proceedings of the 1st International Conference on Electronics and Information Management,* August 1994.

Fortier, P., and G. Sawyer. "DISWG: A New Player in NGCR Open Systems Standards." *Computer Standards and Interfaces.* In press.

Fortier, P., and J. Sieg. "Simulation Analysis of Early Commit Concurrency Control Protocols." In *Proceedings of the SCS Annual Simulation Symposium,* April 1995.

————. "Recovery Protocols for Real-Time Database Management Systems." In *Proceedings of the International Conference on Information Management (ICIM94),* May 1994.

Gallagher, L. "Object SQL: Language Extensions for Object Data Management." In *Proceedings of the International Society for Mini- and Microcomputers, CIKM-92,* 1992.

Gallmestier, B., and C. Lanier. "Early Experience with POSIX 1003.4 and POSIX 1003.4a." In *Proceedings of the IEEE Real-Time Systems Symposium*, December 1991.

Garcia, O. D., and P. M. D. Gray. "Semantic-Rich User-Defined Relationship as a Main Constructor in Object-Oriented Databases." In *IFIP TC2 Conference on Database Semantics: Object-Oriented Databases*. Amsterdam: North-Holland, 1990, pp. 144–154.

Garcia-Molina, H. "Using Semantic Knowledge for Transaction Processing in a Distributed Database System." *ACM Transactions on Database Systems*, vol. 8, June 1983, pp. 186–213.

Garcia-Molina, H., D. Gawlick, J. Klein, K. Kleissner, and K. Salem. "Modeling Long-Running Activities as Nested Sagas." *Bulletin of the IEEE Technical Committee on Data Engineering* 14(1), March 1991.

Garvey, T. et al. "Toward a Tool to Detect and Eliminate Inference Problems." In *Proceedings of the 6th IFIP Working Conference on Database Security*, Vancouver, British Columbia, August 1992.

Gibbs, S., C. Breiteneder, and D. Tsichritzis. "Data Modeling of Time-Based Media." In *Proceedings of the ACM SIGMOD Conference. SIGMOD Record* 23(2), June 1994.

Goguen, J. A., and J. Meseguer. "Security Policy and Security Models." In *Proceedings of the 3rd IEEE Symposium on Security and Privacy*, April 1982, pp. 11–20.

Gordon, K. "DISWG Database Management Systems Requirements." NGCR SPAWAR 331 2B2, Alexandria, VA, 1993.

Graham, M. "Real-Time Data Management." *IEEE Technical Committee Real-Time Systems Newsletter* 9(1/2), Spring/Summer 1993.

Graubart, R. D. "The Integrity-Lock Approach to Secure Database Management." In *Proceedings of the 5th IEEE Symposium on Security and Privacy*, Oakland, CA, April 1984, pp. 62–74.

Graubart, R. D., and K. J. Duffy. "Design Overview for Retrofitting Integrity-Lock Architecture onto a Commercial DBMS." In *Proceedings of the 6th IEEE Symposium on Security and Privacy*, Oakland, CA, April 1985, pp. 147–159.

Graubart, R. D., and J. P. L. Woodward. "A Preliminary Naval Surveillance DBMS Security Model." In *Proceedings of the 3rd IEEE Symposium on Security and Privacy*, Oakland, CA, April 1982, pp. 21–37.

Gray, J., and A. Reuter. *Transaction Processing: Concepts and Techniques.* San Mateo, CA: Morgan Kaufmann, 1993.

Greenberg, I. "Distributed Database Security." Technical Report AO02, SRI International, April 1991.

Grohn, M. J. "A Model of a Protected Data Management System." I. P. Sharp Associates Ltd., Technical Report ESD-TR-76-289, June 1976.

Gupta, R. *Object-Oriented Databases with Applications to CASE, Networks, and VLSI CAD.* Englewood Cliffs, NJ: Prentice Hall, 1991.

Hamacher, V., Z. Vranesic, and S. Zaky. *Computer Organization,* 2d ed. New York: McGraw-Hill, 1984.

Haritsa, J. R., M. J. Carey, and M. Livny. "On Being Optimistic about Real-Time Constraints." In *Proceedings of the ACM PODS Symposium,* April 1990.

Haritsa, J. R., M. Livny, and M. J. Carey. "Earliest Deadline Scheduling for Real-Time Database Systems." In *Proceedings of the IEEE Real-Time Systems Symposium,* December 1990.

Hennessy, J., and D. Patterson. *Computer Architecture: A Quantitative Approach.* San Mateo, CA: Morgan Kaufmann, 1989.

Herlihy, M., and J. Wing. "Linearizability: A Correctness Condition for Concurrent Objects." *ACM Transactions on Programming Languages and Systems* 12(3), July 1990.

Hinke, T., and H. Delugach. "Aerie: An Inference Modeling and Detection Approach for Databases." In *Proceedings of the 6th IFIP Working Conference on Database Security,* Vancouver, British Columbia, August 1992.

Hinke, T. H., and M. Schaefer. "Secure Data Management Systems." System Development Corp., Technical Report RADC-TR-75-266, November 1975.

Honeywell Inc. "Lock Data Views." Technical Reports, 1989.

Hsiao, D. K. "Heterogeneous Database Systems." In *Handbook of Database Management Systems.* Edited by P. Fortier. New York: McGraw-Hill, 1996.

———. "Supercomputers Built with Microprocessors versus Supercomputers Built without Microprocessors." In vol. S of *Encyclopedia of Microcomputers.* New York: Marcel Dekker, 1995.

——. "Federated Databases and Systems: Part II—A Tutorial on Their Resource Consolidation." *International Journal on Very Large Data Bases*, vol. 1, no. 2, September 1992.

——. "Federated Databases and Systems: Part I—A Tutorial on Their Data Sharing." *International Journal on Very Large Data Bases*, vol. 1, no. 1, June 1992.

——. "Object-Oriented Database Management—A Tutorial on Its Fundamentals." In *Proceedings of the Second Far-East Workshop on Future Database Systems*, Kyoto University, April 1992.

——. "A Parallel, Scalable, Microprocessor-Based Database Computer for Performance Gains and Capacity Growth." *IEEE MICRO*, December 1991.

Hsiao, D. K., and M. N. Kamel. "Heterogeneous Databases: Proliferations, Issues, and Solutions." *IEEE Transactions on Knowledge and Data Engineering*, vol. 1, no. 1, March 1989.

Huang, J., and J. Stankovic. "On Using Priority Inheritance in Real-Time Databases." In *Proceedings of the IEEE Real-Time Systems Symposium*, December 1991.

Huang, J., J. Stankovic, D. Towsley, and K. Ramamritham. "Experimental Evaluation of Real-Time Transaction Processing." In *Proceedings of the IEEE Real-Time Systems Symposium*, December 1989.

Hughes, D. "ZIP-RTDBMS: A Real-Time Database Management System." Technical Report PRISTG-93-011, ANSI DBSSG PRIS-TG, San Diego, CA, 1994.

Hull, R., and R. King. "Semantic Database Modeling: Survey, Applications, and Research Issues." *ACM Computing Surveys*, vol. 19, no. 3, September 1987.

Hung, S., and K. Lam. "Locking Protocols for Concurrency Control in Real-Time Database Systems." *SIGMOD Record*, vol. 21, December 1992, pp. 22–27.

IEEE. *Portable Operating System Interface (POSIX)—Part 1: System API; Ammendment 1: Real-time Extension*. New York: IEEE, 1994.

IITA Task Group. "Information Infrastructure Technology and Applications." National Coordination Office for HPCC, Executive Office of the President, February 1994.

ISO/IEC. "RDA—Part 1: Generic Model, Service, and Protocol." Technical Report 9579-1, ISO/IEC, Washington, DC, 1993.

———. "RDA—Part 2: SQL Specification." Technical Report 9579-2, ISO/IEC, Washington, DC, 1993.

Jaeger, U., and J. Freytag. "An Annotated Bibliography on Active Databases." *SIGMOD Record*, vol. 24, no. 1, March 1995.

Jagadish, H., D. Lieuwen, R. Rastogi, A. Silberschatz, and S. Sudarshan. "DALI: A High-Performance Main Memory Storage Manager." In *Proceedings of the 20th VLDB Conference*, Santiago, Chile, 1994.

Jajodia, S., and V. Atluri. "Alternative Correctness Criteria for Concurrent Execution of Transactions in Multilevel Secure Database Systems." In *Proceedings of the 13th IEEE Symposium on Research in Security and Privacy*, May 1992, pp. 216–224.

Jajodia, S., E. Bertino, and V. Atluri. "Achieving Stricter Correctness Requirements in Multilevel Secure Databases." In *Proceedings of the 14th IEEE Symposium on Research in Security and Privacy*, May 1993, pp. 135–147.

Jajodia, S., and B. Kogan. "Concurrency Control in Multilevel Secure Databases Based on a Replicated Architecture." In *Proceedings of the 11th IEEE Symposium on Security and Privacy*, Oakland, CA, April 1990, pp. 360–368.

———. "Integrating an Object-Oriented Model with Multilevel Security." In *Proceedings of the 11th IEEE Symposium on Security and Privacy*, Oakland, CA, April 1990, pp. 76–85.

Jajodia, S., and R. Sandhu. "A Novel Decomposition of Multilevel Relations into Single-Level Relations." In *Proceedings of the 12th IEEE Symposium on Security and Privacy*, Oakland, CA, April 1991, pp. 300–313.

———. "Polyinstantiation Integrity in Multilevel Relations." In *Proceedings of the 11th IEEE Symposium on Security and Privacy*, Oakland, CA, April 1990, pp. 104–115.

———. "Database Security: Current Status and Key Issues." *SIGMOD Record*, vol. 19, no. 4, December 1990, pp. 123–126.

Jajodia, S., R. Sandhu, and E. Sibley. "Update Semantics for Multilevel Relations." In *Proceedings of the 6th Computer Security Applications Conference*, Tucson, AZ, December 1990, pp. 103–112.

Jayant, M. J. C., R. Haritsa, and M. Livny. "Dynamic Optimistic Concurrency Control." In *Proceedings of the IEEE Real-Time Systems Symposium*, December 1990.

Jensen, C. D., R. M. Kiel, and R. D. Verjinski. "SDDM—A Prototype of a Distributed Architecture for Database Security." In *Proceedings of the 5th International Conference on Data Engineering*, Los Angeles, CA, 1989, pp. 356–364.

Keefe, T. E., and W. T. Tsai. "Multiversion Concurrency Control for Multilevel Secure Database Systems." In *Proceedings of the 11th IEEE Symposium on Security and Privacy*, Oakland, CA, April 1990, pp. 369–383.

Keefe, T. E., W. T. Tsal, and J. Srivastava. "Multilevel Secure Database Concurrency Control." In *Proceedings of the 6th International Conference on Data Engineering*, Los Angeles, CA, February 1990, pp. 337–344.

Keefe, T. E., W. T. Tsai, and B. Thuraisingham. "A Multilevel Security Policy for Object-Oriented Systems." In *Proceedings of the 11th National Security Conference*, Baltimore, MD, October 1988.

Kim, W. "UniSQL/X Unified Relational and Object-Oriented Database System." In *Proceedings of the ACM-SIGMOD International Conference on Management of Data*. *SIGMOD Record*, vol. 23, no. 2, June 1994.

————. "Observations on the ODMG-93 Proposal for an Object-Oriented Database Language." *SIGMOD Record* 23(1), March 1994.

Korth, H., E. Levy, and A. Silberschatz. "A Formal Approach to Recovery by Compensating Transactions." In *Proceedings of the 16th VLDB Conference*, 1990.

Korth, H., and A. Silberschatz. *Database Systems Concepts*, 2d. ed. New York: McGraw-Hill, 1991.

Kulkarni, K. "Object-Orientation and the SQL Standard." *Journal of Computer Standards and Interfaces*, vol. 15, 1993.

Kung, H., and J. Robinson. "On Optimistic Methods for Concurrency Control." *ACM Transactions on Database Systems* 6(2), 1981, pp. 213–226.

Kuo, T.-W., and A. K. Mok. "SSP: A Semantics-Based Protocol for Real-Time Data Access." In *Proceedings of the IEEE Real-Time Systems Symposium*, December 1993.

————. "Application Semantics and Concurrency Control of Real-Time Data-Intensive Applications." In *Proceedings of the Real-Time Systems Symposium*, December 1992.

Lampson, B. W. "A Note on the Confinement Problem." *Communications of the ACM*, vol. 16, no. 10, October 1973, pp. 613–615.

Lee, J., and S. H. Son. "Using Dynamic Adjustment of Serialization Order for Real-Time Database Systems." In *Proceedings of the IEEE Real-Time Systems Symposium*, December 1993.

Lehoczky, J., L. Sha, and J. Strosnider. "Enhancing Aperiodic Responsiveness in a Hard Real-Time Environment." In *Proceedings of the IEEE Real-Time Systems Symposium*, 1987.

Leu, P., and B. Bharat. "Multidriven Signal Timestamp Protocols for Concurrency Control." *IEEE Transactions on Software Engineering* SE-13(12), December 1987.

Lin, K., and M. Lin. "Enhancing Availability in Distributed Real-Time Database." *SIGMOD Record* 17(1), March 1988.

Lin, Y., and S. Son. "Concurrency Control in Real-Time Databases by Dynamic Adjustment of Serialization Order." In *Proceedings of the IEEE Real-Time Systems Symposium*, December 1990.

Liskov, B. "Overview of the Argus Language and System." Technical Report, Programming Methodology Group Memo 40, MIT, Cambridge, MA, February 1984.

Little, T., A. Ghafoor, C. Chang, and P. Berra. "Multimedia Synchronization." *Bulletin of the IEEE Technical Committee on Data Engineering* 14(3), September 1991.

Liu, C. L., and J. W. Layland. "Scheduling Algorithms for Multiprogramming in a Hard-Real-Time Environment." *Journal of the ACM*, vol. 20, 1973, pp. 46–61.

Liu, J., K. Lin, W. Shih, A. Yu, J. Chung, and W. Zhao. "Algorithms for Scheduling Imprecise Computation." *IEEE Computer*, vol. 24, May 1991.

Locke, C. "Best Effort Decision Making for Real-Time Scheduling." Ph.D. Thesis, Carnegie Mellon University, Pittsburg, PA, May 1986.

Loomis, M. "Client/Server Architecture." *Journal of Object-Oriented Programming* 4(9), February 1992.

Lunt, T. E. "Multilevel Security for Object-oriented Database Systems." In *Proceedings of the 3rd IFIP Workshop on Database Security*, Monterey, CA, 1990, pp. 199–209.

————. "Aggregation and Inference: Facts and Fallacies." In *Proceedings of the 10th IEEE Symposium on Security and Privacy*, Oakland, CA, April 1989, pp. 102–109.

Lunt, T. E., D. E. Denning, R. R. Schell, M. Heckman, and W. R. Shocldey. "The SeaView Security Model." *IEEE Transactions on Software Engineering*, vol. 16, no. 6, June 1990, pp. 593–607.

Lunt, T. E., and E. B. Fernandez. "Database Security." *SIGMOD Record*, vol. 19, no. 4, December 1990, pp. 90–97.

Lynch, N. A. "Multilevel Concurrency—A New Correctness Criterion for Database Concurrency Control." *ACM Transactions on Database Systems*, vol. 8, December 1983, pp. 484–502.

Manola, F., and G. Mitchell. "A Comparison of Candidate Object Models for Object Query Services." Technical Paper, ANSI X3H7-94-32v1, Waltham, MA, 1994.

Marks, D. "Inference Problem in MLS Database Systems." In *Proceedings of the 6th Rome Laboratory Workshop*, Maine, June 1994.

Marks, D., L. Binns, and B. Thuraisingham. "Hypersemantic Data Modeling for the Inference Analysis." In *Proceedings of the 8th IFIP Working Conference on Database Security*, Hildesheim, Germany, August 1994.

Material Data Management Centre. *COBOL: Journal of Development*. Quebec: Material Data Management Centre, 1968.

McCarthy, D. R., and U. Dayal. "The Architecture of an Active Database Management System." In *Proceedings of the 1989 ACM SIGMOD International Conference on the Management of Data. SIGMOD Record* 18(2), June 1989, pp. 215–224.

McKellar, B., and J. Peckham. "Representing Design Objects in SORAC: A Data Model with Semantic Objects, Relationships, and Constraints." In *Proceedings of the 2nd International Conference on Artificial Intelligence and Design*, June 1991.

Melton, J. "Accommodating SQL3 and ODMG." X3H2-95-161, American National Standards Institute, Technical Committee X3H2 Database, April 1995.

————, ed. "ISO-ANSI Working Draft: Call-Level Interface (SQL/CLI)." X3H2-95-085, American National Standards Institute, Technical Committee X3H2 Database, March 1995.

————, ed. "ISO-ANSI Working Draft: Database Language (SQL3)." X3H2-95-084, American National Standards Institute, Technical Committee X3H2 Database, March 1995.

————, ed. "ISO-ANSI Working Draft: Framework for SQL (SQL/Framework)." X3H2-95-083, American National Standards Institute, Technical Committee X3H2 Database, March 1995.

————, ed. "ISO-ANSI Working Draft: Persistent Stored Modules (SQL/PSM)." X3H2-95-086, American National Standards Institute, Technical Committee X3H2 Database, March 1995.

————, ed. "ISO-ANSI Working Draft: SQL Global Transactions Interface (SQL/Transaction)." X3H2-95-088, American National Standards Institute, Technical Committee X3H2 Database, March 1995.

————, ed. "ISO-ANSI Working Draft: SQL Host Language Bindings (SQL/Bindings)." X3H2-95-087, American National Standards Institute, Technical Committee X3H2 Database, March 1995.

————. "Accommodating SQL3 and ODMG." Technical Report ISO X3H2, ANSI X3H2, Salt Lake City, UT, September 1994.

Melton, J., and A. Simon. *Understanding the New SQL: A Complete Guide*. San Mateo, CA: Morgan Kauffman, 1992.

Mili, A. "Towards a Theory of Forward Error Recovery." *IEEE Transactions on Software Engineering* SE-11(8), August 1985.

Minet, P., and S. Sedillot. *Integration of Real-Time and Consistency Constraints in Distributed Databases: The SIGMA Approach*. New York: Elsevier Science Publishers, 1987.

Mitre Corporation. "OMG Request for Comment Submission: IDL => ADA Language Mapping Specification." OMG Document Number 95-5-16, June 1995.

Mohan, C., and I. Narang. "Aries/CSA: A Method for Database Recovery in Client/Server Architectures." In *Proceedings of the ACM SIGMOD Conference. SIGMOD Record* 23(2), June 1994.

Moniz, D., and P. Fortier. "Simulation Analysis of Real-Time Database Buffer Management." In *Proceedings of the SCS Multiconference*, April 1996.

Moore, M. *Low-Level Language Constructs for Predictable Databases*. Syracuse, NY: Softec, 1994.

Morgenstern, M. "Security and Inference in Multilevel Database and Knowledge Base Systems." In *Proceedings of the ACM SIGMOD Conference*, San Francisco, CA, May 1987.

Moss, J. "Nested Transactions: An Approach to Reliable Distributed Computing." Ph.D. Thesis, Massachusetts Institute of Technology, Cambridge, MA, 1981.

Nakazato, H. "Issues on Synchronizing and Scheduling Tasks in Real-Time Database Systems." Ph.D. Thesis, University of Illinois at Urbana-Champaign, 1993.

Nijssen, S., and D. Halpin. *Conceptual Schema and Relational Database Design*. Englewood Cliffs, NJ: Prentice Hall, 1989.

OMG. "CORBA Services Common Object Services Specification." OMG Document Number 95-3-31, March 1995.

O'Neil, P. *Database Principles, Programming, and Performance*. San Mateo, CA: Morgan Kaufmann, 1995.

Ozsoyoglu, G., and R. Snodgrass. "Temporal and Real-Time Databases: A Survey." *IEEE Transactions on Knowledge and Data Engineering*, vol. 7, no. 4, August 1995.

Ozsu, T., and P. Valduriez. *Principles of Distributed Database Systems*. Englewood Cliffs, NJ: Prentice Hall, 1991.

Pang, H., M. Livny, and M. Carey. "Transaction Scheduling in Multiclass Real-Time Database Systems." In *Proceedings of the IEEE Real-Time Systems Symposium*, December 1992.

Papadimitriou, C. "Serialization of Concurrent Updates." *Journal of ACM*, October 1979, pp. 631–653.

Peckham, J., and P. Fortier. "Operating Systems Support for Next-Generation Database Management Systems." NGCR-DISWG-94-11, June 1994.

Peckham, J., and F. Maryanski. "Semantic Data Models." *Computing Surveys* 20(3), September 1988.

Peckham, J., F. Maryanski, and S. Demurjian. "Towards the Correctness and Consistency of Update Semantics in Semantic Database Schema." *IEEE Transactions on Knowledge and Data Engineering*. In press.

Peterson, J. *Operating Systems Concepts*. Reading, MA: Addison-Wesley, 1983.

Pritchard, J. "ANSI SQL3 Condition Handling Change Proposal." X3H2, 95-163, March 1995.

Prichard, J., L. DiPippo, J. Peckham, and V. Wolfe. "RTSORAC: A Real-Time Object-Oriented Database Model." In *Proceedings of the 5th International Conference on Database and Expert Systems Applications*, September 1994.

Pritchard, J., V. Wolfe, and P. Fortier. "SQL/RT: Real-Time Database Extensions to the SQL2 Standard." *Journal of International Standards and Interfaces*, 1996.

Pu, C. "Relaxing the Limitations of Serializable Transactions in Distributed Systems." *Operating Systems Review* 27(2), April 1993, pp. 66–71.

Pu, C., and A. Left. "Epsilon-Serializability." Technical Report CUCS-054-90, Department of Computer Science, Columbia University, 1991.

Pu, C., W. Hseush, G. E. Kaiser, K.-L. Wu, and P. S. Yu. "Distributed Divergence Control for Epsilon Serializability." In *Proceedings of the 13th International Distributed Computing Conference*, June 1993.

Pugh, W., ed. *Proceedings of the ACM SIGPLAN Workshop on Language, Compiler, and Tool Support for Real-Time Systems. ACM SIGPLAN*, 1994.

Rajkumar, R. "Task Synchronization in Real-Time Systems." Ph.D. Thesis, Carnegie Mellon University, 1989.

Ramamritham, K. "Real-Time Databases." *International Journal of Distributed and Parallel Databases* 1(2), 1993.

———. "Real-Time Databases." *International Journal of Distributed and Parallel Databases*, vol. 1, no. 1, 1992.

Ramamritham, K., and E. Chrysanthis. "In Search of Acceptability Criteria: Database Consistency Requirements and Transaction Correctness Properties." Technical Report, 91-92, Computer Science Department, University of Massachusetts, December 1991.

Ramamritham, K., and C. Pu. "A Formal Characterization of Epsilon Serializability." *Transactions on Knowledge and Data Engineering*, 1993.

Rasikan, D., and S. H. Son. "A Secure Two-Phase Locking Protocol." In *Proceedings of the 12th Symposium on Reliable Distributed Systems*, October 1993.

Richey, J. "Condition Handling in SQL Persistent Stored Modules." *SIGMOD Record*, vol. 24, no. 3, September 1995.

Roarke, M. *EagleSpeed: A Real-Time Database Manager*. Syracuse, NY: Martin Marietta, 1995.

———. "RTDM: A Real-Time Database Management System." Technical Report PRISTG-93-012, X3 DBSSG PRIS-TG, San Diego, CA, 1993.

Rosen, S. "Electronic Computers: A Historical Survey." *ACM Computing Surveys* 1, 1969.

Rubinovitz, H., and B. Thuraisingham. "Design and Implementations of a Query Processor for a Trusted Distributed Database System." *Journal of Systems and Software*, April 1993.

Rumbaugh, J. "Relations as Semantic Constructs in Object-Oriented Language." In *Proceedings of the ACM OOPSLA*, October 1987.

Rumbaugh, J., M. Blaha, W. Premerlani, F. Eddy, and W. Lorensen. *Object Modeling and Design*. Englewood Cliffs, NJ: Prentice Hall, 1991.

Schwartz, P. M., and A. Z. Spector. "Synchronizing Shared Abstract Types." *ACM Transactions on Computer Systems*, vol. 2, 1984, pp. 223–250.

Senerchia, J. "A Dynamic Real-Time Scheduler for POSIX 1003.4a–Compliant Operating Systems." Master's Thesis, Computer Science Department, University of Rhode Island, 1993.

Sha, L. "Priority Inheritance Protocols—An Approach to Real-Time Synchronization." Technical Report CMU-CS-87-181, Carnegie Mellon University, Pittsburg, PA, Febuary 1987.

———. "Modular Concurrency Control and Failure Recovery—Consistency, Correctness, and Optimality." Ph.D. Thesis, Carnegie Mellon University, Pittsburg, PA, 1985.

Sha, L., E. Jensen, R. Rashid, and J. Northcutt. "Distributed Cooperating Processes and Transactions." In *Proceedings of the SIGComm Symposium*, August 1983.

Sha, L., J. Lehoczky, and E. D. Jensen. "Modular Concurrency Control and Failure Recovery." *IEEE Transactions on Computers* 37(2), 1988.

Sha, L., R. Rajkumar, and J. P. Lehoczky. "Concurrency Control for Distributed Real-Time Databases." *SIGMOD Record*, vol. 17, March 1988, pp. 82–98.

Sha, L., R. Rajkumar, S. Son, and C. Chang. "A Real-Time Locking Protocol." *IEEE Transactions on Computers* vol. 40, July 1991, pp. 793–800.

Sheth, A., and J. Larson. "Federated Database Systems." *ACM Computing Surveys*, September 1990.

Shin, K. "Introduction to the Special Issues on Real-Time Systems." *IEEE Transactions on Computers* C-36(8), August 1987.

Simovici, D., and R. Tenney. *Relational Database Systems*. New York: Academic Press, 1995.

Singhal, M. "Issues and Approaches to Design of Real-Time Database Systems." *SIGMOD Record* 17(1), March 1988.

Smith, G. W. "Modeling Security-Relevant Semantics." In *Proceedings of the 11th IEEE Symposium on Security and Privacy*, Oakland, CA, April 1990, pp. 384–391.

Snodgrass, R. "TSQL2 Language Specification." *ACM SIGMOD Record*, vol. 23, March 1994, pp. 65–86.

Son, S. H., ed. "Predictability and Consistency in Real-Time Database Systems." In *Advances in Real-Time Systems*. Englewood Cliffs, NJ: Prentice Hall, 1995, pp. 509–531.

———. "Real-Time Database Systems: A New Challenge." *IEEE Technical Committee on Data Engineering Quarterly Bulletin* 13(4), December 1990, pp. 51–57.

———. "Real-Time Database Systems: Issues and Approaches." *SIGMOD Record* 17(1), March 1988.

Son, S. H., and B. Thuraisingham. "Towards a Multilevel Secure Database Management System for Real-Time Applications." In *Proceedings of the IEEE Workshop on Real-Time Applications*, New York, May 1993.

Son, S., S. Yannopoulos, Y. Kim, and C. Iannacone. "Integration of a Database System with Real-Time Kernel for Time-Critical Applications." In *Proceedings of the International Conference on Systems Integration*, June 1992.

Spector, A. "Support for Distributed Transactions in Tabs Prototype." *IEEE Transactions on Software Engineering* SE-11, June 1985.

Stankovic, J. "Misconceptions about Real-Time Computing: A Serious Problem for Next-Generation Systems." *IEEE Computer*, vol. 21, October 1988.

———. *Real-Time Computing Systems: The Next Generation*. New York: IEEE Computer Society, February 1988.

Stankovic, J., and K. Ramaritham. "The Spring Kernel: A New Paradigm for Real-Time Operating Systems." *ACM Operating Systems Review*, vol. 23, July 1989, pp. 54–71.

Stankovic, J., and W. Zhao. "On Real-Time Transactions." *SIGMOD Record* 17(1), March 1988.

Stone, H. *Introduction to Computer Architecture*. New York: SRA Inc., 1980.

Stonebraker, M. *Readings in Database Systems*, 2d ed. San Mateo, CA: Morgan Kaufmann, 1994.

———. "Operating System Support for Database Management." *Communications of the ACM* 24(7), July 1981, pp. 412–418.

Stroustrup, B. *The C++ Programming Language*, 2d ed., Reading, MA: Addison-Wesley, 1991.

Tannenbaum, A. S. *Structured Computer Organization*. Englewood Cliffs, NJ: Prentice Hall, 1976.

Tansel, A., J. Clifford, S. Gadia, A. Segev, and R. Snodgrass. *Temporal Databases: Theory, Design, and Implementation*. Database Systems and Applications Series. Redwood City, CA: Benjamin-Cummings, 1994.

Teng-Amnuay, Y. "A Categorization Scheme for Concurrency Control Protocols in Distributed Databases." Ph.D. Thesis, Iowa State University, 1984.

Thomas, R. "A Solution to the Concurrency Control Problem for Multiple Copy Databases." In *Proceedings of the IEEE CompCon Conference*, New York, 1979.

Thuraisingham, B. "Multilevel Security for Information Retrieval Systems." *Information Management Journal*, January 1995.

———. "Current Status of R&D in Trusted Database Management Systems." *SIGMOD Record*, vol. 21, no. 3, September 1992, pp. 44–50.

――――. "The Use of Conceptual Structures for Handling the Inference Problem." In *Proceedings of the 5th IFIP Working Conference on Database Security*, Shepherdstown, VA, November 1991.

――――. "Recursions Theoretic Properties of the Inference Problem." Technical Report, MTP 291, The Mitre Corporation. Version presented at the 3rd Computer Security Foundations Workshop, Franconia, NH, June 1990.

――――. "Security Checking in Relational Database Systems Augmented with Inference Engines." *Computers and Security*, December 1987.

Thuralsingham, B., and W. Ford. "Security Constraint Processing in a Multilevel Secure Distributed Environment." MTR 1123, The Mitre Corporation, Bedford, MA, April 1992. Version published in *IEEE Transactons on Knowledge and Data Engineering*, April 1995.

Thuraisingham, B., W. Ford, M. Collins, and J. O'Keeffe. "Design and Implementation of a Database Inference Controller." *Data and Knowledge Engineering Journal*, December 1993.

Thuraisingham, B., and A. Kammon. "Secure Query Processing in Distributed Database Management Systems—Design and Performance Studies." In *Proceedings of the 6th Computer Security Applications Conference*, Tucson, AZ, December 1990, pp. 88–102.

Thuraisingham, B., H. Rubinovitz, and David A. Foti. "Design and Implementation of a Distributed Database Inference Controller—I." MTR 92B0000168, The Mitre Corporation, Bedford, MA, December 1992.

Tokuda, H. "Compensatable Atomic Actions in Object-Oriented Operating Systems." In *Proceedings of the Pacific Computer Communications Symposium*, October 1985.

Tokuda, H., and C. Mercer. "ARTS: A Distributed Real-Time Kernel." *ACM Operating Systems Review*, vol. 23, July 1989, pp. 29–53.

Tokuda, H., T. Nakajima, and P. Rao. "Real-Time Mach: Towards a Predictable Real-Time System." In *Proceedings of the USENIX Mach Workshop*, 1990, pp. 1–8.

Tokuda, H., and M. Rotera. "An Integrated Time-Driven Scheduler for the Arts Kernel." In *Proceedings of the 8th IEEE Phoenix Conference on Computers and Communications*, March 1989.

Ullman, J. *Principles of Database Systems*. Rockville, MD: Computer Science Press, 1982.

Ulusoy, O., and G. Belford. "Real-Time Concurrency Control in Distributed Database Systems." *IEEE Technical Committee on Real-Time Systems Newsletter* 3(1), February 1991.

Varadharajan, V., and S. Black. "A Multilevel Security Model for a Distributed Object-Oriented System." In *Proceedings of the 6th Computer Security Applications Conference*, Tucson, AZ, December 1990, pp. 68–78.

Vasta, J. *Understanding Database Management Systems*. Belmont, CA: Wadsworth, 1985.

Vossen, G. "Bibliography on Object-Oriented Database Management." *ACM SIGMOD Record* 20(1), March 1991.

Watson, P. "The Challenge of Response Time Management in Real-Time Distributed Systems." In *Proceedings of the IEEE 4th Israel Conference on Computer Systems and Software Engineering*, June 1989.

———. "An Overview of Architectural Directions for Real-Time Systems." In *Proceedings of the 5th Workshop on Real-Time Software and Operating Systems*, 1988.

Weihl, W. "Local Atomicity Properties: Modular Concurrency Control for Abstract Data Types." *ACM Transactions on Programming Language and Systems* 11(2), April 1989.

———. "Commutativity-Based Concurrency Control for Abstract Data Types." *IEEE Transactions on Computers*, vol. 37, December 1988, pp. 1488–1505.

Wells, D. L., J. A. Blakely, and C. W. Thompson. "Architechture of an Open Object-Oriented Database Management System." *IEEE Computer*, vol. 25, October 1992, pp. 74–82.

Whang, K. Letter from the special issue on multimedia information systems issue editor. *Bulletin of the IEEE Technical Committee on Data Engineering* 14(3), September 1991.

Widom, J. "Set-Oriented Production Rules in Relational Database Systems." In *Proceedings of the 1990 ACM SIGMOD International Conference on the Management of Data*, 1990, pp. 259–270.

Woelk, D., and W. Kim. "An Object-Oriented Approach to Multimedia Database Systems." In *Proceedings of the ACM SIGMOD Conference*, Washington, DC, 1986.

Wolfe, V., L. Cingiser, J. Peckham, and J. Prichard. "A Model for Real-Time Object-Oriented Databases." *IEEE Technical Committee on Real-Time Systems Newsletter* 9(1/2), Spring/Summer 1993.

Wolfe, V., S. Davidson, and I. Lee. "RTC: Language Support for Real-Time Concurrency." *Journal of Real-time Systems* 5(1), March 1993.

Wolfe, V. F., L. C. DiPippo, J. P. Pritchard, and P. Fortier. "The Design of Real-Time Extensions to the Open Object-Oriented Database System." In *Proceedings of IEEE Workshop on Object-Oriented Dependable Systems*, October 1994.

Wong, M., and D. Agrawal. "Tolerating Bounded Inconsistency for Increasing Concurrency in Database Systems." In *Proceedings of the 11th Principles of Database Systems Symposium*, 1992, pp. 236–245.

Wu, K.-L., P. S. Yu, and C. Pu. "Divergence Control for Epsilon-Serializability." In *Proceedings of the International Conference on Data Engineering*, 1992.

Yang, Q., A. Vellaikal, and S. Dao. "MB+ Tree: A New Index Structure for Multimedia Databases." In *Proceedings of the International Workshop on Multimedia Databases*, New York, 1995.

Yu, P., K. Wu, K. Lin, and S. Son. "On Real-Time Databases: Concurrency Control and Scheduling." In *Proceedings of the IEEE*, January 1994.

Zdonik, S., and D. Maier, eds. *Readings in Object-Oriented Database Systems*. San Mateo, CA: Morgan Kaufmann, 1990.

Zhang, A., M. Nodine, B. Bhargava, and O. Bukhres. "Ensuring Relaxed Atomicity for Flexible Transactions in Multidatabase Systems." In *Proceedings of the ACM SIGMOD Conference*, June 1994.

Zhao, W., K. Ramamritham, and J. Stankovic. "Preemptive Scheduling under Time and Resource Constraints." *IEEE Transactions on Computers*, vol. C-36, August 1987, pp. 949–960.

———. "Virtual Time CSMA Protocols for Hard Real-Time Communication." *IEEE Transactions on Software Engineering* SE-13(8), August 1987.

———. "Scheduling Tasks with Resource Requirements in Hard Real-Time Systems." *IEEE Transactions on Software Engineering*, vol. SE-13, May 1987, pp. 564–577.

ADDITIONAL READING

Accredited Standards Committee. "X3-Information Processing Systems, Projects Manual." July 1993.

Accredited Standards Committee. "X3 Information Processing Systems, Standards Evaluation Criteria." December 1992.

Accredited Standards Committee. "X3-Information Processing Systems, Master Plan (Operational)." X3/SD-1B, January 1991.

Advanced Launch Systems Information Segment Unified Information System Concept and Reference Architecture. Aerospace Report no. TOR-0090(5561-02)-1, March 15, 1990.

Application Portability Profile (APP). "The U.S. Government's Open System Environment Profile-OSE/1 Version." Systems and Software Technology Division, Computer Systems Laboratory, National Institute of Standards and Technology, Gaithersburg, MD, revised October 1992.

Database Technology Assessment for Modeling and Simulation. Presented August 11, 1992, to the Defense Science Board Summer Study on Modeling and Simulation, Iris Kameny, WD-6166-DR&E.

Department of Defense. "Trusted Database Interpretation." 1991.

IDA Paper P-2457. "A Survey of Technical Standards for Command and Control Information Systems." September 1991.

Proceedings of the ACM 1994 Conference on Multimedia Database Management Systems, San Francisco, CA. Summary published in *ACM SIGMOD Record*, March 1995.

Technical Reference Model for Information Management, Version 1.3. Defense Information Systems Agency, Center for Information Management, July 31, 1992.

X3/SPARC/DBSSG/OODBTG Final Report, September 17, 1991.

Index